SHORT
OF THE
GOAL

SHORT
OF THE
GOAL

U.S. POLICY AND
POORLY PERFORMING STATES

Nancy Birdsall
Milan Vaishnav
Robert L. Ayres
editors

CENTER FOR GLOBAL DEVELOPMENT
Washington, D.C.

Short of the Goal: U.S. Foreign Policy and Poorly Performing States may be ordered from:
BROOKINGS INSTITUTION PRESS
c/o HFS, P.O. Box 50370, Baltimore, MD 21211-4370
Tel.: 800/537-5487; 410/516-6956; Fax: 410/516-6998
Internet: www.brookings.edu

Library of Congress Cataloging-in-Publication data

Short of the goal : U.S. policy and poorly performing states / Nancy Birdsall, Milan Vaishnav,
    Robert L. Ayres, editors.
    p.   cm.
    Summary: "Analyzes U.S. policy toward poorly performing states that are ineligible for
new U.S. foreign assistance programs and examines the role of specific policy instruments
in building state capacity to prevent deterioration and collapse"—Provided by publisher.
    Includes bibliographical references and index.
    ISBN-13: 978-1-933286-05-1 (pbk. : alk. paper)
    ISBN-10: 1-933286-05-9 (pbk. : alk. paper)
    1. United States—Foreign economic relations—Developing countries. 2. Economic
assistance, American—Developing countries. 3. Infrastructure (Economics)—Developing
countries. I. Birdsall, Nancy. II. Vaishnav, Milan. III. Ayres, Robert L. IV. Center for
Global Development. V. Title.
    HF1455.S545   2006
    338.91'7301724—dc22   2005028731

9 8 7 6 5 4 3 2 1

The paper used in this publication meets minimum requirements of the
American National Standard for Information Sciences—Permanence of Paper for
Printed Library Materials: ANSI Z39.48-1992.

Cover photograph: Wolfgang Kaehler/Corbis

Cover by Sese-Paul Design

Typeset in Adobe Garamond

Composition by Cynthia Stock
Silver Spring, Maryland

Printed by R. R. Donnelley
Harrisonburg, Virginia

 **Center for Global Development**

The Center for Global Development is an independent, nonprofit policy research organization dedicated to reducing global poverty and inequality and to making globalization work for the poor. Through a combination of research and strategic outreach, the Center actively engages policymakers and the public to influence the policies of the United States, other rich countries, and such institutions as the World Bank, the IMF, and the World Trade Organization to improve the economic and social development prospects in poor countries. The Center's Board of Directors bears overall responsibility for the Center and includes distinguished leaders of nongovernmental organizations, former officials, business executives, and some of the world's leading scholars of development. The Center receives advice on its research and policy programs from the Board and from an Advisory Committee that comprises respected development specialists and advocates.

The Center's president works with the Board, the Advisory Committee, and the Center's senior staff in setting the research and program priorities and approves all formal publications. The Center is supported by an initial significant financial contribution from Edward W. Scott Jr. and by funding from philanthropic foundations and other organizations.

Contents

Preface   ix

Part I. Introduction

1   *A Mismatch with Consequences: U.S. Foreign Policy
    and the Security-Development Nexus*   1
    JEREMY M. WEINSTEIN AND MILAN VAISHNAV

Part II. Narratives of State Deterioration

2   *Life Support or Assisted Suicide? Dilemmas of
    U.S. Policy toward the Democratic Republic of Congo*   53
    PIERRE ENGLEBERT

3   *The Dysfunctional State of Nigeria*   83
    PETER M. LEWIS

4   *Indonesia as a Poorly Performing State?*   117
    ANDREW MacINTYRE

5   *Reforming Central Asia*   144
    MARTHA BRILL OLCOTT

6 *No Quick Fix: Foreign Aid and State Performance in Yemen*   182
SHEILA CARAPICO

7 *Burma-Myanmar: The U.S.-Burmese Relationship and Its Vicissitudes*   209
DAVID I. STEINBERG

8 *Making Peace Perform in War-Transition Countries: El Salvador, Guatemala, and Nicaragua*   245
SUSAN BURGERMAN

9 *Failing and Failed States: Toward a Framework for U.S. Assistance*   285
CAROL LANCASTER

Part III. Tools of State Building

10 *Aid through Trade: An Effective Option?*   309
ARVIND PANAGARIYA

11 *Toward Best Outcomes from Foreign Direct Investment in Poorly Performing States*   334
THEODORE H. MORAN

12 *The Persisting Poverty of Strategic Analysis in U.S. Democracy Assistance*   376
DAVID W. YANG

13 *U.S. Military and Police Assistance to Poorly Performing States*   412
ADAM ISACSON AND NICOLE BALL

Contributors   461

Index   463

Preface

I n July 2004, the Center for Global Development released a report entitled *On the Brink: Weak States and U.S. National Security.* Prepared by a high-level, bipartisan commission of former officials and scholars of U.S. foreign policy and of development, the report emphasized that the economic and political well-being of the world's many weak states is a security as well as a moral imperative and offered concrete recommendations for changes in U.S. foreign policy and development architecture to address the challenge weak states pose for their own peoples and for the global system.

On the Brink was informed by a series of studies commissioned by Robert Ayres, one of the coeditors of the present volume. The completed studies, prepared in 2004 by leading scholars with expertise in particular countries or in policy issue areas such as trade and aid, make up this volume. *Short of the Goal* serves as a worthy companion piece to the commission's 2004 report, which, by necessity, was tightly argued, heavily focused on policy recommendations, and short on illustrative background.

The publication of *Short of the Goal* is certainly timely. In a January 2006 speech on transforming U.S. foreign policy, Secretary of State Condoleezza Rice underlined the challenge the United States faces in helping to transform the world's many weak or poorly performing states into "responsible sovereigns." Providing in-depth reviews of individual countries, the authors detail the complexity of that challenge. In their frank assessments of past mistakes, they suggest many lessons for readers interested in assessing current U.S. efforts at nation building.

The first chapter by Jeremy Weinstein and Milan Vaishnav in an initial section serves as a primer for academics, policymakers, and students interested in the developing world's weak states. They discuss the definition of weak states, the causes and consequences of their weakness, and the options in foreign policy terms for the United States. The second section consists of a series of case studies by contributors with regional and country expertise covering Central America, the Democratic Republic of Congo, Indonesia, Myanmar, Nigeria, and Yemen. These chapters highlight the roots of state weakness and the role of the United States and the international community in addressing (or in some cases, exacerbating) the origins of their weakness. In the third and final section experts explore the potential—exploited and unexploited—of various policy instruments for addressing the problems weak states pose. The policy instruments addressed include the potential role of foreign assistance, trade and market access, foreign direct investment, security assistance, and democracy promotion.

An early and ongoing project of the Center has been the analysis of the implementation of the U.S. Millennium Challenge Account (MCA), a foreign aid program for reasonably well-governed but poor developing countries. In many ways, weak states are a more daunting development challenge. In addition to the work reflected in this volume and in the Commission's report, ongoing analysis by Steven Radelet of nation building in Liberia under that country's newly elected president and by Stewart Patrick on the links between weak state capacity and global threats are adding further to our stock of expertise and, we hope, the Center's ability to be helpful in the search for effective policy and better practice—in the interests of improving people's lives in poor countries as well as improving global security.

I am particularly grateful to three people for their work on this volume. Robert Ayres is a veteran of the World Bank and a senior fellow at the Center in 2002–03 before going to American University. I thank him for his willingness to take on what was then virtually uncharted territory for development economists. Jeremy Weinstein, a postdoctoral fellow at the Center in 2003–04 and currently on the faculty of Stanford University and a nonresident fellow of the Center, directed our project that led to the Commission's report on weak states and U.S. national security. He made central contributions to this volume in his comments to contributors on their draft essays, in his advice to me, and, of course, as coauthor of the initial chapter. Milan Vaishnav, who assisted Jeremy on the work of the Commission and is now a graduate student, shepherded this volume to its final stages. Without each one of these three collaborators, there would be no volume.

My coeditors and I thank Lawrence MacDonald, the Center's director of communications and policy, and his publications team. Yvonne Siu, our publications coordinator, and her predecessor, Noora-Lisa Aberman, deserve special credit for coordinating with the publisher and the contributing authors and anticipating and preparing for every detail, major or minor, in the publication process. We also thank all the contributors for their collaboration and in some cases their patience with what has been a long but worthwhile process.

Last, but certainly not least, I and my coeditors thank the William and Flora Hewlett Foundation for its generous support of this volume and our Chair of the Board and founding benefactor, Edward W. Scott Jr., for his interest in and support of our work on this central development issue.

Nancy Birdsall
President
Center for Global Development
Washington, D.C.

PART I

Introduction

1

A Mismatch with Consequences: U.S. Foreign Policy and the Security-Development Nexus

JEREMY M. WEINSTEIN AND MILAN VAISHNAV

Looking back, few would argue that it was a good idea for the United States and its allies to disengage from Afghanistan after the Soviet Union withdrew in 1989. Various *mujahideen* factions, many organized and funded with the support of the United States and Pakistan during the 1980s, fought to fill the power vacuum that was left, and civil war continued unabated until the Taliban, a guerrilla group intent on imposing a highly restrictive form of Islamic law, captured the Afghan capital, Kabul, in 1996. The Taliban regime quickly became an international pariah by providing safe haven for al Qaeda leader Osama bin Laden when he was expelled from Sudan. Until the September 11, 2001, terrorist attacks on New York and Washington, however, few realized Afghanistan's central role as a base for the recruitment and training of terrorists from Islamic fundamentalist groups around the world.

Afghanistan's role as a source of support for al Qaeda raised two pressing issues for policymakers. The first—how to combat terrorist groups and the regimes that harbor them—animated a wide-ranging international debate following the 9/11 terrorist attacks. The United States adopted a new doctrine of *preemption*, explicitly committing itself to "act against emerging threats before they are fully formed."[1] The war against Iraq was the first U.S. military demonstration of that principle in action. Heightened international pressure on the regimes of North Korea, Iran, Syria, and Libya, among others, to abandon their efforts to obtain weapons of mass destruction and provide material support to terrorist groups also followed.

The second issue—how to prevent the collapse of governments in the developing world—has received far less attention. Failed states represent the ultimate disintegrative force. Incapable of providing even the most basic public goods to their citizens, governments find themselves confronted by opposition forces that challenge their legitimacy and monopoly on the use of force. The instability generated in such an environment poses a threat to neighboring states and to entire regions as civil conflict spills across borders, spreading disease, criminal activity, and conflict, and refugees seek safety wherever they can find it. Afghanistan demonstrates that the political vacuum predominating in such environments also creates the conditions for the spread and growth of terrorist groups.

But the challenge is not only one of how to prevent state collapse. More broadly, international peace and security now depend, in part, on the capacity of governments in the poorest countries to meet the needs of their citizens and to become responsible members of the international community. They must be capable of patrolling their borders; monitoring the inflow and outflow of people, resources, and money; and preserving internal security. State weakness, not simply state collapse, is therefore a pressing concern for policymakers. And it is an affliction of the world's poorest countries in particular.[2]

This volume explores the causes and consequences of state weakness in the developing world. It focuses on the set of states that we term *poorly performing states*—states that exhibit a combustible mix of poverty and deficient government institutions that appreciably raises the risk of a collapse into conflict. It presents a series of country studies to elucidate the causes of poor performance in different environments and to describe how the U.S. and international actors have engaged (or failed to engage) governments in failing states, with what consequences. It then offers the critical insights of policy experts on how five instruments of U.S. foreign policy—assistance, trade policy, encouragement of direct investment, police and military assistance, and promotion of democracy—can be used to strengthen states and to reduce the likelihood of collapse in the poorest countries.

In this chapter, we define what is meant by a *poorly performing state*, using a taxonomy of state performance based on the criteria for U.S. government Millennium Challenge Account (MCA) assistance. The MCA provides a useful method for grading countries on their economic, political, and social performance. However, in the case studies in this volume, authors use variety of names for poorly performing states, including "weak," "fragile," and "failing." The range of terms used to describe poor performers illustrates the complexity and difficulty of precisely defining and assessing gradations of state weakness.

Redefining "Pivotal" States

The purpose of this volume is to explore the puzzling disjunction between the changing nature of the security threats emerging from the poorest countries and the response mounted by U.S. policymakers. U.S. policy in the developing world has traditionally revolved around the strategy of identifying "pivotal" states. A pivotal state is defined as a "hot spot that could not only determine the fate of its region but also affect international stability."[3] During the cold war, the United States provided military assistance, development aid, and political cover to many regimes and rebel groups to help impede Soviet expansion. That approach, the so-called domino strategy, was justified on the grounds that preventing the fall to communism of particular states would prevent its spread to neighboring governments as well; it was the pivotal states approach in action.

In the post–cold war period, a policy of narrow, selective engagement with developing nations has continued to dominate national policymaking. During the 1990s, interventions were mounted to avert genocide and ethnic cleansing in the Balkans, while international crimes of equal or greater enormity were ignored in Rwanda, Sierra Leone, and the Democratic Republic of Congo. Massive infusions of financial assistance flowed to stem the collapse of the Mexican, Russian, and the Asian economies, while overall foreign assistance to the poorest countries declined. The administration of George W. Bush made this pivotal states strategy explicit in its 2005 National Security Strategy for Africa, suggesting that one of its core strategies would be to promote progress in "anchor" states.[4]

The problem is that by explicitly targeting pivotal states in the developing world, U.S. policy risks leaving too many other countries behind. If the costs of U.S. disengagement were to be borne entirely by the inhabitants of the poorest countries, such a strategy might be practical, albeit morally questionable. However, state collapse has the potential to undermine U.S. national security as well.

Why do poorly performing states pose a threat to U.S. national security? Three particular channels often are cited. First, *illicit transnational networks* strategically target weak governments and porous borders, which enable them to move money, people, weapons, and drugs around the globe; weak states thus become a priority in the fight against terrorists and criminal syndicates. This is the case of Afghanistan.

Somalia provides another glaring example. Following the failed U.S. and UN humanitarian intervention in 1993, both parties gradually disengaged from Somalia, leaving the country consumed by battles between regional and factional warlords. The resulting near-total dissolution of central government authority made Somalia an attractive haven for al Qaeda in the late 1990s. A 2003 UN report pointed to the central importance of Somalia as a training ground, transit point, and escape route for the organizers of terrorist attacks on an airliner and beach resort in Kenya.[5] Without an effective central government or regional leadership able to monitor the flow of goods, services, and persons, Somalia continues to represent a serious threat to U.S. interests.

Illicit trade networks thrive in insecure environments and tend to spill across borders. Following the dissolution of the Soviet Union, the illicit flow of small arms and light weapons increased throughout Central Asia as small-scale entrepreneurs, often protected by friends in government, sought profits on the international illegal arms market. The availability of cheap weapons fueled wars in the region; moreover, these networks have successfully equipped armed groups as far away as sub-Saharan Africa. Porous borders have made the implementation of rigorous export controls difficult, and Western governments have been slow to respond to the emerging challenge. Failure to stem the tide of arms at its source has resulted in a flood of weapons downstream to armed groups that oppose U.S. regional interests in the developing world.

Second, poorly performing states undermine regional and global stability through *spillover effects*, which transcend the boundaries of individual countries. Collapsing states often spawn wider regional conflicts; unrestricted cross-border trade in drugs fuels insecurity and criminality at home and in neighboring states; and infectious diseases cross borders unchecked through expanding local and global networks of trade and migration.

Entire regions have been engulfed following conflicts that first appeared to be isolated to individual countries. Take Liberia, for example. Most international actors, including the United States, ignored Liberia as Charles Taylor took advantage of the breakdown of the state to institute his own brand of ruthless authoritarian rule. From his base in Liberia, Taylor was largely responsible for inciting a decade-long civil war in Sierra Leone, providing material aid to the rebels in Côte d'Ivoire, and funding antigovernment dissidents in Guinea. The stability of West Africa has been compromised, while early intervention might have made a difference. The United States later found itself challenged by various members of the international community to commit precious military resources to correcting the damage done.

Third, reversing the decline of weak states is central to allaying *regional insecurity.* Nigeria, Pakistan, and Sudan, for example—all fairly characterized as poorly performing governments—can be positive influences for stability and reform among their neighbors if they can escape from the trap of poverty and poor performance. On the other hand, a setback in democratic progress or reversion to conflict in key states can threaten regional advancement and undermine U.S. geopolitical strategy.

Recent developments in Bolivia threaten to shake the foundations of other democratic, pro-Western governments in the Andean region. In 2002, suffering from endemic poverty and regional economic malaise, the Bolivian government appealed to the United States for emergency assistance to maintain basic public services and social investments. President Gonzalo Sanchez de Lozada was rebuffed and then deposed by popular protests less than a year later. The ouster of Sanchez de Lozada, the fourth elected Latin American president to be driven out of office by the opposition in only four years, represents a dramatic setback to U.S. regional objectives and a force for destabilization in much of the Andean region. It could also presage a surge in a host of illicit activities, including an increase in new coca cultivation in the Bolivian countryside.

The key point is that while U.S. selectivity in engaging with the developing world has its benefits, it also has its costs. National security concerns increasingly challenge U.S. policymakers to address even the most difficult environments to prevent a host of transnational threats from taking root.

A Mismatch with Consequences

At the same time that U.S. security concerns dictate a more inclusive strategy of engagement with the poorest countries, U.S. and multilateral policy instruments are becoming more selective. In an effort to increase the effectiveness of new investments, policymakers have sought to restrict them to nations whose governments already have demonstrated sound policy choices and established transparent institutions of government. This approach means that weak and failing states are explicitly excluded from programs to promote development.

The most prominent example of the trend is the Millennium Challenge Account. Proposed by President George W. Bush and authorized by Congress, the MCA promises to deliver substantial new flows of foreign assistance to low-income countries that are "ruling justly, investing in their own people, and encouraging economic freedom."[6] Central to the design of the MCA is its commitment to providing assistance only to select countries whose governments already have established the policies and institutions most conducive to development. This approach is a response to U.S. recognition that fifty years of assistance has failed to produce substantial economic development in many parts of the world and to the growing academic consensus that assistance provided in good policy environments produces better results.[7] A transparent public process that includes quantifiable indicators of progress is planned for recipient countries, making it difficult for policymakers to employ MCA funds for political rather than development purposes.

While the MCA offers the opportunity to incorporate cutting-edge reforms in the administration and delivery of foreign assistance, its scope suggests a marked focus on the "best performers" and away from the most troubled states in the developing world. Its proposed $5 billion annual budget represents a 50 percent increase over the $10 billion 2002 U.S. foreign aid budget and a 9 percent expansion in global development assistance.[8] However, the new funds, while substantial, will not be invested in the environments that are most conducive to the basing of terrorist networks and criminal groups and most at risk of collapse.

The MCA is not the only policy instrument that emphasizes selectivity in distributing benefits. The African Growth and Opportunity Act (AGOA), passed by Congress in 2000 and revised in 2003, offers preferential one-way access to U.S. markets to African countries that have established or are making continual progress toward "market-based economies; the rule of law and political pluralism; elimination of barriers to U.S. trade and investment; protection of intellectual property; efforts to combat corruption; policies to reduce poverty, increasing availability of health care and educational opportunities; protection of human rights and worker rights; and elimination of certain child labor practices."[9] These preconditions are defined in the legislation, but determining whether a country has made or is making progress toward pro-development institutions is the prerogative of the U.S. president and the U.S. trade representative. In practice, political considerations play a role in determining eligibility. Nonetheless, the emphasis on these prerequisites for participation has so far led to the exclusion of critical weak and failing states including Angola, Burundi, Liberia, Togo, Sudan, and Somalia, among others.

The rationale behind selectivity is fairly simple. True selectivity provides the strongest possible incentives for governments to set in place the economic policies and transparent institutions conducive to development. By directing the flow of resources to good performers, selectivity also helps to ensure that resources are used effectively to reduce poverty and promote continued reform. But the shift toward selectivity, especially if replicated broadly across other U.S. and multilateral policy instruments, entails a number of problems.

The first problem is that the funds and market access offered may not be significant enough to further deepen reform. This is a particular challenge for the MCA, which, as long as it remains a small percentage of total foreign assistance provided in the developing world, will find it hard to provide strong incentives for institutional reform in difficult environments. More likely, given its limited geographic scope and overall financial scale, the MCA will only be able to demonstrate the degree to which aid is more effective in good environments. In poorly performing states where political and economic arrangements favor a select few and corruption provides a major source of income, the marginal contribution to GDP of potential assistance from the MCA is unlikely to alter those arrangements.

Second, selectivity may exclude states that are simply too poor to institute the political and economic reforms necessary for growth. On the economic front, this situation has been called the "poverty trap."[10] Such countries are unable to provide even the most basic public goods—the health services, education, and physical infrastructure essential for long-term growth. Because growth is a fundamental requirement for reducing poverty, states find themselves in a vicious cycle of poverty, disease, and conflict. The poverty trap has a political dimension as well. In many autocratic political systems, leaders have little incentive to adopt better policies or undertake reform. A recent analysis of the political roots of poverty concluded that "under many of the least politically inclusive systems, good policy is bad politics, and bad policy can be good politics."[11] Political leaders may have little interest in taking advantage of benefits offered by international actors, even though such reforms might be in the best interest of the population at large.

The third problem posed by selectivity is that the United States simply cannot afford to ignore the countries excluded from the MCA and other selective programs in the short term. Security concerns are paramount, and the United States will need to design new programs and dedicate new resources to building state capacity in poorly performing states. Leaving them to their own devices is a recipe for instability and state collapse—both of which threaten U.S. geopolitical interests and, potentially, the security of Americans at home.[12]

On the Other Side of the MCA

The developing world comprises countries that exhibit considerable diversity in their economic performance, the nature of their political regimes, the effectiveness of their government institutions, and their likely development prospects. Policymakers have sought to separate the good from the poor performers in order to target countries where aid is likely to be most effective. But no widely accepted measure of performance exists. Performance can be graded along a multifaceted continuum, and distinguishing good policy environments from bad ones is not an uncontroversial task.

In order to identify the countries of interest to the contributors in this volume, we started with a simple question: which states find themselves excluded from—or in our terminology, "on the other side of"—the MCA?

The Bush administration proposed a selection methodology that determines whether a country qualifies for MCA funding on the basis of three main factors:[13]

—Income. To be eligible to compete for MCA funds, a country must fall under a certain income threshold, which is anticipated to increase gradually over time. In the program's first year, countries with a per capita income of less than $1,435—which also were eligible to borrow from the World Bank's concessional lender, the International Development Association—competed for MCA funding. This delimits a set of sixty-three countries, after subtracting twelve countries otherwise deemed ineligible under U.S. law to receive U.S. foreign assistance for a host of political and security reasons.

—Performance. For each of the three prodevelopment principles outlined in the design of the program, the administration proposed sixteen indicators to be used to assess a country's commitment to "ruling justly, investing in [its] own people, and encouraging economic freedom." These indicators are outlined in table 1-1. For each of the three dimensions of performance, the administration identified a set of quantitative indicators that would be publicly available in order to enable transparent cross-country comparisons. The six indicators that measure "ruling justly" include assessments of a country's commitment to protecting civil liberties and political rights; establishing rules and institutions that reinforce the rule of law and inhibit corruption; and promoting the effective delivery of public services. The four indicators that measure "investing in people" include assessments of the immunization

Table 1-1. *Dimensions of Performance*

Dimension/Indicator	Key questions
Ruling justly	
Civil liberties	To what extent do citizens enjoy basic rights?
Political rights	To what extent do people participate freely in the political process?
Voice and accountability	To what extent does the country have free and fair elections, a representative legislature, fair legal systems, a free press, and a minimal role for the military?
Government effectiveness	To what extent does the country have a high-quality civil service and effective government bureaucracies?
Rule of law	To what extent does the country have fair and predictable rules for contract enforcement, dispute settlement, the protection of property rights, and the disposition of criminal law?
Control of corruption	To what extent is public power used for private gain?
Investing in people	
Spending on public primary education	What is the level of public spending on primary education?
Primary school completion rate	What percentage of graduation age children successfully complete primary school?
Spending on health	What is the level of public spending on health?
Immunization rate	What percentage of children receive immunizations for tetanus and measles?
Establishing economic freedom	
Country credit rating	What is the perceived risk of government default?
Inflation	What is the rate of inflation?
Regulatory policies	To what extent is the economic environment constrained by burdensome regulations, inadequate bank supervision, excessive controls on trade and investment, excessive restrictions on capital flows, and ponderous legal restrictions on ownership?
Budget deficit	To what extent does the government run a large fiscal deficit that must be financed by borrowing?
Trade policy	To what extent does the government set in place tariffs and quotas that restrict trade?
Days to start a business	How burdensome are the costs and procedures required to start a business?

Source: Authors' calculations.

rate, spending on public primary education, the primary school completion rate, and spending on health. The six indicators proposed to measure "economic freedom" include a country's credit rating, inflation rate, regulatory policies, budget deficit, trade policy, and support for business development.

—Corruption. Corruption is one of the key performance indicators in the "ruling justly" dimension. To emphasize its importance, however, the administration proposed eliminating any countries that score below the median on the measure of corruption. Corruption is thus counted twice, and it is a hard constraint on qualifying for MCA assistance.

The administration proposed using a "hurdles" approach to determine whether a country qualifies for MCA assistance. This approach requires countries to score above the median (the hurdle) on half of the indicators in each of the three dimensions of performance. In addition, the hard constraint on corruption means that a country must score above the median on that measure in order to qualify, regardless of how well it performs on the other indicators. Of sixty-three eligible countries, sixteen qualified for MCA assistance in the program's first year.[14]

Who Are the Poor Performers?

One can debate the relative merits of the administration's approach to measuring performance, but it provides a useful tool for describing poor performers. Table 1-2 lists the countries that, using the administration's proposed ranking method, should not qualify for MCA funding in the program's first year, assuming a strict adherence to the indicators.[15] As mentioned, the administration exercised discretion in several cases, deeming countries eligible that did not qualify on the basis of the indicators and vice versa. Therefore our list of "who should qualify" is slightly different from who actually qualified—the variation due to the administration's use of discretion. In addition, we include countries that are otherwise deemed ineligible for U.S. assistance due to statutory restrictions in order to survey the entire universe of low-income developing countries

It is helpful to divide these countries into four main categories. The first category includes the *worst performers*, those that performed poorly on all three dimensions of performance. Governments in these countries failed to set in place institutions to protect political rights and civil liberties; to dedicate public resources to making critical investments in health and education; and to lay the foundation for economic growth by establishing policies and institutions conducive to private sector growth. Sixteen countries, twelve of which are in sub-Saharan Africa, constitute the set of worst performers.

Table 1-2. *The Other Side of the MCA*

Category	Dimensions of poor performance			
	Ruling justly	Investing in people	Promoting economic freedom	Controlling corruption
Worst performers				
Afghanistan	X	X	X	X
Angola	X	X	X	X
Burundi	X	X	X	X
Central African Republic	X	X	X	X
Chad	X	X	X	X
Comoros	X	X	X	
Congo	X	X	X	X
Guinea	X	X	X	
Guinea-Bissau	X	X	X	
Haiti	X	X	X	X
Laos	X	X	X	X
Liberia	X	X	X	X
Myanmar	X	X	X	X
Sierra Leone	X	X	X	X
Somalia	X	X	X	X
Sudan	X	X	X	X
Struggling on many fronts				
Cambodia	X	X		X
Cameroon	X	X		X
Congo	X		X	X
Côte d' Ivoire	X	X		X
Ethiopia	X		X	
Niger	X	X		X
Nigeria	X	X		X
Togo	X	X		
Zambia	X		X	X
Zimbabwe	X		X	X
Near-misses				
Azerbaijan	X			X
Bosnia and Herzegovina	X			
Burkina Faso			X	
Djibouti	X			
East Timor			X	
Eritrea			X	
Gambia	X			X
India		X		
Kiribati			X	
Kyrgyz Republic	X			X
Mozambique		X		X

(continues)

Table 1-2. *The Other Side of the MCA (continued)*

	Dimensions of poor performance			
Category	*Ruling justly*	*Investing in people*	*Promoting economic freedom*	*Controlling corruption*
Nepal		X		
Pakistan		X		
Papua New Guinea		X		X
Rwanda	X			
São Tome and Principe			X	
Solomon Islands			X	X
Tajikistan	X			X
Tanzania		X		X
Tonga			X	
Uganda	X			X
Uzbekistan	X			X
Yemen	X			
Stung by corruption				
Albania				X
Bangladesh				X
Bolivia				X
Georgia				X
Indonesia				X
Kenya				X
Malawi				X
Moldova				X
Good Performers				
Armenia				
Benin				
Bhutan				
Cape Verde				
Ghana				
Guyana				
Honduras				
Lesotho				
Madagascar				
Mali				
Mauritania				
Mongolia				
Nicaragua				
Senegal				
Serbia and Montenegro				
Sri Lanka				
Vanuatu				
Vietnam				

Source: Authors' calculations based on MCA data compiled by Steven Radelet and Rikhil Bhav-nani for the 2004 MCA selection process. Data available at www.cgdev.org.

The second category, governments that are *struggling on many fronts*, includes countries that performed poorly on two of the MCA's three dimensions of performance. An additional ten countries appear in this category, including Côte D'Ivoire, Ethiopia, Nigeria, and Zimbabwe. Only one non-African country, Cambodia, falls into this subset of states.

The third category includes so-called *near-miss states*, which failed to pass the hurdle on only one of the three dimensions of performance described above. This group of twenty-three countries is highly diverse, including five Central Asian states, India, Pakistan, and Yemen, and a number of other African countries. Ten of the twenty-three near-miss states, even if they made progress on the missing dimension, would still fail to qualify for the MCA because they exhibit high degrees of corruption.

The fourth category, states *stung by corruption*, includes those whose governments have demonstrated a commitment to protecting political freedom, making key investments in social sectors, and establishing the conditions for growth but that nevertheless have failed to counteract corruption among public officials. Eight governments are stuck in this position, on the verge of good performance.

These four categories represent the countries "on the other side of the MCA." The first three comprise the countries that we refer to as *poorly performing states*. These states exhibit poor economic performance and widespread poverty, and they are ruled by governments that, through lack of either will or capacity (or both), fail to guarantee political freedom, provide the foundation for economic activity and stability, and dedicate their resources to key investments in public goods. Some of these forty-nine states are implementing necessary and critical reforms on key dimensions of performance, but by and large, they are fragile and pose significant challenges to U.S. policymakers.

The MCA is not unique in using a set of static indicators to categorize performance. The World Bank employs a similar method in its program for "low-income countries under stress" (LICUS), identifying three dimensions of poor performance that substantially overlap with those of the MCA: poor service delivery, poor economic management, and limited participation by citizens.[16] A static approach makes it possible to compare countries with one another on the same, transparent indicators, at a single point in time. However, an alternative approach employed by the Overseas Development Institute in a new study more fully incorporates the dynamic evolution of particular indicators in assessing performance. This approach analyzes performance in terms of whether a country has been able to do "better or worse than before."[17]

The snapshot indicators used by the MCA reveal the poor policy environments and weak institutions that characterize poorly performing states, but they reveal little about the causes of poor performance. Before identifying the factors that put states on a path toward deterioration and collapse, we first explore the key characteristics of poorly performing states.

Looking in more detail at the four categories of states reveals a number of interesting variations. Table 1-3 summarizes some key differences between these states and the good performers.

The Worst Performers

Nearly 240 million people live in the sixteen worst-performing states. It is important to note that these states, which had an average per capita GDP of just over $300 in 2001, are the poorest of the low-income economies. They receive slightly more than twenty-three dollars per person of U.S. foreign aid, and they are among the most highly indebted, when considering debt-to-export ratios. The worst-performing economies have grown at an average of 2 percent per year, only slightly outpacing population growth, which averaged around 2 percent in low-income countries between 1980 and 2000. The worst performers are highly dependent on the export of primary commodities (including petroleum, coffee, cashews, and uranium), and nearly one-quarter are dependent on a *single* commodity for more than 50 percent of their export earnings. Politically, the worst-performing governments exhibit the outmoded political regimes of a previous era. They tend to be authoritarian or semi-authoritarian regimes that fail to protect civil or political rights and make only tentative steps toward the establishment of political freedoms. Most important, perhaps, the worst performers are conflict-ridden states; nearly 50 percent experienced a major war between 1998 and 2003.

Those Struggling on Many Fronts

An additional 288 million people live in the ten states that are struggling on at least two of the three MCA dimensions. These countries are slightly richer than the worst performers, with an average per capita income of $428. Like the other poorly performing states, they display limited economic growth, although their situation is better than that of the worst performers. Interestingly, this set of states receives an even smaller share of development assistance per capita ($19), and 50 percent of the countries in this category are highly dependent on the export of single primary commodities, including coffee, petroleum, and uranium. Politically, their ratings on civil liberties and political rights are only slightly better than the worst performers, indicating

Table 1-3. *Some Characteristics of Poorly Performing States*

Characteristics	Worst performers	Struggling on many fronts	Near misses	Stung by corruption	Good performers
Total population (millions)	237.315	288.598	1,409.243	438.174	194.127
Number of countries	16	10	23	8	18
Economic indicators					
Average per capita GDP (dollars)	302.25	427.60	409.00	594.75	565.60
Average annual GDP growth 1990–2001 (percent)	1.97	2.61	2.71	0.76	3.59
Development assistance Per capita (dollars)	23.40	19.38	37.79	40.13	62.60
Percent of countries dependent on a single primary commodity for 50 percent or more of export earnings	25	50	17	12	5
Political indicators					
Average civil liberties rating[a]	5.31	5.00	4.05	3.63	2.94
Average political rights rating[a]	5.94	5.30	4.41	3.25	3.06
Percent of countries experiencing major war since 1998	44	20	17	0	11

Sources: Central Intelligence Agency, *The World Factbook* (Washington, 2003); World Bank Group, *World Development Indicators* (Washington, 2003); Paul Cashin and others, *How Persistent Are Shocks to World Commodity Prices?* IMF Staff Paper 47.2 (Washington: 2000); PRIO/Uppsala Conflict Database (2003); Steven Radelet and Rikhil Bhavnani, "MCA Data for the 2004 Selection Process" (2004).

a. On a scale of 1 to 7; 1 = best.

stunted progress toward greater freedom and institutionalized democracy. Twenty percent of states in this category have experienced a major civil war in the last five years.

Near Misses

The 1.4 billion people who live in countries showing mixed progress in establishing institutions and policies conducive to development have slightly higher per capita incomes and annual GDP growth than the worst-performing states. Governments of these states receive higher levels of development assistance and are less reliant on the export of primary commodities. Although the countries in this category have very mixed records, on average they have shown substantial progress in protecting civil liberties and political freedom. Nonetheless, major civil conflicts have not left this group un-scathed, with nearly 20 percent experiencing significant conflict between 1998 and 2003.

The Good Performers and Those Stung by Corruption

The fourth category, *those stung by corruption*, we do not consider poor per-formers. Aside from levels of corruption, they are largely indistinguishable from the so-called "good performers." Thus, while those *stung by corruption* find themselves "on the other side of the MCA," they are discussed here with the good performers. The good performers and those states that demonstrate solid commitments on all three dimensions but are plagued by corruption exhibit substantially better outcomes than the low-income, poorly perform-ing states. Per capita income in the good performers is nearly double that of the worst performers, with average annual GDP growth of 3.6 percent, likely outpacing population growth. In addition, their per capita development assistance is nearly triple that of the worst-performing states (indicating selec-tivity already at work). The good performers, in particular, are also more highly diversified economically and less sensitive to the exogenous shocks to commodity prices that threaten the socioeconomic stability and fiscal balance of the poorly performing countries. Politically, both categories of countries are more democratic and less prone to conflict, suggesting stark differences between the good and the poor performers on political dimensions as well.

Four Stages of State Deterioration

While the empirical measurement of performance provides a useful list of countries for illustrative purposes, it does little to help us identify the key fac-tors that contribute to state deterioration and collapse. For that, we turned to the theoretical literature for guidance.

First, we needed to be clear about the dependent variable of interest. The ultimate outcome of concern to policymakers is state failure. Here, we define state failure in simple terms: a failed state is one in which the government faces a significant armed challenge to its authority by one or more rivals. In such an environment, a government exhibits a limited capacity to deliver the most basic public goods to the population. Security is the most essential public good, and a government in a failed state finds itself challenged by armed insur-gency, communal unrest, and political instability—all of which impede the delivery of other essential public goods, including health care and education. The environment is characterized by rising criminality, weakened institutions,

Figure 1-1. *The Dynamics of State Failure*

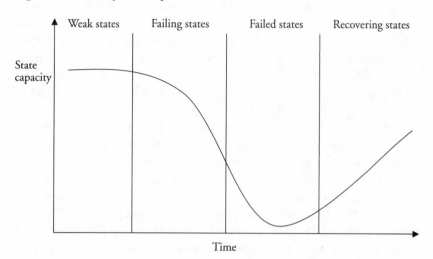

limited or destroyed infrastructure, and rampant corruption. Another important characteristic is that the government of a failed state has little capacity to effectively monitor and control its borders, facilitating the illicit flow of people, money, drugs, and arms. Outward indicators of state failure include the collapse of a political regime, the loss of substantial segments of territory, and violence that results in a significant number of civilian deaths.

Of the low-income countries, the *worst performers* exhibit the highest incidence of state failure. Slightly less than half of these states experienced a large-scale civil conflict between 1998 and 2003, while the others have been afflicted with unconstitutional regime changes (coups in the Comoros and Guinea-Bissau), low-level instability and violence (Chad and Somalia), and repressive authoritarian dictatorships (Liberia and Myanmar).

But state failure is an extreme condition—the ultimate result of sustained deterioration in the state's capacity and legitimacy or of reversion to conflict following an abbreviated recovery. Intermediate stages of state deterioration exist along the path to and from state failure. Figure 1-1 plots the dynamics of state deterioration over time, pointing to other zones of state weakness that merit attention. Introducing a dynamic element enables us to point to *weak states*, which exhibit underlying risk factors for collapse; *failing states*, where warning signs of conflict are visible; *failed states*; and *recovering states*, where, following the end of hostilities, conditions for improving state capacity are gradually being put in place but reversion to conflict is possible.

States *struggling on many fronts* and the *near-miss* countries fall into a variety of categories. One subset includes states in recovery. Bosnia, Cambodia, East Timor, and Haiti all have emerged from significant civil conflicts and are in the process of rebuilding their government institutions. Another subset includes failing states, which perform poorly across the dimensions outlined in the MCA and have highly visible signs of conflict on the horizon. Côte d'Ivoire and Nepal face growing challenges from armed groups, and each is threatened with the loss of total control over some of its territory. Pakistan, Rwanda, and Zimbabwe also exhibit worrying signs, as authoritarian leaders struggle to maintain their monopoly on political power through constitutional and extra-constitutional means.

On the other hand, some countries in these middle categories are exhibiting substantial progress in building sustainable democracies, such as Kenya, while others are establishing the types of institutions conducive to poverty reduction and growth, such as India and Uganda. But even the majority of states characterized as *struggling on many fronts or near-miss* give cause for concern on at least one of the key MCA dimensions—ruling justly, investing in people, or promoting economic freedom. For example, in Nigeria successive democratic elections have brought an end to decades of military rule, yet President Olusegun Obasanjo has failed to set in place the institutional architecture and economic policies needed to promote private sector development, and he has not reined in widespread corruption. Few of the near-miss states are on the verge of collapse, yet the sources of their weakness portend continued state deterioration unless they make substantial policy changes.

The question is this: What causes state capacity to deteriorate? Why do some governments lose both capacity and legitimacy? How are others able to maintain control and stability when their capacity is weakened or their legitimacy challenged?

The Causes of State Deterioration

To organize our thinking about the causes of state failure, we found it helped to distinguish between "ultimate" and "intermediate" outcomes. Ultimately, we were concerned with the collapse of governments—situations in which a political regime is confronted by a credible armed challenge within its borders. To make sense of the conditions under which states fail, we focused on three key determinants: geography, income, and institutions.

Geography relates to the impact of a country's physical location, characteristics, and natural resources—for example, latitude, proximity to water, terrain, climate, and stores of such natural economic assets as oil and minerals. *Income*, which represents the absolute level of wealth in a country and an assessment of how it changes over time, characterizes the economic situation confronting the population and the government. *Institutions* refer to a country's formal and informal governing arrangements—from systems to protect property rights to the political institutions established to govern to non-state community institutions.

State deterioration is a gradual process, and two of the key determinants of collapse, income and institutions, are endogenous factors that co-evolve with conflict and change over time. A country's economic condition has important implications for the nature of the political institutions that emerge and their resilience in the face of change. However, there is growing recognition that the quality of formal and informal institutions also plays a critical role in shaping economic outcomes. Understanding intermediate outcomes and their relationship to one another is essential for making sense of the stages of state deterioration. We start with geography, an influence that can plausibly be called exogenous.

Geography

Geography plays an important role in determining the likelihood of state failure and the outbreak of conflict through a number of channels. Its direct impact is felt in two ways. First, the nature of the terrain plausibly shapes the ease with which armed groups can effectively organize a credible challenge to the government.[18] A mountainous, forested country poses a substantial challenge to the capacity of its government to establish sovereignty and effective control over large swaths of territory. Second, the endowment and quality of natural resources, especially oil and minerals, raises the value of the "prize" to be had if armed groups can capture the state.[19] The incentives geography provides for insurgent groups to seek control of the state are particularly pronounced in environments where centralized control is necessary to extract resources effectively.

Geography also shapes state failure through two other channels. First, geography is a key determinant of the income of a country. Its natural resources may not be marketable, depriving a country of a critical source of income. The quality of the soil and the amount of rainfall may not be conducive to growing crops, weakening the agricultural sector of the economy. The climate shapes the likely exposure of citizens to some diseases, making geography an important determinant of the quality and quantity of human capital. Geography also has an impact on the extent to which a country can trade in world markets. Distant, landlocked countries face an uphill road trying to integrate into trading networks.

Second, geographic conditions affect the development of institutions. It is argued that environments plagued by disease, for example, led colonists to set up "extractive institutions" that transferred natural resources from the colony to the colonizer and failed to protect local property rights or to set in place checks and balances against government expropriation.[20] Many former colonies are still stuck with the remnants of legal systems and institutional structures developed during the colonial period. Sizable resource endowments, particularly in oil and minerals, are associated with the development of rent-seeking and rent-distributing institutions.[21] In such environments, if the government is capable of controlling the extraction of resources, it has few incentives to establish a social contract with the population.

The rich literature on the role of geography illustrates its critical role in shaping economic outcomes, political institutions, and the likelihood of conflict. Arguably exogenous, geographic influences are the deepest determinants of state failure and the most difficult to influence though policy. But geography is not the final word. Even with "bad" geographic endowments, some countries manage to avoid state deterioration and collapse, as in the case of Botswana, a mineral-rich, landlocked country in southern Africa. So it makes sense to look more closely at other key determinants of state failure.

Income

The significance of poverty as a driver of state collapse is an emerging theme in the literature on civil conflict and instability. In a 2003 study, Paul Collier and his colleagues at the World Bank argued that low-income countries face a risk of internal conflict that is around 15 times higher than the risk in countries that belong to the Organization for Economic Cooperation and Development (OECD).[22] Others have replicated their results, finding that $1,000 less in per capita income is associated on average with a 41 percent greater annual chance of onset of civil war.[23]

Poverty may make state failure more likely through two distinct paths. In the first, low and declining income, especially if poorly distributed, tends to create a pool of impoverished and disaffected young men who are easily recruited by armed opponents of the state. Economic alternatives for such potential combatants may be nonexistent or substantially worse than those promised by an armed group. Low per capita income also is associated with a second path to failure. Financially, organizationally, and politically weak central governments make insurgency more feasible and more attractive to leaders of armed groups, and they tend to lack the capacity to impede the growth of opposition.

Poverty, then, seems to be an important variable in predicting the likelihood of state deterioration. But that begs the question of what causes poverty. Here the interrelationships between the key variables become more visible.

Rodrik divides the "deep" determinants of economic performance into three categories.[24] One is the extent of a nation's integration into the world economy. The difficulty of accessing and participating in world markets is determined in part by the physical location of a country, but it is also a function of a government's policy choices. Openness to trade leads to specialization, technology transfer, capital flow, and the sharing of management expertise—in short, it is a key route to prosperity. The State Failure Task Force, which produced a CIA-sponsored study on the correlates of state failure, found that low levels of trade integration nearly doubled the odds of state collapse, perhaps by reducing the level of income.[25]

We have already explored Rodrik's second category, geography. Some of the same factors that raise the likelihood of state collapse also affect a country's development prospects. Resource endowments are both a blessing and a curse. They offer the prospect of an income stream to sustain economic growth, but their presence invites exploitation and makes it more difficult to build high-quality institutions that are favorable to economic development. Climatic conditions also influence growth by affecting the productivity of the land, and they are believed to have influenced the nature of the institutions that were constructed during colonial times, which still influence government economic policies in some countries today.

So Rodrik's third category, institutions, matters a great deal in economic performance. Economists increasingly believe that some institutional forms are more favorable to development than others—in particular those that protect property rights, preserve judicial independence, and develop the bureaucratic capacity to deliver public goods. And key geographic conditions, including a tropical climate and the presence of natural resources, seem to impede the development of exactly those types of institutions, thereby creating a major constraint on growth. What are the other key determinants of institutional quality?

Institutions

Our brief review of the literature illustrates the pivotal role of institutions in creating the conditions for state deterioration and collapse on one hand and a path to successful development on the other. Because institutions come in so many shapes and sizes, it is important to pinpoint the exact institutional arrangements that heighten the risk of state collapse in order to more efficiently identify the factors that lead to those arrangements.

Four types of arrangements stand out. The first is partial autocracy, often referred to as semi-authoritarianism, in which the government has adopted some of the key facets of democracy (including regular elections and legal opposition parties) but leaders maintain strict control over the governing institutions, creating in effect a stalled transition to democracy.[26] These institutions are particularly unstable under a second type of arrangement, which exists when leaders formalize the permanent exclusion of minority groups, as in countries where one ethnic group is dominant and controls the reins of government.[27] Looking at institutions in a dynamic sense points to a third unstable arrangement, in which new regimes, enmeshed in an immediate transition to democracy, face much higher risks of conflict.[28] A related, fourth result is that any political instability in governing arrangements (toward or away from democracy) makes state collapse more likely.[29]

So the message is pretty clear. Nondemocratic, exclusionary governments, particularly when they have unleashed the forces of democratic opposition by taking some tentative steps toward political opening, face the highest risk of collapse. The dynamics of transition exacerbate instability even if political reforms might ultimately produce more stable institutions. Political environments of this sort stand in marked contrast to the governing regimes and institutions seen as favorable to good economic performance. So why do some countries fail to get the institutions right?

One answer is that it is just plain hard to do. That is true particularly where geography impedes the establishment of stable, transparent, and long-term government institutions that protect property rights and formalize a social contract with the citizenry. It is already apparent that tropical climates and natural resource endowments leave countries at a distinct disadvantage on this front.

A second challenge to institution building is that countries need to grow in order to develop stable and effective government bureaucracies. Poverty itself is an impediment to institutional development. Many used to argue that democratic, accountable government institutions were a luxury of rich countries, but there is increasing recognition of the fact that democracy can thrive in poor countries.[30] It is just that the transition to democracy in poor countries is inherently unstable, and governments find it difficult during the transition to raise the resources they need to govern and to manage conflicts over the distribution of goods and services, which are heightened by broad, open participation in governance.[31]

It also is clear that poverty creates incentives for the construction of weak, opaque, and unaccountable institutions. Political clientelism tends to be the norm, with politicians using state resources to provide jobs and services to narrow constituencies; politicians also may use their control of state resources for personal benefit.[32] Bratton and van de Walle use the term *neopatrimonialism* to refer to such arrangements, in which individuals rule by dint of their personal prestige and power, granting few rights and privileges to the citizenry.[33] Neopatrimonial governments tend to have a strong executive, a weak judiciary, and an inefficient or corrupt civil service—precisely the institutions thought to impede development. When the state has deteriorated substantially, new forms of governance take hold that benefit even smaller and narrower constituencies and find ways to integrate themselves into the legal or illicit global economy.[34] The implication here is that economic growth is critical to, if not a precondition for, institutional development, as it increases demand for stability, new and fairer rules, and a more effective civil society capable of disciplining the governing elite.

If geography and poverty work against the development of effective institutions in poorly performing states, what's left? How can countries with the cards stacked against them push for institutional change?

Only tentative offers can be answered here, but there appears to be an important role for the international community to play. One cannot ignore the dramatic growth of electoral democracies in the past thirty years.[35] Whereas only 39 of 142 countries (28 percent) were electoral democracies in 1974, now fully 121 of 192 countries (63 percent) are holding regular elections. While the march of democratic progress, one of the defining trends of the late twentieth century, has many causes, it clearly was spurred by major pro-democracy investments by developed countries, changing norms and beliefs in the international community, and significant outside (and inside) pressure on nondemocratic regimes to change their ways.

The problem is that international pressure has taken institutional development only so far, succeeding in making a place for elections and opposition parties but fundamentally failing to upset the authoritarian equilibrium that predominates in the poorest countries. Transitions to democracy have often been shallow, and many of the new electoral democracies still have not established an independent judiciary and other institutions to check abuses of power, protect civil and political freedoms, and unleash the potential of civil society. At the same time that elections have become more common, the proportion of liberal democracies—those governments with a deeper commitment to transparency and accountability—has fallen markedly. Ottaway calls this the rise of "semi-authoritarianism" and defines it as one of the key challenges of our time.[36] But transforming such institutions is no easy task, as she admits. Institutions are not easily replaced or reformed, especially when their current inhabitants have strong incentives to preserve them. So Ottaway returns to the underlying conditions, suggesting that international pressure and assistance be combined in efforts to reinvigorate economies, address deep political polarization, reaffirm the capacity of the state, and push for a more balanced distribution of power.

Interrelationships of Determinants of State Failure

As figure 1-2 demonstrates, the relationships among the core determinants of state deterioration and collapse are complex. State failure is a product of multiple influences, some of which are largely exogenous (geographic factors), while others, such as economic performance and quality of institutions, are partly endogenous—the result of policy choices and political decisions.

One challenge is that intermediate outcomes—including the level of income and the nature of institutional arrangements—while susceptible to reform, change slowly. Progress on economic performance can help to create the conditions for more transparent and accountable governance, although economic failures merely promote the continuation of personalistic, corrupt political regimes. The establishment of high-quality institutions can lay the foundation for dramatic improvements in economic performance, but the rise of semi-authoritarianism and the threat of regime instability are likely to impede the investment necessary for economic development. Progress on economic growth and institutional change are interrelated and reinforce one another, but change takes time and often fails to be sustainable.

Moreover, state collapse and conflict have feedback effects on income and institutions. Conflict weakens the economy, damages infrastructure, and creates uncertainty, impeding investment. Conflict also weakens the foundations of the state, threatening the existing regime and challenging the rules and arrangements that govern social and economic behavior. Once a government fails, its risk of future collapse increases. The poverty trap proposed by Sachs is more fairly a cycle of poverty, weak governance, and instability.

Given these powerful feedback effects, the questions become clearer. Why do some weak states collapse, while others remain mired in poverty and repression? Which arrows in figure 1-2 matter most and why? Are countries

Figure 1-2. *Causes of State Deterioration*

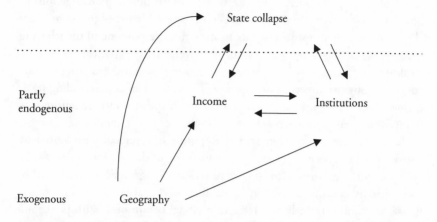

with poor geographic endowments doomed to repeat the cycle of poverty, weak governance, and instability? Can economic growth prevent state failure even if transparent and accountable institutions are not established? Can such institutions stem the tide of state deterioration in the absence of growth?

And the implications for policymakers are obvious. If some countries are too poor and too weak to avoid a slide into conflict, are programs that target the relatively well off and strong the answer? How can incentives for change be created? How can outside actors break the negative equilibrium that emerges in such coountries?

The Country Studies

The country studies included in this volume open a window into the interrelationship of core determinants of state deterioration and collapse, complementing what we have been able to glean from cross-country empirical evidence. Part I features seven country studies, each of which engages a country expert in the task of identifying specific causes of poor performance (and collapse, if applicable) and exploring the dynamics of U.S. policymaking and influence in attempts to shape a country's trajectory. Some broad themes are worth highlighting as an introduction to the studies.

— *The privatization of state resources for personal gain has serious consequences for performance.*

Although corruption takes different forms in different environments, the channeling of state resources for private gain is one key cause and consequence of state deterioration and collapse. Across the seven country studies, unique forms of such "privatization" appear: dictators distributing patronage to supportive constituencies, militaries providing special benefits to the military elite, governments capturing gains from natural resources and distributing them as private rewards, and collapsing governments exploiting their own weakness to further distribute economic power through the sharing of state control to buy off threats to their power. The absence of countervailing institutions—formal or informal—allows such corruption to thrive and to sow the seeds of further state weakening and collapse.

Take the case of the Democratic Republic of Congo, as presented by Pierre Englebert. To many, Congo is emblematic of the phenomenon of state collapse, although the author points to its surprising resilience (reflected in most citizens' continued belief in its viability) in the face of its own structural weaknesses and extremely adverse international conditions. With per capita GDP in 2000 at one-third of its 1960 value and buffeted by years of internal conflict, Congo is a profile in mismanagement and predation. But Congo's failure to deliver economic growth and political rights to its population has come under two forms of government—the powerful, centralized dictatorship of Joseph Mobutu and the decentralized control of warlords of the post-Mobutu era. What the two forms of government shared, however, was an abiding commitment to using the state or state-like institutions to reward certain individuals and small groups. Under Mobutu, the government asserted unchallenged control of the national polity and economy, making the generation of wealth entirely dependent on access to political office or on the president's good graces. Mineral wealth and patronage continually fed this beast. In the wake of Mobutu's demise, rebel leader Laurent Kabila sought to replicate his national system of predation, but Kabila was constantly challenged by armed groups in the east and north that began to carve out regions of control for their own exploitative purposes. State weakness, rather than state strength, enabled corrupt elites of the ruling government and armed groups to continue looting the country's resources at the expense of the population. An equilibrium of predation still dominates Congo and the country's poverty continues, even as the faces at the helm change.

Such state-sponsored predation is exacerbated in countries that are rich in resources, such as Congo and Nigeria. As Peter Lewis explains, Nigeria's oil wealth changed the basic calculus of its governing elites, shifting their concern from revenue generation to distribution of proceeds from the sale of oil derived mainly from abroad. Political competition thus focuses on gaining access for one's own group to state resources and limiting the claims of other groups. Democratic deficits result in these *rentier* states, and the development of organized opposition groups that appeal to national (rather than communal) and public (rather than private) goals is suppressed. In his chapter on Myanmar, David Steinberg tells a similar story about a different governing institution—the military. Amid great poverty, Myanmar's military rulers exist in a "self-constructed cocoon" with access to well-managed and well-equipped educational and health institutions, food and staples at subsidized prices, and housing and jobs provided through military-run commercial operations. The wealth generated from the country's natural resources, foreign direct investment, foreign assistance, and the drug trade has gone to finance increasing the power and scope of the military, with benefits only narrowly distributed to the population.

While corruption is characteristic of many failing states, it is not a sufficient condition for state deterioration and collapse. Indonesia, for example, prospered under the rule of General Suharto, even in an environment of political clientelism and corruption. Andrew MacIntyre hypothesizes that Suharto's effective state bureaucracy managed to keep corruption at tolerable levels, making sure that it did not become too expensive or so unpredictable as to deter investment. Organized, controlled corruption, he suggests, can coexist with poverty-reducing growth, if the state has the incentive and capacity to control it.

—*International actors play a part in creating and replicating poorly performing governments.* The country studies point to the critical role of the international community in supporting, emboldening, and replicating ineffective governments in weak and failing states. Three distinct patterns can be drawn out.

The first pattern is the standard cold war–era story of superpower support for tin pot dictators, in which geostrategic interests trump development considerations. The rise of Mobutu in Congo and the Burmese military dictatorship both can be linked to U.S. strategic investments in stemming the spread of communism in the developing world. But such *realpolitik* considerations were not limited to preventing the spread of Soviet influence. The U.S. and other international actors have taken a permissive attitude toward unconstitutional regime change and rule in Nigeria and Indonesia, primarily because they have been more concerned with protecting access to vital energy sources (in Nigeria) and maintaining regional stability (in Indonesia). This pattern continually repeats itself: recent examples include U.S. backing for Laurent Kabila and his son Joseph in Congo, both of whom took power unconstitutionally in 1997 and 2001, respectively. The problem here is that such transitions, while they may remove bad regimes, do little to change the incentives for local elites to exploit state resources and so feed corruption.

The second pattern is described in Sheila Carapico's chapter on Yemen. There, instead of propping up personalistic dictatorships, the international donor community has been constructing unwieldy, illegitimate state structures that are no more than the "sum of past aid projects." Infusions of foreign assistance to the governments of both North and South Yemen, before their unification, led to the organization of highly centralized states and enshrined public sector dominance of the economy; access to political power became a key channel for wealth accumulation. Carapico details how eight to ten aid agencies competed with one another in the water sector in the 1980s, building parallel national government institutions to manage supply and demand, and by 1997 ironically recommended a return to indigenous, local water management.

Martha Brill Olcott elucidates the third pattern in her description of reform trajectories in Central Asia. Western aid-givers, she argues, began to believe that states in Central Asia were not really "ready" for political and economic reform given their experience under Soviet rule, effectively giving autocrats an out—allowing them to centralize power, restrict civil liberties, and institutionalize corruption in the transitional years. Here, support for dictators was not explicit, as in Congo and Burma. Yet the rhetorical commitment of the United States and other international partners to democratic opening was never realized in practice. Political stability has been the result— four of the five men at the helm in 1991 are still in charge—but at the cost of rising authoritarianism, the crushing of political discontent, and the plundering of public resources.

—*Policy choices cannot be ignored.* Because poverty is such a critical determinant of state deterioration, the role of economic policy choices in determining a state's trajectory should not be underestimated. Good policy choices are characteristic of the resilient countries described in this volume.

In Indonesia, Suharto used his autocratic authority to make the country grow. MacIntyre describes how the government, in conjunction with the International Monetary Fund, implemented a dramatic macroeconomic stabilization program that introduced responsible fiscal management, a stable exchange rate, and an open capital account. A flood of foreign investment followed. Suharto took the revenues from the oil boom of 1973 and invested heavily in key public goods including roads and infrastructure, education, and health. When commodity prices dropped, the Suharto regime unleashed a host of liberalizing reforms, leading to a boom in manufactured exports and increasing diversification of the economy. MacIntyre explains that although many highly contentious policy reforms and adjustments were required, the Suharto government used its autocratic authority to make rapid changes without too much instability.

Olcott uses the divergent reform trajectories of Kazakhstan and Kyrgyzstan on one hand and of Uzbekistan on the other to demonstrate the importance of making economic adjustments to reduce poverty and increase state capacity. Kyrgyzstan was the first post-Soviet state to engage in financial restructuring. Kazakhstan exhibited a strong banking sector and pro-investment policies quickly after independence. Both countries moved rapidly to privatize ownership of land, reorganize the social safety net, invest in education, and bring spending under control. They have grown faster than their neighbors, and in spite of some political backsliding, Olcott argues that neither faces imminent threat of failure.

She explains that Uzbekistan, on the other hand, faltered under the leadership of President Islam Karimov, who employed decisionmaking models from the Soviet era. His restrictions on private ownership and trade have devastated the Uzbek economy and severely undermined the reform efforts of other Central Asian states that rely on its domestic market, industrial sector, and transportation networks. The Uzbek government now finds itself largely cut off from international assistance, with a growing threat from radical Islamic forces in the country.[37] One need only look at the economic policy choices adopted by the Burmese military government, the Nigerian government during its oil economy's boom-and-bust cycle, and Mobutu's policies of "Zaireanization" for further evidence of the harm done by poor economic policy choices.

Political leaders' ability to shape their own trajectory is not limited to choices about the economy. Political policy choices can also make a difference. For example, in the late 1990s, Indonesia was hit with two radical shocks—the Asian financial crisis and the breakdown of the Suharto regime. MacIntyre argues that severe economic pressure from the economic reversal in 1997 upset the delicate balance of political forces that had kept the Suharto regime afloat. With the collapse of a highly centralized and effective autocratic bureaucracy, Indonesia experienced an upsurge in various forms of deadly violence, including armed regional uprisings. In addition, the popular discontent unleashed by the democratic opening gave rise to a highly fractious and weak political system—the exact reverse of what predominated under Suharto's rule. MacIntyre argues that the limited progress in reversing Indonesia's decline after Suharto is a key consequence of weak political institutions, the high turnover among political elites, and the inability of the executive and legislative branches to reach agreement on policy reforms. While it is too early to say, key institutional reforms—including the establishment of direct presidential elections, which brought president Susilo Bambang Yudhyono to power in 2004, and consolidation of the party system—promise to address the underlying causes of weak national leadership that have threatened Indonesia's recovery.

While Indonesian reforms made greater centralization and executive power the priority for achieving stability, Nigeria provides an example of political policy choices that institutionalized greater decentralization. Lewis argues that following the devastating civil war in Biafra, the Nigerian government obtained a broad social peace by transforming the political system—instituting two tiers of state and local governments, establishing a new formula for allocating central government revenues, and setting in place constitutional changes to preserve communal diversity in appointments and distributive policies. In subsequent years, Lewis shows how predatory political leaders mismanaged those new institutions. Nonetheless, Nigeria as a state has shown resilience in the face of communal tensions. National political institutions that protect the rights of competing groups are undoubtedly part of its limited success.

—Transitional periods are critical, yet reformers face an uphill battle. Weak and failing states are especially vulnerable to exogenous shocks, and it is during transitional periods that downward trends may be initiated, reinforced, or reversed. Yemen provides a good example. Carapico argues that the newly unified Yemen of 1990—North and South Yemen were brought together largely to maximize the economic gains from their joint production of oil from common deposits—was particularly susceptible to exogenous shocks, dependent as it was on international assistance and foreign direct investment. Carapico shows how the Yemeni government's vote in the Security Council against the Gulf War of 1990 was devastating to Yemen, leading to the loss of most sources of revenue, including private remittances and international aid and investment flows, in the period that followed. The domestic economy went into a tailspin and southern separatists emerged, with the goal of attempting to recapture access to resources by establishing their own state. Weak government bureaucracies propped up by international financing collapsed, and fighting broke out.

Indonesia provides another example. MacIntyre points to the exogenous shock of the Asian financial crisis as the key impetus for the collapse of the Suharto regime. Economic insecurity exposed the lack of national consensus around Suharto's increasingly rigid dictatorship, and his collapse unleashed pent-up demands from across the archipelago, giving rise to criminal and political violence of unforeseen proportions.

The challenge is that when existing arrangements are upset, the competition for power tends to reflect the patterns of behavior exhibited by the previous governing regime. Weak governments tend to replicate themselves.

The collapse of the Soviet Union eliminated the West's need for Mobutu in Congo. As Englebert shows, Mobutu was deprived virtually overnight of the sustained flow of funds that had propped up his political regime. Laurent Kabila then mounted his armed challenge, greeted with cheers from the Congolese population and the international community. Yet Englebert argues that on arrival in Kinshasa, Kabila tried to install a system of personal rule similar to that of Mobutu, albeit with a slightly revised set of beneficiaries. Political openings in societies organized around state predation may be merely opportunities for new coalitions of individuals to capture control of the state.

Even when new forces embrace political and institutional change, the problems left by their predecessors can be a serious impediment to reform. Lewis demonstrates that President Obasanjo, Nigeria's first elected president in twenty years, faced an uphill battle. The institutions of government were depleted by years of mismanagement and plundering, resources were scarce, huge debts were left by departed dictators, and new democratic freedoms released communal tensions that Nigeria's untested political institutions were unprepared to handle. The most serious problem, Lewis suggests, is that Nigeria is characterized by a "social dilemma"—one in which individuals pursue individual interests at the expense of collective welfare. This equilibrium, developed over time and reflecting communal tensions, is difficult to change even when reform advocates emerge.

—The replacement of an individual ruler can make a big difference if it is accompanied by formal institutional change. It is clear that past patterns of state deterioration and predation have remarkable staying power. Even when political change occurs and rulers are replaced, we find that new leaders replicate past patterns of poor performance. Simply look at the experiences of Myanmar, Congo, Nigeria, Yemen, and Uzbekistan. The international community has been all too comfortable with shallow regime change, especially in the poorest countries.

The country studies suggest that stemming the tide of state deterioration requires much more substantial action than installing a revolving door for changes of autocratic, predatory leaders. Formal institutional reforms supported by a new political consensus can reduce political elites' incentives to exploit the state, thereby arresting deterioration.

Susan Burgerman's essay on the experience of postconflict reconstruction in Central America provides some critical pieces of evidence. Although she is careful to elucidate the fundamental challenges still facing the recovering states there, her review of the postconflict experiences of El Salvador and Guatemala points to a critical lesson: formal constitutional, legislative, and institutional reforms laid the foundation for peace, growth, economic diversification, poverty reduction, and increasing political freedom in the 1990s.

Postconflict peace accords made this type of radical change possible. In looking at the Salvadoran accords, Burgerman describes the fundamental electoral and security sector reforms agreed to and mandated by the competing parties. Political parties were given a greater voice in electoral decision-making and voter registration; a new, independent electoral tribunal was established; the police function was separated from that of the armed forces; and major reforms were launched to promote judicial independence. The Guatemalan accords also codified substantial institutional changes in both political parties and the security sector, while the negotiation process provided an opportunity for civil groups to build capacity and express their opinions about future political structures. While substantial impediments to fully formed democratic institutions remain in both countries, parties from across the political spectrum have largely respected the institutional changes made, and progress in development has followed. Indeed, in 2004 five Central American countries negotiated a free trade accord with the United States—something that would have seemed entirely implausible in the mid-1990s.

Burgerman's discussion of the experience in Nicaragua sounds a note of caution. While the postconflict environment provides a unique opportunity to formalize changes in institutions, that opportunity can be quickly lost if a settlement does not mandate reform and provide the political push to implement it. In Nicaragua, Burgerman explains, there was no negotiation agenda and the peace agreement failed to commit the government to the reintegration of all parties, to reform in the security sector, and to political development. Burgerman concludes that without a negotiation process and a firm commitment to reform in the postconflict period, no clear political consensus emerged and Nicaragua struggled its way through the 1990s with a highly polarized polity and weak institutions.

The Central American cases provide important examples of recovering states and how best to use the postconflict period to lay the foundation for state reconstruction.

—*Changing the political incentives that give rise to poor performance is not easy and may require willingness to depart from past practices.* The country studies do little to increase confidence that significant changes in the domestic practices of poorly performing governments can be brought about by standard diplomatic practices. Indeed, the clearest cases of positive change, those in which states emerged from a period of extended state deterioration or avoided sliding into failure, seem to be a consequence of idiosyncratic developments.

Nigeria's emergence as a democratic power in West Africa did not result from underlying changes in the incentives shaping political behavior in the country. Indeed, Nigeria, which still has a petroleum monoculture, battles intense communal politics and is withering under the competing demands of different ethnic groups, regions, and political factions. However, it did emerge from years of international isolation and decline when its dictator, Sani Abacha, died suddenly, providing some wiggle room for reformers to take a stab at democratic governance. It is too early to know whether it will succeed.

Indonesia's transformation from benevolent dictatorship to nascent democracy and now, slowly, to a consolidated democracy was helped along by a series of unforeseen developments: the Asian financial crisis, gradual recovery, and increasing international attention to the region following the terrorist attacks of September 11, 2001, and the Bali nightclub bombing of October 12, 2002. The Indonesian government is now mounting substantial institutional reforms, which MacIntyre sees as critical to preventing any further state deterioration, with the active support and attention of the United States and other international actors.

Across the country studies, however, the diplomatic actions of external actors have more consistently only reinforced the process of state deterioration, albeit with different faces at the helm of government. Englebert's story of Congo's cycling through predatory leaders shows U.S. support for the next "reformer" every time. In Myanmar, U.S. support for the military dictatorship in the 1970s and 1980s turned into a policy of total isolation, one that has heightened the irrational fears of the regime and led to greater consolidation of military control.

These case studies pose questions rather than offer answers regarding the utility of constructive engagement compared with that of isolation as a strategy for shaping state behavior in the worst-performing states. But as Englebert makes clear in his plea for a reevaluation of the tendency to simply continue the flow of assistance, or "life support," to failing states, the very notion of sovereignty is at stake in thinking about how to prevent state collapse. To the extent that the problems of poverty and institutional weakness are self-reinforcing and that regime change only replicates mismanagement and pre-dation, the international community may need to fundamentally rethink its commitment to protecting, first and foremost, the sovereignty of states. In many of these environments, what is needed is a new social contract between the population and its government—one difficult to form unless institutions are entirely upended and renegotiated, as in the case of postconflict Central America.

U.S. Policy toward Poor Performers

The country studies that make up Part I of the volume offer useful lessons to policymakers on the primary causes of poor performance. Part II evaluates the appropriateness and effectiveness of policy levers currently used by U.S. policymakers charged with formulating strategies toward poorly performing states. What is the role of the international community, specifically the United States, in engaging poorly performing governments? What policy instruments are likely to play an important role in building the capacities of such states and preventing a slide into failure? Experts in five distinct policy domains offer answers to these questions in their examination of five tools commonly employed by policymakers: foreign assistance, trade and market access, foreign direct investment, security sector assistance, and promotion of democracy.

Foreign Assistance

Carol Lancaster argues that U.S. foreign assistance can help encourage reform and reward progress in poorly performing states where the political elites are willing to make good policy choices. Where the elites aggressively resist reform, foreign assistance may have little if any impact in the short term.

Lancaster presents a set of guiding principles for building an enlightened foreign assistance policy designed to prevent state failure. She argues for a policy that is comprehensive and sustained, one with the heft to positively influence the cost-benefit calculations of political elites who stand in the way of political and economic reform. Wary of cookie-cutter approaches, she warns that U.S. assistance programs must be designed and implemented on a case-by-case basis, adjusting the ratio of carrots to sticks to reflect the incen-tive structures in a given country and the particular factors that render a gov-ernment prone to institutional deterioration. Lancaster also cautions that there may be cases in which foreign assistance by itself (irrespective of the amount) will not be sufficient to prod elites to adopt sensible policies. Here, other approaches—including military intervention—may be more suitable and should remain on the table.

She argues that if assistance is to be used effectively, these principles must be accompanied by corresponding organizational changes within the U.S. government. She recommends establishing a permanent entity within the State Department—led by a senior-level director—that would be responsible for providing U.S. government leadership on weak and failing states. Such an entity would be complemented by a counterpart at the National Security Council, lending White House credibility to the effort. With a high-level mandate, improved coordination, and perhaps most important, political will at the highest levels, the U.S. government could reverse the bureaucratic inertia that has plagued serious engagement with poorly performing states. She concludes by emphasizing that while getting the U.S. house in order is necessary, "going it alone" is not likely to be productive. A revamped U.S. approach must be linked to a strengthened international capacity for responding to state failure. She calls for the creation of a small international organization to take the lead in conducting early warning operations and coordinating bilateral and multilateral efforts in weak and failing states. Such a body would be the natural locus for coordinating activities to eliminate international incentives for poor performance, such as the Kimberley process on conflict diamonds, multilateral efforts to counteract money laundering, and much-talked-about initiatives on transparency in the extractive industries.

It is heartening to note that several of Lancaster's central recommendations have either been implemented or are under serious consideration by the highest levels of the executive branch of the U.S. government. With support from Congress and at the direction of the National Security Council, the State Department established the Office of the Coordinator for Reconstruction and Stabilization in July 2004 to "lead, coordinate, and institutionalize U.S. government civilian capacity to prevent or prepare for post-conflict situations, and to help stabilize and reconstruct societies in transition from conflict or civil strife."[38] The office has an initial staff of approximately thirty-five people, with representatives from U.S. government agencies such as USAID; the Departments of Defense, Justice, and the Treasury; and the CIA. The office is a positive though modest start in enhancing U.S. civilian capacity in this area. The office hopes to increase its staff to eighty employees and has asked for $100 million in the fiscal year 2006 budget to finance its operations;

however, budget shortfalls threaten to limit the effectiveness and sustainability of the office.

USAID has also taken modest steps toward increasing the visibility of poorly performing states in its day-to-day operations. In August 2004, USAID issued its Fragile States Strategy, which seeks to "imbed a fragile states business model" within the agency. Among other things, the strategy proposes the creation of contingency financing mechanisms for rapid response teams that could be mobilized and deployed to crisis areas and for new early warning and strategic planning capacities within the agency.

Finally, the Department of Defense has proposed sweeping reforms that would elevate the priority that poorly performing states receive within the massive Pentagon bureaucracy. A recent Defense Science Board study advised the secretary of defense that the Pentagon had not focused sufficiently on operations in postconflict or crisis environments—"stability operations" in Pentagon parlance—and that more, not fewer, countries such as Haiti, Afghanistan, and Iraq will surely be on the military's agenda in the coming years. In response, Secretary of Defense Donald Rumsfeld has ordered a major Defense Department strategy review to recommend organizational changes that would further institutionalize and prioritize stability operations within the department.

Individually, these reforms reflect increased recognition of the fact that state failure is a growing threat to U.S. security interests. Collectively, however, they do not amount to the coherent strategy recommended by Lancaster, nor do they address the problem of diffusion of responsibility. In order to implement coherent policies on poorly performing states, the U.S. government will need to adopt a "whole-of-government" approach that integrates the skills and talents of USAID, the Departments of State and Defense, and at least a dozen more government entities ranging from the Department of Agriculture to the Peace Corps.

Trade and Market Access

Arvind Panagariya's chapter on trade policy contends that deficiencies in governance, not barriers to trade, are at the root of economic failure in poorly performing states. Panagariya points out that over the past few decades, developing countries have all enjoyed similar levels of market access, yet there has been significant divergence in their growth rates. Countries that have experienced significant growth have done so because of the economic policy choices they have made, not the preferential market access they have been given.

If U.S. policymakers wish to provide greater market access to poorly performing states, Panagariya believes that they should do so by concentrating their energies on full-scale multilateral liberalization rather than the use of unilateral trade preferences or bilateral free trade agreements. He argues that multilateral liberalization is more favorable for several reasons. First, poorly performing states are more reliant on regional and neighboring country markets than on U.S. or European Union markets. Unlike unilateral or bilateral arrangements, only multilateral liberalization will reduce the barriers to trade in key developing countries. Second, under a multilateral regime, developed countries cannot pick and choose the imports that they grant preferential treatment. Under existing unilateral trade preference arrangements, the U.S. and the EU have been highly selective in deciding precisely which imports can enter their markets at low (or zero) tariff rates. Unilateral arrangements such as the United States' African Growth and Opportunity Act and the EU's Everything but Arms initiative, for example, have intentionally excluded imports in "sensitive" sectors such as agriculture, apparel, and textiles. Under a multilateral regime, developed countries could not impose such barriers to key exports of the developing world such as rice, sugar, cotton, footwear, and textiles. Finally, a global multilateral regime provides positive incentives for the poor performers to liberalize their own markets *and* for developed countries to fully open their markets to sensitive textile and apparel imports from developing countries.

Panagariya's suggestion that preferential arrangements are not a panacea, particularly for the worst-performing states, is an important contribution to the debate. Yet new empirical research on the impact of the African Growth and Opportunity Act—an initiative designed to grant sub-Saharan Africa substantial access to U.S. markets—provides some evidence of the utility of one-way arrangements. William Cline calls AGOA "a major achievement," with more than 75 percent of exports from eligible countries now entering the United States duty free. In addition, non-oil exports from AGOA-eligible countries to the United States have rapidly increased in recent years, rising by 3.8 percent (relative to non-oil exports from other non-OECD countries) in the period following the AGOA's implementation.[39] In addition to the obvious cases of Nigeria and South Africa, the AGOA has also yielded several other success stories. For instance, exports to the United States from the tiny African nation of Lesotho have almost doubled in the past few years, jumping from $215 million in 2001 to nearly $400 million in 2003. Since AGOA's inception, the garment and textile industry has exploded in Lesotho: in 2003 textiles or apparel accounted for approximately 99 percent of the country's exports to the United States. According to the U.S. trade representative, thanks to AGOA, 2003 marked the first time in Lesotho's history that private sector manufacturing employment exceeded government employment.[40]

Even Panagariya admits that with greater product coverage, more flexible rules of origin requirements, and an extended time horizon, the development impact of unilateral arrangements (such as AGOA and the Office of the U.S Trade Representative's Generalized System of Preferences) could be substantially enhanced, with real benefits to the poorest countries.

Foreign Direct Investment

Conventional wisdom often holds that the poorest countries are unlikely to attract significant foreign direct investment (FDI) in the nonextractive and noninfrastructure sectors. In contrast to that gloomy prognosis, Theodore Moran argues that the challenges of luring investors, generating economic growth, and reducing poverty "have proven quite surmountable" for several poor countries. Citing Mauritius and the Dominican Republic as examples, he commends the use of export processing zones (EPZs), which, if implemented properly, can attract FDI by eliminating duties on capital expenditures, providing competitively priced infrastructure, and otherwise shielding foreign investors from adverse operating conditions.

However, establishing EPZs that offer enticements to foreign investors is not enough to generate investment. According to Moran, host countries must also let foreign investors decide where to locate such zones, allowing them to choose sites with ready access to economic centers and modestly skilled workers. Perhaps more important is that a key determinant of the success or failure of EPZs is the degree to which host countries pursue sound economic policies that help establish an inviting investment climate. A stable macroeconomic environment with a low rate of inflation and a steady exchange rate, access to duty-free imports and reliable infrastructure (roads, ports, and so forth), and a reliable legal-regulatory framework go a long way toward attracting and sustaining foreign direct investment.

However, it is likely that even under the best circumstances foreign investors will be hesitant to invest in many poorly performing countries. For that reason, Moran concludes that developed countries like the United States must play a role in encouraging FDI through a package of incentives that might tip the scales for investors reluctant to accept the risk of putting their money in potentially unstable environments. Specifically, Moran urges the U.S. government to make better use of existing mechanisms such as the

Overseas Private Investment Corporation (OPIC), one of the United States' quasi-official export credit agencies, which are either underutilized or precluded from supporting many types of foreign direct investment in the developing world. Currently, legislative statute forbids OPIC from providing political risk insurance or loan guarantees to companies investing in "sensitive sectors" (such as textiles, footwear, electronics, and so forth) and prohibits support for foreign companies with a substantial presence in the United States. Moran provides a compelling case for revision of the OPIC's mandate and practices to facilitate greater investment in sensitive sectors and support for foreign companies with a large presence in the United States. Moran also proposes utilizing other agencies of the U.S. government, such as the Foreign Commercial Service and the Foreign Service, to more effectively identify potential foreign investment projects, not just export opportunities.

Security Sector Assistance

In their review of U.S. military and police assistance to poorly performing states, Adam Isacson and Nicole Ball argue that internal political crises in these countries feed the unhealthy growth of security forces. Police and military institutions are highly embedded in these countries' economies, political systems, and even social services, making it impossible to think of the security sector outside of a development context. Reforming social services in many of these countries without addressing the role of the security sector often results in only partial or unsustainable reforms. Isacson and Ball suggest that reforming the security sector in poorly performing states must be part and parcel of a larger, more comprehensive strategy to address deficiencies of governance.

Isacson and Ball examine the U.S. provision of security sector assistance to four subgroups of poor performers: frontline states in the "war on terrorism"; other states of strategic importance; lower-priority countries; and countries that receive low levels of security assistance due to legislative or policy bans. They find that the frontline states—such as Afghanistan, Pakistan, the Central Asian states, and so forth—account for a disproportionate share of U.S. security sector assistance. According to the authors, twenty-nine of the forty-seven countries that fall into these four subgroups received less than $2 million in U.S. security assistance between 2000 and 2004. Moreover, weapons and equipment transfers are largely reserved for frontline states and, to a lesser degree, for states of strategic importance, while the remaining poor performers receive only modest amounts of peacekeeping training, technical assistance, and educational programming.

The authors also challenge the wisdom of America's current security sector policies on a number of other fronts. They criticize the tendency to focus on short-term gains (equipment transfers to frontline states) at the expense of long-term objectives (civilian oversight of the military and democratic accountability). They argue that this lopsided approach has serious negative consequences, including the overall effect of "making weak states weaker." Isacson and Ball express concern that providing massive amounts of material assistance to security forces with questionable reputations in the short term may reduce the leverage that the United States has over them in the long term; inadvertently increase regional insecurity; and reward corrupt elites who flout the rule of law with impunity. An important byproduct of recent trends, they write, is a shift away from civilian programs run by the Departments of Justice and State and by USAID toward a much greater role for the Department of Defense. The net result is a security assistance policy that lacks transparency and coherence and that ultimately is governed by the Pentagon rather than by U.S. officials "charged with guaranteeing the full spectrum of U.S. interests." Isacson and Ball recommend that the State Department reclaim its leading role—as legislated in the Foreign Assistance Act—in setting security assistance policy.

It is an undeniable reality that the United States will always provide large amounts of foreign assistance to countries that it deems necessary to protecting its national security; a cursory look at U.S. aid programs to Israel and Egypt demonstrates the point. Security concerns, such as the threat of terrorism or "loose nukes," will require continued provision of large security assistance packages to frontline states and states of strategic importance. However, in providing security sector assistance to those countries, the United States should preserve a healthy balance between short-term security priorities and the longer-term goal of improving their civilian security and border control agencies and increasing the transparency of their security budgets and military resources.

Promotion of Democracy

The final chapter, on assistance in promoting democracy, begins with the premise that successful development is as dependent on sound political choices as economic ones—if not more. That sentiment is clearly echoed in work undertaken by the World Bank on the influence of good governance on the effectiveness of aid as well as in the United Nations' recent emphasis on democracy and good governance as preconditions for human development.[41]

As David Yang points out, there is an active debate about the efficacy of U.S. efforts to promote democracy. While Yang hails the USAID's existing Democracy and Governance (DG) framework, which underpins U.S. strategic planning for democracy assistance, he argues that USAID's weak analysis of in-country governance has resulted in unfocused and ineffective programming. Using Haiti, Kenya, and Cambodia as case studies, he demonstrates that U.S. programs have yielded limited results "that reflect a conceptually shallow approach to democracy promotion."

In Haiti, USAID was forced to implement its democracy and governance programs in a daunting political environment, one in which President Jean-Bertrand Aristide was mired in a deadlock with his political opponents, who accused Aristide's supporters of rigging the 2000 parliamentary elections. While the DG framework identified the key political issues of the day, Yang believes that it contained no real analysis of the nature of the problems or the actors and institutions that must be involved in crafting a solution. In Yang's estimation the USAID mission made no mention of existing or possible reform activities in the five areas of the framework (consensus, rule of law, competition, inclusion, and governance). As a result of vague (or absent) analysis, the resulting programming—in civil society, elections, governance, and rule of law—was "at once comprehensive and superficial." Lacking a democracy strategy that focused on specific results, USAID provided aid across the board by devising cookie-cutter programs that lacked creativity or selectivity. For instance, Yang heralds USAID's decision to fund a new nationwide coalition of civil groups yet argues that the USAID mission should have had a better understanding of the coalition's target. If USAID had analyzed specific ways in which Aristide had clamped down on political and economic freedoms, according to Yang, it could have distinguished among the ways in which the media, nongovernmental organizations (NGOs), and political parties could be reformed and strengthened.

To be fair, the cases examined by Yang represent three of the more difficult environments in which to implement democracy programs. For example, Yang describes USAID's efforts in Kenya as "a donor casting many seeds to the wind in the hope that some will find fertile soil." Yet one could tell a very different story about USAID's work in Kenya. USAID-financed NGOs established the Kenyan Anti-Corruption Coalition, which has worked toward drafting a new anticorruption law to replace the previous law, which was ruled unconstitutional. USAID also provided crucial assistance to civil groups that have assumed a parliamentary watchdog role—including monitoring and influencing important budget proceedings. However, quantifying the success of USAID's work is difficult because democratic progress and change rarely happen overnight and causal relationships are not always easy to decipher.

Yang offers several proposals for how the United States might overhaul its strategic planning process for delivering democracy assistance to ensure that it is tackling the most critical issues, working with the most effective reformers, and targeting the right institutions. He calls for renewed emphasis on strong analysis that can act as the foundation for a refined DG framework and that ranks issues by their importance. Yang also believes that USAID should adopt the framework as official agency policy—to strengthen its implementation—and require senior agency officials in Washington to review and scrutinize the framework, particularly the analytical portions.

Appropriateness and Effectiveness of U.S. Policy Levers

Earlier, we highlighted several key themes that emerged from the country studies, which attempt to diagnose the causes of poor performance across a wide array of states. A review of the five chapters on policy instruments reveals four key lessons that might inform future U.S. engagement with poorly performing states in the developing world.

—*Reforming governance should be a central objective of U.S. policy in poorly performing countries.* The chapters in this volume present compelling evidence that political and economic policy decisions made by elites have tremendous influence on a country's development. When governments make poor policy choices, their development prospects suffer, and despite donors' best intentions, governance failures make it very difficult to realize gains. It comes as no surprise, then, that U.S. policy instruments have had a marginal impact, at best, when elites stood in the way of positive reform and progress.

Yet if the intent to reform and pursue sound policies exists, these policy instruments can be quite effective. Lancaster cites the example of U.S. foreign assistance to South Korea, which struggled in the 1950s to achieve results in the context of a poor policy environment, including a government opposed to reform. In the 1960s, when reform-minded Park Chung Hee assumed power and adopted pro-growth policies, aid contributed to rapid progress in development. Lancaster cites similar experiences with U.S. foreign assistance in Tanzania, Ghana, Bolivia, and Vietnam. Arvind Panagariya refers to analogous examples in the trade arena. From the 1950s to the 1970s, most developing countries pursued isolationist economic policies that shunned integration in the global trading regime. But a few—namely Asian nations such as Korea, Taiwan, Singapore, and Hong Kong—decided to play in global markets, and the result was sustained economic growth. Their experience was then replicated in Indonesia, India, Vietnam, Chile, and Uganda. In his chapter on foreign direct investment, Theodore Moran also argues that willingness to reform and establish a sound policy environment is a prerequisite for growth and development. Moran cites as recent examples the experiences of two low-income countries, Madagascar and Lesotho. Both made decisive reforms to liberalize their economies and provide tangible incentives to foreign investors. Madagascar awarded EPZ status to foreign investors regardless of where in the country they chose to base their operations; as a result, 120 firms set up shop in Madagascar within the first five years. Similarly, Lesotho managed to employ similar incentives to attract fifty-five foreign-export-oriented manufacturing firms to initiate operations in-country.

When the intent to reform is lacking, policymakers will have to dig deeper for another set of tools that may make a difference in such environments. These might include sanctions, diplomacy, and even military intervention. And as Lancaster points out, there may be cases—such as Zimbabwe—where no amount of foreign assistance will be able to convince the leader and the entrenched elites to change course and adopt prudent policies.

A willingness to take risks is crucial to any strategy for counteracting further state decline and collapse. Lancaster argues for continuing assistance to poor performers "where the performance of governments is not so bad" that any efforts to improve socioeconomic progress are doomed to fail. She believes that such aid is crucial, so that when improvements in governance finally arrive, the country has sufficient human and economic resources to take full advantage. Aid over the long term may also help tilt the cost-benefit calculations of elites toward implementing reform. As education and civil systems are strengthened, the demand for better governance also will increase.

—*Policy instruments have varying impacts depending on the nature of the political and economic environment in which they are deployed.* When constructing country strategies, U.S. policymakers must resist the temptation to generalize about all poor performers. While many poor performers exhibit common characteristics, each country is different—its demographics, particular fault lines, and sources of instability can vary greatly. Policy instruments, such as foreign assistance or debt relief, are likely to have different impacts in different contexts.

Arguing that inadequate situation-specific analysis has been the Achilles heel of U.S. democracy promotion efforts in poorly performing countries,

David Yang posits that a more strategic and in-depth analysis of a country's institutions, key actors, and cross-cutting issues is necessary if the United States is to avoid cookie-cutter democracy programs. According to Yang, the analytical weakness of USAID's DG framework renders its programs "vague and often unjustified."

Yang's discussion of USAID's programming in Cambodia throughout the 1990s illustrates his point well. Though USAID noted in Cambodia the absence of the rule of law and an inclination to resolve disputes on the basis of wealth and political power rather than impartial justice, it failed to analyze which Cambodian political parties took part in the corruption or how ruling elites wielded their power and influence over judicial civil servants. The mission then proposed to provide assistance to civil groups to help foster transparency and greater accountability, yet did not state whether such groups were capable of carrying out impartial monitoring activities that could be linked with government reform initiatives.

Isacson and Ball warn of the unintended consequences that may result from the infusion of U.S. security assistance to security forces in Tajikistan, Turkmenistan, and Uzbekistan—staunch allies in the war on terrorism. Security forces in these countries have committed serious human rights violations and continue to subvert the rule of law. U.S. post-9/11 assistance has only strengthened their hand. "The kind of assistance offered these countries," write Isacson and Ball, "is at best inappropriate and ineffective; at worst, it is counterproductive." In 2002 the United States funded a stepped-up border security program in Tajikistan to prevent the spread of weapons of mass destruction and to curb narcotics trafficking. The following year, the State Department's Bureau of International Narcotics and Law Enforcement reported that Tajik officials are likely involved in the trafficking of illicit goods and that corruption among law enforcement officials runs rampant.

In her chapter on foreign assistance, Lancaster cites the importance of identifying a country's particular risk factors for collapse but, at the same time, recognizes the difficulties in doing so. She mentions ongoing work by the State Failure Task Force, which has produced a number of reports on the factors that contribute to state failure—with a particular emphasis on the impact of the quality of governance on state weakness. Lancaster also commends the work of USAID, which has attempted to categorize risk factors into clusters, such as root causes, facilitating factors, and regional or international factors. This ongoing work offers a promising starting point for identifying when, why, and how states fail, but the bottom line is clear: the U.S. government should continue to invest in research and policy analysis that seeks to identify the conditions under which particular policy interventions are effective in preventing, mitigating, and responding to state failure.[42]

—The U.S. government must be organized and equipped to develop coherent polices toward poorly performing states. Because poor governance stands in the way of progress in many of these environments, fundamental change often requires powerful incentives for reform. In practical terms, the United States needs to speak with one voice on policy matters; dedicate part of the bureaucracy to focus on the problems of these states; issue a high-level mandate to prioritize this set of countries in policy development and implementation; and set in place flexible policy instruments. Only then will U.S. policy have enough muscle and influence to address the challenges faced by the poor performers.

This begins with a better organizational focus in the U.S. government. At present, no specific agency has responsibility for identifying, monitoring, or responding to weak and failing states. Lancaster cites the need for an organizational locus for preventing and reversing state failure and proposes setting up a permanent bureau within the Department of State as well as corresponding entity at the National Security Council that can identify weak and failing states and develop appropriate response strategies. In addition, the U.S. government does not speak with a unified voice on development issues; in fact, it often speaks in contradictory ones. Isacson and Ball describe how, as a result of the atrophying of civilian agencies, U.S. security sector assistance is increasingly being channeled though the Defense Department. Security packages often end up serving short-term goals rather than long-term development imperatives that are, formally, under the purview of the State Department.

If preventing state failure is to be a foreign policy priority, development deserves high-level attention within the bureaucracy. Though the Bush administration has made development a central pillar, along with diplomacy and defense, of U.S. national security, the president's cabinet has no U.S. government advocate for development. The fragmentation of U.S. development policy, the decline of USAID, and the lack of a coherent development budget have hampered U.S. foreign assistance efforts. The U.S. government needs a high-level advocate for development with a political mandate and a seat at the table in key interagency forums.

Finally, the U.S. government must have a high degree of leverage—in terms of carrots and sticks—when dealing with poor performers. When a country is moving away from authoritarian rule, the United States needs the flexibility to provide rapid economic and political assistance to bolster a nascent democratic government. Likewise, as a country emerges from violent conflict, the United States needs to promote the reconstruction process by jump-starting its war-torn economy. This flexibility entails taking advantage of old instruments in new ways. For instance, David Rothkopf argues for greater use of the Overseas Private Investment Corporation in the poorest countries. OPIC is precluded from providing risk insurance or guarantees to investments in "sensitive sectors" (textiles, apparel, and so forth) and can deliver services only at commercial rates; both restrictions impede its capacity to make a difference in the poor performers.[43] At the same time, U.S. policymakers must have the appropriate sticks at their disposal to dissuade decisionmakers from straying from reform or exploiting their control of the state to create private wealth. Without sufficient positive and negative inducements, U.S. policy can prove ineffective, if not damaging.

—*Policymakers must take a long-term perspective when dealing with poor performers.* There are no quick fixes when it comes to transforming the world's poorly performing countries. Engendering economic growth, creating more transparent and accountable institutions, and institutionalizing civilian control over the military are difficult and complex tasks that require patience and persistence. A purist foreign policy that engages the good performers while shunning the poor performers is both unrealistic and shortsighted. Though the direct impact of U.S. democracy programs is difficult to quantify, the 2002 election of President Mwai Kibaki in Kenya demonstrates that investments in democracy and civil society can bear fruit over the long haul. The election was most certainly a popular endorsement of his campaign pledges to curtail corruption and invest in social development—seeds that were sown by U.S.-sponsored democracy and governance programs throughout the 1990s. Moran argues that success in attracting foreign direct investment has required a trial-and-error approach. In Mauritius, providing foreign investors with tax incentives to initiate export operations initially yielded little benefit until the government adopted more aggressive economic reforms and offered investors enhanced flexibility. Isacson and Ball warn of the danger of short-term thinking in the delivery of U.S. security assistance to those countries considered most critical in the U.S.-backed war on terrorism. Even when dealing with these states, they write, "it is not in Washington's interests to simply write checks, ship weapons, and transfer lethal skills." A long-term vision that places short-term goals within a broader framework of U.S. objectives regarding democracy and governance is necessary to ensure the effectiveness of U.S. engagement. Finally, Arvind Panagariya writes that one of the major disadvantages of the West's penchant for unilateral trade preferences is that despite their political utility in the short term, they can give poor countries serious disincentives to liberalize their trade regimes. Because unilateral trade preferences are by definition nonreciprocal, beneficiary countries can receive increased access to developed country markets irrespective of the protectionist nature of their trade policies. That leaves developed countries, such as the United States, with little further leverage to challenge developing countries to continue on the path of political and economic reform.

Conclusion

The ubiquity of weak, failing, and failed states is as astonishing as it is regrettable. A cursory glance at the headlines from the world's leading newspapers on any given day is perhaps the most sobering evidence of the phenomenon. Afghanistan's nascent, embattled transitional government struggles to consolidate its power over the vast hinterlands of its territory and to jump-start its sputtering economy. The international community heralds the start of a new era of peace in war-torn Liberia—the scourge of West Africa throughout the 1990s. New beginnings are also on the horizon in Sudan—which has suffered Africa's longest civil war, at a cost of more than 2 million casualties—as the country's warring parties struggle to agree on the terms of peace. Zimbabwe, under the tyrannical reign of Robert Mugabe, inches closer toward the brink of disaster, its economy in shambles and its society coming apart. Almost daily, disconcerting talk is heard of an impending implosion in an increasingly ungovernable Pakistan.

Despite the absence of a one-size-fits-all palliative for the problems of weak states, new investments in poor performers, a more effective policymaking apparatus, and a more coherent strategy could go a long way toward improving U.S. capacity to better identify, respond to, and prevent state decline and failure. The analyses offered here provide a starting point—a foundation on which U.S. policymakers can build such a strategy. In an increasingly uncertain world, one thing U.S. policymakers can count on is that developing countries that are not making progress will not disappear. In this era of greater interconnectedness, poorly performing states will become more visible and more important as a strategic priority of the United States.

Notes

1. See *The National Security Strategy of the United States*, introduction (Washington: White House, 2002).

2. Center for Global Development, *On the Brink: Weak States and U.S. National Security*, Report of the Commission on Weak States and U.S. National Security (Washington, 2004); Stuart Eizenstat, John Edward Porter, and Jeremy M. Weinstein, "Rebuilding Weak States," *Foreign Affairs* 84 (January-February 2005): 134–46.

3. See Robert S. Chase, Emily B. Hill, and Paul Kennedy, "Pivotal States and U.S. Strategy," *Foreign Affairs* 75 (January-February 1996): 33–51.

4. The anchor states include South Africa, Nigeria, Ethiopia, and Kenya. See the president's Africa policy at www.whitehouse.gov/infocus/africa/.

5. United Nations, Report of the Panel of Experts on Somalia Pursuant to Security Council Resolution 1474 S/2003/1035 (New York: 2003).

6. See the president's March 2002 speech at www.whitehouse.gov/news/releases/2002/03/20020314-7.html.

7. See Craig Burnside and David Dollar, "Aid, Policies, and Growth," *American Economic Review* 90 (September 2000): 847–68. This consensus is not without its detractors. For instance, Michael Clemens, Steven Radelet, and Rikhil Bhavnani ("Counting Chickens When They Hatch: The Short-Term Effect of Aid on Growth," Working Paper 44 [Washington: Center for Global Development, 2004]) found that once aid is disaggregated on the basis of the plausible timeframe of its impact, there is a positive, causal relationship between "short-impact" aid and growth, irrespective of a country's level of income or the quality of its institutions and policies.

8. See Steven Radelet, *Challenging Foreign Aid: A Policymaker's Guide to the Millennium Challenge Account* (Washington: Center for Global Development, 2003), p. 1. Congressional appropriations for the MCA have lagged behind the administration's requests, and the Millennium Challenge Corporation (the governing body of the MCA) also has been slow to disburse funds. Despite its slow pace, the establishment of the MCA has greatly influenced the "selectivity" debate among OECD countries.

9. For the AGOA legislation, see www.agoa.info.

10. See Jeffrey D. Sachs, "The Strategic Significance of Global Inequality," *Washington Quarterly* 24 (Summer 2001): 187–98

11. See Bruce Bueno de Mesquita and Hilton L. Root, "The Political Roots of Poverty: The Economic Logic of Autocracy," *National Interest* 68 (Summer 2002): 27–38.

12. Center for Global Development, *On the Brink*.

13. See Radelet, *Challenging Foreign Aid*, chapter 2, for further elaboration.

14. Sarah Lucas and Steven Radelet, *An MCA Scorecard: Who Qualified, Who Did Not, and the MCC Board's Use of Discretion* (Washington: Center for Global Development, 2004). The board of the MCC, in determining which countries would receive assistance in the program's first year, deviated from a strict application of the indicators by exercising discretion in seven cases.

15. We are grateful to Steve Radelet and Rikhil Bhavnani of the Center for Global Development for sharing and explaining their data on the Millennium Challenge Account, which provide the foundation for our taxonomy.

16. See the World Bank, *World Bank Group Work in Low-Income Countries under Stress: A Task Force Report* (Washington: 2002).

17. See Joanna Macrae and others, *Aid to 'Poorly Performing' Countries: A Critical Review of Debates and Issues* (London: Overseas Development Institute, 2004).

18. See James Fearon and David Laitin, "Ethnicity, Insurgency, and Civil War," *American Political Science Review* 97 (February 2003): 85

19. Ibid.; Paul Collier and others, *Breaking the Conflict Trap: Civil War and Development Policy* (Washington: World Bank, 2003), p. 60.

20. Daron Acemoglu, James A. Robinson, and Simon Johnson, "The Colonial Origins of Comparative Development: An Empirical Investigation," *American Economic Review* 91 (December 2001): 1369–1401.

21. See Terry Karl, *The Paradox of Plenty: Oil Booms and Petro-States* (University of California Press, 1997); Michael Ross, *Timber Booms and Institutional Breakdown in Southeast Asia* (Cambridge University Press, 2001); and Nancy Birdsall and Arvind Subramanian, "Saving Iraq from Its Oil," *Foreign Affairs* 83 (July-August 2004): 77–89.

22. See Collier and others, *Breaking the Conflict Trap*, p. 5.

23. See Fearon and Laitin, "Ethnicity, Insurgency, and Civil War," p. 83.

24. See Dani Rodrik, *In Search of Prosperity* (Princeton University Press, 2003).

25. See Jack A. Goldstone and others, *State Failure Task Force Report: Phase III Findings* (McLean, Va.: Science Applications International Corporation [SAIC], 2000).

26. See Marina Ottaway, *Democracy Challenged: The Rise of Semi-Authoritarianism* (Washington: Carnegie Endowment for International Peace, 2003). For empirical results on the relationship between regime type and conflict, see Fearon and Laitin, "Ethnicity, Insurgency, and Civil War," p. 85, and Havard Hegre and others, "Toward a Democratic Civil Peace? Democracy, Political Change, and Civil War, 1816–1992," *American Political Science Review* 95, no. 1 (March 2001), p. 42.

27. See Collier and others, *Breaking the Conflict Trap*, p. 57.

28. See Jack Snyder, *From Voting to Violence: Democratization and Nationalist Conflict* (New York: W. W. Norton, 2000).

29. See Fearon and Laitin, "Ethnicity, Insurgency, and Civil War," p. 85.

30. See Adam Przeworski and others, *Democracy and Development: Political Institutions and Well-Being in the World, 1950–1990* (Cambridge University Press, 2000), pp. 2–3.

31. Ibid., p. 269.

32. See Robert Bates, *Markets and States in Tropical Africa* (University of California Press, 1981); Richard Joseph, *Democracy and Prebendal Politics in Nigeria* (Cambridge University Press, 1987).

33. See Michael Bratton and Nicolas van de Walle, *Democratic Experiments in Africa: Regime Transitions in Comparative Perspective* (Cambridge University Press, 1997), p. 61.

34. See William Reno, *Warlord Politics and African States* (Boulder, Colo.: Lynne Rienner, 1999).

35. See U.S. Agency for International Development, *Foreign Aid in the National Interest* (Washington: 2001).

36. See Ottaway, *Democracy Challenged*.

37. Post-9/11, the situation has become considerably more complicated because Uzbekistan's proximity to Afghanistan has rendered it a "key strategic partner" in the U.S.-led war on terrorism.

38. U.S. Department of State, *Office of the Coordinator for Reconstruction and Stabilization Fact Sheet* (Washington: 2005).

39. William R. Cline, "Trading Up: Strengthening AGOA's Development Potential," *Center for Global Development Policy Brief* 2, no. 3 (Washington: Center for Global Development, 2003).

40. U.S. Department of Commerce, *U.S.–Sub-Saharan Africa Trade Statistics* (Washington, 2003); U.S. Trade Representative, *Comprehensive Report on U.S. Trade and Investment Policy toward Sub-Saharan Africa and the Implementation of the African Growth and Opportunity Act* (Washington, 2003).

41. See Daniel Kaufmann, Aart Kray, and Pablo Zoido-Lobatón, "Governance Matters," World Bank Policy Research Paper 2196 (Washington: World Bank, 1999); and UN Development Program, *Human Development Report 2003: Millennium Development Goals: A Compact among Nations to End Human Poverty* (New York: 2003).

42. See *State Failure Task Force Report*. See also U.S. Agency for International Development, *U.S. Foreign Aid: Meeting the Challenges of the Twenty-first Century* (Washington: 2004) and *USAID Fragile States Strategy* (Washington: 2005).

43. David J. Rothkopf, *The Price of Peace: Emergency Intervention and U.S. Foreign Policy* (Washington: Carnegie Endowment for International Peace, 1998).

PART II

*Narratives of
State Deterioration*

2

Life Support or Assisted Suicide? Dilemmas of U.S. Policy toward the Democratic Republic of Congo

PIERRE ENGLEBERT

Although occasionally referred to as a failed state, the Democratic Republic of Congo (henceforth, Congo) has been surprisingly resilient in the face of its own structural weaknesses and extremely adverse international conditions.[1] Its avoidance of failure, in contrast to Somalia, for example, is in fact equally if not more remarkable than its dreadful performance as a state. Certainly Congo's institutions are dysfunctional, serving purposes diametrically different from those for which they were created, but they are not failed, as they do fulfill some functions and remain the object of a large social consensus. No doubt Congo is performing poorly, unable for the last five years to assert effective control over its own territory. But it is not failed, as neither rebel groups nor occupying foreign armies have promoted secessionist or irredentist aims, pledging instead their allegiance to the idea of Congo.[2] Unquestionably, the Congolese state has been incapable of preventing the salience and polarization of ethnicity among its populations, but it has not really failed at the nation-building exercise, as its citizens simultaneously continue to display rather fervent nationalist sentiments.[3] Although Congo is a rather dubious member of the family of sovereign states, it can thus be better understood as a stunningly deviant case of the genre rather than a failed one.[4]

The author gratefully acknowledges the excellent research assistance of Rebecca Hummel in the preparation of this chapter.

This chapter begins by describing Congo's long-term trajectory, from its independence as a state in 1960 to its current condition of institutional and economic decrepitude. It then argues that the Congolese state may in fact be little more than a private enterprise of economic predation hiding behind a smokescreen of international sovereignty. While predation at the hands of the political elite bankrupts the state, the international recognition of its sovereignty (with its concurrent flows of aid and investments) has repeatedly saved it from complete failure and allows for its reproduction. Congo poses therefore a very serious policy conundrum for the United States and other Western donors. On the one hand, indefinitely maintaining Congo on life support in the interest of avoiding Afghanistan-like chaos postpones or eschews a more profound and much needed reconfiguration of its political structures. On the other hand, the dangers that a total failure of the state would represent, the country's potential for triggering regional conflicts, and its dire human rights record militate for continued involvement. For the United States as for the Congolese, the dilemma may lie between short-term equilibrium predatory underdevelopment and the deferred but uncertain promises of political reconfiguration.[5] This chapter discusses these issues as well as alternative policy options for the United States.

A Poorly Performing Congo

Whichever way one looks at it, Congo is a basket case. Moreover, while conventional wisdom suggests that its crisis is a relatively recent creation of the post–cold war world, a look at historic trends offers a picture of long-term decline that started as early as the 1970s. Congo's developmental failure is even more stunning in view of its prodigious natural resources, including large quantities of copper, cobalt, gold, diamonds and other minerals, massive hydroelectric potential, oil, fertile lands, and dense forests. The contrast between its endowment and its performance suggests an acute case of the "resource curse."[6]

Figure 2-1 provides a damning snapshot of forty years of mismanagement and predation, showing real gross domestic product in 2000 slightly below its level in 1960 and per capita gross domestic product at about a third of its 1960 value. Only the 1960s and early 1970s provided an era of relative development, with GDP growth averaging 6.9 percent a year despite the tumult of the immediate postindependence era, thanks in part to favorable trends in commodity prices. Decline promptly set in, however, as annual growth averaged 0.2 percent in the 1970s, the equivalent of –1.8 percent in

Figure 2-1. *Democratic Republic of Congo, Real GDP Indexes, 1960–2000*

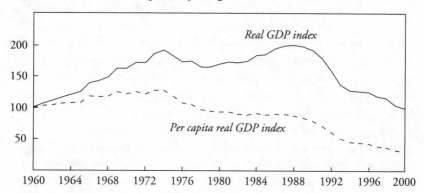

Source: International Monetary Fund, *International Financial Statistics* (Washington: various years); Economist Intelligence Unit, *Democratic Republic of Congo: Country Reports* (London: various years).

per capita terms. The years 1975 and 1976, which followed the "Zaireaniza-tion" episode in which the state seized the assets of foreigners to redistribute them to cronies of President Mobutu (who mostly plundered them for the benefit of their short-term consumption), show declines of 5 percent each. The 1980s failed to register any significant improvement, with continued negative per capita growth as population increased by 3.4 percent a year.[7]

Congo's economic deterioration accelerated sharply from the late 1980s onward, under Mobutu's still little contested stewardship and before West-ern donors stepped up their pressure for democratization. The economy eventually all but collapsed in the 1990s under the combined weight of army lootings, mining infrastructure deterioration, dried-up aid flows, and political chaos. Particularly stunning were the early 1990s, with real GDP contracting by, respectively, 12.3 percent, 10.4 percent, and 13.5 percent in 1991, 1992, and 1993. From 1990 to 1999 Congo lost no less than 44 per-cent of its productive capacity, and individual incomes, weak to begin with, fell by a combined 74 percent. Compounding this apparently endless con-traction of the economy, monetary policy kicked into high gear (as the eco-nomic crisis and Mobutu's international isolation deprived him of the usual means of his patronage policies), and inflation entered four-digit territories and beyond to reach an astounding 23,000 percent in 1993. Although it has since abated, no regime has yet since managed to reduce it below an annual doubling of prices.

Not surprisingly, Congo's long-term economic decline has been accompanied by a deep deterioration of its social sectors. After peaking in 1987 at fifty-one years, life expectancy diminished to about forty-six years in 2000. Child mortality rates increased throughout the 1990s to reach 162 per thousand live births in 2000. Gross primary school enrollment, having reached 98 percent on the eve of independence,[8] maintained levels above 90 percent until the mid-1980s, before contracting and falling to less than 50 percent in the late 1990s. All these numbers compare very unfavorably to average figures for Africa and for low-income countries around the world.[9]

Congo's economic and social collapse of the 1990s is a story of catastrophic governance, as Mobutu's system of personal rule unraveled when the end of the cold war deflated his international currency with the West.[10] According to the annual report of the Banque du Zaire, 95 percent of the country's 1992 budget was earmarked for Mobutu's own discretionary spending, and the government failed to allocate any public monies to education or to pay teachers' salaries.[11] Over the same period, the perceived quality of the state and its institutions remained dismally low, averaging a score of 2 (on a scale of 0 to 10) on a compound index of good governance, which captures freedom from corruption, bureaucratic quality, extent of rule of law, risk of expropriation, and government's commitment to its contractual obligations.[12] Although this had been true for most of the Mobutu years, by the 1990s the state had become an open enterprise of domination and exploitation of the Congolese people, and political rights and civil liberties remained all but nonexistent despite Congo's official "transition" to democracy. According to the Freedom House Gastil Index of political and civil liberties, Congo was among the world's poorest performers, scoring 6.5 throughout the 1990s on a scale from 1 (perfectly free) to 7 (perfectly not free).

The Path of Political Decay

Congo's poor performance as a state has also been most visible recently in its failure to provide peace and security to its citizens and in its occasional propensity to be the cause of their insecurities. The power of the state no longer reaches much beyond Kinshasa. Despite the formal reunification of the country brought about by the Global and Inclusive Agreement of December 2002 among the government, the rebels, and the civilian opposition and the withdrawal of some foreign troops in the second half of that year, most of Congo's territory has remained either under de facto control of the two main rebel groups—the Mouvement de Libération du Congo

(MLC) and the Rassemblement Congolais pour la Démocratie (RCD-Goma)—and of their foreign backers, Uganda and Rwanda, or it has been run on behalf of the government by troops from Angola and Zimbabwe, particularly in the Kasai and Katanga provinces. The relative disengagement of foreign troops has actually coincided with an increase in local insecurity, as competing groups, including the infamous Mai-Mai militias in the east, have vied for political control of regional centers.[13] Although all of them continue to embrace and promote the idea of their state, the Congolese have been at war with themselves since 1998.

For all the chaos and misery of recent years, political violence actually started in the early 1990s as Mobutu let his unpaid troops loose, and several regions experimented with autonomy from Kinshasa. These episodes were marked by a rise in ethnic-based violence (largely manipulated by Mobutu), particularly between populations from the Katanga and Kasai provinces and among different groups of alleged autochthonous and nonautochthonous populations in the Kivu and Orientale provinces. The unleashing of political violence in the 1990s marked in fact the fin de reigne of the Mobutist state, the ultimate failure of a system that for thirty-two years had repressed the contradictions of Congolese society under the tight lid of personal rule.[14]

Mobutu Sese Seko seized power in November 1965, after five years of Congolese independence marked by sheer chaos.[15] Only days after the country was emancipated from Belgian colonialism, in June 1960, large segments of its army mutinied, and the Katanga province announced its secession, followed in 1961 by the secession of the "Great Mining State of South Kasai." Meanwhile, after a mere few weeks, the central government in Kinshasa disintegrated, with President Kasavubu and Prime Minister Lumumba dismissing each other before the latter was eventually arrested and assassinated in early 1961. Following Lumumba's dismissal, his supporters organized a rival government based in Stanleyville, in the east of the country, from 1960 to 1962, while other radical opponents of the regime organized rebellions and revolutions throughout the eastern and central regions from 1963 onward. The secessions were eventually terminated under the influence of a UN intervention, while the numerous rebellions were put out with significant help from foreign powers, including Belgium, France, and the United States. The enduring deadlock among politicians in the capital, however, led to the Mobutu takeover of 1965, with considerable blessing from the United States.[16]

After a few years during which occasional violent political struggles continued for control of the state, Mobutu eventually pacified the entire country

and silenced virtually all expressions of its political, ethnic, and cultural pluralism, while building an absolutist state based on his own personal and arbitrary rule. In essence, Mobutu pacified Congo, which he would later rename
Zaire, at the cost of its very plural nature. In saving the state from disintegration, he stifled all expressions of its social and political diversity. Political parties were banned, and all activities were regrouped under the banner of the
single party, the Mouvement Populaire de la Révolution (MPR). The powers
of customary chiefs were undermined, as were those of unions, student
groups, and regional elites, who were arbitrarily relocated throughout the
country. Opponents were treated with a mix of repression (including several
high-profile executions in the regime's earlier years), isolation, and co-option
in the regime's structure of patronage.[17] Private avenues for wealth accumulation were progressively obliterated as control of the economy by the state
increased. As a result, all wealth soon became dependent upon access to the
state, to political office, or to the good favors of the president; and what the
latter gave he could take back.

Mobutu was able to maintain his system of economic and political domination—and the consequent integrity of Congo/Zaire—because of his access
to the country's vast mineral wealth and to the financial flows of international patronage. He oversaw the nationalization of the country's main
cobalt, copper, and diamond mining companies (Gécamines and MIBA) and
transferred to himself vast agricultural and mining estates. Internationally, he
successfully marketed his regime as a stalwart of anticommunism, a role
deemed particularly important by the United States because of Congo's con-
tiguity to Angola. This guaranteed Mobutu substantial aid flows and budgetary support as well as military interventions by his Western patrons against
the occasional armed insurgencies, with little conditionality as to political
behavior. Access to these resources allowed Mobutu to reproduce his rule
while turning potential opponents into clients. Borrowing from Bayart's
metaphor of the "politics of the belly," Mobutu fed Zaireans into submis-
sion.[18] Mindful of the misery they had experienced from 1960 to 1965, most
of them embraced his system.

Yet as successful as the Congolese experiment was with respect to
Mobutu's power, it contained the seeds of its own destruction. The Mobutist
state, weakened by the very corruption that kept its ruler in power, came
crashing in 1989 as the collapse of the Soviet system all but annihilated the
Western need for Mobutu. Deprived virtually overnight of the international
flows of funds that contributed to his domestic networks of patronage and
having failed to convince the West of his willingness to carry a good-faith

transition to democracy, Mobutu had to resort increasingly to the direct exploitation of diamonds and to giving his main clients and other regional elites their own access to the country's resources.[19] This approach further weakened the state apparatus and unleashed violent instances of regional competition. The state itself was effectively privatized as Congolese elites simultaneously embarked on a formal exercise of "transition to democracy" and an informal race against time for stripping public assets. It is against this background of diluted political power and reversion to the chaos of the early 1960s that Laurent-Désiré Kabila started his rebellion in October 1996, which would take him to Kinshasa by May 1997, with considerable help from Rwanda and other regional powers.

With significantly less talent than his predecessor and with ideological choices that soon deprived him of important foreign sponsors, Kabila by and large attempted to replicate Mobutu's system of personal rule, albeit with an even greater dose of arbitrariness. He too personally appropriated assets of the state and let his cronies engage in similar behavior. He was unable, however, to maintain a truly integrative patrimonial state and faced a widespread insurgency-cum-invasion in August 1998 in which rebel groups in the east allied with Rwanda and Uganda in an attempt to overthrow his regime. This failed after Kabila called upon Zimbabwe and Angola to intervene militarily in his defense, which the latter did in exchange for significant strategic advantages and the former did for material incentives.[20] After three years of presiding over a country partitioned by rebel and foreign forces, Kabila was assassinated in January 2001, possibly on behalf of disgruntled diamond traders, disadvantaged domestic factions, or displeased neighbors. In a pattern not uncommon among personal rulers, he was promptly replaced by his son, Joseph Kabila. The latter has since demonstrated much greater acumen at regaining foreign supporters, has rebuilt the foundations of a reunified patrimonial Congo, and has negotiated the reinsertion of rebellious elites into the system of state spoils. In doing so, however, he appears to have also reproduced the very structure of authority based on plundering and sharing the country's resources that was responsible for its underdevelopment and poverty.[21]

Public Institutions for Private Predation

Since the maturation of the Mobutu system of power in the mid-1970s, the Congolese state has essentially been a structure of private predation hiding behind the façade of a public institution. From the Mobutu years to today, the state has been held together by becoming itself a resource, access to which progressively became the main objective of political elites and their clients, in exchange for their political allegiance. The capacity to use the weak state as an instrument of predation is in fact the most crucial element behind the logic of its survival.

Predation begins with the head of state, for whom the exercise of political power calls for large amounts of resources. Mobutu's was well known.[22] Laurent-Désiré Kabila relied on a similar system. He treated Congo as one vast resource available for plunder. His COMIEX company entered several commercial deals under the umbrella of the state after his takeover in 1997.[23] He was also involved in diamond smuggling, as suggested by the discovery of gems in his office upon his assassination. Although more discreet, Joseph Kabila and his entourage have followed the same approach: several of his associates were named in the 2002 UN report on the illegal exploitation of Congo's resources, and his budget for 2003 allocates more discretionary funds to the presidency than to agriculture, fisheries, mines, social affairs, urban affairs, environment, justice, reconstruction, and human rights combined.[24] But while the corruption of top elites is common across the region and many parts of the world, it is its widespread nature that defines the political system in Congo. Many people benefit from the elites' corrupt policies and provide the foundations for this system to function relatively unchallenged from within and for the state to remain unaffected by its de facto privatization in the hands of political elites.

All over the country, weak state institutions are being systematically hijacked for private gain, with the paradoxical effect that Congo's public institutions are both nonperforming and yet enduring. Ministries, state agencies, provincial administrations, and other bureaucratic appendages of the state are used by state elites, their employees, and citizens in general as sources of private benefits. People with parcels of state authority, however limited, can market them and extract resources from their fellow citizens, while others, not directly associated with the state, can also benefit from these practices. This is probably most obvious in the field of customs and border controls, where individual exactions are most visible, as well as in the multiplicity of state agencies in charge of security, which essentially extort payment from citizens by offering to reduce their harassment. Through some multiplier effect, these practices benefit a large number of intermediaries, who make a living as "facilitators": sellers of the ubiquitous stamps that make documents official, street-side vendors who photocopy the required paperwork, handlers who negotiate the many checkpoints at airports, and so forth.

Consider the following examples.[25] Although most citizens suffer from the domination exerted upon them by the national intelligence agency, the Agence Nationale des Renseignements (ANR), a sufficiently large number of them benefit from its predation to prevent any significant challenge to its exactions. On a visit to Lubumbashi, this author had to deal with the ANR to obtain an arrival permit, a permit to travel to the neighboring city of Likasi, and a permit to depart Lubumbashi. At each occasion, the permit required several hours of transactions, payments, the photocopying of travel documents, the involvement of the protocol services of the University of Lubumbashi, and the intervention of a local facilitator hired for this purpose. In short, the demands of the ANR generated substantial economic activity although it did not perform any security function per se. Similarly, at Kinshasa's Ndjili airport, people frequently use the services of private "protocol" agents to negotiate the many layers of controls. These facilitators are de facto business partners with security personnel. They make a living from the potential arbitrariness of airport authorities.

The same logic applies across state agencies. Preserving an instrument of patronage is the main reason, for example, why the rebel movement RCD-Goma has maintained local administrations in the territories it controls.[26] With respect to the court system, "corrupt" judges and clerks decide cases based on the respective payments of plaintiffs and defendants. Parastatal companies are also used as instruments of individual accumulation. Although the production of the giant mining company Gécamines has come to a virtual standstill since the mid-1990s and its employees no longer get paid, politicians and businessmen (a tenuous distinction in Congo) continue to translate its legal existence into joint venture contracts with foreign companies, from which they accrue substantial income. There were recently about twenty-three such joint ventures.[27]

While corrupt behavior weakens the state, the weakness of the state facilitates corrupt behavior, that is, the hijacking of public institutions for private ends. Public roads provide a physical illustration of this pattern. When driving between Congolese cities, one encounters numerous stretches of severely deteriorated roads. At the location of significant potholes or some other major obstacle, it is not uncommon to come across virtual roadblocks of local youth, armed with shovels and demanding payment for their "maintenance" of the road. In fact, far from repairing or providing maintenance work on the road, they symbolically throw a shovel of dirt into the hole as the car approaches, guaranteeing over the long run that the road remains in bad repair, as happens with other dimensions of Congo's decayed but enduring statehood. Really fixing the road would deprive these local youth of this immediate revenue, a quasi-taxation of travelers. Hence the road with its pot-holes is a resource to them. It is the road's very weakness that allows them to turn it into a resource. From a longer-term perspective, they would probably benefit from fixing it and encouraging traffic, facilitating thereby their vil-lage's participation in local trade networks. But from a short-term, individual perspective, they find greater benefit in turning the decayed public road into a private resource. Note, however, that these young men are by no means part of Congo's elite. On the contrary, they are at the bottom of the social ladder. Yet whereas one would be tempted to see them as victims of Congo's failed development, their actions show them also to be predators, who use one effect of state incapacity—bad roads—as the instrument of their predation.

The complex relationship between Congo's poor governance and its poverty is thus structured around the phenomenon of predation by which individuals hijack public institutions in order to exploit them for private gains. Individual strategies for coping with state weakness, by transforming the state into a private resource, contribute to its maintenance and prevent collective institutional improvements. In Congo's climate of great scarcity, the economic returns to the preservation of weak and dysfunctional institu-tions are therefore sufficient to stifle efforts at improved governance. The fact that Congo is poorly performing is what benefits the current elites, who can hijack state institutions. As a result, it is in their interest to maintain Congo as a weak state so as to benefit from its failures. In essence, Congo and bad governance go hand in hand. Hence it is important to acknowledge the empirical fact that bad governance and state decline were already prevalent under Mobutu. As a result, it may be futile to try to promote better gover-nance in Congo without changing the elites' incentive structure, as if the poor performance of current institutions were a temporary affliction of the system. For, in fact, it is the system.

The possibilities of predation afforded by the weak state are in large part what endears it to many Congolese, whether they be in pursuit of wealth or hoping to escape poverty.[28] To some extent, these economic opportunities account for the prevalence of nationalistic sentiments among the Congolese, which coexist with strong and polarized parochial identities. The transforma-tion of the weak state into an instrument of predation would not be possible, however, if it were not for the state's sovereign status. First, the recognition of Congo's international sovereignty by outside powers confers on the state a certain capacity to impose itself upon its citizens without systematic recourse to violence.[29] State agents derive domestic power from the evidence of their international legitimacy. This is in part why visits of African heads of state abroad and their meetings with other heads of state tend to receive disproportionate coverage in their national press. Second, international sovereignty shields weak governments from outside interference, as they can raise the principle of nonintervention in their domestic affairs against outside attempts to check their excesses. Only in the most outrageous cases of genocide and crimes against humanity is this principle bent in international law. There is, however, no international legal recourse for domestic populations when it comes to daily economic exploitation at the hands of a sovereign state. Third, international sovereignty allows governments to present predation as policy (as was the case with Zaireanization in the 1970s) or as law (as happened with the stripping of the minority Banyarwanda populations of their Congolese citizenship in 1981). As such, it confers the seal of legality to robbery and persecution. Fourth, international sovereignty entitles regimes to official development assistance, which fuels their networks of patronage and funds the transformation of the state into a resource. Fifth, and finally, international sovereignty facilitates foreign direct investments from which local elites benefit, as there is considerable straddling between political and business circles. These investments are often conditional upon guarantees of insurance and arbitration, access to which depends on the sovereign status of the recipient country.[30]

The international recognition of Congo's sovereignty thus favors its remaining a nonperforming state. Foreign policies that promote governmental claims to sovereignty, such as budgetary assistance or support for its diplomatic initiatives and for the defense of its territorial integrity, maintain the incentives for the Congolese to reproduce their weak state and guarantee by and large that Congo will remain weak, even though the objectives of support may be to strengthen it. In the short run it may appear that bolstering the Congolese state improves its performance. Mobutu, for example, looked like a positive influence on Congo in 1965 after five years of civil war. In 2003 too the departure of foreign troops and international support for Congo's territorial integrity seem to augur more peaceful days ahead. Yet Mobutu hid Congo's weakness under the absolutism of his personal rule and did not fix it (arguably, he worsened it). As for the current promotion of national unity under Joseph Kabila, heavily sponsored by South African diplomacy, it is more likely to substitute Congolese oppressors for Rwandan or Ugandan ones than to provide the foundations for a lasting reconstruction of Congo as a nation-state. By providing a rationale for reopening the faucets of foreign aid, it may once more put Congo on life support and provide an extension of its lease on life, while in fact only postponing the next serious crisis and any possibility of a cure.

Without international recognition of its sovereignty, the maintenance of the Congolese state as an instrument of predation would be considerably more difficult. Elites intent on maximizing their power and their access to resources would be forced to look elsewhere, to alternative political strategies. These could either yield a partition of Congo or force the establishment of a new Congolese social contract. At several times in Congo's history, political elites have chosen to play regional rather than national cards and have initiated or promoted secessionist movements. These include the secession of the Katanga province from 1960 to 1963, the creation of the Great Mining State of South Kasai from 1961 to 1962, as well as movements with secessionist overtones in Stanleyville in 1960–62 and 1964, in Kivu since independence, and among the Bakongo around 1960.[31] A second wave of such movements hit in the early 1990s when Kasai Oriental all but broke away from the state and when Katanga politicians proclaimed their autonomy from the Tshisekedi government in Kinshasa.[32] These two broad waves of regionalist impulse, in the early 1960s and early 1990s, coincided with periods of weak sovereignty for Congo/Zaire. In the first case, the chaos of Congo's accession to independence, the rapid mutiny of its army, the political deadlock between Kasavubu and Lumumba, and the aversion of Western powers to Lumumba promoted doubts among several politicians and their constituencies that Congo would survive and continue to be recognized as a sovereign entity and made regional gambles for independence worth their while.[33] In the second case, the displeasure of the West at Mobutu's recalcitrance to democratize led to a dramatic curtailment of foreign aid (from US$1.4 billion in 1990 to US$168 million in 1993) and a concurrent reduction in the economic returns to sovereignty, making local strategies of power relatively more appealing. These secession episodes are often dismissed as foreign ploys to balkanize Congo, and foreign influences have indeed contributed to their dynamics. But upon closer observation, the calculations of local elites in their quests for power and resources seem equally crucial in explaining them.

Secessions need not be the Congolese's only alternatives to their current situation, however. It could well be that confronted with deflated sovereignty and without the possibilities of predation, the Congolese would choose to remain a single people. For such an outcome to overcome the predatory legacy of Congo, however, it would require a new social contract, an exercise in which the Congolese have never had a chance to partake. The numerous occasions of national dialogue that have paved the country's history have always taken place under the promise of state predation for those who could adroitly negotiate their insertion into the state system and have, therefore, always created a set of biases against the consideration of Congo's true pluralism and the means to acknowledge and build upon it. This was true when the Brussels Round Table of 1960 rejected federalism and pushed a tiny group of "modernized" elites to embrace the idea of Congo from which they would benefit in the forthcoming elections. Kasavubu, for example, rejected his autonomous pursuits for the Bakongo in exchange for the country's presidency. It was true again at the Lovanium conference of 1961, where representatives from the government, secessionist regions, and rebel movements reshuffled ministerial portfolios among themselves under UN auspices.[34]

The co-option of opposition elites by the Mobutu government and the appetite of the delegates for the material advantages of their situation also led to the failure of the Sovereign National Conference of 1991–93. A similar logic prevailed over the so-called Inter-Congolese Dialogue undertaken in 1999 under the framework of the Lusaka Cease-Fire Agreement, which culminated in the Global and Inclusive Agreement of 2002. All these conferences have failed to generate a consensual societal project, consumed as they have been with the sharing of the spoils of the state by their delegates. On one occasion only, in 1964, did the Congolese come up with a new constitution of their own that reconciled the idea of Congo with the reality of its social pluralism, adopting a broadly decentralized system based on twenty-one autonomous provinces. Although widely approved by referendum in large segments of the country in June–July 1964, the Luluabourg Constitution of 1964 was suspended and revoked after Mobutu took power in 1965. The Congolese people have never again had a chance to make decisions about the nature of their state.

It is a matter of interpretation whether the historic failure of social contracting and self-determination in Congo derives from the biased incentives of its political elites or betrays an absence of desire or capability of the Congolese to live together. At any rate, from the Brussels Round Table of 1960 to the Sun City conference of 2002, Congolese political negotiations have demonstrated the lack of perceived common interests among Congo's constituent groups and their understanding of the state as a finite resource that they need to compete for rather than as the instrument of a joint political project. Congolese history testifies thereby to the lack of substantive significance of the nation. Moreover, Congo's dialectics of integration and polarization has revealed the crucial role of Western decisions of recognition and support in altering the incentive structure faced by Congolese elites in their dealing with the state. The next section turns to the practical implications of this leverage for U.S. policy toward Congo.

Why Put Humpty Together Again?[35]

The United States has played a significant role in Congo's history since 1960, albeit not as significant as—and more complex than—the majority of the Congolese seems to believe. The United States was instrumental in the death of Patrice Lumumba in 1961, the repression of several rebellions in the 1960s, the rise of Mobutu to power in 1965, and his thirty-two-year tenure.[36] The Congolese remember this well. They more easily forget that the United States also contributed to the UN intervention in the 1960s that preserved the national integrity of their country and was instrumental in Mobutu's downfall, suppressing aid to an insignificant trickle after 1991 and facilitating Laurent-Désiré Kabila's accession to power. This section begins therefore with a historical overview of U.S.-Congolese linkages, before moving on to current U.S. foreign policy issues vis-à-vis Congo.

The United States was relatively more involved in the decolonization of Congo than with other African countries, because of its strategic importance and fears that the administration of the first prime minister, Patrice Lumumba, would usher in a client state of the Soviet Union. The fear of "losing" Congo to the Soviets underlined the timid American support to the Katanga secession in June 1960, but the United States promptly reverted to a policy of support for Congolese territorial integrity after Lumumba's political and later physical elimination (in which it was indirectly involved, together with Belgium).[37] After struggling to make sense of the convoluted dynamics of Congolese politics, the United States encouraged the rise to power of Mobutu in November 1965 and thereafter often chose to ignore the increasingly repressive nature of his regime as the price for stability in the country. Mobutu visited the United States on several occasions and was the guest of Presidents Kennedy, Nixon, Reagan, and Bush, a relatively preferential treatment for an African head of state. While vice president in the Reagan administration, George Bush also visited Zaire, together with the U.S. ambassador to the UN, Jeane Kirkpatrick, in 1982.[38] Nevertheless, relations between the two countries were occasionally difficult and followed a see-saw pattern of collaboration and strain, especially after the mid-1970s. Both the Carter and Clinton administrations were in fact rather hostile to the Mobutu regime.

Financial flows between the United States and Congo provide a barometer of their bilateral relations. Net inflows of U.S. official development assistance

Figure 2-2. *U.S. Aid to Democratic Republic of Congo, 1960–2000*

US $million

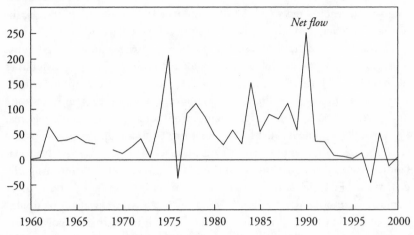

Source: Organization for Economic Cooperation and Development, *Geographical Distribution of Financial Flows to Developing Countries* (Paris: various years).

to Congo hovered below US$50 million a year in the 1960s before reaching both higher volume and much greater volatility in the 1970s and 1980s (see figure 2-2). For these two decades, variations in U.S. aid inflows seem to follow dramatic policy changes and political events in Congo with a lag of a few years. For example, the adoption by the Mobutu government in 1974 of Zaireanization policies that confiscated and redistributed the assets of foreigners was followed by a crash in aid to negative levels in 1976, down from more than US$200 million in 1975. Ironically, the Zaireanization policies had been all but abandoned, amid complete failure, by 1976. This period also marked a low point in U.S.-Congolese diplomacy as Mobutu accused the Central Intelligence Agency of plotting to overthrow him in 1975. After marking a recovery that paralleled a warming of relations between the two countries, U.S. aid dried up again in the latter part of the Carter administration, which was very skeptical of the Mobutu regime although it did provide support in 1978 during the so-called Shaba II crisis for fear of Soviet expansionism, a theme that Mobutu consistently exploited in his relations with the United States. Nevertheless, by the end of the Carter years, U.S. aid flows had again sunk to below US$50 million a year, while Congo was facing a massive financial crisis, accumulating debt arrears, and experiencing a complete loss of economic credibility among donors and international private concerns.[39]

Aid recovered throughout the 1980s, however, under Republican administrations, to reach a record US$250 million in 1990 under President Bush. Mobutu recovered much of his perceived usefulness as cold war dynamics regained the ascendancy in Washington under the Reagan and Bush administrations. By the time the cold war came to an end, however, so did Mobutu's utility to the United States, and U.S. aid flows came crashing down to US$35 million in 1991. From that period onward, the United States, like other Western donors, made foreign aid conditional on democratic reforms. Paradoxically, although Zaire had by then turned to a multiparty system, was enjoying greater civil rights, and saw the convening of a Sovereign National Conference to draw a new constitution, U.S. aid remained all but insignificant from 1991 onward. The reason for this reduction in aid at a time of democratic reforms was to punish Mobutu for his Machiavellian manipulations of the democratic transition and pressure him to surrender power. The first year of the Kabila regime then saw some apparent optimism from the United States, with aid inflows returning to US$50 million 1998, but the outbreak of civil war yet again that year brought development assistance to a new standstill.

Despite Congo's considerable natural resources, U.S. direct foreign investments have been much more limited over time than usually perceived, in large part because of the considerable political risks that Congo represents and because of state control over the main mineral sectors for long periods of time.[40] Capital outflows from the United States have in fact been insignificant, at least from a U.S. point of view, averaging US$1.0 million annually from 1966 to 1969, US$7.1 million in the 1970s, –US$7 million in the 1980s and –US$2.9 million in the 1990s (see figure 2-3). U.S. investments started climbing after Congo adopted a new investment code in 1969 but collapsed after the erratic economic policies of the mid-1970s, never to recover. The frequent negative figures, suggesting net flows from Congo to the United States, could equally represent U.S. investors pulling assets out of Congo or Congolese elites investing in the United States. The arrival to power of Kabila in 1997 brought new optimism among U.S. investors, who brought US$58 million to the country in 1998, only to run for cover the next year.

Trade relations between the United States and Congo remained quite marginal to both countries until Congo began exploiting its offshore crude oil in the early 1970s (see figure 2-4). Since then, the United States has

Figure 2-3. *U.S. Direct Investment in Zaire-Congo, 1966–2000*

US $million

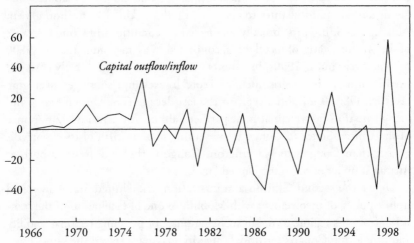

Source: U.S. Department of Commerce, Bureau of Economic Analysis (www/bea/doc/gov).

Figure 2-4. *U.S.-Congo Trade, 1960–99*

US $million

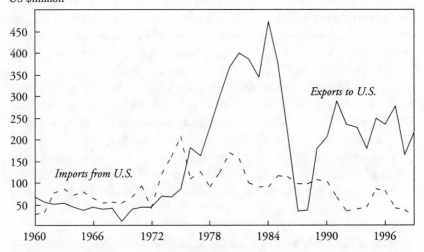

Source: International Monetary Fund, *Direction of Trade Statistics* (Washington: various years).

recorded an almost systematic trade deficit with Congo, importing on average about US$250 million worth of goods, mostly composed of crude petroleum, refined copper cathode, and some gems, while exporting manufactured goods and some foodstuffs to the tune of about US$100 million a year. Although U.S. imports, broadly unaffected by conditions in Congo because of the offshore status of its oil wells, continued to average more than US$200 million a year in the 1990s, its exports to Congo have been severely curtailed by the country's impoverishment and foreign exchange shortages, averaging less than US$50 million a year for the last decade. The United States and Congo are thus not essential trade partners, although the relative importance of the United States to Congo (representing about a fifth of its exports) is greater than Congo's to Washington (Congo is the sixth most important African supplier of oil to the United States).

Under the second Clinton administration, the United States switched from a policy of involvement with Mobutu to one of facilitation of the transition from his regime to the next. Its rationale of pursuing regional stability and promoting Congo's territorial integrity may have stayed the same, however. The main difference was that, by 1996, a dying Mobutu and his regime were greater liabilities than assets for the region. Fearful of a dismemberment of the country as the AFDL (Alliance of Democratic Forces for the Liberation of Congo) rebellion began, the United States did caution Uganda, Rwanda, and Burundi against direct involvement in the fighting in early 1997, but its preferences for the rebel coalition soon became clear.[41] On May 4, as Kinshasa was about to fall, the United States managed to set up a meeting between Mobutu and Kabila, with South African assistance, to ease the transition and avoid violence in Kinshasa, but the meeting failed. The U.S. ambassador to Congo, Daniel Simpson, then urged the Congolese government to surrender and let AFDL troops enter Kinshasa. After the AFDL takeover on May 17, the United States was briefly seen as the closest Western sponsor of Kabila, and a mission from the U.S. Agency for International Development (USAID) visited Congo barely two weeks into the new regime to discuss the resumption of foreign aid.[42] Kabila's ideological rigidities and his own erratic nature prevented the establishment of a sustained positive relationship, however, and the 1998 invasion/rebellion against Kabila, initiated by Rwanda, led to a further deterioration, given Washington's sympathy for the Kigali regime.

From the point of view of the policy interests of the United States after September 11, 2001, the perceived closeness between Washington and Kigali represents a liability to the extent that it has encouraged anti-American

Table 2-1. *Congolese Public Opinion toward Other Countries and the United Nations, 1996, 1998, 2000, 2001*

Date of survey			
December 1996 [a]	*May 1998* [b]	*October 2000* [c]	*December 2001* [d]
Positive public opinion (three top answers)			
Belgium (43%)	South Africa (60%)	Libya (71%)	Belgium (26%)
France (32%)	United Nations (30%)	Angola (68%)	Angola (15%)
United States (26%)	Belgium (30%)	Zimbabwe (68%)	Zimbabwe (12%)
Negative public opinion (three top answers)			
Rwanda (74%)	France (68%)	Rwanda (87%)	Rwanda (33%)
Burundi (69%)	Rwanda (58%)	Burundi (85%)	United States (28%)
United States (53%)	United States (54%)	United States (56%)	France (10%)

Source: Bureau d'Etudes et de Recherches Consulting International, various years.

a. In December 1996, the question asked for respondent's opinion on these countries "with respect to the events that have taken place in the east," namely the Rwandan/AFDL invasion.

b. In May 1998, the only options were South Africa, the United Nations, Belgium, Rwanda, France, and the United States.

c. In October 2000, the question was, "What opinion do you have of the following countries?" The percentages here reflect the top three answers for "good" and for "bad" among Kinshasa respondents.

d. In December 2001, the question was, "What is the foreign country whose actions toward our country you most (least) appreciate?" Answers were open ended.

sentiments.[43] The United States is believed to share responsibility for the Rwandan invasion of 1998 and for the war that has since divided Congo. The Congolese are certain that tiny Rwanda could not have invaded and occupied them so decisively without U.S. political and military support.[44] In addition, there is widespread conviction among Congolese that the United States is promoting a partition of Congo (to benefit Rwanda), a claim for which there is apparently no historical or contemporary evidence.[45] Since 1996, Rwanda and the United States systematically appear together in the top three least popular countries among the Congolese public, while Belgium, the former colonial overlord, is often in the most popular group (see table 2-1).

Despite the marginality of Islamic minorities in Congo, Libya is also a popular country among the Congolese, for it is seen as standing up to the United States. There is even anecdotal evidence that the al Qaeda leader Osama Bin Laden draws symbolic support among the mostly Christian eastern Congolese, who have lived under de facto Rwandan occupation since 1998.[46]

The combination of negative public opinion vis-à-vis the United States and weak state capabilities may provide a fertile environment for the coalescence of anti-U.S. interests. The relative political clout of the Lebanese community in Kinshasa, believed by some to have been associated with Kabila's assassination (and violently repressed for it), may well add another dimension of concern to U.S. security interests. Furthermore, Congo's uranium resources—the very ones that fueled the Hiroshima and Nagasaki explosions of 1945—represent a serious challenge to the nuclear nonproliferation agenda of the United States. Not only is uranium present in significant quantities in Katanga, but in addition the University of Kinshasa actually hosts a working nuclear reactor—which, however old and weak, is capable of enriching uranium (albeit not to weapons grade). Two uranium rods went missing from this reactor in 1997, in the waning days of the Mobutu regime. One was later found in Rome as it was about to be sold to the mafia, but the other one is allegedly still missing. In a testimony to dysfunctional institutions, the current director of the reactor believes the rods may have been stolen "when his predecessor lent out his keys."[47] Not surprisingly, Congo was believed in 2002 to be a target of alleged Iraqi efforts to procure nuclear material.[48]

The lack of effective territorial control by either the Kinshasa government or the numerous rebel groups, compounded by the country's sheer vastness, may also facilitate the recruitment and the organization of militias or similar groups with anti-Western agendas. Although Congolese populations are mostly Christian or profess syncretic beliefs derived from Christianity and local religious practices (limiting thereby the potential for fundamentalist Islamic movements to take root), the forbidding nature of local geographical features and the density of forests in peripheral regions such as the Haut-Congo, Equator, or even Kivu provinces make the establishment of camps or remote communities a relatively easy matter. Bear in mind, after all, that Laurent-Désiré Kabila ruled over a ministate in the Hewa Bora region of South Kivu from 1967 to the late 1980s, out of reach of Mobutu's forces, living off the land, smuggling across the Tanzanian border, exploiting local peasants, and occasionally taking Western hostages for ransom. If this was possible at a time when Kinshasa was deemed in control of its territory, it is certainly possible today. Trade linkages with the Horn of Africa (where Islamic fundamentalism has a significant presence) and beyond, favored by the occupation of Ugandan forces in the Ituri region, have also opened up significant parts of Congo to the Middle East, as illustrated by the prevalence of dubais, taxi vans imported from the Arabian peninsula.

The fragility of Congo also matters well beyond the idiosyncratic security concerns of the United States in the post-9/11 world. Given its central location in Africa (bordering on nine countries), its resource wealth, and the overlapping distribution of its populations with neighboring states, events in

Congo predictably affect the entire region. The very collapse of the Mobutu regime and the bankruptcy by the mid-1990s of his system of plunder facilitated the takeover of Rwandan refugee camps in Kivu by extremist Hutu militiamen and brought about the first Rwandan invasion of 1996. In addition, the very incapacity of the state to rule without polarizing its populations and to defend itself led to the Rwandan/Ugandan/Burundian invasion of 1998 together with the progovernment interventions of Angola, Zimbabwe, and Namibia. For when Congo folds, it sucks in neighboring states that use its territory either to address their own political unrest (Angola, Rwanda, Burundi) or to supplement their incomes (Uganda and Zimbabwe). Preserving Congo as a functioning state therefore permits the containment of violent conflicts from other countries of the region.

Aside from such realist preoccupations, a poorly performing Congo also matters in terms of its toll on human lives and human rights. Political predation and conflict make for nasty living conditions. It has been estimated that more than three million Congolese have died since 1998 as a direct or indirect consequence of warfare. In fact, according to the International Rescue Committee, Congo's has been "the most deadly war ever documented in Africa, indeed the highest war death toll documented anywhere in the world during the past half-century."[49] The lives of the surviving Congolese have been miserable since the early 1990s. Corruption, poverty, lack of education, army and rebel lootings, dictatorial leadership, privatized public institutions, harassment of opponents, and intimidation of citizens deny security and dignity to the majority of Congolese. This desolation breeds individual and communal disengagement from state structures, further weakening the country's social fabric and its institutional capacity.[50] There is therefore a normative case, if not a moral imperative, for restoring some level of bona fide law, order, and accountability to Congo.

While a poorly performing Congo constitutes a U.S. foreign policy concern for rather intuitive reasons, what the United States can do about it is another matter altogether. On the one hand, Congo's mix of institutional weakness, predation, and anti-American sentiment seems to suggest the need for reconstruction and assistance. It is true indeed that recent pacification efforts have significantly reduced violent mortality throughout the country and especially in the east, except for a few pockets in Ituri and the Kivus.[51] Promoting peace, the reunification of political elites, institutional reconstruction, and territorial integrity has been the conventional U.S. foreign policy response to Congo's conundrum, including in the present crisis. The USAID, for example, currently has a democracy and institutions strengthening program in Congo (other Western donors, including the European Union, the World Bank, France, and Canada, also have government capacity building programs).[52] U.S. diplomacy has also supported the efforts, since 2002, of South African president Thabo Mbeki to find a political settlement among the main Congolese factions. President Bush headed a special session of the UN Security Council on Congo on September 13, 2002, in the presence of President Kabila and eight other African heads of state. The next day he also presided over a meeting between Kabila and Rwanda's president Kagame. He met again with Kabila during the latter's visit to the UN in September 2003. The United States sent strong signals, after the semifailure of the Sun City Inter-Congolese Dialogue among government, rebels, and civil society in April 2002, that it would support a peace process that would not challenge the leadership of President Kabila during the transition phase. In doing so, it created additional incentives for rebel leaders to negotiate with Kabila about sharing the spoils of the state, as opposed to pursuing other strategies of self-determination, and facilitated the Global and Inclusive Agreement of December 2002, in which most factions came together.

Attempts by elites at reconstructing the Congolese state have also been handsomely rewarded by the West. Although the United States has not so far resumed significant aid flows, it has sponsored the resumption of aid to Congo by the World Bank and the International Monetary Fund, which started immediately after the announcement in April 2002 of a power-sharing alliance between the government and the MLC rebels (which later proved stillborn). The IMF agreed to a US$700 million, three-year, multisector emergency program, while the World Bank, which had suspended operations since 1993, came back en force in May 2002 with a US$450 million package as partial funding for the three-year "multisector emergency rehabilitation and reconstruction program," most of which was earmarked for infrastructure. The Bank also agreed to a US$45 million budgetary aid to the government.[53] As a member of the Paris Club of official bilateral creditors, the United States also agreed in early September 2002 to forgive Congo 80 percent of its bilateral debt, or US$8.49 billion in principal arrears, interest arrears, and interest on these arrears, and US$490 million of principal and interests coming due between July 2002 and June 2005.[54] In August 2003, the IMF and the World Bank also agreed to grant Congo HIPC ("heavily indebted poor country") status, which qualifies it for about US$10 billion in debt relief, despite a still precarious macroeconomic performance.[55] As the *Financial Times* notes, "the [Congolese] government is now winning widespread backing from abroad" in return for putting together national institutions.[56]

Yet if the maintenance and reproduction of Congo indeed guarantees its very weakness and its very incapacity to function as a state, then these policies of life support and encouragement to national reunification may not be optimal. To some extent, the United States has tried to strengthen the Congolese state ever since the early 1960s and has little to show for it. Despite Congolese misperceptions, U.S. policy has indeed almost always supported Congolese territorial integrity. Yet Congo has been in a state of perpetual crisis and on a steady path of decline maybe because of its very nature as a state. There is no reason to believe that policies that promote good governance, civil society, and democratic transitions within the framework of the Congolese state will yield better results now than before in Congo's history. As discussed, bad governance may well be an intrinsic dimension of Congolese politics. In addition, the U.S. preference for civil society organizations in state formation and democratic transition processes contrasts with the relative absence of civil society standing up to the state in the Tocquevillian sense. In Congo as in many other African states, much of civil society is the self-labeled waiting area of sidelined or future political elites. As for democratic transition, it has been used by Congolese elites as a legitimating discourse vis-à-vis the Western world since the early 1990s, but it has rarely corresponded to genuine local dynamics. The contradiction of further sponsoring unreformed Congolese statehood is well captured by Jeffrey Herbst's comment on Western opposition to the redesign of some African states: "The international community acts like creditors who, having seen their investment lost by a company without a viable business, seek to reinvest in the same company after bankruptcy has been reached but without demanding a restructuring that would protect their investment."[57]

It could arguably make more sense for the United States to consider Congolese sovereignty for what it truly is—an instrument for the domination of the mass of the Congolese by a small group among them—and facilitate a deeper reconfiguration of the state based on a genuine process of social contracting among the Congolese people, and not only its elites, though it is unclear how this latter exercise would be managed. A decentralized, bottom-up process of popular consultation may be part of the answer. Jeffrey Herbst's idea of "decertification" of nonperforming states—akin to a removal of their sovereign status—should also be given consideration in the Congolese context.[58] Another important option, also mentioned by Herbst, is the recognition of new states. Although no part of Congo is currently fighting for international state status, recognition of Somaliland, for example, would transform the incentives of Congolese regional politicians to play the game of national politics and may unleash the voicing of regional political prefer-ences.[59] The West was keen on recognizing new states in the wake of the col-lapse of the Soviet Union. Its resistance to such a policy in the African con-text suggests a preoccupying distinction between its responses to the consequences of Soviet and Western imperialisms. There are no guarantees, of course, that hypothetical new states, born from the ashes of Congo, would perform any better than Congo. After all, state formation through the ages has often taken place at the cost of corruption, domination, and violence. Yet if such deviances are inevitable to state formation, they may stand a better chance of producing results in states endowed with manageable geographical, historical, and demographic features.

These comments should not be construed as suggesting that the United States must actively promote changes in Congo's territorial definition. They do support the idea, however, that the United States should make it possible for the Congolese to do so if they wish, opening up the realm of the possible and breaking the cycle of the politics of the belly, in which political and iden-tity aspirations are sacrificed on the altar of the state-as-resource.[60] Lest this seems unduly bold and insurmountable, one should consider how Leopold II of Belgium single-handedly carved Congo out of Central Africa in the 1880s.[61] Certainly such a political project would have appeared to face insur-mountable obstacles back in the 1870s.

Bearing in mind, however, that such radical options are unlikely to be implemented in the short run, what are the remaining policy instruments available to the United States to prevent the reproduction of a weak Con-golese state? A different type of policy conditionality for foreign aid might provide one alternative. Following the logic of the Bush administration's Mil-lennium Challenge Account, the United States (and other donors) should attach more substantial conditions to development assistance than mere political reunification and promises of democratic transition. Foreign aid could be made conditional upon demonstrably improved institutional effec-tiveness, rather than postcolonial territorial continuity irrespective of where the unification of the state stands at the time. By substituting a norm of insti-tutional effectiveness to the prevailing norm of political reconciliation, donors could shift the incentives for Congolese elites away from maintaining the state without regard for its capacity and toward building institutions with less regard for predation.

The crux of such an approach, however, lies in the donor's willingness to support a wide range of local actors, as long as they develop accountable and effective institutions, be they the government or rebels, public agencies or nongovernmental organizations, traditional authorities or church groups. Taking their rationality for granted, Congolese elites would choose the type of political action that maximizes the development of institutional capacity to the extent that these actions would also maximize their access to the rents of foreign aid. Although elites might still pursue their access to these rents for their private benefit, they would be forced to do so in a context that neutralizes the advantages of sovereignty associated with state weakness and makes personal interest compatible with aggregate welfare. The fear that such signals from donors might result in territorial partition should not be exaggerated, given the high costs for politicians of mobilizing people away from the state in view of the uncertainty of such new political dynamics. It is more likely that these new aid incentives would lead to cooperative strategies among successful local efforts, in order to benefit from economies of scale, leading in time to a mosaic of local institutional successes, which may well provide lasting foundations for effective state building.

Short of challenging the institutional status quo, the United States and other donors still have the option of containing some excesses among the Congolese leadership. As discussed earlier, Congo's political system encourages ethnic polarization. The resulting prevalence of racism in Congolese politics and its propensity for violence and pogroms manipulated by political elites can be curbed by the threat of sanctions. There is a contradiction in the international prosecution of political leaders like Serbia's Slobodan Milosevic and Rwanda's génocidaires while Congolese elites who regularly stir hatred of certain minorities (like the Tutsi of eastern Congo, or Kasaians in Katanga) and among ethnic groups (like Hema and Lendu in the Ituri region) are rewarded with recognition and aid. In 1998, for example, after the second invasion of Congo by Rwanda, foreign minister Abdoulaye Yerodia called upon the Congolese to attack people of Tutsi ethnicity, calling them a "pest to be exterminated" on national radio. Today, Yerodia is one of four vice presidents in Congo's transition government. If the United States is serious about promoting human rights, it should demand that such politicians be removed from power and prosecuted. Human rights violations based on racism also contribute to maintaining Congo as a weak state by diluting the meaning and value of citizenship for the majority of Congolese. Given this fact, penalizing it would no doubt contribute to strengthening public institutions.

In conclusion, there is a range of possible policy options for the United States. This chapter argues that the default policy of constructive engagement with current authorities and within current political structures, while providing short-term benefits, contributes to maintaining the problem to the extent that the trouble with Congo may be Congo itself. When considering the merits of yet another round of national reconciliation, it should be borne in mind that Humpty was sitting on a wall to begin with—hardly a stable position to build upon—and that, in the end, all the king's horses and all the king's men couldn't put him together again. One radical option is to deflate the benefits of national sovereignty for Congolese elites by withholding recognition or making it conditional on effectiveness, in order to encourage them to pursue potentially more robust local strategies of power. Short of this, the sovereignty of Congo may be preserved while foreign aid is conditioned upon institutional effectiveness rather than national reconciliation. In the short run, the United States can at least improve the daily lives of Congolese citizens and promote Congo's societal cohesion by penalizing the frequent recourse to racism and ethnic polarization among Congolese politicians.

Note

1. Jack A. Goldstone and others, *State Failure Task Force Report: Phase III Findings* (McLean, Va.: Science Applications International Corporation [SAIC], 2000); Robert Rotberg, ed., *State Failure and State Weakness in a Time of Terror* (Cambridge, Mass.: World Peace Foundation, 2003).

2. Congolese rebel groups, which have waged war against the central government since 1998, have always made explicit their demands for participation in power and have never developed secessionist, separatist, or revolutionary agendas. As for the foreign armies, in relative retreat since the latter half of 2002, their governments pledged to maintain the territorial integrity of Congo in the Lusaka Cease Fire Agreement of 1999. Occasional accusations of Rwandan irredentism are mostly the work of Congolese government propaganda and do not stand the test of Rwanda's policies in Congo's eastern region, especially its repression of segments of the population of Rwandan origin.

3. For evidence of Congolese nationalism, see the opinion polls of the Kinshasa-based Bureau d'Etudes et de Recherches Consulting International (BERCI), November 1998, according to which 89 percent of the Congolese oppose the idea of partition of their country.

4. As Rotberg, *State Failure and State Weakness,* argues, state failure implies not only a lack of institutional functionality but also an absence of popular legitimacy and the rise of alternative political allegiance among significant segments of their populations. On this account, Rotberg is mistaken in listing the DRC among failed states, in contrast to Sudan or Somalia.

5. On the idea of, and potential for, reconfiguration of the African state, see Richard Joseph, ed., *State, Conflict, and Democracy in Africa* (Boulder, Colo.: Lynne Rienner, 1999); and Leonardo Villalon and Philip Huxtable, *The African State at a Critical Juncture: Between Disintegration and Reconfiguration* (Boulder, Colo.: Lynne Rienner, 1998), particularly Catherine Boone's chapter. On the possible leverage of foreign powers in matters of African state reconfiguration, see Jeffrey Herbst, *States and Power in Africa: Comparative Lessons in Authority and Control* (Princeton University Press, 2000), chap. 9.

6. See Michael Ross, "The Political Economy of the Resource Curse," *World Politics* 51 (January 1999): 297–322.

7. International Monetary Fund, *International Financial Statistics Yearbook 1997* (Washington: 1997), p. 312.

8. James S. Coleman and Ndolamb Ngokwey, "Zaire: The State and the University," in *Nationalism and Development in Africa: Selected Essays,* edited by Richard Sklar (University of California Press, 1994), p. 309.

9. Unless otherwise indicated, figures are from World Bank, "World Development Indicators CD-Rom and Country Data Profile" (http://devdata.worldbank.org/external/CPProfile.asp?CCODE=ZAR&PTYPE=CP [January 2003]).

10. On Mobutu's system, see Crawford Young and Thomas Turner, *The Rise and Decline of the Zairean State* (University of Wisconsin Press, 1985); Thomas Callaghy, *The State-Society Struggle: Zaire in Comparative Perspective* (Columbia University Press, 1984); and Michael Schatzberg, *The Dialectics of Oppression in Zaire* (Indiana University Press, 1988).

11. See William Reno, *Warlord Politics and African States* (Boulder, Colo.: Lynne Rienner, 1998), p. 153.

12. Calculated from *Political Risk Service, Inter-Country Risk Guide Data Set* (East Syracuse, N.Y.: 2000).

13. "Leaving the Quagmire," *Africa Confidential* 43, no. 19 (2002): 3–5.

14. Crawford Young, "Zaire: Anatomy of a Failed State," in *History of Central Africa: The Contemporary Years since 1960,* edited by David Birmingham and Phyllis M. Martin (London: Longman, 1998).

15. For a factually detailed summary of Congo's history, see Georges Nzongola-Ntalaja, *The Congo from Leopold to Kabila: A People's History* (London: Zed Books, 2002).

16. At the time of his takeover and for some years thereafter, Mobutu received payments from the CIA.

17. Particularly interesting is the case of Nguza Karl-i-Bond, a Lunda politician from Katanga, who served as foreign minister before seeking exile in the United States, where he testified against the regime before Congress. He returned to Washington a few years later, however, this time as Mobutu's ambassador, before serving as prime minister and eventually establishing his own party in the 1990s.

18. Jean-François Bayart, *The State in Africa: The Politics of the Belly* (London: Longman, 1993).

19. Reno, *Warlord Politics and African States,* pp. 159–62.

20. See John F. Clark, ed., *The African Stakes of the Congo War* (New York: Palgrave Macmillan, 2002).

21. According to the United Nations, members of Kabila's administration illegally transferred an estimated US$5 billion worth of state assets to themselves and their foreign partners between 1998 and 2002. See United Nations Security Council, *Final Report of the Panel of Experts on the Illegal Exploitation of Natural Resources and Other Forms of Wealth of the Democratic Republic of Congo,* S/2002/1146, October 16 (New York: United Nations, 2002).

22. See Michela Wrong, *In the Footsteps of Mr. Kurtz: Living on the Brink of Disaster in the Congo* (London: Fourth Estate, 2000).

23. See, for example, *Africa Research Bulletin: Economic, Financial and Technical Series* 138, no. 9: 14928.

24. Digital Congo, "Budget 2003 réaménagé: J. Kabila et les vice-présidents trop gourmands" (www.digitalcongo.net [September 18, 2003]).

25. These remarks are based on fieldwork in Congo in July 2001, October–November 2001, and April 2002.

26. Denis Tull, "A Reconfiguration of Political Order? The State of the State in North Kivu (DR Congo)," *African Affairs* 102, no. 408 (2003): 429–46.

27. Digital Congo (www.digitalcongo.net [May 3, 2002]).

28. For grassroots Congolese, who may fall out of the networks of predation and find themselves systematically on the predated side of history, the state also remains a resource to the extent that it offers a minimum level of certainty about public life, the opportunity to form relatively stable expectations about where power and resources lie, and a modicum of reduction of transaction costs as they go about their lives. Political uncertainty, warlords, insurgencies, and the like, on the other hand, blur the cards of politics for common people and complicate, if not endanger, their daily lives. State stability is therefore an intrinsic resource in the lives of people who have to struggle for survival, as it represents an anchor in their volatile and vulnerable life. This helps account for the widespread attachment of the Congolese to their state, despite its predation and dysfunctionality.

29. Robert Jackson and Carl Rosberg, "Why Africa's Weak States Persist: The Empirical and the Juridical in Statehood," *World Politics* 35, no. 1 (1982): 1–25.

30. This discussion on the benefits of sovereignty for a weak state like Congo draws upon Pierre Englebert, "Why Congo Persists: Sovereignty, Globalization, and the Violent Reproduction of a Weak State," Queen Elizabeth House Working Paper 95 (Oxford University, February 2003).

31. Bruce Baker, *Escape from Domination in Africa: Political Disengagement and Its Consequences* (London: James Currey, 2000).

32. On Kasai, see "Zaire: A Provincial Gem," *Economist*, April 27, 1996; and Howard French, "A Neglected Region Loosens Ties to Zaire," *New York Times*, September 18, 1996, p. A1. On Katanga, see miscellaneous issues of Economist Intelligence Unit, *Country Report: Zaire/Zambia*, from 1992 to 1994.

33. See J. Gérard-Libois, *La sécession katangaise* (Brussels: CRISP, 1963).

34. See Isidore Ndaywel È Nziem, *Histoire Générale du Congo* (Paris: Duculot, 1998), p. 593.

35. See John Prendergast and David Smock, "Putting Humpty Dumpty Together: Reconstructing Peace in the Congo," special report (Washington: United States Institute of Peace, August 1999); and I. William Zartman, "Putting Humpty-Dumpty Together Again," in *The International Spread of Ethnic Conflict: Fear, Diffusion, and Escalation*, edited by David Lake and Donald Rothchild (Princeton University Press, 1998). Zartman's allusion to Humpty Dumpty refers to solutions to ethnic conflict in general, not to the DRC per se.

36. See Stephen R. Weissman, "The CIA and U.S. Policy in Zaire and Angola," in *American Policy in Southern Africa: The Stakes and the Stance*, edited by René Lemarchand (Lanham, Md.: University Press of America, 1978); Elise F. Pachter, "Our Man in Kinshasa: U.S. Relations with Mobutu, 1970–1983; Patron Client Relations in the International Sphere," Ph.D. dissertation, School of Advanced International Studies, Johns Hopkins University, 1987.

37. On the United States and the Katanga secession, see Gérard-Libois, *La sécession katangaise*. On the assassination of Patrice Lumumba, see Ludo De Witte, *L'assassinat de Lumumba* (Paris: Karthala, 2000).

38. Michael Schatzberg, *Zaire: Mobutu or Chaos? The United States and Zaire, 1960–1990* (Lanham, Md.: University Press of America, 1991), p. 69.

39. For details on this period, see Young and Turner, *Rise and Decline of the Zairean State*, pp. 378–95.

40. The Congolese frequently argue, however, that their poverty is due to the exploitive nature of international investments.

41. Economist Intelligence Unit, *Zaire Country Report*, 2d quarter, 1997, p. 27.

42. Economist Intelligence Unit, *Zaire Country Report*, 3d quarter, 1997, p. 27.

43. Few in Congo seem to appreciate how U.S. support for Rwanda has considerably eroded since Rwanda and Uganda engaged each other in fighting inside the Congolese city of Kisangani in 2000. For example, the United States abstained in 2002 from an International Monetary Fund board vote on a poverty reduction loan to Rwanda ("Leaving the Quagmire").

44. See, for example, Digital Congo (www.digitalcongo.net [September 27, 2002]), according to which "Congo's aggressors do not have the means to wage war. The Pentagon used them to balkanize the subcontinent and better exploit it" (author's translation). ("Actualité: Bill Clinton revient sur le lieu du crime après avoir endeuillé la République Démocratique du Congo.")

45. As mentioned earlier, U.S. support for the Katanga secession in 1960 was extremely short-lived and represented its aversion for Lumumba rather than a preference for an independent Katanga. From 1961 onward, the United States was the main engineer of the UN intervention and of the preservation of Congolese territorial integrity.

46. Author's fieldwork observations.

47. Jane Flanagan and David Wastell, "War-Torn Congo Is Target in Baghdad's Hunt for Uranium," *Daily Telegraph,* September 29, 2002.

48. Ibid.; Colette Braeckman, "Irak: Dans quel pays Bagdad a-t-il tenté de faire son shopping?" *Le Soir,* September 30, 2002; "Leaving the Quagmire." The apparent fallacy of similar claims about Niger undermines such allegations, however.

49. International Rescue Committee, *Mortality in the Democratic Republic of Congo: Results from a Nationwide Survey* (New York: April 2003), p. i.

50. Baker, *Escape from Domination in Africa*.

51. International Rescue Committee, *Mortality in the Democratic Republic of Congo*.

52. U.S. Agency for International Development, Congo, "Congressional Budget Justification 2003" (www.usaid.gov/cg/program.html [January 2003]).

53. Déo Mulima Kapuku, "La Référence Plus" (www.digitalcongo.net [May 6, 2002]).

54. Digital Congo, "Le Club de Paris annule 4,64 milliards de dette de la Rd Congo" (www.digitalcongo.net [September 13, 2002]).

55. For details of the decision, see Africa Research Bulletin: Economic, Financial, and Technical Series 40, no. 7 (2003): 15741–43.

56. William Wallis, "Kabila Resolves to Overcome 'Shadows' Looming over Congo," *Financial Times,* September 23, 2003, p. 4.

57. Herbst, *States and Power in Africa*, p. 258.

58. Ibid., pp. 264–65.

59. Somaliland, which seceded from Somalia in 1991, has been peaceful and relatively well managed yet has failed so far to be recognized by any foreign country.

60. See Bayart, *The State in Africa.*

61. See Adam Hochschild, *King Leopold's Ghost: A Story of Greed, Terror, and Heroism in Colonial Africa* (Boston: Houghton Mifflin, 1998).

3

The Dysfunctional State of Nigeria

Peter M. Lewis

Nigeria's travails, while hardly unique within the developing world, are surely exceptional in their scope and persistence. Mass poverty, economic stagnation, endemic corruption, political instability, weak institutions, and social conflict can be found in many countries, and viewed in this light, Nigeria might seem unremarkable. Yet the scale of Nigeria's developmental failure and the ironies surrounding its malaise place the country in sharper relief. It is not appropriately regarded as a "failed" (much less "collapsed") state, if by that term we mean a system that lacks major attributes of sovereignty or cohesion. In Nigeria, the state exercises a modicum of political control, there is a basic level of public institutions, and much of the population accepts some notion of common identity and national authority. Nor should Nigeria be characterized as a "poor" country, lacking the resources or capital necessary for economic and social development. During the last three decades, Nigeria has generated about US$500 billion in petroleum exports, much of which has accrued as revenue to the central government.[1] Many of the country's leaders, professing aspirations for development, have spent prodigiously on infrastructure, production, and social services.

There is no question, however, that Nigeria has failed profoundly as a state, a nation, and an economy. Central authorities cannot provide stable governance, in the sense of effective legitimate rule and essential public goods. The country's boundaries may provisionally be settled, but the basis of political community—the idea of Nigeria—is fiercely contested. Economically, Nigeria has experienced a steady decline since the oil windfall peaked more than twenty years ago. Slow growth and a rapidly rising population have yielded dramatic increases in poverty. Confronted by these challenges, Nigerians have repeatedly attempted to overhaul the nation's politics, resulting in cycles of civilian and military government and perennial efforts at institutional change. The country's restiveness and economic deterioration are especially poignant when considered in light of its opportunities and assets. The restoration of civilian rule suggests new opportunities for addressing problems of governance and the economy. Democratic reforms, however, are hesitant, uneven, and factious, beleaguered by economic stagnation and rising social conflict. Recent trends attest more powerfully to the intractability of the problems than to the prospects for renewal.

From the vantage point of the United States, Nigeria's predicament embodies troubling contradictions. Historically, relations between the United States and Nigeria have been accommodating, if sometimes tense. Since its independence in 1960, Nigeria has steered a moderate course in foreign affairs, adopting a nonaligned stance while generally sustaining cordial relations with most western nations. Although disagreements have periodically arisen between Nigeria and the United States, there is no deep ideological or historical source of tension to impair bilateral relations.[2] Furthermore, the two countries have a substantial trade and investment relationship. For three decades, Nigeria has been an important supplier of high-grade oil to the United States. The rising significance of Nigeria to U.S. energy needs and the presence of a large Nigerian immigrant community in the United States bolster links between the states. Nigeria has also emerged in the past decade as an anchor for regional security in West Africa, through its leadership of regional peacekeeping efforts, such as in Liberia and Sierra Leone.

Yet Nigeria's turbulence, poor governance, and economic decay pose major challenges for U.S. policy in the region. Indeed, the infirmity of the state itself forms the primary dilemma in bilateral relations. While the two countries have only moderate differences over alliances, international norms, and multilateral concerns, the greatest problems arise in responding to Nigeria's instability and stagnation.[3] The prospects of political breakdown and autocracy are especially worrisome in a region where democratization is fragile and internal conflicts are frequent. Nigeria is Africa's most populous state, and it has the largest Muslim population in sub-Saharan Africa. Social turbulence, particularly in the oil-producing Niger Delta and in the Muslim-majority states of the northern region, poses risks that are especially salient to the United States; government instability and religious polarization take on added significance in the wake of the September 11 attacks. Terrorism has largely been absent from Nigeria, but the possibility of radicalization among the Muslim community is a matter of concern for many Nigerians, as well as interested observers in the United States.[4]

On behalf of regional security, Nigeria has taken on responsibilities and risks largely eschewed by major outside powers. Its interventions in Liberia and Sierra Leone were of limited effectiveness, however, leaving open the issue of how to guarantee a more durable regional security structure. Economically, the United States has had contentious relations with various Nigerian governments over issues of debt and economic policy reform. The country's continued economic stagnation and endemic corruption impede U.S. commercial relations with Nigeria and more generally hinder economic development in West Africa. Weak governance and economic frailty also underlie the leading irritants in the U.S.-Nigerian relationship: narcotics trafficking, financial fraud, and money laundering. In addition, the rising incidence of HIV-AIDS in Nigeria accentuates humanitarian problems and the health risks inherent in global interactions.

The interests of the United States would obviously be better served by a stable, democratic, and prospering Nigeria, a state that could manage its internal divisions, provide for the welfare of its citizens, promote accountable government, and constitute a stabilizing influence in the region. This suggests a forward-looking policy of engagement on the part of the United States, to encourage political revitalization and economic reform. Unfortunately, our trade relations with Nigeria, so heavily concentrated in the energy sector, frequently eclipse other aspects of the bilateral relationship. For those in the U.S. government and private sector focused chiefly on energy concerns, the bilateral relationship is driven by the need to maintain a hospitable investment climate and stable conditions for production and export. These goals do not necessarily coincide with the broader objectives of promoting better governance and economic performance, especially when trade interests draw the United States closer to authoritarian rulers or stand in the way of needed reform.

This chapter contends, however, that a more diversified and flexible policy toward Nigeria is needed to advance both U.S. goals and Nigeria's long-term developmental prospects. In particular, policies that emphasize democratic development, broad-based economic growth, and social accommodation can better facilitate long-term stability. These objectives call for active engagement with Nigeria on a number of levels, with greater emphasis on institutional development rather than relations with particular leaders, and increased willingness to balance cooperation with pressure in such key areas as corruption, human rights, and conflict alleviation. More diversified economic engagement will expand the range of investment and trade. Linkages with civil society are crucial, since Nigeria's vigorous domain of nongovernmental organizations (NGOs) and its substantial professional middle class are potential forces for better governance and economic performance. The United States can best ensure a positive long-term relationship with Nigeria by clearly signaling to elites its preferences on governance and the economy and by allying with Nigerian advocates of accountable government, human rights, social justice, and a competitive economy.

The Dimensions of Developmental Failure

Nigeria faces developmental challenges in the economic, political, and social dimensions. Though analytically distinct, these problems are integrally related.[5] Economic stagnation arises from a generalized crisis of governance, just as poor economic performance contributes to the infirmities of the state. The weakness of central political authority, and the insecurity of rulers, exacerbates social tensions and undermines capital formation. Nigeria's deep communal divisions significantly impede state formation and economic growth and are themselves aggravated by political uncertainty and privation. I first recount the central problems of Nigeria's postcolonial development, and then analyze the sources of poor performance.

A Stalled Economy

Economically, Nigeria has been on a roller coaster in the decades since independence, culminating in a long period of stagnation following the apex of the petroleum boom. The problems of flagging growth, rising poverty, and widening inequality arise from several factors, including an unfavorable economic structure, detrimental policies, adverse political conditions, and negative external shocks.

Nigeria's economy grew modestly in the early years of independence, under a pragmatic policy regime linked to an open economy based on agriculture. Significantly hampered by the devastating civil war (1967–70), economic growth in the first decade of independence averaged 2.9 percent.[6] The country then entered a heady period of volatile expansion during the decade-long oil windfall of the 1970s. Postwar recovery coincided with a buildup of oil production, and the economy expanded by an impressive average of 9 percent from 1970 to 1975, achieving an overall average of 7 percent for the decade. The massive inflow of resources sent public spending on infrastructure and social programs soaring, alongside an ambitious (though ill-fated) program of state-led industrialization. Revenues fluctuated with the vagaries of world prices, however, and state expenditures were supplemented by extensive international borrowing.[7]

The boom gave way to an equally dramatic bust in the first half of the 1980s, as oil markets flagged and the country's financial position deteriorated. Export revenues plunged by 53 percent between 1980 and 1982 (from US$27.1 billion to US$12.7 billion), dropping another 60 percent by 1986.[8] Meanwhile, the value of external debt grew as commitments accumulated, short-term borrowing increased, and interest rates escalated. Foreign obligations increased from US$5.1 billion in 1978 (14 percent of GDP) to US$17.6 billion by 1983 (50 percent of GDP), reaching US$29 billion by 1987 (124 percent of GDP). Between1980 and 1987, Nigeria's gross domestic product declined at an average rate of 1 percent a year. The downturn began under the Second Republic, whose politicians were loathe to curtail spending or undertake politically costly adjustment measures.[9] In the throes of the oil markets' collapse, the civilians were ousted by the military, but the regime of General Muhammadu Buhari avoided essential policy reforms as the economy spiraled downward.

Another coup brought General Ibrahim Babangida to power, promising decisive action to revive the economy. Babangida entered into a standby agreement with the International Monetary Fund (IMF) and initiated a package of policy reform in cooperation with the IMF and the World Bank. The government's stabilization efforts, embodied in the Structural Adjustment Program (SAP), yielded an interlude of recovery. Macroeconomic reforms, aided by a fortuitous surge in oil prices during the Gulf War, boosted growth to an average of about 6.6 percent from 1988 through 1992. Thereafter, however, Nigeria experienced a decade of stagnation. Oil prices dropped soon after the war, and the Babangida regime veered toward economic indiscipline and malfeasance.[10] Political uncertainty gripped the country after the abortive 1993 transition to democratic rule, giving way to the predatory autocracy of General Sani Abacha. During Abacha's rule, prodigious corruption, political insecurity, and the deterioration of public institutions served as a brake on investment and growth. From 1993 to 1998, Nigeria managed an anemic 2.5 percent average rate of growth. Since the transition to civilian rule in 1999, performance has generally been lackluster, though the economy has been intermittently buoyed by higher world oil prices. The elected government moved inconsistently in its early years to impose fiscal discipline and pursue needed policy changes.

To summarize, Nigeria's aggregate economic growth from 1961 through 1998 averaged 3.6 percent, while the country achieved merely 2.2 percent average growth in the period from 1981 through 1998, significantly below the annual rate of population increase (about 2.9 percent). These trends, especially in a context of increasing income inequality, yielded a substantial increase in poverty. From 1961 through 1998, per capita GDP increased by a scant 0.7 percent annually, providing for little advance in living standards.[11] Average incomes have in fact declined during the last two decades, by slightly less than 1 percent a year. Despite the general scarcity of statistics in Nigeria, credible figures show that the incidence of poverty has escalated steeply since the end of petroleum boom. The rate of poverty (those at or below two-thirds of mean expenditure levels) expanded from 28 percent in 1980 to 71 percent in 1999.[12] Similarly, measures of income distribution (whether using the Gini index or household income shares) describe a society where inequality is rising and income disparities are quite high by international standards. Other indicators of social welfare are even harder to come by, though available statistics show declining primary and secondary school enrollment during the late 1980s, as well as diminished access to such amenities as clean water.[13]

Nigeria's major economic fluctuations since the early 1970s have closely followed changes in global oil markets. The emergence of a petroleum "monoculture," in which a single export provides nearly all foreign exchange and government revenue, renders the economy highly sensitive to external shocks and hinders the emergence of internal sources of growth.[14] The failure to diversify from this narrow export base is an important underlying source of Nigeria's economic stagnation. At independence, the country inherited a reasonably heterogeneous export economy, based on a range of agricultural commodities and solid minerals. The sparse manufacturing sector consisted mainly of final consumption goods produced in a few urban centers and constituted no more than 6 percent of GDP. Crude oil production grew rapidly in the early 1970s, and by middecade petroleum exports accounted for 75 percent of state revenues and more than 95 percent of foreign exchange.[15] In the wake of the oil windfall, agricultural exports atrophied and non-oil mining collapsed. Manufacturing grew rapidly in the boom era, spurred by massive state investments and protectionist measures. Subsequently, however, declining public revenues, import constraints, and inconsistent reform fostered deindustrialization, leaving Nigeria's export profile and productive structure little changed from the patterns that obtained three decades earlier.

Deficits of Governance

Nigeria's crisis of governance is equally conspicuous. Ruling elites and public institutions have not provided essential collective goods, such as physical infrastructure, the rule of law, or legitimate symbols of state authority and political community. One of the most contentious problems is democracy. Nigerians tenaciously maintain aspirations for democratic rule, as evidenced in the recurring political struggles since independence and in public attitudes toward government.[16] Democracy has proven elusive if not chimerical, as cycles of civilian and military government have been punctuated by false starts, failed transitions, and recurring challenges to stable rule.[17] Elected regimes have faltered over precarious institutions, factionalism among elites, and pervasive corruption. The First Republic, a parliamentary system put in place by the departing British colonists, suffered from an institutional design that encouraged ethnic segmentation and invidious regional competition for power. The regime quickly succumbed to communal polarization, political conflict, and social strife. The military stepped into the maelstrom with a coup in 1966. But the officers were themselves vulnerable to ethnic antagonism, leading to a countercoup and the ensuing civil war. Over the next thirteen years there was a succession of "corrective" military regimes, promising a return to democracy but deferring political reform until 1979, when General Olusegun Obasanjo handed power back to the civilians. The Second Republic, a presidential regime modeled on the American system, fared worse than its predecessor, lasting merely four years. Massive corruption, mismanagement, political chicanery, and epidemic violence quickly eroded the regime's ability to govern and undermined the legitimacy of the democratic system in the eyes of the public. Once again, the armed forces stepped in with promises of remedial action.

Despite their reformist pretensions, military regimes have proven no more capable than the civilians at resolving central challenges of state building and development. The turbulent military interventions of 1966 yielded nearly a decade of rule by General Yakubu Gowon, who prosecuted the civil war, sought to address problems of national unity, and presided over the early years of the petroleum boom. His dilatory response to pressures for democratization, and mounting evidence of corruption amid the oil windfall, prompted further intervention by senior officers. General Murtala Muhammad replaced Gowon in July 1975, promising rapid movement toward a transition to civilian rule, greater economic probity, and administrative reform. Only six months later, Murtala was assassinated in a failed coup attempt and was replaced by his second in command, Olusegun Obasanjo, who continued the regime's programs. Apart from overseeing the transition to civilian rule, the Murtala-Obasanjo government advanced an ambitious program of state-led industrialization and expansive social provision.

The four-year civilian interregnum was terminated in 1983 by General Muhammadu Buhari, amid popular hopes that his regime would overhaul the corrupt shambles left by the Second Republic. In the event, Buhari's regime instigated a new era of military dominance that proved more corrosive to state capabilities, economic development, and social stability than its predecessors. The tenures of Buhari (1983–85), Ibrahim Babangida (1985–93), and Sani Abacha (1993–98) traced a downward spiral of repression, arbitrary rule, economic predation, and the erosion of such central institutions as the military, the central bureaucracy, major services, and infrastructure.[18]

With the ouster of the regime of General Buhari (and his close associate General Tunde Idiagbon), whose autocratic style and economic ineptitude dissipated popular support, General Babangida pledged essential political and economic change, delivering a schedule for transition to democratic rule along with a program to stabilize the economy. The reformist impulse was fleeting, however, as Babangida repeatedly postponed and amended the political program, wavered on economic reform, and soon jettisoned even the pretense of stable management. The general employed coercion to quell opposition, while his regime was shadowed by evidence of prodigious corruption. The nadir of Babangida's rule was his abrogation of the democratic transition in June 1993, when he annulled the results of a presidential election that had been widely regarded as fair by a nation anxious to return to civilian rule.[19] The ensuing crisis provoked widespread uncertainty, ethnoregional antipathy, and further economic decline. Babangida was induced to depart, leaving a flimsy civilian caretaker committee in his wake, which was scrapped in a matter of weeks by the defense minister, General Sani Abacha.

Abacha, with none of the finesse or political alacrity of his predecessor, displayed an even more dictatorial and venal style of rule. He wielded the state security apparatus to intimidate, harass, jail, or murder political opponents and contrived a political "transition" that would perpetuate his own rule as a civilian president. After briefly tinkering with populist economic policies, the regime returned to a semblance of orthodox measures, but fiscal indiscipline and unalloyed economic predation left the economy in the doldrums. Abacha is estimated to have amassed a fortune of perhaps US$6 billion in a mere four and a half years, largely embezzled from the public treasury or diverted from state-owned enterprises and projects. The speed and magnitude of plunder at the center was mirrored by accelerated decline of the education and health systems, public administration, utilities, and domestic fuel supplies. Social and political tensions intensified as the general's "self-succession" seemed imminent. Abacha's unexpected death in June 1998, officially attributed to a heart attack, opened the way for reformers in the military to pursue political change. General Abdulsalami Abubakar, selected by the ruling military council, elaborated a program to return Nigeria to civilian rule. The regime adhered to its expeditious schedule of transition, transferring power to an elected civilian regime in May 1999. The newly elected president was Olusegun Obasanjo, the retired general who had handed power to the politicians of the Second Republic two decades earlier.

The resumption of civilian rule has brought many improvements in the climate of popular participation and human rights in Nigeria. In other areas of governance, the changes have been less favorable. The regime is burdened by the accumulated depredations of preceding rulers, manifest in a depleted treasury, a huge debt overhang, dilapidated public institutions, endemic corruption, and simmering social antagonism. The first presidential term has seen little progress on the chronic problems of the economy, while communal violence has exploded in myriad conflicts across the country. A contentious and largely inexperienced political class shows little capacity to address the country's pressing economic and social challenges.

National Integration and Disintegration

The rising trend of violence underscores the deep divisions in Nigerian society and the enduring dilemmas of national cohesion and identity. Nigeria's borders, a colonial inheritance, contain at least 250 ethnic and linguistic groups (some put the number closer to 400), with rough parity among Muslims and Christians. Communal competition is relatively concentrated, however, as three groups—the Hausa-Fulani in the northwest, the Yoruba in the southwest, and the Igbo in the southeast—together constitute about two-thirds of the population. This pattern is overlaid by religious identities, as the northern half of the country is majority Muslim, while the southern portions are predominantly Christian.[20] The early years of the republic were dominated by intensifying competition among the three major ethnoregional groups, each of which controlled a sectional political party and a discrete region within the federal structure. A mounting political crisis from 1965 to 1967 led to collapse of the democratic regime, the federal structure, and eventually the nation itself, with the economy an ancillary casualty. Federal victory in the civil war, which quelled the Biafran (Igbo) bid for secession, upheld the territorial integrity of the state, though at great human cost, including more than a million deaths. For most Nigerians, the conflict affirmed the nation's boundaries as a political entity, if only by default. Yet the terms of national community, still tenuously defined, became more contentious with the development of the oil economy and the political assertion of additional groups and identities.[21]

Throughout the 1970s and 1980s, Nigerian governments obtained social peace through a combination of institutional reform, fiscal redistribution, and patronage, periodically supplemented by coercion. The federal system was transformed by replacing the regional structure with two subnational tiers of states and local governments and changing the formula for the allocation of central revenues. The number of states grew steadily (from twelve in 1966 to thirty-six three decades later), and these changes along with the formal devolution of petroleum revenues provided a degree of stability to the system. The constitutional reforms leading to the Second Republic provided for communal diversity in personnel appointments and distributive policies, while a decisive compromise in the 1979 constitution allowed for the exercise of civil shari'a law in Muslim-majority states. These formal mechanisms to balance sectional interests and regulate the distribution of federal resources were supplemented by the expedient use of patronage to secure elite compliance and furnish instrumental benefits to politically strategic communities. During this period, national equilibrium was aided by Gowon's reconciliatory stance in the wake of the civil war, and by the flood of oil revenue that substantially assuaged distributive concerns.

By the middle of the 1980s, however, the decline of central resources was hampering the use of patronage to obtain sectional accommodation, and new sources of communal tension arose. The proliferation of states and the strategies of competing political parties gave rise to political assertion by ethnic minorities that often challenged the tripartite contention among the major ethnic groups. The communities of the southern Niger Delta, the center of Nigeria's oil production, were increasingly visible, as were various groups in the heterogeneous Middle Belt of the country, and non-Hausa minorities in the northern states. These groups and others exerted new pressures for redistribution and identity.[22] Moreover, the 1980s witnessed growing religious assertion in Nigeria and the accentuation of a north-south divide along confessional lines. Religious cleavages were sharpened by the rising influence of fundamentalist leaders within the Islamic community, as well as the expansion of evangelical Christianity. An unbroken succession of northern Muslim rulers for two decades (1979–99) contributed to both regional and religious polarization, especially disaffection by southern Christians and within the Yoruba heartland.

The 1990s witnessed a marked deterioration of national cohesion and stability. Apart from economic factors and authoritarian rule, several policy decisions were especially corrosive. In 1986 Nigeria's membership in the Organization of Islamic Conference (OIC) came to light and was viewed with particular suspicion by non-Muslims, since it had apparently been undertaken secretly by an earlier military regime. In addition, the governments of Generals Babangida and Abacha undertook ill-considered partitions of state and local governments in 1989, 1991, and 1996, fostering boundary conflicts in the affected communities and giving rise to further tensions over communal balance at the national level. Furthermore, Babangida's abrogation of the 1993 elections and the arrest of the putative winner, Chief M. K. O. Abiola, a Yoruba Muslim, outraged the population of the southwestern states, deepening disaffection between the Yoruba minority and the central government. His successor, General Abacha, aggravated these tensions by jailing Abiola, harassing prominent Yorubas, and crudely suppressing dissent—for example, through the assassination of Abiola's wife and the peremptory executions of Ken Saro-Wiwa and other Ogoni activists from the Niger Delta. Abacha also supervised an opaque, convoluted constitutional reform in the mid-1990s, which exacerbated communal tensions. Beneath the rough stability imposed by military repression, growing discord was manifest in episodes of religious strife, recurrent violence in the southwestern states and the Niger Delta, intercommunity conflicts in the Middle Belt, and confrontations between the authorities and Islamists in several northern cities.

Turmoil followed in the wake of the 1999 transition to civilian rule. In the four years of the first administration, more than forty incidents of communal violence nationwide claimed an estimated 10,000 lives.[23] The violence took many forms: interethnic conflicts in several southern cities; religious confrontations in major urban areas in the north; property clashes among communities in the southwest, the Middle Belt, the northern states, and the Niger Delta; and political violence in numerous locales. The move by a dozen governors in the northern states to expand the writ of shari'a law from voluntary use in civil matters to mandatory application in the criminal domain was a major catalyst of violence and had destabilizing effects throughout the country. Other conflicts arose from such diverse sources as land and chieftancy disputes, electoral rivalries, and grievances toward government.

Public disorder was exacerbated by the uncertain political terrain, a rising sense of insecurity, and the actions of opportunistic politicians. The central administration responded sporadically to social unrest but generally failed to construct a reliable framework for addressing conflict.

Explaining Poor Developmental Performance

Economic malaise, weak governance, and communal polarization speak to a profound social dilemma at the heart of Nigeria's political economy. Public choice theorists define a social dilemma as a situation in which actors pursue individual or particular utilities at the expense of collective welfare, and where it is not possible for a third party to resolve the tension between individual and collective interest. In other words, the self-interested behavior of individuals and groups leaves everyone worse off than would a cooperative solution, yet political authorities or institutions are unable to induce coordination for common goals.[24] This essential problem of collective action highlights the political obstacles to resolving the country's developmental challenges. In the economic realm, investment and capital formation are stymied by pervasive distributive struggles among ruling groups, and consequently no regime or power center within the state has been capable of overseeing a project of growth and transformation. Politically, elite division and instability erode the foundations of governance. The alternation of civilian and military regimes, each troubled by internal discord and uncertainty, is inimical to effective leadership, the consolidation of capable institutions, or the provision of essential public goods. In the social domain, a striking aspect of Nigeria's communal politics is the absence of a broad social compact that would establish consensus on national identity and the meaning of citizenship. Such an accord is necessary for the development of institutions to manage intergroup relations, yet efforts at accommodation have repeatedly been eclipsed by invidious communal contention.

By framing the problem of Nigerian development as a social dilemma, I focus attention on governance. Additional factors are obviously relevant. Economists have rightly drawn attention to how the flawed policy choices of various governments have contributed to slow growth. Jeffrey Sachs, for instance, has observed four types of crises in poorly performing states: a "poverty trap," implying that a low level of resources hampers growth; state bankruptcy, in which the government faces chronic fiscal crisis and insolvency; liquidity crises, where abrupt changes in capital flows create transitory shortfalls; and transition crises, which emerge in circumstances of regime change, where institutional turbulence disrupts policymaking and exchange relations.[25] Nigeria clearly reflects two of these syndromes: state bankruptcy, attributable mainly to policy choices rather than external shocks; and a transition crisis arising from domestic political and economic disruption. In view of the country's abundant petroleum revenues, it is difficult to ascribe its poor performance to a poverty trap, and its isolation from global capital markets obviates the type of liquidity crisis associated with the Asian financial downturn. There is little question that the country's decades-long economic stagnation has been instigated and protracted by harmful government policies, but this observation fails to explain why Nigeria's various rulers have selected and maintained policies that were demonstrably harmful to development. Answering this question calls for consideration of the political context of policymaking and market relations.

Sachs, along with others, has also emphasized the geographic foundations of underdevelopment in the tropics generally, and in Africa in particular. Adverse endowments of climate, soil, and disease and limited integration in global trade have contributed to slow growth and lagging productivity.[26] These conditions undeniably hamper many countries, but it is important to ask why contemporary governments have not undertaken public health measures, agricultural reforms, or trade initiatives to surmount an unfortunate geographic inheritance. Other lines of analysis, focusing on structural and historical factors, run up against a similar problem. Many authors have emphasized Nigeria's colonial legacy and the problems of economic dependence.[27] It has also been suggested that states with dominant resource-export sectors confront special impediments to growth.[28] These factors are important to an understanding of Nigeria's developmental performance, yet in each instance one can observe significant variation in performance among countries with similar structural conditions or historical legacies. These differences in performance can be attributed to policy choices, arising from the particular political conditions of different countries and regions.

What accounts for the political syndrome at the heart of Nigeria's lagging development? The underpinnings are found in the structure of communal competition, the evolution of a rentier economy, and the course of institutional degeneration.

Communal Competition

Nigeria exhibits substantial ethnic fragmentation. There are hundreds of ethnic groups, including dozens that are politically significant.[29] Communal competition, however, is highly concentrated among the three largest ethnolinguistic groups (Hausa-Fulani, Igbo, and Yoruba), although these demarcations are frequently offset by broader regional divisions and by the participation of smaller groups (for example, Tiv, Ijaw, Nupe, Kanuri, Edo, Efik, among others). Competition and conflict have been shaped by different economic attributes and resources for collective action.[30] During the colonial era, British policies reinforced disparities between northern and southern populations. Southern peoples had greater access to modern education, commercial opportunities (by virtue of coastal access and urbanization), and integration in the colonial administration. By contrast, the Northern Region, under the colonial doctrine of indirect rule, remained under the sway of traditional authorities in the Emirates; Muslim religious, judicial, and educational institutions; and prevailing agrarian structures. In the postcolonial era, these historical patterns of socioeconomic development yielded substantial advantages for southerners in entrepreneurship, administrative experience, and education. The consolidation of three regional governments controlled by distinct ethnically oriented parties served to reinforce and politicize these disparities.

Paradoxically, the Northern Region, despite lagging educational and economic resources, proved most adept at collective action on behalf of sectional interests.[31] Elites linked to the emirate system retained influence throughout the colonial era, and they built upon common religious and cultural identities to forge an effective political network during the years of nationalist mobilization. Northern elites coalesced in the 1950s under the Northern People's Congress (NPC), organizing a voting block and wielding legislative discipline to achieve dominance of the postindependence parliamentary system. The Northern Region held a plurality of legislative seats, whereas dissension among southern groups prevented a countervailing regional coalition. The growing influence of northerners in the armed forces, especially after the civil war, bolstered regional supremacy.[32] Over the four decades following independence, politicians and military officers from the northern states held executive posts for twenty-seven years; the country was continuously governed by northern Muslims from 1979 through 1999. These regimes furnished a semblance of inclusion through expedient political alliances, selective appointments, and patronage, but most southern groups and non-Muslim northern minorities felt marginalized and excluded.[33]

Communal competition is defined by these polarities of political and economic power. The persistence of social and economic disparities along the north-south divide has prompted northern rulers to use political power to pursue their goals of geographic redistribution. Northern elites have consistently favored statist strategies as a means of directing economic resources

and opportunities toward "disadvantaged" regions and mitigating the pre-
sumed advantages of the south. Groups in the south are more frequently
(though not uniformly) proponents of economic liberalization, as they perceive advantages in an environment of relatively competitive markets. All,
however, share basic assumptions about political and economic competition.
First, access to the state is viewed as essential for sectional opportunities and
claims on resources. Strategies for communal advancement therefore focus on
securing control of government or gaining important representation through
electoral office, cabinet appointments, the civil service, or public enterprise.[34]
Having a "son of the soil" in high position is the only assured channel for
advancing group interests. Second, the coincidence of political and economic
power enables a particular sectional group to consolidate its dominance.
Political authority is therefore seen in instrumental, zero-sum terms: state
positions are used to direct resources towards one's own group, while denying
access to competitors. Elites in power are motivated not only by the patronage demands of their particular constituencies, but also by a desire to prevent
other groups from building an economic base that could yield competitive
political resources.

To sum up, communal competition in Nigeria has created a proliferation
of points of access to state resources, while forming a set of mutual vetoes
among groups over market access and distribution. The resulting political
stalemate is antithetical to economic development. Without a stable governing coalition across communal lines, it is largely impossible to organize concerted state action on behalf of growth and capital formation.[35] For political
leaders, time horizons are short, economic decisionmaking is particularistic
rather than general, and discretion over resources is prized above institutional
credibility. Distributive pressures on state actors impel the immediate disper-
sal of resources, hindering the cooperation over broader policies or institutional changes that would enhance investment and exchange.

The Rentier State

The emergence of the oil economy significantly increased the political
impediments to development. The growth of oil exports created a rentier
state, a government relying principally on revenues from resource rents.[36]
Nigeria's fiscal transformation occurred suddenly in the early 1970s, with far-
reaching effects on public finance, economic strategy, distributive politics,
and private economic activity. In the first decade after independence, the federal structure and a varied export profile produced substantial fiscal decentralization. The three regions, each with different cash crops and minerals,

retained their own export revenues.[37] Their budgetary autonomy, and the reliance of regional governments on local production, created incentives for promoting and sustaining output across the economy. These incentives shifted abruptly with the advent of petroleum exports. First, revenues became substantially centralized in the hands of the federal government, and the fiscal discretion of the central authorities was greatly increased. The replacement of regions by states limited the fiscal autonomy of subnational government, and the subsequent growth of petroleum exports quickly overshadowed other revenue sources. The precipitous decline of non-oil exports spurred the concentration of resources at the center.

A second set of effects is associated with the "Dutch disease," a syndrome of price distortions and structural changes in resource-exporting economies that are generally adverse to growth.[38] Briefly, countries experiencing a resource windfall see a shift in relative prices as nontradable goods (for example, construction and services) appreciate relative to tradables (for example, cash crops and manufactured goods). The appreciation of the exchange rate causes imports to become cheaper and lowers returns on exports. This creates disincentives for investment in productive sectors such as agriculture and (non-oil) industry, and thus reduces their competitiveness and economic flexibility. The dynamics of the Dutch disease are frequently associated with inflation, a proliferation of prestige projects, accelerating urbanization and crime, and heightened corruption.[39] These are certainly evident in Nigeria.

Paradoxically, state bankruptcy (defined by Sachs as an inability to service external debts) is a common problem for resource exporters. In Nigeria, the windfall prompted steep growth of public spending, and fiscal expansion quickly outpaced the increase in revenues. Large commitments to ambitious capital projects as well as a growing public sector wage bill made it difficult to adjust spending in response to periodic declines in revenue. The gap was bridged through foreign loans, producing a large debt overhang by the 1980s. A sense of fiscal myopia also comes into play: leaders' perspectives (and incentives) shifted so dramatically with the initial windfall that they regarded the gains as permanent, despite abundant evidence of volatility. In the face of revenue shortfalls and rising external obligations, policymakers have regularly behaved as if exports would provide a bailout. Occasional boosts in revenues from favorable oil market shocks have not provided fiscal deliverance but simply added to a mounting trend of insolvency.

The rentier state draws revenues primarily from a foreign-dominated enclave; state resources are therefore divorced from domestic output. This shifts the basic concern of governing elites from revenue generation (through taxation and expansion of the economic base) to the distribution of proceeds derived mainly from abroad.[40] An independent revenue base reduces the pressures on ruling groups to maintain general conditions for production and allows them to use their fiscal discretion to bolster political power. A key to this strategy is expansion of the public sector, which allows leaders to use employment, subsidies, public works, and development spending in the course of building patronage networks.

The growth of government largesse increases the state's role in conflicts over distribution among elites and average citizens. For politicians and military officers, the stakes of winning and losing political office are significantly heightened. For the public, the state becomes a font of resources and the gatekeeper of economic opportunities. For business elites, in particular, opportunities are multiplied through the government's role in allocating petroleum rents and the copious growth of the state sector. Business gravitates toward government contracts, licenses, quotas, and employment and auxiliary relationships with state enterprise. The rentier state fosters a rentier economy, in which the principal avenues of accumulation are found in access to politically mediated rents and state elites are the central arbiters of resource distribution and market entry.[41] As a corollary, fiscal discretion, a lack of accountability, and abundant pressures for special preferences generate massive corruption throughout the state and private sectors.

The Decline of Institutions

An additional factor, particularly in the wake of the oil boom, has been Nigeria's course of institutional decline.[42] This is both a manifestation of poor governance and a cause of further deterioration in governance. Although the effects of institutional weakness are sometimes difficult to distinguish from other effects, there is no question that the degeneration of major state institutions has been an important factor in the poor developmental performance of the past two decades. Nigeria, like most postcolonial countries, had weak institutional foundations at independence, and the process of institution building in the early years of the new state was slow and uneven. The petroleum boom was a period of rapid institutional expansion. The precipitous growth of the civil service and a proliferation of public enterprises in the 1970s and 1980s magnified the challenges of institutional design and local staffing.[43] The burgeoning state became overextended, and public institutions descended into inefficiency, disarray, and corruption.

The situation worsened markedly in the 1980s, as resources declined and political instability further eroded government capacities. The slump in the oil market gave rise to fiscal shortfalls, salary arrears, and the deterioration of essential services. Under the Second Republic, the resource gap was aggravated by budgetary indiscipline and epidemic corruption. Following the civilians, the Buhari regime implemented stringent austerity measures in response to dwindling export revenues and rising debt, including large-scale retrenchment in the civil service and state enterprises. This trend continued under Babangida, whose Structural Adjustment Program called for further cuts in public employment and subsidies, along with widespread liberalization and divestiture of state firms. From the 1980s forward, therefore, the situation has been characterized by increasing resource constraints, faltering public services, and pervasive insecurity within state agencies.[44]

State bankruptcy, however, is only one facet of the picture. A notable deterioration in professionalism and organizational cohesion within the armed forces was equally apparent during the 1980s. Internal divisions and instability had long afflicted the military, as reflected in two coups in 1966, the 1975 action by Murtala, and the unsuccessful revolt that took Murtala's life. Several years later, in the aftermath of Buhari's coup, internal weaknesses in the military had clearly multiplied; indeed, the Buhari-Idiagbon regime was ousted in just twenty months. Babangida put down two major revolts in his first five years in power, both of which suggested a disturbing fragmentation of the military along factional, ethnic, and generational lines. Moreover, corruption within military regimes became increasingly conspicuous. Officers grew more openly interested in continued political control and were less concerned with presenting a rationale of reform.[45] The persistence of military rule politicized the armed forces, and the attractions of power at the fountainhead of oil wealth intensified venal impulses throughout this crucial institution.

These pathologies were evident in the dictatorship of Sani Abacha, who fashioned his regime around an agenda of economic predation and political domination. Abacha personalized power to an unprecedented degree by employing widespread repression, encouraging a cult of personality, and manipulating the political process to perpetuate his rule. Historically, Nigeria's military regimes have been relatively collegial, as leaders worked within consultative processes and wider decisionmaking institutions. Abacha moved decisively toward the creation of a "sultanistic" regime, based upon personal rule and a monopoly of patronage.[46] His efforts to gather power at the center—eschewing consultation, bypassing, manipulating or remaking state institutions, and plundering resources—accelerated the decline of major instruments of governance. The education and health systems, starved of funds and wracked by professional protests and government repression, grew moribund; the traditionally independent judiciary, manipulated by autocratic rulers and short of resources, became increasingly ineffectual and corrupt; the civil service was organizationally weak, demoralized, and suffused with misconduct; and the banking system, following a hasty, politically inflected, liberalization in the early 1990s, descended into full-blown financial crisis. The declining legitimacy of the military and other leading public institutions further undermined the capacity to govern. Mounting antigovernment violence and social conflict were further indications of a state in crisis.[47]

With Abacha's demise and the subsequent transition to civilian rule, the trend of institutional decline has been arrested, though hardly reversed. The institutions bequeathed to the new administration were enfeebled by years of mismanagement and plunder, and the civilians have neither the resources nor the programs to revive services and overhaul the machinery of government. The Obasanjo government has restored a modicum of fiscal control and transparency, while promising to stem corruption. The new democratic institutions, however, bring additional problems, not least of which are the untested nature of the party system, the legislature, and many elected offices, as well as inexperience among much of the political class. Tensions between the presidency and the National Assembly have impaired budgeting and spending, while major reforms have stalled in the assembly or in subsequent bureaucratic implementation. Institutional malaise is evident in the poor state of public services and government functions, as well as the intractable political wrangling that seems to block effective reform.

Summary

This analysis underscores the domestic political constraints on development. Background factors of Nigeria's geography, history, and international position frame the essential challenges of development. The principal external shocks of recent decades, arising from energy and capital markets, are also of great importance. However, it is the policy response of Nigerian governments to these structural conditions and exogenous factors that lies at the heart of the problem. Nigeria's poor developmental performance therefore requires political solutions, though since the civilian transition, promises of reform and political reconfiguration have been overshadowed by increased turbulence and uncertainty. This context must inform the United States' relations with Nigeria.

Engaging Nigeria

Nigeria's profound challenges are necessarily a matter of concern for the United States.[48] The country commands attention by virtue of its sheer size and regional position. With 137 million people, Nigeria accounts for about half of the total population and gross domestic product in the West African subregion; continentwide, one in five Africans is Nigerian. The country is a major trading partner with its neighbors, a crossroads of migration, and a leading security influence in the fifteen-member Economic Community of West African States (ECOWAS). Nigerian forces constituted the bulk of the ECOWAS Monitoring Group (ECOMOG) that played a decisive role in peacekeeping and security operations in Liberia and Sierra Leone during the 1990s. Nigeria continues to exert diplomatic and security influence in West Africa, notably through its pivotal role in facilitating the 2003 departure of Charles Taylor from Liberia. The government has interceded widely in crises in Côte d'Ivoire, Darfur, Zimbabwe, and Congo and has taken the lead in continental initiatives such as the New Partnership for African Development (NEPAD).

Another central interest is the country's increasing prominence in global energy markets in general, and trade with the United States in particular. Nigeria is currently the fourth largest producer in the Organization of Petroleum Exporting Countries (OPEC), with daily production of about 2.3 million barrels of low-sulphur crude oil as well as rapidly growing natural gas output. It is a major supplier to the United States, accounting for 8–10 percent of American oil imports, and conversely imports between US$500 million and US$1 billion of goods from the United States each year.[49] Its strategic significance is heightened by growing concerns over America's dependence on Middle Eastern energy, especially as Nigeria's proven reserves of oil and gas have risen substantially in recent years and a large liquefied natural gas complex has come on stream.

A burdensome international debt, currently around US$33 billion, is an important issue in bilateral relations. Beginning in the early 1990s, various Nigerian governments placed explicit or de facto caps on debt service, resulting in arrears on foreign debt that exceed US$19 billion. The majority is owed to Paris Club creditors, with Britain, Germany, Japan, and France heading the list.[50] Since 1999 the Obasanjo government has placed a high priority on lobbying the United States for a cancellation of Nigeria's foreign debt, the centerpiece of a desired "democracy dividend" from creditor governments in the G-7. Though not included in the Bretton Woods institutions' heavily indebted poor countries (HIPC) initiative, Nigeria has sought a parallel arrangement on debt reduction from its creditors, which was eventually agreed in July 2005. When fully implemented, the agreement would provide for cancellation of two-thirds of Nigeria's external debt.

Religion has not previously been a significant factor in bilateral relations between Nigeria and the United States, though its salience has increased since September 11. With at least 60 million Muslims, Nigeria is generally regarded as a Muslim majority country.[51] As of this writing, there is little evidence of Nigerian involvement in international terrorist activities, though domestic Islamist groups are quite active and religious polarization has increased sharply in recent years. Issues of economic development are increasingly intertwined with concerns about the country's stability and security. The preponderantly Muslim northern states are among the poorest and most economically stagnant areas of the country, giving rise to conditions that nurture religious extremism. The movement begun in 1999 by twelve northern governors to expand shari'a law in their states has been one of the most divisive trends in the period since the transition to civilian rule.

Apart from trade, financial, and regional interests, the United States has significant links to Nigeria based on culture and community. Several hundred thousand people of Nigerian origin are U.S. citizens or permanent residents, and many Americans trace their ancestry to the area that is present-day Nigeria. These ties are certainly more extensive than those with any other African country.

Other linkages are more problematic. Since the late 1980s, Nigerian criminal networks, encouraged by domestic economic malaise and the military authorities' permissive attitude toward corruption and lawlessness, have moved aggressively into international enterprise. Their leading activities are drug trafficking and financial fraud. A thriving traffic in opiates and cocaine channels these drugs from producer countries to North America and Europe. Initially couriers traveled directly from Nigeria, but syndicates now use third countries as conduits. In the mid-1990s, U.S. drug enforcement authorities estimated that Nigerian networks transported as much as 60 percent of the heroin available in the United States. In addition, fraudulent activities have flourished in the past decade, forming a shadow economy that provides significant foreign exchange. Nigerian letters soliciting collaboration in money laundering and corrupt activities (known colloquially as "419" letters, from the Nigerian criminal code for fraud) began to blanket the United States and many European and Asian countries toward the end of the 1980s, supplemented recently by e-mail messages. By some estimates, these scams defraud credulous respondents of hundreds of millions of dollars annually. The proceeds from fraud, drug trafficking, oil smuggling, and other illegal activities naturally create a large need for money laundering through numerous banks and other businesses. The Nigerian government has only tentatively addressed these concerns.

Most recently, public health concerns have come to the fore. Current epidemiological evidence suggests that Nigeria's HIV prevalence is high (at 5.9 percent for adults) and rising. While this is considerably lower than the adult prevalence in South Africa (about 20 percent), Nigeria's larger population means that the number of people infected is rapidly approaching that in South Africa.[52] The prospect of a catastrophic increase in HIV-AIDS obviously carries severe consequences for social and economic stability in Nigeria, which will reverberate in the West African subregion. Nigeria is therefore likely to command a large share of attention and resources as the U.S. government expands health assistance in Africa. In addition, the considerable flow of people between Nigeria and the United States could have implications for public health in the United States.

A Cooperative Legacy

Relations between Nigeria and the United States have historically been marked by cooperation and a degree of affinity. In the decades after independence, Nigerian governments defined a pragmatic stance in continental and global affairs. In the 1960s and 1970s, Nigeria maintained cordial diplomatic and economic relations with the United States, while U.S. investment and trade grew significantly. Nigeria did not play a prominent role in the cold war, adopting balanced approaches to most international alliances and political issues. In some areas, Nigeria's position did diverge from that of the United States. Like many African countries in the 1970s, Nigeria was a supporter of the UN movement for a New International Economic Order and an advocate of independent continental action on such issues as recognition of the Popular Movement for the Liberation of Angola (MPLA) government in Angola and opposition to apartheid in South Africa. The federal government turned to the Soviet Union for military assistance during the civil war and subsequently maintained aid and trade relations. At the same time, major American oil firms and other companies were rapidly expanding their activities in the country, and Nigeria looked to the United States as a model for its new democratic institutions in 1979. The United States generally took a neutral view of Nigeria's frequent regime changes until the 1990s, and there were few other political or trade issues to create discord in the bilateral relationship. General Babangida's commitment to democratization, and his cooperation with multilateral financial institutions on economic reform, helped to keep relations on a cooperative footing for much of his tenure.

Crisis and Dissension

Nigeria's abortive transition to democracy in 1993 precipitated a historic rift in relations with the United States. General Babangida repeatedly revised the transition schedule and extended it several years beyond the original deadline. Meanwhile, as his regime grew increasingly autocratic and corrupt, the public intensified its impatience for the military to depart from power. The 1993 presidential election was set against the backdrop of democratization elsewhere in sub-Saharan Africa and during the early months of the Clinton administration. This conjuncture of international events influenced the repercussions of the political crisis.

The presidential poll held on June 12, 1993, was regarded by domestic and international observers as surprisingly fair and transparent, given Nigeria's checkered history of flawed elections.[53] Returns indicated a decisive 59 percent majority for M. K. O. Abiola, yet Babangida halted the official release of election returns and annulled the poll, citing legal and procedural problems that were largely of his own creation. The annulment was greeted with widespread public indignation, particularly in Abiola's southwestern constituency. Demonstrations erupted in Lagos and other southwestern cities, and the violent police response caused dozens of casualties. The aspiring civilian politicians entered into a flurry of maneuvers to salvage the transition. The United States, Britain, and the European Union criticized the annulment, suspended military assistance, and suggested further paring their aid. Domestic and external pressure induced Babangida to leave office in August, turning over power to an ineffectual civilian caretaker committee that was soon replaced by General Abacha.

Abacha's political intransigence, growing abuses of human rights, and flagrant corruption aggravated tensions in bilateral relations and intensified the regime's disfavor abroad. Several months after the general's seizure of power, Chief Abiola called for recognition of his own electoral mandate, whereupon he was jailed. This provoked an extended strike by the powerful oil workers unions, which was quelled with the arrest of their leaders. Not long afterward, retired General Obasanjo and several other prominent Nigerians were detained in connection with an alleged coup plot. The regime's international standing reached its nadir in November 1995, when Ogoni activist Ken Saro-Wiwa and eight compatriots were summarily executed after a highly irregular murder trial. Nigeria was suspended from the Commonwealth, and the United States joined several other countries in extending sanctions on travel, aid, and (nonenergy) trade. Over the next two and a half years, Abacha's isolation deepened amid a pall of domestic repression, assassinations of opposition figures, and efforts to create a compliant party system that would regularize the general's rule in civilian garb. U.S. ambassador Walter Carrington, a vocal critic of the autocratic regime and a candid partisan of the prodemocracy opposition, became virtually persona non grata in Nigeria. Foreign assistance dwindled to a token health program and modest aid to nongovernmental organizations engaged in human rights and democratic activism.

Despite an increasingly confrontational political relationship, however, major American oil firms continued to operate normally, even expanding investments in some areas. Petroleum companies and other large investors vigorously opposed harsher sanctions against Nigeria, especially the prospect of an oil embargo. The Clinton administration, already ambivalent about the effectiveness of petroleum sanctions, essentially removed this option from consideration.

Diplomatic pressure and peripheral sanctions had little appreciable impact on Abacha's behavior, but the United States and other major powers appeared to have few other points of leverage.[54] Policymakers in Washington were constrained by their considerable stakes in trade and investment, as well as by concerns for security cooperation in the subregion, where Nigeria's role was crucial. These interests essentially trumped concerns over democracy, human rights, and economic reform.

The Challenges of Normalization

Relations between Nigeria and the United States normalized quickly upon Abacha's death. His successor, General Abdulsalami Abubakar, relaxed political restrictions, freed political prisoners, and elaborated a scheme for transition to civilian rule. The United States opened dialogue with General Abubakar and sought consultation with Chief Abiola, who collapsed and died during a meeting with visiting State Department officials only a month after Abacha's demise. This dramatic turn of events did not impede the transition program, however, and Washington continued to engage with the military government throughout the transition process. Elections were held in February 1999, and the administration of President Obasanjo was inaugurated that May. In addition to regularizing diplomatic relations, the United States lifted visa restrictions on Nigerian officials, rescinded limits on aid and trade, and ended the embargo on military cooperation. Foreign assistance from the United States grew exponentially, from less than US$7 million in 1998 to US$109 million by 2001.[55] This represented a precipitous increase in virtually all areas, notably democracy and governance, economic policy reform, health, education, and infrastructure. After the transition, the Department of Defense initiated a training program in peacekeeping operations for five Nigerian battalions, accompanied by an enlarged program of cooperative military education.[56] With the accord of the United States, Nigeria was able to resume borrowing from the World Bank, and the government concluded a new standby arrangement with the IMF in August 2000. All these initiatives displayed engagement with Nigeria over key areas of political and economic reform, military conversion, and basic needs in health and education.

Another important dimension of the bilateral relationship has been the personal interaction between President Obasanjo and American leaders. At the time of the transition, hopes ran high in Washington that Obasanjo's presidency could be a watershed for Nigeria. Obasanjo, although previously a military ruler, had voluntarily ceded power to civilians (for the first time in Nigerian history) and had subsequently spent twenty years as a private citizen. During that time, apart from running a livestock farm, Obasanjo marked a career as an international statesman. He was a member of the Commonwealth Eminent Persons Group appointed to lead antiapartheid initiatives, a founder of the African Leadership Forum, and a charter member of the anticorruption group Transparency International. His activities on behalf of governance and development, as well as his experience as a political prisoner under Abacha's regime, led many to expect that he would tackle Nigeria's challenges conscientiously. President Clinton pointedly included Nigeria in his second tour of sub-Saharan Africa, and Obasanjo was the first African leader received at the White House by George W. Bush, following which the Nigerian president made additional visits to Washington.

Paradoxically, the rapport between U.S. officials and President Obasanjo, desirable though it may be, also complicates U.S. approaches toward Nigeria's fragile civilian regime. The president has presented a new face for Nigeria abroad and has cooperated with the United States in key areas, notably antiterrorist efforts after September 11. Domestically, however, Obasanjo has been an increasingly controversial figure in light of a languishing economy, proliferating social violence, and episodic human rights violations by security forces. He has been at loggerheads with several governors and much of the legislature and has survived two impeachment efforts in the National

Assembly—the most recent launched by his own party caucus. He was reelected by a substantial majority in 2003, though domestic and foreign observers raised questions about the integrity of the election and survey data showed declining public approval of the executive. The administration's lackluster performance, including in areas of direct interest to the United States (for example, corruption and the economy), raises the possibility that more assertive U.S. engagement might be appropriate.

A related problem—recently seen also in U.S. relations with Russia, Mexico, and Indonesia—is the challenge of balancing personal links with a specific leader against other forms of bilateral engagement. The United States obviously has an interest in cooperating with sympathetic leaders in large, troubled democracies, and there is no necessary contradiction between these high politics and broader interactions between nations. Yet the United States has too often banked on particular leaders in crisis-ridden states. An important challenge for American policy toward poorly performing states is to identify elite groups, elements of civil society, and leading public institutions that can serve as agents of stabilization and reform, and to build a diverse array of linkages with these sectors. Nigeria presents significant opportunities in this area, as there is a history of involvement by American nongovernmental organizations, business groups, universities, and an array of government institutions that can serve as a basis for diversified engagement.

Beyond Normalization

The decline of governance, social stability, and economic performance in Nigeria throughout the 1990s led many observers, Nigerians included, to view the country as a failing state. The demise of Abacha's regime closed a long, discouraging chapter of predatory dictatorship. The return of civilian rule, accompanied by promises of political and economic reform, suggests prospects for arresting the downward trajectory of recent decades. Nigeria's crisis-ridden civilian regime is nonetheless burdened by a listless economy, weak governance, and deteriorating domestic security. While some of these problems may be linked to underlying structural problems and the legacy of earlier regimes, aspects of civilian politics and the shortcomings of the leadership are equally culpable. Nigeria vividly illustrates the challenges of reforming governance in a poor, turbulent society amid partial democratization. The main levers of change reside in the creation or rehabilitation of critical institutions, the emergence of new social coalitions to sustain a reform agenda, and potential shifts in the composition of political elites and the incentives of leaders. Such transformations in the nature of the state and the economy can only be brought about by domestic factors, since Nigeria's size, complexity, and independent revenues will inevitably limit the influence and leverage of outside actors. At the same time, Nigeria is not isolated from the rest of the world (in contrast to, say, Burma or Zimbabwe). The country's myriad trade, investment, and financial relations, along with its involvement in regional and international organizations and its traditional diplomatic and aid relationships, therefore furnish points of external influence and assistance.

The United States confronts important challenges in moving the relationship with Nigeria beyond postauthoritarian normalization to engagement on issues of improved governance and better developmental performance. This calls for a commitment of resources and people on critical issues pertaining to democratic development, economic policy change, the alleviation of social conflict, and reform of the rentier state. Unfortunately, rather than intensifying engagement around a broad agenda of reform, U.S. interest in Nigeria appears to have receded both politically and financially, while the focus of the bilateral relationship has largely shifted to a few functional issues, including energy, counterterrorism, health, and education. This approach is partly a consequence of America's current U.S. global priorities, but it also reflects previous disappointments in seeking to promote reform in Nigeria. It is clearly risky to allow short-term exigencies to drive the bilateral relationship, as the symptoms of political decay—manifest in corruption, transnational crime, terrorism, and escalating humanitarian needs—will likely be exacerbated in the absence of underlying improvements in government and the economy. Immediate concerns over security and energy must be balanced with continued attention to larger structural issues if the United States is to significantly address the basic syndrome of developmental failure.

The tools that can be brought to bear on these issues are diverse in scope, although, frankly, limited in their potential impact. Sanctions were employed during the 1990s against military rulers who abused human rights and resisted democratic reform, even though the critical step of embargoing Nigerian oil was never seriously contemplated. These political, diplomatic, and commercial restrictions had limited effects in altering the behavior of leaders or inducing regime change. In the current setting, such confrontational measures are simply unthinkable as means to influence leaders who are working within democratic institutions and pursuing cooperation with the United States in important economic and security areas. Furthermore, the centrality of trade and investment in the petroleum sector is an unavoidable fact that eclipses other considerations in U.S. policy, and therefore constrains the repertoire of policy approaches.

Within these constraints, however, the United States has an array of official and nongovernmental relationships with Nigeria that provide avenues of influence and leverage. A starting point at the official level would be to improve the scope and quality of U.S. representation in Nigeria.[57] During the past decade, the United States' mission in Nigeria has had chronic difficulties in securing adequate numbers of capable, experienced staff. The closure of U.S. facilities outside Lagos and Abuja has also reduced the scope of representation in, engagement with, and information about a complex and important country. Apart from the basic issue of establishing an appropriate diplomatic presence, the tenor of bilateral interactions should also be more finely tuned to changing needs and circumstances in Nigeria. Within the context of a generally cooperative relationship, it is reasonable to consider the use of quiet diplomatic pressure to encourage progress in key policy areas, such as corruption, minority rights, or military conversion.

U.S. aid to Nigeria is another obvious channel of influence. Nigeria's abundant oil revenues dwarf any development assistance, thereby limiting its relative significance, but these transfers still provide a potential conduit for influencing policy, bolstering performance, and affecting the priorities of leaders. In recent years U.S. assistance has fluctuated widely in both volume and composition. From a peak of US$109 million in 2001, total estimated allocations for 2004 had been diminished by more than a third, to about US$65 million. Moreover, resources shifted during this period, as U.S. priorities gradually retreated from political and economic reform and gravitated toward health and education. Allotments for democracy and governance dropped by more than two-thirds (from US$17 million to US$5 million) and for agriculture and economic growth by more than half (from US$20 million to US$9 million). Meanwhile, assistance to child survival and health programs doubled from US$23 million to US$46 million, about half of which is a large new commitment to basic education. Military and security assistance, which peaked around 2001, has dwindled to a small allotment for counterterrorism and other security assistance. Overall, U.S. policymakers reduced commitments and resources for political and economic reform to token levels. There is no question that the visible dividends from assistance to democratization and economic reform have been sparse and uneven, and that the country's ability to effectively use external assistance is limited. Nonetheless, in view of Nigeria's importance and the potential stakes of its political failure, there is a strong case for sustaining engagement on critical areas of reform and for making long-term investments in institutions essential to better governance.

Continued attention to economic policy reform should be a basic component of the bilateral agenda. The first civilian administration under President Obasanjo evidenced chronic problems of economic management, as it failed to chart a clear policy agenda, regularly lagged on budgets, and eventually concluded a reform program with the IMF that was soon abandoned as the government missed essential targets. A distracted executive, a weak economic team, and legislative obstruction compounded the liabilities of feeble institutions and policy drift. The second Obasanjo administration displayed new resolve on the economy shortly after its inauguration in 2003, renovating the economic team and unveiling an ambitious new program of policy and institutional reform. Regrettably, these new commitments coincided with a substantial reduction in U.S. economic support funds and other assistance for economic growth, emblematic of a more general disengagement with a country that is seen as a poor prospect for economic change. Here again, there is a case for continued involvement with Nigeria, so that U.S. policymakers can respond to opportunities for advancing reform. U.S. commitments could include higher levels of technical assistance and financial support for critical institutions of economic management, including macroeconomic policy units, regulatory agencies, the anticorruption and privatization commissions, and improved budgeting and procurement functions.

As noted earlier, the civilian government has been concerned with the question of debt relief. Obasanjo and other senior leaders have raised the issue regularly in meetings with the U.S. government, seeking an arrangement comparable to the debt reduction mechanism under HIPC. In the absence of any credible commitment by Nigeria to economic reform or macroeconomic stability, the United States initially foreclosed the possibility. With the acceleration of policy reform and anticorruption efforts during Obasanjo's second term, the Paris Club was able to reach an agreement that would effectively write off two-thirds of Nigeria's external debt. Debt cancellation offers a means of reducing Nigeria's financial constraints without requiring new resources in the form of bilateral aid. It may also furnish political dividends to the Nigerian government in sustaining difficult policy changes and offer incentives for continued reform.

Private business can also provide support for economic reform and restructuring. Petroleum corporations, which obviously play a central role in Nigeria's politics and economic affairs, can be catalysts for reform. One of the most intriguing initiatives to arise from the NGO community recently is the "publish what you pay" campaign. This calls upon petroleum companies to make public their tax and royalty payments to the government, thereby aiding fiscal transparency and presumably undermining the corrupt diversion of funds by public officials. This concept has been taken up more formally by the Blair government in Britain, which has launched an Extractive Industries Transparency Initiative (EITI). Nigeria signed on early to the EITI framework, and the government has formally launched its own domestic initiative. Corporate executives have been cautiously receptive to this proposal. Most appear willing to disclose their payments, as it could potentially reduce criticism and suspicion of collusion with corrupt government officials. On the other hand, none is willing to unilaterally declare potentially sensitive business information: each will move when the others do and will disclose only what the others disclose. The U.S. government has played a relatively passive role in these efforts, but nongovernmental organizations can help to further coordinate actions among companies as they move toward implementation. Other potential areas of reform include harmonizing corporate security with general human rights standards (especially in the Niger Delta) and fiscal reforms that would allow taxes and royalties to flow directly to state and local governments, bypassing the federal coffers in Abuja. Such initiatives could attenuate the pathologies of the rentier state and lessen the adverse impact of oil production in the southern communities.

Continued aid for political reform is essential if the United States hopes to retain leverage or exert a significant impact on improving the climate for democracy in Nigeria. Direct, concerted, and sustained support for democratic consolidation is appropriate and salient as a focus of bilateral relations. The United States can encourage broader aid for institutional reform. It can also foster links between the two governments that would allow for assistance to the legislature, the judiciary, the Independent National Electoral Commission (INEC), selected offices within the executive, and other departments and agencies in critical areas of state performance.[58] Electoral reform is an especially urgent arena, particularly as Nigerians look to 2007 elections that promise to be highly contentious. Continued efforts to reform the military and restructure civil-military relations are also integral to political change. Engagement with Nigeria's armed forces should be revisited and move beyond intermilitary linkages and technical training into important areas of civil-military relations, with the participation of civilian agencies and NGOs.

The large domain of nongovernmental linkages between Nigeria and the United States furnishes immediate and fruitful avenues of engagement. Numerous interactions among NGOs, business associations, religious institutions, universities, and the media provide important channels for dialogue, cooperation, and assistance. This realm of activity has broad relevance for domestic conflict resolution, intercommunal relations, political accountability and improved governance, changes in economic policies and institutions, popular welfare, and the development of human capital. Indeed, the nongovernmental arena is the central source of constituencies for reform and countervailing social forces that can begin to impose accountability on rulers and shift incentives toward better performance. Engagement with Nigeria's diverse and vibrant civil society is essential, as it can furnish important catalysts of democratization, social accommodation, and economic revival. In view of the many daunting challenges facing Nigeria, and the limited capacities of the United States to effectively address these problems, careful and attentive engagement in pursuit of reform is likely to yield the most constructive relationship with this important but troubled state.

Notes

1. Exports and revenues are calculated from the Central Bank of Nigeria, Annual Report and Statement of Accounts (various years).

2. The vicissitudes of U.S.-Nigerian relations are covered by Robert B. Shepard, *Nigeria, Africa, and the United States* (Indiana University Press, 1991).

3. See, for example, Peter M. Lewis, Barnett Rubin, and Pearl Robinson, *Stabilizing Nigeria: Incentives, Sanctions and Support for Civil Society* (New York: Council on Foreign Relations, 1998); and Gwendolyn Mikell and Princeton N. Lyman, "Critical U.S. Bilateral Relations in Africa: Nigeria and South Africa," in *Africa Policy in the Clinton Years: Critical Choices for the Bush Administration*, edited by J. Stephen Morrison and Jennifer G. Cooke (Washington: Center for Strategic and International Studies, 2001).

4. See Peter M. Lewis, "Islam, Protest and Conflict in Nigeria," Africa Notes 10 (Washington: Center for Strategic and International Studies, December 2002).

5. These linkages are variously addressed by Richard Joseph, *Democracy and Prebendal Politics in Nigeria: The Rise and Fall of the Second Republic* (Cambridge University Press, 1987); Tom Forrest, *Politics and Economic Development in Nigeria*, 2d ed. (Boulder, Colo.: Westview Press, 1995); and Eghosa Osaghae, *Crippled Giant: Nigeria since Independence* (Indiana University Press, 1998).

6. GDP growth rates are calculated from World Bank data.

7. This economic history is recounted by Douglas Rimmer, "Development in Nigeria: An Overview," in *The Political Economy of Income Distribution in Nigeria*, edited by Henry Bienen and V. P. Diejomaoh (New York: Holmes and Meier, 1981).

8. Export revenues and external debt are calculated from World Bank data.

9. Forrest, *Politics and Economic Development in Nigeria*, pp. 165–79.

10. The uneven course of reform is analyzed by Peter M. Lewis, "From Prebendalism to Predation: The Political Economy of Decline in Nigeria," *Journal of Modern African Studies* 34, no. 1 (1996).

114   *Peter M. Lewis*

11. Per capita GDP is calculated from World Bank data.

12. O. O. Akanji, "Incidence of Poverty and Economic Growth in Nigeria," paper prepared for the International Association for Official Statistics conference, "Statistics, Development, and Human Rights," Montreux, Switzerland, June 6, 2000.

13. Data on income inequality are summarized in the WIDER/UNU World Income Inequality Database, available at www.undp.org/poverty/initiatives/wider/wiid.htm. Data on social welfare are from World Bank, *African Development Indicators 1998/99* (Washington: 1999).

14. See, for example, Henry Bienen and Alan Gelb, "Nigeria: From Windfall Gains to Welfare Losses?" in *Oil Windfalls: Blessing or Curse?* edited by Alan Gelb (Oxford University Press, 1988).

15. Forrest, *Politics and Economic Development in Nigeria,* p. 134.

16. The Afrobarometer research network has collected data on political attitudes in Nigeria. See Peter Lewis, Etannibi Alemika, and Michael Bratton, "Down to Earth: Changes in Attitudes toward Democracy and Markets in Nigeria," Afrobarometer Working Paper 20 (Michigan State University, August 2002).

17. These dynamics are discussed by Osaghae, *Crippled Giant;* and Larry Diamond, "Nigeria: The Uncivic Society and the Descent into Praetorianism," in *Politics in Developing Countries: Comparing Experiences with Democracy,* 2d ed., edited by Larry Diamond, J. Linz, and S. M. Lipset (Boulder, Colo.: Lynne Rienner, 1995).

18. Lewis, "From Prebendalism to Predation"; Richard Joseph, "Nigeria: Inside the Dismal Tunnel," *Current History* 95, no. 6 (1996); Diamond, "Nigeria"; and Osaghae, *Crippled Giant,* p. 312.

19. Detailed in Peter M. Lewis, "Endgame in Nigeria? The Politics of a Failed Democratic Transition," *African Affairs* 93 (July 1994).

20. James S. Coleman, *Nigeria: Background to Nationalism* (University of California Press, 1958).

21. Rotimi Suberu, *Federalism and Ethnic Conflict in Nigeria* (Washington: U.S. Institute of Peace, 2001).

22. Rotimi Suberu, *Ethnic Minority Conflicts and Governance in Nigeria* (Ibadan: Spectrum, 1996). On the Niger Delta, see Human Rights Watch, *The Price of Oil* (New York: 1999).

23. An overview is provided by Bronwen Manby, "Principal Human Rights Challenges in Nigeria," paper prepared for the conference "Nigeria: Unity, Governance, Law, and Conflict," Kennedy School of Government, Harvard University, December 12–14, 2002.

24. See, for instance, Elinor Ostrom, "A Behavioral Approach to the Rational Choice Theory of Collective Action," *American Political Science Review* 92, no. 1 (1998): 1.

25. Jeffrey D. Sachs, "The Strategic Significance of Global Inequality," *Washington Quarterly* 24, no. 3 (2001).

26. John Luke Gallup, Jeffrey D. Sachs, and Andrew D. Millinger, "Geography and Economic Development," Working Paper 6849 (Cambridge, Mass.: National Bureau of Economic Research, December 1998).

27. See, for instance, Bade Onimode, *Imperialism and Underdevelopment in Nigeria* (London: Zed, 1982).

28. See, for instance, D. Michael Shafer, *Winners and Losers: How Sectors Shape the Developmental Prospects of States* (Cornell University Press, 1994); and Michael Ross, "The Political Economy of the Resource Curse," *World Politics* 51 (January 1999).

29. The importance of ethnic fragmentation is emphasized by William Easterly and Ross Levine, "Africa's Growth Tragedy: Policies and Ethnic Divisions," *Quarterly Journal of Economics* 112, no. 4 (1997).

30. The structures and evolution of communal politics in Nigeria are elaborated in Robert Melson and Howard Wolpe, eds., *Nigeria: Modernization and the Politics of Communalism* (Michigan State University Press, 1971).

31. This is emphasized by Michael Watts and Paul Lubeck, "An Alliance of Oil and Maize? The Response of Indigenous and State Capital to Structural Adjustment in Nigeria," in *African Capitalists and African Development*, edited by Bruce Berman and Colin Leys (Boulder, Colo.: Lynne Rienner, 1994).

32. See, for instance, P. C. Lloyd, "The Ethnic Background to the Nigerian Crisis," in *Nigerian Politics and Military Rule: Background to Civil War*, edited by S. K. Panter-Brick (London: Athlone Press, 1970); and Robin Luckham, *The Nigerian Military: A Sociological Analysis of Authority and Revolt 1960–67* (Cambridge University Press, 1971).

33. Eghosa Osaghae, "Managing Multiple Minority Problems in a Divided Society: The Nigerian Experience," *Journal of Modern African Studies* 36, no. 1 (1998).

34. Joseph, *Democracy and Prebendal Politics*.

35. Watts and Lubeck, "An Alliance of Oil and Maize?"

36. The model of the rentier state is elaborated by Terry Lynn Karl, *The Paradox of Plenty* (University of California Press, 1997); and Kiren Aziz Chaudhry, *The Price of Wealth: Economies and Institutions in the Middle East* (Cornell University Press, 1997). See also Osaghae, *Crippled Giant*, pp. 28–29.

37. Gerald Helleiner, *Peasant Agriculture, Government and Economic Growth in Nigeria* (Homewood, Ill.: R. D. Irwin, 1966).

38. See Alan Gelb, "Adjustment to Windfall Gains: A Comparative Analysis of Oil Exporting Countries," in *Natural Resources and the Macroeconomy*, edited by J. P. Neary and S. van Wijnbergen (Oxford: Basil Blackwell, 1986); and Alan Richards and John Waterbury, *A Political Economy of the Middle East*, 2d ed. (Boulder, Colo.: Westview Press, 1998).

39. The broader syndrome is treated in Michael J. Watts, ed., *State, Oil, and Agriculture in Nigeria* (Berkeley, Calif.: Institute of International Studies, 1987).

40. Jane Guyer, "Representation without Taxation: An Essay on Democracy in Rural Nigeria, 1952–1990," Working Papers in African Studies 152 (African Studies Center, Boston University, 1991).

41. Watts, introduction to *State, Oil, and Agriculture*, p. 16; see also Karl, *The Paradox of Plenty*.

42. Pat Utomi, *Managing Uncertainty: Competition and Strategy in Emerging Economies* (Ibadan: Spectrum, 1998), p. 307.

43. Anthony Kirk-Greene and Douglas Rimmer, *Nigeria since 1970* (London: Hodder and Stoughton, 1981), p. 118.

44. Forrest, *Politics and Economic Development in Nigeria*, pp. 177, 226.

45. Diamond, "Nigeria"; and O. Aborisade and Robert J. Mundt, *Politics in Nigeria* (New York: Longman, 2001), pp. 98–99.

46. Lewis, "From Prebendalism to Predation." See also H. E. Chehabi and Juan Linz, "A Theory of Sultanism: A Type of Nondemocratic Rule," in *Sultanistic Regimes*, edited by H. E. Chehabi and Juan Linz (Johns Hopkins University Press, 1998).

47. Lewis, Rubin, and Robinson, *Stabilizing Nigeria*. See also Osaghae, *Crippled Giant*, pp. 312–13.

48. Mikell and Lyman, "Critical U.S. Bilateral Relations."

49. Data on energy exports are drawn from the Energy Information Administration, available online at www.eia.doe.gov/emeu/international/nigeria.html. Data on U.S. exports to Nigeria are provided by the Bureau of the Census, available online at www.census.gov/foreign-trade/balance/c7530.html.

50. Despite widespread defaults, the government has attended to the "lenders of last resort" by keeping current with payments on Brady bonds and World Bank debt.

51. Without a credible census providing information on religious identity, it is impossible to estimate religious balance with any certainty. Common estimates, however, hold that about 50 percent of the population is Muslim, about 45 percent is Christian, and the rest practices traditional African religions or has some other religious affiliation.

52. Comparative data are provided by the United Nations Program on HIV-AIDS, available online at www.unaids.org/hivaidsinfo/statistics/fact_sheets/index_en.htm.

53. Lewis, "Endgame in Nigeria?"

54. See Lewis, Rubin, and Robinson, *Stabilizing Nigeria;* and Mikell and Lyman, "Critical U.S. Bilateral Relations," pp. 80–81.

55. See "Press Briefing by Senior Director for African Affairs Gayle Smith and Assistant Secretary of State for African Affairs Susan Rice," U.S. Embassy, Abuja, Nigeria (August 26, 2000).

56. Variously estimated at US$42 to US$88 million. Partial figures are provided by the Center for International Policy, at www.ciponline.org/Africa/aid/nigeria.htm. See also Human Rights Watch, "Military Revenge in Benue: A Population under Attack," April 2002, p. 22.

57. See Mikell and Lyman, "Critical U.S. Bilateral Relations," pp. 82–83.

58. The importance of institutional linkages is emphasized by Princeton N. Lyman and Linda Cotton, "Reviewing U.S.-Nigeria Relations: New Links to Reinforce Democracy," *ODC Viewpoint* (Washington: Overseas Development Council, March 2000).

4

Indonesia as a Poorly Performing State?

Andrew MacIntyre

In the years since the historic upheavals of 1998, Indonesia has struggled with the twin challenges of rebuilding its economy and constructing a viable framework for democratic governance. This has been a turbulent period, with prolonged economic difficulties, weak and frequently changing political leadership, and widespread problems of sectarian violence that have called the very territorial integrity of the republic into question. These recent travails have brought greater international attention to the country than did the three decades of rapid economic growth and strict but stable authoritarian rule under former president General Suharto. Understandably, there has been much worried discussion in policy circles within the United States and elsewhere about whether Indonesia, rather than embarking on a new and optimistic democratic era, is in fact in danger of becoming caught in a stagnant or even downward developmental trajectory. Is Indonesia, the fourth most populous country in the world, at risk of developing that combustible mix of economic stagnation and systematically weak governance that characterizes the phenomenon of poorly performing states?

The aim of this chapter is to assess Indonesia's developmental trajectory, giving particular emphasis to outlining the economic and political challenges the country is wrestling with, and to reflect upon the implications of Indonesia's trajectory for U.S. policy. I begin with an overview of Indonesia's past record of economic and political development and then focus on the contemporary situation and whether Indonesia is appropriately considered a poorly performing state. For this purpose, I outline the key economic and political problems Indonesia has been experiencing and analyze the underlying reasons for these problems. The chapter concludes with a review of the terms of U.S. engagement with Indonesia today.

Indonesia's Developmental Record

Indonesia has always been a hard country to govern. It has a large population (currently 220 million), as an archipelago it is geographically disparate, and as a society made up of multiple ethnic, religious, and linguistic groups it is also culturally disparate. (For example, Indonesia has the unlikely distinction of having both the world's largest Muslim population and the world's largest Melanesian population.) These basic physical and demographic characteristics help to explain episodes of sharp conflict and violence that have periodically erupted in various parts of the country over its approximately half-century history as an independent state. As well, Indonesia is a poor country, with per capita income of US$690.[1] Notwithstanding these difficulties, Indonesians have generally thought of themselves as a loosely cohesive and inclusive society, with great economic potential deriving from their rich and diverse natural resource endowments. Figure 4-1 charts gross domestic product (GDP) per capita for Indonesia and for low-income, lower-middle-income, and upper-middle-income countries, as classified by the World Bank. It shows that while Indonesia's absolute level of income per capita is higher than the average for the poorest grouping of countries, since the upheavals of 1998 Indonesia has no longer kept pace with the average for lower-middle-income countries.

Indonesia's overall developmental trajectory since independence in 1945 has been starkly episodic, with marked swings over time in its progress on either (or both) the economic and political dimensions of development. Following independence and the eventual departure of the Dutch, Indonesia struggled with the need both to bind the nation together within a framework of democratic governance and to stimulate economic development. Notwithstanding the early mood of optimism deriving from the success of the country's long nationalist struggle for independence, developmental progress was slow. The constitutional framework in place through much of the 1950s compounded the difficulties by fragmenting authority and blurring political accountability. With over twenty parties in the parliament,

Figure 4-1. *Comparative per capita GDP Trends, 1992–2002*

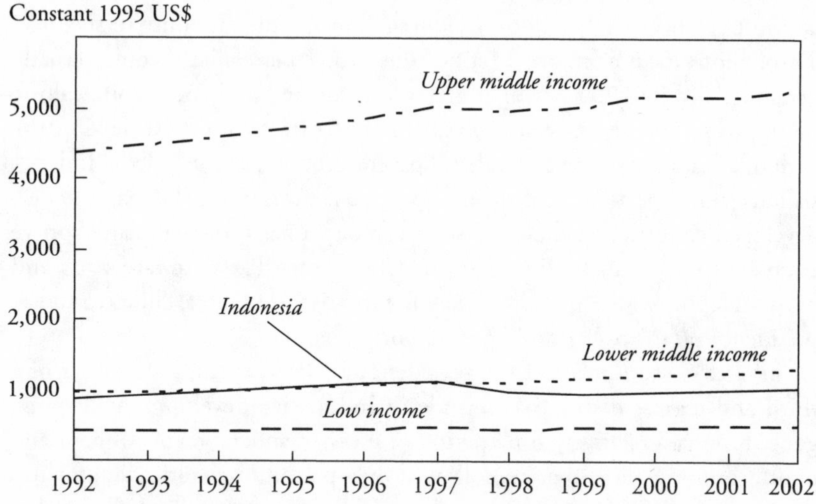

Constant 1995 US$

Source: International Economic Databank, Australian National University (calculated from World Bank and IMF raw data).

coalition governments were inherently unstable, forming and dissolving in rapid succession.[2] This was scarcely an environment conducive to effective economic policymaking. Not surprisingly, economic progress during these early years was modest. Unfortunately for Indonesia, worse was to follow.

By the latter 1950s Indonesia's political system was coming under increasingly severe strain. With the national government functioning very weakly and economic gains only limited, geographic and social divisions became sharper and finally triggered armed rebellion in several regions. As the situation deteriorated, the country's president and preeminent nationalist leader, Sukarno, moved to take control of the government. Backed by the army, he pushed to suppress the rebellions and overturn the constitution. This marked the onset of authoritarian rule in Indonesia. In 1959 Sukarno proclaimed the inauguration of what he termed "guided democracy" and "guided economy."

For the next half decade Indonesia bore all the hallmarks of a poorly performing state that was trending dangerously downward. Sukarno presided over an increasingly erratic dictatorship, kept afloat by an unlikely (and inherently unstable) coalition of the army and the Communist Party. Policy management was a largely haphazard amalgam of socialist-style economic policies, couched within a wider context of an anti-Western diplomatic crusade and military harassment of neighboring Malaysia. Inflation grew alarmingly on the back of uncontrolled government spending. Private investors, both local and foreign, began to abandon Indonesia, causing the economy to stagnate. Throughout most of the first half of the 1960s, per capita income actually declined, and by 1965 both per capita income and daily per capita caloric intake were among the very lowest in the entire world.[3] Reviewing the period, a leading international development economist concluded: "Indonesia must surely be accounted the number one failure among the major underdeveloped countries."[4] These pressures came to a head following an abortive coup attempt (allegedly linked to the Communist Party) in late 1965 and mass violence, which paved the way for the rise of General Suharto to the presidency on the back of military support.

Suharto's assumption of the presidency in 1966 marked the onset of a third and no less distinctive episode in Indonesia's development. Having gone through a relatively brief period of messy democratic government and poor economic performance, followed by a period of chaotic dictatorship and even worse economic performance, Indonesia now embarked on what would prove to be a long period of stable but strict authoritarian government and remarkably strong sustained economic growth. The defining characteristics of the Suharto era—the New Order, as the regime styled itself—were controlled political stability and rapid aggregate economic advancement. In both respects then, this was a very sharp contrast with what had immediately preceded it. Quite quickly, Indonesia pulled back from exhibiting all the symptoms of a poor performer.

Politically, the foundation of Suharto's regime was the control of and support from the military. In the early years this enabled him to crush the Communist Party and then to achieve a much firmer grip on the bureaucracy. The former was achieved through violence and repression, the latter through a systemic move to place military officers in all key state institutions, all the way down to the village level.[5] Once the Communist Party had been eliminated and the bureaucracy increasingly refashioned as an effective policy instrument in the hands of the presidency, Suharto and his key security planners were able to set about a wider restructuring of Indonesia's political landscape.

For an authoritarian regime, the New Order was surprisingly constitutional in the sense of sticking to the letter of the law, even if not its spirit. Through a series of subsidiary political laws, Suharto was able to work within the country's constitutional framework to bring about a radical centralization of power. A key element in this were strict legal controls on political parties and the press. These gave the government formal power to restrict and co-opt all political parties and to set the parameters for public debate. Elections were regular events but were always carefully managed so that the ruling party, Golkar, won by a large majority. The parties (including Golkar) had little independent life of their own and yielded a rubber-stamp parliament. A similar strategy of co-optation and control was extended into civil society via a corporatist network of interest groups. Overall, the net effect of these institutionalized controls was a radical and systemic centralization of power within the executive branch, and around the presidency in particular.[6]

For the first time in the country's history, the writ of the national government ran clearly and reasonably effectively into most parts of the republic. This had important consequences for the extension of basic transport and communications infrastructure as well as health and education systems into outlying areas of the archipelago. What it did not do, however, was promote or protect political freedoms. The extreme manifestation of this was the outright military suppression of secessionist movements in East Timor, West Papua, and Aceh. The political controls of the Suharto era were much more thoroughgoing and systematic than they had been under Sukarno. Also in stark contrast with the Sukarno period were the extraordinary economic gains during the Suharto period.

The economic transformation during the three decades of Suharto's rule was truly remarkable. Indonesia's transformation from its status as an archetypical developmental basket case in the mid-1960s began with a dramatic macroeconomic stabilization program in conjunction with the International Monetary Fund, a program that is frequently cited as one of the most successful in the twentieth century.[7] With the introduction of responsible fiscal management, a stable exchange rate, an open capital account, and more broadly the support of the United States and other key Western countries, Indonesia was once again able to attract investors. In a remarkably short period of time economic growth picked up strongly, on the back of natural resource exports, major productivity gains in the agricultural sector, and foreign investment in the manufacturing sector (mostly from Japan). Through the 1970s and early 1980s industrial development was largely on the basis of import substitution, rather than manufacturing for export markets.

The boom in oil prices from 1973 meant that the government found itself in an increasingly comfortable fiscal position. As might be expected, the oil boom generated substantial waste and profligacy, with a significant portion of the windfall gains being pumped into inefficient state industrial enterprises or, worse, contributing to deepening corruption problems in the regime. And yet even more remarkable than the graft and sometimes spectacular mismanagement, Indonesia also used a large portion of the oil revenue to invest heavily in key public goods: roads and infrastructure, education and health. As is now well understood, resource booms can often be economic and political curses. By the standards of the developing world, Indonesia used its oil resources to remarkably good effect.[8] Along with patronage networks and pervasive corruption, a defining feature of economic policy management was a strong and enduring commitment to what might be described as growth-promoting economic policies.

In the mid-1980s, following nearly two decades of sustained rapid growth, Indonesia was forced to restructure its economic model. The catalyst for change was a looming balance-of-payments crisis stemming from the collapse in global commodity prices (especially oil) and a realignment of the major international currencies. Indonesia's falling export earnings were mostly denominated in U.S. dollars—and the dollar itself was falling—but its foreign debt obligations were largely denominated in yen and in European currencies, which were rising. Driven by this crisis, Indonesia unleashed a burst of liberalizing economic reforms in the late 1980s. The manufacturing and financial sectors were substantially deregulated, and many disincentives to foreign investment were removed. These were major and highly contentious policy adjustments, but with control over policy highly centralized around the presidency and the scope for organized political opposition limited, rapid policy change was possible. The result was a boom in manufactured exports as labor-intensive products such as textiles and footwear took off, soon surpassing many of the country's traditional commodity exports. On the basis of these far-reaching changes, Indonesia was able to enjoy yet another decade of very strong economic growth and a broadening and deepening of its industrial capabilities.

By the mid-1990s Indonesia had notched up extraordinary economic progress. Real per capita GDP had more than trebled from its level in the late 1960s, and the country was well under way in transforming itself from an agriculture- and commodity-based economy to an increasingly industrial economy.[9] Between 1965 and 1995, the share of agriculture in the Indonesian economy dropped from 56 percent to 17 percent. Manufacturing, on the other hand, rose from 8 percent to 24 percent. The service industry also rose, although more marginally: from 31 percent to 41 percent.[10] While not matching the spectacular economic trajectories of such East Asian economies as Korea and Singapore, by comparison with both its own past and the aggregate record for low-income developing countries, Indonesia's economic and

Table 4-1. *Comparative Development Indicators, Indonesia and Low-Income Country Average, 1991–96*

	1990	1991	1992	1993	1994	1995	1996
GDP growth rate							
Indonesia	9.0	8.9	7.2	7.3	7.5	8.4	7.6
Low-income country average	3.1	0.8	1.1	1.6	2.5	5.5	5.6
Illiteracy rate[a]							
Indonesia	20.4	19.6	18.8	18.0	17.2	16.4	15.7
Low-income country average	45.4	44.7	43.9	43.1	42.3	41.5	40.7
Life expectancy[b]							
Indonesia	61.7	n.a	62.7	n.a.	n.a.	64.1	n.a.
Low-income country average	57.2	n.a.	57.7	n.a.	n.a.	58.4	n.a.
Vehicles per capita[c]							
Indonesia	15.7	17.0	17.6	18.3	19.9	21.3	22.5
Low-income country average	8.9	11.1	11.4	11.5	11.3	11.8	12.6

Source: World Bank, *World Development Indicators, 2002.*
a Illiteracy rate; adult total (percent of people aged 15 and above).
b. Life expectancy: life expectancy at birth, total (years).
c. Vehicles per capita: vehicles per 1,000 people.

welfare gains were remarkable indeed. A comparison between Indonesia's performance and the average for low-income countries through the 1990s—up until the financial crisis—tells the story (see table 4-1).

Inevitably, economic progress under Suharto was not all that the regime claimed it to be. To mention some of the more conspicuous shortcomings beyond deep-seated corruption, the institutions of economic governance remained very weak and there were widely perceived problems of inequity, with a growing income gap between a small superelite and the middle class— to say nothing of the poor.[11] And without doubt there were major human rights abuses inflicted by the military, particularly in the regions of East Timor, West Papua, and Aceh. Serious flaws notwithstanding, extraordinary economic advances—with job creation, poverty reduction, and improved living standards—were in fact made under the Suharto regime, as was brought into stark relief by the very developmental setback resulting from the financial crisis of 1997–98. The Asian financial crisis marked a dramatic interruption of Indonesia's developmental trajectory, triggering a radical economic reversal and the collapse of the military-based regime of Suharto. In effect, 1998 marked the end of the third major episode in Indonesia's postindependence developmental history.

In considering Indonesia's own developmental history—and certainly when comparing Indonesia's developmental history to that of most Latin American, Middle Eastern, and African countries—one of the great questions is how this extraordinary result of sustained high economic growth over three decades was achieved. Economists rightly point to the policy framework of the Suharto regime: generally sound and stable macroeconomic management, significant investment in human capital and infrastructure (education, health, transportation, and so on), sectoral trade and investment policies that facilitated huge productivity gains in agriculture, and subsequently the rapid growth of labor-intensive export industries.[12] (Allowing for variation in natural resource endowments, a roughly comparable story can be told for the other Asian developing economies that experienced sustained rapid economic growth through the latter part of the twentieth century.)[13] But lying behind an answer that emphasizes policy settings is another more basic question: *Why* did Indonesia under Suharto adopt and sustain a policy mix that was, in broad terms, strongly conducive to growth?

This is not the place for a full discussion of the question, but a brief answer would point to a range of domestic political factors as well as international variables, most of which pertained in one form or another in the other high-growth Asian economies. In Indonesia, the central elements of this can be summarized as follows: leadership that defined its own political survival in terms of delivering improved economic outcomes (in essence, a conservative regime responding to an earlier challenge from the Left by the Communist Party); an institutional framework of government that heavily centralized power in the executive branch, thereby facilitating relatively coherent and decisive and policy action regardless of opposition; and an international environment (initially shaped by cold war calculations) that yielded U.S. and Japanese support and, in particular, access to U.S. and Japanese capital and consumer markets.[14]

Indonesia Today: A Poorly Performing State?

The primary concern of this chapter is to assess current developments in Indonesia in light of the wider concern about poorly performing states. What we learn from a review of Indonesia's developmental record is that there have been very marked swings in its performance. Through much of the 1950s Indonesia muddled along before deteriorating markedly under Sukarno's erratic dictatorship. In retrospect, Indonesia can be thought of as a glaring example of a poorly performing state through the first half of the 1960s.

Subsequently, under the institutionalized authoritarianism of the Suharto regime, it became more stable, secured effective territorial control of the archipelago, and experienced extraordinary economic progress. The developmental deficit of the Suharto period lay in the absence of any significant progress in building meaningful channels for public participation and political accountability.

What of Indonesia today? In the years since the fall of Suharto in 1998, Indonesia has been in a state of flux as it struggled with an array of daunting economic and political problems. Were these problems to continue unchecked, the country would unambiguously be on a worrying developmental trajectory once again. The key analytical issue here is how we should assess the nature of Indonesia's recent difficulties and the extent of progress in overcoming them. In addressing this, I begin by outlining Indonesia's developmental performance during the post-1998 years and highlighting key economic and political problems, before turning in a more analytic direction to examine the underlying reasons for these problems and offer some thoughts on their likely trajectory.

In economic terms, having enjoyed an average rate of real GDP growth of 7 percent over thirty years, in the post-Suharto period Indonesia has been able to manage only about 3 percent growth. (If we include the catastrophically bad years of 1998 and to a lesser extent 1999, the average is much lower.) Indonesia no longer looks like a high-performing developing economy. It is the only one of the Asian crisis economies yet to regain precrisis GDP levels.[15]

One way of capturing the practical significance of this dramatically lowered economic performance is to recall that, during the long period of high growth, the work of careful labor market economists suggested that Indonesia could not afford to grow any slower than about 5 percent annually if there were to be enough jobs to absorb the many new, young entrants to the job market each year.[16] In other words, continued strong economic growth was necessary just to cope with population growth and the approximately two million new entrants to the workforce each year. With economic growth having been very much lower for half a decade, it takes little imagination to anticipate the accumulating social and political problems associated with young people unable to find work, despite having completed their schooling.

If we draw back from aggregate economic indicators and look at three specific variables that have come to be viewed as bellwether issues—corruption, foreign investment, and bank restructuring—there is much to be worried about. On corruption, whether one looks at the large independent surveys of corruption across countries or anecdotal accounts from seasoned observers of Indonesia over many years, the consistent picture to emerge is one of problems being as bad or worse than they were under the Suharto regime.[17] This is not to say that the governments of Megawati Sukarnoputri and her two predecessors have been more venal than that of Suharto (though, certainly, none have been pure), but that corruption has become so unpredictable that investors can no longer understand the rules of the game.[18]

This connects directly to a second alarming trend: the collapse of investment in Indonesia. In 1997 total investment as a percentage of GDP stood at 33 percent. Subsequently it has fallen steadily and stood at just 14 percent in 2003.[19] And within overall investment, foreign investment has virtually collapsed. Although most developing countries have seen foreign direct investment decline from the peak of 2000, the share of the shrinking pie that Indonesia commands has fallen very sharply. And in Indonesia, alone among the main Asian crisis economies, aggregate indicators of investment risk have deteriorated markedly.[20]

Bank restructuring and reform is widely seen as essential to any sustained economic recovery in Indonesia. The financial crisis plainly revealed the fundamental institutional weaknesses of the Indonesian banking sector, but progress in addressing these problems has been intermittent at best. The greatest headway has been achieved under Megawati's administration, but much remains to be done. Reduction in nonperforming loans has ground to a halt, with the central bank postponing the scheduled introduction of a 5 percent prudential requirement on nonperforming loans.[21] And with bank balance sheets in poor condition, very little in the way of new investment lending has been initiated. If Indonesia's economic recovery is to be closer to the reasonably quick turnarounds of Thailand, Malaysia, and South Korea than the desperately disappointing record of Japan, then renewed strong progress with banking reform is essential.

Protracted economic problems over the half decade following Suharto's demise are one source of serious concern about Indonesia's developmental trajectory; another is the extended political turbulence of this time period. In the immediate post-Suharto years, the country's social and political problems seemed to grow, not decline, and the initial euphoria surrounding the idea of a new democratic dawn proved short-lived.

The most dramatic manifestation of this was the upsurge in a variety of forms of deadly political violence. One of these has been ethnic and religious violence between neighboring communities, such as the bloody battles between Christian and Muslim communities in Maluku, Kalimantan, and

Lombok. In some instances, as was made clear in the wake of the October 12, 2002, bombing of two tourist nightclubs in Bali, Indonesian militants have been working in tandem with international Islamic terrorists.[22] Another variant has been bombings—particularly in Jakarta—as a result of intra-elite political battles. Yet another form of serious political violence have been the smaller scale, though frequent, ad hoc attacks against members of the local Chinese communities in towns across Java. Finally, there have also been renewed armed regional uprisings by groups rebelling against a history of military oppression and seeking independence for the provinces of Aceh and Papua. The genesis of these different forms of violence ranges from previously repressed ethnic and religious sensitivities arising from the country's diverse social makeup, the legacy of earlier enforced population resettlement programs, to internecine conflict among security agencies and the shadowy maneuverings and provocations of downwardly mobile members of the old political elite.[23] Although the causes are still not well understood, the violence in all its forms has been as shocking to external observers as it has been to Indonesians and has led to a questioning of what it means to be Indonesian: whether the notion of Indonesia as a coherent nation still makes sense.

A distinct but kindred set of political problems relates to civil or criminal violence and lawlessness. One dimension of this is growing concern about criminal violence and organized crime, with police being unable or unwilling to do anything effective about it.[24] The impunity with which such criminal groups operate was dramatically underlined in 2003 when, following investigative reports about a particular group by a leading news magazine, the magazine's headquarters were stormed and management assaulted by thugs while the police stood by. An even more problematic variant on criminal violence is extortion by individual police and army units desperate to raise money to fund themselves. Informal or off-budget funding of the security forces—as distinct from sheer personal graft—has always operated in Indonesia. But again, in the years since the collapse of the old regime, the problem seems to have become rampant and increasingly pernicious. (It is commonly estimated that 40–60 percent of the military's operating expenses are met by off-budget sources.) The problem was thrown into sharp relief by an incident involving the giant U.S. mining company Freeport, in which two Americans and an Indonesian were killed in an ambush, apparently by a local military unit unhappy with the level of payment it was receiving from the company.[25]

A final key area in which the country has been experiencing serious and systemic political problems is the erosion of the authority of the national government in provincial areas. Under Suharto the writ of the national government was in force through nearly all of the archipelago. Indeed, in fiscal terms, Indonesia was one of the most centralized large states in existence, much more so than, say, China. As pent-up political pressures exploded post-Suharto, the national political elite moved reluctantly to devolve significant authority to the local level. (Political leaders chose not to empower provincial-level governments, for fear that this might encourage secession, particularly in the provinces rich in natural resources.) There are many serious questions about how this process of devolution will work out, with concerns that there will be even less transparency and accountability at the local level and that overall service delivery will suffer as a result. But beyond these problems, there have been the increasingly frequent incidents of local authorities disregarding the rules and directives of Jakarta, that is to say, the wilful neglect of legally valid decisions by the central government (for instance, local authorities in Kalimantan deciding to impose additional unauthorized taxes on mining companies or to restrict the operation of mining companies in particular ways despite explicit and legally valid instructions to the contrary from the central government). Or the national government deciding to privatize a state-owned cement factory by selling a controlling share to the large Mexican firm CEMEX, only to see a local government in Sumatra (where a large production facility of the state-owned firm was located) deciding to resist the central government's decision and (quite unlawfully) assert control of the factory itself.[26]

To summarize, while Indonesia has certainly made important progress over the past seven or eight years in promoting individual political freedoms, there have also been clear setbacks. The country's economic trajectory has declined and national government has become weak and incoherent. This record is a source of concern to both Indonesians themselves and policymakers elsewhere, given the country's pivotal status in Southeast Asia and its wider significance in the Muslim world, both as a model of an inclusive and tolerant Muslim society and, more pointedly, as a focal point for Islamic terrorists.

Explaining Poor Performance

How should Indonesia's developmental record since the fall of Suharto be assessed? What are the key causal factors that explain the disappointing economic performance and the even more worrying signs of weak governance? Although, inevitably, a multiplicity of factors have been at work to generate these outcomes, three basic drivers stand out: the radical dislocation associated with the twin shocks of the Asian financial crisis and the breakdown of the Suharto regime, an inhospitable external economic environment, and severely dysfunctional national political institutions. The interaction of these three factors accounts for much of the difficulty the country has experienced. I address each in turn.

Having suffered two huge and simultaneous shocks (a truly radical economic reversal and the sudden unravelling of a long-standing authoritarian regime), it was inevitable that Indonesia should be substantially set back and need at least a few years to recover. Recall that the effects of the Asian financial crisis were much more devastating in Indonesia than anywhere else in the region. In 1996, the year before the crisis broke, GDP growth in Indonesia stood at 7.6 percent; in 1998 it stood at −13.1 percent.[27] This was a catastrophic reversal, reputedly the most dramatic recorded anywhere in the twentieth century.[28] In addition to producing massive destruction of wealth and social dislocation, the ensuing tangle of unpaid debt and insolvent banks was bound to freeze the financial and corporate sectors of the economy for some time. While the number of people thrown into poverty was not as great as initially feared (with rural villages serving as something of a social safety net for the urban disposed), overall income per capita levels have still not returned to precrisis levels.

And while less easily calibrated, the political dislocation was also extreme. From the rubble of the Suharto regime, Indonesia needed to construct a new and democratic framework for politics, with student and other mass protest groups demanding dramatic change.[29] But beyond an almost universal recognition that a way had to be found to make democracy work, there was uncertainty on many fronts. Controls were lifted on political parties (causing over a hundred new parties to mushroom almost overnight), the press was set free, the student movement had found a powerful voice, the military drew back from its support for Golkar, and Indonesia shocked the world by suddenly announcing that it would allow the people of East Timor to determine their future in a UN-supervised referendum. In short, on the political front too, it was inevitable that Indonesia would need several years to grapple with the enormous challenge of building a new and democratic system of government. Furthermore, the twin challenges of economic and political reconstruction fed back upon and complicated each other. Deep political uncertainty compounded the problems of economic recovery, and a stalled economy compounded the problems of political recovery.

The second basic problem adding to Indonesia's woes at this time was an unfavorable international environment. With economic growth rates down across much of Asia relative to precrisis conditions, the Japanese economy still in recession, and the U.S. economy moving slowly as well, Indonesia faced a much less hospitable international environment for economic recovery. Demand for a range of Indonesian exports was reduced in a number of key markets. Similarly, the supply of external capital from traditional sources was diminished, and China was soaking up a very large proportion of the investment that was still flowing in Asia.[30] I do not mean to suggest that Indonesia suffered uniquely because of inclement international economic conditions, only that the external environment made Indonesia's challenges significantly harder. We have only to refer to China's continued strong economic growth amid less favorable international conditions and, even more tellingly, South Korea's extraordinarily rapid economic turnaround after being hit hard by the financial crisis to realize external conditions alone were not a determining factor. To understand why Indonesia made such slow progress in tackling its problems we must turn to the third of the three broad causal factors: weak national governance.

Slow progress on much-needed policy reforms has been a key factor in Indonesia's weak economic rehabilitation and festering social and political problems. On countless issues, ranging from reforming the banking sector to tackling extremist religious violence, the country's national political leadership has made inadequate progress. To be sure, some of the major policy problems Jakarta has faced are truly very difficult. For example, coordinating financial settlements on corporate debt among thousands of Indonesian corporations and international creditors is, by its very nature, extremely complex. However, even the more organizationally tractable tasks, such as selling off corporations whose debt had been formally assumed by the state, have proved to be arduous. The special high-powered agency created to handle this task (the Indonesian Bank Restructuring Agency) was subject to countless delays, blockages, and leadership changes. Similarly, the challenge of forcing those banks that remained viable after the crisis to accept their losses and clean up their balance sheets has proved difficult. Reform tasks of this type and magnitude are always inherently difficult politically. Nevertheless, Indonesia has made very slow progress, whereas countries such as Korea and Malaysia have moved much more effectively to deal with these problems and to move on.[31]

Why has Indonesia had such difficulty with making progress on policy reform? Popular explanations lay the blame on the weakness or incompetence of successive presidents. But this is superficial. Whatever the personal limitations of individual incumbents of the presidency, larger forces have been at work, in particular the debilitating effects of rapid turnover of leadership positions in the executive branch, lack of coordination among relevant ministers in developing policy positions, and problems of disagreement within the executive branch and, even more, between the executive branch and the legislature. These have all had deeply corrosive effects on the quality of national governance. In terms of turnover, neither the first nor second incumbent to succeed Suharto (Habibie and Wahid) lasted even twenty-four months in office, and in some ministerial posts turnover has been more rapid still. The Megawati administration was the first that ran its full course. Similarly, in varying degrees all three administrations have suffered from weak coordination among relevant cabinet ministries, reflecting in part differing party affiliations among ministries and in part an inability of presidents to impose their will. And even where the executive branch has reached a conclusion on a preferred way ahead, all too frequently this has been stalled or sidetracked as a result of an inability to reach agreement with the legislature.

Lying behind this multiplicity of governance problems has been an acutely dysfunctional institutional framework for national politics. For much of the transitional period the way national politics was structured by the constitution and the party system was so unhelpful as to render the always difficult task of national policy leadership all but impossible. To be sure, all three incumbents of the presidency since Suharto have suffered from major weaknesses and foibles, but the deeper and more powerful problem has been the severely problematic political institutions.

It is widely recognized and understood that transitions to democracy are bumpy and messy processes, particularly where there has been a long history of authoritarian rule. Equally, it is well understood that the dynamics of democratic government are necessarily slower and more cumbersome than autocracies precisely because they are designed to ensure executive accountability to the public. Yet we also know from comparative studies that democracies vary greatly in the ways in which they are configured and operate.[32] Regrettably, the particular configuration of Indonesia's political architecture during the transitional years following Suharto has been one of the most unfortunate imaginable. The essence of the problem has been a severe fragmentation of decisionmaking authority and confused lines of accountability. Under Suharto authority was radically centralized; after Suharto it swung to the opposite extreme, with authority highly diffused.[33]

We do not need to detour here into the arcane details of constitutional design to appreciate the essential elements of the problem. Americans understand well that the processes of bargaining and compromise between the executive branch and legislature can be awkward and take time. In Indonesia, this process was compounded by a multiplicity of parties. As Brazilians understand well, this makes the business of government much more complicated. In Indonesia, the situation was compounded even further by the fact that the president was directly dependent upon the parties in the legislature for his or her appointment and continued survival in office. That is, the president was appointed by the parliament (rather than being directly elected) and, furthermore, could be readily removed by the parliament. Under Suharto this was not an issue, as he controlled all the parties and other appointed members of the parliament through various direct and indirect means. However, with the rescinding of formal controls on the parties after Suharto's fall, they suddenly sprang to life and multiplied. This fundamentally changed the dynamics of national governance. Given the reality of a multiparty system, to win the presidency it was necessary to construct a multiparty coalition to secure a majority and then to reward members of this coalition with cabinet posts. But because the parliament could also readily remove the president from office, the president's ability to impose discipline on the cabinet or to bargain effectively with legislators over bills was very limited. Quite simply, the president could not afford to isolate the parties that put him or her into office. With such a multiplicity of actors and such ambiguity about accountability lines, all too often the net effect was deadlock and confusion. Further, with the president rendered so weak, the political actor with primary responsibility for tackling big national problems was in no position to do so.

This extraordinarily dysfunctional political framework made weak national governance a certainty. No matter whether the issue was bank restructuring or responding to religious and ethnic tensions, the essential task of national decisionmaking became excruciatingly difficult. It was all too easy for anyone inside or outside government to veto or derail coherent action. If a minister or the president sought to take specific measures to tackle a glaring problem—say, deliberate efforts by extremist elements to inflame religious tensions in the strife-ridden Maluku islands—supporters of the extremists, or groups that might stand to benefit indirectly from the ramifications of the extremists' actions, could derail the possibility of government action by playing upon either the partisan divisions with the cabinet or, if necessary, the president's vulnerability to removal from office.

To summarize, the argument here is that once we take account of these underlying factors (truly radical shocks, inclement international economic conditions, and a profoundly unhelpful political framework), then Indonesia's weak performance since 1998 becomes much more understandable. This argument has important analytic and policy implications, for it points in a very different direction from the popular and alarmist interpretations of Indonesia's future in the immediate post-Suharto years. The argument here is that Indonesia is not doomed to follow a Yugoslavia-like path of inescapable ethnic and religious conflict leading to an eventual national breakup. Nor is it necessarily the case that Indonesia has now been abandoned by investors indefinitely. To be sure—and as we have seen—there is no shortage of evidence to encourage such interpretations. This is particularly the case for the first three years following Suharto's fall. Nevertheless, the argument presented here is that these two radical shocks—the inclement international economic conditions and an acutely dysfunctional national political structure—account for a large part of Indonesia's diminished developmental performance over this period.

There is a further important step to this argument. Amid all the gloom about Indonesia, there has been crucial—if little heralded—progress in reforming the very institutional problems that were generating such weak national policy leadership. During 2002–03 formal agreement was reached on further streamlining some of the key institutions in the country's political architecture: the establishment of direct presidential elections and the independence of presidential tenure from the legislature; and consolidation of the party system and the electoral system.[34] This is important progress, for it opens up the possibility of tolerably effective governance. Indeed, we have already seen these institutional changes begin to exert some effect; with Megawati safe from removal from office, for example, a more coherent and coordinated approach has been facilitated in at least some policy areas.[35] For example, substantial progress is being made on the macroeconomic front with a major reduction in the overall public debt burden and reforming the legislative framework for public finance. The new politics of economic policymaking—indeed, of policymaking generally—that is now emerging is markedly more hopeful than it has been in the recent past. There is now significantly greater scope for forging agreement and legislative action on key issues.[36] Constitutional adjustment is by no means the panacea for all of Indonesia's problems, but it does at least make it more possible for the country's elected representatives at the national level to come together in a moderately coherent and effective manner for the purposes of hammering out policy compromises on the big issues of the day.

Plainly, Indonesia still faces large challenges. The familiar pessimistic assessments of contemporary Indonesia are not without foundation: I do not wish to minimize the scale of the challenges still before Indonesia nor pre-tend that there is no risk of political or economic progress being derailed. For all the historic progress with reform of the country's national political institutions, a widespread sense of cynicism and resignation now infuses public attitudes toward national politics. Partly this reflects normal processes of deflated expectations about democracy in transitional settings, and partly it reflects dashed hopes after the serial failure of successive administrations and the policy immobilism associated with this. More broadly, it also reflects near-universal dismay that corruption seems an even more cancerous problem now than under the old regime. It is important to be clear, then, that democracy in Indonesia remains fragile. Public commitment to sustaining democracy will not endure indefinitely in the face of governmental incapacity, all the more so given the enduring political strength of the military. Even as the military withdraws from the center of the formal political stage, its informal influence is once more on the rise as a result of its active combat role in Aceh and its expanding off-budget business operations and illicit rackets. And if we add to this list the many complex problems of implementing the devolution of power from the national government to provincial and district governments as well as the even more challenging problem of the systemic weakness of the country's legal system, the challenges do indeed appear daunting. But this brings us back to the fundamental importance of a tolerably effective national government, since in the absence of this none of these problems can be addressed coherently. Public skepticism notwithstanding, the recent reforms directed at restructuring the country's national political architecture mean that there is now some basis for expecting more effective policy leadership than has been the norm for most of the post-Suharto period.

Indonesia and Instruments for U.S. Engagement

During the three decades of the Suharto regime U.S. policy toward Indonesia was friendly, supportive, and remarkably low profile. Particularly during the early years, Washington welcomed the political stability and rapid economic growth that the regime brought, along with its staunch anticommunist credentials. The United States thus sought to support economic development in Indonesia through bilateral aid activities as well as through multilateral initiatives via the Inter-Governmental Group on Indonesia, the World Bank, and the International Monetary Fund. Politically, the emphasis was on nurturing relations with the armed forces. But with the regime settling in and with core U.S. policy interests seemingly in hand, Indonesia came to attract less and less attention. So low profile did the relationship become over time that informed observers began to worry that Washington had forgotten about Indonesia.[37]

This changed as the 1990s progressed. In part this reflected shifting U.S. policy priorities in the post–cold war period, with key developing countries coming to attract greater attention either in economic terms as "big emerging markets" or in politico-security terms as "pivotal states."[38] U.S. policymakers came increasingly to see Indonesia as both of these. In addition, however, there were also Indonesia-specific factors that caused the country to become a source of growing worry for Washington. Bilateral irritants (such as human rights and trade concerns) were emerging as issues of contention toward the end of the Suharto regime, but the big forces for change were the financial crisis that erupted in 1997, the separation of East Timor from the rest of the republic in 1999, and the challenge of global terrorism in the wake of the September 11, 2001, attacks in the United States. Individually and collectively these three developments have pushed Indonesia into a position of much greater prominence on the U.S. policy radar screen. Each demonstrated powerfully how developments in Indonesia had the potential to seriously impact U.S. interests. Particularly important today is Washington's concern (shared by Indonesia's neighbors) that Jakarta take effective steps to tackle extremist Islamic groups operating boarding schools (*pesantren*) that are suspected of being regional training grounds for new cohorts of terrorists to follow in the footsteps of a number of individuals now known to have been involved in the September 11 and Bali attacks.[39] In this new environment, it is no longer imaginable that a major summary statement to Congress by an assistant secretary of state for East Asian and Pacific affairs would make no mention of Indonesia or that a major Defense Department report on Asia would make no mention of Indonesia—as was occurring as late as the mid-1990s.[40]

In the half decade following Suharto's fall Indonesia has once again experienced serious developmental difficulties that are suggestive of some of the characteristics of poorly performing states. The symptoms are not as severe as they had been in the mid-1960s, but they are certainly serious enough to command attention. The argument advanced here, however, is that it would be a mistake to draw the conclusion that Indonesia is now incapable of serious developmental progress and is thus at risk of falling backward into a dangerously degenerative condition. Indeed, for all the numerous difficulties the country is struggling with, it is remarkable that so much progress has been made over this period of time.[41] Indonesia has had to rebuild a shattered economy and a destabilized polity and to do so in a time of deteriorating international economic conditions and in the context of a transitional political framework, in which authority became so fragmented that the possibilities for coherent policy action were severely circumscribed. Indeed, given all of this, in some ways the more remarkable point is that the things have not turned out worse for Indonesia.

For all the distressing internal conflict and violence and for all the worrying problems of corruption and criminal activity that erupted following Suharto's departure, it is important to keep sight of the fact that ethnic and religious tensions and violence appeared to ease during 2002–03, that efforts to enshrine shari'a (Islamic law) in the constitution failed, that there has been growing official recognition of equal status for Indonesia's Chinese minority, and, most important, that these have been happening along with the ongoing consolidation of democracy (the reforms to the structure of national government, the devolution of power to local government, and the continued reduction of the military's direct role in the government). In the circumstances, these are powerful achievements. They speak to the underlying durability of both the shared conception of the Indonesian republic as a coherent nation and the common commitment to building a framework for open and accountable government that reflects the vibrant plurality of Indonesian society.

Indonesia, in the midst of historic adjustments, faces formidable challenges. Even though the primary determinants of its developmental trajectory will be internal to the country itself, there is scope for the international community to assist the situation. With the United States increasingly conscious of Indonesia's strategic significance within Southeast Asia in traditional geopolitical terms and in the war on terrorism, and with the United States also increasingly sensitive to the significance of Indonesia as both the largest Muslim country in the world and the most promising example of a broadly tolerant, pluralistic, and democratic society in the Muslim world, there can be little doubt that it is powerfully in the interests of the United States to see Indonesia move to a stronger developmental trajectory.[42] The record of the past few years offers some grounds for optimism, for in a number of important areas U.S. policy instruments appear to have made significant contributions. Others are more ambiguous, and in some cases there are grounds for believing that U.S. policy initiatives are actually injurious to Indonesia's developmental effort.

On the positive side, in a number of areas it has been possible for U.S. development assistance projects to make significant contributions. Some of these have been obvious and natural targets for U.S. aid. For instance, a range of USAID projects have focused on deepening democracy through providing technical assistance to support ongoing constitutional fine-tuning (such as the issue of direct presidential elections); helping to foster "demand" for democratic government by supporting nongovernmental organizations that play a key role in articulating public grievances and advancing the notion of public accountability of officials; supporting the expansion of an independent media; and facilitating the political decentralization drive with projects to promote political and administrative capacity at the local government level. Similarly, on the economic front, a range of valuable projects have focused on, inter alia, facilitating the resolution of outstanding corporate debt through the Jakarta Initiative; providing specialist technical assistance to key agencies; and providing support for regulatory reform drives in areas ranging from trade policy to rice production to the drafting of a new companies law.[43]

Not all priority areas have been as susceptible to developmental assistance as these. For instance, there is universal agreement on the fundamental importance of strengthening the courts and legal processes. And while USAID has indeed mounted projects in this area, it is widely understood that this is an area that requires long-term behavioral change on a number of dimensions that will likely take a generation to accomplish. Other difficult areas include the challenge of connecting with Muslim constituencies and the question of resuming military aid to Indonesia. The former—an obvious priority, given both the war on terrorism and the general desire to smooth the path for social tolerance and pluralism in Indonesia—proves to be deceptively difficult. Thus far the emphasis has been on reaching out to moderate elements within the Indonesian Muslim community. But this can be a double-edged sword, leaving progressive Muslim leaders easy targets for their militant rivals seeking to discredit them as being little more than puppets on Washington's financial strings. Similarly, the question of resuming military-to-military cooperation via the International Military Education and Training (IMET) program is also problematic. The case for engaging Indonesia's military is strong, since in any scenario for Indonesia's short- and medium-term future, the military is critical to its developmental prospects.[44] Further, given both its national security powers and the alleged involvement of some officers in at least tacit support for Muslim extremists, the military is likely to be critical to Washington's drive against terrorism. But here, too, there are inescapable ambiguities that bedevil any attempt to assist Indonesia. Not only has the military been associated with serious human rights abuses and political actions that seem inimical to democracy, in some respects the police (now an independent agency) has a more impressive track record as a partner in the war on terrorism, given its impressive strides in pursuing the Muslim extremists responsible for the October 12 bombings in Bali. There is no simple answer to this problem. Working with the military is, almost certainly, essential to advancing U.S. efforts to contain terrorism, but if it comes at the price of simply disregarding the deeply problematic track record of particular sections of the military, it will likely prove counterproductive.

Finally, in one conspicuous case, it is hard to avoid the conclusion that U.S. policy carries significant, if unintended, negative implications for Indonesia. I refer here to the preferential regional trading arrangements that Washington has negotiated with, among others, Singapore and Australia. Regardless of any wider arguments for or against these initiatives, they are likely to have a negative impact on Indonesia. Along with any trade-diversion effects, under rules-of-origin requirements, Singapore will need to separate out goods coming from Indonesia for re-export to the United States, as these will be subject to less favorable treatment than goods originating in Singapore. This is unwelcome news for Indonesia. Of course, such initiatives are not intended to harm Indonesia (or any other country in the region). Although it is subject to powerful domestic political constraints within the United States, those responsible for U.S. international interests might ponder the potential importance of trade policy as an instrument for engagement with a country like Indonesia as a means of facilitating the flow of U.S. trade and investment with Indonesia.[45] The burden of discussions about development assistance is typically upon the policies of the recipient country and the way in which donor countries can contribute to refinements in these policies. But given the enormous importance of the U.S. economy as a market for exports and as a source of investment, it is also appropriate to consider how U.S. policies affect the prospects for developing countries—all the more so as protectionism and economic nationalism come more to the fore in countries like Indonesia.

Conclusion

Indonesia is a notable case for considering the problems of poorly performing states, given the sharp swings in its developmental trajectory over time. In the early 1950s it was, like many newly independent countries, muddling along with weak and fragmented governance (albeit of a generally democratic nature) and modest economic growth. As political and economic difficulties accumulated, this situation was overturned by the country's founding president, Sukarno, who imposed authoritarian rule. His chaotic dictatorship only deepened the country's problems and had severely negative consequences for the economy. During this phase—the late 1950s to the mid-1960s—Indonesia was in many ways a prime example of the dangerously degenerative consequences of weak governance and a sickly economy. Eventually the situation deteriorated so far that the military was able to move against Sukarno and claim power for itself. Thereafter, in a stark break with the past, strong and systematic authoritarian controls were imposed, enabling Suharto's new regime to enforce stability across the archipelago. This paved the way for strongly pro-growth economic policies to drive a thirty-year boom and industrial transformation, before the regime finally unravelled amid the upheaval of the Asian financial crisis. More recently we have seen Indonesia struggle to rebuild itself economically and politically in particularly challenging circumstances.

Viewed in its entirety, Indonesia's developmental record thus offers an important illustration both of how poorly performing states can readily slide into more dire circumstances and of how even acute situations can be salvaged. (In 1964 or early 1965, no one inside or outside Indonesia could have guessed that within a few years the country would be enjoying sustained strong economic growth.) But the model that was so successful in economic terms, and for so long, could not endure indefinitely given its shallow base of public consent. And in the wake of the regime's dramatic collapse, the country has faced an uphill battle to rebuild. Also of analytic and policy interest are the ambiguities of Indonesia's current situation.

Indonesia's problems today are numerous and serious, but the situation is not dire. Thanks primarily to its own internal reform efforts, but also aided by constructive policy engagement in certain areas by the United States and other providers of development assistance, the country is now showing signs of slowly emerging from a deeply worrying period of flux. But just as there is ambiguity in assessing Indonesia's developmental performance over the past years, so too there is ambiguity in considering the likely character for the period ahead. Given the recent progress with restructuring the national political institutions, there are good grounds for expecting that Indonesia will experience stable and moderately effective government and moderate economic growth. A stable developing country with a viable form of democratic government and economic growth in the 3–4 percent range is above the status of low-income poorly performing states. And yet it is by no means a situation about which one can be sanguine either.

A trajectory of only moderate economic growth will not allow Indonesia to regain the rapid pace of developmental progress it once enjoyed. In practical terms, this means that improvement in living standards will be slow and that we may well see the deterioration of public infrastructure, such as public health and education systems and roads in outlying areas. If this is correct, a growing gap is likely to emerge between Indonesia and the more strongly performing economies of East Asia. The best hope is that Indonesia will be able to continue its record of broadly successful institutional reform at the national political level and extend this to the next wave of institutional challenges: regional government and the legal system. Better institutions will permit better governance, and better governance will permit more rapid economic progress. Primary carriage of these issues inevitably lies with Indonesia itself, but this is something to which the United States has shown it can make a significant and positive contribution.

Notes

1. This is the figure for 2001. World Bank, *World Development Indicators, 2002.*

2. Herbert Feith, *The Decline of Constitutional Democracy in Indonesia* (Cornell University Press, 1962).

3. Hal Hill, *The Indonesian Economy since 1966* (Cambridge University Press, 1996), pp. 1–3; John Bresnan, *Managing Indonesia* (Columbia University Press, 1993), p. 1. For a full accounting of the period, see Bruce Glassburner, ed., *The Economy of Indonesia: Selected Readings* (Cornell University Press, 1971).

4. Benjamin Higgins, *Economic Development* (New York: W. W. Norton, 1968), p. 678, as quoted in Hill, *The Indonesian Economy since 1966,* p. 1.

5. Harold Crouch, *The Army and Politics in Indonesia* (Cornell University Press, 1978).

6. For a fuller discussion of the issues see Andrew MacIntyre, "Political Parties, Accountability, and Economic Governance in Indonesia," in *Democracy, Governance, and Economic Performance: East and Southeast Asia,* edited by Jean Blondel, Takashi Inonguchi, and Ian Marsh (Tokyo: United Nations University Press, 1999).

7. Hill, *The Indonesian Economy since 1966,* p. 3.

8. Alan Gelb, ed., *Oil Windfalls: Blessing or Curse?* (Oxford University Press, 1988).

9. The best overview study of the Indonesian economy through the Suharto period is Hill, *The Indonesian Economy since 1966.* For a comparative perspective, see I. M. D. Little and others, *Boom, Crisis, and Adjustment: The Macroeconomic Experiences of Developing Countries* (Oxford University Press, 1993).

10. World Bank, *World Development Indicators, 2000.*

11. For a critique of development progress under Suharto, see Jonathon Pincus, *Class Power and Agrarian Change: Land and Labour in Rural West Java* (London: Palgrave Macmillan, 1996).

12. Hill, *The Indonesian Economy since 1966;* David Cole and Betty Slade, *Building a Modern Financial System: The Indonesian Experience* (Cambridge University Press, 1996); Radius Prawiro, *Indonesia's Struggle for Economic Development* (Oxford University Press, 1998).

13. World Bank, *The East Asian Miracle* (Oxford University Press, 1993).

14. No single study brings all these variables together. Although not dealing with Indonesia, the best comparative overview of this subject remains Stephan Haggard, *Pathways from the Periphery: The Politics of Growth in the Newly Industrializing Countries* (Cornell University Press, 1990).

15. Measured in local currency, GDP per capita at the end of 2002 was still about 10 percent below the 1997 level and about 3 percent below if measured in dollars. See World Bank, *Indonesia: Maintaining Stability, Deepening Reforms* (2003), pp. 1, 3.

16. The rule of thumb used by policymakers in the Economic Planning Agency (BAPPENAS) is that about 400,000 jobs are created with each additional 1 percent in GDP growth; with the workforce growing by about 2 million each year, an annual growth rate of 5 percent would be necessary to employ the new entrants. For a wider discussion of the socioeconomic ramifications of the economic dislocation created by the crisis, see Aris Anata, ed., *The Indonesian Crisis: A Human Development Perspective* (Singapore: Institute for Southeast Asian Studies, 2003).

17. See, for instance, Transparency International's Corruption Perception Index for 2002 and 1997 (www.transparency.org) or other declining statistical indicators (for instance, World Bank, *Indonesia: Maintaining Stability, Deepening Reforms,* table 40 (statistical annex); the analysis of seasoned economic observers such as Prema-chandra Athukorala, "Survey of Recent Developments," *Bulletin of Indonesian Economic Studies* 38, no. 2 (2002): 143–45; and journalistic accounts such as Antara Newsagency, "Mega Admits Legal Graft Worse than Ever," December 16, 2002; "World Banker Assails Indonesia's Corruption," *New York Times,* August 28, 2002.

18. Another of the fascinating puzzles the Indonesian case reveals is the question of corruption. Under Suharto, Indonesia was characterized by pervasive corruption combined with sustained strong private investment and growth. In the half decade since, Indonesia has been characterized by pervasive corruption and disappointing investment and growth. The recent experience is less puzzling; the combination of deep corruption and strong growth under Suharto is more intriguing. How was it that pervasive cronyism and corruption coexisted with extremely good aggregate economic outcomes for so long? Again, this is not the place for an extended discussion of the subject. But briefly, a key element to the puzzle seems to have been that the president had both the incentive and the capability to ensure that, although graft flourished, it did not become either so expensive or so unpredictable as to deter investors. Central to this was the institutional ability to monitor and punish agents who acted in a sufficiently capricious manner as to deter significant numbers of investors. Putting it crudely, subsequent to Suharto's fall Indonesians have learned that there is a malady even worse than organized corruption: disorganized corruption. For a fuller discussion of these themes, see Andrew MacIntyre, "Institutions and the Political Economy of Corruption in Developing Countries," paper prepared for the workshop on corruption, Centre for Development, Democracy, and the Rule of Law, Stanford University, January 31–February 1, 2003 (http.apseg.macintyre.anu.edu.au); and Andrew MacIntyre, "Institutions, Property Rights, and Corruption in Indonesia," in *Corruption: The Boom and Bust of East Asia,* edited by J. E. Campos (Ateneo University Press, 2001).

19. The data are from Standard Chartered Bank, quoted in John McBeth, "Bombed Economy," *Far Eastern Economic Review,* November 14, 2002.

20. World Bank, *Indonesia: Maintaining Stability, Deepening Reforms*, p. 17.

21. Ibid., p. 6.

22. International Crisis Group, *Al-Qaeda in Southeast Asia: The Case of the "Ngruki Network" in Indonesia*, briefing paper (Brussels: 2003).

23. International Crisis Group, *Communal Violence in Indonesia: Lessons from Kaliman-tan*, Report 19 (Brussels: 2001); International Crisis Group, *Tensions on Flores: Local Symptoms of National Problems*, briefing paper (Brussels: 2002).

24. "Unchecked Thuggery Could Lead to Organized Crime," *Jakarta Post*, March 17, 2003.

25. For an easily accessible discussion of these issues, see "A Military Mafia," *Newsweek*, August 26, 2002; and "TNI Nothing More than Mercenaries," *Jakarta Post*, March 17, 2003.

26. Athukorala, "Survey of Recent Developments," pp. 145–48, 155–56.

27. World Bank, *World Development Indicators, 2002.*

28. Hal Hill, *The Indonesian Economy in Crisis: Causes, Consequences, and Lessons* (Singapore: Institute of Southeast Asian Studies, 1999).

29. Kevin O'Rourke, *Reformasi: The Struggle for Power in Post-Suharto Indonesia* (Sydney: Allen and Unwin, 2003); Dwight King, *Half-Hearted Reform: Electoral Institutions and the Struggle for Democracy in Indonesia* (Westport, Conn.: Praeger, 2003).

30. Andrew MacIntyre and Budy Resosudarmo, "Survey of Recent Developments," *Bulletin of Indonesian Economic Studies* 39, no. 2 (2003): 133–56.

31. Stephan Haggard, *The Political Economy of the Asian Financial Crisis* (Washington: Institute for International Economics, 2000).

32. Arned Lijphart, *Patterns of Democracy: Government Forms and Performance in Thirty-Six Countries* (Yale University Press, 1999); Gary Cox and Matthew McCubbins, "The Institutional Determinants of Policy Outcomes," in *Presidents, Parliaments, and Policy*, edited by Stephan Haggard and Matthew McCubbins (Cambridge University Press, 2001); Andrew MacIntyre, *The Power of Institutions: Political Architecture and Governance* (Cornell University Press, 2003).

33. For a wider discussion of these issues, see MacIntyre, *The Power of Institutions.*

34. For valuable overviews and analyses of the continuing political reforms, see the various reports of the National Democratic Institute: Andrew Ellis and Etsi Yudhini, *UU Pemilu 2003: Observations on Some Key Issues* (Washington: National Democratic Institute, 2003); Andrew Ellis and Etsi Yudhini, *Indonesia's New State Institutions: The Constitution Completed, Now for the Detail . . .* (Washington: National Democratic Institute, 2002).

35. Of course, many factors play into judgments about the relative success of different administrations. My point here is simply that the fact that Megawati has had to worry much less about the possibility of removal from office by her political opponents has had a powerful effect on her ability to promote coherence and purposefulness within the cabinet and to bargain with the legislature over policy. To be sure, Megawati's administration has suffered from a range of problems, but it has been less subject to the debilitating incoherence and gridlock of her predecessors.

36. This theme is developed further in MacIntyre and Resosudarmo, "Survey of Recent Developments."

37. John Bresnan has written of American "amnesia" about Indonesia, and in an often repeated remark, Paul Wolfowitz (previously a U.S. ambassador to Jakarta) said that

Indonesia was the important country the United States knew least about. John Bresnan, "Indonesia," in *The Pivotal States: A New Framework for U.S. Policy in the Developing World,* edited by Robert Chase, Emily Hill, and Paul Kennedy (New York: W. W. Norton, 1999), p. 25.

38. The former term comes from Garten and the latter from Chase, Hill, and Kennedy. See Jeffrey Garten, *The Big Ten: Emerging Markets and How They Will Change Our Lives* (New York: Basic Books, 1999); Robert Chase, Emily Hill, and Paul Kennedy, eds., *The Pivotal States: A New Framework for U.S. Policy in the Developing World* (New York: W. W. Norton, 1999).

39. Zachary Abuza, *Militant Islam in Southeast Asia: Crucible of Terror* (Boulder, Colo.: Lynne Rienner, 2003); International Crisis Group, *Jemaah Islamiyah in Southeast Asia: Damaged but Still Dangerous,* Report 63 (Brussels: 2003).

40. Winston Lord's fifteen-page testimony at his 1993 confirmation hearing did not mention Indonesia once, and the Department of Defense report "United States Security Strategy for the East Asia–Pacific Region" (February 1995) was scarcely better. See Bresnan, "Indonesia," p. 25.

41. A broadly similar conclusion was reached by the veteran head of USAID's Indonesia office, Desaix Terry Myers, in a valedictory speech at the end of a second tour of duty in Indonesia, March 17, 2003. See Desaix Terry Myers, "More Progress than Meets the Eye: The Role of U.S. Assistance in Turbulent Times," Open Forum report (Washington: USINDO, 2003).

42. Matthew P. Daley, "U.S. Interests and Policy Priorities in Southeast Asia," testimony by the Deputy Assistant Secretary of State for East Asian and Pacific Affairs before the House International Relations Committee, Subcommittee on East Asia and the Pacific, March 26, 2003.

43. For an overview of projects, see USAID, *USAID/Indonesia Annual Report FY 2002* (March 2002). It should be noted that much valuable developmental assistance work is also done by U.S. nongovernmental organizations. For example, in the area of political reform, the National Democratic Institute, the International Foundation for Electoral Systems, and the International Republican Institute have made very important contributions.

44. For an informed and cogent summary of the case in favor of reengagement, see John Haseman, "Engage Indonesia's Military," *Far Eastern Economic Review,* March 20, 2003. But see also International Crisis Group, "Resuming U.S.–Indonesia Military Ties," briefing paper (Brussells: 2002).

45. For a thoughtful general critique of the problem, see Bernard Gordon, "A High-Risk Trade Policy," *Foreign Affairs* 82, no. 4 (2003): 105–18.

5

Reforming Central Asia

MARTHA BRILL OLCOTT

I t is many years, now, since the USSR collapsed, resulting in, among other things, the emergence of five independent states in Central Asia—and many years, too, since the United States and the international financial institutions began to actively seek to influence developmental outcomes in this region. This chapter looks at how these countries have fared in this period and at the effectiveness of the role of the United States and of international financial institutions in achieving their desired outcomes in this part of the world.

There is always a danger in rendering such a judgment at a fixed point in time, much like predicting the path of a bird photographed in flight. One never knows what comes next, whether the bird will soar or will plummet to the ground. Much the same can be said about the situation in Central Asia. Many who have advised these governments look at the current situation in places like Kyrgyzstan and Tajikistan and say that to dwell on what is negative in the current situation is to ignore improvements that will inevitably soon be measurable. Similarly, those who have been part of international missions that have reduced activities or closed up shop where their advice has been ignored, such as in Uzbekistan and Turkmenistan, often claim that current growth figures disguise imminent economic crises.

Evaluating developments in Central Asia is a highly subjective exercise, a classic case of whether or not to call the glass half empty or half full. One can look very critically at decisions that were made in each of these five countries and paint far rosier alternative scenarios as to what might have been achieved, given the economic starting points and education levels of the populations that lived in these states. At the same time it is possible to argue that as bad as things are, far worse might have been expected as a result of the economic collapse caused by the demise of the USSR and the risk of interethnic violence inherent in the region.

To be sure, the percentage of the population generally accepted as living in poverty has increased in four of the five countries, and no serious observer places much credibility in statistics originating in the fifth country, Turkmenistan. At the same time, though, there are no reports of famine in the region, and however idiosyncratic the state-building strategies of some of these states have been, none of these countries seems about to implode from within, nor is the prospect of interstate conflict a seemingly immediate one.

For those living in Central Asia, though, it is little consolation that things might have been worse, and things are bad enough that the World Bank already considers Uzbekistan, Kyrgyzstan, and Tajikistan to be "poorly performing states." Only oil- and gas-rich Kazakhstan is something approximating a success story in the region, for although Turkmenistan's government reports average wages and per capita gross domestic product (GDP) that are high enough to keep them off the list of troubled states, these official statistics are highly suspect. Even Kazakhstan is underperforming, a point reinforced in a World Bank study on the impact of systemic corruption on the Kazakh economy.

A question that comes readily to mind is who is to blame for the disappointing performance of many of these states. Is it the leaders who failed to follow the advice of the international community and either rejected the macroeconomic stabilization programs proposed to them or failed to implement them in a conscientious enough fashion, turning a blind eye to the corruption that surrounded them? Or is it in large part the fault of the international financial and assistance community, who dashed into a region that they knew little about with a lot of assumptions about how best to move these societies from point A to what the outside world saw as the desired point B?

For those living in the region an even more important question is not which states are poorly performing but whether the underperformance of all or even some of these states puts their long-term economic well-being or that of their neighbors at risk. Certainly the underperformance of a state like Uzbekistan, which sits at the center of the Soviet-era transportation hub for all four neighboring states, has had enormous consequence for the economic recovery of the region's smallest economies, those of Kyrgyzstan and Tajikistan, inflicting a further geographic isolation that was not factored in by the Western experts who devised their macroeconomic stabilization programs.

The thesis of this chapter is that the underperformance of all three of these states puts their long-term economic well-being at risk and that the underperformance of Uzbekistan in particular poses a threat to the security of neighboring states. I argue, though, that there is no simple explanation for why these states have performed so poorly. The boundaries of these Stalin-era administrative creations were not set with an eye to self-sustaining economies, and in fact Soviet economic policies were designed to reinforce the economic dependency of the constituent parts. But geography alone holds only part of the answer. The initial frameworks of economic decision-making employed after independence were often flawed as well. U.S. advisers and Western financial institutions raced into the region prepared to apply lessons learned elsewhere, with little consideration of whether these experiences were applicable in the economic and geographic conditions of Central Asia. For their part, Central Asian leaders often felt that they knew better and could therefore ignore any advice that clashed with their own worldviews or that was not consistent with the interests of their families or those of their closest associates.

Moreover, I argue that although a shared perception held by international observers and local leaders of the poorly performing states developed over time that economic and social problems were either growing or only slowly abating, neither group was willing to fundamentally change its approach. This remains true today, despite the heightened importance of these states in U.S.-sponsored security arrangements. No priority is given to substantially increasing the resources available to help solve these nations' developmental problems, and this in turn creates few incentives for the region's leaders to change their ways.

Why Look at Central Asia?

The events of September 11, 2001, clearly brought home the risks associated with ignoring state collapse. While not every failing state will become a refuge for terrorist groups with global reach, as Afghanistan did, every failing state poses a risk to the security of its own citizens and usually to those living in

Table 5-1. *Key Economic Indicators, Five Central Asian Countries,*
Various Years

Indicator	Kazakhstan	Kyrgyzstan	Tajikistan	Turkmen-istan	Uzbek-istan
Gross national income (US$ billion, 2001)	20.1	1.4	1.1	5.1	13.8
Gross national income (per capita US$, 2001)	1,360	280	170	950	550
Private sector percent of gross domestic product (2001)	60	60	45	25	45
Population (millions, 2001)	15	5	6	5	25
Urbanization (percent)	56	34	28	45	37
Population density (people per sq. km.)	5	26	44	11	61
Average annual growth rate per capita (percent)	13.5	4.2	4.1	18.4	2.6
Unemployment (percent, 2001)	11.0	3.2	20.0	a	0.6
Poverty rate (percent, 2001)	26.0	55.0	83.0	34.4	n.a.
Land area under permanent crops (percent, 1999)	0.1	0.3	0.9	0.1	0.9
Irrigated land as percent of cropland (1997–99)	7.6	75.0	82.4	106.2	88.3
Hectares of cropland per capita (1997–99)	1.99	0.28	n.a.	n.a.	n.a.
Food production index (1998–2000; 1989–91 > 100)	61.0	115.9	53.8	134.0	116.2

Source: World Bank, *World Development Indicators, 2003.*
a. Every Turkmen citizen is guaranteed employment; therefore, an official unemployment rate does not exist. According to a household survey, unemployment was 19 percent in 1998.
n.a. Not available.

neighboring states as well. Developments in Afghanistan had an impact on the lives of many Central Asians years before their influence was felt in New York City and Washington. Similarly, state failure in one Central Asian state would produce a rapid ripple effect in neighboring countries and could greatly magnify the global security risks emanating from the South Asian region. The economic data reproduced in tables 5-1 and 5-2 show a region that may be heading toward crisis and provide ample incentive to examine and rethink the developmental strategies that have been pursued in this part of the world.

Table 5-2. *Average Annual Growth Rate, Five Indicators,*
Five Central Asian Countries, 1990–2001
Percent

Indicator	Kazakhstan	Kyrgyzstan	Tajikistan	Turkmen-istan	Uzbek-istan
Gross domestic product	–2.8	–2.9	–8.5	–2.8	0.4
Agriculture	–6.5	2.1	–5.8	–3.2	0.9
Industry	–6.9	–8.5	–13.2	–6.7	–2.6
Manufacturing	n.a.	–14.1	–12.6	n.a.	n.a.
Services	3.1	–3.9	–1.1	–3.2	4.0

Source: See table 5-1.
n.a. Not available.

An examination of the situation in Central Asia also offers a good opportunity to examine the assumptions behind some of the leading paradigms that have been applied to the problems of transition in postcommunist societies and to ask whether we erred more by initially treating these states as all quite similar or by later choosing to see the Central Asian states as relatively unique.

Initially, "transitologists" viewed all postcommunist countries as going through similar, if not identical, processes of economic and political transition. As the transition in Central Europe began before that in Central Asia, people with experience in the former hurried to apply their expertise in the latter. But when they found their successes from Central Europe hard to duplicate, they began arguing that the transitions in the Central European states, as well as in the Baltic republics, were really quite different from those of the post-Soviet Central Asian states, because the former group of countries had a history of prior statehood that the others (save Russia) lacked. The nature of their interwar experiences in particular explained why many of these Central European states had an easier time transforming their centrally planned communist economies into market-based ones and seemed to be making relatively smooth transitions to democratic or quasi-democratic political systems.

By the mid-1990s it was clear that the post-Soviet Central Asian states were proceeding more slowly with reform than had the countries of Central Europe, but it was not self-evident that differences in their history were the cause. Some of the blame obviously lay with decisionmakers in the Central Asian states, who proved more unyielding to Western advice than their counterparts elsewhere. But much of the responsibility also lay with foreign advisers, who generally applied a cookie-cutter approach to reform. When this approach failed to result in the desired outcomes, doubts were raised on the wisdom of the goals rather than on the process of implementation. Western sources of aid began arguing that many of the post-Soviet Central Asian states were not "ready" for political and economic reform, given their long experience under the Russian and Soviet colonial "yoke," views that were encouraged by Central Asia's ruling elite. These apologists of failed reform hid behind simplifications of history that were no less crude than the earlier renderings of Soviet scholars.

Information that got in the way was conveniently forgotten, such as the fact that by many macroeconomic indicators two Central Asian states, Kazakhstan and Kyrgyzstan, were ahead of the other post-Soviet Central Asian states or at least nearly keeping up to Russia. Kyrgyzstan was the first of these states to engage in financial restructuring, and Kazakhstan has one of the two strongest banking sectors among the Central Asian Soviet successor states, having received positive investment ratings more quickly than did Russia. Both Kazakhstan and Kyrgyzstan have introduced private ownership of land, albeit with some restrictions, and both countries have reorganized pension systems, health care systems, and education systems in an effort to make them financially self-sustaining.

Nonetheless, despite these areas of high performance, Western observers have not been willing to hold any of the Central Asian nations to the same standards that were applied in Central Europe, allowing them to hide behind the curtain of their "Asianness" and to emphasize the importance of a "history of prior statehood." But given the strong performance of a number of Asian economies, the invocation of Asianness is a slippery concept. It is one that is generally used by the Central Asian leadership to justify a model of economic development that is partnered with strong one-man or oligarchic rule and that sees little value in political liberalization until some very distant future.

The absence of prior statehood is an even more amorphous idea, as the region's leaders simultaneously stress the newness of their nations as well as the ancientness of their peoples. Here too history has been rewritten to create an argument of "statehood restored." The Kyrgyz even planned to commemorate the 2,200th anniversary of statehood in 2004.[1] At the same time, few in the region would disagree with the claim that the ideological glue of nationalism based on "statehood denied" was in relatively short supply. It is less clear how important nationalism is in predicting success in economic and political reform. In Russia, nationalism has been both a complicated and complicating factor, as it is difficult to separate what was Soviet from what was Russian, making both potentially destabilizing to the redefined Russian state. Georgia and Armenia, states that view independence as "statehood restored" (regardless of how the broader international community views it) have had economic and political transitions as difficult as post-Soviet states in Central Asia.

There were small nationalist movements throughout Central Asia in the late Soviet period; the largest proportionally was in Tajikistan, the largest in absolute numbers was in Uzbekistan, and the smallest in both absolute and proportional terms was in Turkmenistan. Ordinary Central Asians also had complex feelings about both Russian domination and Soviet rule, which they saw as overlapping but not identical. Most of the nationalist movements in Central Asia were movements for cultural and political autonomy and became independence movements only after it was apparent that the USSR would not survive.

This does not mean that Central Asians were less fit to build states than were their counterparts in other parts of the Soviet Union. Levels of educational attainment in Central Asia were somewhat lower than in most other parts of the Soviet Union, but they were very high when compared with most non-European countries. The majority of Central Asians lived in rural areas, but each republic had an industrial sector, and factories were frequently located in rural settings. More important, the gap between rural and urban was easily breeched through the mobility provided by Red Army service, through universal access to merit-based higher education, and through the hospitality provided by even distantly related urban family members bound by obligations of kinship. If anything, the gap between urban and rural was much smaller in Central Asia than in Russia or other European parts of the Soviet Union, where there were not always the same cultural supports for upward mobility.

Structural distinctions play a larger role than cultural ones in explaining the developmental pattern in Central Asia. The nature of the transition in Central Europe after the dissolution of the USSR was fundamentally different from that of other areas of the former Soviet Union. For Central European states, the end of communism meant throwing off the influence of a powerful foreign power that largely dictated local economic and political conditions. A much more difficult transition was being attempted in Central Asia, as a vertically integrated whole was being divided into parts.

True, in Central Europe Czechoslovakia split into the Czech and Slovak republics in 1993, but that was a very simple division compared to the experience of the USSR as a whole, which included lopping off three republics from the USSR and then dividing the remaining whole into twelve uneven parts, each of which received a fragment of a previously integrated economy. It is often argued that the whole of an economy is much more than the sum of its parts, and the economies of many of these newly independent post-Soviet republics became less valuable when they were severed from the rest of the country. Even resource-rich republics that stood to gain from integrating directly with the global economy faced a difficult transition period before the value of their assets could be realized, given the relative geographic remoteness of the Central Asian and Caucasian states.

The transition to a market economy was a great deal more complicated in the Central Asian post-Soviet states than in Central Europe, where varying degrees of private ownership had survived forty years of communist rule and where it was sometimes possible to have hard currency. A restrictive form of cooperative ownership was introduced in the 1980s, where virtually none existed before. Even then, those engaged in newly legalized forms of foreign trade had limited access to hard currency. But these conditions left the Central Asian states no more or less prepared for the transition to the market than the other post-Soviet states, save for their geographic isolation. In fact, Uzbekistan, much like Azerbaijan and Georgia, seemed better prepared for the transition to a market economy than many other parts of the Soviet Union, because in Uzbekistan (and these other states) there was capital accumulation in the Soviet period, through the functioning of the gray economy.

One could say that the Uzbeks are natural entrepreneurs, as tens of thousands of Uzbeks found ways to bend the rules in the Soviet period to accumulate capital, selling goods that they themselves produced or had managed to steal from the state. They were so successful that a parallel economy existed in Uzbekistan alongside the formally sanctioned Soviet one, with surcharges for goods and services levied on top of the official Soviet price structure, effectively reflecting what the market would bear.[2] Within a few years of independence, though, President Islam Karimov decided to restrict the development of an entrepreneurial class, largely for political reasons.

By contrast, the two countries in the region that have gone the furthest with market reforms, Kazakhstan and Kyrgyzstan, seemed to have the least preparation for it. Although the Kazakh elite in particular had been skilled at managing the old Soviet economic system to both personal and republic advantage,[3] neither the Kazakhs nor the Kyrgyz were particularly entrepreneurial, nor did either have a history of private property ownership. In fact, the opposite was true: in a nomadic culture, land is for communal usage, and even livestock were largely held in common. Yet both of these countries embraced comprehensive macroeconomic reforms and privatization programs, which have enjoyed reasonable success. This further calls into question some of the assumptions about what Central Asians could or could not be expected to do and makes the question of why Kyrgyzstan is a considered a poorly performing state a particularly important one.

Who Is to Blame for Central Asia's Poor Performance?

There is no simple answer to this question. As the following case studies make clear, several factors are at work, and these played out differently from country to country. Part of the blame for Central Asia's poor performance rests with the approach applied by the international developmental community, which sent experts to the region who had little knowledge about local conditions but who had no lack of confidence about their ability to suggest appropriate strategies of reform. Some of the assumptions made about what it would take to sustain economic growth in Kyrgyzstan, as well as in Tajikistan, were unjustly optimistic and failed to consider the isolation of the region and the potentially crippling interdependence of these states.

This lack of local experience proved quite costly in, for example, Kyrgyzstan, which accepted international guidance rather uncritically. The international community used Kyrgyzstan as a laboratory for reform, and President Akayev felt compelled to accept the advice, largely because of the paucity of economic alternatives. This approach paid off. Per capita international aid in Kyrgyzstan, as table 5-3 shows, was the highest in the region, twice its nearest competitor and five and even ten times more than other Central Asian states.

The reforms were also undermined by corruption, which is endemic in the region, reaching from presidential administrations down to the local level of government. Reformers hold out hope that as the capacity of these political systems increases, through structural reforms that penetrate to the most local level of government, corruption will begin to lessen. Patterns of economic growth will be sustained, they argue, allowing governments to raise the revenues necessary to finance restricted social welfare systems. There is no question, though, that corruption is sufficiently pervasive as to be a major challenge to economic development in all five Central Asian countries. The Transparency International Corruption Perceptions Index of 2003 assigns both Kazakhstan and Uzbekistan a country rank of 100, awards Kyrgyzstan 118th place, and Tajikistan 124th (which it shares with Azerbaijan). Turkmenistan is unranked because of the unavailability of data.[4]

Table 5-3. *Average International Aid per Capita, Five Central Asian Countries, 1994–2001*
US$

Country	World Bank	International Monetary Fund	RDB	Asian Development Bank	U.S. Agency for International Development
Kazakhstan	9.6	−0.6	2.7	29.9	17.5
Kyrgyzstan	10.8	3.9	9.8	4.4	29.7
Tajikistan	3.8	2.5	1.0	28.7	7.8
Turkmenistan	1.3	0	0.9	...	6.9
Uzbekistan	1.7	0.7	1.1	29.9	3.5

Source: See table 5-1 and the websites of the international funding institutions.

Corruption was a factor in Central Asian life throughout the last decades of the Soviet period, and whether it is an inherent part of Central Asian culture is a question of considerable debate. The Transparency International figures support the conclusion of most observational data: that corruption has worsened since independence. With the removal of the overlords in Moscow, the perquisites of power increased in both relative and absolute terms, fed by direct access to hard currency and to the money available from the ability to regulate investment as well as both legal and illegal trade. This is especially true of oil- and gas-rich states like Kazakhstan and Turkmenistan, but even in the poorer states there has been no shortage of opportunities for corruption among the ruling elite everywhere in the region.

Corruption in Kazakhstan largely centers on the president and his family, and an ongoing investigation into the Kazakh oil industry in U.S. district courts in New York City has already resulted in two arrests of American businessmen.[5] President Nazarbayev has admitted to the existence of Swiss bank accounts that held some US$2 billion; he maintains that this money was deposited abroad as a way to protect the funds, a claim few believe. But Nazarbayev, whose son-in-law is the number-two figure in the state oil and gas company, is not the only one to profit from abuses in the sale of Kazakhstan's oil. Shady transfer transactions are the source of most of the US$2,011 million of goods sent from Kazakhstan to the Bahamas in 2002, a trade that the Kazakh government and state oil company have been unable to control.[6] The shift from state control to partial private control of Kazakhstan's gold, chrome, copper, coal, and steel industries has not been done transparently and has been the source of repeated rumors and controversy as to who in power profited from it.[7] The economies of both Kyrgyzstan and Kazakhstan may be able to withstand the negative effects of corruption. As table 5-1 shows, both have experienced high growth rates in recent years, and both have strong private sectors. Unlike Kyrgyzstan, Kazakhstan is a potentially wealthy state—and a diverse one economically, as well. Moreover, the creation of a National Fund in 2000 to invest windfall income from mineral resource development may further stimulate the diversification of the Kazakh economy.

There is simply no dependable statistical information coming out of Turkmenistan that can be used to approximate the scale of unregulated or illegal economic activity, as much of it centers on one person, the country's president, Saparmurad Niyazov. The country's key export, gas, is sold in a part barter arrangement, in which the seller is the Turkmen state, as represented by Niyazov, and the purchaser is Russia's Gazprom. All other foreign trade is also subject to Niyazov's approval, and his power is effectively unchecked.

The drug trade is at the center of corruption in Turkmenistan and Tajikistan and is a major source of corruption in Kyrgyzstan and probably in Uzbekistan as well. In the last three cases the state has been partially suborned through payments made by drug traffickers, while in Turkmenistan, the state (or more accurately, the president) seems to have captured the trade. Even in Tajikistan, the scale of the drug trade is large enough to fully eclipse most forms of legitimate business, although this is not reflected in the country's official statistics or the evaluation of them offered by its major financial advisers.[8]

Bad decisionmaking has reinforced the damage done by pervasive patterns of corruption. The refusal to take aggressive steps to reduce corruption is sometimes justified in part as a "strategy" of development in which key members of the regional elite are given an incentive to support the political incumbent. This is an explanation for at least some of the corruption in the cotton economy of Uzbekistan and Turkmenistan, as local elites were permitted to pocket some of the profits of this state-dominated sector, in the interests of stability. It is also a reason why the Rahmonov government in Tajikistan turned a blind eye to drug trading organized through the city government of Dushanbe. Obviously this is a questionable as well as dangerous way to maintain stability, encouraging the creation of a spiral of corruption rather than a stable platform from which to build a development strategy.

While all the regimes have preached the importance of stability, in most cases there has been a high turnover of local elite, and frequently this has not served the cause of increased professionalization. The ranks of the regional elite have been thinned to dysfunctional levels in Turkmenistan, while the sums of money involved in Tajikistan's drug trade have left the central government in incomplete control. The persistence of rent-seeking behavior of local elites, and their passing on of the spoils, has created enormous disincentives for governments in Central Asia to introduce local election of regional leaders. The Kyrgyz and Kazakhs have begun the slow transition to election of district leaders, with election of governors said to gradually follow.[9]

In general, Uzbekistan's status as a poorly performing state owes much to the decisionmaking models applied by President Islam Karimov, a Soviet-era economist who ran the state planning bureau of Uzbekistan (Gosplan) from 1966 to 1983.[10] As such, Karimov believed himself an expert in the workings of the global market, and his harsh political regime created little incentive for advisers with Western training to argue against Karimov's isolationist policies. He understood political economics in Marxian terms and feared that the nascent entrepreneurial class in Uzbekistan would be successful in their adaptation to market conditions and demand political power commensurate with their economic power.

As important was Karimov's fear of the social consequences of a rapid deregulation of the economy. In the early 1990s radical Islamic groups were gaining in popularity, especially in the densely populated Ferghana Valley, where over 60 percent of the population was under twenty-one. The civil war in Tajikistan, which was at its bloodiest in 1992–94, created a frightening specter for Karimov (and his fellow Central Asian leaders) of what could happen if the struggle for political power spun out of control. For Karimov, though, the problem was more than just imitation. He feared that Uzbekistan would become a place of refuge for Tajikistan's displaced religious elite, as well as its masses, and that the influx of ethnic Uzbeks or ethnic Tajiks from Tajikistan posed a threat to Uzbekistan's own delicate ethnic balance. But Karimov overestimated how far Uzbekistan's hard currency earnings, from gold sales as well as from cotton, would go to maintain the country's social welfare system.

Moreover, Karimov's decision to restrict private ownership and to retain strong state control led to a strict trade regime, as Tashkent's policies of price supports created strong incentives for the export and resale of basic commodities bought on the Uzbek market. To prevent this the Karimov regime effectively sealed off the country from trade with neighboring states. Uzbekistan, the region's previous transportation and communications hub, shares borders with Kazakhstan, Turkmenistan, Kyrgyzstan, and Tajikistan, and passage through Uzbekistan was vital for traders in the latter two countries to reach markets in Russia and Kazakhstan.

Uzbekistan had the capacity to become an important regional producer of processed foods, clothing, and textiles, but Karimov's policies hurt hopeful Uzbek entrepreneurs and those in Kyrgyzstan and Tajikistan as well, diminishing the impact of wide-reaching economic reforms, in the former country in particular. While Karimov's isolationist policies were driven primarily by his understanding of the country's economic and political security needs, there was an element of spite in these policies as well. After bombings in Tashkent in 1999, allegedly done by the Islamic Movement of Uzbekistan (whose members took refuge in Tajikistan and then entered Uzbekistan from Kyrgyzstan), the Uzbeks literally fenced themselves off from their neighbors by delineating and then mining their borders.

The development of a strong regional market—reaching from Central Asia into western Siberia, down into Afghanistan and even eastern Iran—would have been to the benefit of all five Central Asian states. But the atmosphere of competition that dominated in the region made this a near impossibility. The region's five presidents competed among themselves for international preeminence, with the rivalry being especially keen among Islam Karimov of Uzbekistan, Nursultan Nazarbayev of Kazakhstan, and Saparmurad Niyazov of Turkmenistan, all of whom served together in Mikhail Gorbachev's last politburo. In true Soviet fashion—and even Kyrgyzstan's Askar Akayev and Tajikistan's Emomali Rahmonov had held vetted posts in the USSR—Central Asia's leaders substituted "virtual" cooperation for real economic cooperation.[11] In 1994 they created a Central Asian Cooperation Organization, which, however, lacked the authority and institutional capacity to manage economic relations among the member states.[12]

The existence of the Central Asian Cooperation Organization has done little to improve trade among the member states, largely because of Uzbekistan's policies. In 2002 the International Monetary Fund rated Uzbekistan a 9 on a scale of 1 to 10, with 10 representing the most restrictive trade policies possible. By contrast, Kyrgyzstan and Tajikistan are each rated 1.[13] Even within the current difficult trade environment, the three poorly performing states remain important partners for each other, accounting for 13 percent of total exports and 14 percent of imports; when Kazakhstan is added, regional trade amounts to almost 20 percent of Kyrgyzstan, Tajikistan, and Uzbekistan's trade total.[14] Given the limited purchasing power of the populations of these states it would be a mistake to romanticize the capacity of each of them to serve as a market for any of the others, but a freer trade regime would have provided greater (and in some cases critical) markets both for start-up small- and medium-sized enterprises and for existing firms trying to make the transition to market conditions. Some of the Soviet-era economic linkages were clearly unprofitable and ill suited to market conditions, but others made good economic and geographic sense.

The relative importance of regional cooperation has been a much debated question among economic observers of the region, who rightfully point to the need for each of these states to orient itself to a global market, especially with regard to the development of its natural resources. But this argument minimizes the importance of the local regional market for creating employment and opportunities for economic diversification. This market is not insubstantial: it includes at least 75 million people when neighboring parts of Russia are included, and it could be reached without great transportation costs if cross-border transit were improved. Transportation costs to more distant markets in the United States, Asia, and Europe are quite high, much higher than from China or Pakistan, both of which are competing producers with lower labor costs. Here the opportunity costs have been experienced everywhere in the region, except for Kazakhstan, where since 1998 in particular there has been a synergy between Russian and Kazakh capital, especially in agrobusiness.

As we see in the more detailed accounts provided below, the failure to appreciate the importance of the regional market diminished the potential success of the developmental paradigm that was being imposed on Tajikistan and Kyrgyzstan in particular, making the economic targets necessary to minimize long-term debt virtually unattainable. Moreover, the nature of the debt (much of it was going to foreign consultants and to the purchase of foreign equipment) created an atmosphere of distrust toward Western institutions, which will continue to influence domestic politics throughout the region.

Kyrgyzstan: Eager to Reform and Failing to Thrive

Kyrgyzstan is classified as a low-income, highly indebted country by the World Bank, but it has been the most receptive country in the region to international advice. Kyrgyzstan is the best performing of the poorly performing states in the Central Asia region.[15]

Specialists in the international financial community find it easiest to work with the Kyrgyz, who bring the highest degree of professionalism to their work. But one result of this is that Kyrgyzstan has the highest debt-to-income ratio in Central Asia (table 5-4). While some of this debt is the result

Table 5-4. *External Debt Management, Four Central Asian Countries, 2001*[a]

Country	Debt as percent of GNI (present value of debt)[b]	Debt as percent of exports of goods and services (present value of debt)[b]	Total external debt (US$ thousand)	Total debt as percent of GNI
Kazakhstan	67	134	14,372,200	39
Kyrgyzstan	91	223	1,716,700	150
Tajikistan	83	120	1,085,600	125
Uzbekistan	40	138	4,627,100	. . .

Source: See table 5-1.

a. Turkmenistan is not included because its statistics gathering is held faulty.

b. The present value of debt is the sum of short-term external debt plus the discounted sum of total debt service payments due on public, publicly guaranteed, and private nonguaranteed long-term external debt over the life of existing loans.

of unpaid energy bills to neighboring countries, most of it is a result of external borrowing. One positive aspect to this debt is that it has forced the country into debt restructuring programs. In addition, the Paris Club in March 2002 gave international financial institutions a critical lever to press the government of Kyrgyzstan into greater fiscal responsibility.[16] Current assistance money is also being much more closely supervised than previous funds in order to prevent the kind of pilfering of assistance money that is said to have occurred in the first seven or eight years of independence. However, debt service is the highest in Central Asia (91 percent of gross national income and 223 percent of the value of exports of goods and services; see table 5-4).

Kyrgyzstan has a very small economy, with little prospect of significant expansion. In 2001 its gross national income was $1.4 billion, or $280 per capita. At the same time, though, Kyrgyzstan (which, like all of the Central Asian countries, experienced a decline in its gross domestic product for the period 1990–2001) has had a faster rate of recovery than some of its neighbors (tables 5-1, 5-2). In addition, the privatization of small- and medium-sized enterprises has been effectively completed (approximately 60 percent of the population is engaged in this sector, which produces 43 percent of the national product). By July 2002 the overall level of privatization had reached 69.7 percent; although there is still only limited legal protection of private property, the Kyrgyz government has pledged to improve this protection as part of its poverty reduction strategy for 2003–05.[17]

The withdrawal of the state from the economy in Kyrgyzstan has not been without costs for the country's population. According to the government of

Table 5-5. *Kyrgyzstan Regional Overview, by Oblast*
Percent

Oblast	Total population	Population living in poverty[a]	Share of region's GDP	Unemployment
Batken	8.0	41.2	3.8	9.1
Jalal-abad	18.3	55.0	14.2	18.7
Osh	24.5	56.1	11.7	16.3
Talas	4.2	67.3	3.8	3.0
Issyk Kul	8.5	55.2	17.0	8.3
Naryn	5.2	70.4	4.1	11.8
Chui	16.1	29.2	21.2	16.0
Bishkek City	15.9	29.5	24.3	16.3

Source: Government of Kyrgyzstan: National Poverty Reduction Strategy, 2003–2005; Comprehensive Development Framework of the Kyrgyz Republic to 2010; Expanding the Country's Capacities, National Poverty Reduction Strategy 2003–2005; Regional Development in the Kyrgyz Republic, chapter 5. Available on the World Bank website.

a. A region is considered to have extreme poverty if 21.3 percent of its population is poor.

the Kyrgyz Republic, 47.6 percent of the population was living in poverty in 2001, pockets of poverty being unevenly distributed across the country; 88 percent of the population lives on under US$4 a day.[18] Unemployment in Kyrgyzstan, as elsewhere in the region, is difficult to measure as so much of employment still goes on off the books, to avoid the payment of taxes.[19]

One of Kyrgyzstan's burdens is closing the gap between north and south, a gap that is geographical as well as cultural and economic (table 5-5).[20] The country's ruling elite has always come disproportionately from the more industrialized north, whereas more than 40 percent of the population lives in the more densely populated, predominantly agricultural south. This population density as well as its predominantly young age make the question of poverty and unemployment a question of national security.[21] The government strategy for alleviation of poverty is sensitive to these regional factors, and poverty levels in the south are being reduced faster than the republic average.

While the international community is now gearing up to help Kyrgyzstan fight the country's poverty problem, there is still no broad public recognition of the fact that it helped to contribute to it through the sums of money that Kyrgyzstan borrowed in the process of trying to reinvent its economy along market-driven principles. Certainly the government of Kyrgyzstan could have been more responsible in administering the international funds that it received. Unfortunately, there is no systematic study of how much money went astray; most of the worst abuses seem to have been in the allocation of foreign credit by the government to favored entrepreneurs under highly favorable terms, which effectively allowed them to accumulate personal capital at state expense.

But the sums allocated, and most of the guidelines on how this money was to be spent, were set by the international institutions funding projects in the country, and the leadership of the country had very little bargaining clout to press for more grants, aid, and loans. The size of the awards to Kyrgyzstan was determined in large part by international advisers' unrealistic expectations about how rapidly Kyrgyzstan's economy would grow, and these expectations further fueled the naive assessments of the Kyrgyz. There was reason to hope that by being "first through the gate" on questions of economic investment the Kyrgyz would attract foreign capital. In conditions of freer trade, Kyrgyzstan would have had a smoother economic recovery. But the Kyrgyz and their international advisers both underestimated the inherent fragility of the Kyrgyz economy and overestimated the country's capacity to compete in the global market.

It is clear that not all of the earlier unfounded assumptions have been sufficiently discredited. Food security is still a priority, and the Kyrgyz government deserves a great deal of credit for promoting the most wide-reaching agricultural reforms in the region. But there are real limitations as to how much growth in the agricultural sector Kyrgyzstan can hope to achieve. As table 5-1 shows, Kyrgyzstan's food production has improved considerably since independence, more than in any other country in the region (with the exception of Turkmenistan, whose figures are suspect). But the amount of cropland available per person is limited (.28 hectares) and cannot be increased substantially without changes in the water distribution pattern to downstream states. Nevertheless, both the International Development Association and the International Monetary Fund have criticized the Kyrgyz for failing to develop measures to create an environment for greater private sector participation.[22]

Some further expansion of light industry is possible, and an improved legal environment, combined with Kyrgyzstan's favorable tax regimes (Kyrgyzstan's tax is under 20 percent), will give Kyrgyzstan an edge should regional trade restrictions ever be reduced. But it is hard to envision Kyrgyzstan's industry developing a strong regional presence, given the increasingly commanding position occupied by new or substantially reorganized Kazakh and Russian enterprises in the region. While Kyrgyz government economists offer both optimistic and less optimistic scenarios for growth, they recognize that the former would require a dramatic change in the trade and investment climate in the region. But even the more pessimistic scenarios (that gross domestic product will attain a growth rate of 5 percent annually, as opposed to 7 percent in the alternative scenarios) will be difficult to achieve.[23]

Still, the country's principal economists hold out hope that Kyrgyzstan will develop into a regional transport center, serving as a "doorway" to China, as both countries are World Trade Organization (WTO) members. Kyrgyzstan has used substantial amounts of foreign assistance money toward improving transport linkages within the country, to the Tajik border, and to the Chinese border, but the failure to develop a strong regional demand for trade has meant that these road improvements have led to little new revenues for transit traffic through Kyrgyzstan.[24]

A number of structural impediments to expanding trade are caused by Russian and Kazakh displeasure over the Kyrgyz decision to enter the WTO unilaterally. Russia and Kazakhstan subject Kyrgyz goods to high fees and bribes to move goods across borders and intranational checkpoints in Kazakhstan and Russia. Road transport costs from Kyrgyzstan are estimated to average 10–15 percent of total costs, of which only about one-third are fuel costs.[25] Both Russia and Kazakhstan favor a uniform tariff system among states partnering in a free trade regime, at least until 2005, and both of these states are important trading partners of Kyrgyzstan.[26]

Kyrgyzstan also had overly optimistic plans to substantially expand its gold mining sector. The extraction of any of these deposits would entail substantial environmental risks, and the Kyrgyz population has become increasingly more ecologically risk averse in the aftermath of cyanide-related deaths caused by working in the country's large Kumtor field.[27]

Plans to seek major international investment to expand Kyrgyzstan's hydroelectric industry are also problematic. Soviet development schemes posited the development of gigantic new power stations in both Kyrgyzstan and Tajikistan, and the building of any of these would substantially increase the export potential of the countries involved. But the development of hydroelectric power is irrevocably tied to the larger question of control of access by downstream users of the Syr Darya and Amu Darya rivers, whose headwaters lie in Kyrgyzstan and Tajikistan, respectively. Under current economic conditions, for Kyrgyzstan or Tajikistan to unilaterally divert large quantities of water to export-oriented hydroelectric projects would be to risk war with Kazakhstan and Uzbekistan. The one likely investor in both Kyrgyzstan and

Tajikistan is Russia's energy giant UES, which is trying to unify the Russian and Central Asian energy grids in order to sell Russia's surplus energy in Europe. This quasi-government entity would provide a secure environment for the expansion of Kyrgyz and Tajik hydroelectric industries but would not maximize local income potential.

There is a similar situation in the gas sector, wherein Russia's Gazprom is making a bid to acquire assets throughout Central Asia, planning to reinvest regional profits in local transport networks. This too would likely lead to little new economic growth for the Kyrgyz, as plans for developing new Kyrgyz oil and gas fields are relatively capital intensive, given the small size of these deposits and the abundance of energy in neighboring states.

Tourism is another area that the government of Kyrgyzstan has targeted for growth with little prospect of achieving its goals. Tourism currently accounts for nearly 4 percent of the country's gross domestic product. Although the Kyrgyz would like to encourage "exotic" tourism by Europeans and Americans and recreational tourism by South Asians, the country has virtually no international connections with the outside world and a real dearth of first- and second-class tourist facilities.[28] The Kyrgyz are in direct competition with Kazakhstan's larger and better developed leisure industry, which is being built to serve the needs of that country's large expatriate business community.

Finally, Kyrgyzstan's poverty alleviation strategy is undermined by the pervasive atmosphere of corruption in the country. While the country's anticorruption policy claims to target everyone, in reality the president and his family and his close associates and their families are all effectively immune from prosecution. How corrupt the members of the Kyrgyz ruling class have been is of course a matter of debate, but they are perceived as corrupt, and this helps fuel the corrupt behavior of others. Although opposition politicians' claims that the ruling class has a stranglehold over Kyrgyzstan's economic life may be exaggerated, President Akayev's relatives have accumulated a great deal of economic power, and the family's empire has sometimes grown through forcing legitimate businessmen to abandon their property.[29] The increased professionalization of the security services and the judiciary will do little to keep those who are "above the law" from meddling in the economy without constraint, as currently the president of Kyrgyzstan and his immediate family are exempt from legal prosecution.

Although initially President Akayev was considered a hero because of his ability to garner so much international assistance to Kyrgyzstan, now these same policies are the cause of a great deal of public criticism, in large part because of growing rumors about the corrupt nature of the regime. The Kyrgyzstan of today is a less open society than it was a decade ago, in part because of the poorer-than-expected performance of the economy. Clamping down on political opposition is reducing public criticism of the president, but it is not increasing public confidence in the government, nor is it increasing public support for economic reform.

It is hard to predict whether the failure of the current Kyrgyz government's poverty alleviation strategy will be the source of serious social or political unrest. Leading local economists believe that the income of the Kyrgyz population is twice as large as indicated by the official statistics, given how much of the population hides income to avoid taxation. Certainly life around the capital city of Bishkek indicates the existence of a small but growing middle class as well as a very small upper class. But at the same time, it is clear that the economic recovery of the country is disproportionately in this city and the surrounding Chui oblast.[30] One of the consequences of this is the growing problem of internal migration, from the poorer and more densely populated regions to the capital. Internal migrants are said to account for 83 percent of the new population in Bishkek, contributing to a growing housing, employment, and crime problem in the capital.[31] Kyrgyzstan is also falling deeper into the opium and heroin drug nexus that originates in Afghanistan and trades through Tajikistan and Kyrgyzstan and then on to Russia and Europe.

Many also blame the unevenness of Kyrgyzstan's economic recovery for the growth in popularity of extreme religious groups, like Hizbut Tahrir, which advocates the creation of an Islamic caliphate. Although Hizbut Tahrir has been declared illegal in both Kyrgyzstan and Uzbekistan, it is attracting membership from among both Uzbek and Kyrgyz youth in the south of Kyrgyzstan. One of its reported attractions to these young men is the group's payment to them of betweenUS$50 and US$100 a month for leafleting. Hizbut Tahrir is centered in Uzbekistan, where it is the subject of a campaign to eliminate it, in part because the group is rumored to have financial ties to Osama bin Laden.

The treatment of religious and secular opponents has brought considerable international criticism of the Akayev regime in recent years. In general, dialogue with the Kyrgyz government on questions of political reform has grown more strained, leading those in the development community who see the creation of a democratic polity as a condition for securing economic reform ever more pessimistic about Kyrgyzstan's chances. Yet for now, at least, Kyrgyzstan seems to have largely maximized its chances for international recovery, through taking Western advice, be it good or bad, and by being diligent enough in applying it that the Paris Club nations rescheduled large amounts of the ensuing debt.

Tajikistan: Can Its Failing Economy Be Helped?

Generally considered among the very poorest of the Soviet republics, Tajikistan has the smallest gross national income in Central Asia (see table 5-1). In 1998 the Tajik government began to work closely with advisers from international financial institutions to devise and execute a policy of macroeconomic reform. The results are not encouraging, and there is reason to question the capacity of the Tajik government to make them work.

Most who have studied the economy of the country have little confidence in the government's capacity to break a poverty cycle begun under Soviet rule and accelerated by years of civil war, despite the modest goals the government has set for itself, hoping to drop poverty levels to 75 percent by 2006 and to 60 percent by 2015.[32] In 2001 only 56 percent of all able-bodied citizens were reported to be employed, but there is strong reason to distrust these statistics. The three top sources of income for the population of Tajikistan are participating in the illegal drug trade, working for foreign-sponsored nongovernmental organizations (NGOs), and remittances from migrant laborers working largely in Russia.[33] The relative ranking of the three income sources varies somewhat from year to year. Of the three sources, only income from NGO jobs would be reported.

It is hard to identify a realistic strategy for Tajikistan to reverse the destructive trends in its economy. Many of these trends are the result of the devastating civil war, begun in the waning days of the USSR and not really concluded until the signing of a peace agreement among most of the regional factions in 1997. The war is estimated to have cost about US$7 billion, and it left one of the poorest economies of the former Soviet Union in virtual ruin.[34] Projects designed to help the country rebuild have added substantially to Tajikistan's debt to neighboring states, much of it accumulated during the civil war.[35] But the legacies of the civil war also make it difficult for Tajikistan to discharge this debt. In part the problem is one of human resources: there has been an enormous outflow of talented people of all nationalities, and even ethnic Tajiks are reluctant to return home if they have any other economic choices.

All the other Central Asian countries were able to begin the process of state building with a relatively complete bureaucratic apparatus. While this had many minuses, as many bureaucrats were ill prepared for their new tasks, the presence of functioning bureaucracies that penetrated down to the local level made the delivery of social services much easier, even if they were to be financed in new ways. The regional nature of the fighting made it seem imperative to the winning side to largely redefine the country's administrative units, and many talented people were pushed from their positions simply for backing the wrong side.[36]

One further result of the war is that there is substantially less trust of government in Tajikistan than elsewhere in the region, and this lack of trust has further exacerbated the government's difficulties in collecting revenues, even from legitimate businesses. Money from the drug trade has also helped fund a commercial revival, especially in the capital city of Dushanbe, and most of those engaged in construction, the service industry, and retail trade keep two sets of books to hide employees and revenues from government inspectors. As a result, Tajikistan is likely to have a lingering account deficit.

Although patronage is a problem throughout the region, the Tajik government has been more vulnerable than other countries to its pressures, which complicates privatization in particular. By November 2001 only 359 of 1,500 medium-sized and large state enterprises had been privatized, in part because the government was incapable of creating a transparent tender process. Privatization has also been hampered by unrealistically high prices, the paucity of solvent bidders, and the almost total unavailability of credit.[37] Many state-held assets also have little appeal to a commercial buyer.

The economic prospects of Tajikistan are thus very bleak. As with so many of these countries, the agricultural sector has increased in importance, but the country is trapped in the conundrum of whether to grow cash crops (mostly cotton) or food (table 5-1). But Tajikistan has not demonstrated the ability to become an efficient food producer. Part of this is the result of the deterioration of agriculture during the civil war years, but it also is a reflection of the almost completely unreformed nature of Tajikistan's agriculture. The Soviet-era industrial base is also in disarray. Factories have closed, and the country's major export facility, the Turzunsade Aluminum Smelter, requires considerable investment. Most of the supervisory class has left the country, and the skills of the labor force are deteriorating. Given the current state of education in the country, the skill level of the workforce seems certain to deteriorate further.

A generation of Tajiks is largely being abandoned to manage as they can, with far less access to education and social services than their parents had. Nearly 80 percent of children of the poorest families lack any material assistance from the state. The educational system of the country is in complete disrepair; over 50 percent of all schools nationwide require capital investment, and not surprisingly the worst schools are found in rural areas.[38] Since 1990, enrollment ratios in primary and secondary schools have been declining; the gender balance in the schools is changing as well, as parents send sons to school in preference to daughters. This same pattern is said to exist in much of Turkmenistan and Uzbekistan and even in parts of Kazakhstan and Kyrgyzstan. But in Tajikistan, the number of places in secondary schools is dropping too, with fewer places available in 1999 than in 1990, although the high school age population has increased by 12 percent.[39]

Tajikistan is the most geographically isolated of the Central Asian countries. Before independence more than 80 percent of Tajikistan's freight left the republic through Uzbekistan. Allegedly, as part of an effort to keep Tajik goods from competing with goods from the Uzbek market, the government of Uzbekistan has made the movement of road freight across their territory quite difficult, forcing the Tajiks to ship through Kyrgyzstan, a more arduous route, and to sell their goods in the much smaller and well-sated Kyrgyz market. This has been especially bad news for Tajikistan's formerly prosperous Sogd (Leninabad, previously known as Khujand oblast), which used to be economically fully intertwined with Uzbekistan. Trade across Tajikistan is also a physical challenge. In general, Tajikistan's highway system is in the worst repair of any of these countries. Tajikistan is served internationally by CART Tajikistan, the state-owned airline company, which offers very limited service to neighboring countries, regular service to Russia, and limited service to Turkey (and sometimes on to Germany).

Much like Kyrgyzstan, Tajikistan has unrealized potential as an energy exporter, but by continuing Soviet-era practice, Tajikistan limits the production of hydroelectric power in favor of importing gas from Uzbekistan (paid for in part through barter arrangements), which is a constant source of debt for Tajikistan.[40] Like the Kyrgyz, the Tajiks are working closely with Russia's UES in the hopes that a consolidated Russian-dominated electric grid will give a weak state like Tajikistan more clout to transform water into hydroelectric power. But the end result is likely to be a Tajik hydroelectric system that is under Russian control, with less economic benefit to Tajikistan than expected.

Tajiks would like to encourage foreign investment in telecommunications. But the density of telecommunications in Tajikistan is the lowest in the Commonwealth of Independent States (CIS).[41] This isolation has made Tajikistan receptive to the spread of extremist ideologies as well as prey to the further criminalization of the economy. Tajikistan already has many of the features of a narcostate, and with the revitalization of opium and heroin production in Afghanistan this trend is certain to continue. Twice as much heroin has been seized along the Tajik border in 2003 than was seized a year previously, and there is no evidence that interdiction rates have improved.[42]

The evolving Tajik political system is unable to serve as a check on these developments, even with projected increases in spending on border security. In the face of the deteriorating social and political situations President Rahmonov has been accumulating more power in his hands, and he sponsored a 2003 referendum that exempts him from earlier term limits. As long as Rahmonov is in office, there is likely to be little serious effort to attack the political corruption that is at the core of the Tajik state, which is bad news for those who would like to use legal means to address Tajikistan's poverty.

Uzbekistan: Refusal of Reform

The government of Uzbekistan has had a rather schizophrenic attitude toward reform, initially courting the international financial institutions, then distancing itself from the World Bank and the International Monetary Fund, and then courting them again but without real enthusiasm. In 1996 Uzbekistan decided to stop meeting targets in the macroeconomic stabilization program that it had negotiated with the IMF. In the aftermath of September 11, 2001, when prospects for more U.S. and other international assistance were raised, the Uzbeks once again pursued engagement, only to back away again for nearly two more years. Finally, in October 2003 Uzbekistan agreed to accept the provisions of IMF article 8 and to move to a freely convertible currency.[43] However, years of nearly draconian restrictions on trade, combined with the government's policies of import substitutions, have led to the deformation of many aspects of Uzbekistan's economy, including the magnitude of the country's debt burden, which was 40 percent of the gross national income in 2001 (table 5-4).

At the center of the problem was the Uzbek government's decision to maintain Soviet-era state purchase and price support systems in agriculture; state control was facilitated by maintaining a multiple exchange rate system, albeit with some modifications. This was in violation of article 8 of the IMF agreement, but Uzbekistan's president maintained that he better understood the nature of his country's economy than foreign specialists did and that his approach to Uzbek economic development was more likely to lead to success.

It may well be that neither side fully understood the needs of the Uzbek economy, and certainly both were talking past each other for many years in a series of negotiations frustrating to all concerned. From 1996 on, the government pursued "step-by-step" exchange-rate unification but always put off the final convergence of the multiple exchange rates, a problem that the government promised to rectify in a December 2001 letter of intent to the managing director of the IMF. The letter was designed to cover a six-month period, ending on June 30, 2002. In this letter, the Uzbek government agreed to a series of structural reforms, including exchange rate unification and a step-by-step elimination of the state procurement system for raw cotton and grain. In these two sectors Uzbek farmers (who are still largely organized in collective or communal farms) have production targets set and are offered seriously deflated purchase prices for their harvest.[44] In return the IMF and World Bank agreed to help the Uzbek government meet projected budget deficits if the latter kept to the agreed upon timetable for structural adjustments. The Uzbek government also made the commitment to liberalize the country's highly restrictive trade policy.[45]

The Uzbek government never qualified for the additional assistance, having failed to meet the agreed upon targets. By late 2002 the IMF and the World Bank both had reached new levels of frustration in dealing with the Uzbek government, in large part because of the introduction of a series of new tariffs and other trade restrictions, which led to the virtual collapse of the fledgling wholesale trade network in the country and further hampered trade with neighboring states (leaving millions of dollars in goods on trucks that were blocked en route to Uzbekistan). Much of this drama played out against the backdrop of strong international criticism at the 2003 European Bank for Reconstruction and Development (EBRD) annual meeting, which the Uzbeks had fought hard for the privilege of hosting.

The question of whether or not to sharply quicken the pace of structural reforms was a divisive one among the Uzbek ruling elite. Proreform economists within governing circles argued that Uzbekistan's state-dominated economy must inevitably make way for market forces and that to delay the transition would put the country at greater risk, given the continuing impoverishment of the Uzbek population. But even promarket reformers were clearly frightened about what a unified exchange rate would mean for the standard of living of ordinary Uzbeks. In purchasing power parity terms, per capita gross domestic product was $2,460 (somewhere between that of Kyrgyzstan and Tajikistan, at $2,750 and $1,170, respectively).[46] A country strategy report from the European Bank for Reconstruction and Development argues that Uzbekistan has avoided the extreme levels of poverty prevalent in some of the other poor CIS countries, with a government-reported national poverty rate of 27.5 percent.[47] The expectation is that this rate will increase if economic reforms are pursued aggressively.

However, it is hard to know what the official poverty rate measures mean, as anecdotal information, including this author's own observations from considerable travel in Uzbekistan, argues for a sharp deterioration in the standard of living.[48] Many blame the increasing restrictions on the illegal "shuttle" trade between Central Asia and China, which brings cheap goods into the country. But in much of the country even the items from the unregulated trade are beyond the reach of many people's finances. This despite the fact that the government of Uzbekistan has placed a strong emphasis on maintaining the social welfare net, spending 7 percent of GDP in 2001 on health and education and 6 percent on social transfers.

Many argue that this money is not being spent effectively, that too much money is spent on salaries, and that many benefits are extended wastefully to rich and poor alike (including family subsidies, cheap gas and electricity, and subsidized rent). There is also substantial controversy about the use of local councils of elders (*mahalla* councils) to distribute relief aid to poorer families. Although they are generally seen as doing a good job in at least identifying families with genuine need, some Western experts argue that poverty assistance could be more equitably managed through a state-supported professional social service.[49] The schools are used to target assistance to children, and at the beginning of the school year specific grades nationwide are targeted for distribution of books, backpacks, and even boots and winter coats. School lunches are an important source of nutrition for Uzbek children, meager though they sometimes are. The high overhead in the schools, though, is another source of criticism for the Uzbek government.

It is hard to know, then, why Uzbek reform was further delayed between 2001 and 2003. Part of the explanation may be the rumored ill health of the country's president and what some see as his weakening hold on power. Corruption is as serious a problem in Uzbekistan as elsewhere in the region, although the repressive nature of the regime makes detailed information about it more difficult to come by. But there is no question that the existing system of partial state purchase of cotton (and to a lesser extent of grain) at less than world market price benefits several people close to President Karimov as well as privileged members of the Soviet-era regional elite. Similarly, fortunes have been made on the disparity between the different values of the Uzbek som. Part of the answer for the delay in reform is the fear among the elite as to what freeing the Uzbek market, and privatizing key sectors of the Uzbek economy, would mean for social stability in the country. The principal arguments against exchange-rate unification are that prices would increase, as would unemployment. Most outside observers believe these fears to be exaggerated. Official unemployment in Uzbekistan in 2001 was 0.6 percent, and the EBRD estimated that the introduction of a unified exchange rate would lead to the loss of between 150,000 and 250,000 jobs and create an official unemployment rate of 3–4 percent of the workforce.[50]

There has also been concern that economic reform would inevitably lead to the introduction of private landownership, something that many in the country believe would create near-revolutionary levels of public dissatisfaction in Uzbekistan, where 63 percent of the population lives in rural areas, population density is high, and agriculture is dependent upon irrigation.[51] Added to this is the country's ecologically damaged environment, with salinization of soil and pollution of water supplies a commonplace problem in rural areas. These problems trace their origin to Soviet-era agricultural practices and especially to the overcultivation of cotton (with heavy dependence on irrigation and fertilizers), which date from this period—and which are generally viewed as responsible for the shrinking (and impending demise) of the Aral Sea.

Uzbekistan missed the opportunity to cut back on the cultivation of cotton in the first years of independence, and instead the "dependency" of Russia's textile industry on Uzbekistan's cotton was reaffirmed—but on market terms, which gave the Uzbeks hard-currency earnings. It would be politically inexpedient for the Uzbek government to drastically alter this relationship in the short term, making the introduction of private agriculture more difficult than would have been the case if agricultural diversification had been introduced a decade earlier. But even Uzbek economists are coming around to the idea that the staged privatization of agriculture is necessary.

The decision to move toward the convertibility of currency could be a boost to Uzbekistan's struggling private sector, especially if existing trade restrictions are removed. But much of the enthusiasm has been beaten out of Uzbekistan's entrepreneurial class, and many have abandoned the idea of doing business in Uzbekistan. The World Bank estimates that small- and medium-sized enterprises account for only 15 percent of the country's GDP but provide 41 percent of the total employment. These figures are at sharp variance with official Uzbek statistics, which claim that these enterprises account for 35 percent of the country's GDP and that 78 percent of Uzbekistan's population is employed in the private sector. This latter figure, though, includes all those employed in collectivized agriculture. But however the number is calculated, the realities of doing business in Uzbekistan are to the disadvantage of the private sector. A March 2003 report by the EBRD maintains that 99 percent of smaller Uzbek firms are not engaged in any form of private trade.[52] This is an astonishing figure, given the former fluidity of the Soviet-era borders in Central Asia and the dominant role that Uzbeks used to play in the markets of neighboring countries. There are many reasons for this outcome, including most prominently the difficulties of securing access to hard currency, which has remained problematic even as the gap between rates has narrowed and despite the introduction of laws designed to provide freer access to foreign exchange.

There is also the question of the security of private property. Many of those engaged in the private sector lost their property in 1993–95, when some of the early privatizations were rejected as illegal. A November 2002 decree, signed well after the Uzbek government recommitted itself to meet the goals of macroeconomic reform, sent shudders through the Uzbek small business community. This decree seemed to open the door to the renationalization of any enterprise that changed its principal line of economic activity since privatization occurred. When one adds to this the high (and varying) levies on both the import and the export of goods, and the difficulty of maneuvering through the multitiered Uzbek bureaucracy to get the various licenses necessary for a business to function, it is surprising that anyone has the energy or patience to run a privately owned enterprise in the country.[53] Under the prevailing economic conditions it is hard to gauge how much of Uzbek entrepreneurialism remains and how successful the country will be in penetrating a Central Asian market that is now filled with competitors' goods. Some Uzbek capital fled the country in the early 1990s: Uzbek entrepreneurs do play a role in Kyrgyzstan, Kazakhstan, and Tajikistan, but these markets are dominated by members of the titular ethnic community, and those Uzbeks who have ended up in neighboring countries may find Uzbekistan's own market difficult to penetrate.

Reformers in the Uzbek government understand that there are no quick fixes for the economic stagnation created by a decade of vacillating on questions of economic reform. Establishing a single exchange rate for the Uzbek som opens the door to the strengthening of the country's private sector and may stimulate the development of a local entrepreneurial class, whose existence might stimulate necessary political reforms. However, the relative impoverishment of the population over this same period, and the growth of radical Islamic forces in their midst, makes the process of reform riskier than it would have been if starter earlier—and the outcomes less obvious.

Could the International Community Have Been More Effective in Central Asia?

The international community could have been a more effective presence in Central Asia, but this would have required changing the basic assumptions of international assistance, which is designed to spur development rather than to pay the costs associated with economic transition. Simply put, the scale of international assistance was too small to induce Central Asia's leaders to do things that they did not want to do (see table 5-5). This money was largely designated for technical assistance, to jump-start the transition process rather than to fund it. A large percentage of the money went to pay the salaries and overhead of foreign advisers and for the purchase and shipment of equipment coming from foreign countries.

Central Asia's leaders quickly understood that international assistance was not an investment in their economies so much as an incentive for them to integrate into the global economy under terms that foreign advisers (with limited experience in Central Asia) defined as advantageous to the region. Although Central Asian leaders had little experience with the global economy, they had a deep understanding of what it took to remain on top of their own societies, and reformers—reluctant reformers and nonreformers alike—have managed to do just that. There has been a remarkable degree of political stability in Central Asia.

Much of the Western advice that was offered was couched in terms of national interest, but for all of these men, and those who surrounded them, national interest was a major consideration only if it coincided with personal interest. In Kazakhstan and Kyrgyzstan, the case for economic reform clearly did, as it provided President Akayev with a focus for economic activity that his poor country otherwise lacked. Moreover, it also provided jobs for the Kyrgyz, both in government and in the NGO sector. For much the same reason President Rahmonov of Tajikistan also became, in 1998, a proponent of economic reform, but he never leveled the playing field for international institutions, allowing reform to go forward in the shadow of the drug economy and other criminal activities that occupied many key figures in the country.

The way that the international financial institutions distribute money in the region (the balance between overhead and money dispersed directly to the sectors or projects targeted) is a controversial topic in Kyrgyzstan and Tajikistan. In both countries, a great deal of ill will has been generated by the need to pay off debts (which include salary reimbursements for specialists, who are paid ten or even twenty times more than locals), and there is also anger in these countries that a class of privileged locals are being supported by Western grants.

The case of Kazakhstan is a bit different. Economic reform was understood as the only path to a desired outcome: foreign investment in Kazakhstan's oil and gas sector. Without that, President Nazarbayev feared that his country would not be able to sustain its independence but would in some form or another be swallowed up by Russia. But when investment was secured he quickly slowed the pace of reform, at least those reforms that might impede his ability and that of those closest to him to enjoy the fruits of these investments. Even so, Kazakhstan is as close as the region comes to a success story. It shows no signs of becoming a failing state. Partly this is because of its oil revenue, but that has also been a source of many of its political problems. The reasons for Kazakhstan's relative success are largely grounded in the complexity and diversity of the Kazakh economy.[54] But the kind of economic direction that Kazakhstan received has been a real plus.

At the same time, the international community could have been more assertive in both Kazakhstan and Kyrgyzstan, pressing for more legal transparency and better protection of private property. Legal reform programs in both of these countries (programs sponsored by the U.S. Agency for International Development) are drastically underfunded, given the costs involved in reforming judicial systems. Both countries have been far more receptive to U.S. engagement in judicial reform than in the also critical area of parliamentary reform. In both countries too, substantial increases in the amount of funding going to local government reform would make an enormous difference in helping to sustain economic reforms.[55] However, while such increases might have mitigated corrupt practices, especially at the lower levels, at best they would only have muted corruption at the top of these regimes. The amount of foreign direct investment in a state like Kazakhstan or Turkmenistan, investment that could reach as high as US$60 billion in the oil and gas sector alone, dwarfs the money available for economic or political reform programs.

President Niyazov of Turkmenistan is simply not as bright as President Nazarbayev and, unlike Nazarbayev, did not allow bright people close to him, either. He did not understand that gas wealth was harder to capitalize on than oil, given the dependence of gas providers on securing access to a specific market. He overestimated his ability to dictate the terms of the development of Turkmenistan's fossil fuel industry and was eventually forced to accept Russian-dictated terms for the sale of his gas. But given that the alternative routes for Turkmenistan lay through Iran and Afghanistan, both of which were effectively unavailable for geopolitical reasons, Niyazov stood to gain little from accepting international direction of his economy. Moreover, continued dependence upon Russia has not hampered (and may even have strengthened) Niyazov's primary goal, that of creating a form of rule more totalitarian than that of Stalin. At the same time, Turkmenistan is well on the road to becoming a policy-poor but resource-rich state, although the liberties that the Turkmen government takes in reporting its basic economic statistics make it hard for anyone to figure out just how close to this designation the country is in actuality.

With President Niyazov in charge, Turkmenistan will be difficult to influence. Overall, though, the United States could have been a far more aggressive and effective champion in the region. U.S. foreign assistance in general is only a tiny fraction of the U.S. budget, and assistance for Central Asia accounts for only a small fraction of that, reducing the kind of moral authority that the United States could have exercised in the region.

The situation of Uzbekistan is the most complex in the region and the one in which the West lost the greatest opportunity to influence outcomes by devoting more resources. While eager to use support from the West to distance Uzbekistan from Russia, President Karimov was also deeply suspicious of Western models of economic and political reform, which linked one to the other. Karimov's personal preference was to see Uzbekistan develop along the lines of China, with a state-managed economy existing side by side with a small private sector. But more than anything he feared social disorder, and given Uzbekistan's proximity to Afghanistan and Tajikistan, both of which were in turmoil in the early 1990s, this was no empty concern. Had the West come into Uzbekistan with a comprehensive reform package of five to ten times the size of what was offered, enough to bolster the Uzbek social welfare system through a three- to five-year transition period, then the Uzbek government might have been willing to pursue economic and even limited political reform. Such reform would have been made even more palatable if it had been accompanied by increased spending in the security sector as well.

Helping Uzbekistan to reform was not a Western priority in the early 1990s, nor was it a real priority as late as 2003. Although the International Monetary Fund and the World Bank are likely to assist Uzbekistan in making structural reforms, they are not bound by commitments made in 2002, as the Uzbek government did not meet the agreed upon deadlines. But new resources for Uzbekistan and all the other Central Asian states are likely to be difficult to come by, given the escalating reconstruction costs in Afghanistan (which are only a small fraction of the sums requested for rebuilding Iraq). In addition, the U.S. administration believes that the situation in Afghanistan is stabilizing, which makes Central Asia's needs seem less acute. U.S. bases in Kyrgyzstan and Uzbekistan are slated to move from "hot" to "warm" status, and U.S. assistance has declined in several categories. Even now the international community could do more with the money it spends in the region. Assistance programs emphasize national rather than regional goals. This national tilt becomes even more pronounced in organizations like the UN Development Program, which gives a priority to local ownership of projects, with the host governments encouraged to come with a shopping list of their own. Had more money been on offer, some of the decisionmaking weight of local ownership might have been muted.

Uzbekistan's lack of interest in improving the conditions of regional trade meant that projects with a regional emphasis were not a priority. A freer trade regime within Central Asia would have led to the largest gains in border regions of Uzbekistan, where Uzbekistan's decision to close its borders forced long-time linkages to be artificially broken. Yet by the time the international financial institutions began to make free trade a priority—when they began to focus more attention on the Central Asian states in the aftermath of September 11—it was too late to redress the current situation. This does not mean that current programs designed to regularize customs procedures and other technical problems associated with trade, as well as constant pressure to create a common tariff structure for the most frequently traded commodities, will not eventually yield results. However, a lot more could be done to create additional incentives for regional cooperation, including the creation of special loan funds that earmark money for cross-border businesses being set up by private entrepreneurs. Such a project would have the additional advantage of helping to reduce tensions in the border regions, especially if funding does not discriminate against ethnic minorities.

But the development of freer trade through the region (whether through regional initiatives or the less likely entrance of all the Central Asian states into the World Trade Organization) is not about to come any time soon.

Moreover, when it does come, it will be too late to serve as a stimulus for helping the weaker economies develop industries that take advantage of a regional market, both for selling their goods and for securing components necessary for production. The opportunity to do this in a fashion timely enough to help significantly alleviate poverty in Kyrgyzstan and Tajikistan is likely already lost. And the longer Uzbekistan keeps its borders closed, the more difficult it will be for private entrepreneurs to develop small- and medium-sized enterprises, and the more difficult it will be for these entrepreneurs to break into the Central Asian and southern Siberian market.

One of the tragedies of Central Asia is that things were not so terrible in the region at the time of independence. The trajectories of development were certainly negative in the mid-1990s, but three of the states (Kazakhstan, Kyrgyzstan, and Tajikistan) now show signs of recovery. And the two states that are not recovering adequately, Uzbekistan and Turkmenistan, are not in danger of imminent collapse. But international financial institutions and developmental agencies think in terms of the life of the project, about realistic targets; people living in the region think in terms of their lives and the lives of their children. Using the first yardstick, there is reason for some optimism in two of the three poorly performing states in Central Asia, and even in Uzbekistan forces favoring economic reform may soon come to power. But individuals are moved to action by the criteria of the second yardstick.

No one working in Central Asia has yet found a way to bring these two perspectives together. And until someone does, the short-term fallouts from long-term projects can create real long-term problems.

Notes

1. See www.eurasianet.org/resource/kyrgyzstan/hypermail/200212/0034.shtml.

2. Nancy Lubin, *Labour and Mobility in Central Asia* (Cambridge University Press, 1987).

3. Much of this was the product of the friendship between Leonid Brezhnev and the head of the Kazakh Communist Party, Dinmuhammad Kunaev. For a detailed account, see Martha Brill Olcott, *The Kazakhs* (Stanford University Press, 1995), pp. 228–29, 232–35, 250–54.

4. Transparency International Corruption Perceptions Index 2003 (www.transparency.org).

5. In September 2003, J. Bryan Williams, a former ExxonMobil executive, was sentenced to nearly four years in prison after pleading guilty to tax evasion in connection with a U.S. Justice Department investigation into alleged bribery in oil deals in Kazakhstan in the mid-1990s. James Giffen, a U.S. merchant banker and a special adviser to

President Nazarbayev, was indicted on bribery charges. Joshua Chaffin, "ChevronTexaco Quizzed as Kazakh Bribery Proof Widens," *Financial Times,* September 11, 2003, p. 1.

6. Bahamas exports were 20.7 percent of total exports in 2002. Economist Intelligence Unit, *Country Profile,* August 12, 2003.

7. Olcott, *The Kazakhs,* pp. 166–68.

8. See also Martha Olcott and Natalia Udalova, "Drug Trafficking on the Great Silk Road: The Security Environment in Central Asia," Working Paper 11 (Washington: Carnegie Endowment for International Peace, March 2000).

9. In Kazakhstan, the first parliamentary elections were held in 1999. The latest local elections to regional, district, and city councils were held on September 20, 2003. In Kyrgyzstan, President Akayev signed a special decree to fix the date of the local elections in the country. Radio Free Europe/Radio Liberty reports, 2001–03.

10. Karimov started work at the State Planning Bureau of Uzbekistan in 1966, where he was chief specialist and later deputy chairman. In 1983 he was appointed minister of finance of the UzSSR (//uzland.narod.ru/fact/karimov.htm).

11. Nursultan Nazarbayev was elected first secretary of the Kazakh Communist Party in 1989 and served as chairman of the Kazakh Supreme Soviet from 1989 to 1990 and as president of the Kazakh SSR from 1990 to 1991. In 1991 he became independent Kazakhstan's president. Nazarbayev had his term extended to 2000 by a nationwide referendum held April 30, 1995. His last reelection was held January 10, 1999, a year before it was previously scheduled. Askar Akayev was first elected president of the Kyrgyz SSR on October 28, 1990. On October 12, 1991, Akayev ran uncontested for president of independent Kyrgyzstan. Akayev was reelected as president in December 1995 and again on October 29, 2000. Emomali Rahmonov served as the head of state and Supreme Assembly chairman of Tajikistan from November 19, 1992, until November 6, 1994, when he was elected president. He was last reelected on November 6, 1999. Saparmurad Niyazov, then first secretary of the Communist Party of Turkmenistan, was elected president of the Turkmen Soviet Socialist Republic on October 27, 1990. Niyazov was elected president of independent Turkmenistan in June 21, 1992. In January 1994 Niyazov's rule was prolonged until 2002; on December 28, 1999, his rule was extended indefinitely. Islam Karimov, then first secretary of the Central Committee of the Uzbek SSR, was elected president of Uzbekistan in December 1991. President Karimov's original term was extended for an additional five years by a national referendum held on March 2, 1995. He was last reelected on January 9, 2000.

12. Kazakhstan, Kyrgyzstan, and Uzbekistan, the founding members, were later joined by Tajikistan. Turkmenistan refused to join because of the country's foreign policy of "positive neutrality." Until 1998 it was called the Central Asian Union. Then it was named Central-Asian Economic Community. Finally in February 2002 it was transformed to the Central Asian Cooperation Organization. See also Anders Aslund, Martha Brill Olcott, and Sherman Garnett, *Getting It Wrong* (Washington: Carnegie Endowment for International Peace, 1999).

13. Kyrgyz tariffs average 5 percent, Tajik, 8 percent, and Uzbekistan, 19 percent, with tariffs on some commodities important to regional trade set at 100 percent. Constantine Michalopoulas, "The Integration of Low-Income CIS Members in the World Trading System," paper prepared for the Commonwealth of Independent States (CIS-7) conference in January 2003, p. 24.

14. As quoted in ibid., p. 13. Michalopoulas uses 2000 trade data, p. 14. IMF break-downs for 2001 do not provide necessary by-nation data for updating these calculations (see p. 23).

15. Kyrgyzstan was listed in the third quintile in the 2001 Country Policy and Institutional Assessment of International Development Association countries, with Uzbekistan and Tajikistan both being in the fifth quintile. "Linking IDA Support to Country Performance, Third Annual Report on IDA's Country Assessment and Allocation Process," April 2002 (//worldbank.org/ida).

16. In part because of this the European Union Commission decided to nearly double its assistance to Kyrgyzstan; the UN Development Program has switched from a project-based to a program-based approach; the Asian Development Bank has signed a three-year memorandum of understanding with the government of the Kyrgyz Republic; the World Bank is providing closer supervision through a new regional office in Almaty; the Islamic Development Bank has promised to begin a direct investment program; the European Bank for Reconstruction and Development has committed to larger scale projects in agriculture, energy, and telecommunications; and Switzerland, Germany, Japan, and the Scandinavian countries have committed to increased bilateral assistance.

17. "Comprehensive Development Framework of the Kyrgyz Republic to 2010, Expanding the Country's Capacities, National Poverty Reduction Strategy, 2003–2005," pp. 88, 94. Available on the World Bank website.

18. UN Development Program, *Human Development Report, 2003,* p. 248.

19. World Bank, *World Development Indicators, 2003,* p. 27.

20. Batken, Osh, and Jalal-abad and Talas oblasts (the south) are separated from the country's capital city of Bishkek, and the oblasts of northern Kyrgyzstan (Chui, Issyk Kul, and Naryn) are separated by a series of mountains (with three passes at over 3,000 meters in elevation) and are linked by a highway that was made year-round only after independence.

21. The registered unemployed in this region numbered 60,522 in 2001: 5 percent were sixteen or seventeen years old, 11 percent were eighteen to twenty-one, 22 percent were between twenty-two and twenty-eight, 34 percent were twenty-nine to thirty-nine, 23 percent were forty to forty-nine, 5 percent were fifty to fifty-four, and 6 percent were fifty-five and older. This area also suffered interethnic riots in 1990, since Uzbeks comprise over a third of the population of southern Kyrgyzstan; they live largely in ethnic enclaves in this border region. (My own observations bear this out: during extensive travels in the region I have seen hundreds of illegal Uzbek traders and itinerant Uzbek workers.) Although the formal statistics of the two countries do not bear this out, the standard of living in Kyrgyzstan is considered much higher than in Uzbekistan. For 2001 per capita income in both countries, see table 5-1.

22. IMF and IDA staff, "Kyrgyz Republic: Joint Staff Assessment of the Poverty Reduction Strategy Paper," January 24, 2003, p. 27.

23. The scenarios are predicated on a volume of investment of 20 percent of GDP, but investment dropped by 2 percent in 2001. "Comprehensive Development Framework of the Kyrgyz Republic to 2010, Expanding the Country's Capacities, National Poverty Reduction Strategy, 2003–2005," p. 152. Available on the World Bank website.

24. Many of the linkages within the country were necessitated by Uzbekistan closing access points that linked the principal cities in the southern oblasts of Kyrgyzstan and by

the fact that transit from north to south in Kyrgyzstan was generally accomplished on roads that passed through both Kazakhstan and Uzbekistan. Foreign assistance money included funds from the European Bank for Reconstruction and Development and the Asian Development Bank.

25. Michalopoulas, "The Integration of Low-Income CIS Members in the World Trading System," p. 44.

26. In 2002 Russian and Kyrgyz tariffs were reported to have been harmonized to only 14 percent, as compared with 60 percent between Russia and Tajikistan and 85 percent between Russia and Kazakhstan (and 95 percent between Russia and Belarus). See ibid., p. 28. According to Michaloupolas (p. 29), the Kyrgyz Republic has yet to decide to seek a World Trade Organization waiver to adopt the Eurasian community's higher external tariffs instead of the WTO-mandated lower ones. (Kyrgyzstan is also part of the Eurasian Economic Community, a loose customs union including Russia, Kazakhstan, Tajikistan, and Belarus. Kyrgyzstan was permitted to keep this prior membership as part of its accession terms.)

27. The Kumtor field is situated in the Issyk-Kul region, 4,000 meters above sea level and 60 kilometers from the Chinese border. On May 20, 1998, a truck transporting sodium cyanide crashed there. As a result, twenty tonnes of its load fell into the river Barskoon, causing the contamination of the river. The contamination spread to the Issyk Kul Lake, the main tourist attraction in Central Asia. The serious health impacts of the toxic spill were magnified by the extensive use of sodium hypochlorite solution to neutralize the toxic compound. For more details, see "Poisoned Gold, the Kumtor Goldmine in Kyrgyzstan" (www.zpok.hu/~jfeiler/kumtor/).

28. There is only one luxury-class hotel in the country, which averages only about 25 percent occupancy despite low business and international government rates.

29. Akaeyev's cousins Askar Sarygulov and Dastan Sarygulov initially headed the State Privatization Committee and the country's state-owned gold company, Kyrgyzaltyn, respectively. Akayev's son Aidar and his Kazakh son-in-law Adil Toygonbaev are considered to be the dominant figures in the economy, controlling the distribution of fuel oil, alcohol, tobacco, local real estate ownership, media, hotels, and casinos. David Stern, "Kyrgyz President Admits Relative Sells to U.S. Base," *Financial Times,* July 22, 2002.

30. The city of Bishkek enjoys oblast status, which has allowed the city residents to further profit from the local economic recovery.

31. Khalida Rakisheva, "Impact of the Internal Migration upon the Poverty Problem," paper prepared for the World Bank conference on poverty in Central Asia, Issyk Kul, June 2003.

32. IDA and IMF staff, "Republic of Tajikistan," p. 4; Government of Tajikistan, "Poverty Reduction Strategy Paper" (Dushanbe, June 2002), p. 12.

33. The size of the Kyrgyz migrant labor population in Russia is also increasing, therefore competing with the Tajiks for Russian jobs.

34. It is estimated that 60,000–100,000 people were killed in the war and that about a tenth of the population became internally displaced. International Crisis Group, "Tajikistan: An Uncertain Peace," Asia Report 30 (December 24, 2001).

35. In mid-2003 Tajikistan's external debt was estimated to be US$1billion. About 75 percent of Tajikistan's external debt stock is owed or guaranteed by the public sector. Russia is Tajikistan's single largest bilateral creditor. Other major bilateral creditors include

Kazakhstan, Belarus, and Uzbekistan. Economist Intelligence Unit, *Country Profile, Tajikistan*, September 1, 2003.

36. Tajikistan now consists of Gorno-Badakhsahn autonomous oblast, Sogd oblast (formally Leninabad), Khatlon oblast (formally Kurgan Tiube and Kulyab oblasts), the city of Dushanbe, and rayons of republican subordination (formerly Dushanbe oblast).

37. Government of Tajikistan, "Poverty Reduction Strategy Paper," p. 27.

38. Ibid., p. 22.

39. Ibid., p. 21.

40. Some US$40 million as of July 1, 2003, US$33 million of which is householder debt. Asia-Plus Information Agency, Dushanbe, in Russian 900 gmt (July 16, 2003).

41. There has been virtually no investment in television relay and broadcast facilities and limited use of satellite dishes, leaving Tajik viewers and listeners with little choice. The number of listeners is also declining, for as Soviet-era television sets and radios break, many people—especially those in the countryside—do not have the money to replace them with new foreign electronics. This situation is common in the poorer areas of the Central Asian republics but is a particular problem in as isolated a country as Tajikistan. The density of telecommunications is 9.3 telephone sets for every 100 urban residents and 0.6 sets for every 100 rural residents.

42. According to the Drug Control Agency under the Tajik president, in 2002 Tajikistan seized about seven tonnes of heroin and opium. Interfax Central Asia, March 3, 2003.

43. In October, Uzbekistan officially lifted all currency restrictions, including required currency purchases by firms and individuals and the use of multiple exchange rates. The national currency unit became convertible on October 15, 2003. All convertibility restrictions on payments and transfers for current international transactions, and deals were canceled starting October 8, 2003. Radio Free Europe/Radio Liberty reports on Central Asia, 2003.

44. The letter of intent promised that 30 percent of the cotton harvest would be purchased from farms at state procurement prices, another 20 percent would be purchased at negotiated prices, and the remaining 50 percent would be freely disposed of by the farmers at their discretion. (Grain production was to be disposed of in much the same way, but at 25, 25, and 50 percent.)

45. The commitment was to simplify the import tariff system in 2002 by limiting the number of items subject to trade restrictions and eliminating the system of ex ante registration of import contracts by the end of 2002. See the letter of intent signed by Rutam Azimov, deputy prime minister and minister of macroeconomics, and by Mamarizo Nurmuradov, minister of finance, and Faizulla Mulladjanov, chairman of the Central Bank of Uzbekistan, on January 31, 2001 (www.imf.org/external/np/loi/2002/uzb/01/index.htm).

46. By contrast, Kazakhstan and Turkmenistan were at US$6,500 and US$4,320, respectively. UN Development Program, *Human Development Report, 2003*, pp. 279–80.

47. EBRD, "Strategy for Uzbekistan," approved by the board of directors March 4, 2003, p. 16.

48. In 1998, 19 percent of the Uzbek population lived on less than US$1 a day and 44 percent lived on less than US$2 a day. World Bank, *World Development Indicators, 2003*, p. 60. Children, always the pride of an Uzbek household, now often walk around in tattered and dirty clothing, as baths as well as soap have become a luxury for many. The

quality of footwear has deteriorated strikingly as well, among all sectors of the population. In November 2001, I was brought, in a middle-class section of Tashkent, to a mosque at which women were receiving religious instruction, and not a single pair of shoes left at the door were in normal repair.

49. EBRD, "Strategy for Uzbekistan," p. 17.

50. Ibid. The EBRD also estimated that Uzbekistan would be able to maintain this growth rate, given the country's rich resource base. Ibid., p. 28.

51. Irrigated cropland is 88 percent of the total, one of the highest irrigation rates in the world.

52. International Finance Corporation/SECO.

53. EBRD, "Strategy for Uzbekistan," pp. 27–28.

54. For a detailed explanation, see Martha Brill Olcott, *Kazakhstan: Unfulfilled Promise* (Brookings, 2002).

55. The U.S. Agency for International Development and the UN Development Program both have projects in this area.

6

No Quick Fix: Foreign Aid and State Performance in Yemen

SHEILA CARAPICO

F ew of the world's poorest countries better exemplify American interests in government performance than Yemen. Long overshadowed by its oil-rich Persian Gulf neighbors, Yemen gained attention as both an occasional target and a natural haven for militant regional paramilitary groups (including but not limited to al Qaeda). Headlines were made at a time when development analysts were already worried about ecological and economic stresses exacerbated by the strains of structural adjustment and critical water scarcity. In view of these circumstances, analysts began wondering if Yemen is an example of the combustible mix of poor governance and economic stagnation that could blow up or melt down. Realizing that the stability, safety, and welfare of the most populous and poverty-stricken country on the Arabian Peninsula matter, the Bush administration promised substantial U.S. assistance for the first time in Yemeni history. The question is, can American aid fix Yemen's problems?

This cautionary tale by an old Yemen-watcher is divided into four parts. After reviewing sources of military-political and socioeconomic insecurity and prospects for their amelioration, it traces the effects of past international aid programs, first at the level of international relations and then at the level of infrastructural and institutional development. It describes and analyzes how Soviet and Eastern European security assistance, fat subsidies from Arab neighbors during the oil boom, loss of both communist and Gulf aid between 1989 and 1991, and statist institution-building efforts by the World Bank and Western donors all affected state budgetary allocations, institutional development, and ultimately performance. The caution is that just as past bilateral and multilateral assistance ultimately centralized authority in executive institutions, an infusion of security assistance may tip the delicate balance between the state and civil society; among the executive, legislative, and judicial powers; between the military and the civilian arenas; between the public and private sectors; or between the political center and the localities. My greatest fear is that in an effort to ward off the Somali scenario of chaos American policies may bolster the Saddam model of dictatorship. In any case, there are no quick fixes to Yemen's national security problem that do not address government performance in the areas that matter most to households. And these too are not easy.

Security Dilemmas

Yemen offers a series of enigmas to the outside observer. On the one hand in cross-national comparison it lags behind most other countries on virtually any development indicator and shares certain disturbing social and ecological similarities with famously collapsed states like Somalia and Afghanistan. Yet by most narrative accounts Yemen enjoys a kind of political equilibrium, some prospects for democratization, and possibilities for economic stabilization led by its infant oil industry. Its people hardly resist modernization but, to the contrary, are always migrating and trading abroad, improvising roads and electricity, clamoring for schools, and demanding progress.[1] In the field of international security, although the combined effects of poverty, unruliness, and regime acquiescence left room for small-scale paramilitary groups to operate inside the country, the Yemeni government has embraced the American war on terrorism, cooperating with U.S. authorities in the pursuit of al Qaeda and its affiliates. Having all but ignored this poor, unstable corner of Arabia in the past, Washington now regards Sana'a as an ally against an elusive common enemy.

Yemen is not a failed state but a new state, a teenager, born only in 1990 of the marriage of two weak, unstable governments in their twenties: North Yemen, or the Yemen Arab Republic, based in Sana'a, where military officers deposed the last imam in 1962; and South Yemen, where revolutionaries seized power in Aden after the British departure in late 1967 and later declared the People's Democratic Republic. The two Yemens merged in 1990, only to face off again in a brief conventional civil war in 1994. Having reduced Aden's governance institutions to rubble, the victorious Northern army overran what had been South Yemen for the first time. Rather than in the process of breaking, then, Yemen is a state in the making. National legislative and judicial institutions are not well rooted; the executive branch rules in conjunction with the armed forces, manipulating elections and the administration of justice to its own advantage.[2] Greatly strengthened in the past half-decade, the central government's authority still is not uncontested, either in the North or in the South. Border agreements with neighboring Saudi Arabia and Oman were drawn finally in the 1990s after decades of negotiations.[3] Basic services and systems of taxation, representation, and law enforcement are all under construction.

Long notorious for its Wild West frontier, where bloodless kidnappings and hijackings were commonplace, Yemen became a rather natural haven for groups later associated with al Qaeda for several reasons. Its wide-open plains, towering mountains, and obscure valleys along a mostly unpatrolled 1,400-kilometer boundary with Saudi Arabia offered many excellent hideouts. Osama bin Laden and several associates have Yemeni roots, especially in the distant southeast province of Hadramawt. Like other Middle Eastern governments (including those of Israel, Saudi Arabia, and Egypt), Sana'a had encouraged radical Islam as a counterweight to its socialist rivals up until the 1994 civil war, when veterans and admirers of the much-glamorized anti-Soviet Afghan jihad joined the North Yemeni army in the sacking of the former South Yemeni capital of Aden. As elsewhere, the clampdown on leftists and Marxists emboldened right-wing fanatics, who attacked socialists, beauty parlors, and even ("idolatrous") Islamic shrines in the mid-nineties. Moreover, Yemen had an unusually liberal immigration policy especially for fellow Arabs and Muslims.

So it is not surprising that groups known locally as, variously, Afghan-Arabs, salafis, Wahhabis, the Aden-Abyan Islamic Army, al Qaeda, and other general and specific names were able to make homes, conduct military training, toss the occasional bomb, and spread propaganda inside Yemen. Nor is it surprising that Yemeni intelligence was no better able than the FBI, the CIA, or the authorities in Hamburg, Germany, to detect the extent of its internal al Qaeda network until they all began comparing notes. The Yemeni government's initial reaction to the *Cole* incident was as to another in a series of bombings in and around Aden, not as another in a series of attacks on Americans. Between October 2000 and September 2001, Sana'a began to uncover connections between a radical fringe within its borders and international terrorism.

Until then, the U.S.-Yemeni relationship remained at arm's length. The United States never invested heavily in Yemen, nor have Yemenis seen the United States as a benefactor. A few early showpiece projects like the Kennedy Water System for Taiz notwithstanding, American generosity was pretty paltry. Yemen was twice punished with the suspension of U.S. aid for opposition to Israeli or American military actions against fellow Arabs. The number, cost, and visibility of U.S. programs pale in comparison to Chinese roads, Kuwaiti hospitals, Saudi schools, and World Bank consultants. And the American corporate presence, led since the mid-1980s by Hunt Oil of Texas, was nothing compared with the massive American business community in neighboring Saudi Arabia. On the other hand, hard hit by suspension of aid from both Warsaw Pact and Arab Gulf donors, Sana'a has been desperately seeking American approval. Parliamentary elections in 1993, 1997, and 2003 drew some positive publicity. But for the most part the government of President Ali Abdallah Salih failed to convince the United States of its importance until Americans came under attack in Yemen. Anxious to be treated like Pakistan, not Afghanistan, in the wake of September 11, 2001, the Salih administration is keener than ever to curry American favor and to use it to domestic political advantage.

Yemen appeared on Washington's radar screen after internal security, always precarious, deteriorated from frontier lawlessness to deadly paramilitary operations against Yemeni and international targets.[4] Although Somalia-bound American sailors were targeted in Yemen in the early 1990s, the first incident to warrant wide international coverage was the kidnapping of sixteen Western tourists in the district of Abyan on December 28, 1998—four of whom died in a botched rescue mission by the Yemeni government. Explosions aboard the USS *Cole* in Aden harbor in October 2000 and the French tanker *Limburg* in 2002—costly especially in terms of inflated insurance premiums for the shipping industry, a potential growth sector for investment and revenues—gave the country a reputation as a site of international terrorism.[5] Assassinations of three Baptist medical missionaries and a prominent Yemeni socialist politician in late 2002 and protests against the American invasion of Iraq in early 2003 threatened another sector slated for growth, tourism, as the country appeared increasingly dangerous.[6] These and other signs of a high-risk, low-security environment multiplied disincentives to private investors, including resident Yemenis, Yemenis living abroad, and foreign companies.[7] Security trepidations and constant contestation of land rights hampered further oil, gas, and mineral exploration so essential to scenarios for income growth.

The American and Yemeni militaries have joined forces to patrol Yemen's borders and coasts and to share intelligence. After Yemen opposition to the Saudi-U.S. alliance against Iraq in the 1990–91 Kuwait War severely strained U.S.-Yemeni relations, the Yemeni government took several steps to improve its image in Washington. It welcomed the U.S. navy to Aden, implemented an unpopular austerity package recommended by the International Monetary Fund, mended fences with Saudi Arabia, and began issuing tourist visas to Israeli Jews. Evidence of a closer relationship included FBI participation in the investigation of the attack on the USS *Cole* in 2000, Yemeni president Ali Abdallah Salih's Washington visit in November 2001, Vice President Dick Cheney's trip to Yemen in March 2002, the resumption of military education and training, and Yemeni approval of the U.S. Hellfire missile strike on a vehicle carrying al Qaeda operatives inside Yemen in November 2002. By that time the United States was already providing military assistance in the form of training, special forces and security specialists, and materials to support Sana'a's own counterterrorism campaign. Everyone expects this cooperation to expand in coming years into hundreds of millions of dollars. As in the past, therefore, events in the larger world arena—this time the September 2001 attacks and the occupation of Iraq—are influencing domestic policies via government budgets.

Depending on how you look at it, Yemen is either a fledgling polyarchy or an imperfect dictatorship. Among Arab states it is widely considered one of the more promising "emerging democracies," in which a relatively laissez-faire policy betokens some prospects for political as well as economic liberalization. Token female parliamentarians, contested multiparty elections, and freewheeling public discourse make it look more enlightened than most of its neighbors. All the political parties—including the ruling General People's Congress, the conservative, religiously based Reform Party, the Yemeni Socialist Party, and the smaller parties—at least pay lip service to electoral representation, universal suffrage, human rights, and the rule of law. But although democratic practices in parliament, the press, and the courts are sometimes vivacious, they are hardly robust. The same clique has ruled from Sana'a since the late 1970s. After the civil war the liberal unity constitution was amended to reconcentrate power in the central executive and to restrict the authority of the elected legislature. The parliamentary elections of April 2003 served to consolidate the ruling party's strong majority.

Still, North-South fissures endure, and the North itself is riven by center-periphery tensions often cast in tribal idiom. Although the regime resorts to more bargaining than brutality in its quest to consolidate control, the military already governs. Loyal army, air, republican guard, internal security, and now coast guard forces police more effectively than ever. Armed forces moved against political paramilitary groups long before the *Cole* bombing, chasing the Abyan-Aden army out of Aden, conducting sweeps in other regions, expelling hundreds of non-Yemeni Arabs, and closing some paramilitary camps. New laws and death sentences seem to have curbed kidnappings, and scores of suspected militants have been rounded up or gunned down. Some regions can resist army incursions, but direct military challenges anywhere in the country have been crushed.

Tempting though it is for the United States to concentrate on counterterrorism and state-strengthening measures, I fear that a sudden, security-driven infusion of resources and expertise into selected security institutions risks reinforcing authoritarian tendencies. Surveillance agencies or antiterrorism squads can be disproportionately empowered by dollars and elite training. This influences the power of the military-security apparatus over civilians and also power struggles within the military regime. An important example of this has already happened: after the Yemeni army fatally botched an attempt to rescue kidnapped Western tourists around Christmas 1998, a new special forces unit was established under the command of the president's son and successor-designate, Ahmad Ali Abdallah Salih, to deal with quick strikes and hostage situations. The U.S. military's efforts to strengthen these special forces have fed rumors in Yemen that the Bush administration approves of the presidential succession from father to son and favors the special forces over other branches of the military and their officers.

Nor, whatever the immediate exigencies, are the demonstration effects of high-powered remote-control executions, like the Hellfire attack, conducive to the rule of law. Human rights and due process had already been violated in the prosecution of the domestic war against regime opponents in the 1990s, though outright extrajudicial killings that could be pinned on the government were unusual. The unfortunate precedent is not likely to be offset with a few human rights conferences or help with elections administration if the net gain in resources engorges a police state. Economic logic can justify an investment in stability in order to lure private investors. But if Yemenis perceive a trade-off between utilities and the military, or experience governance as more surveillance than responsiveness, this strategy could backfire on both the government and the United States. People expect both security (within legal parameters) *and* a decent standard of living.

Socioeconomic Insecurities

Although location gives it a strategic importance that landlocked countries in resource-poor environments lack, Yemen's development conundrum echoes that of other poorly performing states described in this volume. The lack of financial and technical wherewithal to deliver essential services to more than 18 million people scattered over a vast terrain perpetuates a vicious cycle of poverty. Private investment capital remains scanty, scared, and small scale, while the terms of structural adjustment have raised the costs of investment and reduced the level of consumption. Civil war, elite corruption, and disproportionate spending on domestic security have all drained public coffers. All in all, the peculiarities of Yemen's internal and external affairs notwithstanding, it is similar to other so-called basket cases, desperate for any sort of finance. While national leaders have not managed resources well, the economy has also borne the brunt of regional and global forces beyond its control.

By virtually any comparative indicator Yemen now fits the profile of poor performance. It scores among the poorest performers in the world on five major indicators: civil and political liberties as reported by Freedom House; the UN Development Program human development index; negative gross domestic product per capita growth during the 1990s; the proportion of the population living on less than a dollar a day; and the World Bank's measure of rule of law, including things like contract enforcement. The United Nations puts Yemen in the group of forty-nine countries that have been iden- tified by the UN as least developed in terms of their low GDP per capita, weak human assets, and high economic and trade vulnerability.[8] Life expectancy seems to be declining (despite negligible known AIDS cases).[9] With birth rates outstripping economic growth, widening inequality, and bad risk ratings—all despite being an oil exporter—prospects for affluence seem dim.

It was not always so. As explained more fully below, in the 1970s and 1980s foreign aid supplemented by labor remittances enabled urban and rural households to acquire electrical power, running water, imported goods, and better access to schools and medical attention. On the eve of unification the North, with a per capita income of over US$600 a year, was close to "grad- uating" into the World Bank's middle-income category. Then, due primarily to exogenous factors that suspended both aid and remittances, the economy crashed. The poverty rate doubled during the 1990s, while real GDP per capita tumbled to about US$300. Once rather rare, malnutrition now plagued nearly half of young children, a serious deterioration of nutritional standards from a generation earlier, when indigenous grains, vegetables, and dairy products were dietary staples. Whereas 1990s' parents had experienced great gains in literacy in their school years, their children were crammed into crowded, crumbling classrooms. Households that secured water and electricity hookups not long before now found themselves unable to pay for these services. New fees made hospitals inaccessible to the burgeoning poor. Cities, which had seemed to offer a better life, had become crowded, messy, anomic places. High aspirations were dashed, prompting people to take to the streets on numerous occasions.

Environmental disaster looms in southwestern Arabia, heretofore a semi-arid, temperate region of self-sufficient agriculture and herding known historically as Arabia Felix. The calamitous shortage of clean water, water delivery services, and new water sources to meet mounting urban demand is undermining the agricultural economy to such an extent that World Bank experts anticipate social conflicts over contesting claims to water. The urban centers served by huge public water corporations have drained their hinterlands even as the availability of household water delivery is a major incentive for rural-to-urban migration. International experts point out that overirrigation and overcultivation of *qat*, a cocaine-like shrub that is the country's most profitable alpine cash crop, grown entirely for the domestic market, is lowering the water table throughout the central highlands.

Profligate pumping for other crops and purposes in the coastal regions is intensifying the salinization of groundwater. These conditions endanger production and jeopardize social relations among neighboring villages and between cities and rural areas. The water sector is an example: in instituting agencies for the central control of ground and surface resources, donors inadvertently disrupted intricate local water laws in favor of corruption-prone central bureaucracies by assuming the latter's eminent domain rather than exploring the question.[10]

Some optimists in the donor community point to economic and political liberalization as well as growth in the nascent oil and gas sector. International financial analysts have approved of modest steps toward privatization and compliance with World Trade Organization standards. Government deficits were brought under control. Small declines were posted in fertility, infant mortality, and illiteracy. Population growth rates peaked at 3.9 percent and then inched downward. Actual GDP growth, fueled by the petroleum sector, fluctuated in the range of 3–8 percent a year from the mid-1990s onward, prompting the World Bank to report "recovery" even as the non-oil economy remained "sluggish."[11] Donors and planners attributed the economic crisis of the early 1990s to the triple shock of the 1991 Gulf War, the drought, and the 1994 civil war but hoped that strategic, environmental, and oil-price conditions would become more auspicious. A great deal depends on petroleum revenues, and great hopes are pinned on returning Aden to its former glory as a world-class shipping hub—that is, on exogenous variables.

It is easy to blame political leaders and the ruling class for poor management of the economy.[12] Noting that Yemen ranks below most of its neighbors in regulatory framework, government effectiveness, rule of law, and its handling of corruption, World Bank experts enumerated problems, including poor domestic security, arbitrary regulations, lack of clear property rights and other legal uncertainties, high taxes, corruption, smuggling, inefficiencies in public service delivery, weak contract enforcement, and an absence of mechanisms for settlement of business disputes.[13] Along with other contemporary donors, the World Bank has also criticized Yemen for a bloated public service, excessive public management, and bad decisionmaking in such sectors as electrical power and water resources management. Yet these criticisms of past policies overlook the role of the World Bank and bilateral donors in guiding development decisionmaking.

Erratic Development Finance

Like many other poor performers, Yemen's macroeconomy is buffeted by regional and global geopolitical forces beyond its control.[14] It is not (or not simply) that Yemen is the victim of large amorphous forces of globalization, nor apart from the colonial era in South Yemen is it a classic case of dependency. Its strategic position in the lower Arabian Peninsula—between the Suez Canal, the Horn of Africa, the Indian Ocean, and the Persian Gulf—places the country along key fault lines in the international system. Via the mechanism of military and economic aid, Yemen felt the impact of the cold war and inter-Arab conflicts in every bone of its rather skeletal state structure(s). Events like the waxing and waning of Soviet power, the rise and fall of oil fortunes in neighboring Arab Gulf states, and the Kuwait War of 1990–91 directly affected what was spent for what purposes and where. This was not bilateral dependence on a single rich patron that deliberately maneuvers outcomes but a sort of multilateral pegging of fortunes to a capricious world system. Here we examine two historic periods, before and after unification, when events elsewhere directly affected the domestic political economy.

Boom and Bust in the Two Yemens

For at least a generation, while communist, Arab, European, and Asian donors were feeling generous, Yemen enjoyed significant improvements in standards of living. Roads, ports, schools, hospitals, and utilities were installed with generous cold war, Arab Gulf, and multilateral aid packages. The population per physician dropped from nearly 60,000 to 6,000 in North Yemen in the twenty years after 1962. In the postcolonial People's Democratic Republic of (South) Yemen (PDRY), where the British had established some services and revolutionaries promised better, the population served by each doctor fell from nearly 13,000 to about 4,000.[15] The percentage of children in school in the North rose from 9 percent to 79 percent during this period, a remarkable achievement made possible by a combination of local efforts and Saudi-Kuwaiti largesse.[16] In the PDRY, half of all girls attended secondary schools, double the rate for colonial Aden, and the number of mothers losing infant children each year dropped from 197 to 120 per thousand live births. North Yemen cut infant mortality too, though female secondary school attendance rose only from a very low 3 percent to 12 percent.[17] The urban proportion of the PDRY's population swelled from 30 percent to 42 percent, and city dwellers in North Yemen increased from only 5 percent in the early 1960s to nearly 25 percent by the late eighties.[18]

By 1995 half of all Yemenis had access to safe water and sanitation.[19] Literacy rates were about two-thirds for men and one-quarter for women.[20] Many of these advances sprang directly from foreign finance and expertise. The transportation sector, for instance, was improved by contributions from the United States, the Soviet Union, and the People's Republic of China. South Korean companies paid by Saudi Arabia paved the major arteries of the North Yemeni road network. The Russians and the World Bank worked on port development for Aden and the Northern port of Hodeida.

Such external largesse was a function of superpower competition and the extraordinary riches of nearby oil-exporting states. Postcolonial South Yemen was backed financially by communist governments, Arab neighbors, and even the World Bank. Between 1968 and 1980, the USSR disbursed over US$150 million to the PDRY, or about a third of its total aid receipts for the period; it was spent for irrigation works, a thermal power station, a joint fishing enterprise, port facilities, public health, and oil exploration.[21] Hundreds of millions more went to arms, which were exported on easy long-term credit. China provided about US$84 million, especially for road construction, a textile factory, and agricultural development. East German experts trained police and security forces.[22] Bulgaria, Czechoslovakia, Albania, Hungary, and Poland also sent commodity credits and technical experts. Hundreds of Socialist Party members studied in Eastern Europe. The state socialist model was clearly preferred, and it showed in public investments.

Aden was not entirely dependent on communist resources and models, however. Perhaps surprising in light of its socialist aspirations, the World Bank's International Development Association (IDA) provided about a third of the PDRY's development loans in the 1970s and more in the 1980s. Official grants from Kuwait and other Arab countries had reached US$125 million in 1982, and total transfers from OPEC countries from 1973 through 1981 were estimated at US$399 million.[23] Although the Soviet Union and China were extending about half of all new development loans, Arab sources (directly or indirectly through multilateral organizations) generated most of the remainder.[24] By the late 1980s loans and grants from Arab sources far surpassed ruble transfers. Overall, South Yemen gradually moved from dependence on communist states to dependence on Arab and multilateral sources. Still, the demise of European communist states left Aden bereft. In the end (following an intraparty bloodbath in 1986), the state ceased to exist.

The picture in the aspiring capitalist North was not as different from the socialist South as one might expect. During the cold war, North Yemen's fortunes too were enhanced by global and regional power politics. The USSR, China, and the United States vied for influence via large infrastructural projects in the 1960s, when few other countries were getting aid from all three superpowers. Subsequently, the World Bank, the United Nations, West Germany, the Netherlands, and Japan became active donors. The United States (which branded the PDRY a terrorist state) had only a small U.S. Agency for International Development mission in Sana'a, which was suspended between 1967 and 1972 on account of the Arab-Israeli conflict, and its Yemen policy was always tempered by American deference to Saudi interests.[25] Between 1973 and 1982, gifts, grants, and loans from Arab oil exporters outstripped all other sources, although as the main supplier of weaponry, the Soviet Union was also Sana'a's principal creditor, holding nearly half of outstanding debt in 1986.[26] Hundreds of North Yemenis, civilians as well as officers, also studied in communist Eastern Europe (as they did in Western Europe and North America, though Yemen was very marginal to the United States, in economic terms, especially compared to Saudi Arabia).

The Saudi kingdom exercised considerable influence over its southern neighbor by providing weapons, petroleum supplies, direct-grant budgetary subsidies, turnkey construction projects, salaries for teachers recruited else-where in the Arab world, covert payments to individuals and factions, and easy access to work permits for Yemenis.[27] Estimates of total annual Saudi payments range between about US$400 million and US$1 billion during the oil boom, when Iraq, Kuwait, and other Arab OPEC (Organization of Petroleum Exporting Countries) donors also helped keep Sana'a afloat finan-cially. For a while Iraq was the largest financier of government projects. OPEC sources provided some US$1.4 billion between 1973 and 1981 (almost all financial rather than technical assistance).[28] OPEC assistance lev-eled off after 1981. Saudi Arabia and the other Persian Gulf states funded North Yemen heavily because of its poverty and proximity and as part of their regional anticommunist strategy. So in the cold war standoff between Sana'a and Aden, Saudi Arabia represented Western interests by backing the North. Washington recognized a Saudi sphere of influence in Yemen most visibly when, during an inter-Yemeni border skirmish in 1979, "the United States cooperated with Saudi Arabia to greatly expand the security assistance program to the Yemen Arab Republic by providing F-5 aircraft, tanks, vehi-cles, and training."[29]

Before unification, then, both Yemeni republics dealt with a mixed bag of benefactors. The American role was negligible. Moscow held nearly half of both governments' debts, mostly for military equipment, a major factor in their budgets. China, Czechoslovakia, East Germany, Hungary, and Bulgaria accounted for another fifth of Aden's outstanding debt and a fraction of the North's. Japan and Western Europe lent funds for projects in the North but not the South. The World Bank and Arab Gulf states favored Sana'a over the PDRY, but supplied credits to both.[30] In short, both Yemens depended on international aid rather than any special patron. Although a good deal has been written about dependence on a single bilateral donor, often the United States, this situation has been less investigated and may be characteristic of other poorly performing states. But Yemen had then and has now rather more strategic salience than many other poor countries.

External Shocks to a Unified Yemen

Unification in 1990 was a product of domestic politics intersecting with a seismic global shift and clear economic incentives. Yemeni unity roughly coincided with the demise of the Soviet Union, the Warsaw Pact, the cold war, and the Berlin Wall and just preceded German unification. Negotiations between Sana'a and Aden, intermittent for over two decades, now offered each regime a means of survival.[31] Economic logic also played a role. Texans and Russians prospecting on their respective sides of the inter-Yemeni frontier discovered common oil deposits in the 1980s. Soon the two nascent state petroleum companies merged into a Yemeni oil investment corporation. For all intents and purposes, state socialism and state capitalism had converged. Cost-benefit analysis favored joint ventures in electrical power, mutual road connections, and countrywide adventure tourism, antiquities tourism, commercial fishing, export agriculture, and certain manufactures. There was some hope that the law and order mentality of the PDRY would have a settling effect on the rampant petty entrepreneurship of the North. Initially, then, the plan was that oil, economies of scale, and redevelopment of Aden as a free port could offset dwindling external public assistance. It might have worked but for a number of setbacks.

The discovery of commercially viable oil deposits in 1984 had signaled new-found possibilities to attract international direct investment. Even in the heyday of British Aden, when the port was a major naval hub between the Suez Canal and India, few foreign investors were ever attracted to Yemen. A British Petroleum (BP) refinery was Yemen's only significant commercial venture even in the colonial era, and no large private investments in any sector survived anywhere in Yemen in the tumultuous 1970s. In 1984, when the Dallas-based Hunt Oil Company found commercially viable petroleum deposits near Marib in southeastern North Yemen, prospects for attracting foreign private investment improved for the first time since 1962. Vice President George Bush attended Hunt's going-on-line celebrations in 1986, underscoring American interest in Yemen's petroleum sector. Soon Exxon, and then a consortium of South Korean firms, bought into Yemen-Hunt; Texaco, Elf Aquitaine, Total, Canadian Occidental, and USSR firms negotiated to drill for Yemeni oil. The Soviet company Technoexport made a major find in 1986 at Shabwa across the border from Marib.

The oil sector generated subcontracting opportunities for suppliers and builders such as the U.S. firm that built a small modular refinery near Marib and a Lebanese-Italian-German group that laid the pipeline. There were new commercial finds in 1987, 1988, and 1989, mostly south of the inter-Yemeni border, including the major Hadramawt concession that went to Canadian Occidental.[32] Soon there were discussions of refurbishing the old BP refinery at Aden and of exporting via a revitalized Aden port. Given discoveries under their common border and the increasingly clear advantages of cooperation,[33] the two Yemeni public petroleum companies merged their operations into the joint Yemen Company for Investment in Oil and Mineral Resources. This company signed a production agreement in late 1989 with an international consortium consisting of Hunt and Exxon, the Kuwait Foreign Petroleum Exploration Corporation, Total, and two Technoexport subsidiaries.

Aspirations for growth led by oil and shipping were dashed within a couple of months after unification by the fighting in the Gulf in 1990–91, however. By mere luck of the draw, newly unified Yemen held both the "Arab seat" and the rotating chair of the Security Council when the U.S.-backed resolution authorizing force to dislodge Iraq from Kuwait came up for a vote. When Yemen voted no, Secretary of State James Baker admonished it for what he called an expensive mistake. And indeed it was, for Saudi Arabia and the other Gulf monarchies reacted angrily. Ultimately the war disrupted the private remittances and international public finance that heretofore kept all of Yemen afloat.[34] In the clash among its most generous Arab benefactors, Yemen lost hundreds of millions of dollars from Kuwait, Saudi Arabia, other Gulf Cooperation Council monarchies, *and* republican Iraq, not to mention the token US$30 million a year or so from the United States. Moreover, Saudi Arabia suspended work visas for most Yemenis, sending some 750,000 to 800,000 people (male workers or traders and some families) over the border.[35]

A hefty one-time infusion of migrants' savings notwithstanding, the combined loss of public (aid) and private (remittance) access to hard currency sent the domestic economy into a tailspin.[36] Urban services, most conspicuously in the Red Sea port city of Hodeida, were overwhelmed by the influx of returnees. Exacerbated by drought and the financial costs of relocating officials from Aden to Sana'a, by 1993, despite modest oil sector growth, real per capita income was 10 percent lower than in 1989. Unemployment was more than 25 percent, and the inflation rate hit 50 percent. Public sector employees went unpaid for months. The current account deficit for 1990–93 topped US$3 billion. Central Bank reserves plummeted to the equivalent of a month's import bills. The debt overhang, measured by the ratio of debt to GDP, barely noticeable a few years earlier, was 200 percent, among the highest in the world. Now the International Monetary Fund was recommending stringent adjustment measures.[37]

Declining aid receipts, the concomitant free fall in hard currency reserves, and depressed oil prices forced the riyal downward in the early 1990s, exacerbating the zero-sum reasoning that led to the civil war of 1994.[38] Neighboring Gulf monarchies rewarded the Southern socialists' separatist aspirations with covert payments.[39] In the end, Sana'a's army encircled the rebels in Aden and disabled the city's main water supply. With some help from irregular "volunteers," the army plundered the city's public infrastructure, systematically destroying the files of the former PDRY ministries of planning, housing, justice, social security, labor, and security. It also looted foreign consulates, UN agency compounds, the Red Cross, oil company offices, hotels, museums, prisons, factories, port warehouses, and selected private homes.[40] Later the central banks, the national airlines, and other public companies were merged and the pace of privatization of PDRY enterprises accelerated. Note the destruction of institutions and services as the physical manifestation of the old PDRY state.

Victorious over the socialists, Sana'a begged for hundreds of million of dollars to reconstruct what had been destroyed. Talks with the World Bank and the International Monetary Fund focused on reducing a cumulative combined public debt of between US$8 billion and US$10 billion, especially the Russian portion of the debt. And indeed receipts surged from a little over US$200 million in 1995 to more than twice that amount the following year. Virtually the entire increase came from the International Monetary Fund and the World Bank's International Development Association (IDA), in conjunction with the Economic, Financial, and Administrative Reform Program (EFARP). Now multilateral assistance, including Arab and European Union funds and especially the IDA, accounted for over three-quarters of external financing. The IMF's contribution soared from near zero to nearly 30 percent. Whereas past loans and grants covered projects, usually involving physical construction, the EFARP focused on programs leading to debt reduction.[41] While donors, led by the World Bank, the Netherlands, and Germany, expressed faith in development cooperation, new aid was hardly on the generous terms of an earlier era.[42] As poverty, inflation, and unemployment skyrocketed, households, social services, and enterprises faced their own deficits. Spending on education slipped from 19 percent to 16 percent of the government budget.[43] The burden fell disproportionately on the unemployed, landless peasants, and female-headed households.[44]

Petroleum, the economy's potential savior, generated much-needed but unreliable revenues. By the mid-1990s oil earnings of about US$300 million a year covered around half of a leaner, meaner state budget. This was nowhere near enough to halt Yemen's fall into the ranks of the world's poorest countries nor to reduce the government's need for foreign grants and loans to cover its expenses. Although as a small, non-OPEC exporter Yemen had no control over them, world prices increasingly drove government accounts, the balance of trade, and national income. Other sectors were still ignored by large multinational corporations and were barely attractive to Yemenis living abroad. Therefore, a policy favoring privatization and foreign investment notwithstanding, the state's share of the economic pie was actually expanding because oil rents replaced migrants' remittances as the main source of earned foreign exchange.[45] Aid per capita slipped from US$22 to US$15 between 1997 and 2000, rising again following the reinstatement of a U.S. economic aid package worth about US$56 million in 2000. Debt service increased from 2.6 percent to 3.2 percent of the value of exports in the same three years.[46] Domestic tax collection remained moribund. Rises in world prices for oil in 2000–03, combined with a slight increase in rates of production, boosted gross national income, per capita gross domestic product, and earnings from exports. With no significant nonfuel exports, however, a steep rise in oil prices would sustain economic growth.

Public Sector Growth

Foreign aid affected not only the economy as a whole but also budgetary and policy decisions that determined the distribution of resources in society. This section explains the decisive impact of international development assistance in a country without the wherewithal to create basic socioeconomic infrastructure. When state construction projects began in the 1970s there was a colonial legacy in Aden but not, really, in the rest of South Yemen; the Northern imam heretofore maintained only the most minimal civil service and public works. Bilateral and multilateral assistance enabled both fledgling governments, but especially the North, to build institutions as well as infrastructure. This is how the state structures grew—one aid project at a time— and it is how public sectors came to dominate both Yemeni economies. East German training of domestic security forces, Soviet credits for arms purchases, World Bank loans to public corporations, billions of dollars spent on a nationwide power grid, Saudi funds for conservative education, and too many uncoordinated projects in the water sector all left a direct imprint on an inchoate bureaucratic structure. Thus when the World Bank and other donors criticize centralization and the large state share in the economy, they are implicitly repudiating at least some of their own past institution-building efforts. I demonstrate this point with respect to the power and water sectors in North Yemen (both sectors being essential to meeting basic human needs, to stimulating economic development, and to affording citizen appraisals of government performance), in which substantial international investments have only partly solved some problems while creating others.

Let us focus on North Yemen, the larger and surviving partner, embarking on state construction from scratch with a capitalist model in mind. Quite simply, the state sector, including its bureaucracy and its public corporations, came to resemble what one expatriate called "the sum of past aid projects." In national plans recommended by donors to rationalize investments, foreign public sector loans and grants were expected to cover the lion's share of new investment and a very high proportion of spending in such sectors as education, power, water, and even manufacturing. Indeed, with North Yemen's acute shortages of technical expertise, anticommunist bent, empty public coffers, and perennial instability, only the influx of international assistance can explain the engorgement of the state sector. How else could a coup-ridden government with negligible domestic revenues amass such a relatively large centralized public sector so quickly? Consider the period between the late 1960s and the early 1980s when North Yemen experienced the improvements in standards of living cited above and the institution building explained below, along with a civil war, a military coup, two subsequent presidential assassinations, domestic insurrection, Saudi antipathy, and skirmishes with South Yemen.

It may at first seem incongruous that five-year plans, normally thought of as a socialist mechanism, were introduced into North Yemen by "bastions of neoliberal orthodoxy" like the World Bank. The Bank's very first order of business was the establishment of a North Yemen Central Planning Organization to compile a national three-year plan.[47] In the process, the Bank, the UN Development Program (UNDP), and the Kuwait Fund collaborated to enlarge the Central Planning Organization to manage hundreds of externally funded projects. The UNDP, the IDA, the Kuwait Fund, and West Germany provided technical experts to ghostwrite the ambitious five-year plan, 1976–81, beautifully published in a 924-page hard-bound English version that devoted an entire subchapter to listing needs for foreign experts.[48] In this plan, foreign loans and grants were to cover roughly half of all investments; at least three-quarters of government investments; and nearly all new projects in power, water, education, health, and other civilian sectors.[49] It was an ambitious program that would create massive bureaucracies to manage centralized universal public services.

In the electrical power sector, the World Bank took the lead in replacing the jumble of private, cooperative, and municipal generators—which had begun to light most towns and some villages in the evenings—with a nationwide power grid.[50] Since electricity consumption surged steeply (from near zero) during the affluent 1970s, and in consideration of technical snafus that plagued early municipal suppliers, a nationwide megaproject was recommended. Under a series of multimillion-dollar loans, steam turbine engines were installed in the Red Sea near the port city of Hodeida and a network of high-tension transformers to supply hundreds of thousands of homes and businesses in the northern half of North Yemen. In 1988 the Arab Fund approved a second grid to serve the Taiz region of the Yemen Arab Republic and Aden in the South, where the aging Soviet-built thermal plant needed refurbishment.

Huge investments in centralization notwithstanding, the grid never operated very well. By the mid-1990s the Yemen General Electric Company (YGEC) was wired to only a third of households, and power outages forced businesses and hospitals to maintain backup generators. In retrospect, using sea-powered generators in a country soon discovered to be endowed with oil, liquid natural gas, and solar potential seemed shortsighted.[51] Power stations on both sides were damaged on the first day of the 1994 civil war. The North-South network recommended in the 1980s was completed in 1997, with funding primarily from the Kuwait-based Arab Fund for Social and Economic Development.[52] As creditors, the Paris Club urged the YGEC to phase out subsidies, sell shares to the private sector, and break up the national monopoly; other consultants drew up a master plan for electricity and gas calling for more loans and contracts to enable the YGEC to alleviate scheduled rolling blackouts and unscheduled brownouts.[53]

All of this was very political. North Yemen's nationwide grid was part of the centralization of heretofore local services into a public corporation. The Aden-Taiz link was a step toward unity. Blowing out power stations was later a tactic of war. Blackouts and brownouts in the vanquished South caused such bitterness that the Netherlands embassy took the lead in upgrading the system in the far southeastern Hadramawt region to assuage political tensions there. Power failures are still not uncommon in the urban centers, and many communities remain off the "national" grid. Not surprisingly, those same communities are wont to resent government interference in local affairs. Erratic electricity supplies discourage investors and technology users while reminding everybody that the government is not working properly.

The water sector was a different story. Whereas electricity is widely considered a natural monopoly, the water sector in a semiarid, mountainous country is naturally decentralized. Yemen's traditional water resource management mechanisms—canals, cisterns, shallow wells, spate systems, and other devices tailored to each microenvironment—were ecologically elegant, separating every drop of water by use: drinking, cooking, livestock, bathing, irrigation. Private and community water rights, with minute provisions for drinking and irrigation, were a central feature of both Islamic and tribal law: water management was a crucial part of the agrarian order. But household supplies fell unhealthfully short of World Health Organization standards. New pumping and drilling technology introduced in the 1970s revolutionized water utilization. Even collectively, international developers can hardly be blamed for all the profligate pumping that now threatens long-standing aquifers, since municipalities and farmers were often wasteful. Still, a range of donor agencies contributed to the strange, ultimately counterproductive development of water management bureaucracies. And when the concept of eminent domain applied by foreign donors to water resources enabled national agencies to pump farm water to the cities, this wreaked havoc with a critical feature of indigenous Islamic or tribal law.

Water engineers were quick to recognize both the peril of overpumping and the disfunctionality of the hydraheaded water bureaucracy assembled through "institution-building" projects.[54] The National Water and Sewerage Authority (NWASA) was established in 1973 at the urging of lenders to assume oversight of huge urban delivery systems under construction in Sana'a, Taiz, and Hodeida. Later, NWASA expanded, was moved from one ministry to another, and then became a semiautonomous public corporation, like the electricity company, with a large well-paid professional staff in a huge central office.[55]

The management of the rural water supply—for three-quarters of the population spread out over mountainous, semiarid terrain—was another matter. As each of eight or ten donor agencies introduced its own unique technology, management systems, and accounting methods to a different selected counterpart bureaucracy established and trained for this purpose, units and outposts of the Rural Water Supply Department proliferated. More water agencies were initiated by other international development agencies in the Ministry of Agriculture, the Civil Aviation Authority, the federation of development cooperatives, the Central Planning Organization, and the Ministry of Oil and Mineral Resources' Geological Survey Division (the latter an American Trojan horse). By the mid-1980s, at the urging of the UNDP, a cabinet-level Supreme Water Council began requiring private drillers to obtain signatures from each of several water commissioners. On one level the state was asserting its ownership of natural water (and mineral) reserves; on another, a new state class enjoyed unprecedented opportunities for private enrichment. Both levels encouraged heavy water usage.

Another way in which international development agencies facilitated over-exploitation of water resources was by constructing large-scale, capital-intensive Ministry of Agriculture irrigation schemes intended to stimulate cultivation of semitropical crops like citrus fruits in an otherwise semiarid climate.[56] Cheap credits for private irrigation and import policies discouraging production of indigenous drought-tolerant cereals in favor of exotic fruits and vegetables for export also contributed to heavy water utilization. While Yemeni policymakers, corrupt bureaucrats, wildcat entrepreneurs, and ordinary farmers smitten with a new technology made enough of a mess on their own, international experts recommended and funded some terrible policy decisions.

By 1995 annual freshwater withdrawal was estimated at a phenomenal 136 percent of total water resources, second in the world only to neighboring Saudi Arabia.[57] Yet half of Yemeni households had no access to safe water, and the per capita water supply was among the most meager in the world. In 1997 IDA, UNDP, and the Netherlands formed the Multi-Donor Group for Yemen Water to study and help alleviate a perilous water shortage. One recommendation—no longer ecologically or institutionally practical, though repeated in a number of reports—was a return to local, indigenous water management.[58] It was certainly too late for Taiz, where the Kennedy Water System (built by USAID and improved by the World Bank and other funders) drew from wells in a verdant valley to supply a city whose population grew tenfold in less than two decades. The verdant farms are gone, and yet neighborhoods in Taiz go thirsty or buy water retail. This project and others based on the principle of eminent domain for public works—such as roads and oil fields—also had unforeseen consequences for the practice of religious and common law in the Taiz region and elsewhere. Always contested but subject to a substantial body of Quranic law and communal tradition, water rights were an inherently local matter of inestimable value. The nationalization of water rights for urban use, however rational or justified in terms of public policy, undermined important legal practice and rights without replacing them with an alternative legal structure. The implicit trade-off was a promise of urbanlike services including a different sort of "right" to utilities. But villagers saw a net drain of resources to the urban centers, resources of which water is the most vital.

Similar effects were to be found in other important sectors. Foreign aid enabled the Ministry of Education to centralize and nationalize schools, while Gulf funding of primary, secondary, and higher education helped shape the curriculum at all levels. Saudi aid for education was especially capricious, first assisting the ministry and Sana'a University but later aimed at private parochial schools and colleges. Both the health and education ministries became sprawling central bureaucracies. One development expert called the Ministry of Agriculture "a clearing house for foreign aid." Thanks to access to transnational credits and tenders, the Ministry of Public Works owned what was for a time the largest company in the country. "Capitalist" and "communist" donors alike funded agricultural projects and industrialization until the state had become the principal source of new investments in both sectors. Overall—indeed, rather surprisingly—the state's share of large enterprises in the "capitalist" North was not much less than in the PDRY (although petty trade flourished in the former and languished in the South).[59]

The emergence of a technocratic elite within the executive branch of government to manage what became the Ministry of Planning, the water and power corporations, ministries of public works and education, and other important central institutions was directly connected to study-abroad possibilities. A political leadership otherwise composed of semiliterate officer-tribesmen had not envisioned national development plans, nationwide power grids, or curricula. These were planned, funded, and executed by donors and staffed by a new class of foreign-educated technocrats. The World Bank, consistently the leading financier and policy adviser, designed and financed some of the very same public corporations its economists wished to see privatized, decentralized, and streamlined. Overall, then, the cumulative effects of the institution-building efforts of a dizzying array of donors was the accumulation of public sector entities controlled by the central executive. Unlike oil rents that enter the general coffers of the kleptocracy, or for that matter migrants' remittances that used to evade bureaucratic siphoning, aid programs channel resources to particular institutions and individuals whose political and economic fortunes are thereby greatly enriched. Substantial investments naturally affected the distribution of values in a resource-poor environment.

Conclusions

Clearly Yemen faces many obstacles to security and prosperity. It is a new state with a long-entrenched regime but incomplete sovereignty. It has not all that much oil and even less water. Popular aspirations have been repeatedly elevated and dashed, and millions of teenagers face an uncertain future. Regular elections have not produced regime change but only reinforced the monopoly of the ruling General People's Congress. Even without detailing how Sana'a and Riyadh encouraged the Islamist right as a counterweight to the socialist left, fed subsidies to key tribal militia, or subverted law and order, and even assuming optimal political will on the part of the Salih administration, it is easy to see that improving governance and government performance would be a tall order. Providing universal access to electrical power and water alone is still a daunting yet indispensable task, essential to meeting basic human and entrepreneurial needs; the inability to deliver power and water even with significant sustained international investment represents a fundamental kind of state malfunction.

This chapter makes four main points. First, the United States can no longer afford to ignore problems of law and order in southwestern Arabia because they impinge on Red Sea shipping and the stability of the entire peninsula. While in the short run Yemen is unlikely to either blow up or melt down, its relative tranquility is fragile and unfinished. Second, deteriorating utilities and inadequate services matter not because misery and frustration necessarily breed terrorism but because infrastructure represents the physical and social girding of the state apparatus and the main criteria by which ordinary men and women assess government performance. Third, Yemeni states' ability to offer citizens basic services in exchange for governance has hung on decisions of external donors in light of capricious global and regional circumstances—in a boom-bust cycle. Finally, bilateral and multilateral donor programs have always been statist by definition, greatly expanding the power, wealth, and bureaucracy of the central executive and, in many sectors, contributing to unwieldy, ineffective public agencies and corporations. Thus external donors, led by the World Bank, must share responsibility for creating an institutional structure that is both too big and not big enough.

It is still not clear whether the current consortium of the United States, the World Bank, Japan, the Netherlands, Germany, other European countries, the European Union as such, UN agencies, and presumably soon some Arab OPEC governments can or will help lift Yemen out of the ranks of the world's poorest and poorest performing countries. Perhaps a unified condominium of donors is an improvement over the past multiplicity of competing models from the point of view of rational policymaking. On the other hand, pressures from international creditors to raise prices for basic commodities and services have been greeted with street demonstrations and other forms of protest. Other Arab, African, and Asian governments have learned that prosecution of economic austerity measures and a simultaneous security crackdown risk kindling popular support for right-wing causes. Outside of widespread opposition to American policies regarding Israel and Iraq, Yemen is by no means a hotbed of anti-American or anti-Western sentiment (I detected outrage at the murder of the Baptists but not over the Hellfire assassination; and Islamists in the Reform Party angry over the 2003 elections' ballot count complained to American and European delegations). Such sentiments may be stoked if Washington and the West are seen as conspiring with an extractive national security state responding to external powers, as for instance when FBI operatives were reportedly "crawling all over Aden" in the *Cole* investigation as Yemeni forces were conducting dubious mass arrests.

This conclusion offers no specific policy recommendations. If anyone knew how to fix Yemen's water and electricity problems, they would have done it in California by now. Guns and cowboy-tribesmen are not necessarily more of a problem in rural Yemen than in Wisconsin. Primary schools and teacher education are surely needed, but we know from Egypt that mass education does not automatically boost economic performance. Having seen so many projects that seemed reasonable on technical grounds at the time of implementation result in deleterious long-term consequences, I am not urging more, less, or even different American programs in Yemen but only asking donors and experts to be aware of the political and policy implications of institution-building programs.

Notes

1. Elsewhere I credit civic initiatives with major contributions to the process of state formation. Without contradicting myself here, I examine effects of past donor efforts at state construction. See Sheila Carapico, *Civil Society in Yemen: A Political Economy of Activism in Modern Arabia* (Cambridge University Press, 1998).

2. See Iris Glosemeyer, "Parliamentary Elections in Yemen 1997," in *Elections in the Middle East and North Africa,* edited by Sven Behrendt and Christian-Peter Hanelt (Munich/Gütersloh: Bertelsmann Foundation, 1998); Ahmed Abdul Kareem Saif, "A Legislature in Transition: The Parliament of the Republic of Yemen 1990–91," Ph.D. dissertation, University of Exeter, April 2000.

3. On the issues and terms, see Richard Schofield, "The Last Missing Fence in the Desert: The Saudi-Yemeni Boundary," in *Yemen Today: Crisis and Solutions,* edited by E. G. H. Joffee, M. J. Hachemi, and E. W. Watkins (London: Caravel Press, 1997).

4. On security issues in the face of paramilitary attacks, kidnappings, and other problems, see International Crisis Group, "Yemen: Coping with Terrorism and Violence in a Fragile State," *Middle East Report* 8, January 8, 2003.

5. For background, see Sheila Carapico, "Yemen and the Aden-Abyan Islamic Army," *Middle East Report Online,* October 18, 2000 (www.merip.org/mero/mero101800.html); Charles Schmitz, "Investigating the *Cole* Bombing," *Middle East Report Online,* September 6, 2001 (www.merip.org/mero/mero090601.html).

6. World Bank, *Yemen Economic Update,* Issue 11, December 2002. For more on the political assassinations, see Sheila Carapico, Lisa Wedeen, and Anna Wuerth, "The Death and Life of Jarallah Omar," *Middle East Report Online,* December 31, 2002 (www.merip. org/mero/mero123102.html).

7. World Bank, "The Republic of Yemen Economic Growth: Sources, Constraints and Potentials," Report 21418-YEM, May 31, 2002.

8. See www.unctad.org/templates/webflyer.asp?docid=2026&intitemid=1397&lang=1.

9. USAID, "Yemen Briefing" (www.usaid.gov/regions/ane/newpages/one_pagers/yemen01a.htm).

10. This problem has been recognized and addressed by the government of Yemen, which, in consultation with donors, passed the Eminent Domain Protection Law in 1995. See World Bank, "Resettlement Policy Framework for the Yemen Urban Water Supply and Sanitation Project," draft, January 22, 2002 (www–wds.worldbank.org/servlet/WDSContentServer/WDSP/IB/2002/02/16/000094946_02020504022427/Rendered/INDEX/multi0page.txt).

11. World Bank, "Yemen Country Brief" (///lnweb18.worldbank.org/mna/mena.nsf/Countries/Yemen/6C89A1E20F9D3F4D85256B7400726EF6?OpenDocument).

12. Charles Schmitz, "Whose Failing? State, Business, and the IMF in Yemen," paper prepared for the MESA Annual Conference 2002, Washington, considers the wisdom of International Monetary Fund advice. My focus here is more historical.

13. World Bank, "The Republic of Yemen Economic Growth: Sources, Constraints and Potentials," citing Daniel Kaufmann, Aart Kraay, and Pablo Zoido–Lobaton, "Aggregating Governance Indicators," World Bank Policy Research Working Paper 2195, October 1999.

14. To paraphrase Karl Marx and credit Andre Gunder Frank, it can be said that leaders in places like Yemen mismanage, but not under conditions of their own making.

15. World Bank, *World Development Report 1989,* table 28.

16. Ibid., table 29. The 79 percent figure is inflated by the large number of adults belatedly attending schools.

17. Ibid., table 32.

18. Ibid., table 31.

19. Ibid., table 6.

20. Central Planning Organization, *Statistical Yearbook 1992* (Sana'a, 1993), p. 14.

21. Fred Halliday, *Revolution and Foreign Policy: The Case of South Yemen, 1967–1987* (Cambridge University Press, 1990), pp. 199–200.

22. Stephen Page, *The Soviet Union and the Yemens: Influence in Asymmetrical Relationships* (New York: Praeger, 1985), pp. 26–27.

23. These figures are from, respectively, Gerd Nonneman, *Development, Administration, and Aid in the Middle East* (New York: Routledge, 1988), p. 103; Richard P. Mattione, *OPEC's Investments and the International Financial System* (Brookings, 1985), p. 148.

24. World Bank, "People's Democratic Republic of Yemen, Special Economic Report: Mid–Term Review of the Second Five–Year Plan, 1981–85," June 4, 1984, p. 12.

25. On the history of this relationship, including diplomatic relations and the oil industry, see Ahmed Noman Kassim Almadhagi, *Yemen and the United States: A Study of a Small Power and Super-State Relationship, 1962–1994* (London: I. B. Tauris, 1996).

26. Central Yemen Bank, "Percentage of External Public Loans from Major Donors" (Sana'a: June 30, 1987). On Soviet military aid, see Richard Nyrop and others, *Area Handbook for the Yemens* (U.S. Government Printing Office, 1977), pp. 233–39.

27. For an analysis of Saudi influence, see F. Gregory Gause, *Saudi-Yemeni Relations: Domestic Structures and Foreign Influence* (Columbia University Press, 1990).

28. Mattione, *OPEC's Investments and the International Financial System*, p. 148. Note that unlike Northern donors the Gulf donors did not subcontract work to their own contractors but rather asked for international bids and tenders. Saudi-financed roads, for instance, were built by South Korean workers.

29. Department of State, Bureau of Near Eastern Affairs, "Yemen Background Note," January 2002 (www.state.gov/r/pa/ei/bgn/5302.htm).

30. Data from Bank of Yemen, Aden, December 12, 1983, and Central Yemen Bank, Sana'a, June 30, 1987. That the data are several years apart makes little difference in the long time frame for accumulated debt; in addition, they are consistent with the data in World Bank, *World Debt Tables, 1986–87*, pp. 410, 414.

31. As their tumultuous, interconnected history reveals, many domestic political forces were at work. Gregory Gause, "Yemeni Unity: Past and Future," *Middle East Journal* 42, no. 1 (1988): 33–47; Gregory Gause, "The Idea of Yemeni Unity," *Journal of Arab Affairs* 6, no. 1 (1987): 55–81; Mark Katz, "Yemeni Unity and Saudi Security," *Middle East Policy* 1, no. 1 (1992): 117–35.

32. Simon Edge, "Yemen: *MEED* Special Report on Oil and Gas—Upstream Joy Masks Doubts Downstream," *MEED*, April 3, 1990. In Arabic, see Ahmad Qa'id Barakat, *al–Naff al–Yaman* (Sana'a: Afif Center, 1991); Ahmad 'Ali Sultan, *al–qtid al–Jumhuriyyah al–'Arabiyyah al–Yamaniyyah* (1988), available at Post Office Box 1128, Sana'a.

33. See Robert Burrowes, "Oil Strike and Leadership Struggle in South Yemen: 1986 and Beyond," *Middle East Journal* 43, no. 3 (1989): 437–54.

34. On Yemeni-Saudi relations in the 1990s, see Petroleum Finance Market Intelligence Service, *Yemen: Border Disputes and Relations with Saudi Arabia* (Washington: 1992); Mark Katz, "External Powers in the Yemeni Civil War," in *The Yemeni War of 1994: Causes and Consequences*, edited by Jamal al–Suwaidi (London: Saqi Books: 1995), pp. 81–93; Gwen Okruhlik and Patrick Conge, "National Autonomy, Labor Migration, and Political Crisis: Yemen and Saudi Arabia," *Middle East Journal* 51, no. 4 (1997): 554–65

35. See Nora Ann Colton, "Homeward Bound: Yemeni Return Migration," *International Migration Review* 27 (Winter 1993): 870–82.

36. Nicholas Van Hear, "The Socioeconomic Impact of the Involuntary Mass Return to Yemen in 1990," *Journal of Refugee Studies* 7, no.1 (1994): 18–38; Marc Lucet, "Les rapatries de la crise du Golfe au Yemen: Hodeida qatre ans apres," *Monde Arabe Maghreb-Mashrek*, no. 148 (April–June 1995): 28–42.

37. International Monetary Fund, "Republic of Yemen, 1993 Article IV: Consultation," September 18, 1993.

38. Thomas B. Stevenson, "Yemeni Workers Come Home: Absorbing One Million Migrants," *Middle East Report* (March–April 1993): 15–20; Jeffrey Ian Ross, "Policing Change in the Gulf States: The Effect of the Gulf Conflict," in *Policing Change, Changing Police*, edited by Otwin Marenin (New York: Garland, 1996); Eric Watkins, "Yemen's Riots Prompt Talk of Reform," *Middle East International* 444 (February 19, 1993): 18.

On the civil war, see Charles Schmitz, "Civil War in Yemen: The Price of Unity?" *Current History* (January 1995): 33–36; David Warburton, "The Conventional War in Yemen," *Arab Studies Journal* 3, no. 1 (1995): 20–44.

39. See Carlos A. Parodi, Elizabeth Rexford, and Elizabeth Van Wie Davis, "The Silent Demise of Democracy: The Role of the Clinton Administration in the 1994 Yemeni Civil War," *Arab Studies Quarterly* 16, no. 4 (1994): 65–76.

40. Jemera Rone and Sheila Carapico, "Yemen: Human Rights in Yemen during and after the 1994 War" (New York: Human Rights Watch, October 1994).

41. Nader Fergany, "Human Development, Poverty, and Structural Adjustment in Yemen," paper prepared for the conference "Yemen: The Challenge of Social, Economic, and Democratic Development," Center for Arab Gulf Studies, University of Exeter, April 1–4, 1998.

42. "Yemen: Development Partners Affirm Support," October 17, 2002 (//web.world-bank.org/wbsite/external/news/0,,contentmkd%3a20071483~menupk%3a34463~pagep k%3a34370~pipk%3a34424~thesitepk%a4607,00.html). Country participants in the donor's conference were, in alphabetical order, France, Germany, Hungary, Iran, Italy, Japan, Malaysia, the Netherlands, Oman, Poland, Qatar, the Russian Federation, the United Kingdom, and the United States. Among other participants were Arab Fund for Economic and Social Development, Arab Monetary Fund, Kuwait Fund for Arab Economic Development, OPEC Fund for International Development, European Commission, Islamic Development Bank, Saudi Fund for Development, UN Development Program, UN Children's Fund, UN Population Fund, International Monetary Fund, International Finance Corporation, Adventist Development Relief Agency, Benevolence International Foundation, CARE, Handicap International Belgium, Mercy International, OXFAM, and World Bank.

43. Al-Maytimi, "Efforts of Economic Program and Structural Adjustment," p. 7. Meanwhile, private domestic and foreign contributions to private education, especially conservative Islamic education, increased. See Mutahar A. Al-Abbasi, "Education Sector in Yemen: Challenges and Policy Options," paper prepared for the conference "Yemen: The Challenge of Social, Economic, and Democratic Development," Center for Arab Gulf Studies, University of Exeter, April 1–4 1998.

44. See, for instance, Mouna H. Hashem, "Poverty Reduction Strategies in Yemen: A Social Exclusion Perspective," paper prepared for the conference "Yemen: The Challenge of Social, Economic, and Democratic Development," Center for Arab Gulf Studies, University of Exeter, April 1–4 1998.

45. Charles Schmitz, "Politics, State, and Markets: Lessons for Yemen from the East," paper prepared for the conference "Yemen: The Challenge of Social, Economic, and Democratic Development," Center for Arab Gulf Studies, University of Exeter, April 1–4 1998.

46. World Bank, "Yemen: Country Data File, 2002."

47. For a review of early planning history, see UN Economic Commission for Western Asia, *Summary of the First Five-Year Plan of the Yemen Arab Republic* (Beirut, 1977).

48. North Yemen Central Planning Organization, *The First Five-Year Plan, 1976/77–1980/81* (Sana'a: Prime Minister's Office, 1977), pp. 809–50. On the role of donors, see Klaus Konig and Friedrich Bolay, "The Evaluation of an Administrative Cooperation Project in North Yemen and Its Significance for German Aid Policy," *Public Administration and Development* 2 (1982): 225–37.

49. Military spending was never included in the national plans but accounted for at least half of all government expenditures in both systems.

50. I took part in the twenty-two-community national rural electrification feasibility study undertaken by National Rural Electric Cooperatives, an American concern, under contract with the World Bank.

51. Ahmad Kaid Barakat, "The Energy Sector and Development: Present Situation and Prospects," paper prepared for the conference "Yemen: The Challenge of Social, Economic, and Democratic Development," Center for Arab Gulf Studies, University of Exeter, April 1–4, 1998

52. Commercial Data International, *Country Review Yemen 1998/99* (Houston: 1998), p. 28.

53. Hisham Khatib, "The Yemeni Energy Sector and the Yemeni Economy," paper prepared for the conference "Yemen: The Challenge of Social, Economic, and Democratic Development," Center for Arab Gulf Studies, University of Exeter, April 1–4, 1998.

54. See two reports by Zohra Merabet, "A Survey of Water Activities under Foreign Assistance in the Yemen Arab Republic," October 1980, prepared for USAID Yemen; and "A Survey on Development and Management of Water Resources in the Yemen Arab Republic," May 1980, prepared for the German Volunteer Service.

55. David Althus Garner, Edwin Connerly, and John Blumgart, "Institutional Development Assessment Report, 28 October–5 December, 1985: Final Report to USAID/Sana'a" (Washington: Management Systems International, 1985).

56. Christopher Ward, "Yemen's Water Crisis" (www.al–bab.com/bys/articles/ward01.htm).

57. World Bank, *World Development Report 1997,* table 10.

58. Christopher Ward, "Practical Responses to Extreme Groundwater Overdraft in Yemen," paper prepared for the conference "Yemen: The Challenge of Social, Economic, and Democratic Development," Center for Arab Gulf Studies, University of Exeter, April 1–4, 1998.

59. For more evidence of this, see Sheila Carapico, "The Economic Dimension of Yemen Unity," *Middle East Report* 184 (1993): 9–14.

7

Burma-Myanmar: The U.S.-Burmese Relationship and Its Vicissitudes

David I. Steinberg

Myanmar is in crisis.[1] An interlocking set of political, economic, and social problems faces the present military government, known as the State Peace and Development Council (SPDC). Some of these problems, such as minority issues, were inherited as early as independence in 1948 and inherent in the formation of the state at that time. Some evolved from the civilian administration (1948–58, 1960–62), and some from the previous military government (1962–88). Many problems have been exacerbated by the military regime since the coup, in 1988, that brought the present government to power.

The present state of the Burmese economy is the worst since independence. The World Bank has designated Myanmar a "low-income country under stress," indicating especially severe developmental problems.[2] The political stalemate between the ruling military and the opposition National League for Democracy (NLD), led by Nobel laureate Aung San Suu Kyi, forestalls significant reforms in any sector, and the tenuous ceasefires with a multitude of minority groups are fragile. Relationships between the majority Burmans, comprising two-thirds of the population, and multitudes of various minorities remain the most enduring of issues with which any administration in Myanmar must cope. It is an issue that must be addressed at the National

Convention, which is tasked with developing a new constitution for the state, but satisfaction among all parties under any formula is most unlikely.

Burma was a state without ever being a nation with an overarching ethos that promoted national unity. Ethnically fragmented, Burma following independence from British rule on January 4, 1948, experienced a plethora of problems. The Union of Burma was a constitutional parliamentary government led by a disparate coalition of civilians in the Anti-Fascist People's Freedom League (AFPFL), a political party that had been formed against the Japanese at the close of World War II. Although it experienced rebellions from the left and some ethnic strife, its bicameral legislature constitutionally allowed minority representation. Its economic policies were moderate and democratic-socialist, representing the Burman need to retrieve economic power that had been held by foreigners (Europeans, Indians, and Chinese) in the colonial era.

To forestall civil war as the AFPFL political coalition fragmented, the military took over in 1958 for eighteen months in an action approved by the parliament in what was called a constitutional coup, and as it promised, it returned the country to civilian rule after a free election in which the military's preferred civilian party lost. The next two years of civilian rule under Prime Minister U Nu economically and politically failed. He established Buddhism as the state religion. Although Buddhism had always been given special status, this move angered some of the powerful minorities, some of which were Christian, others that were Muslim. The military believed the state was fragmenting, which was unlikely at that time but which gave the military the excuse for decisive action.[3] The civilian leadership was arrested and civilian institutions, such as the legislature and the courts, were abolished. This second military coup in 1962 ushered in what was evidently viewed as perpetual military rule by its elite.

Authoritarian repression has been evident in Burma-Myanmar since that time. Before the coup of 1988, Burma from 1962 to 1974 was ruled by a military junta through decrees of the Revolutionary Council led by General Ne Win. A rigid socialist system was introduced under the military-led Burma Socialist Programme Party (BSPP) shortly after the coup. Socialism was to provide both legitimacy and a secular national ideology around which the whole state could rally and replace the still-revered Buddhism as the societal focus.

After extensive political propaganda, a new constitution was formulated, elections were held, and a single-party mobilization system was established under a 1974 constitution modeled on Eastern European precedents. This was a unitary, centralized state, enforced with power located within the BSPP, which meant military control. Even the modest autonomy previously granted the minorities was rescinded. The periphery was without effective voice. A unicameral legislature, the Pyithu Hluttaw, was a means to legitimate military authority. A single slate of BSPP candidates for election was proposed from the center, and no choices were permitted. Although "elected" representatives were obligated to return to their constituencies to learn the problems of their electorate, the system did not work, as fear prevented criticism of the military hierarchy and its policies and programs.

General Ne Win was the most influential, if not the most efficacious, of the state's leaders. He was first deputy head of the army at independence, then commander in 1949, minister of defense and sometimes deputy prime minister under civilian rule, then head of the 1958–60 caretaker government, chairman of the Revolutionary Council from 1962, and then from 1974 continued his preeminent role as president of the state until 1980. When he retired from that position, he remained the commanding influence in society through his personal entourage and as chairman of the party until 1988. He was as thoroughly powerful as any dictator in the modern world.[4] In March 2002 he was effectively marginalized with the arrest and later conviction of his grandsons and son-in-law in a purported attempted coup that seemed to outside observers questionable. Ne Win's influence was over, and he died in his Rangoon home in December 2002.

Yet in the period from 1962 to 1988, when the World Bank, the Asian Development Bank, Japan, the United States (after 1979), the Federal Republic of Germany, and other donors were most active, the socialist policies of the government, and the absence of political and other rights denied by a ubiquitous military intelligence system, were not issues in their assistance programs.

The BSPP regime failed through economic incompetence, political repression, and minority disaffection, leading to the third military coup, on September 18, 1988, which was designed to shore up the military as the ruler in spite of the earlier failed political and economic programs by the previous military-led government. That military administration changed its name from the State Law and Order Restoration Council (SLORC) in 1997 to the SPDC, but its top leadership remained intact. This fall from political and economic grace—a functioning if creaky democracy with a well-educated elite and an economy with the potential for growth and development—has been precipitous and tragic for its diverse peoples, who remain among the poorest in Asia.

The nexus of political repression, internal rebellions, whimsical and whimsically administered economic policies and programs, social dislocation, and deprivation make Myanmar a case of not only arrested development but also development denied in spite of the potential. The internal traumas spill across borders, affect international relations, and cause humanitarian concern worldwide. All these raise international questions over the future of the state and its peoples.

The Promise

Once called Burma, now officially known as Myanmar, that area of mainland Southeast Asia in ancient times was known as Suvannabumi (the Golden Land), a land filled with promise. From the earliest geographic references, in the second century, the region was considered fortunate. Natural resources were abundant, the area was sparsely populated for its size, famines were unknown in contrast to India and China, and the social system seemed more benign than in many other states. Women in traditional Burma were the equal of men, not subject to foot binding as in China or suttee as in India, and their status was said by European travelers in the early nineteenth century to be higher than that of women in Europe at that time. Burma in the nineteenth century was regarded as the most literate society between Suez and Japan. A late-nineteenth-century guidebook to Burma noted that the traveler who arrived in Rangoon from Calcutta would breathe a sigh of relief as he or she walked down the gangplank.

If in the mid-1950s one were to have speculated on which of the countries of Asia had the greatest opportunity and prospects for economic and social development, Burma would have been rated at the top. It had been the largest rice exporter in the world just before World War II (3.123 million tons in 1940), and an exporter of oil. It held 75 percent of the world's teak reserves and the world's best jade and rubies and even unexplored mineral wealth. Burma had an excellent higher education program, relatively equitable income distribution, extensive English language skills, and a functioning democracy with a British-based legal system and well-trained Burmese lawyers. The status of its women was high. Burma seemed placed for takeoff and participation in the world. It had, to be sure, been devastated by World War II and by a variety of political and ethnic insurrections after independence in 1948. These rebellions reflected the heritage of arbitrary, colonial-imposed boundaries and administration that separated minority areas from Ministerial Burma, or Burma proper, where the Burmans lived. Yet it had held together and seemed on the road to recovery. Foreign aid organizations of all stripes and pedigrees competed for Burmese attention, as Burma was wooed by all in the cold war. Burma also had a glorious explosion of architectural achievement beginning with the eleventh century at Pagan, an ancient capital and one of the most important historic sites in contemporary Southeast Asia. Its Buddhism to the outside world seemed benign and offered a softer, more humane, approach to the developmental process.[5]

Even in the period of the military caretaker government (1958–60), when democracy was suspended and during which the *tatmadaw* (armed forces) came to temporary power to prevent what might have developed into a civil war between opposing civilian politicians, those eighteen months were universally regarded as ones of accomplishment and success.[6] Law and order were restored, cities were cleaned up, prices were autocratically lowered in the bazaars, a border agreement was signed with China, and the hereditary authority of the minority Shan *sawbwas* (maharajas) was legally, if not socially, rescinded. The *tatmadaw* expanded the Defense Services Institute, a military-run and -owned conglomerate of many industries that appeared to be extremely effective.[7]

After the military voluntarily relinquished power to a civilian administration, as it had promised, international academics and theorists used the Burmese example as a prime case in the generic study of the military as the most important developmental force in the third world because it was allegedly rational, goal oriented, and developmentally inclined. In retrospect, although one may fault the theoreticians for perhaps being unconsciously influenced by the perceived need of the West to support authoritarian governments in the midst of the cold war, the Burma case offered a certain realistic example of effective military government. This taste of power and its successful conclusion gave the military confidence that it could administer the country and run the economy and, thus, influenced their future role, although with devastating results. The difference may have been in the temporary and effective mobilization of effort in contrast with the later expectation of perpetual military control.

Then why, after such promise, has Burma-Myanmar become a failing or dysfunctional state, or one whose economy has collapsed?[8] Why has Burma-Myanmar never even approached reaching its potential and, instead, had a per capita gross domestic product of US$151 in 2001, below that of Laos (with US$330) and Cambodia (one of the least developed countries in the world, with US$270)? Why did it take thirty years (1945–75) for its per capita income to reach pre–World War II levels? Was it economic policies, issues of governance, internal unrest, some or all of these or other factors that have led to promise denied?

What also has caused Burma-Myanmar to have episodically troubled relations with the United States? Was it primarily the cold war? This quintessential neutral state, whose ambassador to the United Nations, U Thant, became the secretary-general of that institution because of Burma's centrality to East-West struggles, was buffeted by conflicting ideological and political forces, prompting the severance of U.S. economic assistance programs on three occasions.

Why, indeed, should the United States once again be interested in this state, ignored for almost three decades? What national interests, if any, prompt the United States to consider or reconsider its diplomatic and economic relations, and how does the history of such interaction color the expectations and realities of both sides? What does the latest involvement of the United States in the region, the war on terrorism, mean to the future of Burmese society, growth, and equity and its contacts with its neighbors and the nations beyond its periphery? Can the United States do anything to assist political and economic change in Burma-Myanmar?

The Reality

Soothsayers picked the date and time of independence and predicted a planned and prosperous future for Burma; U Nu's *pyidawtha* (cool, or happy, land) development program of moderate socialism was the goal. They were proven wrong about the future. Burma's past promise belies Myanmar's present reality.

Myanmar is not in a state of collapse; rather, if collapse indicates a previously economically developing or developed state, then it is precollapsed. As a set of some 67,000 essentially self-contained villages, it could limp along at barely subsistence levels if the state did not make egregious demands on its peasantry. Its recently burgeoning urban population is less dependent on urban services because most have strong and recent ties to the hinterland.

One-quarter of the population of Myanmar, according to the World Bank in 1999, lives below the poverty line and an equal percentage subsist at it, indicating that even a slight economic downturn would pauperize them. Income disparities are growing and becoming increasingly obvious. Rampant and fluctuating inflation—some 30 percent in 2002 but underreported by the state by an estimated 100 percent by knowledgeable observers—destroys living standards, and civil servants cannot live on their salaries.

Malnutrition, even hunger, exists; the extent is not known, but it is thought to be spreading and intensifying. Official statistics, always questionable and optimistic in Myanmar and subject to significant regional differences, indicate that the average family spends 71 percent of income on food alone, of which 20 percent is on rice. Infant mortality is higher than in any other country in the region except Laos and Cambodia.[9] Wasting affects 30 percent of children under ten years of age. The country's health care is said to be the world's second worst.

Educational standards have declined through school closures (sometimes for years), truncated schedules, inadequate teachers and facilities; a quarter of school-age children do not attend primary school, and only a third of them complete it. Per capita spending in constant currency on education has diminished even as the government has expanded the numbers of students at all levels of education. Private "tutorial" schools have been established to do what the public sector was intended to do—provide education and pay teachers—but these are expensive and the province of the relatively well-off.

Social service spending (health and education) in Myanmar is the lowest in the region as a percentage of the national budget, and its military budget is the highest. Foreign aid is minuscule; except for humanitarian assistance, it is mostly from China. In 1997, when foreign economic assistance to Myanmar was about US$1 per capita, it was US$14.70 in Vietnam, US$41.70 in Cambodia, and US$82.40 in Laos.[10] The minority areas, through both revolution and neglect, have been denied developmental opportunities. Through a web of tenuous ceasefires (in which, however, the former insurgents retain their arms), the government has access to many of those areas, but in some it is regarded as much the same as a foreign occupying army with its negative implications. Myanmar's military rulers exist in a self-constructed cocoon, isolated from most of the trauma associated with civilian life. The 450,000 troops plus their dependents have their own well-managed and -equipped educational and health facilities, their own distribution mechanisms for food and staples at subsidized prices, housing for dependents and jobs for many of them at military-run commercial factories and establishments, and even their own religious institutions. The Burmese military is a state within a state.

Yet this isolation is only half real. Although largely insulated from external social vicissitudes, the military's power pervades the state to a degree remarkable on any world scale. It can continue because it mandates its own budgets and is autonomous in its internal affairs. It also directly administers the government at all levels and controls the civil service, which is clearly subordinate to the military command. Civil society was essentially emasculated from

1962 to 1988, although since then it has been allowed to expand in apolitical spheres. No pluralistic centers of political power or influence exist beyond the purview of the state except those in direct revolution. It barely tolerates a titular opposition, composed of ten political parties, of which the over-whelmingly important one is the NLD, led by Aung San Suu Kyi. These par-ties are effectively prohibited from normal political and organizational activi-ties, and many members have been arrested.

The military still offers the greatest opportunities for the advancement of youth, since there are so few others. All avenues of social mobility—educa-tion, mass organizations, the *sangha* (monkhood)—are under military super-vision. Civil society, in a contradiction of the term, exists on the sufferance of the military command structure; it is, to paraphrase, alive and well and con-trolled by the government. The private business sector of any consequence is closely monitored and needs military acquiescence to succeed.[11] Capital for private economic activities and agricultural improvements is lacking, and incentives are generally absent, as the government owns all the land. Careers for the educated in business are still nascent. The ubiquitous Union Solidar-ity and Development Association (USDA) with some 16 million members, or about 38 percent of the total population, reaches virtually into every fam-ily, is mandated as under military control, and has some quasi-military train-ing as well as general educational functions. It was formed as an alternative to the BSPP, which had failed, and is likely to be used to support the military's position and views in any potential "civilianized" administration.[12] It is also used to turn out crowds for government-organized demonstrations.

The military has its own "private sector" as well, one distinct from public economic activities, the State Economic Enterprises, which it also controls. These include the operation of commercial factories under the Ministry of Defense's Office of Procurement that produce for the civilian market as well as for the military itself: the Myanmar Economic Holdings Corporation, formed as an autonomous organization under the Companies Act, and the Myanmar Economic Corporation, founded under a special edict. These two massive, military-run conglomerates will be outside of control of any future civilian administration. Together they have dozens of joint ventures with for-eign firms and employ hundreds of thousands of workers in a wide variety of businesses and industries.

Burmese industry is at the most elementary level of industrialization, swamped by cheaper and better goods smuggled or now legally imported from China and Thailand and further hindered by past jejune economic policies. Politically, although a member of the Association of Southeast Asian

Nations (ASEAN), the regime is regarded as a pariah in much of the industrialized world because of its political repression.[13]

Yet some of the military's national goals and programs, stripped of their excessive rhetoric, are unexceptionable. National unity, better health care and education, and preservation of national culture could be the goals of any developing state. Yet the methods the military employs to achieve these ends are leading to failure. The government believes with reason that its impressive accomplishments in building infrastructure of all sorts have been unappreciated outside Myanmar. But in some sense, the *tatmadaw* perhaps unconsciously equate construction with legitimacy, a very tenuous basis for noncoercive governance.[14]

The Causes

Some observers posit one of two causes for Myanmar's faltering. Foreign observers blame internal Burmese economic policies, and many Burmese (especially those in the military) blame foreign interference. Both are partly correct, but neither cause separately or together is an adequate explanation. Internally, macro- and micro-economic policies have been inept and ineptly administered. Externally, there have been problematic foreign influences. It is easy, but perhaps simplistic, to point to the failed economic policies of the governments of Burma-Myanmar, both civilian and military, as the primary forces of economic failure. There is no question that these policies have been more than instrumental in Burma-Myanmar's plight and may even have been the precipitating factors. But these policies are based on fundamental attitudes, which prompted the introduction and acceptance of these policies, not to mention the whimsical changes that continue to affect them.

All the sequential economic policies of the state since independence have failed. Moderate socialism under civilian leadership (1948–58, 1960–62) was poorly administered. Then doctrinaire and autarkic socialism (1963–72) under the military miserably miscarried under an already weakened bureaucracy, further purged by the military of its most knowledgeable civilian members. This was followed by a modified approach to socialism and the pursuit of foreign assistance (1972–88) and finally by the abandonment of the socialist system in 1988 (but not *dirigiste* attitudes toward the private sector) and the introduction of what was said to be a market economy and openings to foreign investment. All have been problematic in conception and execution.

A concatenation of policies has had calamitous effects on the economy, the quality of life, and foreign investment. These include internal planning and management that have been destructive of Burmese potential, exacerbated by poor macroeconomic policies such as the continued expansion of the money supply, which has fueled inflation (prices in the bazaar by the summer of 2002 had risen about fifteen times since 1988). Generally repressive agricultural production and procurement policies forced paddy sales to the state at far below market prices.[15] Excessive spending on defense (real levels of expenditure are hidden and probably total half of the government's budget), three demonetizations (the last and most disastrous in 1987 and one of the fundamental causes of the people's revolution of 1988), and arbitrary changes in economic investment and trade policies, together with ubiquitous and necessary corruption for lower level civil servants, all contribute to the problems.

The failure of economic, and with it social, performance by all governments of Burma-Myanmar also cannot be attributed alone to external events, although they have contributed to the economic malaise and are often blamed by Burmese nationalists. The optimistic miscalculations (by American advisers to that government) on the world price of rice following the Korean War were detrimental to Burmese economic planning and the delivery of social services; rice exports were less than half of those planned, and prices were lower. Later, the isolation of society and the withdrawal of most foreign economic assistance negatively affected development. Internal rebellions were sometimes surreptitiously assisted from abroad and denied the government effective economic control over perhaps a third of its land area. All Burma's neighbors and Britain and the United States indirectly supported these rebellions for a generation following independence, each for its own nationalistic objectives—the United States to encourage Chinese Nationalist troops to "retake" the mainland, the Thai to protect their frontier, the Chinese to spread communism, the Bangladeshi (East Pakistanis before them) to protect Muslims in the Arakan, and others as well.

These factors resulted in a perceived need for very high military expenditures, and a military rationale of security that remains internally, not externally, focused. The growing costs of imports and the low prices of Burmese exports, the sanctions imposed by the United States, and the Asian financial crisis of 1997 that effectively cut Asian direct foreign investment into Myanmar, all were factors in the economic doldrums into which Burma-Myanmar sank. The latest foreign influences on the economy have been the U.S. sanctions of 1997 and 2003 and the 2003 freezing of Burmese assets, which affects all U.S. dollar transactions going through U.S. banks. But these were not the sufficient or primary causes, which had roots in society itself and in its history.

More basic to an understanding of the dynamics of Burma-Myanmar as a failing economic state are deeply ingrained attitudes toward governance, permeating internal and external economic relations. These stem from a profound sense of vulnerability and a lack of cohesiveness that result in extreme nationalistic, even xenophobic, reactions to economic, social, and political issues. This vulnerability, not unusual in a state that once experienced a colonial occupation, seems to be more pervasive and has lasted longer in Burma-Myanmar than in many other societies because of unresolved ethnic issues and an unfortunate colonial history that is continuously exploited, and embellished, as a cause of current and past woes. Fundamental concepts of governance and power also detrimentally affect social, political, and economic progress.

Burma-Myanmar is a state yet not a nation. The military, echoing the writing of General Aung San who brought independence to Burma, continuously invokes the unity of the diverse peoples of society who have been together "in weal and woe." Yet the British separation of Ministerial Burma (essentially, the Burman ethnic areas) from the peripheral frontier areas (of minority peoples), which were governed separately on the Indian model (and until 1937 Burma was a province of India and governed first from Calcutta and then from Delhi), further split a society fomenting a lack of ethnic understanding, with suspicions and animosities that remain. Some two dozen ethnically based rebellions were prevalent in the peripheral areas when the SLORC took power in 1988. Within the space of a few years, the SLORC engaged in a series of negotiations, with about three-quarters of them resulting in ceasefires. The minority groups were allowed to retain their arms and to engage in traditional agriculture. The central government is attempting to supply social services to these groups and giving economic investment opportunities (mining, logging) to some.

By using ascriptive notions of ethnicity common in nineteenth-century Europe, and in claiming that the Shan, the Karen, and other groups are ethnic categories embodying living social formations with unique and independent histories, ethnic labels became reified into claims for the existence of political nations within Burma other than that recognized as the "Burmese" state.[16]

The numerous attempts by both civilian and military governments to create an overarching national ethos that could unite these diverse peoples have yet to succeed. With at least one-third of society composed of non-Burmans of various levels of political sophistication, population, religion, and potential economic influence, the appeals of Buddhism as the unifying force (although highly important among Burmans) were nationally unsuccessful, even divisive among significant Christian or Muslim populations. Then socialism as the secular ideology also failed, although it was strenuously pushed by the military, which saw it as having the potential (that Buddhism lacked) to unify the state and to help the state move forward economically. With the demise of socialism as ideology in 1988 (although the state's role in the economy remains pervasive), the present focus by the military on the military itself as the central and unifying element of society has yet to prove itself. History has been rewritten, massive military-related museums built, the past romanticized to show the military's efficacy and *cetena* (good will, actions taken with loving kindness).[17] The vulnerability of national unity, the cardinal element in the military's national goals, remains their most vital concern. The attempted imposition of a national ideology—from communism in the former centrally planned economies, to *juche* (autonomy, self-reliance) in North Korea, to *pancasila* in Indonesia—has failed. It is unlikely that the present emphasis on the military as the unifying force will rally the people, in spite of mass mobilization under military auspices.

This vulnerability is expressed through a fear of foreigners and their influence in society and economy. This attitude, based on historical memory, is understandable, though not unique among former colonies of the great imperial powers. Without exaggeration, it is accurate to state that during the colonial period the Burman population lost control not only over the political processes but also over their own economy. Europeans controlled the big businesses, and the British imported Indians to staff the bureaucracy, to take jobs as skilled professionals, to fill manual labor jobs, to man much of the military, and to work as subsidized indentured labor in the expanding rice-based economy of the Irrawaddy Delta. Indians controlled much of the trading and credit systems as well. Rangoon, Burma's capital, was as much an Indian as a Burmese city. In 1930, 53 percent of the population was Indian. The influx of Chinese both overland from Yunnan Province and by sea from South China filled the bazaars. The Burmans then were not only subordinated in governance, they were also relegated in large part to be mortgaged agricultural workers and petty traders in the bazaars. Although a small percentage of upper-class Burmans had the resources to be educated in England (and later became important in the politics of Burma), they were a limited and elite group.

Thus it was not primarily the Fabian socialism of the London School of Economics that influenced Burmese society, although that school of thought was fashionable at the time of the rise of Burmese nationalism and the struggle for independence and seemed to support Burmese and Buddhist interests.

It was rather the need—economically, socially, intellectually, and emotionally—to get the economy back under Burman control.[18] This has remained a cardinal element of Burmese thinking and is still evident after the 1988 demise of socialist policy and the openings to the private sector, both indigenous and foreign, wherein the government maintains a strongly *dirigiste* attitude toward all businesses. Suspicion of the development of autonomous centers of power in the business community, foreign and domestic, that could subvert control by the center seems also to be prevalent. In spite of some Burmans, including those in the military in their private capacities, making money in trading, there remains a strong suspicion of such activities as exploitive of the population. So in the caretaker government period, the army could simply force merchants to lower prices. As U Nu, civilian prime minister and devout Buddhist, remarked, capitalism bred greed, which was not a good Buddhist concept.

This negative attitude toward foreign intervention and control is not only prevalent in the sphere of economics but was and still is also evident in policy dialogue with foreigners on more fundamental issues and on attitudes toward foreign economic assistance. Pervasive in official announcements is also the belief that Burmese culture (more accurately, Burman culture) is under threat from the imposition of deleterious foreign influences (read, U.S. popular culture) and that subversion of society is the aim of foreigners through intermarriage of different "races" with the Burmans.[19]

The perceived vulnerability of the Burman population and authorities to the role of foreigners was exacerbated by the actual and implicit influence and support given by foreign entities to the internal rebellions that plagued the state then—and that continue at a more modest level. Surrounding states, in an earlier era after independence, contributed support to a variety of insurrections: Bangladesh (East Pakistan) to the Muslim rebels in the Arakan (Rakhine), India to the Nagas in northwest Burma and to some of the Chin, the Chinese to the Burma Communist Party, and the Thai at various levels to a variety of insurrectionist "buffer states" along the western Thai littoral (to protect the conservative government in Bangkok from the "radical" regime in Rangoon). British elements have been accused of fostering independence among the Karen, and the United States covertly supported the remnant Chinese Nationalist (Kuomintang) troops who retreated into Burma in 1949–50.

The relationships between individual minority peoples and their ethnic peers across international frontiers have been significant as well, because the borders of the state imposed by the colonial powers were ethnically arbitrary and took no account of ethnicity. Thus the minorities had stronger external ties than did the Burmans, who were the only major ethnic group completely contained within the state. There is a Shan (Tai) autonomous region in Yunnan (Sipsong Banna), and there are, for example, more Kachins in China than in the Kachin state in Burma, more Nagas than are in India (Nagaland). The Chin in Burma are part of the Mizo group in India (Mizoram), the Karen and Mon straddle the Thai border, and the Arakanese are closely related by religion and culture to the Bangladeshis. This outward orientation was made more acute by the fact that Christian populations were in contact with international Christian movements and that Burmese Muslim groups were subject to Middle Eastern influences. Such outward orientation increased the Buddhist Burman sense of isolation, already exacerbated by the political and economic policy of cutting off the country from the outside world. Significantly, the higher ranks of the military have been stripped of minority officers, and promotions to higher ranks seem to require Buddhist allegiance.

Critical to effective governance in the modern world is a pervasive Burman political culture that affects both modernization and development. Power is conceived of as limited, not infinite, so sharing or delegating it (individually, institutionally, geographically) becomes difficult. As a zero-sum game, to share it is to lose it. Power thus becomes highly personalized, with loyalty not to institutions but to leaders. This results in factionalism; the development of entourages in highly structured and hierarchical relationships; a system of rent seeking to grease the skids of such entourages; control of information (and thus the sponsorship of orthodoxy and control over media and publishing); and the discouragement of pluralistic centers of power (which are in danger of developing in a growing civil society with significant local autonomy and an influential private business sector). Some argue that Burmese politics are atavistic.[20]

These tendencies are reinforced by a military command system that makes more taut the hierarchical structure and in which the leadership—the single individual who eventually emerges at the apex of the hierarchy—is insulated from external education and concepts, operates with only a limited understanding of external administration and norms, and whose decisions are not to be contradicted, even questioned, yet who is often shielded from unpleasant but vital information as data are manipulated.[21]

Further, the Burmese fear of foreigners and lack of understanding of their operations have been made more evident and palpable through both world developments and their impact on Burma-Myanmar. Although Japan has been the primary donor to Burma-Myanmar since independence in 1948—supplying more than half of all bilateral and multilateral economic assistance (US$2.2 billion until 1988)—it is the United States, with its industrialized influence and military power, about which the government seems most concerned.[22]

U.S. Interests in Burma-Myanmar

To the United States, Burma was a British preserve until World War II, except for American Baptist missionaries who, mostly in the nineteenth century, worked effectively among non-Burman, non-Buddhist groups, some of whom readily responded to their new teachings. The United States significantly contributed to the campaign to wrest Burma from the Japanese, who had occupied that country early in World War II.[23] At an emotional or ideological level, President Franklin Roosevelt was interested in freeing the colonies from their colonial masters throughout Asia, but little real action took place in that regard. U.S. interests in Burma were essentially a product of the cold war.

The defeat of the Kuomintang Nationalist government in China in 1949 and the formation of the People's Republic of China in 1950, together with the Korean War that same year, gave immediate focus to the anticommunist sentiment in the United States, which had already become apparent in Europe and in the American military occupation of South Korea (1945–48). An official investigative team was sent from Washington in 1950 to the countries of Asia, including Burma, to see what types of assistance the United States might provide to stem this perceived communist advance (communist-inspired uprisings in Burma, the Philippines, Malaya, and Vietnam). Although the magnitude of such aid and the administration of its provisions were nowhere comparable to the U.S. Marshall Plan that had assisted Western Europe in its recovery from World War II for similar anticommunist reasons, the precedent had been set, and U.S. foreign assistance programs soon followed.

Burma was the first country to recognize the People's Republic of China (PRC), and since that time, in spite of problems in the relationship, Burma may have felt it had to be neutral in the cold war and in the Sino-Soviet dispute, but it was always a neutrality in the shadow of a vast China and with an eye on the Chinese reaction. Given the long, indefensible border with China and China's massive population, Burma has always been vulnerable.[24] The U.S. aid program started soon after Burmese independence, but because of covert U.S. and Taiwanese support to the nationalist troops that had fled from Yunnan into Burma (and who, with U.S. prodding, hoped to "re-invade" China and overthrow the People's Republic), the Burmese government under U Nu was fearful that the Chinese would pursue them into Burmese territory over which the Burmese central government (and indeed Shan state government) had little or no control. In spite of vehement but misleading U.S. denials that the Central Intelligence Agency (CIA) was funding Kuomintang (KMT) troops, the Burmese government stopped the U.S. aid program.[25]

In 1956 the program was restarted, and it lasted through the coup of 1962 and into the beginnings of the socialist period. It was again stopped in 1964 by mutual agreement because of rigid socialist policies and disagreement about projects, especially the siting of the proposed new road to Mandalay.[26] With a change in foreign assistance policy at the first BSPP Congress in June–July 1971 when the decision to seek foreign aid was endorsed, and following the end of the Vietnam War in 1975, the Burmese may have felt more comfortable in requesting the restart of U.S. assistance in 1978.[27] Because the previous agreement between the U.S. and Burmese governments on the administrative aspects of the assistance program was never terminated but was just held in abeyance, the program could then easily be resuscitated. That program, focused on basic human needs, lasted until the coup of 1988, when it was once again ended by the United States.[28]

The cold war and the perceived threat of Chinese expansion were not the only reasons the United States sought to continue good relations with Burma.[29] Rangoon, with both Chinese and Soviet embassies active there, was a useful listening post for observing the Sino-Soviet split, and both countries had foreign assistance programs.

The United States was also concerned with the trade in heroin, which was flooding the United States from Burma. Stopping the production and supply of opium—which was converted into a morphine base and then into heroin—became a U.S. priority, so the United States supplied equipment and helicopters to carry out narcotics surveillance and interdiction. The equipment was to be used solely for antinarcotics activities, but it became apparent that it was used against the Karen rebels, who shot one down, and also used to transport military officials on non-narcotics-related trips.

Burmese heroin production at that time supplied some 75 percent of the world market (that "honor" now goes to Afghanistan), but the opium was grown in remote areas of the country over which the central government had no control. The narcotics trade was able to fuel the supply of arms to various insurgent groups. Although the Burma Communist Party (BCP) eschewed opium production in its territories as long as it was supported by the PRC, when that support stopped, the BCP went into production in the Wa tribal areas. This production continues today, although it is significantly lowered. The U.S. State Department's periodic reporting on narcotics in Burma indicates that although the local military must either acquiesce to or be involved in the production or movement of narcotics, it has no evidence that the central Burmese authorities directly benefit from the trade. Nonetheless, according to some observers, narcotics principals who have surrendered live undisturbed in Rangoon and have invested in legitimate businesses there.[30] The United States calls this money laundering. Myanmar is engaged in an extensive antiopium campaign. Production has dropped to 850 tons in 2001 from 2,500 tons at its peak some years earlier, and the Burmese government has destroyed about 8 percent of production.[31]

Since the failed people's revolution against the BSPP military regime, the coup of 1988 designed to shore up military control over society, and the end of the cold war, U.S. interests have been refocused. U.S. concerns from 1988 through the end of the Clinton administration concentrated on the absence of political rights in Myanmar, including the military's denial of the results of the May 1990 elections, which were swept by the opposition NLD led by Aung San Suu Kyi (who had been under house arrest since July 1989). When she received the Nobel Peace Prize in 1991, she became an international symbol of the fight against political oppression. Essentially, U.S. policy from 1988 through 2001 was on a single track: human rights. Economic, strategic, narcotics, even humanitarian issues were not pursued. The human rights policy was in part dictated and supported by an effective human rights lobby in the United States and the industrialized world; the lobby comprises various nongovernmental organizations and expatriate Burmese and is mobilized in large part through the Internet. Reflecting the views of Aung San Suu Kyi, these activists have advocated a boycott on tourism, trade, investment, and NGO activities as providing support to and legitimating that military junta. Some of these positions, such as on NGO operations, have been modestly modified.

Had not the military coup been so brutal in 1988 in repressing the popular riots throughout the country, the United States and the industrialized world would have welcomed the most important economic policy change by the military since 1962: the abandonment of socialism and the opening of the economy to both the foreign and domestic private sectors. Private interests, both U.S. and international, did exploit Burmese natural resources, most specifically oil and natural gas. The Burmese themselves became a controlled, literate, productive, and low-cost labor force for the production of, for example, textiles and garments. Prompted by Congress (in which no member could be seen to be voting in favor of a "pariah regime"), which in turn was spurred by human rights groups and activists, the United States imposed sanctions in 1997 on all new U.S. investment in the country (an arms embargo had existed since the coup of 1988, and the foreign assistance program, which had been focused on basic human needs, had also been closed down) as punishment for the suppression of political rights.[32]

Although the U.S. government, especially the legislative branch that was effectively lobbied by articulate and well-coordinated human rights groups, was reluctant to become economically engaged, other countries were not so reluctant. Until the Asian financial crisis of 1997, which effectively dried up investment in Myanmar, since much of it came from the ASEAN states, approved foreign investment totaled more than US$6 billion (actual projects were probably one-third of that total). Investment has since restarted, and Myanmar is increasingly used as a site for garment production, as other states used Burma's quotas for export to the United States.[33] This came to an end with U.S. sanctions in 2003, but Burma's share of textiles into the United States would have dropped in any case with the end of the Multifiber Agreement on December 31, 2004.

As the internal economic, social, and political ills of Myanmar spread across the borders in the region, the neighboring states and the United States began to pay more attention. Some 130,000 Karen and fewer Mon refugees, fleeing political repression and war, are in camps in Thailand along the Myanmar border. Perhaps one million illegal workers from the Shan state and other areas are either seeking employment or are moving under forced evacuation from what has become free-fire zones, in which the military tries to deny to Shan rebels the bases of local support. Drug trafficking, the exploitation of women for prostitution, and the rapid and alarming spread of HIV-AIDS, where the highest rates in Thailand and China are along the Myanmar littoral, have become regional concerns. The World Health Organization estimates that there may be 420,000 cases; the government, after years of denial, admits to 180,000.

Aung San Suu Kyi, the NLD, and their supporters abroad had vigorously campaigned against humanitarian assistance, foreign investment, and tourism because of supposed benefits to the military and its legitimation. With the deepening of the crisis and the release of Aung San Suu Kyi from virtual house arrest in May 2002, this attitude has been modified. The need for increased humanitarian assistance to Myanmar mainly through international NGOs, often but not always under the UN Development Program umbrella, has been understood both by the military and the opposition.

Burmese authorities have permitted international NGO activities under individual ad hoc arrangements; now several dozen NGOs have operations in the country, many with resident offices and local staffs. These organizations work with local apolitical groups focusing on everything from rural development, health, nutrition, and education, to microcredit projects and community development. Such international groups offer no threat to local or national authorities. Some are encouraged by the government to work with local arms of state-sponsored organizations, such as the USDA, but in general even groups at the local level have a degree of marginal, noncontroversial autonomy on some local problems. The rationale behind this effort in overall developmental terms is the re-creation of local civil society organizations, which eventually could have a positive impact both on development and on the growth of pluralism in society.

Opium production has decreased markedly in Myanmar, partly due to weather but mostly to the increased efforts of the Burmese government. Yet the shift has been away from poppy production and its agricultural base as a subsistence crop for upland farmers to the chemical production of methamphetamines, which have flooded Thailand and have become a political issue there. Thus continued major production of methamphetamines indicates that the central government cannot or will not control the trade. The Thai estimate that from 700 million to 1 billion tablets were smuggled into Thailand from Myanmar in 2001. Through the United Nations program, the United States has been supporting their antinarcotics efforts. In early 2003, the Thai Thaksin government began a major crackdown on the illegal Thai trade in narcotics, with the resulting death of an estimated 3,000 people: alleged dealers, others associated with the trade, and innocent bystanders. Thai civil rights groups have protested these actions.

Of less concern, but of great potential importance to the United States, is the strategic place of Myanmar. Myanmar is a nexus of potential rivalries among China, India, and the ASEAN states. In the Sino-Indian War of 1962, Burma flanked the still disputed border between those two countries. Although China may not feel a threat from India, the reverse is not true. Indian defense minister Fernandes announced in the late 1990s that China was India's potential enemy. Chinese penetration of Myanmar has been extensive, in the supply of military materiel (some US$2 billion in arms and equipment), the training of officers, the construction of infrastructure, a growing influence on the economy, and massive illegal migration into the country to take advantage of clear economic opportunities that are denied to provinces in Southwest China, such as Yunnan.[34] Senior General Than Shwe, chairman of the SPDC, went to Beijing in January 2003, where he received approval for US$200 million in loans and US$5 million in technical assistance grants. Of concern to India and to Japan (which views China's preeminent role in Myanmar as strengthening the PRC) as well has been the apparent effort by China to gain access to the Bay of Bengal and the Malacca Straits.[35] India, which for several years following the coup of 1988 pursued a strong anti-SLORC policy, changed to a policy of accommodation because of the likelihood of continued military control and the apparent rise of Chinese influence. The entry of Myanmar into the ASEAN in July 1997 was, many say, in part prompted by ASEAN concerns to limit Chinese influence in Myanmar as much as by Burmese interests in tapping into ASEAN direct investment in that country and increased international legitimacy. In early 2003 a classified U.S. report was leaked to *Jane's* in London indicating that, in the aftermath of Indian-U.S. cooperation in antiterrorist activities, these two countries agreed to form a strategic association to counter potential Chinese influence in the region.

Thailand, with which the United States has a defense treaty, has had a delicate relationship with Burma-Myanmar. The Burmese destruction of the Thai capital of Ayuthia in 1767 still causes deep resentment,[36] and although the Democratic Party government of Thailand under Chuaan Leekpai pushed for more pluralism and better human rights in Myanmar, the government of Prime Minister Thaksin Shinawatra (who was elected in 2001) had closer relations with the Burmese military. In May–August 2002, a proxy war was fought along the border, which was closed from May 22 to October 15, 2002, to the economic detriment of many on both sides, as the Thai-supported Shan state army fought against the Burmese-supported Wa troops over the trafficking of methamphetamines. At the same time, the antipathy of the United States toward the regime in Rangoon is interpreted by that government as an effort to overthrow it because Myanmar is the weakest link in the containment policy of the United States toward China.[37]

As the economic conditions in Myanmar deteriorated—caused by bad management, unpredictable swings in economic policies, ubiquitous corruption, the Asian financial crisis of 1997, and the sanctions and voluntary withdrawal of some foreign investment—the plight of the Burmese peasantry became a focal point for foreign donors. The UN specialized agencies resident in Myanmar released a statement in June 2001 noting that the situation had reached crisis proportions and called on potential donors to respond to this as quickly as possible with more humanitarian assistance. In June 2000, various international NGOs resident in Myanmar issued a statement of operating principles essentially eschewing any political intent in their programs.

The perceived vulnerability of the Burmese to U.S. intervention in the eyes of the Burmese military leadership, no matter how far-fetched and illogical to Americans given the paucity of U.S. vital interests in that country, is still palpable in high-level Burmese military circles. In 1988 stories circulated about a U.S. aircraft carrier sent to the Bay of Bengal to prevent the coup, although some argue that if it were there, it was to evacuate resident Americans in the wake of the riots, which at that time seemed out of hand. Burmese military intelligence in the mid-1990s interviewed many prominent Burmese and asked which side they would be on if there were an American invasion. When they were told several years later that the United States has no national interest in invading or intervening militarily in that country, responsible Burmese officials respond noting the examples of Afghanistan, Kosovo, Iraq, Haiti, Panama, and Grenada.[38] The fear of U.S. military action, however unrealistic to foreign observers, is palpable to the Burmese leadership. U.S.-Thai military exercises ("Cobra Gold") excite the Burmese. Fear of U.S. intervention may be a factor in the 2005 movement of critical Burmese ministries (defense, home affairs, information, industry, and so on) to the central Burmese town of Pyinmana.

The United States has been the international leader opposed to the military regime in Myanmar. It imposed sanctions and refused to nominate an ambassador (there is a U.S. embassy with a chargé d'affaires). It has denied visas to high-ranking Burmese officials and their families and has stated that the Burmese are not in compliance with U.S. antinarcotics desiderata (even of a lowered bar legislated to enable Mexico to qualify). The U.S. Department of State and members of Congress have complained about human rights and the illegitimacy of the military since it refused to recognize the results of the 1990 elections and essentially vetoed any potential multilateral assistance on political grounds (should Myanmar meet the economic requirements of those organizations). These policies were pursued through the end of the Clinton administration. Some of these policies were initiated by Congress, others by the administration, especially prompted by the close association of U.S. Secretary of State Madeleine Albright with Aung San Suu Kyi. Whatever the source, the Clinton administration did not seem prepared to use up any political ammunition with Congress to fight for policy changes that were less stark in their approach to the Burmese military.

Until 2002 the position of the United States has been to demand that the Burmese authorities recognize the results of the May 1990 election and thus allow the NLD to take control of the government. This has been tantamount to saying to the junta, Get out of power and then the United States will talk to you. This obviously has not been effective. The result of this policy and the polarization of attitudes toward that country has been the lack of any nuanced, moderate policies designed in the first instance to assist the Burmese peoples in dealing with their economic plight. Even the information that is available to the outside world becomes simplistically polarized between that emanating from the Burmese military justifying its actions (or lack thereof) and that from the opposition doing the same. Dialogue for years has been impossible.

U.S. Interests in Burma-Myanmar: Terrorism and Changing Patterns of Relations

In October 2000, the military began a quiet, unannounced dialogue with Aung San Suu Kyi, who was under a modified house arrest at that time. Fostered and encouraged by Ambassador Tun Sri Razali Ismail, the UN secretary-general's personal representative, and backed by Prime Minister Mahathir of Malaysia, this tentative effort at confidence building was well along at the time of the September 11, 2001, attacks on the United States and the subsequent U.S. war on terrorism. These two events, the dialogue and the response to the September 11 attacks, were on parallel paths, which seemed to have merged in 2002.[39]

The United States sought to expand the search for terrorist cells and training facilities throughout the world, and significantly one important focus was Southeast Asia. Indonesia was the world's largest Muslim country, and one that was said to harbor such cells, but radical Islam had been held in political check by former president Suharto, who recognized that these tenets were destabilizing both to his country and to his regime.[40] The bombing of discotheques frequented by foreigners in Bali in October 2002 gave new urgency to these worries. Southeast Asia became another center of U.S. concern. This was also the case in the Philippines, in which an active Muslim rebellion had been under way for decades. The United States sent in troops as trainers to the southern Philippines, and supplied equipment, in what has yet to be demonstrated as an effective operation and that seemed more a political statement by the United States than a strike at core al Qaeda organizations. Singapore had unearthed an evident al Qaeda plot to attack

U.S. naval personnel in that country after U.S. troops discovered plans to do so in Kabul.

"Terrorism" has become a popular designation in Myanmar, with meanings varying according to the political position of each party. So the Burmese government calls all dissidents terrorists, and the opposition in that country calls the government terrorists. On the occasion of the visit to Myanmar of the Vietnamese president, Tran Duc Luong, May 5–8, 2002, both countries issued a joint statement of cooperation against terrorism. Shortly thereafter, the annual ASEAN Senior Officials Meeting on Transnational Crime took place in Kuala Lumpur, May 15–17, 2002. The Burmese indicated that there was no evidence that drug money was used to finance international terrorist groups. This meeting was followed by the ASEAN Special Ministerial Meeting on Terrorism, although Myanmar indicated that it was not necessary at that time to join in the trilateral pact on antiterrorism signed by Malaysia, Indonesia, and the Philippines.[41]

Myanmar, suspicious of U.S. intentions but fearing a U.S. intervention, demonstrated an interest in improving U.S. relations and was quick to respond in a positive manner to U.S. interests in antiterrorism. The government is said to have supplied the United States with any intelligence information that the Burmese might have, allowed military overflights to the Middle East, and taken steps to protect physically from terrorist attack the very vulnerable U.S. embassy building in downtown Yangon by sealing off that portion of the street on which the embassy is situated. The Burmese government spokesman said, "We then subsequently learned that some of these individuals [Muslim rebels in the Arakan] were actually trained by the Taliban in Afghanistan, as well as in terrorist training camps in the Middle East. The Myanmar government, practicing zero-tolerance policy in such matters, vigorously confronted the activities of this group threatening the national as well as regional security. While the government of Myanmar and the United States have had differences in the years past, we are pragmatically in full agreement that terrorists must be given no sanctuary."[42]

A videotape acquired by CNN from al Qaeda in Afghanistan purports to show Burmese being trained by that group inside Burma.[43] Any involvement with al Qaeda was denied by the Arakan Rohingya National Organization and by the Muslim Liberation Organization of Burma.[44] But some Muslims feel that their coreligionists in Myanmar have been oppressed. According to the August 1996 edict issued by al Qaeda, "Massacres in Tajikistan, Burma, Kashmir, Assam, the Philippines, Fatani, Ogaden, Somalia, Eritrea, Chechnya, and Bosnia-Herzegovina have taken place," and Osama bin Laden is said to have boasted of having agents in a variety of countries, including Burma.[45]

Burmese motivations for cooperation were probably fourfold: the generalized suspicions of the Burman military authorities toward the Muslims in the country, the fear of U.S. intervention should it be demonstrated that there were al Qaeda cells in the country, a useful and internationally acceptable rationale for cracking down on Muslim groups in insurrection, and a general attempt to improve relations with the United States. It may also be relevant that this served the Burmese strategic purposes as well, since the Chinese had expressed interest in cooperation with the United States on the war on terrorism because of their vulnerability to the fundamental Islam of the Muslim Uighur population in Xinjiang Province. On August 1, 2002, Myanmar signed the U.S.-ASEAN Joint Declaration for Cooperation to Combat International Terrorism at a meeting in Brunei, which the U.S. secretary of state attended.

More fundamentally, the Burman-Muslim relationship has been uneasy since the colonial period. Although official Burmese statistics indicate that about 4 percent of the population is Muslim, Muslim sources say the figure may be as high as 10 percent. Buddhist-Muslim riots broke out in the 1930s as a result of charges that the Muslims were defaming Buddhism. Whatever may have been the immediate religious causes of the attacks, more fundamental economic rivalries certainly have played an underlying role, especially during the depression era, when Burma was hard hit. There have been vicious charges for decades that Muslims are out to subvert the Burman "race" by paying Muslim men to marry and convert Burman Buddhist women: the higher the status of the women, the higher the reward.[46] Most important, there has been continuous trouble in Rakhine state (Arakan) with the extensive Muslim population there. The area on the Burma side of the Burma-Bangladesh (formerly East Pakistan) border is essentially Muslim territory. There has been since Burmese independence a Muslim autonomy or independence insurrection in that area, supported first from East Pakistan and funded with Middle Eastern monies. Suspicion of Muslims has been traditionally important and has been exacerbated by these separatist movements. Harassment and attacks by the Burmese military in the late 1970s, ostensibly checking on citizenship and related matters, led to an exodus of some 200,000 Muslim refugees from Burma into Bangladesh; they were repatriated by the United Nations only after considerable time. A similar problem arose in the early 1990s, resulting in another movement of about 200,000 Muslims into Bangladesh, where some 20,000 still remain after the others were repatriated under UN auspices. There were also anti-Muslim riots in Sittwe (Akyab).

Violence against Muslims has also been apparent in other areas, most recently in Toungoo, Prome, and Pegu in 2001 and in a variety of other cities.[47] In May 2001, more than a thousand people led by monks attacked Muslims and their shops, homes, and mosques in Toungoo. In Prome in October 2001, and in February 2001 in Akyab (Sittwe), riots broke out, resulting in curfews in both cities.[48] Although reports have often said that the destruction of mosques and the burning of Muslim homes were triggered by personal incidents, not by political motivation, there are charges that the military may have deflected and focused dissatisfaction against the regime and its economic failures on to an unpopular minority.[49] Yet it is also obvious that the military has been fearful that such religious antagonisms might get out of hand. It suppressed all reporting and mention in the controlled press of the Taliban's destruction of the large Buddhist statues in Bamiyan, Afghanistan, for fear of Burman Buddhist violent actions against Muslims and their property. Yet reports indicate that some fourteen people were killed, and much larger, unconfirmed estimates indicate that perhaps hundreds have died.

Burmese government cooperation with the United States and the beginnings of an improvement in relations, however tentative, had come with the Bush administration's temporary tempering of policy toward Myanmar. In its February 2002 assessment of the previous six-month situation in Burma-Myanmar by the U.S. Department of State, for the first time there was a movement away from the ritual of demanding that the military step aside and honor the results of the May 1990 election and bring the NLD into power. In that document, the May 1990 election was not mentioned, and instead the U.S. Department of State called for progress in the process of democratic governance and improvement in human rights and indicated that the United States would respond positively to such changes.

This quiet yet substantial change, modifying the personal diplomacy that had developed between Madeleine Albright as U.S. secretary of state and Aung San Suu Kyi, opened the way for the release of "the lady," as she is referred to in Rangoon, from house arrest in May 2002. It seems apparent that with Aung San Suu Kyi having access to key U.S. congressional figures, if she had not acquiesced to such a change in advance, there would have been an outcry from Congress.[50] This has not happened, although the United States has not yet changed its policies on other aspects of the relationship with the regime, such as sanctions and withholding an ambassadorial appointment to Rangoon.

Frustration with the lack of anticipated dialogue, and perhaps prompted by pressures from the Republican-controlled Congress following the November 2000 elections in the United States, the administration quietly readjusted its policies in late November,[51] reverting to its insistence on honoring the results of the May 1990 election and refusing to recognize that Myanmar was in compliance with the anti-narcotics criteria, criteria that had been lowered to accommodate Mexico's compliance and with which Myanmar would have complied.

The year 2003 brought further regression in the developed world's relations with Myanmar. The United States took the lead in protesting the regime's actions. Myanmar had already been buffeted by a bank crisis in the spring, when a type of pyramid scheme by bank-related financial institutions that had offered 5 percent interest a month on investments collapsed. Then, as Aung San Suu Kyi continued to make government-approved travels throughout the country that met with enthusiastic responses, including those in minority areas, the military appears to have ordered their controlled civil groups to ambush the opposition motorcade one night in Central Burma. In the resulting melee on May 30, 2003, the government claimed that four people had been killed, but opposition and other credible observers claim some seventy had died. Aung San Suu Kyi was barely saved from harm and was then whisked into "preventive detention," which once again became house arrest. Although the government claimed that the opposition fomented the disturbances, this was not credible. Observers indicate it was ordered from on high. The dilemma facing the government was whether to release Aung San Suu Kyi and placate international opinion. She might have demanded justice for the deaths of her supporters—and thus further embarrassed the regime. The previous dialogue was not only over, the level of distrust and acrimony had fallen to new lows.

In response, the U.S. Congress quickly passed the Burmese Freedom and Democracy Act of 2003 on July 28, 2003, followed by an executive order. The measures imposed had long been advocated by Senator Mitch McConnell, who had become the Republican whip and thus of singular importance to the Bush administration. These introduced sanctions against all Burmese imports into the United States, extended the ban on higher-level travel by Burmese officials of the USDA, and froze Burmese assets. This sweeping legislation stopped the export of Burmese garment manufactures (worth some US$356 million and the second-largest foreign exchange earner—after natural gas—of the state) and also halted the activities of most financial transactions from most countries (as they often went through U.S.

banks), including temporarily the payments of foreign embassies in Myanmar and the humanitarian activities of nongovernmental organizations, most of which operate in U.S. dollars. Even educational materials were not exempt from import restrictions, although this was rescinded a month later. Although Myanmar began operating in other currencies, and NGOs were granted licenses to operate in the country, these acts were emotional reactions that forced the nationalistic military rulers into articulated resistance. To resolve this dilemma, a solution that involves face-saving measures for all three parties—the military, the NLD, and the United States—needs to be sought. For the first time, higher-level military and civilians were calling for some form of foreign adjudication.

Future Issues for Burma-Myanmar

The gentle glacial thaw in Burmese-U.S. relations was welcomed as long as it lasted, and although it seemed as slow as global warming, it was over by the late spring of 2003, when confrontation and mutual recrimination became the norm. The Malaysian prime minister Mahathir, in an August 2002 investment trip to Myanmar, advocated a slow and deliberate return to democracy, and this was echoed by Prime Minister General Khin Nyunt. The situation has since deteriorated.

The global hegemony of the United States in terms of its superpower status gives it only limited leverage in various regional situations, and Myanmar is one such case. Because of the war on terrorism, the United States will have to pay more attention to the ASEAN countries, to which the United States has generally responded only in times of stress, as in Indonesia during the Asian financial crisis of 1997 and the fall of Suharto. This, and the slow, but now defunct, movement toward some form of political accommodation within Myanmar, might have meant a greater and more positive role for the United States, although this possibility has now definitely faded. The United States vigorously and publicly lobbied against Myanmar's entry into the ASEAN in July 1997 at its meeting in Kuala Lumpur. The United States agreed in the summer of 2002 to support an anti-AIDS education campaign to which both the military and the NLD agreed in principle. But to enable the United States to resume full, normal relationships with Burma-Myanmar will require extraordinary measures. The Republican leadership in Congress has vigorously opposed amelioration of the U.S. policies, and such attitudes have been reinforced by the seeming intransigence of the SPDC leadership, specifically Senior General Than Shwe, toward political liberalization.

It is relatively simple to impose sanctions on any regime; it is extremely difficult to remove them because there is a tendency for the goal posts, as the Burmese have said, to be moved and more demands placed on a target administration based on the political agendas in the sanctioning country. Any solution to the political problems of Myanmar will require compromise and likely fall far short of the absolutist human rights and justice positions demanded by some of the most vocal of the opposition supporters abroad. When the NLD compromises in some manner, these supporters may feel betrayed as they have regarded the Burma-Myanmar cause as one of the most clear-cut moral political issues in the world. Convincing a U.S. administration to use up political good will with Congress on Burma-Myanmar, when it is one of the lowest priorities on the complex Asian policy agenda facing the administration, is highly unlikely.

Chinese relations with Myanmar will come in for more scrutiny. The Burmese may be fearful of China's potential role, but they may play their "China card" by arguing for greater U.S. flexibility on Myanmar political issues in return for limiting Chinese influence. If they were to take such an approach, they may find that Chinese penetration is already too extensive to be pushed back. Whether the United States characterizes its relationship with China as "containment" or "strategic competitor," it will have to examine more closely Myanmar's relationship to China and its importance as the prime example of Chinese economic and security influence and expansion in Southeast Asia. Myanmar has become a strategic nexus in Southeast Asia.

Because of their influx, access to credit through informal channels, and knowledge of international markets, the Chinese may compose the future middle class in Myanmar, with the danger that the Burmese once again will see their economy slip under foreign control. China needs to be convinced that the present stasis will lead to instability in a country that the Chinese have said is in their direct national interest and, thus, that Myanmar must reform in some appropriate manner. For political progress a timetable is needed, but the Burmese authorities have been most reluctant to agree to such an approach, although they have been asked many times by a variety of governments. It is likely that whatever compromise evolves over time, the military will retain veto power over the essential issues facing what it regards as state survival. This should come as no surprise, as this as been the situation since Burmese independence in 1948. The issues on which compromise is unlikely and that the military will want to control, in addition to prevention of retaliation against individual army officers for crimes committed, are the autonomy of the military and its budgets and operations, the independence of the military-controlled private industrial and business interests, and most important, the unity of the state.

Although international attention has been focused on immediate political and human rights issues, the most intractable problem facing that country is the development of some fair and equitable (to all parties) distribution of power and the assets of the state among the various ethnic groups in the country. This is a problem no administration has yet resolved, and it is likely to be the most difficult of issues. This requires at the same time, or as a result, the formulation of an ethos that will move the country from a state to a nation. It is likely that such an ethos cannot be mandated by a government all too prone to intervene in the ideological and intellectual activities of its citizenry. It is evident that the most effective means to garner such support is through fears of an external enemy, real or imagined. This was the case in 2002 with the Thai-Myanmar border dispute. The potential role of the United States as such a danger is always in the background.

The dilemma for foreign governments is whether isolation or engagement will alleviate or solve the present impasse in Myanmar. The United States, often backed by the European Community, believes that isolation will topple the military, while Japan, Thailand, and the ASEAN countries consider that engagement will be more effective. Neither approach has proven adequate to the task as of the summer of 2003, but the history of Burma-Myanmar suggests that isolation is less likely to be effective. The Burmese believed they could retreat into isolation, as theirs was a rich country. This is no longer true, and isolation is no longer possible. General Ne Win could cut the country off in 1962; General Than Shwe cannot do so today. International news pours into the country through television dishes, through tourists, and through international publications (though censored). The resource base of the state has been mismanaged and is not as productive as it once was, and demographics have changed the country's population. Globalization and the advancement of all of Myanmar's neighbors, and their attractions for jobs and goods and services, are now too important. Isolation is not an internal option and is a questionable external one as well.

Since 2004 the situation has deteriorated. Prime Minister Khin Nyunt, head of military intelligence and the junta member responsible for and most interested in international relations, was dismissed for tolerating corruption, tried, and found guilty but given a suspended sentence. His large entourage was dismissed, limiting the capacity of military intelligence to prevent terrorist-type bombings in Rangoon and Mandalay in the spring of 2005. The junta in July 2005 determined that it would not host the 2006 ASEAN summit, as ASEAN was under strong pressure from the United States and the European Union to prevent this, but the military continues to claim that it will adhere to its road map of completing the National Convention, formulating a new constitution, holding a referendum on it, and then having a multiparty election leading to what it calls disciplined democracy. Until the constitution is completed, there is every indication that Aung San Suu Kyi will remain under house arrest. This effectively limits any improvement in U.S.-Burmese relations. The movement of government ministries upcountry to Pyinmana may be an indication that the military is turning more inward, relying on its own resources and assistance from China and India.

The United States is usually suspect—treated with suspicion as advocating the breakup of the state. Minimally, the United States together with the countries bordering Myanmar could publicly reaffirm the territorial integrity of the state. This is, of course, simply reaffirming the status quo, but it might prove to be a useful reminder that the United States regards the development of a viable, prosperous, and united Burma-Myanmar as in the U.S. national interest.

It is also apparent that if there were to be a road map or a set of benchmarks, the United States should not simply list all the reforms that it feels are needed, but rather it should indicate specific reactions that would follow from positive Burmese actions. This has already begun in the field of antinarcotics programs, in which the United States has indicated the specific steps needed for the U.S. administration to certify that Burma is in compliance with its antinarcotics criteria. Such changes in Myanmar might include a joint SPDC-NLD movement on a new constitution, a timetable for its completion, the release of political prisoners, the announcement of new elections, economic reforms and stabilization efforts, and so on. The United States then could sequentially, as each action is announced or takes place, lift the ban on visas for high officials; nominate an ambassador; agree to lift restrictions on Myanmar seeking World Bank, International Monetary Fund, or Asian Development Bank support if Myanmar meets their economic criteria; agree to the removal of sanctions; and at some point provide an appropriate level of foreign assistance.

At the same time, the United States should encourage, or offer no objections to, NGOs working in that country on humanitarian assistance projects; it should also support Japanese efforts to increase humanitarian support.[52] But full-scale developmental assistance from any source should be dependent on changes in economic policies. One lesson from the aid programs of the 1970s and 1980s was the lack of substantive economic policy changes in that period: too much unrestricted assistance was provided without concurrent economic progress. Admiral Dennis Blair's proposal to fund antiterrorism training for the Burmese in Defense Department programs, to establish "a few effective connections with the newer elements of the military could (also) make a difference in our ability to ameliorate both change and the future in Burma."[53]

Change is inevitable in Burma-Myanmar. It may be slow and tortuous, but it will come. But to delay considering the future of that society while awaiting reform would be unconscionable. There is a need to begin now with capacity building. The country has lost 1 percent of its educated population (not counting refugees and migrant workers) through legal and illegal emigration to escape political repression, through ethnic discrimination, and through economic stasis. It cannot now manage expanded programs in basic human needs, in economic planning, in public administration (including administration by minority groups in their own areas), in business administration, and in the management of the foreign aid process itself. Training, internally and externally, is needed now, without waiting for reform, for if one awaits reform to begin such training, there will be a hiatus that would be detrimental to improving the lives of the citizens when the inevitable political change occurs. It is in training that the United States has comparative advantages, and it is here that some form of U.S. developmental assistance might be appropriate and useful.

Whatever the solutions to the problems of Burma-Myanmar, optimistically there is likely only to be an amelioration of the problems rather than a resolution of the critical issues facing the state. Neither the military, nor the NLD, nor an amalgam of the two will easily resolve the issues. If that time comes, they will be dealt with in Burmese fashion: the opposition would probably say *bama-lo* ("in the Burmese manner"), and the government might well counter *myanmar-lo* ("in the Myanmar manner"), but whichever it is, it will come from the efforts of the Burmese peoples and will not be imposed by foreign powers or organizations, no matter how benevolent their motivations.

Notes

1. In 1989 the Burmese military, following the coup of 1988, changed the name of the country from Burma to Myanmar, the latter a written form of the name of the state. Since the opposition believed the military regime to be illegitimate, it has refused to accept this change. The use of either term has become a surrogate indicator of political persuasion. The United Nations uses Myanmar, the United States prefers Burma. In this chapter, Myanmar is used for the state from 1988 on and Burma for previous periods; both are

used together to indicate continuity. Burmese is used as an adjective and as the designation of all citizens of the country, while Burman refers to the dominant ethnic group. These terms are used without political implication. Other names have been changed as well, such as Yangon for Rangoon, although the latter is used here for the sake of familiarity.

2. In December 1987, Burma was designated by the UN as a "least-developed nation," at its request, allowing it to receive more favorable loan terms. This designation was inappropriate, as Burma's literacy rate was too high to qualify, but the "effective" literacy rate was readjusted downward to enable it to conform to the UN criteria.

3. Under the constitution of 1947 the ethnic compromise allowed the large and powerful Shan state and the smaller Kayah state to opt for independence after ten years and a referendum. Although the option was unrealistic, the British required such encouragement of unity before it would grant independent status to the whole country.

4. After the coup of 1962 Ne Win was in legal and extralegal command of the state until his "retirement" from the party in 1988, after which he still exerted influence over critical decisions until 2002, or so many Burmese believe.

5. In the volume *Small Is Beautiful: Economics as if People Mattered* (London: Blond and Briggs, 1973), E. F. Shumacher articulates an alternative approach to development, largely based on the Burmese model and ideal.

6. The umbrella Anti-Fascist People's Freedom League (AFPFL), in power since independence, split because of personal loyalties. The military told civilian prime minister U Nu that they had to take over to prevent civil war; U Nu then had legislation passed making their temporary role constitutional.

7. Military personnel salaries and facilities were not cost-accounted, so whether in strict economic terms these ventures were sustainable is not known. At the close of their rule in 1960, the military published a volume on their accomplishments entitled *Is Trust Vindicated?* It obviously was in military eyes. The picture on the dust jacket of the volume was Hercules cleaning out the Augean stables.

8. Per capita income and most economic data in Burma-Myanmar are notoriously unreliable because of a combination of factors: the difficulty of collecting statistics, multiple exchange rates, an undocumented but vigorous black market (which may be larger than the formal economic sector), and manipulation of data for political purposes.

9. In 1999 infant mortality was said to be 47.1 per 1,000 live births, but this figure is suspiciously low, given the lack of medical care and the inability of the state to monitor diseases and deaths. Singapore's infant mortality, in stark contrast, was 3.3 the same year. UN Economic and Social Commission for Asia and the Pacific, Statistical Division, 2001. The CIA *World Factbook 2002* gives Burma's infant mortality for 2002 as 72.11; other estimates are 71 for infants and 105 for children under five.

10. Asian Development Bank, *Country Economic Report, Myanmar*, vol. 2 (Manila, 2001).

11. Kyaw Yin Hlaing, "The Politics of Government-Business Relations in Myanmar," *Asian Journal of Political Science* 10, no. 1 (2002).

12. The model seems to be Suharto's GOLKAR, a mass organization supporting the military, which eventually became Suharto's political party.

13. More accurately, perhaps, it is a pariah not only because of its human rights record but also because after it called for a free election, in which its favored party disastrously lost, it refused to recognize its results. Ironically, the regime may have been more tolerated

abroad had there been no election and simple repression, for expectations would have been lower. The ubiquitous repression from 1962 to 1988 prompted little world attention, as Burma took itself off the world's radar screen. For the past decade or so, however, more worldwide attention has been focused on human rights.

14. The incessant construction about the country has resulted in many new bridges, roads, railroads, dams, and irrigation facilities. Although this may be an investment for the future, the costs for such construction must be exceedingly high in an economically fragile state and are probably accomplished by the excessive and secret printing of currency and by the use of corvée labor. Critics question whether some of those funds might have been better used for social products of more immediate use.

15. In early April 2003, the government announced it would no longer purchase paddy from farmers under forced procurement procedures. The state uses such foodstuffs for the military, as a benefit to civil servants, and for export. The purpose of this liberalization may have been to stave off rural discontent, but some required procurement at less than market rates has been reinstituted.

16. Robert Taylor, *The State in Burma* (University of Hawaii Press, 1987), p. 286. The military claim there are 135 "races" in Myanmar. This figure is from a colonial period analysis of various linguistic groups and dialects. Until it suited their purpose after 1988, the military had denied the existence of minority problems.

17. When this important Buddhist concept is employed to explain, and inherently justify, military actions as it often is, the implication is that the benevolent motivation behind the action cannot be questioned in the Buddhist context.

18. There are interesting parallels between the birth, importance, and implementation of socialism in Burma and in Tanzania, although they seem to have been parallel, not causal, phenomena.

19. This has had obvious political implications against Aung San Suu Kyi, whose husband was British, but it also is used against the Muslim community, which is accused of intentionally subverting the Buddhist population. Those "foreigners," who are not of the indigenous ethnic groups, must prove that their ancestors lived in Burma before 1824, the time of the First Anglo-Burman War, which brought Indians into part of the county (the Arakan and Tenasserim regions, which were ceded to England as a result). Otherwise, they become second-class citizens under the 1982 Nationalities Act and are not eligible for certain government positions and educational opportunities.

20. Maung Maung Gyi, *Burmese Political Values: The Socio-Political Roots of Authoritarianism* (New York: Praeger, 1983).

21. The isolation of General Ne Win from unpleasantness was apparent, and this is said to be the case with Senior General Than Shwe, chairman of the SPDC. General Ne Win remarked in 1986 that the government had to stop lying with statistics. Anecdotal evidence points out that production figures, for rice for example, were politically mandated, in one case to rise 10 percent in one year, and this increase was so reported. Personal communication from Myanmar official.

22. David I. Steinberg, "Japanese Aid to Burma: Assistance in the *Terenagashi* Manner?" In *Managing Japan's Foreign Aid. Power and Policy in a New Era,* edited by Bruce Koppel and Robert Orr (Boulder, Colo.: Westview Press, 1993).

23. In the 1990s, some of the U.S. survivors of the Burma campaign raised funds for an agricultural school for the descendants of the Kachin, who helped them during the war.

24. It is said that General Ne Win was against any family planning programs because he wanted to increase Burma's population relative to that of China. Chinese control of, and immigration into, Yunnan Province bordering Burma only took place during the Ch'ing Dynasty (1644-911), and their expansion into northern Burma was said to have been halted by virulent malaria in that region.

25. The results of the Kuomintang (KMT) incursion were numerous. Although many were evacuated, many remained in Burma and supported themselves by expanding the opium trade, which had been legal on a small scale before. Many of the KMT troops moved to Northern Thailand, where they continued this trade and became wealthy and influential in some of the northern provinces. In order to fight the KMT and to keep the Chinese communist troops out, the Burma army moved in and began to administer areas of the Shan state, thereby gaining both the experience in management and the conviction that they could do a better job than civilian politicians and the civil service. Later, however, a joint PRC and Burmese offensive was launched against the KMT remnants.

26. The original Kipling "Road to Mandalay" was, of course, the Irrawaddy River.

27. Although evidence is lacking, it seems possible that the Burmese informally asked the Chinese their views on inviting the United States to provide assistance, and the Chinese, who were interested in improving relations with the United States at that time, concurred. The author was the leader of the USAID team that explored and recommended the reopening of the aid program. See David I. Steinberg, *Burma's Road toward Development: Growth and Ideology under Military Rule* (Boulder, Colo.: Westview Press, 1981).

28. David I. Steinberg, *Burma: The State of Myanmar* (Georgetown University Press, 2001).

29. Chinese Nationalist and early PRC maps included northern Burma as part of China, so these fears were not as farfetched as might be imagined later.

30. Other authorities might dispute this claim. In June 2002, the Burmese government passed an anti-money-laundering bill with the strong approval of the United States. This is not ex post facto legislation, however. The Burmese authorities deny all involvement in the drug trade and claim they are doing all in their power to stop it.

31. See *Myanmar Opium Survey* (Government of Myanmar, 1996). The government is involved in what it calls the New Destiny Project, which aims to eliminate opium production altogether by 2015.

32. Some members of Congress wanted an imposition of sanctions on all past and future investment, but the administration reached a compromise on only future investment. Trading, as contrasted to investment, was still allowed until the sanctions imposed in the summer of 2003.

33. The total imports of textiles from Burma in 2001 were about US$420 million, of which US$356 million were to the United States. Most of the factories are owned by Chinese, Taiwanese, and Korean firms. Foreign investment *approvals* by the Burmese government are over US$7 billion, but perhaps only one-third of that amount has actually been invested, and new investment has virtually been stagnant since 2003. The overall foreign investment figures usually quoted for Myanmar are not accurate. Since almost all Chinese investment does not go through the Myanmar Investment Commission, the Chinese contribution to the total is misleadingly small: cumulatively, Chinese investment may be the largest of any country. Chinese illegal immigration into Myanmar has been extensive, and

investment in businesses, hotels, and real estate are sizable, especially in Mandalay and the area to its north.

34. Thomas M. Carroll, "China's Penetration into Burma: Extracting Meaning from the Buildup of Burma's Infrastructure," master's thesis, Georgetown University, July 2001. Mandalay, the seat of Burman culture, is now said to be one-quarter Yunnanese Chinese, and Lashio in the Shan state is about 50 percent Chinese.

35. John W. Garner, *Protracted Contest: Sino-Indian Rivalry in the Twentieth Century* (Washington University Press, 2001); *Jane's Foreign Report*, April 3, 2003.

36. Thailand, in spoken Burmese, is still called Yodiya. In June and July 2002 the English-language-controlled press in Myanmar referred to Thailand as Yodiya, an apparent insult resulting from what should have been a minor military dispute along the border.

37. Lt. Colonel Hla Min (a government spokesman), "Political Situation of Myanmar and Its Role in the Region" (Yangon: Office of Strategic Studies, Ministry of Defense, 1998).

38. Personal communication from a military official, Rangoon. In the summer of 2003, military authorities undertook a one-to-three-month paramilitary training program for males under fifty years old. At least in one area, people were told that this was so that they could put up resistance to the Americans and buy time until the Chinese came to their aid.

39. David I. Steinberg, "Myanmar: Reconciliation in the Process?" in *Southeast Asian Affairs 2003* (Singapore: Institute of Southeast Asian Studies, 2003).

40. Suharto used the doctrine of *pancasila* as a national ideology, thus foreclosing the imposition of an Islamic state. The call for a more fundamental Islamic administration was a primary cause of the Aceh rebellion in north Sumatra, along with the sharing of Aceh's considerable contribution to Indonesia's exports through its extensive energy resources.

41. *Straits Times*, Singapore, May 21, 2002.

42. Agence France-Presse, August 8, 2002, quoting Myanmar Information Committee Information Sheet C-2311 (I/L) of August 7, 2002. The Indian press has been concerned about an international Muslim group called Tabliq, supposedly supported by the Pakistanis and operating in Myanmar. *Boston Herald*, December 26, 2001.

43. This is disputed by Bertil Lintner (Asia Pacific Media Services Limited, October 1, 2002), who asserts that the camps were inside Bangladesh and run by the Rohingya Solidarity Organization (RSO); personal communication from Bertil Lintner. This group's activities in Chittagong, Bangladesh, have been monitored by the Burmese authorities, who have noted that in May 1994 Rohingya rebels have received training, funds, and rewards from supporters from a variety of Muslim states, and that same month eight RSO members were sent to Libya for training.

44. Associated Press, August 26, 2002; BBC, August 10, 2002.

45. Rohan Gunaratna, *Inside Al Qaeda: Global Network of Terror* (Columbia University Press, 2002), p. 89; BBC Worldwide Monitoring, August 10, 2002, from the Irrawaddy website.

46. "Over the decades, many anti-Muslim pamphlets have circulated in Burma claiming that the Muslim community wants to establish supremacy through intermarriage. One of these, *Myo Pyauk Hmar Soe Kyauk Hla Tai* (or the *Fear of Losing One's Race)* was

widely distributed in 2001, often by monks. . . . Local Buddhist monks have often been at the center of these campaigns. According to Burmese Muslim leaders, distribution of pamphlets in 2001 was also supported by the Union Solidarity and Development Association (USDA), a government-sponsored mass organization that fulfils a social and political function for the military." Human Rights Watch/AsiaWatch, "Crackdown on Burmese Muslims," briefing paper, October 4, 2002.

47. AsiaWatch, *Crackdown on Burmese Muslims* (July 18, 2002).

48. Ibid.

49. It is charged that in 1967 the Ne Win government redirected popular unrest over deteriorating economic conditions by encouraging rioting against the Chinese at the height of the Cultural Revolution. Several dozen Chinese were killed and many shops were looted.

50. It is of course possible that this change was first suggested by Aung San Suu Kyi and that the United States agreed to it. Senator Mitch McConnell, a longtime foe of the Burmese military, in a statement released on September 13, 2002, called for regime change in both Burma and Cambodia, similar to that advocated by President Bush in Iraq.

51. Speech by Assistant Secretary of State for East Asian and Pacific Affairs James Kelly at the Johns Hopkins University School of Advanced International Studies, November 23, 2002. But a State Department report stated, "Should there be significant progress in Burma in coming months on political transition, economic reform, and human rights, the United States would look seriously at additional measures that could be applied to support the process of constructive change. Absent progress, we will be forced to consider, in conjunction with the international community, additional sanctions and/or other measures." U.S. Department of State, "Conditions in Burma and U.S. Policy toward Burma for the Period September 28, 2002, to March 27, 2003."

52. The term *humanitarian assistance* may be too broadly interpreted, as some have charged that the Japanese have done. Perhaps *meeting basic human needs,* a phrase that was in vogue some years ago, may be more accurate and appropriate and would limit assistance to health, education, agriculture, and so forth.

53. *Far Eastern Economic Review,* June 20, 2002.

8

Making Peace Perform in War-Transition Countries: El Salvador, Guatemala, and Nicaragua

SUSAN BURGERMAN

The governments of El Salvador, Guatemala, and Nicaragua can all be classified as poorly performing, although according to different indicators, to different degrees, and demonstrating important differences in their obstacles to development. A major cause of poor performance in each case is the residual costs of devastating civil wars—civil wars in which the United States directly or indirectly participated. While the horrors of civil war are over, the legacies of political polarization, civil violence, injustice, and public insecurity still impede good governance. Effective governance (defined broadly to encompass provision of citizen security, delivery of basic social services, nonviolent maintenance of public order, and management of public finance and the economy) is severely hampered in all three countries by two areas of institutional dysfunction. First, the political leaderships are dominated by former civil war adversaries, contributing to electoral systems that are highly fragmented, polarized, unwilling to accommodate, and either are poorly integrated into the community or penetrate the community through patronage networks. Second, the public security and justice sectors that, in many instances, engaged in abusive activities during the conflicts are now infiltrated by organized crime; are directed by elites seeking to preserve privilege and impunity; or are too poorly resourced, trained, monitored, coordinated, and managed to respond to current security needs.

It should be noted at the outset that only one of these three countries, Nicaragua, qualifies as a low-income state according to the indicator used by the World Bank (having a per capita gross national income [GNI] of US$825 or under). El Salvador and Guatemala are ranked as lower-middle-income economies, despite the desperate poverty of their rural populations.[1] Even given the variation in economic performance, the three states are examined together because of the light they collectively shed both on the effects of civil conflict on democratic institutions and on the role that the United States can play in postconflict states.

U.S. foreign policy vis-à-vis these states is affected by their civil wars in three ways. First are the important implications for major national U.S. interests, such as bilateral, regional, and multilateral counternarcotics efforts, involvement by corrupt agencies of these states in cross-border contraband and money laundering, and transnational organized crime. Second, the civil wars created refugee flows into U.S. cities that continue unabated in the postconflict period owing to economic contractions, unemployment, and skyrocketing crime and public insecurity. Indeed, in 2002 remittances from emigrants working in the United States accounted for 14 percent of gross domestic product (GDP) per capita in El Salvador, 15 percent in Nicaragua, and over 11 percent in Guatemala.[2]

Third are the political and moral obligations on the part of the United States, which played a role as a "friendly nation" in the Salvadoran and Guatemalan peace processes and had an active role in brokering the end of the Nicaraguan civil war. This involvement carries political and financial commitments to help implement the resulting peace agreements. The U.S. government has in fact been deeply involved in the domestic politics of these states for over a century. It has at various periods built and trained their militaries and continues to provide them with military assistance. It was allied with one side or another in all three civil wars, to the extent of being the major financial support of the Salvadoran military and the Nicaraguan armed opposition. Having been so involved in the civil wars, the marked decrease in U.S. financial commitments during the postwar reconstruction period has led many Central Americans to voice their growing resentment. However, despite the perception that the United States has lost interest, Central American countries do continue to receive U.S. foreign assistance, and the need for such assistance has grown significantly since the late 1990s, as the region has been further devastated by hurricane, drought, and earthquake.[3] The programs and budgets allocated to each country differ, but in all three countries U.S. Agency for International Development (USAID) missions are engaged in following through with the implicit promises of peace.

In the case studies that follow, I focus on government performance as indicated by how well the institutional channels for political representation and the state's public security institutions function. The reason for the focus on the institutions of justice, security, and representation is that their poor functioning was a key source of grievance in the past and in large part set the conditions for violent civil conflict; improved performance in these areas is essential for future development. Following a general overview, I review the conditions that led to civil war in each of the three war-transition countries, examine the postconflict obstacles to government performance, and discuss the impact of U.S. foreign policy on these developments. The concluding section discusses how foreign assistance can help overcome these obstacles.

Overview of Postconflict Central America

The civil wars in El Salvador, Nicaragua, and Guatemala generated a great deal of international attention in the 1980s, owing to publicity from human rights organizations and to the direct involvement of the United States. In terms of human loss alone, these conflicts resulted in around 75,000 dead and over a million displaced in El Salvador (population about 6 million); an estimated 200,000 dead and more than 1.5 million displaced in Guatemala (population about 10 million); and 80,000–110,000 dead and 300,000 displaced in Nicaragua (population about 4 million). The conflicts were settled through internationally mediated talks, beginning with Nicaragua in 1990, followed by El Salvador in 1992, and finally Guatemala in 1996. Peace has proved durable in all three countries, and all three are now governed by elected civilian administrations (all are constitutional republics, presidential systems with unicameral legislatures), which are engaged in promoting sustainable development, with the advice and assistance of international financial institutions and a consultative group of donor states.

El Salvador is the furthest along by World Bank measures, having diversified its economy away from underperforming agricultural exports (primarily coffee) to service industries and maquiladora manufacturing. The peacetime governments have also achieved improvements in social conditions. Between 1990 and 2002, extreme poverty decreased from 31 percent to 15 percent, while overall poverty was reduced more than 27 percent. Malnutrition among children under five was cut from 23 percent in 1993 to 20 percent in 2002, infant mortality dropped from 60 to 39 per 1,000 live births between 1990 and 2002, and access to improved sources of water increased from 66 percent in 1990 to 77 percent in 2002. During that period, income inequality decreased slightly, with improvements mainly in urban centers.[4] Ironically, however, El Salvador also has the highest rates of civil violence in the region and one of the highest homicide rates in the world, which is bound to have a depressing effect on investment, despite modest but fairly steady growth, successful dollarization of its economy, and a mobile workforce.

Postconflict Guatemala is another story. Despite the fact that Guatemala is ranked as a lower-middle-income country, it is second only to Haiti in the Latin American and Caribbean region in inequality of income distribution. GDP growth averaged 4 percent during the 1990s, then stagnated to somewhat over 2 percent between 2001 and 2003, and has not yet recovered. Inflation declined to 7.5 percent in 2004, and external debt is low. However, 56 percent of the overall population (76 percent of the indigenous population) lives in poverty; 16 percent lives in extreme poverty. Inequality in land distribution, a chief and enduring source of violent conflict in Guatemala, has not been alleviated in peacetime even though the problem was directly addressed in the peace accords. With 30 percent adult illiteracy, Guatemala has one of the lowest literacy rate in the region.[5] The vast majority of poor households are in the agricultural sector, producing corn for private consumption and coffee for export. Despite efforts spanning at least two decades to diversify production, especially in textile manufacturing and nontraditional agricultural exports, the economy remains dependent on coffee and therefore vulnerable to a deterioration in world prices. Not surprisingly, the government of this land of extreme inequality is often paralyzed by internal factionalism and corruption scandals.

As noted earlier, Nicaragua is the only one of these three countries ranked as low income, largely owing to the complete economic collapse of the 1980s. The country's governments of the 1990s focused their efforts on economic recovery and privatizing assets that had been nationalized under the previous regime. Nicaragua managed to achieve real GDP growth of 4 percent in 1995 and has maintained a declining but positive growth rate. Between 1993 and 2001, overall poverty fell slightly, from 50 percent to 46 percent nationally (to 68 percent in rural areas), with 15 percent in extreme poverty. Nicaragua is overall the second poorest country in the region, but despite having a higher degree of absolute poverty its income inequality does not exceed the Latin American average.[6] The economy is still based in agricultural production (mainly cotton, sugar, and coffee) and therefore is highly vulnerable to world price fluctuations and, worse, to natural disasters such as 1998 Hurricane Mitch.

The war-transition countries of Central America differ considerably in their economic and political history, but they do share broad similarities. First, they are all within the U.S. sphere of influence. The governments of all three countries during most of the twentieth century could be characterized as military-dominated dictatorships that generally hewed to the U.S. geopolitical strategy. Second, they are small states traditionally dependent on primary agricultural production. In simple terms, oligarchic elites—coffee, cattle, and cotton growers—maintained landownership, control of resources, and political control from independence through the end of the twentieth century and, arguably, to the present. In Guatemala, economic and social inequality coincides with ethnicity: indigenous peoples comprise 49 percent of the population and are concentrated in the areas with the highest levels of poverty and exclusion; 62 percent of indigenous Guatemalan women are illiterate, and 76 percent of indigenous Guatemalans are poor.[7] The problem of racial discrimination in Guatemala is so severe that an entire peace agreement was dedicated to the rights of indigenous peoples.

The causes of civil conflict were broadly similar in each of these countries: perceived extremes of economic and social injustice, the virtual absence of meaningful channels for nonviolent political change, and the use of government security forces to repress opposition. In El Salvador and Guatemala, these conditions led to "unsuccessful" insurgencies (insofar as the armed opposition was unable to capture control of the state). In Nicaragua, guerrilla forces were successful in overthrowing a repressive, corrupt government. These forces formed a socialist government, which then faced an armed opposition—incited by widespread land expropriations that were perceived to be unjust—and harsh dislocations caused by government mismanagement of the economy. They also faced U.S. military support for this antisocialist insurgency.

The twentieth-century political histories of these Central American states differ markedly. Whereas the Nicaraguan political system before the civil war is best characterized as a personalist dictatorship, politics in El Salvador and Guatemala were more institutionalized, in that the military ruled as an institution. This had important implications for how change of government could take place: in Nicaragua, it was a matter of removing a family dynasty from power. In Guatemala and El Salvador, when factionalism within the armed forces and corruption or incompetence in the high command reached an egregious level, the military would enact a self-correction through reformist officer coups, which adjusted the undesirable behavior and allowed the military to retain power. In these cases, the military relinquished the reins of government only through tightly controlled elite pacts.

The postconflict democracies that evolved from this background in El Salvador and Guatemala share at least two similarities: the electoral institutions are polarized and rent by factionalism, and their public security and justice systems are overburdened and corrupt. The result is that public confidence in their democracies has suffered, disenchantment is growing, as are abstention rates. The process of institutional consolidation is further hampered in all three cases by ongoing government corruption.[8]

El Salvador, Guatemala, and Nicaragua share a trait with all postconflict states: they are awash in arms and unemployed young males who are trained to use them. Violent crime has many causes, from inequality and unemployment to posttraumatic stress disorder, but the availability of firearms is a critical factor. Despite this similarity, however, rates of civil violence vary among the three countries. Violent crime is much worse, and therefore more of an impediment to growth and human development, in El Salvador and Guatemala than it is in Nicaragua, although the former states are relatively better economic performers than Nicaragua. As noted above, Nicaragua is ranked on the World Bank's list of lowest income states, while Guatemala and El Salvador are in the middle-income category. However, the latter two governments have much worse performance records in the most fundamental service the state provides: public security. According to statistics for 1998, the homicide rate in El Salvador was 83 violent deaths per 100,000, Guatemala 77, and Nicaragua 13.[9] The economic costs of violent crime are staggering; one analyst estimated that in 1995 the costs directly associated with crime in El Salvador (not counting the opportunity costs of lost revenues and investment) amounted to 13 percent of GDP. In 2001 the costs of crime were on a par with the costs of the earthquake damage.[10]

A factor that distinguishes the Nicaraguan security sector from those in El Salvador and Guatemala is that during the civil war years of the 1980s the Sandinista police and armed forces were creatures of the ruling party but were not used by the state as agents of repression. Despite low rates of public confidence and reports of police abuse, the Nicaraguan National Police developed better community relations and community policing projects than the civilian police forces in El Salvador and Guatemala, which were designed under UN auspices and according to U.S. and European models.[11] All three forces are subject to corrupting pressures, but there is increasing evidence that the Salvadoran and Guatemalan security forces in particular are infiltrated by organized crime up through the highest ranks.

Concerning the role of the United States in these countries, Central America policy during the 1980s was dominated by cold war security concerns to the detriment of other foreign policy goals, such as promoting human and civil rights, democracy, and free trade and assisting lesser developed states to achieve economic growth.[12] The perceived threat of communist incursion in the region led the U.S. government to take sides in the Central American civil conflicts. In both El Salvador and Guatemala, the United States sided with the military-dominated governments against leftist insurgent forces, whereas in Nicaragua it supported an armed insurgency seeking to overthrow the socialist Sandinista government. The wars in El Salvador and Nicaragua held a higher priority on the administration's agenda, received considerably more in military assistance (in the case of Nicaragua, authorized and unauthorized covert lethal assistance), and therefore generated greater controversy in Congress and the interested public than did Guatemala. Foreign aid to the region nearly doubled between 1984 and 1985, with the bulk of the increase going toward military and security assistance in El Salvador.[13]

As the cold war cooled and with the transition from the Reagan administration to that of George H. W. Bush, U.S. strategic interests in Central America took on a more pragmatic posture, and policy priorities in the region shifted from counterinsurgency to democratic consolidation and economic recovery. The Bush administration ended the policy of opposing negotiations with Marxist insurgents and gave its support to the regional and UN mediation efforts. Overall assistance to Central America dropped sharply between 1991 and 1995. El Salvador was in time to benefit greatly from U.S. support for the peace process and accords implementation at the outset, but funding for Guatemala's peace process has suffered doubly from U.S. budgetary pressure on the United Nations, which resulted in a severely limited General Assembly budget for the UN operation, and from the reduced amounts of U.S. foreign aid available to assist with peace accords implementation and reconstruction (although this continues to be a special objective of U.S. development assistance in Guatemala).

The Clinton administration's regional policy priorities in Central America were sustainable development, including environmental protection programs; building democracy, including support for the peace accords implementation; humanitarian assistance, especially the food for peace programs; and assistance for counternarcotics programs.[14] After 1993 direct lethal assistance to the region from the U.S. Defense Department budget had virtually dried up and was replaced at lower spending levels by narcotics control, military

(IMET) and police (ICITAP) training, joint exercises, and joint military civic aid projects (road building and other development assistance).

Relations between the United States and Central American governments are now dominated by an overarching concern with counterterrorism, which partially subsumes and is pursued in tandem with the other pillar of U.S. policy in Central America, interdiction of drug trafficking and other forms of organized crime. Another key issue, albeit one that has received decreasing amounts of policymakers' attention since the September 11 attacks, is immigration, in particular the legal status of Salvadoran immigrants to the United States, whose remittances are the single largest source of foreign income in El Salvador and account for a significant percentage of that country's GDP.[15] Recent diplomatic concerns emphasize trade integration through the Central America Free Trade Agreement (CAFTA) and cooperation on anticorruption measures.

Along with a variety of European Union and UN programs, U.S. government and nongovernmental agencies are deeply involved in peace building in these countries, funding police training through the ICITAP program, judicial and electoral reform through a number of USAID projects, and working directly with communities to overcome years of conflict through projects like the USAID Human Rights and Reconciliation Program in Guatemala. Foreign assistance, primarily through USAID, has become increasingly focused on technical assistance to strengthen democratic institutions and, more recently, to professionalizing civil society organizations, especially in their capacity to advocate for and monitor policy reforms. The effort to build the skills and professional capacity of civil society organizations is now recognized as key to increasing democratic participation. The results of this effort vary with factors such as literacy rates, societal divisiveness, and ultimately the civil organizations' ability to access and influence decisionmaking elites.

Given this snapshot of the postconflict political and socioeconomic context in the region, this chapter examines each country in greater detail with respect to the repercussions of civil war on political and rule of law institutions and the influence of U.S. policy in the region on these developments.

Political Institutions in El Salvador

In El Salvador before 1979 the official party of the military ordinarily won presidential elections; if an opposition party or coalition unexpectedly gained a majority, as happened in 1972, the official party simply won by fraud. During a period of mild opening in the 1960s the military permitted popular unrest, debate over industrial development projects, and demands for agrarian reform to be expressed through partisan politics.[16] Channels for nonviolent citizen participation outside of elections, whether in the form of labor and peasant unions or political parties that represented popular interests, were notably absent.

By the late 1970s gross socioeconomic inequities and blatant electoral fraud had resulted in civil protest. Given the restrictive nature of the Salvadoran electoral system, civil protest became violent protest; meanwhile, guerrilla forces were mobilizing in the countryside. To control the increasingly unstable political situation, a group of reformist junior officers staged a successful coup in October 1979 and formed a ruling junta that initially included members of the civilian left opposition.[17] Opposition members were squeezed out, and the junta became increasingly repressive over the next year, leading most of the remaining center-left civilian opposition to either join the armed resistance or regroup in exile. Confrontation escalated to open civil war in early 1980, when five guerrilla organizations joined forces to form the Farabundo Martí National Liberation Front (FMLN) and initiated a large-scale military offensive.

Under pressure from the Reagan administration, on whose support the Salvadoran military depended, the junta scheduled presidential elections for 1984 and selected two interim civilian presidents to oversee the transition. In the 1984 elections the United States promoted and financed the campaign of the centrist Christian Democratic Party (PDC) candidate, José Napoleón Duarte, who narrowly won against the right-wing candidate of the National Republican Alliance (ARENA) party. It is frequently noted but bears repeating that the elections held in El Salvador during the civil war were not the result of a democratic compromise among domestic actors but were imposed by the Reagan administration in order to overcome congressional reluctance to finance the Salvadoran military's counterinsurgency efforts. Following the restrictive electoral politics of the 1970s, this has contributed to a legacy of sharp partisanship and factionalism and weak popular access to or participation in the Salvadoran political system.

In August 1987, the Central American regional peace process (the Contadora process) produced an accord, referred to as Esquipulas II, which served as the basis for ending the civil wars in all three countries, beginning with Nicaragua. Esquipulas II required the Salvadoran government to permit opposition leaders to return from exile and participate in elections.[18] Several of the returned center-left politicians formed a legal party and registered for the 1988 elections. The 1989 presidential election was won by Alfredo Cristiani, leader of a center-right, modernizing faction of ARENA. By the end of 1989 both the government and the FMLN had requested UN mediation. Negotiations lasted from April 1990 to December 1991, and final peace accords were signed in January 1992.[19]

A number of electoral reforms were mandated by the terms of the Salvadoran peace accords.[20] These provisions were aimed at providing a level field for political campaigns, at increasing participation, and at ensuring the security of campaign workers and candidates. Parties from across the political spectrum were given a greater voice in electoral organization and voter registration. The FMLN registered as a national political party for the March 20, 1994, elections, came in second in the presidential race, and won twenty-one of eighty-four seats in the National Assembly.[21] The accords established a national electoral tribunal and a special commission to review draft amendments to the electoral code. Although these amendments were incorporated into the code in time for the March 1994 elections, fairly serious irregularities in the registration process cast doubt on the tribunal's impartiality and ultimately threatened to disrupt the election.

Technical reforms in registration and voting procedures have been much more gradual. One worrying development is the growing abstention rate, which reached 63 percent in the 2000 elections. Some of this could be attributable to the sheer difficulty of voting for most Salvadorans. Registration, a process that can require several visits, and balloting are located in the largest urban center of each municipality, which often entails a long and arduous trip by bus or on foot for those who live in the countryside. The physical and bureaucratic obstacles are slowly being addressed. However, a 1999 University of Central America poll indicates that at least a third of those who abstained did so because they lacked confidence in their parties and in the political system.[22] The cynicism or lack of confidence is easy to understand. A series of government corruption scandals have roiled the ARENA administrations of Armando Calderón Sol (1994–99) and Francisco Flores (1999–2004). A code of ethics for civil servants was introduced in December 2000 with USAID sponsorship, but there appears to be no political will to enforce it.[23]

Salvadorans have also had to suffer ugly public internal battles, which have come close to disintegrating the major parties, especially ARENA and the FMLN. Electoral politics have become more transparent and stable since the "Elections of the Century" (as the 1994 elections were called), but the parties themselves remain poorly institutionalized. ARENA saw its majority in the National Assembly and at the municipal level decline steadily in the 1997, 2000, and 2003 elections, although it has retained the presidency since

1989. The FMLN, truncated in the mid-1990s by the defection of two original components, picked up a plurality in the assembly and most of the major
municipalities in the March 2000 elections and maintained that lead in 2003
(assembly elections are held every three years). In the 2003–06 legislature,
the FMLN and ARENA combined held slightly more than two-thirds of the
eighty-four-seat total. Three smaller parties—the Christian democratic PDC,
the social democratic CDU, and the right-wing PCN—combined carried
twenty-six seats, or just under one-third. Taking advantage of the internal
fragmentation within the two major parties, the smaller parties on occasion
were able to play a useful role in forming balancing coalitions.[24] Nonetheless,
inflexibility and retaliatory politics on the part of the FMLN and ARENA
leadership and the extreme polarization of legislative politics in El Salvador
frequently result in gridlock on important items that require a majority, such
as international loan agreements (short-term loans require a simple majority,
medium- and long-term loans require a two-thirds majority) and the national
budget (which requires a simple majority).[25]

Protecting the Rule of Law in El Salvador

The mandate to separate policing from the armed forces was a major achievement of the Salvadoran peace process, after decades of political violence per-
petrated by the state security forces. The peace accords outlined a plan to
civilianize public security by disbanding the existing military police units and
replacing them with a single institution, the National Civilian Police, which
integrated equal numbers (in theory) of demobilized combatants from both
the FMLN and the Salvadoran armed forces (the armed forces were downsized by nearly 50 percent) with new recruits who had never served in any
security force. The new force was to operate under the Ministry of the Interior, rather than the Defense Ministry. A new security doctrine was developed that emphasized rule of law and human rights standards, to be instilled
during training at a newly created national police academy overseen by the
UN Observer Mission in El Salvador (ONUSAL).[26]

ONUSAL also undertook what is now known to have been a barely
effective weapons collection from demobilized FMLN combatants. Worse
yet, weapons collection from demobilized military personnel was a complete
failure. Safe reintegration of the roughly 7,500 demobilized FMLN combatants received a great deal of attention following the demobilization period,
but there were severe problems with the retraining and land transfer programs designed for this purpose. There were equally serious problems with
compensation programs for the 28,000 demobilized soldiers. With high

unemployment and underemployment rates, the Salvadoran economy could not absorb the influx of young males trained to do battle. Armed ex-combatants from both sides contributed to the postwar wave of violent crime.

The new civilian police force has not been able to control rising crime, which includes gang violence (gang membership is rising across Central America but continues to be highest by far in El Salvador), kidnappings, and homicides. Nor have they been free from accusations of human rights violations—although nothing comparable to the forces they replaced. The police force is severely underfunded, has a high rate of casualties due to the numbers of firearms available to criminals, and is infiltrated by organized crime. In May 2000, the chief of police publicly admitted that officers had been involved in kidnappings and robberies and instigated an investigation that led to over 1,500 dismissals (nearly 10 percent of the force). Internal oversight mechanisms such as the inspector general's office, although improving, continue to be weak and politicized.[27]

The reforms to the justice administration system mandated by the Salvadoran peace accords focused on judicial independence and legal safeguards for civil and political rights. The National Council of the Judiciary was restructured, a judicial training school was created, and the mechanisms for selecting Supreme Court justices were restructured to make the court less partisan. ONUSAL, in conjunction with the National Council, organized training courses in human rights and due process for justices and magistrates. The mission also assisted in the process of evaluating justices and sending to the Supreme Court lists of those recommended for purgation based on findings of corruption or unprofessional conduct.

Unfortunately, most of the justice sector reforms mandated by the peace accords required constitutional amendment and were held up for most of the decade by the divisive, partisan legislative process. Corruption continues to be a serious obstacle to judicial reform. Beginning in 2000, the attorney general conducted a purge of corrupt officials in the public prosecutor's office that resulted in the indictment of sixty prosecutors, the investigation of sixty judges, and the dismissal of fifty staff members, but the effort did not result in convictions.[28]

International organizations, especially USAID, the United Nations Development Program (UNDP), the Inter-American Development Bank (IDB), and the World Bank, have worked steadily to improve the Salvadoran justice system in the postconflict period. In August 2002, the World Bank approved a US$18 million loan to increase efficiency at the lower court level and public access by reorganizing jurisdictions for better geographic and demographic distribution.[29] The justice system in postconflict El Salvador is more independent of political influence than it was before, and justices and staff are better trained and more professional. But public access to justice is still low, and the perception of class bias and corruption in the judiciary continues.[30]

U.S. Foreign Policy in El Salvador

During the 1980s the U.S. government spent over US$1 billion in direct military assistance and perhaps an even greater amount in economic support funds and security supporting assistance to finance, equip, and train the Salvadoran armed forces. For at least the first half of the decade, El Salvador was the object of intensely polarized battles between the Reagan administration and members of Congress who opposed U.S. intervention in Central American civil wars.[31] Officials who criticized Reagan's Central America policy were accused of being soft on communism, and once a civilian, José Napoleón Duarte, was elected president of El Salvador in 1984, the majority found it convenient to forge a bipartisan policy consensus on the issue and release withheld military funds.

With the end of the Salvadoran civil war in 1992, U.S. assistance shifted rapidly from lethal aid to promoting democratic institutions and implementing the peace accords. A major factor contributing to the relative success of the Salvadoran accords was that international donors, including the United States, placed "peace conditions" on assistance.[32] Congressional priorities for U.S. support during the 1990s were the training and deployment of the National Civilian Police and the demobilization of former security forces, expedition of land transfers to demobilized combatants, and judicial and electoral reforms.[33]

The bulk of international development and emergency assistance funds to El Salvador from 1998 through 2002 was absorbed by recovery from Hurricane Mitch (October 1998) and the January and February 2001 earthquakes. As crucial as hurricane recovery aid is, this has had the adverse effect of redirecting funds away from parts of the country that were less affected by natural disasters but are equally in need of development assistance. International donors committed US$1.3 billion to long-term earthquake recovery (US$1 billion in "soft loans," US$300 million in grants; this amount includes pre-earthquake commitments), of which the United States committed approximately US$168 million.[34] The USAID mission in El Salvador is pursuing current policy priorities through programs to improve access to justice, citizen participation in local government, public service management, government transparency, citizen election oversight, community policing (through special authorization and Economic Support Funds), education, maternal and child health, public health, and environmental protection. The effort to strengthen civil society organizations through grants and skills training has seen results in advocacy for water rights and services, legislation against domestic violence, and anticorruption campaigns.

To conclude, despite external assistance that has been generous in comparison with its neighbors, El Salvador has not yet overcome the legacies of civil war. Democratic consolidation has progressed in El Salvador; the mandated constitutional reforms have largely been enacted, and the former armed opposition has successfully transformed into a political party with a strong electoral and legislative voice. Social policy and economic development efforts have achieved measurable, albeit meager, success, and the process of societal reconciliation appears to be more advanced than in other war-transition countries. But the freely elected administrations of the postconflict period have been led by members of the traditional, and often corrupt, elite. Since the mid-1990s these administrations have been confronted by a legislature that is increasingly dominated by a fractious opposition. The political leadership as a whole has yet to adapt to democratic norms of behavior. Further, the comparatively large numbers of demobilized combatants from both the armed forces and the FMLN, whose reintegration into productive life was partial at best, contribute to the high degree of public insecurity and extremely high rates of homicide.

Political Institutions in Guatemala

Guatemala's electoral institutions were even more constricted than those of El Salvador. From 1966 to 1985, Guatemala had a multiparty system in which the candidates of all major parties were either military officers or civilians nominated with military approval.[35] Military control of electoral politics was institutionalized in the mid-1960s through party registration criteria that forced all legal parties to cooperate with the military on the substance of their programs. The party of the military was not the sole vehicle for the official government candidate, as it was in El Salvador. Instead, the Guatemalan military was able to select an appropriate vehicle from among several parties or coalitions of parties. Economic elites for the most part acquiesced in the military's preponderant political role. The agriculture export oligarchy exercised considerable political influence but did not actively attempt to wrest authority from the armed forces.

In 1979, facing a resurgence of guerrilla warfare in the countryside and popular unrest in urban centers, the government initiated a radical increase in state-sponsored violence targeting opposition politicians. The result was decimation of the incipient political center and moderate democratic left. The worst years of political violence, 1979–84, also saw a fragmentation of the official party system and increasing internal dissent within the military ranks over the threat to institutional integrity from the corrupting influence of government power and over the threat to the military's prestige through mismanagement of the economy. Economic elites began to agitate for a greater role in government. This, combined with growing U.S. pressure to hold elections, caused the military to engineer a carefully controlled transition to civilian rule in 1984—so carefully controlled that significant domains of governmental authority remain in the military's hands to this day.[36]

The Esquipulas peace agreement set the stage for a negotiated settlement between the government and the guerrilla opposition (Guatemalan National Revolutionary Unity, URNG), which, as in El Salvador, was mediated by the United Nations. This process took several years longer than the Salvadoran negotiations (March 1990 to December1996), owing to a lack of real or perceived military stalemate (the army had virtually won the war in 1983) and the continued dominance of the military over civilians in government. Nonetheless, the peace process itself promoted a degree of liberalization; a coalition party of civilian opposition groups, the New Guatemala Democratic Front (FDNG), formed for the November 1995 elections, a full year before the final accords were signed. Six FDNG candidates were elected to Congress, including high-profile indigenous and victims' rights leaders.

The Guatemalan peace accords were far more ambitious than the Salvadoran accords in the types of reform they proposed although less specific in mechanisms to verify compliance and sanction noncompliance.[37] The electoral reforms mandated by the accords are aimed at reinforcing the independence of the Supreme Electoral Tribunal, increasing the level of citizen participation, and decreasing the rate of abstention. Toward these goals, the Electoral Reform Commission was created to report to the Supreme Electoral Tribunal with recommendations to modernize identification documents, electoral registries, and voting procedures; to improve transparency in party publicity and nomination procedures, campaign financing, and media access; to improve public education and information, especially for indigenous communities; and to strengthen the institutional system by professionalizing personnel and increasing the tribunal's budget.[38]

Unfortunately, all of the reforms mandated by the peace accords that required constitutional amendment fell victim to a tragic demonstration of political obstructionism in May 1999. After being held up for nearly two years in Congress, an unwieldy package of fifty proposed amendments (the accords only required twelve) was passed through Congress in October 1998 and submitted to a national referendum for ratification. The parties and reform advocates did little to educate the public about the proposed reforms, and a right-wing, race-based attack campaign was launched two weeks before the referendum linking the reforms to urban middle-class fears of ceding political power to indigenous peasants.[39] The confused and disenchanted population by and large did not vote on the referendum: 81 percent abstained; of the 19 percent of registered voters who placed ballots, 44 percent voted for the reforms and 56 percent voted against. The outcome highlights the rural-urban and ethnic cleavages. Indigenous majority municipalities, almost invariably rural, voted for the reforms; major urban centers voted against.[40] After the referendum, draft legislation for a law on elections and political parties, mandated by the accords and designed to expand opportunities for participation in the electoral process especially among indigenous groups, was presented in Congress but failed to acquire the necessary majority for passage.[41] The measures required by the terms of the accords on constitutional reforms should increase political participation, but they cannot be enacted until the constitutional amendments have been ratified.

Voter abstention historically has been very high in Guatemala, and this relates to an even prior problem, that voter registration has always been very low. Poor registration rates reflect not only apathy and disenfranchisement but also illiteracy and lack of public information among the poor and indigenous; they also reflect the exclusion of much of the population from the body politic. As of January 2002, roughly 10 percent of the rural adult population lacked identity documentation.[42] As in El Salvador, both registration and voting are difficult for those in the countryside because they only take place in the municipal centers. These difficulties only compound the distrust of governmental institutions and the disenfranchisement of indigenous communities, discouraging voter participation.

Despite the comprehensive nature of the negotiated reforms and careful attention to electoral institutions, postconflict Guatemala remained arguably the worst case of an underinstitutionalized party system. Not to mince words, this was because important areas of political authority were retained by antidemocratic forces seeking to enrich themselves and undermine the reform process. The Guatemalan Republican Front (FRG) held both the executive and legislative branches from January 2000 to January 2004. During this period a steady stream of high-level government corruption scandals linked the president, Alfonso Portillo, the president of Congress (and FRG's founder) General Efraín Ríos Montt, members of the presidential security staff, and former and current members of the military high command to organized crime.[43] Despite being under investigation for malfeasance and prohibited by the constitution from serving as president, Ríos Montt (a former military dictator who took power in a 1982 coup) manipulated a Constitutional Court decision permitting his candidacy for the November 2003 presidential elections. He came in a distant third in the first round and was placed under house arrest in early 2004. Meanwhile, no institutionalized political party won the December 2003 presidential runoff. The winning candidate, Óscar Berger, led a coalition of center-right forces (GANA) that won a bare five-seat lead over the FRG in Congress. No single party won enough seats to hold a majority; the centrist PAN and center-left UNE formed a coalition that gave them one seat more than GANA, leaving the FRG in a position to hold the legislature hostage by demanding guarantees that Ríos Montt would not be prosecuted for corrupt practices or for crimes against humanity. Of the leading parties, only the FRG maintained an internally cohesive structure and a national presence.[44] This is not a promising basis for consolidating democracy.

Protecting the Rule of Law in Guatemala

As in El Salvador, the terms of the Guatemalan peace accords restructured, downsized, and constrained the political autonomy of the armed forces. In Guatemala, the army agreed to reduce its force size by one-third (which it did in June 2004, although it only eliminated 2,000 positions, leaving open the possibility of restaffing approximately 10,000), to dissolve its mobile military police force within one year, and to remove itself from internal security functions.[45] A civilian intelligence agency was to be created under the Ministry of the Interior, and the Defense Ministry's intelligence department, associated with many of the worst offenses of the civil conflict, was required to restrict its operations to constitutionally defined military matters. Language concerning the supervision of private security businesses and national arms control—especially important in the long term to civilian security—was included in the accords. Unfortunately, most of these reforms require constitutional amendments and were postponed indefinitely by the May 1999 referendum result. A restructured National Civil Police was also created under the Interior Ministry with a target of expanding force levels from 12,000 to 20,000, with professionally recruited agents to be trained at a new police academy.

The restructured civil police were fully deployed in all regions of the country by August 1999. The target of 20,000 civil police was reached, but this was accomplished by not properly training recruits or vetting and retraining former force members. The government opted for rapid deployment at the expense of quality assurance, because decisionmakers believed that the lengthy delays in deploying the new civilian police force in El Salvador had created a window of opportunity for criminal organization. The new civilian police force was also deficient in recruiting indigenous members; as of early 2005 only around 15 percent of all officers were indigenous, and the force is often criticized as unrepresentative of the greater community. Internal oversight and disciplinary mechanisms lack transparency and independence and are incapable of controlling corruption in the force; external oversight is virtually nonexistent.[46] A police Disciplinary Tribunal was established in January 2004 to address police corruption and abuse. It had resolved a number of the most serious cases by the end of its first year, but the situation continued to worsen.[47]

Despite the relatively efficient deployment schedule, the Guatemalan police have been unable to deal with the postconflict wave of public insecurity. The army uses police inadequacy to justify its continued involvement in internal security, in violation of the peace accord on civil-military relations. Civilian control of the Interior Ministry is also uncertain, as high-level positions are held by former military officials. As of early 2005, Congress has yet to pass the legislation on arms control or private security agencies required by the accords.[48] With a police force and court system incapable of guaranteeing public security, local disputes are often resolved, and criminal justice dispensed, by extralegal means. For example, eighty-eight lynchings or attempted lynchings by vigilante mobs occurred between July 2000 and June 2001, a number that increased the following year.[49] In light of the severity of the lynching problem, the UN Verification Mission in Guatemala (MINUGUA, closed in December 2004) launched a public information campaign in December 2002 to combat vigilante justice and promote arms control.[50] The government's response to lynching (forming a committee and roundtable) has been weak and ineffective.

The crime wave brought a proliferation of criminal gangs, often with either direct or tenuous links to military personnel but with no apparent political motivation behind their activities. More threatening to Guatemala's fragile democracy, since 1998 there have been documented reports of a resurgence of violence with probable political motives, especially against human rights activists, public investigators and defenders, and members of the judiciary. The number of such attacks grew rapidly in 2002 and 2003, as did unrest among former members of rural civil patrols who were demobilized with the peace but began to reorganize to demand payment for the time they spent impressed into military-controlled local militias. Forming a clandestine network (cadena), remobilized former civil patrols have halted commerce on the highways and at one of Guatemala's busiest tourist sites to demand compensation. They have frequently been implicated in lynchings and "social cleansing." Ríos Montt on occasion called on these forces to march on Congress when he needed to flex political muscle.[51] The most effective use of these militias to date took place in July 2003. The Supreme Electoral Tribunal and the Supreme Court had barred Ríos Montt from running for president on constitutional grounds. The Constitutional Court overruled the decision and approved his candidacy; the Supreme Court responded by upholding an appeal and suspending the Constitutional Court's ruling. This resulted in the crisis of July 24–25, when several hundred armed and organized FRG supporters were bussed into Guatemala City, surrounded the electoral tribunal, and rioted through the streets, attacking journalists and offices of human rights and opposition political organizations.

Furthermore, the UN mission found evidence that former URNG combatants were also remobilizing and forming roving criminal posses.[52] The guerrilla demobilization was completed on schedule in May 1997 and pronounced a success—URNG forces numbered under 3,000, so disarming and resettlement took place efficiently and without much difficulty. However, the process of reintegrating former combatants into productive life suffered for lack of a strategy to provide stable employment and housing. Unabsorbed former URNG and civil patrol combatants began taking up their uncollected arms and adding to the spiraling rates of violent crime, and the civilian security institutions grew more militarized in response, with the government deploying joint police-military units for policing operations, creating a vicious cycle of violence.

Guatemala's administration of justice system was addressed in the accord on constitutional reforms, and these reforms were also held up by the referendum debacle. The agreement called for a constitutional amendment to guarantee free and equal access to justice regardless of language or ethnicity, public defense for the poor, judicial independence, prompt resolution of cases, and public provision of mechanisms for alternative mediation. It also called for greatly improved training, appointment, remuneration, and disciplinary mechanisms through the Career Judicial Service Act. MINUGUA worked with UNDP and USAID on projects to train the public prosecutor's office on legal procedures and penal reform. The mission assisted the office of the human rights ombudsman with investigative and management procedures and the Interior Ministry with police and prison reform. It also assisted in improving coordination between police and public prosecutors in criminal investigations. Most of these institution-building programs were funded through international donations to the Trust Fund for the Guatemalan Peace Process.

There have been real advances in the amount of Guatemalan national territory covered by local courts, although they remain poorly coordinated. Administrative reforms have taken place at the national, district, and municipal levels to promote career standards, judicial independence, protection of justices, and coordination of the courts with police investigators. Improvements have been most evident at the local level: case processing has been streamlined, and local case management has been made more efficient and less corrupt. But reformed criminal procedure and penal codes have not prevented ongoing occurrences of arbitrary arrest and illegal detentions, and prisons continue to be overcrowded and underresourced, conditions that occasionally result in deadly prison uprisings.[53] Reforms to the justice system have been woefully ineffective in overcoming corruption and intimidation (including even assassination of members of the judiciary) and have not lessened the impunity of government and military officials. The investigatory system remains inadequate, largely because investigators often work under death threats and systematic obstruction.[54]

U.S. Foreign Policy in Guatemala

Relations between the United States and the Guatemalan government in the 1980s were very different from U.S.-Salvadoran relations during the same period, primarily because the United States appropriated relatively little direct military assistance for Guatemala. Congress had terminated direct military aid to Guatemala in 1978 in response to human rights violations. Because of this, the Guatemalan armed forces did not become dependent on U.S. funding and training in the way that the Salvadoran armed forces did—and it was the dependence on U.S. military aid that eventually led to the Salvadoran military's subordination to civilian authority and cooperation with the peace process, a fact often noted with derision by the Guatemalan military.[55]

Military aid was reinstated in 1986 following the election of a moderate civilian (Vinicio Cerezo, like Duarte a Christian Democrat) but at low levels relative to El Salvador (US$34 million in direct military aid between 1985 and 1995).[56] The Guatemalan armed forces were able to resist becoming dependent on U.S. funding because by the time assistance was reinstated, they had established other arms sources and had developed independent financial portfolios in banking, real estate, and other enterprises.

The effect of the post–cold war shift in geopolitical interests on U.S.-Guatemalan relations was less direct than in El Salvador, but there was a marked increase in the level of U.S. State Department scrutiny and criticism of government human rights abuses under the George H. W. Bush administration. Because of human rights concerns, lethal aid to Guatemala was cut back again, and deliveries were temporarily suspended in December 1990. Appropriations legislation for 1993 prohibited all military aid and required that nonmilitary assistance fund only civilian agencies of government and nongovernmental organizations.

The Clinton administration was proactive in helping to reverse a May 1993 attempted executive coup in Guatemala. It demonstrated its support for the reconstituted democratic government by resuming both military and police training and joint military exercises (although direct military assistance remained suspended).[57] Two years later, in March 1995, a scandal emerged linking the CIA with a military officer suspected of torture and murder, as a result of which remaining military financing, including officer training programs, was terminated.[58] Military training was resumed in 1997. Antinarcotics assistance was introduced in 1996 and continues to be the major channel for defense-related appropriations to Guatemala.

Following the trend in nonmilitary assistance to postconflict Central America, priorities vis-à-vis Guatemala are improving the legal system; improving the quality of education and access to it; providing health care for women, children, and rural families; increasing earning capacity for the rural poor; and managing natural resources and conserving biodiversity. Special emphasis has been placed on implementing the peace accords (according to the U.S. State Department, U.S. commitments to support the implementation of the peace accords totaled over US$260 million between 1997 and 2002) through community assistance, including mental heath provision, literacy and scholarship programs, financial support for resettlement programs, and security sector training.[59] The USAID mission in Guatemala has provided technical training in advocacy to anticorruption, human rights, prodemocracy, women's, and indigenous civil society organizations; it also provided capacity building through a grants project that worked with a network of twenty-five Guatemalan nongovernmental organizations.

Government corruption became a high-profile issue in U.S.-Guatemalan relations during the Portillo administration, to such a degree that the U.S. embassy expressed its concern in a public forum over the influence of organized crime in the Guatemalan armed forces and police.[60] Guatemala was decertified as a cooperative ally in the war on drugs in January 2003, owing to frequent allegations that government and military officials were involved in drug traffic and organized crime.[61]

To conclude, although the peace process in Guatemala created a somewhat less polarized society, it is not a demilitarized one. Recovery and reconciliation have not advanced much; popular confidence in state institutions, especially the security forces still closely associated with years of violent repression, is very low. Democratic consolidation in Guatemala has been badly hindered by peace spoilers in government and an extremely contentious political system. The number of combatants who were demobilized is significantly lower than in El Salvador, but conditions for peaceful and productive reintegration are worse, and the remobilization of former civil servants is adding to widespread violence and lawlessness. There is a ray of hope, however: the mechanisms for civil sector participation—especially of women and indigenous groups—in designing and implementing the accords gave organized civil society a voice for reform that is unprecedented in Guatemalan history. International assistance programs such as that of the USAID mission are seeking to broaden and deepen citizen capacity. This trend holds out promise for reconciliation and potentially for democratic consolidation in Guatemala.

Political Institutions in Nicaragua

Unlike those of El Salvador and Guatemala, the electoral system in Nicaragua was not controlled by the military before the civil war. Rather, the government was monopolized by a dynastic, personalist dictatorship, established in 1936 by Anastasio Somoza García and ruled directly or indirectly by his sons from 1956 through 1979. The Somozas used patronage and crony networks to control a vast amount of national assets. The economic growth period of the 1950s and 1960s created a new middle class, which began to demand a voice in governance, occasionally forming short-lived and mainly unsuccessful political parties.[62] However, in the 1970s the oil crisis and resulting global recession reversed the gains of the previous decades; the emerging middle classes suffered and became even more outraged by the depredations of the Somoza family. Armed opposition movements mobilized throughout the country, and most civil sectors and political organizations had declared their support for the armed opposition by the end of 1978.

The guerrilla forces formally united as the Sandinista National Liberation Front (FSLN) in March 1979; in mid-July they entered Managua. Somoza fled, the National Guard collapsed, and a broad-based junta took charge with the open support of several Latin American governments.[63] The initial direction of the junta was social democratic and not aligned with international powers. However, deep ideological divisions between the FSLN faction and the center and center-left members of the junta led to the exclusion of moderates (including future president Violeta Chamorro) from decisionmaking and, within a year, to their resignation. The FSLN directorate gained dominance in the ruling coalition and began to impose socialist central planning modeled on Cuba.[64] The planned economy was not popular among the productive sectors, from business owners to small farmers, and it was very poorly managed. Assaults on state cooperative farms by bands of armed dissidents began in mid-1981. Within months, the U.S. Central Intelligence Agency had, with assistance from Argentine military trainers, organized the dissidents into a full-scale paramilitary force (counterrevolutionaries, or contras), which launched attacks from camps on the Honduran and Costa Rican borders.[65]

The contra war was politically very costly for the Sandinistas. The government declared a state of emergency in March 1982; it lasted until January 1988, reinforcing U.S. assertions that the Sandinista government was an antidemocratic communist dictatorship. The civil conflict so polarized Nicaraguan politics that even when elections were scheduled for November 1984, there could be no civil debate, much less accommodation, between the political opposition and the Sandinistas.[66] And it cost a great deal in foreign relations. Nicaragua's relationship with the Soviet Union had much the same effect as the Salvadoran government's relationship with the United States: it alienated other Latin American governments, internationalized the domestic conflict by inviting outside intervention, and created a dependence on major power assistance that evaporated with the waning of the cold war. The Sandinistas found themselves virtually abandoned by the Soviet Union in 1988, bankrupt, and with no option but to negotiate with the contras. In compliance with the Esquipulas agreement, the government lifted the state of emergency in January 1988, met directly with contra leaders, and signed a ceasefire in March. Elections were held in February 1990, which proved to be transitional. The presidency was won by Violeta Chamorro, candidate of the

National Opposition Union (UNO), a coalition of fourteen disparate opposition parties, a coalition that began to disintegrate soon after the elections.

In El Salvador and Guatemala, civil war was settled through mediated peace talks that at least addressed, if they could not resolve, outstanding sources of conflict. There was no similar negotiation agenda in Nicaragua, and the settlement did not produce agreements mandating reforms that could mitigate further civil conflict. The peace agreements failed to commit the government to a feasible reintegration scheme and failed to specify measures to verify implementation and sanction noncompliance. The signatories to the accords, both the government and the contra leaders, failed to consult with their constituents to ensure that the agreements were acceptable. Even the terms of disarmament and demobilization were not resolved until after the elections.[67] Combined with corrupt leadership, the lack of a negotiated settlement and reintegration plan goes far in explaining why Nicaraguan politics remained intensely polarized and underinstitutionalized through most of the 1990s.

Once the government and the contra command had agreed on a ceasefire, the Sandinistas and the civilian opposition quickly mobilized their supporters for elections. The contra forces did not participate in the elections, nor were they represented by any of the parties running in the elections, and they had already begun to fragment by the time of the transition. They found themselves with few allies in the UNO government, which was primarily composed of elites from the Pacific Coast bourgeoisie, and eventually the three main contra divisions negotiated separate demobilization deals with Chamorro.[68]

To get the contra factions to disarm, Chamorro made promises to distribute land that her government could not deliver, given the condition of property rights and competing interests from those whose land had been expropriated by the Sandinistas—and whose land claims were supported by the U.S. government. The land transfer policy reflected Chamorro's weak political base and the need to balance the demands of former contra combatants, the farmers displaced from now-privatized state cooperative farms, demobilized Sandinista soldiers, and right-wing members of the UNO coalition. Both Sandinista and UNO officials skimmed inordinate amounts off the top when state assets were privatized. This led to an interesting political realignment over the course of the 1990s, with the upper echelons of parties on both sides making deals to retain their power and assets, to the detriment of their own resentful bases.

The UNO government of necessity focused on economic recovery from the start. By the time of the transition, Nicaragua was US$365 million in debt to the World Bank and the Inter-American Development Bank alone, and total foreign debt was around US$11 billion. The government was able to secure over US$750 million in grants and financing for 1992, but this level of debt could not be managed without assistance from international financial institutions. In order to meet International Monetary Fund and World Bank conditions, Chamorro initiated a major restructuring program that entailed privatizing state assets, shrinking the public sector, deregulating prices, reducing social spending and eliminating subsidies, liberalizing trade and banking, and instituting a "shock therapy" financial stabilization program that managed to bring hyperinflation under control, from 30,000 percent in 1990 to 12 percent in 1994.[69] In a pattern now familiar throughout the developing world, the macroeconomic achievements of structural adjustments were accompanied by a sharp increase in inequality (the GINI index went from 57 in 1993 to 60 in 1998). Unemployment and underemployment rates quickly exceeded 53 percent—rates that did not improve as growth picked up after 1994.[70] The combination of raised expectations with the transition and rapid deterioration in living standards produced social instability and soaring crime rates, all of which contributed to the remobilization of former combatants.

In addition to the polarizing effects of the economic program, Chamorro's ability to promote institutional change was limited by the Sandinistas' majority in the Supreme Court and strength in the National Assembly. A combination of crises over land rights, structural adjustment, and the rearming of demobilized combatants created an extremely unstable situation by mid-decade. Responding to the instability, in 1995 dissident reformist factions in both the UNO and the FSLN pushed through compromise legislation on constitutional revisions that reinforced checks and balances among the branches of government, placed term limits on the executive, and gave the assembly greater powers in economic and taxation policymaking and the power to appoint Supreme Court justices and the comptroller general.[71]

Aside from the severe difficulties associated with recovering from economic collapse, the major impediment to democratic consolidation in post-conflict Nicaragua has been government corruption. Attempts at anticorruption legislation have been unsuccessful.[72] In January 2000, Nicaraguans were treated to a cynical demonstration of corruption when leaderships on both sides joined forces to consolidate political control and protect their rents. The heads of the two leading parties, the FSLN and the Liberal Constitutionalist Party (PLC), passed a constitutional amendment that established joint party control of the comptroller general, the Supreme Court, and the Supreme Electoral Council. It manipulated the electoral laws in such a way as to impede third-party competition and was followed by an electoral law revision that placed prohibitive obstacles in the way of registering new parties and even of forming party coalitions. The amendment strengthened presidential immunity from prosecution and provided an automatic seat in the assembly (also with immunity from prosecution) for outgoing presidents and the candidates who place second in presidential elections.[73] This was not to prevent hypothetical prosecutions. It was well known at the time that the incumbent president, PLC's Arnoldo Alemán, was embezzling money, later calculated at US$95 million, from the state. The other signatory to this pact, FSLN leader Daniel Ortega, had been protected by his assembly immunity from prosecution on charges of molestation brought by his stepdaughter. Ortega placed second in the 2001 presidential election and therefore retained his immunity.[74]

The PLC candidate who won that election and took office in 2002, Enrique Bolaños, had run on an anticorruption platform and quickly overturned Alemán's immunity, thus alienating the rest of his party. Alemán faced prosecution and was sentenced to twenty years of house arrest, despite which he retained control of the PLC. The "Ortega-Alemán pact" was reenacted in the summer of 2005 in an effort regain power using the FSLN's lock on the justice and electoral systems and the PLC's strength in the assembly, prompting diplomatic intervention by the OAS secretary-general and the U.S. deputy secretary of state.[75]

Protecting the Rule of Law in Nicaragua

In Nicaragua, following the 1979 coup, the Sandinista government disbanded the former Nicaraguan security forces (principally Somoza's National Guard) and replaced them with the Sandinista Popular Army (EPS), staffed by FSLN loyalists. A new national police was created under the Interior Ministry; Nicaragua had no history of civilian policing or security independent of the military. The FSLN also created party-controlled militia organizations, neighborhood defense committees, and a number of irregular patrol units, all charged with the defense of the Sandinista revolution. As the contra war heated up in 1981–82, the Sandinistas imposed universal conscription of males between the ages of seventeen and twenty-five, exponentially increasing the size of the army and the military budget. Overall, there was a general militarization of society, as citizens found themselves impressed into local defense organizations.[76] When the war ended, 72,000 Sandinista soldiers, 22,500 contras, and 5,000 police officers were demobilized. The total number of demobilized combatants exceeded the total number of civilians employed in formal sectors in Nicaragua at the time.[77]

As discussed in earlier sections, implementation of the peace accords in El Salvador and Guatemala was verified by UN missions that deployed before a ceasefire; these missions monitored human rights, oversaw the implementation of institutional reforms, and verified the demobilization of combatants. By contrast, missions to Nicaragua from the UN and the Organization of American States (OAS) were traditional peacekeeping operations in that their mandates, with the exception of a joint election observation unit, were limited to overseeing the ceasefire and demobilization operations.[78] The UN operation (the UN Observer Group in Central America, or ONUCA, which was deployed from November 1989 to January 1992) oversaw the demobilization of the contra bases in Honduras and monitored the borders. The OAS mission (the International Commission of Support, or CIAV/OAS, which was deployed from November 1989 to July 1997) verified the much more numerous contra demobilizations within Nicaragua's borders, assisted with the reintegration process, and monitored the 1990 elections. Of the estimated 300,000 weapons that had been delivered either to the contras or the Sandinistas during the civil war, only one-third were collected by the international operations.[79]

Given the lack of jobs or resources available for demobilized combatants, it is hardly surprising that approximately 22,000 former contras and Sandinista Army soldiers remobilized within a year, not as an organized opposition force but as disorganized militias with differing objectives. President Chamorro responded to the remobilization with three general amnesties and forty-one ad hoc side agreements promising a variety of concessions in exchange for arms, including the disastrous land transfer programs (above). Most of the recontras, recompas, and revueltos had disarmed by 1995, but the countryside remained chaotic, and the problems of uncollected arms and unintegrated former combatants led to a 112 percent increase in the rate of violent crime between 1990 and 1995.[80] Violence linked to former combatants has since declined.

Again, the manner of settling the civil war distinguishes postwar Nicaragua from El Salvador and Guatemala. Whereas the peace accords in the other two cases called for the security sectors to be restructured, their doctrines to be redirected, their leaderships to be vetted, their forces to be retrained, and their agencies to be placed under civilian oversight, in Nicaragua security sector reform was not negotiated. Nor was it addressed in the demobilization agreements, although a number of former contras were incorporated into the police units in areas that had heavy contra presence during the war. Following the transition, Chamorro left the army and national police under the command of FSLN leaders in a compromise settlement that angered the contra command, many UNO coalition members, and the U.S. government. It led to demands for full withdrawal of the Sandinistas from the security services. A new military code was passed in 1994 that helped establish formal presidential authority over the military hierarchy. The police over time have become less identified with the Sandinistas but have not been restructured, modernized, or professionalized to adequately confront the postconflict security environment of economic crisis, severe unemployment, and weapons proliferation. That said, the extent of violent crime in Nicaragua is much lower than in the other two war-transition countries, and, although inadequately trained, the police force has had some success in adopting community policing techniques.

Concerning justice administration, the 1996 constitutional reforms in Nicaragua gave legislators the power to appoint Supreme Court justices and increase the court's budget, reforms that should have contributed to making the courts independent and less susceptible to corruption. However, the assembly continues to be dominated by party leaders, who wield centralized control over their benches, leading to a biased selection of Supreme Court officials, who maintain control of lower court justice appointments. Despite a great deal of international training and assistance and the creation of an internal inspection commission, the justice system has remained inefficient, unprofessional, undertrained, highly politicized, and very corrupt.[81]

U.S. Foreign Policy in Nicaragua

Obviously, U.S. relations with Nicaragua during the 1980s were the opposite of its relations with either El Salvador or Guatemala, in that the United States openly supported the antigovernment insurgency. Once the FSLN were clearly in power in late 1980, the Carter administration attempted to influence the new government through increased economic assistance, sending US$15 million in emergency reconstruction aid shortly after the revolution and pushing a US$75 million assistance package through Congress that same year.[82] When Reagan took office in 1981 with a decisively ideological anticommunist foreign agenda, all economic assistance to the Nicaraguan government was cut off. In November 1981, a national security directive detailed a program of direct aggression against the Sandinistas and authorized another US$19.5 million to assist the armed opposition.[83]

In terms of infrastructure and lost production, the devastation caused by a decade of civil war in Nicaragua was much higher than that sustained by either El Salvador or Guatemala.[84] Scarce resources were diverted to the defense budget, which absorbed 55 percent of the national budget in 1986–88. A significant portion of Nicaragua's economic collapse of the 1980s is attributable to U.S. activities. Economic sanctions and a trade embargo imposed in 1985 cost Nicaragua an estimated US$254 million. The administration exerted diplomatic pressure to isolate Nicaragua, recruited other governments to cooperate with the embargo, and vetoed—and successfully lobbied against—World Bank and IDB loans to Nicaragua. The U.S. Department of Defense contributed to the spiraling escalation of hostilities by conducting military exercises just off the Pacific Coast. CIA operations (conducted by CIA personnel, not by Nicaraguan contras) included blowing up oil tanks, pipelines, and transportation and storage facilities; launching helicopter assaults from offshore; and mining harbors.[85] In December 1982, the U.S. Congress passed an amendment that explicitly prohibited the administration from supporting the overthrow of the Sandinista government. The administration violated the prohibition, and after a full ban on U.S. support for the contras was passed in October 1984, the White House resorted to illegal activities to keep the contras in operation, causing a major public scandal that broke in October 1986 (the Iran-contra scandal). Before the illegal operation was exposed, however, Congress reversed the ban and in June 1986 appropriated US$100 million in military assistance for the contras.

The most marked shift in Central America policy between the Reagan and the Bush administrations was toward Nicaragua. While the former maintained a determined policy of overthrowing the Sandinista government at any cost, under Bush the objective was to get the costly situation off the foreign policy agenda. The administration came to an agreement with Congress to appropriate US$66 million in nonlethal assistance for the contras in 1989 and to cut off all funding except for repatriation assistance after that. Foreign aid to Nicaragua was rechanneled to promotion of democratic institutions (especially strengthening opposition parties) leading up to the February 1990 elections. Following the 1990 transition, the United States restored normal diplomatic relations with Nicaragua and expressed its support for the Chamorro government with a rapid and significant increase in financial assistance.

However, economic aid was cut back as sharply for fiscal year 1992 in order to pressure the government on two priority items: unresolved private claims to property that had been expropriated by the Sandinista government, and continued Sandinista dominance of the military and police. US$104 million of the appropriated economic assistance budget was withheld. It was released in 1994 on four conditions: that a human rights code of conduct be imposed on the military and police forces, that efforts be made to reform the judicial system, that outstanding claims to expropriated land be resolved, and that the USAID monitor the use of all assistance to prevent corruption. During this time members of Congress further complicated relations by making an indirect association between a May 1993 explosion in Managua (of a weapons cache containing false identity documents) and the February 1993 World Trade Center bombing. Members of Congress cited the explosion as evidence that Sandinistas were involved in international terrorism and conditioned economic support funds in the 1994 budget on investigations into Sandinista relations with international terrorist groups.[86]

Current priorities for U.S.-Nicaraguan relations are promotion of human, intellectual, and property rights; civilian control of military and police; interdiction of transborder criminal activity such as narcotics traffic, illegal alien smuggling, and international terrorist and criminal organizations; reforms to the judiciary; and governance issues, especially electoral transparency and anticorruption. Claims to expropriated lands continue to be an issue in U.S.-Nicaraguan relations, although the U.S. State Department annually waives the 1994 legislation, conditioning assistance on resolution of those claims. A total of US$93 million was appropriated in 1999–2001 for Hurricane Mitch reconstruction.[87] Between 1990 and 2002, the United States provided Nicaragua with US$260 million for debt relief and US$450 million for balance of payments support. Since 2000, U.S. assistance programs have focused on government transparency, sustainable growth, primary education, and food assistance for families. An important thrust of the governance program is increased citizen participation in decisionmaking; in 2001 USAID granted a total of US$6.2 million to the Supreme Electoral Council to train a consortium of civil society organizations in election monitoring and analysis.[88]

In sum, the crippling legacies of Nicaragua's civil war are not uncontrollable violent crime, ineffective public security systems, and highly polarized electoral politics, as in the other two cases, or residual authoritarian leadership and societal militarization, as in Guatemala. The lack of negotiated reintegration mechanisms and institutional reforms in Nicaragua left the country vulnerable to remobilized political violence during the years following the end of the civil war, and crime rates rose precipitously during the mid-1990s. However, even given underreporting of crime, violent crime is now considerably lower than in the other two countries. The government has pressed forward with efforts to reform the justice administration system, and civil organizations have mobilized to address the problem of government corruption. The major obstacles to governance in Nicaragua reflect unconsolidated democratic norms and institutions, seen especially in the corruption and the cynical manipulation of power among political elites and in the destruction to the economy and national infrastructure caused by the war.

Conclusion

It is now a decade since the civil wars in Central America have ended, but the sustainability of the peace must remain on the U.S. foreign policy agenda. Spillover issues from poor state performance—unimpeded narcotics traffic, money laundering, and transnational organized crime, often involving corrupt government and military officials; the steady stream of immigrants from Central American countries—all have clear national security ramifications. U.S. Coast Guard, Navy, and Army resources are engaged in protecting U.S. borders from drugs and other contraband transshipped through Central America. The possibility of political instability in the region increases the likelihood that internal violence will cross borders and create a new flood of refugees. Political instability also poses a threat to U.S. commercial and financial interests in the region: we are partners in a regional trade agreement (CAFTA), El Salvador has tied its fiscal policy to that of the United States by dollarizing its economy, and U.S. textile and other product manufacturers have plants throughout the region. If the United States had a vital national interest in stability in Central America during the 1980s, it is even greater now, with increased levels of transnational crime and with the regional integration that has directly or indirectly linked the Central American economies with the U.S. economy.

The postconflict political context in El Salvador, Guatemala, and Nicaragua is less restricted, less violently conflictual, and more plural but—especially in Guatemala—still precarious. Poor government performance plays out in different ways in these countries, but it shares a common source: the democratic institutions have not overcome the legacies of social and political exclusion enforced by a repressive state, even where reforms to those institutions have been enacted through peace accords. The major obstacles to better governance are extreme political polarization, continued fragmentation of political parties and other systems for representation, corruption and authoritarian tendencies of political leaderships, mismanagement and corruption in the administration of justice and the police forces, and the lack of societal confidence in state institutions.

One obvious lesson from this study is that although negotiated peace accords can facilitate the process of institutional reform, they do not guarantee that the parties will comply with their agreements. International assistance programs for postconflict states that are not under a form of transitional authority (as was the case in Cambodia, Bosnia, Kosovo, and East Timor) must work within the limitations imposed by the country's domestic politics, and donor states should not have inflated expectations of their ability to influence the process. International assistance programs can make inroads but will not be able to unblock obstacles created by resistant and corrupt elites. And while it is often essential to a program's success to have international donors schedule their assistance so that it is conditional on compliance with reforms, this may not be feasible in cases where withholding funds would threaten other important objectives, such as not further destabilizing a shaky government at a critical juncture.

What are the implications of this study for U.S. policy? At the broadest level, should the United States become involved in civil conflict or "regime change" in other countries, the government must plan to stay the course in the postconflict period and focus assistance on strengthening democratic institutions through agencies such as USAID's democracy and governance program and the National Endowment for Democracy. Aid programs should work with the political parties to create internal mechanisms to ensure their accountability to the electorate; work with local nongovernmental organizations on grassroots voter education and programs to encourage participation in the electoral system; strengthen legal training and oversight agencies in justice administration; and work with local police forces on internal and external oversight. More so than in the lower-income but not war-transition poorly performing states, assistance programs must be designed with a very long timeline to account for necessary reconstruction—not only of the physical and economic infrastructure but also of the weakly consolidated public institutions and of the still-disrupted community networks. And special attention in all cases must be given to arms registration and collection.

Public security and rule of law in general is a product of the proper functioning of a system of agencies and institutions, including police who walk neighborhood beats, police investigators, public prosecutors and public defenders, local courts, the national attorney general, national and constitutional courts, and prisons. Lowering violent crime significantly in poorly performing states requires focused, systemic, long-term assistance to the security sector and justice administration systems plus intervention at the community level to provide mental health and conflict mediation services. Unfortunately, these kinds of programs receive much less public support than the draconian anticrime laws of El Salvador, the vigilante justice of Guatemala, and the death-squad-like social cleansing operations in both countries.

An important consideration when assessing the U.S. foreign policy implications of poor government performance in war-transition states is that U.S. country assistance priorities will vary according to a number of factors not necessarily related to conditions on the ground: at the planning stage priorities will vary with the interests of the current administration; at the mission level priorities will vary with the nature of local partners, the latest mandate from Washington, budgetary considerations, and diplomatic pressure. Even with the best of intentions, U.S. assistance priorities may not reflect local needs. Given budgetary restrictions and political sensitivities, USAID programs should be commended for moving into areas that were not originally part of the development agenda, such as electoral and governance reform. Noteworthy in this regard are USAID/El Salvador's efforts to increase popular access to justice; USAID/Guatemala's program to professionalize civil advocacy organizations; and USAID/Nicaragua's efforts in voter education and mobilization and in political party development. The following recommendations recognize those achievements.

—Justice system reform: experience shows that piecemeal training for individual agencies does not result in improved performance over the long term. Those who design justice administration programs should take a systematic approach to needs assessment that takes the full justice cycle into account: programs should recognize that each phase of the system is an interacting part. One focus should be citizen oversight boards to ensure professional standards and equal access to justice. Another focus should be professional training at each level of the justice system.

—Police reform: this is a very sensitive issue in relations between outside assistance agencies and host governments, but it is vitally important in any postconflict situation to ensure public security. The Department of Justice's ICITAP assistance in training and providing material to transitional police forces should be encouraged in conjunction and cooperation with local civilian oversight groups. Strengthening internal and external police oversight structures should be a focus of USAID's democracy and governance strategy.

—Electoral reform: these programs tend to focus on monitoring the elections themselves, guaranteeing the security of campaign workers, equal access to media and finance during campaigns, assistance with registration, and training election officials in proper administrative practices. But a consistent level of attention to the electoral system should be maintained during the lulls in the electoral cycle. Voter education and the professionalization of citizen oversight organizations are important channels for reform. This includes working with domestic nongovernmental election monitoring teams between campaigns and building mechanisms to keep civil organizations involved in the electoral system, for example by working with the parties to ensure that they are accountable and responsive to their members.

For assistance agencies, the challenge is to create aid programs with built-in incentives that can effectively induce cooperation beyond the time of the administration that negotiated the deal, beyond the short time horizon and faddishness of assistance programs, and beyond changing geopolitical landscapes and shifting congressional attention. To meet this challenge, program designers must be able to answer some fundamental questions: Can points of leverage be found that would provide incentives for government and business leaders to overcome entrenched interests and equally entrenched corrupt behaviors? Are there civil actors with the capacity (in terms of literacy, skills and expertise, cohesion, trust in public agencies) to cooperate and mobilize for development, to work effectively with international project managers, and to engage in democratic participatory politics? Is there sufficient human capital among organized civil actors to provide alternatives to the current set of political elites? In the aftermath of civil war, the answers to these questions will never be solidly positive, but the process of examining them should lead international assistance providers toward imaginative solutions to some of the most contentious and obstinate problems of war-transition states.

Notes

1. See the Country Classification section of the World Bank's website www.worldbank. org/data/countryclass/classgroups.htm. All three countries are ranked by the UN Development Program (UNDP) as being in the "medium human development" category, with Human Development Index—which ranks 177 countries according to life expectancy, literacy, education, and GDP, with the highest rank being 1 (Norway) and the lowest rank 177 (Niger)—rankings of 104 (El Salvador), 112 (Nicaragua), and 117 (Guatemala). See UNDP, *Human Development Report 2005, International Cooperation at a Crossroads: Aid, Trade, and Security in an Unequal World* (Oxford University Press, 2005).

2. From Inter-American Development Bank Office of Evaluation and Oversight, Country Program Evaluation El Salvador: 1992–2004 (Washington: 2005), p. i; Inter-

American Development Bank, IDB Country Strategy with Nicaragua (Washington: 2002), p. 8; Inter-American Development Bank, IDB Country Strategy with Guatemala: 2004–2007 (Washington: 2004), p. 20.

3. According to the Inter-American Development Bank, Hurricane Mitch (October 28–29, 1998) killed an estimated 9,000 people and caused approximately US$6.2 billion in damages; 80 percent of damages were sustained by Honduras and Nicaragua. See Janet Garrido and Kahwa Douoguih, *Responding to Natural Disaster: The Role of the Inter-American Development Bank's Lending in Rebuilding Central America after Hurricane Mitch* (Washington: WOLA and InterAction, 2001). Posthurricane restoration of agricultural production was hindered by a severe drought. Two major earthquakes shook El Salvador on January 13 and February 13, 2001, killed nearly 1,200 people, and left damages of approximately US$1.5 billion, or 12 percent of GDP. See Jack Spence, Mike Lanchin, and Geoff Thale, *From Elections to Earthquakes: Reform and Participation in Post-War El Salvador* (Cambridge, Mass.: Hemisphere Initiatives, 2001).

4. International Bank for Reconstruction and Development and International Finance Corporation, *Country Assistance Strategy for the Republic of El Salvador* (Washington: World Bank, 2005), pp. 2–3.

5. International Bank for Reconstruction and Development, *Country Assistance Strategy for the Republic of Guatemala* (Washington: World Bank, 2005), pp. 3–8.

6. World Bank, "Memorandum of the President of the International Development Association and the International Finance Corporation to the Executive Directors on a Country Assistance Strategy of the World Bank Group for the Republic of Nicaragua" (Washington: 2002), pp. 3-4.

7. Demographic information is from a 1998–99 national survey, cited in United Nations Verification Mission in Guatemala (MINUGUA), "Report of MINUGUA for the Consultative Group Meeting for Guatemala," January 18, 2002, p. 6.

8. Transparency International's 2003 Corruption Perceptions Index ranks Nicaragua at 88 and Guatemala at 100 (ranked from least corrupt = 1, most corrupt = 133), although if only presidential theft were considered Nicaragua would rank considerably lower. By comparison, the same report ranks Honduras at 106, Panama at 66, El Salvador at 59, and Costa Rica at 50.

9. The statistics are from Charles T. Call, "Sustainable Development in Central America: The Challenges of Violence, Injustice, and Insecurity," Centroamérica 2020 Working Paper 8 (Hamburg: Institut für Iberoamerika-Kunde, 2000), p. 9. It should be emphasized that crime statistics in this region are notoriously unreliable, as police units often lack the facilities to collect the data, the central registries fail to properly aggregate them, and an estimated two-thirds of all crimes are unreported.

10. Luis Romano, cited in Spence, Lanchin, and Thale, *From Elections to Earthquakes,* p. 17.

11. Call, "Sustainable Development in Central America," p. 36. In the same paper, Call also discusses the pros and cons of importing the democratic policing model; for further information on this question, see Rachel Nield, "Democratic Police Reforms in War-Torn Societies," *Journal of Conflict, Security, and Development* 1, no. 1 (2001): 21–43; George Vickers, "Renegotiating Internal Security: The Lessons of Central America," in *Comparative Peace Processes in Latin America,* edited by Cynthia Arnson (Washington: Woodrow Wilson Center Press, 1999).

12. For a comprehensive analysis of the politics of Central America policy, see Cynthia Arnson, *Crossroads: Congress, the President, and Central America, 1976–1992* (Pennsylvania State University Press, 1993).

13. Mark P. Sullivan, *Central America and U.S. Foreign Assistance: Congressional Action* (Washington: Congressional Research Service, December 1994), pp. 3–12.

14. Ibid., p. 3.

15. Remittances in 2002 from Salvadorans working in the United States that were transferred through banks and therefore were counted by the central bank totaled US$1.93 billion, or 13.6 percent of El Salvador's GDP. See U.S. Department of State, Bureau of Western Hemisphere, "Background Note: El Salvador," September 2003.

16. Enrique A. Baloyra, *El Salvador in Transition* (University of North Carolina Press, 1982).

17. The most detailed account of these events is found in Tommie Sue Montgomery, *Revolution in El Salvador: From Civil Strife to Civil Peace* (Boulder, Colo.: Westview Press, 1995).

18. On the Central American peace process, see Jack Child, *The Central American Peace Process, 1983–1991: Sheathing Swords, Building Confidence* (Boulder, Colo.: Lynne Rienner, 1992). On the dynamics of Salvadoran politics of this period, see Joseph Tulchin and Gary Bland, eds., *Is There a Transition to Democracy in El Salvador?* (Boulder, Colo.: Lynne Rienner, 1992).

19. On the Salvadoran peace process, see Susan Burgerman, "Building the Peace by Mandating Reform: United Nations–Mediated Human Rights Agreements in El Salvador and Guatemala," *Latin American Perspectives* 27, no. 3 (2000): 65–70.

20. "Mexico Agreement," reproduced in *The United Nations and El Salvador, 1990–1995*, UN Blue Books Series, vol. 4 (New York: United Nations Publications, 1995), pp. 167–74.

21. For a detailed analysis of the 1994 elections, see Jack Spence, David Dye, and George Vickers, *El Salvador, Elections of the Century: Results, Recommendations, Analysis* (Cambridge, Mass.: Hemisphere Initiatives, 1994); also see Tommie Sue Montgomery, "Good Observers, Bad Leaders, and Ugly Politics: Observing Elections in El Salvador," paper prepared for the conference "Multilateral Approaches to Peacemaking and Democratization in the Hemisphere," Miami, April 1996.

22. Cited in Spence, Lanchin, and Thale, *From Elections to Earthquakes*, p. 6.

23. Miren Gutiérrez, "Central America, the Caribbean, and Mexico," in *Transparency International Global Corruption Report, 2001*, edited by Robin Hodess (Berlin: Transparency International, 2001).

24. Spence, Lanchin, and Thale, *From Elections to Earthquakes*, pp. 4–5.

25. My thanks to Pamela Starr for these clarifications.

26. For details of the training and deployment of the new Salvadoran police force, see Gino Costa, "The United Nations and Reform of the Police in El Salvador," *International Peacekeeping* (Autumn 1995); William Stanley, *Protectors or Perpetrators? The Institutional Crisis of the Salvadoran Civilian Police* (Washington: WOLA and Hemisphere Initiatives, 1996); William Stanley and Charles T. Call, "Building a New Civilian Police Force in El Salvador," in *Rebuilding Societies after Civil War: Critical Roles for International Assistance*, edited by Krishna Kumar (Boulder, Colo.: Lynne Rienner, 1997).

27. Spence, Lanchin, and Thale, *From Elections to Earthquakes*, pp. 17–22.

28. Gutiérrez, "Central America, the Caribbean, and Mexico," pp. 153–54.

29. International Bank for Reconstruction and Development, "El Salvador: World Bank Approves $18 Million to Support Judicial Modernization," News Release 2003/043/LCR, August 1, 2002.

30. See especially Margaret Popkin, *Peace without Justice: Obstacles to Building the Rule of Law in El Salvador* (Pennsylvania State University Press, 2000); also Margaret Popkin, with Jack Spence and George Vickers, *Justice Delayed: The Slow Pace of Judicial Reform in El Salvador* (Washington: WOLA and Hemisphere Initiatives, December 1994); and Call, "Sustainable Development in Central America."

31. Susan Burgerman, *Moral Victories: How Activists Provoke Multilateral Action* (Cornell University Press, 2001), chap. 4; Arnson, *Crossroads,* chaps. 3–6.

32. James K. Boyce and others, *Adjustment toward Peace: Economic Policy and Post-War Reconstruction in El Salvador* (San Salvador: UN Development Program, 1995).

33. Sullivan, *Central America and U.S. Foreign Assistance,* pp. 6, 9–10.

34. U.S. Department of State, "Background Note: El Salvador" (September 2003); Spence, Lanchin, and Thale, *From Elections to Earthquakes,* pp. 34–37.

35. Héctor Rosada Granados, "Parties, Transitions, and the Political System in Guatemala," in *Political Parties and Democracy in Central America,* edited by Louis Goodman, William LeoGrande, and Johanna Mendelson Forman (Boulder, Colo.: Westview Press, 1990); Thomas P. Anderson, *Politics in Central America* (New York: Praeger, 1988); Robert H. Trudeau, *Guatemalan Politics: The Popular Struggle for Democracy* (Boulder, Colo.: Lynne Rienner, 1993).

36. Jim Handy, "Resurgent Democracy and the Guatemalan Military," *Journal of Latin American Studies* 18, no. 2 (1986): 383–408; Susanne Jonas, *The Battle for Guatemala: Rebels, Death Squads, and U.S. Power* (Boulder, Colo.: Westview Press, 1991).

37. Burgerman, "Building the Peace by Mandating Reform," pp. 72–77.

38. UN General Assembly, "Agreement on Constitutional Reform and the Electoral Regime," A/51/776, December 7, 1996.

39. David Holiday, "Guatemala's Precarious Peace," *Current History* 99, no. 634 (2000): 80–81.

40. MINUGUA, "Report for the Consultative Group," p. 2.

41. UN General Assembly, "United Nations Verification Mission in Guatemala, Report of the Secretary General," A/58/267, August 11, 2003, p. 3.

42. MINUGUA, "Report for the Consultative Group," p. 3.

43. For an exhaustive analysis of these scandals, see Rachel Sieder and others, *Who Governs? Guatemala Five Years after the Peace Accords* (Cambridge, Mass.: Hemisphere Initiatives, 2002), pp. 7–11.

44. See Rogelio Núñez, "Guatemala ante el nuevo gobierno de Oscar Berger," Observatorio Electoral Latinoamericana, January 13, 2004 (www.observatorioelectoral.org/informes/analisis/?country=guatemala).

45. Adriana Beltran, "WOLA Memo on IMET funding for Guatemala" (Washington: WOLA, May 5, 2005).

46. On Guatemalan police reform, see Rachel Garst, *The New Guatemalan National Civilian Police: A Problematic Beginning* (Washington: WOLA, 1997); Jack Spence and others, *Promise and Reality: Implementation of the Guatemalan Peace Accords* (Cambridge, Mass.: Hemisphere Initiatives, 1998), pp. 30–35; Hugh Byrne, William Stanley, and

Rachel Garst, *Rescuing Police Reform: A Challenge for the New Guatemalan Government* (Washington: WOLA, 2000); and Sieder and others, *Who Governs?* pp. 39–42.

47. U.S. Department of State Bureau of Democracy, Human Rights, and Labor, *Country Reports on Human Rights Practices for 2004* (Washington: Department of State, February 28, 2005) (www.state.gov/g/drl/rls/hrrpt/2004/41762.htm).

48. MINUGUA, "Report for the Consultative Group," p. 18, and reiterated in subsequent reports.

49. UN General Assembly, "Twelfth Report on Human Rights of the United Nations Verification Mission in Guatemala," A/56/273, August 8, 2001, p. 9; MINUGUA, "Report to the Consultative Group Meeting for Guatemala," May 8, 2003. For a geographic breakdown of lynchings, see MINUGUA, "Los Linchamientos: Un Flagelo Que Persiste," Verification Report 16 (July 2002).

50. Scott Hartmann, "MINUGUA Campaign Targets Problem of Lynchings," *UN Wire*, December 13, 2002.

51. See especially Angelina Snodgrass Godoy, "Lynchings and the Democratization of Terror in Postwar Guatemala: Implications for Human Rights," *Human Rights Quarterly* 24, no. 3 (2002): 640–61; David Gonzalez, "Fighters Demands Open Old Wounds in Central America," *New York Times*, August 19, 2002, p. A1; Danilo Valladares, "FRG es responsible," *Prensa Libre*, October 4, 2002.

52. MINUGUA, "Report for the Consultative Group," p. 5; Cynthia Arnson and Dinorah Azpuru, "From Peace to Democratization: Lessons from Central America," paper prepared for the Woodrow Wilson Center for International Scholars, Washington, March 2002.

53. Department of State, *Country Reports on Human Rights Practices for 2004;* General Assembly, "United Nations Verification Mission in Guatemala, Eighth Report of the Secretary General," pp. 6-8; MINUGUA, "Report for the Consultative Group," pp. 16–18; Sieder and others, *Who Governs?* pp. 32–36.

54. See UN General Assembly, "United Nations Verification Mission in Guatemala, Eighth Report of the Secretary General."

55. See Burgerman, *Moral Victories;* Lisa Martin and Kathryn Sikkink, "U.S. Policy and Human Rights in Argentina and Guatemala, 1973–1980," in *Double-Edged Diplomacy: International Bargaining and Domestic Politics,* edited by Peter Evans, Harold K. Jacobson, and Robert D. Putnam (University of California Press, 1993), p. 336.

56. This does not include covert funding through the Central Intelligence Agency or through security supporting assistance and economic support funds, both of which were significant sources of support for the military.

57. Human Rights Watch, *Human Rights in Guatemala during President de León Carpio's First Year* (New York: 1994), p. 114.

58. "U.S. Cuts off Remaining Military Aid to Guatemala," *International Herald Tribune,* March 13, 1995.

59. U.S. Department of State, Bureau of Western Hemisphere, "Background Note: Guatamala," May 2002; U.S. Department of State, "Background Note: Guatamala," September 2003.

60. Julieta Sandoval, "Preocupa influencia de grupos paralelos: Diplomático de EE.UU. se reúne con Efraín Ríos Montt para tartar varios temas," *Prensa Libre*, August 3, 2002.

61. David Gonzalez, "Graft Aggravates Woes Plaguing Central America: Guatemala's Plight Especially Severe," *New York Times,* February 25, 2003, p. A3; also see UN General Assembly, "United Nations Verification Mission in Guatemala, Eighth Report of the Secretary General," p. 4.

62. Virgilio Godoy Reyes, "Nicaragua, 1944–1984: Political Parties and Electoral Processes," in *Political Parties and Democracy in Central America,* edited by Louis Goodman, William LeoGrande, and Johanna Mendelson Forman (Boulder, Colo.: Westview Press, 1990), pp. 179–81.

63. See Jaime Wheelock Román, "Revolution and Democratic Transition in Nicaragua," in *Democratic Transitions in Central America,* edited by Jorge I. Domínguez and Marc Lindenberg (University Press of Florida, 1997).

64. Silvio de Franco and José Luis Velázquez, "Democratic Transitions in Nicaragua," in ibid., pp. 89–91.

65. The majority of contra rank and file was composed of disgruntled agricultural workers from the interior, although the political and military leadership were predominantly former National Guard officers. For demographic and regional analysis of the contra forces, see Deena I. Abu-Lughod, "Failed Buyout: Land Rights for Contra Veterans in Postwar Nicaragua," *Latin American Perspectives* 27, no. 3 (2000): 32–62.

66. William LeoGrande, "Political Parties and Postrevolutionary Politics in Nicaragua," in *Political Parties and Democracy in Central America,* edited by Louis Goodman, William LeoGrande, and Johanna Mendelson Forman (Boulder, Colo.: Westview Press, 1990).

67. These points are made by Rose Spalding, "From Low-Intensity War to Low-Intensity Peace: The Nicaraguan Peace Process," in *Comparative Peace Processes in Latin America,* edited by Cynthia Arnson (Stanford University Press, 1999), p. 41.

68. Abu-Lughod, "Failed Buyout."

69. De Franco and Velásquez, "Democratic Transitions in Nicaragua," pp. 104–06.

70. Figures are from Roland Paris, "Peacebuilding in Central America: Reproducing Sources of Conflict?" *International Peacekeeping* 9, no. 4 (2002): 44–45.

71. David R. Dye, *Patchwork Democracy: Nicaraguan Politics Ten Years after the Fall* (Cambridge, Mass.: Hemisphere Initiatives, 2000), p. 3.

72. See especially Gutiérrez, "Central America, the Caribbean, and Mexico," pp. 154 and 159.

73. Dye, *Patchwork Democracy,* pp. 7–18.

74. See David Gonzalez, "Nicaraguan President Demands Corruption Trial for Predecessor," *New York Times,* August 8, 2002, p. A5.

75. Joel Brinkley, "U.S. Envoy Goes to Nicaragua to Back Embattled Leader," *New York Times,* October 5, 2005, p. A3.

76. De Franco and Velázquez, "Democratic Transitions in Nicaragua," pp. 93–94.

77. Abu-Lughod, "Failed Buyout," p. 45.

78. On the development of multidimensional peacekeeping operations, see Michael Doyle, Ian Johnstone, and Robert C. Orr, eds., *Keeping the Peace: Multidimensional UN Operations in Cambodia and El Salvador* (Cambridge University Press, 1997); Susan Burgerman, "The Evolution of Compliance: The Human Rights Regime, Transnational Networks, and United Nations Peacebuilding," Ph.D. dissertation, Columbia University, 1997.

79. Spalding, "From Low-Intensity War to Low-Intensity Peace," pp. 46–47.

80. Ibid., p. 51; Vickers, "Renegotiating Internal Security: The Lessons of Central America."

81. Dye, *Patchwork Democracy,* pp. 21–26.

82. Peter Kornbluh, "The U.S. Role in the Counterrevolution," in *Revolution and Counterrevolution in Nicaragua,* edited by Thomas W. Walker (Boulder, Colo.: Westview Press, 1991), p. 325; for a detailed look at U.S. policy in Nicaragua during the Carter administration, see Robert A. Pastor, *Not Condemned to Repetition: The United States and Nicaragua* (Boulder, Colo.: Westview Press, 2002); for the Reagan administration's, see Peter Kornbluh, *Nicaragua, the Price of Intervention: Reagan's Wars against the Sandinistas* (Washington: Institute for Policy Studies, 1987).

83. Arnson, *Crossroads,* pp. 75–81; Kornbluh, "The U.S. Role in the Counterrevolution," p. 330.

84. Spalding, "From Low-Intensity War to Low-Intensity Peace," p. 54.

85. Kornbluh, *Nicaragua, the Price of Intervention.*

86. Sullivan, *Central America and U.S. Foreign Assistance,* pp. 11–13.

87. U.S. Department of State, "Background Note: Nicaragua," January 2002.

88. U.S. Department of State, "Background Note: Nicaragua," July 2002.

9

Failing and Failed States: Toward a Framework for U.S. Assistance

CAROL LANCASTER

In 2002 President Bush announced the creation of a US$5 billion Millennium Challenge Account (MCA) to provide aid to those low-income countries that are good performers to help them reduce poverty and develop more rapidly. Good performance includes good governance (upholding the rule of law, protecting human rights, fighting corruption), public investments in health and education, and sound economic policies that encourage private initiative. The creation of the MCA immediately raised the issue of what is to be done for "poor performers"—those countries that did not qualify for MCA monies—and especially the failed and failing (and "fragile") states. Fragile states are those that are unable to provide basic security and services to their populations and appear headed for civil conflict and the collapse of governmental authority and capacity to function. Depending on the criteria for state failure, anywhere between twenty and forty-six states have been categorized as failing or failed.[1]

What is the role of foreign aid in these countries, which suffer from poverty and inequality, are vulnerable to natural disasters and thus needful of aid, but which are also often poorly governed, exhibiting serious social cleavages and civil violence, which compromise the effectiveness of foreign aid in spurring development? This chapter examines these questions, providing a quick overview of U.S. foreign aid generally, examining the role of the United

States in the past in helping poor performers become good performers, and focusing on a new category of poor performers—failing and failed states— asking what role foreign aid should play in these unfortunate countries.

An Overview of U.S. Foreign Aid

Foreign aid, for the purposes of this essay, is defined as a voluntary transfer of public, concessional resources (with at least a 25 percent grant element) from one government to another government of a low-income country or to an international organization or nongovernmental organization working in such a country, one purpose of which is to further development in the recipient country. This is the official definition of foreign aid used by the Development Assistance Committee of the Organization for Economic Cooperation and Development. By this definition, U.S. foreign aid (both bilateral and multilateral) amounted to US$20 billion in 2003 and has totaled US$400 billion between 1948 and 2003.[2]

The principal U.S. aid programs are Development Assistance (including child survival monies), primarily to support economic and social progress in recipient countries; Economic Support Funds (ESF), primarily to support governments with a particular importance to U.S. foreign policy and security concerns; food aid provided under Public Law 480, mainly used for balance of payments support, nutrition intervention, and emergency relief; aid to Eastern Europe and the former Soviet Union to support economic and political transitions in those countries; the Millennium Challenge Account, managed by the Millennium Challenge Corporation to provide aid to "good performers"; and multilateral aid, primarily contributions to the World Bank, the regional development banks, and various UN agencies engaged in development activities.

For fiscal year 2006, the administration requested US$19 billion in aid, US$17 billion of which is bilateral aid. Just over US$2.3 billion in aid was to be concentrated in six countries: Afghanistan, Egypt, Iraq, Pakistan, Jordan, and Israel, reflecting the administration's foreign policy priorities in the Middle East and the war on terror. The rest of bilateral economic assistance was planned for some 120 countries, many of which were low-income ones, including US$1.6 billion to countries in sub-Saharan Africa and more than US$100 million each to Indonesia, Liberia, Haiti, India, Uganda, Sudan, and South Africa.[3] U.S. bilateral aid, especially Development Assistance, is used to further economic growth and agriculture, to improve health and family planning, and to promote democracy. It is also used for humanitarian relief. U.S. aid is provided almost entirely in the form of grants.

The Evolution of U.S. Aid to Poorly Performing Countries

President Bush has defined poor performance in terms of the choices made by governments: choices about how to govern, about how to manage their economies, and about how to spend public resources. This is not, of course, the only way to define performance, and these are not the sole factors affecting the actual performance of economies. But choices are important and are amenable to change. In fact, promoting development is all about choice and change—for example, how to use aid to persuade governments to make choices (and to help them once they have made these choices) is essential to sustained development and poverty alleviation.

This challenge is not new to foreign aid. Much of the history of aid giving by the United States and other governments has been a series of approaches intended to influence governments of poor countries to make choices that will improve the incomes, growth, and quality of life for their citizens. There have been three major approaches to choice and change in the history of aid giving, with one not so much replacing another as being added to earlier ones.

Approach 1: Laying the Foundations for Development

If we mark the start of the modern "development aid era" at 1960, we can identify the first approach to bringing about changes essential for development taking place between that year and 1980. During this period, the major thrust of development aid was to expand the capacity of government to manage its economy through requiring that aid recipients produce development plans (and providing technical assistance where it was needed to produce those plans) and to expand education and health services. Aid was also provided to increase the productive base of the economy, through funding infrastructure and the development and spread of new agricultural technologies and services and through transfers to ease balance of payments constraints. By helping to strengthen the capacity (including the absorptive capacity) of governments and providing training and advice, it was hoped that governments would be able to make the right choices to spur economic and social progress in their countries. Expanding the pool of educated and healthy citizens would, among other things, eventually provide them a pool of individuals who could further increase the capacity for beneficial choices and change.

While a widely held view at this time was that governments were generally committed to making the right choices for the development of their countries, it was also recognized that for a variety of reasons some governments chose not to make those choices. The government of Syngman Rhee of Korea during the 1950s, for instance, chose to manage its economy poorly, pursuing inflationary fiscal policies. The United States put pressure on the Korean government to make policy changes but with little effect. In Latin America, it was recognized that development and democracy would be spurred if there were a more equal distribution of national resources in this most unequal of regions. The Alliance for Progress, initiated by President Kennedy, attempted to tie aid funding to tax and land reforms, but it also had limited success. A further approach during the latter part of this period was using aid to address the basic human needs of the poor (primary education and health care, water and sanitation, primary roads, and agricultural services) in an effort to channel resources to the poor despite governments' reluctance to redistribute national resources. This aid-funded approach improved education and health services, extended infrastructure, and revolutionized agriculture (the "green revolution"). Most of the evidence of aid effectiveness from this period suggests, however, that the "good performers" (such as Korea after 1960, Costa Rica, and Botswana) chose to become good performers for reasons having little to do with foreign aid. And once they decided to manage their economies well, they were able to tap into aid and draw on a pool of educated individuals (whose higher education had often been partly funded with foreign aid).

Approach 2: Aid as an Incentive for Responsible Economic Policies

The debt and balance of payments crises that erupted throughout much of the developing world in the 1980s drew attention to the problems of poor economic policy choices by the governments of many less developed countries. Policy distortions—including overvalued exchange rates; controls on prices, wages, and interest rates; subsidies; tariff and nontariff barriers to trade; weak financial systems; inefficient state-owned enterprises; and large budgetary deficits—had impeded growth and development by reducing the incentives for private entrepreneurs to produce and invest. Aid was increasingly conditioned on governments agreeing to stabilization and structural adjustment programs that would remove these impediments and increase the scope for private economic initiatives. Many governments in Africa and Latin America agreed to such programs, but not all the reforms in those programs were implemented or sustained. (Those most sustained were currency adjustments; those least sustained were the more administratively complex and politically sensitive reforms in the financial sector or civil service.) The World Bank's report *Assessing Aid* concludes that using aid as an incentive for economic policy reforms where government had little commitment to such reforms is generally ineffective.[4]

Approach 3: Aid for Political Reform

At the end of the 1980s, the use of aid to persuade and press governments to improve the quality of governance (often defined in terms of democratization) gained prominence. A confluence of factors led to this shift in emphasis. One was the disappointing outcome of a decade of economic reforms. One of the reasons, it was concluded, that economic reforms had been disappointing was poor governance, meaning a lack of transparency, accountability, and predictability on the part of the governments of poor countries. A 1989 World Bank report gave an early voice to this concept, which echoed work being done in the academy on the role of institutions in promoting or impeding economic growth—in particular, the importance of the rule of law to protect property, including investment.[5] The U.S. government (and eventually other aid-giving governments) took this argument one step further and asserted that democracy was essential for development since it would create an environment in which the public and public interest groups would demand accountability and the rule of law from governments. Another source of the new focus on political reform came from the wave of democratization sweeping Eastern Europe, the former Soviet Union, Africa, and elsewhere. In many ways, democratization was an extension of the human rights movement of the 1970s and 1980s to include political rights.

Whatever the sources of the ideas behind the emphasis on good governance and democracy, aid in support of political reform became an important focus of the U.S. Agency for International Development (USAID) during the 1990s. Aid was used as an incentive for political reform in Kenya, for example, where a group of aid donors withheld assistance until the government there agreed to multiparty elections. Aid was used to further democratic governance, funding efforts to strengthen civil society, the legislature, and laws, to reform the judiciary, to support independent media, to train political party members, to draft new constitutions, and to organize elections.

The consequences of aid in support of democratization are yet to be fully assessed.[6] But anecdotal evidence suggests that, as in the case of other types of intervention, immediate goals are often achieved, such as ensuring free and fair elections and helping to expand and strengthen civil society organizations—

but that the longer term goal of effective democracies is much more difficult to achieve. In Kenya, the government of Daniel arap Moi ruled in a corrupt and often repressive manner even after the adoption of multiparty elections, since the president and his supporters were able to manipulate the political process (and the opposition proved unable to collaborate effectively) so as to remain virtually unchallenged in power for ten years.

What this brief review of the use of U.S. aid to turn poor performers into good performers suggests is that where some portion of the political elite—especially the political leadership—wants to make the choices that turn a poorly performing government into a good performer, foreign aid can be helpful. Where elites are opposed to such changes (often because their own political and economic interests are threatened), as in the case of Korea in the 1950s, Latin America in the 1960s, and much of Africa and the Middle East today, foreign aid may have little impact, at least in the short run, on the difficult choices that are necessary to become a good performer. One of the reasons aid has not been effective against a resistant elite is that it is seldom adequate to alter the calculation of costs and benefits of change that elites must make. Where desired policy and behavioral changes threaten to undercut their economic positions or political power, aid alone has seldom been large enough to alter that calculus.

The U.S. government is now once again considering what policies it should adopt toward poor performers so as to help them become good performers. In 2003 Andrew Natsios, USAID's administrator, listed four categories of poor countries in addition to the good performers qualifying for MCA monies: those that just missed qualifying, those whose governments lacked the commitment to make the choices necessary to qualify, those that were such poor performers that they were failing or failed states, and those the United States wished to support for national security reasons (regardless of performance).[7] For those governments that almost made the good performer class (and presumably had a commitment to doing so), USAID proposed to help them improve where they fell short on the indicators of good performance, such as providing adequate educational services or implementing needed reforms. For the second group of countries, USAID would "continue programs that address global issues such as HIV/AIDS and environmental degradation" but would review "broader development assistance."[8] This remark suggests that foreign aid would be limited to those poor countries that appeared to lack the commitment to become good performers but were not yet in the category of failing states. For the category of failing and failed states, USAID was "actively developing new assistance models that will integrate emergency relief and food with transitional assistance, governance investments, and civil society building."[9]

These categorizations of poor countries suggest a fundamentally new approach to the policies and strategies governing U.S. foreign aid. The remainder of this chapter focuses on the issues raised by this approach and the policies and programs that do exist or should exist to implement it. The first issue involves a further definition of these categories. The second involves policies and programs for poor performers not yet heading toward failure. The third section focuses on failing and failed states. A final section draws conclusions and points toward the future for foreign aid and poorly performing states.

Categorizing States by Performance

Categorizing anything implies that one has clear definitions and concepts or theories regarding the differences among the things categorized. The Bush administration has created the category of good performers on the basis of three broad qualities: good governance, investment in people, and sound economic policies fostering entrepreneurship. Sixteen quantitative indicators have been proposed as the basis for governments qualifying as good performers. It is assumed that good performers can use aid monies effectively to further economic and social progress in their countries.

It is hard to fault the basic idea that more aid ought to be provided to governments that can use it effectively. And the idea of identifying those governments on the basis of objective criteria is attractive. But identifying those governments based on the use of multiple quantitative indicators (some of which, such as the corruption indicators developed by Transparency International, are subjective in any case) risks creating the illusion of false precision and encouraging the gaming of the indicators. Good performance may well *not* be captured by the indicators; and poor performance can easily be missed, as is indicated by some of the countries that nearly qualified as good performers when Steve Radelet applied the indicators to low-income countries. (The fact that Georgia made the list despite a high degree of corruption underlines this danger.) It would be far better to simplify the quantitative basis for qualification as a good performer and supplement it with the judgment of experts.

Another definitional problem arises with the category of failing and failed states. What does *failed state* mean? It is often defined as a state that cannot provide security to its people, control its territory, or offer basic services. But if a government controls three-quarters of its territory, has it failed? If it has chosen to limit social services but controls most of its territory, has it failed? Does a failed state automatically include civil violence? Is failure the cause or consequence of such violence? Is state failure to be judged by other standards, like human rights, abusive government, or repression of minorities? And what are the international implications of state failure? Does it give a right to other governments to intervene militarily or politically or with humanitarian aid? The reason this definition is important is because there is a tendency in official circles to apply the term *failed state* to states that are not liked for their policies, ideologies, or orientation. Was Afghanistan under the Taliban really a failed state? It controlled most of its territory, chose to close its schools to girls, and gave refuge to al Qaeda. It was not an admirable state, but it was also arguably not a failed state. This is not the place to propose definitions, but they are clearly needed to provide the basis for policies vis-à-vis failed states. I focus on the even more difficult problems of defining and identifying failing states below.

U.S. Aid Policies toward Poorly Performing States

What policies should guide U.S. foreign aid to poorly performing (but not failing) states? As we have seen from Andrew Natsios's comment above, USAID appeared to be considering funding activities associated with such transnational problems as HIV/AIDS but phasing out other types of funding. If this is to become the U.S. aid policy toward poorly performing countries, it would be an unfortunate shift. In the past, the United States has funded activities in the areas of health, education, and poverty alleviation in poorly performing states even though their governments were pursuing policies that limited economic and social progress in the short term. U.S. aid to Korea in the 1950s is a case in point. Despite the poor policy environment and the unwillingness of the government to implement needed policy reforms, the United States funded the education of a number of promising young Koreans, particularly in the field of economics. Most of them returned to their country and were available to advise and serve in government when a new president, Park Chung Hee, took power in 1961 and adopted growth-promoting policies. The lesson is that where the performance of government is not so bad that any efforts to expand the basic conditions for economic and social progress are doomed to failure, it makes sense to continue sending aid so that when improvements in governance and economic management come, the country will have the human and physical resources to make rapid development progress.

There are other reasons to continue aiding poor performers. One is that such aid may over the long term help change the calculus by elites of the benefits and costs of implementing economic and political reforms or persuade them of the value of such reforms. Education, especially when combined with gradually improving incomes, can increase the number of citizens who demand improved governance. Strengthening the civil society can increase the numbers of organized groups articulating such interests to government. Aid-funded advisers, interacting with local government officials and other elites, may over time even convince the government of the value of economic and political reforms. Such reforms have taken place over the past several decades in, for example, Tanzania, Ghana, Bolivia, and Vietnam.

U.S. Aid Policies toward Failing, Failed, and Fragile States

A failing state, for the purposes of this essay, is one whose government is losing the ability to provide security and essential services for its population and to protect its borders. A failed state is one in which the government has lost this ability entirely (in some cases, the state has collapsed and civil conflict has erupted, with warring groups competing for power and control of resources). A fragile state is a failing, failed, or recovering state.[10] Various organizations use different estimates for the number of these states: the Carnegie Endowment and Fund for Peace, for example, identify twenty "at risk" states out of sixty "vulnerable" states.[11] The World Bank counts thirty "low income countries under stress," while the United Kingdom's Department for International Development lists forty-six "fragile states of concern."[12]

Failing and failed states have become a source of concern to the United States for three reasons. First, state collapse is usually accompanied by prolonged civil conflict, leaving destitution, death, displaced persons, refugees, and the destruction of economic assets in its wake, creating severe human suffering. Second, civil violence in one country often spills over into neighboring countries, undermining their political institutions, economies, and social harmony and further spreading human suffering. And third, failing and failed states can attract and provide sanctuary to criminal and terrorist organizations as well as spread disease; these problems, in turn, can affect the security and well-being of Americans at home and abroad. The terrorist attacks of September 2001 reminded Americans that problems in distant lands can become problems at home if they are ignored.[13]

A comprehensive U.S. strategy for preventing state failure and for reconstituting failed states requires, first, the ability to identify failing countries.

The second requirement is policies crafted for various ends: to help such countries avoid failure in the first place, to bring an end of a conflict once it has erupted, and to help countries recover from state failure and avoid regressing into violence again.

Identifying Failing States

What are the indicators of state failure? What are the causes of state failure? When does a failing state become a failed state? We do not yet have definitive answers to these questions or even analytically rigorous definitions of state failure. However, in recent years some interesting research has been undertaken on these questions, a portion of it funded by the U.S. government with the intent of developing policies and programs for failing and failed states. For example, the State Failure Task Force, formed under Vice President Gore's leadership and now located at the University of Maryland, has produced a series of reports on factors that contribute to the probability of state failure. At the core of these factors is the quality of governance (a finding of numerous other studies as well). Other factors include inequality, the material well-being of the population, international influences (especially war in neighboring countries), and the ethnic composition of society.[14] The reports of this task force have been interesting, but they do not take us very far in developing strategies to avoid or reverse state failure.

Another way of looking at the causes of state failure is to categorize causal factors according to underlying motives (for example, the motives underlying civil violence), facilitating factors (in this case, the means to commit civil violence, including organization and financing), political and social institutions (such as the policies or weaknesses that create opportunities for civil violence), regional and international factors (such as war in a nearby country), and triggering factors (such as an election, a disaster, an assassination). This approach offers a conceptual framework for predicting state failure and a template for developing policies to prevent it.[15] The USAID's "fragile states strategy" emphasizes the problems of effectiveness and legitimacy that underlie fragility and recommends the following generic policies to address these problems:

—Security: For effectiveness, military and police services must secure the borders and reduce crime. For legitimacy, such services must be provided reasonably, equitably, and without major violations of human rights.

—Political: For effectiveness, political institutions and processes must adequately respond to citizens' needs. For legitimacy, political processes, norms, and leaders must be acceptable to the citizenry.

—Economic: For effectiveness, economic and financial institutions and infrastructure must support economic growth (including jobs), adapt to economic change, and manage natural resources. For legitimacy, economic institutions, financial services, and income–generating opportunities must be widely accessible and reasonably transparent, particularly related to access to and governance of natural resources.

—Social: For effectiveness, provision of basic services must generally meet demand, including that of vulnerable and minority groups. For legitimacy, providers of these services must be tolerant of diverse customs, cultures, and beliefs.[16]

Meanwhile, beginning in 1999, USAID missions in the field were instructed to conduct "conflict vulnerability analyses" as part of their country strategies to provide some indication as to the likelihood that their country might suffer from civil conflict. There was no template, based on a theory of the causes of conflict, to give shape to this analysis, but the agency felt it had to start somewhere to begin to grapple with the problem of conflict. This is a somewhat different focus from identifying failing states, but it certainly is one of the precursors of the effort in that direction.[17] In 2002 USAID established the Office of Conflict Management and Mitigation to provide a focal point of work and leadership in this area.

All of these efforts appear promising, but the U.S. government and USAID are still far from being able to identify failing states in time to reverse state failure. Identifying failing states and understanding why states progress from fragility, to failing, to failure remains one of the significant gaps in addressing the problems of low-income, poorly performing countries.

Conflict Prevention in Failing States

Although no U.S. administration thus far has had an explicit policy of preventing state failure, there have been a number of policy pronouncements on "preventive diplomacy" and efforts, mentioned above, to develop a policy of conflict prevention.[18] At the most fundamental level, the promotion of development and effective democracy is a way of helping to prevent state failure and has been justified as such by USAID since the early 1990s. It is clear that poor countries tend to be more vulnerable to civil conflict and state failure than richer ones—for one thing, their governments tend to be less effective and their populations tend to be under greater economic stress. It is also true that functioning democracies are less plagued with civil conflict and a lack of legitimacy than authoritarian regimes relying on patronage and repression to remain in power. However, these observations do not take us very far, since many poor countries and authoritarian governments avoid state failure, and since some better off, democratic countries (like Colombia) suffer from severe civil conflict and faltering government. (Further, the transition from an authoritarian regime to a democratic regime is especially vulnerable to civil conflict.) What is needed, in addition to general support for development and democracy, are policies and programs designed specifically to address failing states.

First, reversing the fate of a failing state requires changing the choices made by the political elites of the state, choices that lead to the state's failure. Where these elites see good state performance as colliding with their interests and ideologies, good state performance is not likely to be their choice. Second, in addition to changing the calculus of political elites, political institutions also need to change, since they failed not only to constrain those elites from making decisions that led to state failure but also to facilitate conflict resolution. Changing political institutions takes time (and there is not always a lot of time to reverse a failing state) and may include strengthening civil society (as a vehicle for demanding accountability from government) and reforming political institutions. Tactics for achieving these goals include identifying and working with partners in society and, preferably, with political elites committed to reforms. An effective policy must be comprehensive and sustained. Diplomatic pressure, foreign aid, even peace-keeping forces may be required.

These are not easy tasks. The literature on preventing conflict and state failure sometimes seems to assume away the problem of political elites and their interests.[19] Practitioners have at times thought that a single fix here and there might help reverse a slide toward political disaster. This has seldom worked. For example, at one point the United States sought to improve government performance in Liberia under the incompetent, corrupt, and repressive President Doe by sending a team of expatriate fiscal experts to control government revenues and expenditures. The effort was a total failure, and the experts left in frustration after six months. The International Monetary Fund had a similar experience earlier in the former Zaire. In another part of the world, El Salvador, the U.S. government decided in the 1980s to attempt to reform the judiciary (which lacked independence from the repressive military regime in power at the time) as a first step to improving governance. Not much progress was made in upgrading the judiciary, and little change took place in the quality of governance until much greater, across-the-board diplomatic pressures eventually persuaded the army to return to its barracks.[20]

An example of a more comprehensive approach involved Burundi, which threatened to dissolve into communal violence in the early 1990s. The U.S. government appointed Howard Wolpe as special envoy to the Great Lakes in East Central Africa to help further the peace process there. Wolpe, together with other outside actors, including the World Bank, South African peace-keeping forces, and USAID, acted as "calming forces" while negotiations proceeded between the Hutus and Tutsis.[21] Aid was (and still is) necessary to reintegrate a million displaced persons and refugees (another potential source of discontent and violence). The peace process in Burundi remains incomplete, but it seems likely that the involvement of diplomats, peace-keeping forces, and foreign aid has helped prevent large-scale bloodletting, potentially on the order of the genocide in Rwanda in 1994.

Third, state failure can be addressed by removing the international incentives that encourage failing performance. The effort, for example, to limit the sale of "conflict diamonds" by requiring their source to be labeled is a useful initiative that could be extended to other valuable natural resources that can be exported illegally to fund aspiring warlords or corrupt dictators. Greater transparency in international banking and the willingness of international banks to return the ill-gotten gains of autocrats to their treasuries is another important initiative, and it appears to be growing. The application of human rights law by foreign courts to repressive dictators (as in the case of the former Chilean president Pinochet) may also change the calculus of such power elites.

Fourth, because the instruments for preventing state failure differ from country to country as the particular causes of failure themselves differ, these instruments have to be considered case by case. Policies that might have prevented state failure in Somalia in the early 1990s—with its lethal combination of corrupt, repressive, exclusionary government and clan allegiances—would have been different from the policies that may have avoided the civil conflict and near state collapse in democratic, drug-lord-penetrated, historically conflicted Colombia.

Fifth, there may be cases of failing states where no amount of external involvement short of a military conquest will persuade political elites to adopt responsible policies. Zimbabwe under Robert Mugabe appears to be such a country. In this case, the best that can be done with foreign aid is to provide for humanitarian relief and to protect and extend where possible the investments already made in people and economic assets.

This consideration leads to the last one: sixth—do no harm. Foreign governments, including the U.S. government, should avoid exacerbating the problems leading to state collapse. This challenge particularly relates to the allocation of foreign aid, both sins of omission and sins of commission. An example of a sin of omission is Burundi, where (before the current emergency) foreign aid—intended to foster development in the country but channeled through an exclusionary and repressive minority Tutsi government—appears to have increased inequalities and exacerbated tensions that fed conflict.[22] The quintessential case of a sin of commission is the former Zaire, where the over US$1 billion in U.S. aid provided to that country during the regime of Mobutu Sese Seko was in fact intended to avoid state failure in the short run (the regional consequences feared by successive U.S. governments focused on cold war concerns). But by ignoring the deepening problems of governance and economic management, the aid likely increased the probability of state failure over the long term.

Another potential sin of commission is too much aid. Where aid from all sources becomes too large over an extended period of time (several years), incentives are created for public officials and private individuals to spend their productive hours pursuing access to aid rather than producing goods and services. Thus aid can become destructive of development and even social comity. This was arguably the case during the early 1990s in Somalia, where foreign aid exceeded at one point 200 percent of the country's gross national product. One study suggests that when aid surpasses 20 percent of gross domestic product, it is likely to have negative effects on the economy.[23] This percentage will of course be different from country to country, depending on the nature of its political institutions. The percentage is likely to be low in a place like Somalia (before the state collapsed), where government is based on support by and manipulation of clans, primarily through patronage, which aid fueled. A country like Botswana, with more transparent, accountable, inclusive, and democratic political institutions (and a capable civil service), could handle a higher level of aid without negative effects. But these are hypotheses and have yet to be tested.

These cases of aid aggravating tendencies toward state failure are of more than just historical interest. Where U.S. aid is provided with minimal concerns or conditions regarding the nature and performance of governments, that danger can arise. It may be that in the future we will count Egypt and Pakistan—two of the largest recipients of U.S. aid today and arguably exhibiting the problems that often lead to state failure—as failed states for those reasons. This is not to argue that the U.S. government should never provide aid to poorly performing states with high diplomatic priority. But in doing so, there should be an effort to understand and address the root causes of potential state failure within the constraints set by foreign policy imperatives.

Ending Conflict in a Failing State

Once a state has collapsed and conflict has erupted, the policy challenge is to bring that conflict to an end. It is in meeting this challenge that the role of aid is preeminent. It is also in this arena—using aid to support a transition from war to peace—that the most experience with failing or failed states has been gained, not only by the United States but also internationally. Beyond providing humanitarian relief for the victims of war and state collapse, aid can be used to demobilize and retrain troops, to clear the country of mines, to support community-based efforts to overcome past hostilities among warring parties (often ethnic groups), and to reestablish political institutions.

To provide a focus within the U.S. government for aid-funded work in postconflict transitions, USAID established in 1994 the Office of Transition Initiatives (OTI), whose purpose is to "provide fast, flexible, short-term assistance to take advantage of windows of opportunity to build democracy and peace."[24] It lays the foundations for long-term development by promoting reconciliation, jump-starting economies, and helping stable democracy take hold. The OTI began with a mission to address postconflict and transition activities to strengthen peace and democracy and has since worked to evolve principles and best practices. By 2003 the office had worked in twenty-five countries funding and supporting a variety of programs, including community-based organizations, support for media, and conflict management and peace initiatives. Evaluations thus far undertaken by USAID (by independent contractors) of OTI's work have been generally favorable.[25]

USAID has promoted postconflict state resuscitation in addition to the work of the OTI and has published a number of studies, including Krishna Kumar and Marina Ottaway's edited volume, *From Bullets to Ballots: Electoral Assistance to Postconflict Societies*, and Krishna Kumar's edited volumes, *Rebuilding Societies after Civil War* and *Postconflict Elections, Democratization, and International Assistance.*[26] This body of literature, plus that of other scholars, practitioners, and other aid agencies, has begun to recount and analyze the growing experience of foreign aid in this area, providing the basis for a sophisticated set of best practices and policies.

Summing Up

The policies and programs needed to address the problem of failing and failed states are part of a broader approach to problems of poor performance among low-income countries, but they are an increasingly important part of that approach, with the continuing problems of state collapse, the humanitarian costs of the conflicts associated with state collapse, and the dangers that failing and failed states present to the international community generally. This category of states may become a major focus for foreign policy and foreign aid in coming years, especially in a world of terrorism and the transnational problems that can emerge from state failure.

An effective approach to reversing state failure must be a comprehensive one, dealing with the problems of failing states, periods of conflict and chaos, and the postconflict resuscitation of states, economies, and societies. Foreign aid has a role to play in each of these stages, though its role is likely to be most important in the first stage and the final stage. In the first, crucial stage, a good deal more thought and experience is needed to clarify and deepen policies that can help identify failing states and address their problems. Foreign aid alone is seldom enough to reverse the problems of a failing state: diplomatic engagement is also essential (which can be costly and time consuming). In some cases, there may be no effective way to reverse the fate of a failing state, where external pressure and persuasion is inadequate to change the calculus by entrenched political elites of policies and behavior that have put the state on the path of failure.

However, not even this panoply of policies is likely to be adequate to address the problems of low-income, poorly performing states. Three more elements are needed: the organization in the U.S. government designated to address these issues, the political will to do so (and criteria to choose when the United States will and will not mount an effort to prevent state failure), and international collaboration.

Government Organization

The challenge of reversing state failure is a new one, at least in the explicit form discussed here. It involves several U.S. government agencies, primarily the Department of State and USAID but potentially the Department of Defense and others still. If the administration wanted to elaborate such a policy quickly and manage it effectively (including coordinating the involvement of multiple agencies), it would have to consider creating an organizational locus to do so. Where would such a locus be and what might it look like?

The obvious locus of leadership in the U.S. government to address reversing state failure is the Department of State. The locus should be in the form of a permanent organizational entity rather than a coordinator (an individual with a small staff, often regarded as temporary). The locus should be at a sufficiently high level—perhaps a bureau—to have visibility and stature. It should have resources of its own to put behind its initiatives. And a designated official in the National Security Council should be responsible for issues involving state failure, an official with whom this new bureau can collaborate. It would also liaise with USAID's Office of Conflict Management and Mitigation and would work with U.S. ambassadors, USAID mission directors, and possibly Central Intelligence Agency station chiefs to identify failing states and develop strategies for preventing failure, including mobilizing other resources and individuals available to the U.S. government for diplomatic initiatives. When states do collapse and conflict erupts, this bureau could take the leadership in mitigating conflict and in designing an approach to resuscitation (in this latter stage, relying on USAID's Office of Transition Initiatives to respond to opportunities in the postconflict period).

Political Will

The lack of political will on the part of governments has been the main reason that these governments have failed to act to prevent state failure. When the genocide in Rwanda began, there was an opportunity for other countries to act to stop the killings, but the U.S. government, for one, resisted such an intervention and reportedly even opposed terming the killings *genocide* to avoid being obliged to act under international law. The reluctance to intervene in Liberia, a very troubled country with special ties to the United States, is another case in point. Both of these cases would have involved military intervention to stop the violence, but the principles and problems involved with such an intervention apply to a policy of diplomatic and foreign-aid-based interventions as well. The essential deterrents to intervention are the lack of government resources and bureaucratic attention and domestic (perceived or real) political constraints.

Even a superpower like the United States has constraints on the time its officials can put into significant diplomatic initiatives abroad, and even in an era of budgetary exuberance, there are limits to the resources that can be dedicated to preventing state failure. So how does the United States decide where to put its efforts, assuming that it adopts a policy of preventing state failure? And who takes responsibility for those problems of state failure when the United States chooses not to become involved?

The policies of both the Clinton and Bush administrations suggest that active U.S. engagement on these issues occurs only when important U.S. interests are at risk: the threat of illegal drugs being smuggled into the United States from Latin America; a surge in illegal immigration, as in the case of Haiti during the 1990s; the threat of terrorism, as in the case of Afghanistan.

When fundamental U.S. interests are not threatened (Rwanda and Liberia), the U.S. government has been reluctant to take a leadership role in conflict prevention or mitigation. This pattern clearly relates to domestic politics— specifically, the ability of an administration to justify a significant diplomatic initiative to Congress and the public. There may be times when such initiatives are not high profile and so do not engage domestic political attention, as was the case in Burundi. But where they are high profile, domestic politics will intrude.

The criterion of how a failing state is likely to affect U.S. national interests is a logical and essential one for determining when the United States will take the initiative to prevent state failure, but should this be the only criterion? The answer to this question must be no if the United States is to live up to its ideals and international obligations. When there is a threat of massive violence, as in the case of Rwanda, the United States must be prepared to act to prevent or mitigate state failure, collapse, and conflict. And when a U.S. intervention promises to be effective, especially if the costs of that intervention are limited, the United States should also consider taking action.

International Collaboration

No one government is in a position to take on the leadership of all of the problems of failing and failed states. In several areas multilateral approaches are needed, such as in information gathering and monitoring failed states. It would be useful for an international entity to undertake these charges, drawing on information provided both by governments and by its own staff and consultants. On the basis of agreed standards and norms for identifying failing states, such an organization could provide credible reporting and early warnings on failing states that would not have the taint of self-interest. Such an international organization could also act as a coordinating mechanism for the activities of bilateral and multilateral aid agencies in postconflict situations. Without such an organization, it is likely that the fragmentation of activities now evident—plus the lack of definition of and focus on state failure—will continue.

Diplomatic action to reverse state failure must rest primarily with governments (both those in the region of the conflict and those more distant) with the resources and influence to act effectively. Regional organizations and arrangements could be useful in this regard—and have been at times in Latin America and Africa. But in Africa in particular, regional organizations are often too weak or (because of the hesitancy of their member states) unwilling to persuade failing states to change their policies and behavior or also unwilling to provide peacekeeping services. Since these regional organizations are not always able to work effectively to prevent state failures, the United States should not refer such problems to these organizations just to get them off of the U.S. diplomatic agenda.

Conclusion

The issues of how to deal with poor performers and especially with failing states are new ones. The categories themselves are new and still fuzzily defined. Developing comprehensive policies and an organization to address these issues remains a challenge, one that is related to another priority of the Bush administration: nation building. Whether these issues will become a new paradigm in aid giving in the early part of the twenty-first century is unclear. A start, at least, has been made.

Notes

1. The U.S. Central Intelligence Agency proposes twenty; the U.K. Department for International Development proposes forty-six. The Failed States Index, produced by *Foreign Policy* and the Fund for Peace, identifies some forty countries as vulnerable to state failure by varying degrees. See www.foreignpolicy.com/story/cms.php?stody_id=3098.

2. USAID, "US Overseas Loans and Grants" (//qesdb.cdie.org/gbk/ [October 2005]).

3. See USAID, "Congressional Presentation 2006" (www.usaid.gov/policy/budget/cbj2006/summtables.html [October 2005]); Department of State, "FY 2006 International Affairs Budget Request" (www.state.gov/s/d/rm/rls/iab/2006/pdf [October 2005]). The country figures do not include assistance from the MCC.

4. See David Dollar and Craig Burnside, *Assessing Aid* (Washington: World Bank, 1998).

5. World Bank, *Sub-Saharan Africa: From Crisis to Sustainable Growth* (Washington: 1989).

6. An excellent place to start is Tom Carothers, *Assessing Democracy Abroad: The Learning Curve* (Washington: Carnegie Endowment, 1999).

7. Testimony of Andrew S. Natsios, Administrator, U.S. Agency for International Development, "Millennium Challenge Account," before the Senate Foreign Relations Committee, March 4, 2003 (www.usaid.gov/press/speeches/2003/ty030304a.html [December 2005]).

8. Ibid., p. 3.

9. Ibid., p. 4.

10. See USAID, *Fragile States Strategy* (2005), p. 9.

11. See "Failed States Index," *Foreign Policy,* July–August 2005.

12. Ibid., p. 1.

13. It must be recognized that terrorists, criminals, and others may base their activities in states that have not failed. Afghanistan under the Taliban was not a failed state by the

definition used here and elsewhere. The Taliban government was in control of most of Afghanistan's territory and chose to welcome al Qaeda into the country for ideological and financial reasons. It is not the point of this essay to do so, but considerably more rigorous thought needs to be given to the definitions of failed and failing states if the categorizations (often based on whether we like a particular government and its policies or not) are not to defeat U.S. policy goals or simply justify U.S. interventions for reasons other than preventing state failure.

14. See Jack Goldstone and others, "State Failure Task Force Report, Phase III," September 2000 (www.cidcm.umd.edu [May 2004]). For a critique of Goldstone and a review of the literature on state failure, see David Carment, "Anticipating State Failure," January 2001 (www.carleton.ca/cifp/docs/anticipatingstatefailure.pdf [December 2005]). See also Robert Rotberg, ed., *When States Fail* (Princeton University Press, 2004).

15. For an exposition of this approach, see USAID, *Foreign Aid in the National Interest* (2002), chap. 4.

16. USAID, *Fragile States Strategy*, p. 12.

17. A conflict vulnerability assessment for Bulgaria is available on USAID's website, www.usaid.gov.

18. Although there is a degree of overlap in the concepts of preventing state failure and preventing conflict, these are somewhat different. Conflict can erupt even when states are not failing—for example, between states rather than within states. And in theory, states can fail without conflict occurring, though a case of state failure without civil conflict is rare in today's world. It is also unclear whether and when state failure leads to civil violence or when it is the reverse: civil violence leading to state failure.

19. The Development Assistance Committee of the OECD, a club of bilateral aid agencies, has undertaken some useful work on conflict prevention and peace building. See, for example, the committee's publication *Helping to Prevent Violent Conflict: Orientations for External Partners* (Paris: OECD, 2001). However, this document skirts the difficult issue of changing the political calculus of entrenched elites and so seems to ignore the core problems behind failing states.

20. U.S. General Accounting Office, "US Rule of Law Assistance to Five Latin American Countries," GAO, National Security and International Affairs Division 99–195 (1999); also see USAID, "Achievements in Building and Maintaining the Rule of Law," occasional paper, Democracy and Governance Center, November 2002, pp. 68ff.

21. See testimony of Howard Wolpe, Consulting Director, Africa Project, Woodrow Wilson International Center, before the House Subcommittee on Africa, House Committee on Foreign Affairs, April 3, 2003 (www.house.gov/international_relations/108/wolp0403.htm).

22. See International Crisis Group, "A Framework for Responsible Aid to Burundi," *Africa Report* 57, February 21, 2003.

23. Paul Collier, "Aid 'Dependency': A Critique," *Journal of African Economies* 8, no. 4 (1999): 528–45.

24. See OTI website, www.usaid.gov. Other countries and institutions, including the World Bank, Denmark, and the United Kingdom, have followed USAID's initiative and established their own postconflict offices and funds.

25. See, for example, Robert Rotberg, "The First Ten Years: An Assessment of the Office of Transition Initiatives" (Belfer Center Program on Intrastate Conflict, John F. Kennedy School, Harvard University, 2005).

26. See Krishna Kumar and Marina Ottaway, *From Bullets to Ballots: Electoral Assistance to Postconflict Societies* (Washington: Center for Development Information and Evaluation, USAID, 1997); Krishna Kumar, ed., *Rebuilding Societies after Civil War: Critical Roles for International Assistance* (Boulder, Colo.: Lynne Rienner, 1997); and Krishna Kumar, ed., *Postconflict Elections, Democratization and International Assistance* (Boulder, Colo.: Lynne Rienner, 1998).

PART **III**

Tools of State Building

10

Aid through Trade: An Effective Option?

ARVIND PANAGARIYA

W hat trade policy initiatives can the rich countries such as the United States take to assist the poor countries in improving their growth prospects and achieving faster alleviation of poverty? This question has been a subject of research and debate among policy analysts in the area of trade and development for more than four decades. During the Kennedy Round of trade negotiations, developing countries successfully lobbied for the addition of Part IV, titled "Trade and Development," to the General Agreement on Tariffs and Trade (GATT). Under Article XXXVII of this part, developed countries promised to "accord high priority to the reduction and elimination of barriers to products currently or potentially of particular export interest to less developed contracting parties" and to "refrain from introducing, or increasing the incidence of, customs duties or non-tariff barriers on products currently or potentially of particular export interest" to them.

Again, in 1971, under the auspices of the United Nations Conference on Trade and Development (UNCTAD, founded in 1964), developing countries successfully pushed for the adoption of the Enabling Clause by the

I am grateful to Jagdish Bhagwati for numerous discussions that shaped my thinking on the subject matter of this chapter and to two anonymous reviewers for excellent comments on an earlier version.

GATT contracting parties. The clause was initially adopted for ten years but was renewed in 1979 for an indefinite period. It gives legal status to the Generalized System of Preferences (GSP) and the exchange of South-South trade preferences. The GSP provision gives legal status to one-way trade preferences by developed to developing countries, while the provision on South-South preferences freed developing countries from GATT's Article XXIV requirements while exchanging trade preferences among themselves.

Subsequently, encouraged by the 1973 success of the Organization of Petroleum Exporting Countries (OPEC) in increasing oil prices, developing countries called for far-reaching changes in the rules of the North-South engagement under the rubric of the New International Economic Order (NIEO). As a part of this effort, on May 1, 1974, the Sixth Special Session of the UN General Assembly adopted a manifesto entitled "Declaration and Program of Action of the New International Order." Among the measures proposed under the NIEO were the indexation of developing country export prices to developed country manufactures exports, raising official development assistance to 0.7 percent of developed country gross national product (GNP), linking the International Monetary Fund's special drawing rights to development aid, lowering tariffs on manufactures exported by developing to developed countries, creating an international food program, and negotiating the redeployment of some developed country industries to developing countries.[1]

Unfortunately, few of these efforts during the 1960s and 1970s can be said to have contributed significantly to growth and development in the poor countries. Given the best endeavor nature of the commitments in Part IV of GATT and the unwillingness of the rich countries to give one-way concessions, its addition led to the lowering of few barriers facing the products exported by developing countries. On the contrary, the 1960s and 1970s saw the grip of textile and apparel quotas, organized under the rubric of the Multifiber Arrangement in 1974, tighten progressively. The enabling clause did lead to the grant of trade preferences under the GSP and other schemes, but as I discuss later in greater detail, these had at most limited impact on the developing country exports and proved of questionable value.

The NIEO movement was a complete failure. Beyond paying lip service to the proposed agenda, developed countries yielded little. Instead, they chose to delegate the issues of concern to developing countries to the Bretton Woods institutions, in which they held the balance of power. In turn, these institutions went on to aggressively promote liberal trade policies in developing countries themselves. Simultaneously, in the aftermath of the Tokyo

Round (1974–79), developed countries began to insist that developing countries abandon the practice of free riding the multilateral liberalization negotiated by developed countries and become active parties to future rounds of negotiations. The Uruguay Round was launched in 1986 only after developing countries agreed formally to participate fully in the negotiations.

During the last two decades, the NIEO agenda was thus relegated to the background.[2] But following the Uruguay Round Agreement, the process came full circle. Perceptions that developing countries got shortchanged in the Uruguay Round and that the benefits of the agreement went asymmetrically to the rich countries have led to a partial resurgence of the NIEO agenda.[3] Though many of the impractical schemes proposed under the NIEO have been buried for good, moral pressure is being exerted once again for one-way concessions from rich to poor countries through trade and aid. Interestingly, this time around the leadership at the Bretton Woods institutions has joined hands with the United Nations in accusing developed countries of double standards and maintaining trade barriers that hurt developing country interests.

A question that has, therefore, gained salience in the United States is whether the changed circumstances make it more feasible for the nation to deploy trade policy instruments to assist the neediest developing countries, characterized in this volume as poorly performing states, in their endeavor to achieve faster growth and reduce poverty.[4] Is there scope for further expansion of the trade concessions by the United States to these countries; if yes, does the experience to date point to the desirability of such expansion; and if not, are political circumstances favorable to reforms that would make the expansion desirable?

In pursuit of answers to these questions, I examine the scope for and desirability of U.S. assistance to poor performers through three separate trade policy measures: one-way trade preferences as, for example, under the GSP; bilateral trade preferences as under free trade agreements, such as the North American Free Trade Agreement (NAFTA) and the U.S.-Jordan Free Trade Agreement; and multilateral trade liberalization for products of interest to developing countries, as under the Uruguay Round Agreement. Based on the accumulated experience of the past forty-five years, my principal conclusion is that of these three forms of market access, only the last one—multilateral trade liberalization—is both desirable and feasible.

The record of one-way trade preferences by the United States and the European Union (EU) has been quite poor, and there is little reason to believe that this will change in the near future. These preferences have been selective, uncertain, and subject to all kinds of side conditions. On balance, EU preferences have been less arbitrary than those of the United States, but even they have failed to generate significant impact on growth in the beneficiary countries.

Likewise, the potential for free trade agreements between the United States and poorly performing states is limited and their value questionable. Currently, with the attention focused on Latin America, few free trade agreements with poor performers are on the U.S. trade policy radar screen. But even if that were not the case, it is far from clear that two-way trade preferences would succeed where one-way preferences have failed. For example, the U.S.-Jordan Free Trade Agreement has given few reasons for celebration of Jordan's economic development.

Therefore, multilateral liberalization under the auspices of the Doha Round remains the best available option. This liberalization is subject to World Trade Organization (WTO) discipline and cannot be withdrawn at will. It is also free of the trade diversion that plagues free trade agreements. And above all, it has the potential to induce nondiscriminatory liberalization in poor performers themselves.

A final qualification must be added before I proceed to the detailed discussion of these themes. Further opening of developed country markets, no matter what form it takes, can help these countries only in a limited way. Despite all the rhetoric and assertions to the contrary, the bitter and sad truth is that even if developed countries were to open their markets fully without asking for reciprocal liberalization and without any side conditions, few poor performers would succeed in achieving significant growth and poverty reduction purely as a consequence of this opening up. The explanation for the poor growth performance of many of these countries is to be found not in the barriers to their exports in the rich countries—though these barriers do impose a burden on them—but in their own domestic policies and political environment, which governs the internal investment climate.

This conclusion is supported by the fact that though the external environment facing all developing countries has been the same during the past several decades, their performance has been far from the same. Some of them have managed to register much higher growth rates than others. They have accomplished this principally because of their superior economic policies rather than special market access favors granted them. From the 1950s through the 1970s, most developing countries took the pessimistic view that the world economic order was rigged against them and chose inward-looking policies. But countries such as the Republic of Korea, Taiwan, Singapore, and

Hong Kong did the opposite, opting to go for the world markets. The result was spectacular growth on a sustained basis. This experience has been repeated subsequently by such countries as Malaysia, Thailand, Indonesia, People's Republic of China, India, and Vietnam in Asia; Chile in Latin America; and most recently Uganda in Africa.

Barriers to Exports: An Overview

By definition, poorly performing states are countries with low per capita incomes and poor performance along some specified dimensions. This volume defines low-income countries as those having annual per capita incomes below US$1,435 in 2001. This is the level used by the World Bank to identify countries eligible for its concessional lending window, the International Development Association. There are thought to be seventy-four countries that fall below this cutoff point. Invoking the governmental performance criteria narrows down this set further. This volume adopts the criteria of the Millennium Challenge Account, measuring governmental performance along three dimensions: the degree to which governments rule justly, invest in people, and promote economic freedom.

The criteria used to identify poorly performing states are highly correlated with those used to identify the least developed countries (LDCs) by the United Nations.[5] Not surprisingly, four-fifths of the countries categorized as LDCs by the United Nations appear as poor performers on one or many of the dimensions described in this volume. This commonality allows us to exploit the detailed information collected by UNCTAD on LDCs to gain further insight into the economic performance of poorly performing states.

During 1990–98, the real GDP of LDCs as a group grew by 3.2 percent a year compared with 3.4 percent for the low- and middle-income countries and 2.5 percent for the world.[6] This relatively favorable comparison is tempered by two facts. First, the bulk of LDC growth represents growth in one country, Bangladesh, with one-fifth of the total LDC population. Excluding Bangladesh, the growth rate was more modest, at 2.4 percent. Second, the growth rate of population in LDCs was much higher than that in other developing countries. As such, on a per capita basis, LDC incomes grew only 0.9 percent during 1990–98. If we exclude Bangladesh, this figure drops to 0.4 percent. Over the same period, other developing countries grew at 3.6 percent in per capita terms.

Behind these aggregate numbers, there is substantial variance in the performance across LDCs. The top fifteen LDC performers during 1990–98 grew at 2 percent or more in per capita terms. At the other extreme, twenty-two LDCs were either stagnant or declined in per capita terms during that time period. In eleven LDCs suffering armed conflicts and internal instability, real per capita GDP declined at 3 percent or more annually during 1990–98.

The share of LDCs in world trade declined from 3.04 percent in 1954 to a tiny 0.42 percent in 1998. The bulk of this decline took place during the 1960s and 1970s, though there was a slight decline during the 1990s as well. In 1999, LDCs sent 27 percent of their exports to the United States, 37 percent to EU countries, 4 percent to Japan, 1 percent to Canada, 2 percent to other developed countries, 1 percent to each other, and 28 percent to other developing countries. Thus overall they sent 71 percent of the exports to developed countries and 29 percent to developing countries.

Table 10-1 provides the weighted applied tariff rates facing LDCs in various regions of the world in 1999. It is evident from this table that least developed countries faced the highest tariffs in South Asia: 28 percent in agriculture and fisheries and almost 25 percent in manufactures. Corresponding rates in developed countries are 2.1 and 4.4 percent, respectively. All developing country regions impose higher barriers to LDC exports than developed countries.

Table 10-2 offers further details on the status of trade barriers in 1998 facing LDCs in what are termed the Quad countries by the WTO: Canada, the European Union, Japan, and the United States. These four markets account for most LDC exports to developed countries. Among the four markets, the EU offers LDCs the least restrictive trade regime. In 1998 only 3.12 percent of LDC exports to EU members faced any tariffs. In contrast, in the United States 47 percent of LDC exports faced tariffs exceeding 5 percent. A similar pattern is also observed in terms of the proportion of product lines subject to tariffs. Furthermore, LDCs registered positive exports in many more product lines in the EU in than the United States.

The lead enjoyed by the EU in offering trade concessions to LDCs was strengthened following the adoption of the "Everything but Arms" (EBA) initiative by it in February 2001. Under this initiative, the EU introduced duty- and quota-free entry to all products from LDCs, with three important exceptions (plus arms and ammunition, of course). The three excluded products are bananas, rice, and sugar. They are to be given unlimited duty-free access starting January 2006, July 2009, and September 2009, respectively. Currently, two of the products, rice and sugar, are subject to limited tariff-free quotas, which are to be increased annually.

Table 10-1. *Weighted Applied Tariffs Facing Least Developed Country Exports, by Region, 1999*

Export	Developed countries	South Asia	Middle East and North Africa	Latin America and the Caribbean	Europe and Central Asia	East Asia and the Pacific	Sub-Saharan Africa	Quad markets[a]	World
Agricultural and fishery products	2.1	28.3	7.6	14.8	11.9	14.0	11.0	1.7	6.0
Crustaceans (live)	0.7	16.4	15.1	30.0	14.3	9.4	11.5	0.7	1.8
Other fish	1.8	13.8	12.8	14.6	9.6	22.7	19.3	1.8	6.0
Edible fruit and nuts	0.1	38.0	13.0	17.0	8.9	6.4	23.5	0.0	24.0
Coffee and substitutes with coffee	0.0	35.0	16.3	12.7	7.4	0.9	4.5	0.0	1.7
Oil seeds and miscellaneous grain, seeds, and fruits	0.4	33.4	8.1	11.2	5.8	14.1	7.6	0.3	4.4
Other agricultural and fishery products	5.1	13.0	29.2	16.8	18.4	3.2	7.8	5.3	6.9
Minerals and fuels	0.0	6.5	14.4	5.9	0.7	4.5	9.3	0.0	2.9
Ores, slag, and ash	0.0	5.0	12.0	0.0	0.0	1.3	0.0	0.0	0.1
Crude and refined petroleum oil	0.0	30.0	20.0	6.0	3.9	4.5	15.4	0.0	3.6
Other minerals and fuels	0.0	5.0	0.0	5.2	0.0	3.0	10.8	0.0	2.2
Manufactures	4.4	24.7	12.6	10.3	8.0	2.4	7.4	4.5	5.0
Rubber, leather, and footwear products	2.8	13.0	12.7	11.5	13.8	1.4	17.4	2.6	3.4
Wood and wood products	0.4	7.7	11.5	18.1	3.2	2.0	5.8	0.3	2.2
Cotton products	0.3	4.5	11.9	8.4	0.0	2.0	1.0	0.0	2.1
Knitted or crocheted articles	8.3	35.7	16.0	26.3	21.1	1.8	24.0	8.4	8.5
Nonknitted or crocheted articles	7.2	35.5	13.3	20.8	22.9	6.2	13.4	7.2	7.4
Diamonds	0.0	40.0	4.2	4.5	5.0	0.3	0.0	0.0	0.0
Other manufactured products	0.5	34.5	11.2	7.5	1.9	2.7	8.9	0.2	2.0
Other products not elsewhere specified	3.3	28.8	5.2	10.7	7.9	7.5	7.0	2.1	8.3
Total	3.5	25.5	8.9	9.7	9.4	4.5	8.8	3.4	4.9

Source: UNCTAD, "Handbook of Market Access Barriers" (Geneva: United Nations, 2001).

a. Quad markets are Canada, Japan, the United States, and the European Union.

Table 10-2. *Least Developed Country Exports to the Quad Markets, 1998*

Measure	Canada	European Union[a]	Japan	United States
Total least developed country (LDC) exports (US$1,000)	227,677	9,874,807	1,019,120	6,962,416
Total imports in product lines of LDC (US$1,000)	83,670,842	637,766,105	126,378,101	528,279,235
Total imports (US$1,000)	211,085,424	783,684,206	305,438,116	1,015,143,866
LDC share of competitive imports (percent)	0.27	1.55	0.81	1.32
LDC share of total imports (percent)	0.11	1.26	0.33	0.69
Total harmonized system 6 (HS6) tariff lines	758	2,222	545	946
Tariff (HS6) lines with protection	201	55	74	335
Tariff (HS6) lines with protection above 5 percent	181	51	36	282
LDC exports entering duty free (US$1,000)	103,260	9,566,647	498,534	3,596,270
LDC exports dutiable (US$1,000)	124,417	308,160	520,586	3,366,146
LDC exports dutiable above 5 percent (US$1,000)	123,827	308,134	226,274	3,272,917
Share of LDC exports facing protection (percent)	54.60	3.12	51.10	48.30
Share of LDC exports facing tariff >5 percent (percent)	54.40	3.12	22.20	47.00
Share of HS6 lines with tariff (percent)	18.50	4.20	12.10	17.10
Share of HS6 lines with tariff >5 percent (percent)	12.80	3.80	7.60	14.10

Source: UNCTAD, "Duty and Quota Free Market Access for LDCs: An Analysis of Quad Initiatives" (Geneva: United Nations, 2001).

a. Before the "Everything but Arms" initiative.

One-Way Trade Preferences

To assess possible benefits from further expansion of trade preferences by the United States, we must consider three questions: Is there substantial scope for this expansion? If yes, does the experience to date support the desirability of the expansion? And if not, do political circumstance offer an opportunity to reform the system such that the expansion is made desirable? Consider each of these questions in turn.

The Scope for the Expansion of Trade Preferences

The United States offers trade preferences under the GSP, the Africa Growth and Opportunity Act (AGOA), the Caribbean Basin Trade Partnership Act (CBTPA), and the Andean Trade Preferences Act (ATPA). None of the beneficiary countries of ATPA and CBTPA are poor performers as described in this volume. Therefore, the discussion below is limited to the GSP and the AGOA.

The U.S. GSP program was introduced in 1976.[7] Since the program carries an expiration date, it had to be renewed eight times by 2002. The last expiration took place on September 30, 2001, and the last renewal August 6, 2002. The latest renewal validates the GSP until December 31, 2006. Currently, of more than 10,000 items, 4,600 are accorded duty-free status under the program. In 1997 the United States added another 1,700 items to the duty-free list for developing countries, though stricter criteria allow only thirty-five of these forty-nine countries to qualify for the expanded preferences.

The Trade and Development Act of 2000, which contains the AGOA, seeks to expand trade with sub-Saharan African countries. The AGOA offers to the eligible among these countries—many of them poor performers—duty-free and quota-free access to the U.S. market for all products under the GSP, plus 1,800 new items until September 30, 2008. Under special conditions, it also extends duty-free status to apparel, which is subject to high tariffs in the United States. Furthermore, the AGOA eliminates the GSP competitive-need limitation, which can otherwise be invoked to withdraw duty-free status when imports from a country exceed certain limits.

Despite these concessions, there remains considerable scope for the expansion of trade preferences by the United States to poorly performing states. U.S. preferences have fallen far short of those granted by the EU under its EBA initiative. According to UNCTAD, a little more than 45 percent of total LDC exports in 2000 were eligible for better-than-MFN access to the United States market.[8] Although more than 80 percent of all harmonized system 6 (HS6) products qualified for duty-free access that year, if petroleum products are excluded, this share drops down to about 50 percent. Furthermore, not all LDC exports eligible for preferences actually receive preferential treatment. Thus the utilization ratio was about 77 percent in 1998.

Some insight into the nature of excluded products can be obtained by examining the top twenty LDC exports by source country to the United States according to their product classification and preference status (see table 10-3). None of the exporters of manufactures on this top twenty list received any preference. The only preferences received were those on tobacco and perhaps oil. An examination of the products with tariff peaks reinforces this picture. Various apparel items, which are subject to tariff peaks, are excluded from the GSP. The AGOA permits duty-free entry of these items but requires that exporters have a strict visa system to ensure origin. Until April 2001 only two LDCs, Lesotho and Madagascar, were able to fulfill this requirement. Of these two, only Madagascar appears on the list of poorly performing states. Of course, neither of these countries is a big enough exporter to make the top twenty exports list in table 10-3.

Does Past Experience Point to the Desirability of Expansion of Preferences?

If the objective is to see poor performers grow faster, the past offers little support to the concentration of efforts on the expansion of trade preferences.[9] The preferences may make the donor countries feel good, transfer some of the forgone tariff revenue to the beneficiary countries, and may even lead to a marginal expansion of the latter's exports, but the track record of preferences to date gives little reason to conclude that they will make a perceptible difference in growth and poverty to the beneficiary countries.

EU preferences are by far the most extensive of all for developing countries and African countries, although the record of these preferences is disappointing. Under Lomé IV, which was succeeded by the Cotonou Agreement, seventy-one African, Caribbean, and Pacific (ACP) countries, including many poorly performing countries, enjoyed a highly favorable trade regime. Yet a 1997 European Commission "green paper," published as a preparatory step toward the 1998 talks for the extension of Lomé IV, offered a grim assessment. It reported that the share of ACP countries in the EU market had declined from nearly 7 percent in 1976 to 3 percent in 1998. Merely ten products accounted for 60 percent of ACP exports to EU members. Per capita gross domestic product (GDP) in sub-Saharan Africa grew by only 0.4 percent a year, compared with 2.3 percent for all developing countries from 1962 to 1992. At most, a handful of nations—Côte d'Ivoire, Mauritius, Zimbabwe,

Table 10-3. *Top Least Developed Country Exports to the United States, using the Harmonized System of Product Codes, 2000*

Harmonized system 6 code	Product	Value (US$1,000)	Country (% preferential margin)
270900	Petroleum oils and oils obtained from bituminous minerals, crude	2,488,009	Angola (n.a.)
270900	Petroleum oils and oils obtained from bituminous minerals, crude	337,349	Congo (n.a.)
620520	Apparel	193,570	Bangladesh (0)
620342	Apparel	184,549	Bangladesh (0)
650590	Headgear and parts thereof	165,258	Bangladesh (0)
620342	Apparel	155,759	Cambodia (0)
620462	Apparel	152,775	Bangladesh (0)
620630	Apparel	127,913	Bangladesh (0)
610910	Knitted apparel	125,935	Haiti (0)
260600	Aluminum ores and concentrates	116,814	Guinea (0)
30613	Shrimps and prawns	115,046	Bangladesh (0)
270900	Petroleum oils and oils obtained from bituminous minerals, crude	109,067	Zaire (n.a.)
611020	Knitted apparel	106,662	Cambodia (0)
620462	Apparel	85,251	Cambodia (0)
611030	Knitted apparel	80,848	Bangladesh (0)
611020	Knitted apparel	77,042	Bangladesh (0)
710231	Diamonds	73,949	Zaire (0)
610821	Briefs and panties	56,182	Bangladesh (0)
620193	Apparel	55,669	Bangladesh (0)
240120	Tobacco	52,535	Malawi (31.11)

Source: See table 10-2.

and Jamaica, none of which were poorly performing countries—benefited perceptibly from the preferences.

Empirical studies support the broad conclusion that trade preferences have had little beneficial impact beyond the obvious rent transfer accompanying duty-free entry of goods.[10] In his assessment of the impact of the special and differential treatment to developing countries under GATT, John Whalley concluded "that special and differential treatment has had only a marginal effect on country economic performance, especially through GSP. And in the more rapidly growing economies, such as Korea, Taiwan, Turkey, and others, there is little evidence that special and differential treatment has played much of a role in their strong performance."[11] As noted in the introduction, the

limited or complete lack of impact of trade preferences on economic performance is to be attributed principally to domestic policy regimes that discourage
economic activity in general and trade in particular. But many features of the
preference schemes themselves complement this factor by making preferences
largely ineffective. These are discussed below.

SIDE CONDITIONS. Despite the provision in the Enabling Clause that
GSP schemes be unilateral and not require reciprocity from developing countries, donor countries have introduced a considerable element of reciprocity
in them. The U.S. GSP scheme requires that beneficiary countries provide
adequate and effective protection of intellectual property rights and that they
take steps to observe internationally recognized worker rights. There have
been many instances of countries losing GSP benefits on account of a poor
intellectual property rights regime. Countries have also been investigated for
child labor violations.

The AGOA attaches even more elaborate side conditions. Eligibility
requires countries to work toward strengthening market-based economies,
promoting the rule of law and political pluralism, eliminating barriers to
U.S. trade and investment, protecting intellectual property, combating corruption, instituting policies to reduce poverty, increasing the availability of
health care and educational opportunities, protecting human rights and
worker rights, and eliminating certain child labor practices.

On one hand, these conditions seem sensible if the objective is to promote
good governance in these states. And yet they become a hindrance to investments that might help a beneficiary country to take advantage of the preference, for the conditions introduce an element of uncertainty about the continuity of the preferential status. Whenever U.S. producers feel threatened by
competition from a specific beneficiary country, they can lobby for the
removal of the latter from the beneficiary list under the pretext that it is failing to satisfy one or more of the host of governance conditions. There have
been several instances of a U.S. pharmaceutical firm successfully lobbying
against countries it saw as failing to protect intellectual property rights.
Because the preferences are not subject to WTO discipline, such decisions
can be made unilaterally by the United States.

In addition to nonreciprocity, the Enabling Clause requires that preferences be generalized, meaning that they be extended to all products. Nevertheless, given the permissive, rather than mandatory, nature of the clause,
countries have been highly selective in their choice of products, excluding
precisely the products in which developing countries have a comparative
advantage. It has already been noted that both the EU and the United States

give very limited preference in textiles and clothing sectors. Table 10-3 illus- trates graphically how the United States has left the top exports of LDCs out of the preference net. More important, the EU and the United States main- tain strict import quotas on the imports of these products from all significant suppliers under the Multifiber Agreement (MFA). Indeed, it was not until developing countries opted for reciprocal bargains in the Uruguay Round that the United States, the EU, and other developed country markets agreed to dismantle the MFA regime.[12]

This point applies even more forcefully to agricultural exports. Until just a few years ago, virtually all agricultural products remained out of even the more generous EU GSP schemes. Only a few years ago, the EBA initiative, aimed exclusively at LDCs, attempted to bring them into the GSP net. But even this attempt seems to have been more symbolic than real. Thus three major items of potential interest—rice, bananas, and sugar—have been left out of the EBA net. What is surprising is that (the publicity surrounding the EBA initiative notwithstanding) the potential for agricultural exports from the least developed countries is minimal. For example, given the paltry 2,000 tons of annual rice exports by LDCs to EU countries, there is little rationale for the failure of the EU to grant LDCs immediate quota-free entry of that product. A similar point also applies to sugar.

UNCERTAINTIES AND OTHER LIMITATIONS. Uncertainties and other limi- tations further undercut the value of GSP schemes. The schemes are made available for limited periods of time and can expire if not renewed. The U.S. GSP scheme has gone through eight renewals since inception, and there have been breaks during most of those renewals. For instance, the last expiration took place on September 30, 2001, and renewal did not take place until August 6, 2002. Such breaks can be fatal for producers operating on small margins of profit, as is likely among producers in developing countries. The U.S. GSP system also applies a competitive needs limit whereby a country is denied the preference in a product if it exports that product in a value exceeding a specified limit. Currently, this limit is set at US$100 million a year for each tariff line. This provision necessarily discourages countries from taking full advantage of specialization. Finally, the side conditions mentioned above can be invoked to deny a potential competitor the GSP benefit. Within the U.S. system, this often happens in response to complaints by domestic producers whose objective is to place a particularly efficient sup- plier from a developing country at a disadvantage.

These limits and uncertainties discourage potential entrepreneurs from making the necessary investments. Amar Hamoudi of the Center for Global

Development made this point forcefully in the context of the AGOA in a letter to the *Financial Times,* June 6, 2002. To quote him,

> Take the recent case where a consortium of US fruit producers asked the Bush administration to suspend South Africa's AGOA benefits on canned pears, arguing that the expansion of the industry in South Africa threatened to put a handful of Americans out of work. Fruit producers in South Africa protested that AGOA did not induce them to expand production, since the necessary investments were too risky given that the benefits granted by AGOA can be revoked at any time. Producers in Africa can expect that any time they succeed in taking true advantage of AGOA, some special interest group in the US will demand that the benefits be rescinded.

RULES OF ORIGIN. Favorable impact of tariff preferences on LDC exports has often been contained by the rules of origin that such exports must satisfy. In principle, preferences are meant for goods produced in the beneficiary countries, so rules of origin are unavoidable, for in their absence, beneficiary countries would simply import goods from more efficient nonbeneficiary countries and reexport them as their own, pocketing the tariff revenue in the process.

Nevertheless, the rules of origin can be and are chosen in ways that minimize the benefit of the preference to exporters and result in reverse preferences to producers in the donor countries. The commonest such rule makes the preference contingent on a minimum value addition to the product within the exporting country. According to the U.S. GSP scheme, to qualify for duty-free treatment, the cost, or value, of materials wholly grown, produced, or manufactured in the beneficiary developing country plus the direct processing costs there must be at least 35 percent of the product's dutiable value. This requirement can be a major deterrent, since many poor performers are able to perform only simple assembly operations. Indeed, it can discriminate against these states, since larger and richer developing countries are able to take advantage of the preference due to their ability to satisfy the rules of origin—whereas they are not. Effectively, trade can be diverted away from them relative to no tariff preference.

The AGOA rules of origin on apparel also introduce an element of reverse preferences. They require that fabric used in apparel be of U.S. or beneficiary country origin. Such a feature introduces a rent on the fabric made in the United States, especially because few African beneficiary countries produce it. Though this rule of origin is waived for less developed African countries (defined as those with per capita incomes less than US$1,500) in place of a visa requirement, few of them are able to satisfy the latter—and even then there is a strict quantitative limit placed on such exports.

ADVERSE IMPACT ON THE LIBERALIZATION OF BENEFICIARY AND DONOR COUNTRIES. Tariff preferences can also discourage liberalization within the beneficiary countries themselves. As Robert Hudec has noted, "the non-reciprocity doctrine tends to remove the major incentive [the GSP beneficiary country] export industries have . . . for opposing protectionist trade policies at home."[13] Once exporters have achieved free access to the markets of major trading partners, their incentive for using internal liberalization as an instrument of encouraging the partner to open its market disappears. Alternatively, if exporters fear losing GSP status because exports cross a certain threshold (as is true of many GSP schemes), they may be more accommodating of protectionist policies at home.

Econometric research by Caglar Ozden and Eric Reinhardt supports this hypothesis.[14] These authors analyzed a panel data set of annual observations on each of the 154 developing countries ever eligible for the U.S. GSP program, starting in the year of first eligibility (mostly 1976) and continuing through 2000. Comparing those countries remaining on the GSP to those dropped, they find that the countries dropped from the program opened their markets substantially. Specifically, according to their quantitative estimates, the removal from the GSP program had the effect of boosting a developing country's imports by 8 percent of its GDP, cutting its average nominal tariff by 4 percentage points, and reducing the duties it collects by about 1.6 percent of the value of its trade. These findings control for a wide variety of confounds (like geography, income, GDP, and global liberalization trends), and the response rises slightly after correction for the endogeneity of the GSP.

Ozden and Reinhardt offer the example of Chile, whose trade liberalization had come to a standstill by the late 1980s. In 1988 Chile was dropped from the U.S. GSP program for human and worker rights violations. Its finance minister immediately announced a reduction in Chile's average nominal tariff from 20 to 15 percent, his explicitly stated rationale being to compensate for its exporters' loss of competitiveness in the U.S. market by defraying their input costs.

Ironically, preferences have also had an adverse effect on genuine, multilateral trade liberalization by developed countries in products of interest to developing countries. Notwithstanding various strings attached to the preferences, they have helped developed countries promote the image that they have opened their markets to developing countries without reciprocity. More concretely, the fear on the part of the beneficiary countries that multilateral liberalization would erode their preference margin has undercut their incentive to push harder for such liberalization. To some degree, special deals built around trade preferences have allowed developed countries to maintain MFA and high tariffs in apparel, footwear, and fisheries.

Is Reform Possible: The Politics of Preferences

Devotees of preferences may respond to these criticisms by suggesting that the fault lies not with preferences but with their implementation and that what is required is more judicious implementation. That is to say, the GSP must be reformed as per its original conception in the Enabling Clause, making it truly general by bringing all products within the fold, freeing it of reciprocity by eliminating side conditions and ending the uncertainty by ensuring that export success in specific products does not result in the loss of the preference.

If these reforms could be accomplished, the GSP will be worth promoting. But given the politics in the United States, there is little reason to think that such far-reaching reform could ever be achieved. In the introduction, I describe the disappointing history of developing country efforts to obtain one-way concessions from developed countries. The GATT Article XXXVII in Part IV actually committed developed countries to open their markets in products exported by developing countries and to refrain from erecting new barriers in those products. But no progress whatsoever was made with tariff peaks and agricultural protection having disproportionately greater limiting impact on the exports of developing countries. The MFA quotas reinforced these restrictions.

The politics of trade preferences is even worse. The United States clearly sees them as a privilege rather than a right and therefore subject to the use as an instrument of promoting other policy objectives. For instance, given the U.S. failure to bring labor standards into the WTO to date, it is more likely to use preferences as an instrument of promoting labor standards. Given all kinds of side conditions even in AGOA, it is naïve to think that a proper reform of trade preferences is possible even as applied to developing countries. Hence I am skeptical that trade preferences can serve as a genuine instrument of aid.

Of course, even if one considers the hypothetical scenario in which the trade preferences to poor performers are freed of all these abuses, one must take into account the adverse impact of the preferences on trade policies within these countries before reaching a final conclusion on the desirability of such a reform. One must confront the evidence provided by Ozden and Reinhardt that countries that were successful in taking advantage of the preferences also found their own trade liberalization programs slow down.

Two-Way Preferences: Free Trade Areas

An alternative to one-way trade preferences is the free trade area, in which preferences are two-way, which has two advantages over one-way preferences. First, free trade areas in which one or more developed countries participate are subject to the discipline of GATT Article XXIV. This means that some of the abuses of one-way preferences under the Enabling Clause can be contained. For example, substantially all products must be subject to zero duty, and no limits can be placed on the quantity of exports entering the partner country market at zero duty. Nor can the preference be arbitrarily withdrawn in response to domestic lobbying pressures on one pretext or the other. Second, a free trade area agreement forces the developing country participant to open its own market to the developed country partner as well. Therefore, it may be viewed as having a liberalizing impact on the developing country as well.

But these advantages must be weighed against many disadvantages.[15] First, like one-way preferences, free-trade-area preferences are also subject to the rules of origin. The costs of rules of origin are not confined merely to higher prices of inputs sourced from within the union but also include substantial administrative costs. Using firm-level data, Matti Koskinen estimates that administrative compliance costs within the FTA between the European Community and the European Free Trade Association (EFTA), administrative compliance costs ranged between 1.4 percent and 5.7 percent of the value of export transactions.[16] In a similar vein, Peter Holmes and G. Shephard note that the average export transaction from EFTA to the European Community required thirty-five documents and 360 copies.[17] According to the empirical evidence, within NAFTA, even Mexico has not been able to make use of the tariff preference effectively in some of the key sectors due to the rules of origin. Thus, according to Olivier Cadot and others, after we exclude the goods subject to zero external tariffs, Mexico's overall preference utilization rate in the U.S. market in 2000 was 83 percent.[18] But in the textile and apparel sector (HTS2, chapters 50–63), where the margin of preference is the highest and the Mexican comparative advantage greatest, the utilization rate is only 66 percent. Within textiles and clothing, the utilization rate for knitted products (HTS2, chapter 61) was even lower, at 48 percent. The ability of poorly performing states to satisfy the rules of origin is likely to be far more limited than that of Mexico, so that they are unlikely to succeed in taking advantage of the preferences.

Second, side conditions are now increasingly a part of free trade area agreements as well. Within the NAFTA region, these side conditions were introduced through relatively benign side agreements on labor and the environment. But subsequently they began to appear centrally within the free trade area agreements concluded by the United States. Thus the U.S.-Jordan Free Trade Agreement requires the signatories to enforce their labor and environmental regulations and allows trade sanctions in case of noncompliance. The same provision also exists in the free trade area agreement concluded by the United States with Singapore and Chile. Indeed, these latter agreements extend the scope of side conditions further by limiting the ability of Singapore and Chile to use capital controls. The European Union's free trade agreements do not include these conditions, but they are themselves usually a part of broader agreements such as the Euro-Mediterranean Partnership and Cotonou Agreement, which are wide-ranging in scope and include such matters as human rights, democracy, and labor and environmental standards.

Third, given that the imports into many poorly performing states are still subject to relatively high trade barriers, preferential liberalization by them is likely to result in substantial trade diversion. The cost of such diversion must be borne by these countries, since they will be the ones paying the higher price to the union partner in preference to the lower price they would pay to the most efficient supplier of the product in the absence of the free trade area agreement. Thus when liberalization takes place on a discriminatory basis, as is true under a free trade area agreement, the benefits of liberalization are not automatic. We must weigh the losses due to trade diversion against the benefits from trade creation. This point becomes particularly compelling when we consider the fact that politics often results in the rules of origin being tighter in sectors where trade creation threatens the less efficient domestic industry and weaker in sectors where trade diversion is likely to displace the more efficient outside trading partners.

Finally, before embarking on a strategy of aiding specific poor countries through a web of crisscrossing free trade area agreements, the United States carries the responsibility of ensuring that it does not lead to a fragmentation of the entire trading system. Jagdish Bhagwati and Arvind Panagariya draw attention to the growing "spaghetti bowl" of tariffs, whereby the tariff on a product is no longer the simple most-favored-nation tariff but instead depends on the source country.[19] The tariff varies according to the stage of implementation of the free trade area agreement to which the source country belongs and the rules of origin within that agreement. Even after all of these agreements are fully implemented, the differences in the rules of origin across agreements will continue to allow for discrimination in the tariff based on the source country. Andre Sapir has made the dramatic point that the EU already has so many preferential arrangements that its MFN tariff applies uniformly to only six trading partners.[20] Any attempts at helping poorly performing countries further through free trade area agreements will only damage the trading system further.

Even if we choose to ignore these limitations, the political reality is that it will be a long time before free trade area agreements with poor performers even appear on the U.S. trade policy radar screen. The countries with which the United States has concluded the last two such agreements are far from poor: Singapore and Chile. The next set of countries in the queue includes five Central American nations, Morocco, Australia, and several southern African states. Also on the agenda is the Free Trade Area of the Americas. Insofar as free trade agreements are concerned, the U.S. preoccupation is hardly with the states discussed in this volume.

Multilateral Liberalization

Having argued that neither one-way nor two-way trade preferences offer a desirable or feasible approach to help the least developed countries through trade, I now suggest that the best course is the multilateral approach. I reiterate that this is not a cure-all for these states, since the principal barriers to their development are within rather than outside. But if trade can be instrumental in promoting or facilitating faster growth in the presence of sound domestic policies and a stable investment environment, multilateral liberalization is to be preferred for a number of reasons.

First, multilateral liberalization does not carry with it the fear of trade diversion, since it treats all trading partners equally. Nor does it require any rules of origin, since market access is given independently of the origin of the product. Second, the liberalization is a legal obligation and therefore cannot be withdrawn at will. Domestic lobbies have only limited power to temporarily withdraw market access through safeguards and antidumping actions. In the case of small exporters (a quality of virtually all poor performers), even this power is limited. Third, multilateral liberalization has the great virtue that it will also lead to liberalization in some of the large developing countries. Recall that (as shown in table 10-1) the least developed countries, including poor performers, face by far the highest trade barriers among developing countries. Since the latter do not give GSP preferences, and since South-South preferences are limited, liberalization by them could be doubly valuable.

Fourth, in principle, multilateral liberalization has the potential to induce liberalization in poor performers as well, which is a desirable objective. These governments are likely to find it politically less costly to liberalize in the multilateral context since they can mobilize the export interests against import-competing interests in the context of a two-way bargain. Fifth, it is only through multilateral bargains that developing countries will succeed in fully opening markets in developed countries for products such as apparel and footwear, in which they have a comparative advantage. As already argued, this has been one unequivocal lesson of the last forty years of experience. Sixth, at least for now, multilateral liberalization does not carry the risk of side conditions in the form of labor and environmental standards. Though the environment has now entered the WTO negotiating agenda, the mandate is extremely limited, while labor standards have remained entirely outside the WTO purview.

An obvious important reason for pushing ahead with the multilateral approach is its political feasibility. The Doha Round is in progress at present and, at least in the area of industrial products, both the European Union and the United States have placed ambitious liberalization proposals on the table. If the larger developing countries such as Brazil, China, and India could be induced to make similarly bold moves, we have the opportunity to virtually eliminate trade barriers against industrial products. The U.S. proposal calls for complete elimination of these barriers by 2015. To facilitate such an outcome, developing countries could be given a longer phase-out period, say until 2020 under the special and differential treatment mandate in the Doha Ministerial Declaration, and offered adjustment assistance through the instrumentality of the World Bank.

There is one point of caution relating to agricultural liberalization, however, that deserves to be highlighted in the context of the Doha Round. Since 2000, senior officials at various multilateral institutions, especially the World Bank and the International Monetary Fund but also the United Nations, have aggressively promoted the view that agricultural subsidies and protection in the OECD countries hurt the poor countries. But as far as the least developed countries are concerned, this is plain wrong. Subsidies and protections in the OECD countries have kept world prices of agriculture low. This has benefited the countries that import these products but hurt those that export them. As it turns out, by and large least developed countries are net importers of agricultural products. Thus based on 1995–97 trade data, Alberto Valdes and Alex McCalla calculate that of the forty-eight least developed countries at the time, forty-five were net food importers and thirty-three net agricultural importers.[21] The repeal of agricultural subsides and protection in the OECD countries, which would raise world agricultural prices, would actually hurt the least developed countries as a group. Unqualified statements that agricultural subsidies and protection in the rich countries hurt the poor countries, pervasive in the press, do little good to promote the interests of the poor countries as a group. Instead, they principally promote the interests of the richer developing countries in Latin America and East Asia, along with the United States, Australia, and New Zealand.

I hasten to add that this asymmetry is not an argument against the liberalization of agriculture. From the long-run global perspective, there are good reasons to ensure an end to agricultural subsidies and protection under the ongoing Doha negotiations. Nevertheless, the recognition that such liberalization will hurt the majority of the poorest countries is the necessary first step toward working out a balanced bargain as well as preparing for adjustment assistance to these countries. The World Bank clearly has the responsibility to alleviate, through grants-in-aid, the pain that might accompany the rise in agricultural prices.

Concluding Remarks

During the last fifty years, developing countries that pursued outward-oriented policies under a realistic exchange rate and macroeconomic stability—such as the countries in the Far East during the 1960s and 1970 and Malaysia, Thailand, Indonesia, Vietnam, China, India, Chile, and Uganda subsequently—achieved fast growth under the same market access conditions that other countries failed to achieve. Despite high barriers against specific labor-intensive goods in the rich countries, these developing countries succeeded in penetrating the developed country markets. Failure to grow rapidly on a sustained basis has come largely from the failure to adopt sound domestic policies and ensure political stability, which are essential to promote productive investment. Even among the poor countries, the eleven worst failures during 1990–98 that declined by 3 percent annually in per capita terms were all subject to armed conflicts and internal instability.

Thus the hope for countries that do not have their own houses in order is truly limited, indeed. It is tempting to think that favors through trade preferences of one or the other kind that are contingent on good governmental policies may induce the necessary change in behavior in poor performers. I fear this is wishful thinking. Countries that are unable to exploit trade preferences in the absence of the side conditions are unlikely to be able to do so in their presence. Few governments that lack the capacity to enforce contracts and protect property rights to begin with are likely to become capable in these dimensions because trade preferences are available as a reward. Therefore, all the side conditions do is to make it politically easier for the donor country to offer the preferences since they reduce the likelihood that the preference will be used and make it possible to take restrictive action if imports from the beneficiary countries surge.

The upshot of this analysis is that we must be modest in thinking about the role of the U.S. trade policy in assisting poorly performing states. We may think along two possible avenues. First, recognizing that trade preferences are here to stay, what improvements can be made to make them more beneficial to these countries? And second, recognizing that multilateral liberalization offers the best route to promoting access to the U.S. market, precisely what can be done to accommodate the interests of poorly performing states?

Regarding the first question, given how limited the capacity of these states to export is, in the spirit of the "Everything but Arms" initiative, the United States could extend the zero-tariff treatment to all products. To make the preference credible, it could also consider eliminating all side conditions. Furthermore, for all commodities subject to a higher rate of tariff in the beneficiary country than in the United States, rules of origin may be waived entirely. This is because there is no incentive for a third country to export an item to a higher-tariff poor performer for reexport to the United States at zero tariff; direct entry into the United States will result in lower tariff paid. Finally, the United States could commit to maintaining the preference for at least fifteen years or until such time as the preference is eliminated by multilateral liberalization. Only then will potential investors have the incentive to establish production capacity in the otherwise highly risky environment.

On the multilateral front, it is critical for the United States to take the Doha negotiations to their logical conclusion. An immediate area where the United States could give concession to the benefit of poor performers is intellectual property. Virtually none of the countries is capable of taking advantage of the compulsory licensing provisions of the TRIPs Agreement due to the absence of domestic capacity to manufacture drugs. The United States has essentially held up an agreement that would allow these countries to issue compulsory licenses to manufacture drugs to other countries. Poorly performing states would also benefit from an elimination of peak tariffs on industrial tariffs, since these cover labor-intensive products such as apparel and footwear. But my preference would be to push the current U.S. proposal to eliminate all industrial tariffs by the year 2015. As a part of the special and differential treatment, these countries can be given a longer phaseout, say, until 2025.

In the area of agriculture, the removal of these interventions will on balance hurt the least developed countries and perhaps poor performers as a group. Based on the 1999 data, of the forty-nine least developed countries, forty-five were net importers of food and thirty-three net importers of agriculture. These countries would be hurt rather than helped by the increase in prices that would follow the removal of the subsidies and protection. Therefore, it is important that liberalization in this sector be accompanied by adequate compensation to these countries in the form of extra assistance by the World Bank's International Development Association.

Under the Bush administration, the United States has substantially accelerated the move toward preferential trade arrangements. There is not a single poorly performing state currently on the U.S. free trade area agreement list, however. This means that if these countries have any capacity to export to the United States, free trade area agreements stand to divert trade from them. For example, the U.S.–South Africa Free Trade Area Agreement will likely divert imports into the United States from Kenya. Indeed, if the Free Trade Area of the Americas is concluded, trade from Africa and Asia (which contain virtually all poor performers) is bound to be diverted. This fact makes the case for multilateral liberalization under the Doha Round even stronger.

Notes

1. Jagdish Bhagwati, introduction to *The New International Economic Order,* edited by Jagdish Bhagwati (MIT Press, 1977), offers an excellent overview of the NIEO discussions. Also see Robert Looney, "New International Economic Order," in *Routledge Encyclopedia of International Political Economy,* edited by R. J. B. Jones (London: Routledge, 1999).

2. The process of liberalization in developing countries was aided in no small measure by the success of outward-oriented policies in the Far Eastern economies and the failure of inward-looking policies in other parts of the world. Starting in the early 1980s, many developing countries had begun to appreciate the benefits of their own liberalization as well as the futility of insisting on one-way trade concessions from the rich countries.

3. See Arvind Panagariya, "Developing Countries at Doha: A Political Economy Analysis," *World Economy* 25, no. 9 (2002): 1205–33, where I argue that the view that the Uruguay Round hurt developing countries fails to stand up to careful scrutiny. Though the balance of the bargain was in favor of the rich countries, developing countries benefited significantly from the package as well. They benefited from their own liberalization and the liberalization by developed countries, including the removal of the Multifiber Arrangement. The latter was criticized on the ground that it was back loaded. A much unappreciated fact, however, is that many of the uncompetitive developing countries had in fact lobbied for the back loading, since they feared losing their quota captive market to more competitive suppliers such as China. Developing countries also laid down the foundation of future liberalization in agriculture by bringing this sector into the GATT discipline; this was less than what they had hoped for, but it meant progress. Developing countries also benefited from a much stronger dispute settlement arrangement, which allows them to challenge developed countries on near equal footing. The main cost they paid was the TRIPs Agreement (Trade-Related Aspects of Intellectual Property Rights), which was not a win-win bargain and entailed benefits for developed countries at the expense of developing countries.

4. The Center for Global Development, which introduced this category, defines it as countries whose poor economic performance and widespread poverty combine with governments incapable of guaranteeing political freedoms, of providing the foundation for economic activity, and of controlling their territory. The center provides two illustrative lists but does not draw a fixed list even at a point in time.

5. The United Nations introduced this category in 1971. It includes nations deemed structurally handicapped in their development process and in need of the highest degree of consideration from the international community in support of their development efforts. The UN Economic and Social Council, which makes the determination, considers three factors: income, human resource weakness, and economic vulnerability. The income criterion requires that, based on a three-year average, the annual per capita gross domestic product be below US$900. Currently, there are forty-nine such countries, and the list is revised every three years.

6. UNCTAD, *The Least Developed Countries 2000 Report* (Geneva: United Nations, 2000).

7. Many of the details on the U.S. GSP program are taken from GSP Coalition, *The U.S. Generalized System of Preferences Program: An Update* (Washington: Trade Partnership, 2002).

8. UNCTAD, "Duty and Quota Free Market Access for LDCs: An Analysis of Quad Initiatives" (Geneva: United Nations, 2001).

9. This section draws on Arvind Panagariya, "EU Preferential Trade Arrangements and Developing Countries," *World Economy* 25, no. 10 (2002): 1415–32.

10. See R. Baldwin and T. Murray, "MFN Tariff Reductions and LDC Benefits under the GSP," *Economic Journal* 87, no. 345 (1977): 30–46; Gene M. Grossman, "Import Competition from Developed and Developing Countries," *Review of Economics and Statistics* 64 (1982): 271–81; A. Sapir and L. Lundberg, "The U.S. Generalized System of Preferences and Its Impacts," in *The Structure and Evolution of US Trade Policy,* edited by A. O. Krueger and R. E. Baldwin (University of Chicago Press, 1984); Drusilla K. Brown, "Trade and Welfare Effects of the European Schemes of the Generalized System of Preferences," *Economic Development and Cultural Change* 37 (July 1989): 757–76; and

A. Mattoo, D. Roy, and A. Subramanian, "The Africa Growth and Opportunity Act and Its Rules of Origin: Generosity Undermined?" *World Economy* 26, no. 6 (2003): 829–52.

11. John Whalley, "Nondiscriminatory Discrimination: Special and Differential Treatment under the GATT for Developing Countries," *Economic Journal* 100, no. 403 (1990): 1319.

12. Even as the MFA and other quantitative restrictions are dismantled, threats of antidumping and other contingent protection measures loom large. Irrespective of whether or not such threats are carried out and when carried out whether or not they succeed, their mere presence may have a lasting effect on exporters. Thus, for example, though EU attempts to impose antidumping duties on unbleached cotton imports from five emerging markets failed, the attempt itself led to considerable disruption of markets for the developing country exporters that were so targeted.

13. Robert E. Hudec, *Developing Countries in the GATT Legal System* (Aldershot, U.K.: Gower, 1987), p. xx; quoted on p. 2 of Caglar Ozden and Eric Reinhardt, "The Perversity of Preferences: GSP and Developing Country Trade Policies, 1976–2000," *Journal of Development Economics* 78, no. 1 (2005): 1–21.

14. Ozden and Reinhardt, "The Perversity of Preferences."

15. For more in-depth critiques of preferential trade arrangements, see Jagdish Bhagwati, "Regionalism and Multilateralism: An Overview," in *New Dimensions in Regional Integration*, edited by Jaime de Melo and Arvind Panagariya (Cambridge University Press, 1993); Jagdish Bhagwati and Arvind Panagariya, "Preferential Trading Areas and Multilateralism: Strangers, Friends, or Foes?" in *The Economics of Preferential Trading*, edited by Jagdish Bhagwati and Arvind Panagariya (Washington: AEI Press, 1996); Jagdish Bhagwati, David Greenaway, and Arvind Panagariya, "Trading Preferentially: Theory and Policy," *Economic Journal* (July 1998): 1128–48; and Arvind Panagariya, "The Regionalism Debate: An Overview," *World Economy* 22, no. 4 (1999): 477–511. Another work— Arvind Panagariya, "Preferential Trade Liberalization: The Traditional Theory and New Developments," *Journal of Economic Literature* 38 (2000): 287–331—offers a comprehensive review of the theoretical literature on these arrangements.

16. Matti Koskinen, "Excess Documentation Costs as a Nontariff Measure: An Empirical Analysis of the Import Effects of Documentation Costs," working paper (Helsinki: Swedish School of Economics and Business Administration, 1983).

17. Peter Holmes and G. Shephard, "Protectionism in the Economic Community," paper prepared for the eighth annual conference, International Economics Study Group, 1983.

18. See Olivier Cadot and others, "Assessing the Effects of NAFTA Rules of Origin" (University of Lausanne, 2002).

19. Bhagwati and Panagariya, "Preferential Trading Areas and Multilateralism."

20. Andre Sapir, "The Political Economy of EC Regionalism," *European Economic Review* 42 (1998): 717–32.

21. Alberto Valdes and Alex F. McCalla, "Issues, Interests and Options of Developing Countries," paper prepared for the joint World Bank and World Trade Organization conference "Agriculture and the New Trade Agenda in the WTO 2000 Negotiations," Geneva, October 1–2, 1999. This point is made more systematically in Arvind Panagariya, "Trade and Food Security: Conceptualizing the Linkages," paper prepared for the Food and Agriculture Organization conference "Trade, Agricultural Development, and Food Security: The Impact of Recent Economic and Trade Policy Reform," Rome, July 11–12, 2002.

11

Toward Best Outcomes from Foreign Direct Investment in Poorly Performing States

Theodore H. Moran

Can poorly performing states use foreign direct investment to enhance their domestic growth, welfare, and reduction of poverty in ways middle-income developing states have achieved? Or are the difficulties and obstacles simply overwhelming? What are the lessons from low-income states that have been otherwise relatively successful? In what ways must contemporary host authorities become less "poorly performing" to emulate them? How can developed countries help, or hinder, this process?

In the midst of a stark appraisal of failed efforts by many low-income states to attract and use foreign direct investment, this study tries to gather the good news. The ingredients for making a would-be host more attractive to foreign investors—including poorer states without favorable natural resource endowments—are relatively straightforward. And the challenges of achieving at least modest success in pulling in investors and benefiting from their presence, while often difficult, have proven quite surmountable for a diverse array of low-income countries, "even" in the tropics, "even" in Africa.

This chapter begins with an appraisal of the conditions under which foreign direct investment provides the most positive contribution—or, conversely, the least positive (or most negative) contribution—to the host economy.

The second section focuses on the determinants for success and failure in attracting and harnessing nonextractive, noninfrastructure investment, in the experiences of low-income states. From this analysis, it derives lessons for low-income states in the contemporary period. Of particular importance is the question of whether low-income states must permit or tolerate poor worker treatment to secure foreign investment in low-skilled industries, like garments and footwear. This section concludes with analysis of how low-income states can begin to move up the ladder from least-skilled foreign investment activities to more-skilled foreign investment activities, while increasing backward linkages and spillovers into the local economy.

The third section turns to mechanisms by which developed countries can facilitate the flow of foreign direct investment to low-income countries. It offers an appraisal of how U.S. efforts might be strengthened and identifies U.S. obstacles that should be removed.

Most Beneficial and Least Beneficial Foreign Direct Investment

The following is a brief summary of the difficulties associated with natural resource and infrastructure investment, with new evidence about foreign direct investment in manufacturing, assembly, agribusiness, and services as background for examining the prospects for resource-poor, least developed countries.

Foreign Direct Investment in Natural Resources

Foreign direct investment in extractive industries—oil, gas, copper, nickel, bauxite, gold, diamonds, iron ore, and other minerals—can have a dramatic impact on the balance of payments and the tax revenues of the host country where the natural resources are found.[1] While flows of foreign direct investment in natural resources are subject to a certain natural geological determinism, success in attracting investment can be facilitated by the kinds of reconfiguration of investment promotion agencies and minimization of red tape suggested later. Issues of transparency, bribery, and other corrupt practices, however, require special attention.

Conventional wisdom for decades has characterized a rich natural resource endowment as an unambiguously favorable factor for the host country's development, if foreign investors could be found who would exploit the natural resources with responsible environmental and labor practices. Calling this conventional wisdom into question, however, is evidence that favorable natural resource endowments are in general negatively correlated with the growth performance of the countries so endowed.[2]

One explanation for this outcome lies in the likelihood that large resource exports lead to an overvalued exchange rate, which makes it difficult for other indigenous industries to compete in international markets. This is a developing country rendition of what has been called the Dutch disease. Other explanations, however, center on the temptation to use revenues from natural resource exports for personal gain, political payoffs, and other corrupt or quasi-corrupt practices. The presence of natural resources traps the country into a political system that diverts revenues to special interests and uneconomic purposes.[3] Countries like Nigeria, where oil-based income has largely been squandered, readily fit this picture. Countries like Chile, where copper-based income has generally been devoted over time to sensible economic and social endeavors, do not.

To help supervise and provide transparency about the disposition of natural resource revenues, the World Bank helped negotiate an experiment involving Exxon Mobil in Chad. A nine-person committee, including four nongovernmental organization representatives, was given responsibility for monitoring the expenditure of oil revenues, with 80 percent devoted to education, health, and rural development and 5 percent returned to the regions where the oil originates.[4] Technical assistance from the World Bank would underwrite creation of a technically competent auditing agency within Chad. The government of Chad reneged on this agreement, however, provoking a crisis with the World Bank and suspension of lending in 2006.

To enhance transparency in the disposition of natural resource revenues, various nongovernmental organizations—along with George Soros—have urged that investors in extractive industries be required to publicize all taxes and fees paid to host governments before being allowed to list their shares on the U.S. or other major stock exchanges.[5] The British government has launched an initiative to explore options to promote transparency in extractive industries.[6] The Group of Eight meeting in Evian in June 2003 endorsed the objective of improving information disclosure to fight corruption.

To move the international community toward more responsible handling of natural resource revenues will require complex negotiations among home and host governments as well as investors. Private international companies fear, for example, that publicly traded corporations would be placed at a competitive disadvantage to those state-owned companies that still play a large role in the oil industry.[7] They also fear that an international agreement (as opposed to a voluntary compact) might expose them to be sued in U.S. courts under the Alien Tort Claims Act if they operate in countries where there are human rights abuses.

Foreign Direct Investment in Infrastructure

The invitation of international companies to participate in the privatization of infrastructure has also generally been viewed as contributing to developing country growth prospects. The host economy becomes more competitive to the extent it enjoys efficient and reliable water, power, transport, and telecommunication systems. The use of state companies to hold the price of infrastructure services artificially low often has popular appeal, but private ownership and regulatory mechanisms that allow for realistic pricing may provide better and more reliable services—and extend those services to more users, including poor and rural users.[8]

The largely unforeseen challenge with foreign direct investment in infrastructure is determining which parties should be required to absorb commercial risks associated with fluctuations in supply and demand for services or to bear commercial risks associated with fluctuations in foreign or local currency valuations. Foreign investors in Asia and Latin America have typically insisted, as a condition of making an investment, that host authorities make major commitments to supply inputs, or to purchase outputs, and to guarantee the conversion value of payments made in local currency. When host authorities have been unable to meet these commitments due to downturns in the regional or international economy, the resulting defaults have been considered political acts (unwillingness to make good on obligations) rather than commercial acts (inability to make good on obligations).

When Indonesia was incapable of honoring take-or-pay power purchase agreements due to a drop in demand during the Asian financial crisis, for example, the MidAmerican Corporation took the host government to arbitration and won, leading the Overseas Private Investment Corporation (OPIC) to have to make one of the largest payments on political risk insurance ever awarded (US$290 million of a total award of US$572 million) and pursue the government of Indonesia for recovery.[9] Experiences such as these have led to questioning what genuinely constitutes political as opposed to commercial risk and what responsibility international infrastructure investors should assume for the latter.[10] More broadly, experiences such as these have led to reassessment about whether commercial law arbitration procedures constitute a suitable mechanism for dealing with many kinds of contemporary infrastructure investment disputes.

The use of ICSID (International Center for the Settlement of Investment Disputes) and UNCITRAL (United National Center for International Trade Law) arbitration procedures—as specified in most bilateral investment treaties, national investment guarantee agencies (like OPIC), and multilateral bank lending agreements—is in no sense like an appeal to an international supreme court to decide what best serves the public interest. Quite to the contrary, these arbitration procedures focus deliberately on narrow issues of contract compliance and (as in the case of MidAmerican in Indonesia) are likely to place a foreign exchange payment to a foreign investor ahead of all other funding priorities, including importation of food and medical supplies for a population in the midst of crisis.

Foreign Direct Investment in Nonextractive, Noninfrastructure Sectors

The most striking new assessment about the impact of foreign direct investment on development has come in evaluating the pros and cons of foreign direct investment outside of natural resources and infrastructure. Here again the conventional wisdom (that foreign direct investment in manufacturing, assembly, processing, agribusiness, and services is a "good thing" as long as foreign firms do not pollute the environment or engage in unsafe or physically oppressive treatment of workers) has often been misleading.

The "new" discovery is that the impact of foreign direct investment in nonextractive, noninfrastructure sectors takes two quite distinct forms. The data show that there is a fundamental difference between foreign direct investment in projects (often export oriented) serving markets exposed to international competition and foreign direct investment in projects insulated from international competition. In particular, there is a dramatic contrast in performance between subsidiaries that are integrated into the global or regional sourcing networks of the parent multinationals and subsidiaries that are oriented toward protected domestic markets and prevented by mandatory joint venture and domestic content requirements from being so integrated.[11]

As a result, foreign direct investment outside of natural resources and infrastructure has a bifurcated impact on development. Beginning with San-jaya Lall, Paul Streeten, and Grant Reuber, and summarized with additional data by Dennis Encarnation and Louis Wells, cost-benefit analyses of data from eighty-three projects in some thirty developing countries over more than a decade, valuing all inputs and outputs at world market prices, show a majority of the operations generating an increase in the host country's income (from 55 to 75 percent, depending upon alternative shadow-price estimates).[12] At the same time, however, the cost-benefit calculations confirm that a large minority (25–45 percent) was actually subtracted from the host country's income; that is, the developing country would be better off without hosting these foreign investment projects at all.

The principal characteristic differentiating the positive projects from the negative projects is the degree of protection associated with the foreign firms' operations (including domestic content requirements imposed by the host authorities on the foreign investor). Projects without protection (or with low levels of protection) tend to enhance the host country's welfare; projects with high protection detract from the host country's welfare. Export-oriented projects are consistently positive in their contribution to the host country's welfare. The outcomes are not close calls. They are bunched at the extremes, either clearly beneficial or clearly detrimental.

Studies using cost-benefit analysis across sectors in one country point to the same dichotomy. For Kenya, Bernard Wasow examined thirty-five goods produced by fourteen foreign-owned firms within the import substitution framework of the late 1980s. His measurements show that only three of the thirty-five generated benefits to the host economy exceeded their costs. Of these three, only one (a large exporter of processed fruit) made a noteworthy contribution to local economic growth. More than half of the thirty-five siphoned foreign exchange from the economy, rather than saving or earning hard currency. In the protected local setting, many of the foreign plants operated with excess capacity, and if they had expanded output their negative impact on host welfare would have been even greater.[13]

The difference between foreign investment oriented toward a protected host economy and foreign investment oriented toward competitive international markets is even more striking as the foreign investor activities become more sophisticated.[14] The ability to operate with wholly owned subsidiaries that are free to source from wherever they choose takes on more importance for companies that want to incorporate electronic, industrial, or medical components into their global sourcing networks. The evidence shows a particularly potent interaction between parent and subsidiary when the inputs from the subsidiary are integrated into the headquarter's strategy to keep the corporation competitive in international markets, an interaction that is lacking when the subsidiary is forced to operate with domestic content and joint ownership performance requirements. The former interaction typically captures all economies of scale and functions at the international frontier in production, quality control, and management practices, all upgraded on a continuous real-time basis; the latter interaction is subscale, uses older technologies, quality control, and management procedures, and is upgraded more slowly.

Host-Country Measures for Harnessing
Most Beneficial Foreign Direct Investment

Historically, the flow of foreign direct investment to the developing world has been quite concentrated.[15] Over four decades, twenty countries—none of them poor developing countries without favorable natural resource endowments—accumulated 83 percent of the total stock of foreign direct investment in the developing world and economies in transition (see appendix). In 2002 twenty countries—again, none of them poorer developing countries without favorable natural resource endowments—received 82 percent of all foreign direct investment flows in the developing world and economies in transition.

A perusal of international business surveys, moreover, shows that the list of what the multinational investment community considers the ingredients for a good investment climate is long and demanding: low inflation; correct exchange rates; steady economic growth; privatized infrastructure services; high literacy rates; extensive access to the Internet; liberalized trade; low incidences of HIV-AIDS, malaria, and other infectious diseases; little ethnic tension; minimal corruption; stable and transparent political institutions and procedures; independent and capable judicial systems.[16]

As a consequence, there has been a tendency to conclude that the difficulties for poorer countries to join the ranks of countries able to attract and use nonextractive foreign direct investment for development must be staggering and in the case of tropical countries—including most of sub-Saharan Africa, Central America, and the Caribbean—may be almost impossible to overcome. But the evidence indicates otherwise. Two of the most prominent success stories in the literature on foreign direct investment and development are Mauritius and the Dominican Republic. Their accomplishments required straightforward policy reforms, which are readily duplicable.[17]

The Case of Mauritius

Mauritius in the 1960s was dependent on sugar production for 99 percent of its exports. Unemployment was high. Jobs in local industry were limited to sectors protected by import substitution policies. A study commissioned by the British before independence was entitled "Mauritius: A Case Study in Malthusian Economics."[18] Its dismal message was that young workers who were able to secure some education should be urged to emigrate.

In 1975 the government introduced legislation to confer export processing zone (EPZ) status on foreign investors who committed themselves to exporting their output. EPZ status allowed 100 percent foreign ownership and a ten-year tax holiday. But the country continued import substitution policies, subsidized inefficient, state-owned utilities, ran unsustainable budget deficits, and maintained an overvalued exchange rate complete with currency controls and foreign exchange rationing. The pace of foreign investment remained weak.

In 1982 a new political alliance ousted the party that had been dominant since electoral politics had been introduced in 1947.[19] It liberalized the currency, retreated from subsidizing state corporations, and adopted an aggressive policy of voluntary structural adjustment. To help make up for weak infrastructure, foreign investors were granted EPZ status wherever they chose to locate in the island country, often choosing sites where transport and utility services were best.

Led by textile investors from Hong Kong, foreign investment began to expand. Export earnings from manufactures in Mauritius climbed from 3 percent of the total in the early 1970s to 53 percent of the total in 1986, surpassing traditional sugar exports for the first time. Over the entire period from the mid-1970s to the mid-1990s, Mauritius ranked seventh among the fifteen most consistently growing exporters of manufactured products among low- and middle-income countries around the world—less spectacular than Singapore, Taiwan, and Hong Kong but superior to such high performers as Thailand, Portugal, and Israel, with an average annual growth rate of 2.9 percent.[20] By 2000 manufactured goods constituted 70 percent of all exports, totaling more than US$1.2 billion annually and sustaining 80,000–90,000 jobs.[21]

Like most low-income developing countries, Mauritius was initially disappointed by the lack of spillovers and externalities from export-oriented foreign investment and frustrated that the great majority of foreign firms were concentrated in lowest-skilled, labor-intensive operations. In 1985 the Mauritius Export Development and Investment Authority was given responsibility to search out and diversify export-oriented investors, with an aggressive strategy that replaced the earlier Ministry of Industry approach of screening inward investors to determine which would contribute most to import substitution. French, U.K., German, Taiwanese, and Chinese investors began to join the ranks of those from Hong Kong. Taking advantage of a trainable but not highly skilled workforce (4.5 years average schooling), foreign firms with EPZ status began to include light industry, sports equipment, agribusiness, and cut flowers, as well as higher-end garments such as shirting for the London department store Marks and Spencer.

At the same time, Mauritius began to attend to the health of its indigenous business community, reducing regulatory requirements for the establishment of local firms and lowering the corporate tax rate from 35 percent to 15 percent for manufacturers who did not qualify for the EPZ tax exemption. This helped indigenous entrepreneurs to become suppliers to foreign-owned exporters. It also gave them a platform to enter export markets themselves. The data show that indigenous managers and supervisors were able to gain experience in foreign-owned plants and then use this expertise to set up their own companies.[22] By the late 1990s host-country investors represented 50 percent of all equity capital in export-oriented firms.

The Case of the Dominican Republic

The efforts of the Dominican Republic to attract foreign direct investment to EPZs date from the late 1960s, but budget deficits, high inflation rates, and an overvalued exchange rate prevented the country from becoming an export base in the 1970s. Macroeconomic reform in the early 1980s, however, combined with a shift in EPZ strategy began to generate results.[23] Like many host governments, Dominican authorities had initially considered EPZs as a form of employment creation for the most destitute regions of the country, near the border with Haiti. But the combination of a poor infrastructure and an unskilled workforce limited the appeal of such locations to foreign investors. As the government opened up more sites for EPZ activity, closer to Santo Domingo, the number of investors expanded, reaching 178 firms in 1987 and employing some 85,000 workers.

In the second half of the 1980s Dominican authorities adopted a novel approach to the task of trying to upgrade and diversify foreign investor operations: they began to allow private developers to launch new EPZs and to permit international companies in more sophisticated industries to operate both as investors and as promoters. In the model Itabo zone, Westinghouse acted as both zone owner and exporter, soliciting other Fortune 500 companies to set up operations alongside its plants. In the San Isidro zone, GTE (now Verizon) pulled other electronics firms to the Dominican Republic. Private zone developers designed the Las Americas zone for information services. Other private zone operators configured pharmaceutical industrial parks to meet the inspection standards required by the U.S. Food and Drug Administration. Electronics, electrical equipment, medical equipment, metal products, and data processing became the largest new sectors represented, totaling 36 percent of all zone investment in 2000.[24]

While the data on indigenous workers and managers moving from employment in foreign plants to setting up their own firms are not as clear for the Dominican Republic as for Mauritius, 35 percent of all zone companies (166 of 481) were owned by Dominican citizens in 2000.[25] Total zone investment exceeded US$1 billion, total zone employment 197,000, total zone exports US$4.7 billion (80 percent of the country's total exports, and virtually the entirety of its manufactured exports).

Free Trade Zones: Lessons from Mauritius and the Dominican Republic

In Mauritius and the Dominican Republic, the typical effort to attract foreign direct investment in lowest skilled operations centered on creating export processing or free trade zones, but such zones have a very problematic record.[26] The rationale for these zones is to offer foreign investors freedom from duties on the capital equipment and inputs used in assembly operations, to enable them to operate with reliable, competitively priced infrastructure, and to shield them from adverse business conditions that may afflict other parts of the economy (corruption, crime, bureaucratic delay, high taxes, legal uncertainty).

The principal reason that the special zones have failed in low-income countries is that host authorities have simply not delivered these conditions. Ports and airports experience delays. Telecommunications services have been undependable and expensive. Electric power outages have necessitated backup generators. Bonded warehouses (single-factory EPZs with a customs agent at the site) have required graft payments. Duty-drawback arrangements (wherein duties on imported inputs are reimbursed when the final product is exported) invite bribes, to be handled expeditiously. Crime has plagued workers and managers living near the zones.

Beyond providing at least the beginnings of a business-friendly setting, foreign investors need low inflation and a realistic exchange rate. The boom in exports from Mauritius and the Dominican Republic did not take place until exchange rates reflected market conditions. An increasingly overvalued exchange rate in the 1990s in Kenya caused some sixty of the seventy bonded warehouses in the country to cease operations by the end of the decade. An artificially high exchange rate hindered export-oriented investment in Egypt despite extremely generous tax incentives.

Many developing countries have looked to the establishment of EPZs as a policy that might be used for direct poverty reduction. But the requirement for reliable infrastructure has shown that this is often not possible. The decision to locate EPZs in the poorest and most remote regions has seldom resulted in attracting large numbers of foreign investors or generating rapidly growing amounts of exports. For two decades, the most widely analyzed EPZ in all development literature was the zone that the Philippine government established in Bataan in an attempt to attract investors to where the workers were poorest and wages cheapest. But the mountainous area around Bataan was also bereft of good infrastructure, and the Philippine government had to spend millions of dollars to compensate. The Bataan zone generated a sufficiently poor cost-benefit ratio that it became a model of what to avoid.[27]

Much more successful have been policies of permitting foreign investors to qualify for zone status wherever the investors choose to locate (as Mauritius did) or multiplying the zones in proximity to the host country's economic centers with access to at least modestly skilled workers (as the Dominican Republic did). In what is called a buildup rather than a trickle-down strategy, this approach also provides the setting for the most positive experiences in developing local suppliers and generating backward linkages into the local economy.

In fact, to anticipate the argument given later, the most effective zone-led development strategies involve the gradual elimination of special zones, accompanied by progressive improvement in infrastructure services, in the stability and transparency of the institutional regime, in the control of corruption, and in the provision of safety throughout the country. This simultaneously strengthens indigenous business groups, which can become suppliers to foreign-owned exporters, and enables them perhaps to become exporters themselves. Completing the roster of reforms needed for indigenous firms to have a fair chance at becoming suppliers to foreign-owned exporters and perhaps exporters themselves, local firms must have access to competitively priced inputs, requiring steady progress in trade liberalization. At the end of the road, host countries find themselves with most of the key ingredients identified earlier as constituting what the multinational investment community considers a good investment climate.

But case studies of individual countries show that would-be hosts do not have to achieve anything like perfection to be successful in getting started on the road to using nonextractive foreign investment for development. A little macroeconomic, microeconomic, and institutional reform—backed by a consistent trend line—goes a long way. Mauritius and the Dominican Republic are by no means unique among relatively poor developing countries in creating hundreds of thousands of jobs and generating hundreds of millions of dollars of exports from foreign investor operations. In popular parlance, a poor developing country does not have to "become like Denmark" to attract and benefit from foreign direct investment.

Other Country Experiences

Explicitly trying to emulate Mauritius, Madagascar made the decision to liberalize its economy, end an overvalued exchange rate, and establish an EPZ-led growth strategy in 1989.[28] Like Mauritius, Madagascar awarded EPZ status to investors regardless of where they chose to locate. The pace of success in attracting foreign investors was even faster than had been the case in Mauritius, with 120 firms setting up operations in the first five years, in comparison to 100 firms in the first ten years for Mauritius.[29] In 1996 the country had 158 firms, with EPZ employment above 36,000. Between 1994 and 1998 (the most recent year for which data are readily available), exports from EPZs grew from US$64 million (14 percent of all exports) to US$195 million (37 percent of all exports).[30]

Elsewhere in Africa, Lesotho has attracted fifty-five foreign export–oriented manufacturing firms, thirty-eight producing clothing, three producing footwear, four producing electronics, four involved in food processing, and the rest producing assorted products such as umbrellas and plastic goods.[31] The garment sector alone employed approximately 32,000 workers, with exports of US$111 million in 1999, US$140 million in 2000, and US$216 million in 2001. If not somehow blocked by the South African trade unions, according to Sanjaya Lall, Lesotho might be able to integrate its foreign export/manufacturing sector into the South African economy the way Mexico has done via NAFTA, even after the expiration of the Multifiber Agreement in 2005 and the African Growth and Opportunity Act (AGOA) in 2008.[32]

Bangladesh, the Philippines (after it abandoned the Bataan model of placing EPZs in the most impoverished regions and began to allow foreign investors to locate their plants adjacent to the industrial and commercial hubs of the host country), Vietnam, Honduras, and El Salvador have enjoyed various degrees of success.[33] Their country experiences do not suggest that the task of attracting low-skilled, labor-intensive foreign direct investment is easy; but their country experiences do show that the task is highly doable.[34]

The New Model of Investment Promotion

Over the past decade and a half there has been a dramatic transformation in developing country strategy for attracting foreign investors.

In the 1970s and 1980s the predominant perspective among investment promotion agencies in the developing world was that multinational corporations were all-seeing, all-knowing actors ready to jump whenever profitable opportunities presented. Most agencies charged with dealing with foreign investors were devoted to screening those proposals that foreigners presented and then to levying performance requirements upon investors. This heavy-handed approach of screening investment proposals and requiring foreign firms to take on local joint-venture partners and meet domestic content mandates worked only for inward-oriented investment aimed at protected local markets where foreign investors could reap high oligopoly rents for their trouble.

For those host countries that wanted to attract export-oriented foreign investment, the task of attracting multinational investors was much more difficult. Even for the lowest-skill-intensive exports like garments, footwear, and electronic assembly, multinational corporations had to make sure their plants met international standards of quality and reliability. And as export-oriented investment moved into relatively higher skilled operations that would be integrated into a manufacturing corporation's international sourcing network—such as auto parts, plastics, machine tools, industrial equipment, medical devices, and business services—multinational corporations became risk-averse and hesitant about making capital-intensive "irreversible commitments" upon which their standing in international markets would depend.[35] For export-oriented plants, they insisted upon the right to establish wholly owned subsidiaries free from domestic content requirements. And even then they were cautious about building plants in new and untried host countries.

This changed the conceptualization of what was required for investment promotion profoundly. In place of passively waiting for the all-seeing profit seekers to pound on the door, the new task for host authorities became to demonstrate that their country was superior to alternatives elsewhere, when the target investors could not know for sure until they actually had tried the site out. The job of investment promotion agencies became to "market the country" actively and persuasively.[36] In investigating how to go about marketing a country, a study commissioned by the Foreign Investment Advisory Service (FIAS) of the World Bank Group found that host countries that actively courted new investors, provided them with a customized package of concessions oriented toward their specific industry, set up something approximating a "one-stop shop" to speed their approvals, and serviced their needs once they arrived received a statistically significant return on their efforts: for every dollar spent on investment promotion of this kind, the host received a stream of social benefits with a net present value of more than four dollars.[37] The aim became to make approvals as rapid, automatic, and transparent as possible, in place of highly discretionary, case-by-case determinations, which were slow, opaque, and subject to manipulation.

Over the course of the 1990s countries in Latin America and Southeast Asia that wanted both to attract export-oriented foreign direct investment and to upgrade investment from lowest skilled to relatively higher skilled manufacturing and assembly operations devoted increasing attention to the creation of skilled and aggressive investment promotion agencies. The Inter-American Development Bank and the Asian Development Bank have provided training. The Multilateral Investment Guarantee Agency of the World Bank Group (MIGA) created a web-based interactive system (IPANET) that dramatically reduced the search time, effort, and expense for investors to compare countries, compare legislation, and to obtain links to established investors on a real-time basis. Among low-income states, many governments have lagged behind in participating in this new wave of investment promotion and in keeping information sources and other inputs up-to-date.

As the experience of the Dominican Republic shows, a particularly potent discovery has been the role that private EPZ developers can play in identifying, seeking out, and delivering new foreign investors. The use of private operators to create and manage these zones was initially judged to be an unpromising strategy among experts in investment promotion. But the evidence soon demonstrated that the self-interest of the developers in recruiting investors (frequently from the home country of the developer), and in ensuring levels of service that kept investors in a given zone satisfied and growing, matched quite well the goals of the host country.[38] Complementing the use of private developers, a key component of many host countries' proactive strategy to market the country is the role of satisfied investors in attracting other participants from the same industrial sectors. In the Philippines, Texas Instruments, Philips, Toyota, and an array of other high-profile U.S., Japanese, Taiwanese, and European corporations became prime exhibits in helping Philippine authorities to sign up later investors in the same industries. This parallels the part played by companies like Westinghouse and GTE/Verizon in the Dominican Republic. In Latin America and Southeast Asia, investment promotion agencies have used direct web-based access to current investors to enhance the credibility of information about their policies and their economies for potential new entrants.

Sometimes these two components have been combined, as when the host authorities provide a leading international company with both an investment and an administrative stake in a particular industrial park. Zone developers and investors report that they have been able to earn large profits by providing business, managerial, and human resource services to fellow investors. Those fellow investors, in turn, report paying fees three times higher in private zones (the Dominican Republic provides the most extensive evidence) to surround their plants with adequate housing, transport, security, health care, and day care because these facilities help ensure a stable and productive workforce and in addition burnish their corporate image.[39]

The creation of new-generation investment promotion agencies may be difficult, but it is doable. It requires a commitment to transform or eliminate well-entrenched bureaucracies devoted to heavy-handed, case-by-case screening of applications. Investment promotion has a cumulative dynamic: it takes a proactive, efficient agency to attract the early investors and developers; the presence of the early investors creates an opportunity for private industrial park developers to use their home-country networks (in the United States, Europe, Japan, Korea, Taiwan, India) to find new investors; the interaction of established investors and aggressive developers provides comfort and credibility to further investors and more advanced activities. For countries that do not have the resources or the training to launch an effective investment promotion agency, or even to update the information on their websites, this cumulative virtuous cycle never gets started. Investment promotion therefore might be a prime candidate for external assistance and capacity building on the part of developed countries and multilateral lending agencies. The Lesotho National Development Corporation, charged with attracting and promoting foreign direct investment, for example, is 90 percent owned by the Lesotho government and 10 percent by the German Finance Company for Investments in Developing Countries.[40]

Many low-income developing countries are significantly behind the frontier of best practices. In 2000 the FIAS surveyed the process of obtaining the approvals necessary for foreign investors to locate in Namibia, Mozambique, Tanzania, and Uganda.[41] It examined company registration, business licenses, expatriate work and residence permits, tax registration, access to land, construction permits, access to investment incentives, and other licenses and specialized approvals. Rather than one-stop-shop investment promotion agencies designed to facilitate entry, the FIAS reported time-consuming screening by multiple agencies for industrial licenses, for tax holidays, and for expatriate work and residence permits. The result was that it took eighteen months to three years to establish a business and become operational in Tanzania and Mozambique and one to two years in Ghana and Uganda. This contrasts with six months or less in the Dominican Republic, Malaysia, and Thailand. Once again, however, the challenges are not insurmountable. The FIAS found that the system in Namibia compared favorably with best practices around the world, in Windhoek, and in particular around Walvis Bay.[42] Since 2000, investment approval procedures have improved in Mozambique, Ghana, Senegal, and Uganda.

Treatment of Workers in Foreign Direct Investment's Labor-Intensive Jobs

Leaders of poorly performing states have voiced fears to the International Labor Organization (ILO) and others that foreign direct investment in labor-intensive sectors of their countries might push them to adopt poor labor standards.[43]

On the one hand, the labor costs for foreign investors or subcontractors with lowest skill operations—such as making garments or footwear for export—range from 20 percent to more than 200 percent of the profit margin at the production stage. Barriers to entry are low, and competition is great. Managers at this stage are likely to find themselves under strong pressure to keep wages and benefits low in current plants and to be on the lookout for alternative locales where unit labor costs might be lower still. In addition, there is evidence that some international investors (and their home governments) insist upon weak labor standards as a condition of investment. According to the ILO, the governments of Namibia and Zimbabwe, for example, were being told in the mid-1990s that their EPZs would have to be excepted from national labor laws in order to be successful.[44] Pakistan admitted to the ILO that its EPZs had been exempted from some aspects of national labor legislation as a result of pressure from Daewoo.[45] The ambassadors from Japan and Korea intervened with the government of Bangladesh to prevent trade unions from being organized in EPZs where their companies were considering investments; only counterpressure from the United States in the form of a threat to withdraw GSP prevented this from happening.[46] The historical record of workers being fired—or even arrested or murdered—for organizing unions in EPZs is notorious.[47] The early years of the experience with EPZs in the Dominican Republic and the Philippines were wracked with labor strife.

On the other hand, however, the aggregate evidence does not show that poor labor standards attract foreign direct investment. Mita Aggarwal, of the U.S. International Trade Commission, examined the relationship between labor standards and U.S. investment in ten developing countries (China, Hong Kong, India, Indonesia, Malaysia, Mexico, the Philippines, Singapore,

South Korea, and Thailand).[48] Aggarwal finds no association between enforcement of labor standards and level of U.S. foreign direct investment. On the contrary, U.S. investors tend to favor countries with higher labor standards and to invest in sectors within a given host country where labor conditions are superior to—or at least equal to—labor conditions in the rest of the economy. In a study of thirty-six developed and developing countries, Dani Rodrik also discovered no statistical relationship between low labor standards and increasing levels of U.S. foreign direct investment. The evidence points, in fact, in the opposite direction: nations with low labor standards have lower foreign direct investment than might be expected in light of other host-country attributes. These results, proposes Rodrik, "indicate that low labor standards may be a hindrance, rather than an attraction, for foreign investors."[49]

Surveys by the ILO, moreover, consistently find that pay for workers in EPZs is higher than alternatives elsewhere for these workers.[50] Similarly, the U.S. Department of Labor reports that firms producing footwear and apparel generally pay more than the minimum wage and provide working conditions superior to those that prevail in other labor-intensive industries.[51] Other investigations confirm that workers in foreign-owned, export-oriented factories receive higher pay, have better benefits, and have better working conditions than comparable workers in comparable industries. In Mauritius, for example, wages in EPZ companies are higher than in other sectors of the economy and rose in real terms by more than 50 percent between the late 1980s and the late 1990s.[52] In the Dominican Republic, 85 percent of the workers in U.S. firms and 80 percent of the workers in Korean, Taiwanese, and Hong Kong firms report that they acquired their skills exclusively at their current company and opined that they would be either unemployed or earning only 60 percent of their current wages without those skills.[53]

In one of the most carefully designed studies of EPZ workers in the development literature, Mireille Razafindrakoto and François Roubaud find that in Madagascar EPZ workers receive wages and benefits not only better than low-skilled agricultural workers but also better than comparable jobs across the economy. Holding education, professional experience, and tenure in the enterprise constant, they show that EPZ workers in Madagascar earn 15–20 percent more than other workers throughout the country.[54] Edward Graham demonstrates, in fact, that compensation for indigenous workers for foreign affiliates in the manufacturing sector is greater as a multiple of average compensation per worker in the host country's manufacturing sector for lesser and least developed countries than that in middle-income developing countries: in middle-income developing countries the ratio is 1:8; in low-income develop-ing countries the ratio is 2:0, or twice as high as the average compensation in the manufacturing sector of the host country.[55] Thus the contention that host governments have to endorse poor worker treatment to attract foreign investors in labor-intensive industries—or must expect to find their workers receiving substandard wages, benefits, and working conditions when foreign investors arrive—is not supported by the data.

Nor is the perception supported that EPZ-led development is incompati-ble with the existence of trade unions. To be sure, most foreign investors and developers in EPZs have historically been averse to union organizing in EPZs, but in more recent times the evidence is mixed. The Philippines has a bloody history of antiunion repression in its EPZs in the 1970s and early 1980s. By the 1990s, however, as the right to union organizing became recognized and enforced by law in the EPZs, some of the zones with the least-skilled workers witnessed successful unionizing (one-third of the firms in the Bataan zone are currently operating with union contracts); other EPZs with higher-skilled semiconductor and auto parts plants, such as the Cavite and Baguio City zones, have had elections in which workers chose not to form unions.[56] Simi-larly, before 1992 the Dominican Republic exempted its zones from the national labor legislation. With help from the ILO, in 1992 the Dominican Republic began to apply its labor legislation uniformly throughout the econ-omy. As in the case of the Philippines, firms in the Dominican Republic's EPZs devoted to lower-skilled operations sometimes became unionized; firms in EPZs beginning to attract higher-skilled workers tended not to.

In Mauritius, labor regulations applying to EPZ firms were brought into line with national labor regulations elsewhere. Union organizing has been permitted, and approximately 10 percent of workers in EPZ firms are union-ized. In Lesotho, approximately 40 percent of garment workers are registered with the Lesotho Clothing and Allied Workers Union, an organization sup-ported by Dutch funding.[57] Moreover, once host countries begin to move out of the least sophisticated investor operations into slightly more sophisticated investor operations supplying inputs that must meet standards of quality and reliability in international markets—in electronics, plastics, medical devices, auto parts, and the like—foreign investors find that they must take measures (in their own self-interest) to attract and retain superior workers.[58] In these sectors, foreign investors pay workers two to five times more than what is found in garment and footwear industries elsewhere; working conditions are demonstrably superior, sometimes including day care, health care, and edu-cational opportunities associated with work.

And when plants producing more-skill-intensive products are mixed with plants producing less-skill-intensive products, the treatment of workers has improved among all plant-types.[59] Host countries that have begun to add slightly more-advanced investor activities to least-advanced investor activities have experienced a broad process of institutional change in worker-management relations across EPZs and industrial parks. Indeed, the evidence suggests that increases in the number of firms and the upgrading of foreign investor operations constitute the most forceful means that host countries have to improve the treatment of workers. The most powerful remedy for the problems of worker mistreatment as part of the process of the globalization of industry comes from more vigorous and more extensive globalization of industry. In the aggregate, the flow of foreign direct investment to relatively more sophisticated sectors in the developing world—like transportation equipment, electrical machinery, chemicals, and industrial products—is twenty-five times larger each year than it is to less-sophisticated, lower-skilled sectors like garments, footwear, leather products, and sports equipment.

Indigenous Linkages and Spillovers from Foreign Direct Investment

What lessons can poorly performing countries learn from host countries in which backward linkages, spillovers, and externalities have been created by foreign direct investment? What factors are needed for success?

Just as in the earlier discussion of the necessary ingredients for attracting foreign direct investment, the first factor is a stable macroeconomic setting, with low inflation and realistic exchange rates. Indigenous companies cannot tolerate an adverse macroeconomic environment any better than can foreign investors. The second factor is duty-free imports, dependable infrastructure, lack of red tape, and low crime and corruption, backed by reliable legal and regulatory institutions. Accompanying this must be a domestic banking system able to provide competitive financing to local businesses. Survey data of the World Economic Forum and the Harvard Center for International Development suggest that the cost and availability of local financing are widely considered to be among the most important obstacles to the operation and growth of private firms in Africa.[60]

The third factor is availability of capital and reasonably skilled labor (workers, technicians, engineers, and managers). Once again the data show a high payoff to the host country's investment in local education, often not higher than high school and trade school vocational training. Consistent with results from other continents, the findings of Tyler Biggs, Vijaya Ramachandran, and Manju Kedia Shah are that access to formal education (especially technical education at the secondary or high school level) by the owners of indigenous African-owned enterprises in sub-Saharan Africa significantly raises the rate of growth of these enterprises.[61] As with Mauritius and the Dominican Republic, these factors are needed to create the beginnings of an energetic national business community, with experience in meeting standards of quality and price required by open markets and in taking risks to achieve success, rather than relying on favors to protect themselves from competition.

Beyond this, is there a particular role for host governments to try to promote local suppliers or to nurture local supplier relationships? Recent work by the UN Conference on Trade and Development highlights the ability of some host countries to use foreign investors as talent scouts to sort through potential local suppliers by designating a manager in each foreign subsidiary with the responsibility to invite the most promising local firms to participate in management, quality control, and production planning sessions within the foreign subsidiary.[62] The foreign investor recommends to the best local participants what equipment, machinery, and training would best raise local performance. These local participants can then finance the required equipment, machinery, and training through purchase contracts from the foreign investor. The process must be competitive and transparent enough to avoid the danger of cronyism to reward privileged host-country firms. The key is for the host country to be light-handed in manipulating the foreign investors' own self-interest in finding low-cost, reliable suppliers—and not impose onerous requirements to meet domestic content and technology transfer mandates. In middle-level developing countries the stimulation of backward linkages may take the form of contract manufacturing by local firms. In the poorest developing countries, the stimulation of backward linkages may be much more basic, such as maintenance for sewing, cutting, and pressing machines, packaging, and the provision of simple accessories (buttons, trim).[63]

Overall, a strategy to use foreign direct investment for development (including the creation of a vibrant industrial base of indigenous suppliers) requires what might be called a buildup approach to strengthening the host country's economic base rather than a trickle-down approach of channeling rents to privileged recipients. A buildup strategy has a macroeconomic dimension that supports domestic as well as foreign firms with low inflation and a realistic exchange rate, a microeconomic dimension that rewards saving and investment, and an institutional dimension that provides regulatory and legal stability with a minimum of red tape and corruption. It provides domestic as well as foreign firms with reliable infrastructure services. It offers domestic as well as foreign firms access to inputs at internationally competitive prices. Finally, it supplies broad-based access to vocational training and skill development for workers and managers in domestic as well as foreign firms. A buildup strategy does not require separate and differential—and more protective—treatment for low-income developing states than for middle-income developing states, nor does it require reopening the TRIMs Agreement in the World Trade Organization (as some argue) to relegitimate the use of domestic content and trade-balancing requirements on foreign investors.[64]

To be sure, at the end of the day, foreign direct investment cannot be expected by itself (and in isolation from other economic, educational, and health factors) to be a cure-all for the problems of poverty in low-income countries, or even in middle-income countries. But there is a path whereby developing countries can harness foreign direct investment in progressively more important ways to contribute to their growth and welfare. Poorer countries can look to Mauritius, Madagascar, and Lesotho for examples of how to get launched. Countries that replicate the experience of Mauritius, Madagascar, and Lesotho can look to the Dominican Republic and the Philippines for examples of how to diversify their foreign investment base out of least-skilled operations like garments and footwear. Countries that replicate the experience of the Dominican Republic and the Philippines can look to Costa Rica, Malaysia, and Thailand for examples of how to move toward increasingly higher skilled operations, like auto parts, semiconductors, and business services, with expanding layers of indigenous suppliers and increasingly robust spillovers to the local economy.

Home-Country Measures for Providing Most Beneficial Foreign Direct Investment

The two principal ways in which developed countries can facilitate direct investment from the home market to the developing world are via provision of quasi-official political risk insurance and via measures to avoid double taxation of profits earned abroad. Other methods include assistance with identifying investment opportunities, help with creating investment promotion agencies in the host country, advocacy on behalf of foreign investors, and promotion of transparency in payments combined with restrictions on the payment of bribes or other corrupt practices. Home countries may also offer locational incentives to attract multinational investors.

In addition, of course, there is a significant interaction between trade liberalization and the facilitation of foreign direct investment. Multilateral trade liberalization and bilateral or regional trade agreements have as a by-product the stimulation of foreign direct investment flows among the participants. Conversely, developed country agricultural subsidies and protection against imports undermine the ability of international investors to use poor host economies as platforms for export. Antidumping regulations that are filed for reasons other than international price discrimination have the protectionist effect of deterring foreign investment in industries such as processed seafood and fruit juices as well as in manufacturing and assembly operations. (In general, the design of trade policies to support the poorest developing states is left to other chapters in this volume.)

Quasi-Official Political Risk Insurance

All international investors can purchase political risk insurance from private providers, such as AIG, Zurich, or Lloyds of London. The providers offer compensation if host countries take political actions that damage the project covered, such as expropriation or denial of ability to convert local currency into dollars (or other hard currencies). The existence of private insurance policies is often kept secret, so that host authorities do not single out well-covered projects for harsh treatment (knowing that the investor will not actually suffer large losses).

Multilateral lending agencies like MIGA and OPIC also offer compensation, but their "extra" facilitative support for investors comes in the form of deterrence, since host governments are reluctant to require MIGA or OPIC to pay for a loss suffered by a major firm. A claim against MIGA may influence lending decisions of the International Bank for Reconstruction and Development or the International Finance Corporation. A claim against OPIC may result in the U.S. Embassy, the Agency for International Development, the Department of Defense, and other U.S. agencies weighing in on the investor's behalf. Similarly, the host government wants to keep on good terms with the Inter-American Development Bank, the Asian Development Bank, and other multilateral lenders that offer political risk insurance. Some countries—such as Canada, the United Kingdom, and Japan—offer political risk insurance via their export credit agencies.

Besides bringing pressure to bear on behalf of an injured investor, the quasi-official agency—especially MIGA or its counterpart in a regional multilateral development bank, like the Inter-American Development Bank, the Asian Development Bank, or the European Bank for Reconstruction and

Development—can help mediate potential disputes behind the scenes before they become actual claims. Some countries offer quasi-official political risk coverage to any firm that has a significant presence in their home market. Other countries require that recipients of quasi-official political risk insurance be majority owned by home-country nationals.

The performance of developed countries in facilitating foreign direct investment to poorly performing countries should be evaluated as a function of whether the country involved provides home-country firms with access to political risk insurance and guarantees from multilateral lending agencies, provides home-country firms with access to political risk insurance from the country's own political risk insurance agency, and provides all firms with a significant presence in their economy with either or both of these kinds of coverage. U.S. investors can take advantage of the services of MIGA, since the United States is a member of MIGA; New Zealand investors cannot, since New Zealand is not a member of MIGA. All investors with a significant presence in Canada can purchase political risk coverage from Export Development of Canada, whereas only investors with majority ownership by U.S. nationals can purchase political risk coverage from OPIC.

Several aspects of quasi-official political risk insurance must be weighed. Some standards are desirable, others are not. For example, many quasi-official political risk insurers screen projects to ensure that they meet environmental standards, worker treatment standards, and human rights standards (as MIGA and OPIC do), a custom to be encouraged. On the other hand, some requirements are obstacles to outward investment. For example, some insurers are forbidden by the home country to consider projects in "sensitive sectors" of the home economy, such as textile, footwear, electronics, auto parts, steel investors; others may require investors to promise not to lay off workers or close plants in the home country, or promise to consult with local authorities. Also to be weighed negatively is the freedom of some insurers to provide coverage to any project that is commercially viable, including import-substitution projects that are harmful to the host country's development and that rely on trade protection to generate a profit.

Other Home-Country Measures

Home-country authorities may weigh in to the advantage of both foreign direct investors and their host countries in several other ways.

ADVOCACY, ARBITRATION, AND DISPUTE SETTLEMENT. In general, the performance of developed countries in facilitating foreign direct investment to poorly performing countries should be evaluated positively if home-country authorities try to resolve investment disputes in a mutually beneficial fashion. Home governments that intervene on behalf of foreign investors for purposes that contravene core labor standards or other international norms (such as the pressure from the Japanese and Korean governments on Bangladesh to place legal restrictions on freedom of association and right to collective bargaining in export zones) should receive a negative score.

Fundamental questions have emerged about the appropriate framework for the arbitration and settlement of foreign investor–host government disputes, with a growing appreciation of the limitations of commercial law arbitration. Reform of arbitration procedures would include broader provision for assessment of what best serves the public interest of the host state and of the international community and greater attention to distinguishing commercial from political risk.

MECHANISMS TO AVOID DOUBLE TAXATION. A foreign investor may be exposed to double taxation if it is required to pay an income tax or royalty to the host government and also to the home government when the income from the developing country project is remitted or consolidated with its home-country earnings. A tax-sparing agreement, or the use of a foreign tax credit, can avoid this. In addition, a tax-sparing agreement, or the use of a foreign tax credit, helps the developing country to attract foreign direct investment by offering a low tax rate or a tax holiday. If a host country granted a 10 percent tax rate to foreign investors, or granted a "pioneer status" tax holiday to foreign investors, the home country would simply collect the difference between the host country's rate and the home country's rate when the foreign earnings were repatriated or consolidated, if there were no tax-sparing arrangement or foreign tax credit.

Some tax regimes that avoid double taxation are more efficient than others, but the details can be quite complex and it may not be easy to grade alternative efforts. In general, the performance of developed countries in facilitating foreign direct investment in poorly performing countries should be evaluated positively if the sponsor's tax treaties or tax-sparing regimes avoid double taxation.

PREVENTION OF BRIBERY AND CORRUPT PRACTICES. In the past there have been blatant differences among home countries in the way they treated bribery and corrupt practices by home-country investors in overseas markets. The United States considered such practices criminal; other home countries did not consider them either criminal or civil offenses and allowed bribe payments to be considered business expenses. Thus the performance of developed countries in facilitating foreign direct investment to low-income countries should be evaluated in light of the home country's regulations and of its participation in contemporary OECD agreements to prevent bribery and other corrupt practices.

Beyond these OECD initiatives, however, individual governments and firms fear being put at a competitive disadvantage through measures to ensure transparency in payments. The multilateral community has a common interest therefore in establishing standards (perhaps in conjunction with the World Bank and regional development banks) to enhance transparency regarding the taxes and payments made by international investors in ways that can be monitored by external parties.

LOCATIONAL SUBSIDIES AND ASSISTANCE. More and more, home countries offer packages to multinational investors to keep their investments at home; these packages consist of tax breaks, subsidies, free land, below-market office space, and training grants.[65] Ireland was a leader in this. Such U.S. states as South Carolina, Alabama, and Kentucky became active players too, as have the provinces of Canada. European countries (such as Germany, for investment in the former East Germany) have increased their role. Although traditional analysis suggests that multinational investors do not base their locational decisions on tax considerations and that there is little competition between developed country and developing country sites, both of these assertions are being challenged by contemporary econometric research, which suggests that multinational investors are becoming more responsive to locational incentives and that competition between developed and developing countries for such investment is growing.[66] It may be extremely difficult to find accurate and comparable measures of locational incentives, in part because local and national authorities have an interest in concealing or quasi-concealing these measures from their own populaces as well as from outsiders.

The foreign service or the commercial service of some developed countries are trained to help home-country firms to find investment opportunities (as well as export opportunities) in the developing world. Others are not. The performance of developed countries in facilitating foreign direct investment to low-income countries should be evaluated positively if they use these domestic entities to help locate investment opportunities in developing countries—and negatively if they deploy locational incentives to attract or hold international investors.

An Appraisal of the United States on These Measures

By the above measures, the United States does facilitate foreign direct investment flows in many ways. U.S. investors are eligible for political risk insurance via multilateral and regional banks as well as via OPIC. OPIC screens for environmental impact and for worker and human rights abuses. The United States employs a foreign tax credit and has a criminal Foreign Corrupt Practices Act to prevent bribery and other corrupt behavior. U.S. embassies advocate on behalf of foreign direct investors on a regular basis. But it may come as a surprise that in many specific ways the United States does not in fact have a strong record of encouraging U.S. companies to set up labor-intensive operations in least-developed countries, especially when the resulting output might be imported into the U.S. market.

As noted above, the principal instrument of the U.S. government to facilitate foreign direct investment flows to developing countries is OPIC.[67] But OPIC is precluded from providing political risk insurance of financial guarantees to "sensitive sector" investments. By statute, OPIC cannot assist textile and garment projects aimed at exporting more than 5 percent of production to the United States unless a bilateral treaty placing a limit on exports of textiles and apparel to the United States is already in place. By statute, OPIC cannot cover agribusiness projects if the crops involved are "in surplus" in the United States and if more than 20 percent of the output is expected to be exported to the United States. By internal guidance, OPIC has similarly considered all projects in the electronics industry or the automotive industry (including all auto parts) too "sensitive" to support. Similarly, by statute, OPIC cannot support "runaway investments" (any project that results in any job loss even if the net job creation within the United States is strongly positive). It also refuses to finance or insure projects whose exports to third markets might displace exports from the United States. Finally, OPIC has not provided support over the years to U.S. investors interested in setting up EPZs, effectively precluding U.S. companies from playing the investor-developer role that has been such a powerful force in poorer country investment promotion.

Where OPIC has been able to operate in low-income states, it has frequently been able to support pioneering projects with broadly positive social impact that have served as demonstration models to other investors. A relatively modest US$1.9 million political risk insurance policy from OPIC allowed an American investor (Agro Management), for example, to provide chrysanthemum seedlings to farmers in Uganda, to set up buying stations close to the farms, and to establish a communal bank to deposit payments for flower deliveries. By 2001 some 19,000 Ugandan farmers were participating in this export-oriented endeavor. But this is the exception rather than the rule. As a result of statutory and internal policies concerning possible job loss in the United States, no more than 10 percent of OPIC's portfolio is in manufacturing or assembly or in agribusiness. Most investors in labor-intensive sectors simply do not bring their projects to OPIC for consideration. To allow OPIC to return to its original mandate to assist development, OPIC's authorizing legislation and internal policy practices need to be fundamentally revised to prohibit support only for those projects that can be shown to do net harm to the U.S. home economy. This would greatly enlarge the universe of potential investments in nonextractive sectors that OPIC could assist. But an effort to reform OPIC along these lines was defeated in the reauthorization struggle in 2003 as a result of opposition from the AFL-CIO.

The performance of the United States government in facilitating foreign direct investment flows would be improved by other reforms as well. International companies with a major presence in the United States are not eligible for OPIC coverage for the use of their U.S. operations as a base to invest in developing countries unless the companies are majority owned by U.S. investors. Siemens-USA, which employs 90,000 U.S. workers in its U.S. plants (more than in Germany), for example, is not eligible for OPIC coverage. Siemens-Canada, in contrast, is eligible for coverage by Export Development Canada. OPIC's statute should be revised to permit foreign-owned companies with a significant presence in the U.S. economy to be eligible. Another missed opportunity is the underutilized potential of the Foreign Commercial Service (FCS) to facilitate foreign direct investment in low-income states. The FCS does help U.S. firms to spot export opportunities, and the U.S. Foreign Service helps U.S. firms bid on some developing country contracts, but neither has been trained to identify potential foreign investment projects, even though the typical sequence is for an international company first to export to a target market and then to consider investing in a distribution or assembly facility.

Finally, individual state governments in the United States (Alabama, South Carolina, Kentucky) have been at the forefront in the escalation of locational incentives to attract investment and to keep international company plants from leaving. The United States has resisted efforts in the OECD to extend national supervision of investment subsidies to cover subnational authorities. Tax breaks, free land, subsidized office space, and training grants provided to international companies represent a classic example of the prisoner's dilemma: no single government dares refuse to participate, but all would be better off if there were a multilateral agreement to cap (and roll back) these giveaways. The United States could be a prime mover in this endeavor.

Appendix 11A: Foreign Direct Investment, by Host Countries

Table 11A-1. *Foreign Direct Investment, Inflows, by Host Region, 2000–02*
US$ million

Host region	2000	2001	2002
Africa	8,489	18,769	10,998
North Africa	3,125	5,474	3,546
Algeria	438	1,196	1,065
Egypt	1,235	510	647
Libyan Arab Jamahiriya	−142	−101	−96
Morocco	423	2,808	428
Sudan	392	574	681
Tunisia	779	486	821
Other Africa	5,364	13,295	7,452
Angola	879	2,146	1,312
Benin	60	44	41
Botswana	54	26	37
Burkina Faso	23	9	8
Burundi	12	0	0
Cameroon	31	67	86
Cape Verde	34	9	14
Central African Republic	1	5	4
Chad	115	0	901
Comoros	1	0	1
Congo	166	77	247
Congo, Democratic Republic of	23	1	32
Côte d'Ivoire	235	44	223
Djibouti	3	3	4
Equatorial Guinea	108	945	323
Eritrea	28	1	21
Ethiopia	135	20	75
Gabon	−43	169	123
Gambia	44	35	43
Ghana	115	89	50
Guinea	10	2	30
Guinea-Bissau	1	1	1
Kenya	127	50	50
Lesotho	31	28	24
Liberia	−431	−20	−65
Madagascar	70	93	8
Malawi	−33	−20	0
Mali	83	122	102
Mauritania	9	−6	12
Mauritius	277	32	28

Table 11A-1 *(continued)*

Host region	2000	2001	2002
Mozambique	139	255	406
Namibia	153	275	181
Niger	9	23	8
Nigeria	930	1,104	1,281
Rwanda	8	4	3
São Tomé and Principe	2	6	2
Senegal	63	32	93
Seychelles	56	59	63
Sierra Leone	5	3	5
Somalia	0	0	0
South Africa	888	6,789	754
Swaziland	39	78	107
Togo	42	63	75
Uganda	254	229	275
United Republic of Tanzania	463	327	240
Zambia	122	72	197
Zimbabwe	23	4	26
Latin America and the Caribbean	76,792	69,436	43,534
South America	57,248	39,693	25,836
Argentina	11,657	3,206	1,003
Bolivia	723	660	553
Brazil	32,779	22,457	16,566
Chile	3,639	4,477	1,603
Colombia	2,237	2,521	2,034
Ecuador	720	1,330	1,275
Guyana	67	56	44
Paraguay	104	95	−22
Peru	681	1,151	1,462
Suriname	−97	−27	−85
Uruguay	274	318	85
Venezuela	4,465	3,448	1,318
Other	19,544	29,743	17,698
Anguilla	39	33	33
Antigua and Barbuda	33	39	36
Aruba	−144	−319	241
Barbados	19	19	11
Belize	19	40	52
Costa Rica	409	454	642
Cuba	−10	4	4
Dominica	11	12	14
Dominican Republic	953	1 079	961

Host region	*2000*	*2001*	*2002*
El Salvador	173	250	208
Grenada	37	49	41
Guatemala	230	456	110
Haiti	13	4	6
Honduras	282	195	143
Jamaica	468	614	479
Mexico	15,484	25,334	13,627
Montserrat	4	1	1
Nicaragua	267	150	174
Panama	603	513	57
Saint Kitts and Nevis	96	88	81
Saint Lucia	55	22	22
Saint Vincent and the Grenadines	29	21	19
Trinidad and Tobago	472	685	737
Asia and the Pacific	142,209	106,937	95,129
Asia	142,091	106,778	94,989
West Asia	1,523	5,211	2,341
Bahrain	364	81	218
Cyprus	804	652	297
Iran, Islamic Republic of	39	50	37
Iraq	–3	–6	–9
Jordan	787	100	56
Kuwait	16	–147	7
Lebanon	298	249	257
Oman	44	42	40
Occupied Palestinian Territory	62	11	41
Qatar	252	296	326
Saudi Arabia	–1,884	20	–350
Syrian Arab Republic	270	205	225
Turkey	982	3,266	1,037
United Arab Emirates	–515	257	95
Yemen	6	136	64
Central Asia	1,871	3,963	4,035
Armenia	104	70	100
Azerbaijan	129	227	1,067
Georgia	131	110	146
Kazakhstan	1,283	2,823	2,561
Kyrgyzstan	–2	5	–12
Tajikistan	22	9	9
Turkmenistan	131	150	100
Uzbekistan	73	570	65

Table 11A-1 *(continued)*

Host region	2000	2001	2002
South, East, and South-East Asia	138,698	97,604	88,613
Afghanistan	0	1	0
Bangladesh	280	79	45
Bhutan	0	0	0
Brunei Darussalam	549	526	1,035
Cambodia	149	148	54
China	40,772	46,846	52,700
Hong Kong, China	61,939	23,775	13,718
India	2,319	3,403	3,449
Indonesia	–4,550	–3,279	–1,523
Korea, Democratic People's Republic of	5	–24	12
Korea, Republic of	9,283	3,528	1,972
Lao People's Democratic Republic	34	24	25
Macau, China	–1	133	150
Malaysia	3,788	554	3,203
Maldives	13	12	12
Mongolia	54	43	78
Myanmar	208	192	129
Nepal	0	21	10
Pakistan	305	385	823
Philippines	1,345	982	1,111
Singapore	12,464	10,949	7,655
Sri Lanka	175	82	242
Taiwan Province of China	4,928	4,109	1,445
Thailand	3,350	3,813	1,068
Vietnam	1,289	1,300	1,200
The Pacific	118	159	140
Fiji	25	90	77
Kiribati	1	1	1
New Caledonia	22	–1	0
Papua New Guinea	96	63	50
Samoa	–2	1	1
Solomon Islands	1	–12	–7
Tonga	5	1	2
Tuvalu	0	0	0
Vanuatu	20	18	15
Central and Eastern Europe	26,373	25,015	28,709
Albania	143	207	213
Belarus	119	96	227
Bosnia and Herzegovina	147	130	321
Bulgaria	1,002	813	479

Host region	*2000*	*2001*	*2002*
Croatia	1,089	1,561	981
Czech Republic	4,984	5,639	9,319
Estonia	387	542	307
Hungary	1,646	2,440	854
Latvia	410	164	396
Lithuania	379	446	732
Moldova, Republic of	129	156	111
Poland	9,341	5,713	4,119
Romania	1,025	1,157	1,106
Russian Federation	2,714	2,469	2,421
Serbia and Montenegro	25	165	475
Slovakia	1,925	1,579	4,012
Slovenia	136	503	1,865
TFYR Macedonia	177	442	77
Ukraine	595	792	693
Addendum			
Least developed countries	3,427	5,629	5,232
Oil-exporting countries	2,468	8,099	7,364
Developing economies (not including Bermuda, Cayman Islands, Virgin Islands, Bahamas, Netherlands Antilles)	253,864	220 157	178 370

Source: UN Conference on Trade and Development, *World Investment Report 2003: FDI Policies for Development: National and International Perspectives* (annex table B.1) (www.unctad.org/fdistatistics).

Table 11A-2. *Foreign Direct Investment, Inward Stock, by Host Region,*
2000–02

US$ million

Host region	2000	2001	2002
Africa	144,659	157,980	171,032
North Africa	38,082	43,191	48,310
Algeria	3,441	4,637	5,702
Egypt	19,589	20,099	20,746
Libyan Arab Jamahiriya	–4,648	–4,748	–4,844
Morocco	6,758	9,566	9,994
Sudan	1,396	1,970	2,651
Tunisia	11,545	11,667	14,061
Other Africa	106,577	114,788	122,723
Angola	7,977	10,122	11,435
Benin	588	632	673
Botswana	1,821	1,494	1,946
Burkina Faso	149	158	166
Burundi	48	48	48
Cameroon	1,263	1,331	1,417
Cape Verde	174	183	197
Central African Republic	95	101	105
Chad	618	618	1,519
Comoros	24	24	26
Congo	1,893	1,970	2,217
Congo, Democratic Republic of	617	618	650
Côte d'Ivoire	3,407	3,451	3,674
Djibouti	34	37	40
Equatorial Guinea	1,128	2,073	2,396
Eritrea	301	301	322
Ethiopia	941	961	1,036
Gabon	–1,707	–1,538	–1,415
Gambia	216	221	264
Ghana	1,462	1,551	1,601
Guinea	263	265	295
Guinea-Bissau	46	47	48
Kenya	996	1,047	1,097
Lesotho	486	514	539
Liberia	2,516	2,496	2,431
Madagascar	341	434	442
Malawi	183	163	163
Mali	453	576	678
Mauritania	108	101	113
Mauritius	687	719	746
Mozambique	1,094	1,350	1,755

Host region	2000	2001	2002
Namibia	1,230	797	978
Niger	426	449	457
Nigeria	20,184	21,289	22,570
Rwanda	252	256	259
São Tomé and Principe	4	9	11
Senegal	827	859	952
Seychelles	577	636	699
Sierra Leone	19	22	26
Somalia	4	4	4
South Africa	47,418	50,246	50,998
Swaziland	432	479	656
Togo	511	574	649
Uganda	1,255	1,484	1,759
United Republic of Tanzania	1,783	2,111	2,351
Zambia	2,350	2,422	2,619
Zimbabwe	1,085	1,088	1,114
Latin America and the Caribbean	517,421	599,954	643,952
South America	380,061	414,979	441,110
Argentina	72,935	75,989	76,992
Bolivia	5,176	5,839	6,392
Brazil	196,884	219,342	235,908
Chile	44,955	44,693	46,296
Colombia	12,144	16,008	19,375
Ecuador	7,081	8,410	9,686
Guyana	759	815	859
Paraguay	1,311	1,162	867
Peru	10,503	10,669	12,565
Suriname	−719	−746	−830
Uruguay	2,088	2,406	1,291
Venezuela	26,944	30,392	31,710
Other	137,360	184,975	202,842
Anguilla	227	260	293
Antigua and Barbuda	566	606	642
Aruba	816	497	738
Barbados	308	326	338
Belize	269	310	362
Costa Rica	5,206	5,660	6,302
Cuba	74	78	82
Dominica	271	283	297

Table 11A-2 *(continued)*

Host region	2000	2001	2002
Dominican Republic	5,214	6,293	7,254
El Salvador	1,973	2,223	2,431
Grenada	346	395	436
Guatemala	3,420	3,876	4,155
Haiti	215	220	226
Honduras	1,489	1,684	1,826
Jamaica	3,316	3,930	4,409
Mexico	97,170	140,376	154,003
Montserrat	84	85	86
Nicaragua	1,386	1,536	1,710
Panama	6,744	7,257	7,314
Saint Kitts and Nevis	484	572	653
Saint Lucia	804	826	849
Saint Vincent and the Grenadines	489	510	529
Trinidad and Tobago	6,489	7,173	7,910
Asia and the Pacific	1,275,985	1,310,200	1,406,527
Asia	1,272,245	1,306,301	1,402,488
West Asia	69,979	70,035	72,376
Bahrain	5,906	5,986	6,205
Cyprus	3,878	4,530	4,827
Iran, Islamic Republic of	2,474	2,524	2,561
Iraq	−23	−29	−38
Jordan	2,258	2,358	2,414
Kuwait	527	380	387
Lebanon	1,116	1,365	1,622
Oman	2,501	2,543	2,583
Occupied Palestinian Territory	155	165	206
Qatar	1,920	2,216	2,541
Saudi Arabia	25,963	25,983	25,633
Syrian Arab Republic	1,699	1,904	2,129
Turkey	19,209	17,521	18,558
United Arab Emirates	1,061	1,318	1,413
Yemen	1,336	1,271	1,336
Central Asia	16,123	20,856	25,139
Armenia	513	580	680
Azerbaijan	3,735	3,962	5,354
Georgia	423	533	679
Kazakhstan	9,259	12,871	15,354
Kyrgyzstan	439	427	415
Tajikistan	144	153	162
Turkmenistan	913	1,063	1,163
Uzbekistan	697	1,267	1,332

Host region	*2000*	*2001*	*2002*
South, East and Southeast Asia	1,186,143	1,215,410	1,304,973
Afghanistan	17	18	18
Bangladesh	983	1 062	1 107
Bhutan	3	4	4
Brunei Darussalam	3,856	4,383	5,418
Cambodia	1,336	1,449	1,503
China	348,346	395,192	447,892
Hong Kong, China	455,469	419,348	433,065
India	18,916	22,319	25,768
Indonesia	60,638	57,359	55,836
Korea, Democratic People's Republic of	1,046	1,022	1,034
Korea, Republic of	37,106	40,767	43,689
Lao People's Democratic Republic	550	574	599
Macau, China	2,725	2,858	3,008
Malaysia	52,747	53,301	56,505
Maldives	118	130	142
Mongolia	182	225	302
Myanmar	3,178	3,266	3,395
Nepal	97	116	126
Pakistan	6,912	5,536	6,359
Philippines	9,081	10,468	11,579
Singapore	113,431	116,428	124,083
Sri Lanka	2,389	2,471	2,713
Taiwan Province of China	27,924	32,033	33,478
Thailand	24,468	29,158	30,226
Vietnam	14,624	15,924	17,124
The Pacific	3,740	3,899	4,039
Fiji	1,017	1,106	1,183
Kiribati	5	5	6
New Caledonia	146	144	144
Papua New Guinea	2,007	2,069	2,119
Samoa	53	55	56
Solomon Islands	126	114	107
Tonga	21	22	25
Tuvalu	1	1	1
Vanuatu	366	384	399
Central and Eastern Europe	129,169	155,734	187,868
Albania	568	775	988
Belarus	1,306	1,374	1,602
Bosnia and Herzegovina	376	506	828
Bulgaria	2,716	3,410	3,889

Table 11A-2 *(continued)*

Host region	2000	2001	2002
Croatia	3,560	5,049	6,029
Czech Republic	21,644	27,092	38,450
Estonia	2,645	3,160	4,226
Hungary	19,804	23,562	24,416
Latvia	2,084	2,332	2,723
Lithuania	2,334	2,666	3,981
Moldova, Republic of	446	600	717
Poland	34,227	41,031	45,150
Romania	6,480	7,638	8,786
Russian Federation	17,956	20,142	22,563
Serbia and Montenegro	1,319	1,484	1,959
Slovakia	4,634	6,213	10,225
Slovenia	2,809	3,209	5,074
TFYR Macedonia	387	829	907
Ukraine	3,875	4,662	5,355
Addendum			
Least developed countries (LDCs)	35,609	40,867	46,099
Oil-exporting countries	174,176	182,275	189,638
Developing economies (not including Bermuda, Cayman Islands, Virgin Islands, Bahamas, Netherlands Antilles)	2,067,234	2,223,868	2,409,380

Source: See table 11A-1, annex table B.3.

Notes

1. The analysis of the impact of various kinds of foreign direct investment on the host country's physical environment requires much more extensive treatment than is possible here. In general, the focus of this chapter is the positive or negative contribution of foreign investors to the host country's economic welfare (including the treatment of workers) and to the host country's growth prospects.

2. Jeffrey Sachs and Andrew Warner, "The Curse of Natural Resources," *European Economic Review* 45. no. 3 (2001): 827–38.

3. William Ascher, *Why Governments Waste Resources: The Political Economy of Natural Resource Policy Failures in Developing Countries* (Johns Hopkins University Press, 2000); Michael L. Ross, "The Political Economy of the Resource Curse," *World Politics* 51, no. 2 (1999): 297–322.

4. Jerry Useem, "Exxon's African Adventure: How to Build a $3.5 Billion Pipeline—with the 'Help' of NGOs, the World Bank, and Yes, Chicken Sacrifices," *Fortune,* April 15, 2002, pp. 102–09. For a critical perspective on the Chad-Cameroon project, see Ian Gary and Terry Lynn Karl, *Bottom of the Barrel: Africa's Oil Boom and the Poor* (Baltimore: Catholic Relief Services, 2003), chap. 5.

5. See the Publish What You Pay Campaign at www.globalwitness.org.

6. See www.dfid.gove.uk.

7. Jeff Gerth, "U.S. and Oil Companies Back Revised Effort on Disclosure," *New York Times,* September 19, 2003, p. w1.

8. T. Irwin and others, eds., *Dealing with Public Risk in Private Infrastructure* (Washington: World Bank, 1997).

9. Julie A. Martin, with Pamela A. Bracey, "OPIC Modified Expropriation Coverage Case Study: MidAmerica's Projects in Indonesia—Dieng and Patuha," in *International Political Risk Management: Exploring New Frontiers,* edited by Theodore H. Moran (Washington: World Bank, 2001).

10. Charles Berry, "Shall the Twain Meet? Finding Common Ground or Uncommon Solutions: A Broker's Perspective," in *International Political Risk Management: The Brave New World* (Washington: World Bank, 2003).

11. For the detailed evidence and background for the examples that follow, see Theodore H. Moran, *Parental Supervision: The New Paradigm for Foreign Direct Investment and Development* (Washington: Institute for International Economics, 2001).

12. Dennis J. Encarnation and Louis T. Wells Jr., "Evaluating Foreign Investment," in *Investing In Development: New Roles for Private Capital?* edited by Theodore H. Moran (Washington: Overseas Development Council, 1986).

13. For a theoretical analysis of why trade protection, domestic content requirements, or other restraints on competition are likely to lead to a proliferation of subscale and inefficient plants, see H. Eastman and S. Stykolt, "A Model for the Study of Protected Oligopolies," *Economic Journal* 70 (1970): 336–47.

14. See Moran, *Parental Supervision.*

15. Portions of this section draw on Ted Moran, "Attracting Non-Extractive Investment to Africa: Challenges, Success Stories, and Lessons for the Future," paper prepared for the Corporate Council on Africa/Institute for International Economics, Washington, June 2, 2003.

16. *International Country Risk Guide 2002* (East Syracuse, N.Y.: PRS Group, 2002); *Competitiveness Indicators 2002* (Geneva: World Economic Forum, 2002); Klaus Schwab and others, *The Africa Competitiveness Report 2000–2001* (Oxford University Press, 2000); Jeffrey Sachs and Sara Sievers, "Foreign Direct Investment in Africa," in *The Africa Competitiveness Report 1998* (Geneva: World Economic Forum, 1998); William Easterly and Ross Levine, "Africa's Growth Tragedy: Policies and Ethnic Divisions," *Quarterly Journal of Economics* 112, no. 4 (1997): 1203–50; *Global Economic Prospects and the Developing Countries 2003: Investing to Unlock Global Opportunity* (Washington: World Bank, 2002); Aart Kraay, and Jaume Ventura, "Current Accounts in Debtor and Creditor Countries," *Quarterly Journal of Economics* 115 (2000): 1137–66.

17. These case studies can be found in Theodore H. Moran, *Beyond Sweatshops: Foreign Direct Investment and Globalization in Developing Countries* (Washington: Brookings, 2002).

18. The author of the study is James Meade, Port Louis, Mauritius, 1960.

19. Lucie C. Phillips and others, "Foreign and Local Investment in East Africa, Interactions and Policy Implications: Case Studies of Mauritius, Uganda, and Kenya," research paper, Bureau for Africa, Office of Sustainable Development (Washington: U.S. Agency for International Development, 2000). According to *World Development Indicators* (Washington: World Bank, 2004), Mauritius had a GDP per capita of US$1,883 in 1982 (in constant 1995 dollars).

20. Steven Radelet, "Manufactured Exports, Export Platforms, and Economic Growth," CAER II Discussion Paper 43 (Harvard Institute for International Development, Harvard University, 1999), table 3.

21. *International Financial Statistics: Mauritius, 2001* (Washington: International Monetary Fund, 2001).

22. Yung Whee Rhee, Katharina Katterback, and Jeanette White, *Free Trade Zones in Export Strategies* (Washington: World Bank, 1990), p. 39.

23. According to *World Development Indicators* (Washington: World Bank, 2004), the Dominican Republic had a GDP per capita in 1982 of US$1,333 (constant 1995 dollars).

24. National Free Zone Council of the Dominican Republic, *Free Zone Statistical Report Year 2000* (Santo Domingo: 2001), figures 20, 29, 39.

25. Ibid.

26. Dorsati Madani, "A Review of the Role and Impact of Export Processing Zones," PREM-EP working paper (Washington: World Bank, 1999).

27. Peter G. Warr, "Export Promotion via Industrial Enclaves: The Philippines Bataan Export Processing Zone," *Journal of Development Studies* (January 1987): 220–41; Helena Johansson, "The Economics of Export Processing Zones Revisited," *Development Policy Review* 12 (1994): 387–402.

28. Mireille Razafindrakoto and François Roubaud, "Les Entreprises Franches a Madagascar: Economie d'enclave ou promesse d'une nouvelle prosperite? Nouvel exclavage ou opportunite pour le developpement du Pays?" *Economie de Madagascar,* no. 2 (1995): 219–32. According to the *World Development Indicators* (Washington: World Bank, 2004), Madagascar had a GDP per capita of US$275 in 1989 (in constant 1995 dollars).

29. Razafindrakoto and Roubaud, "Les Entreprises Franches a Madagascar," p. 223.

30. Economist Intelligence Unit, *Country Profile 2000: Madagascar,* reference table 12 (London: Economist, 2000).

31. Sanjaya Lall, "Lesotho Integrated Framework Study: Foreign Direct Investment," working paper (Washington: World Bank, 2002). According to the *World Development Indicators* (Washington: World Bank, 2004), Lesotho had a GDP per capita of US$535 in 1998 (in constant 1995 dollars).

32. Lall, "Lesotho Integrated Framework Study."

33. Mauricio Jenkins, Gerardo Esquivel, and Felipe Larrain, "Export Processing Zones in Central America," development discussion paper, Central America Project Series (Harvard Institute for International Development, Harvard University, 1998); Manuel R. Agosin, David E. Bloom, and Eduardo Gitli, "Globalization, Liberalization, and Sustainable Human Development: Progress and Challenges in Central American Countries (El Salvador, Guatemala, Honduras, and Nicaragua)," Occasional Paper UNCTAD/EDM/Misc. 126, 2000 (Geneva: UN Conference on Trade and Development, 2000). Among resource-oriented economies, the list of the more successful of the poorer host countries would include Namibia and Botswana.

34. In an analysis of foreign investment flows from fourteen home countries to forty-five host countries in the early 1990s, for example, S.-J. Wei found that each one-grade increase (on a ten-point scale) in the corruption level was associated with a 16 percent increase in the flow of foreign direct investment, or approximately equal to a 3 percentage point decrease in the marginal tax rate. S.-J. Wei, "How Taxing Is Corruption on International Investors?" *Review of Economics and Statistics* 82 (2001): 1–11.

35. Avinash K. Dixit and Robert S. Pindyck, *Investment under Uncertainty* (Princeton University Press, 1994).

36. This has been likened to trying to convince buyers of a used car that they won't end up with a lemon. Unlike a used car dealer, though, a would-be host country can neither let the prospective investor take a test drive nor share the risk of future failure by offering a lengthy warranty. George A. Akerloff, "The Market for Lemons: Quality Uncertainty and the Market Mechanism," *Quarterly Journal of Economics* 84, no. 3 (1970): 488–500.

37. Louis T. Wells Jr. and Alvin G. Wint, *Marketing a Country: Promotion as a Tool for Attracting Foreign Investment,* rev. ed. (Washington: Foreign Investment Advisory Service of the World Bank Group, 2000).

38. Louis T. Wells Jr., afterword to ibid.

39. Rhee, Katterback, and White, *Free Trade Zones in Export Strategies.*

40. The Lesotho National Development Corporation has begun to divest itself of the management of the country's five major export-oriented industrial estates, subcontracting responsibility to JHI Real Estate Limited, a South African multinational firm. Lall, "Lesotho Integrated Framework Study."

41. James J. Emery and others, "Administrative Barriers to Foreign Investment: Reducing Red Tape in Africa," Occasional Paper 14 (Washington: FIAS, 2000). See also FIAS, "Ethiopia; Foreign Investment Promotion Strategy Framework," draft, December 2000.

42. FIAS indicated that if there could be better coordination of duplicative approvals required from the Namibia Planning Advisory Board and the townships boards, Namibia could well be considered a model for other countries.

43. This section draws heavily upon Moran, *Beyond Sweatshops.*

44. ILO, "African Regional Workshop on the Protection of Workers' Rights and Working Conditions in EPZs and the Promotion of the Tripartite Declaration of Principles Concerning Multinational Enterprises and Social Policy" (Geneva: 1996), p. 11.

45. Kimberly Ann Elliott, "Getting Beyond No . . . ! Promoting Worker Rights and Trade," in *The WTO after Seattle,* edited by Jeffrey J. Schott (Washington: Institute for International Economics, 2000), p. 198.

46. Economist Intelligence Unit, *Bangladesh: Country Report* (London: 2001), p. 19. Bangladesh is now in the midst of a five-year phase in of trade unions in the country's EPZs.

47. ILO, *Labor and Social Issues Relating to Export Processing Zones* (Geneva: 1998).

48. Mita Aggarwal, "International Trade, Labor Standards, and Labor Market Conditions: An Evaluation of the Linkages," Working Paper 95-06-C (Washington: Office of Economics, U.S. International Trade Commission, 1995).

49. Dani Rodrik, "Labor Standards in International Trade: Do They Matter and What Do We Do about Them?" in *Emerging Agenda for Global Trade: High Stakes for Developing Countries,* edited by Robert Lawrence, Dani Rodrik, and John Whalley (Johns Hopkins University Press for the Overseas Development Council, 1996), p. 57.

50. ILO, *Labor and Social Issues Relating to Export Processing Zones.*

51. U.S. Department of Labor, Bureau of International Labor Affairs, *Wages, Benefits, Poverty Line, and Meeting Workers Needs in the Apparel and Footwear Industries of Selected Countries* (Washington: 2000).

52. Radelet, "Manufactured Exports, Export Platforms, and Economic Growth," p. 47.

53. Rhee, Katterback, and White, *Free Trade Zones in Export Strategies,* p. 22.

54. Razafindrakoto and Roubaud, "Les Entreprises Franches a Madagascar," pp. 233–34.

55. Edward M. Graham, *Fighting the Wrong Enemy: Antiglobal Activists and Multinational Enterprises* (Washington: Institute for International Economics, 2000), table 4-2, pp. 93–94. Graham eliminates salaries for foreign managers and supervisors from these calculations.

56. ILO, *Labour and Social Issues Relating to Export Processing Zones,* pp. 23–24.

57. Lall, "Lesotho Integrated Framework Study," p. 9.

58. This hypothesis is tested in Moran, *Beyond Sweatshops,* with positive results.

59. Ibid.

60. Peter Cornelius, "Financial Development and the Liberalization of Financial Services Trade," in *The Africa Competitiveness Report 2000–2001,* edited by Klaus Schwab and others (Oxford University Press, 2000). This finding is also reported in "Economic Diversification and Competitiveness in East Africa: An Analysis of Firm-Level Data from Ethiopia, Kenya, Tanzania, and Uganda" (Washington: World Bank, 2002).

61. Clear land title is a significant factor in determining relative firm growth rates. Access to an initial bank loan or informal loan does not seem to play a role in driving growth but is significant in determining firm size at start-up. Tyler Biggs, Vijaya Ramachandran, and Manju Kedia Shah, "The Determinants of Enterprise Growth in Sub-Saharan Africa: Evidence for the Regional Program on Enterprise Development" (Washington: World Bank, 1998). Vijaya Ramachandran and Manju Kedia Shah, "Minority Entrepreneurs and Private Sector Growth in Sub-Saharan Africa," RPED Paper 086 (Washington: World Bank, 1998).

62. UNCTAD, *World Investment Report 2001* (Geneva: 2001). See also Jenkins, Esquivel, and Larrain, "Export Processing Zones in Central America"; Agosin, Bloom, and Gitli, Globalization, "Liberalization, and Sustainable Human Development."

63. Lall, "Lesotho Integrated Framework Study." In addition, in Bangladesh (also a country with relatively low skill and education levels) many employees of multinational corporations left their garment employers within a few years and set up their own export operations. See Yung W. Rhee and T. Belot, "Export Catalysts in Low-Income Countries: A Review of Eleven Success Stories," Discussion Paper 72 (Washington: World Bank, 1989). More broadly, it should be remembered that the indigenous world-class international machine tool competitors in today's Malaysia grew from local machine maintenance providers who serviced the foreign semiconductor and telecommunications investors. See Rajah Rasiah. "Flexible Production Systems and Local Machine-Tool Subcontracting: Electronics Components Transnationals in Malaysia," *Cambridge Journal of Economics* 18, no. 3 (1994): 279–98

64. The TRIMS Agreement dealt with trade-related investment measures, obliging WTO members to phase out the imposition of required levels of local content on foreign investors and to end the requirement that foreign firms match imports with exports.

65. Kenneth P. Thomas, *Competing for Capital: Europe and North America in a Global Era* (Georgetown University Press, 2000).

66. J. Mutti, *Taxation and Foreign Direct Investment* (Washington: Institute for International Economics, 2003); R. Altshuler, H. Grubert, and S. Newlong, "Has US Investment Abroad Become More Sensitive to Tax Rates?" Working Paper 6383 (Cambridge: National Bureau of Economic Research, 1998).

67. This analysis of OPIC draws on *Reforming OPIC for the 21st Century* (Washington: Institute for International Economics, 2003.)

12

The Persisting Poverty of Strategic Analysis in U.S. Democracy Assistance

DAVID W. YANG

The year 2004 marked the thirtieth anniversary of the so-called third wave of democratization. During the third wave, approximately a hundred countries have embarked on a democratic transition.[1] Given the many difficulties inherent to democratization (as evidenced in the experience of older democracies), many of the newly transitional countries are, not surprisingly, still struggling within a gray zone between consolidated liberal democracy on the one hand and outright authoritarianism on the other.[2] The third wave nevertheless represents the most widespread advance of democracy in world history. Yet until very recently, "democracy" was still a virtually forbidden word in the lexicon of an international development community that had grown too comfortable with the cold war–era maxim that politics does not matter to development. This maxim, although patently false, had been invented as a necessary fiction of sorts so that development cooperation could straddle the East-West and North-South ideological divides of the period.

Even in the late 1990s, when as a U.S. democracy promotion official I used to attend meetings of the OECD's Development Assistance Committee,

The views expressed herein are the author's own. The author wishes to thank Sofia Sebastian and Mina Dadgar for their research assistance.

the preferred multilateral term for democratic governance was "participatory development and good governance." Sitting in the elegant salons at the OECD's headquarters in Paris, I avoided the temptations of diplomatic politeness and proudly used the d-word: "democracy." I did so for several reasons: because I suffer an incurable allergy to bureaucratic euphemism; because the few times I did try to pronounce the Gallic-sounding PDGG acronym, my European counterparts looked at me as if I were trying to play a B-movie version of Gerard Depardieu; and because as an unapologetic Wilsonian I was thrilled to carry the democracy banner back to France (as the president had originally done at Versailles after World War I). But I used the d-word mostly because I believed that in doing so I was defending the U.S. policy of explicitly promoting democracy worldwide.[3]

In the past few years, the development community has caught up with history. Democratic governance is now seen as not only an integral component of human development overall but also one of the main keys to unlocking socioeconomic progress in poorly performing countries.[4] In the foreword to UNDP's Human Development Report 2002, then UNDP administrator Mark Malloch Brown writes, "This [report] is first and foremost about the idea that politics is as important to successful development as economics. Sustained poverty reduction requires equitable growth—but it also requires that poor people have political power. And the best way to achieve that in a manner consistent with human development objectives is by building strong and deep forms of democratic governance at all levels of society."[5]

Examples of the new international consensus about the relationship between democracy and development abound. In the historic "Millennium Declaration" of September 2000, the world's leaders state that "men and women have the right to live their lives and raise their children in dignity, free from hunger and from the fear of violence, oppression or injustice." These rights, they continue, are best ensured by "democratic and participatory governance based on the will of the people."[6] At the International Conference on Financing for Development in March 2002, world leaders issued the equally important "Monterrey Consensus," upon which the Bush administration's innovative Millennium Challenge Account is based. The consensus asserts that "sound economic policies, solid democratic institutions responsive to the needs of the people and improved infrastructure are the basis for sustained economic growth, poverty eradication and employment creation."[7] A 2003 USAID report puts the new consensus into its most blunt and vivid terms yet. "Predatory, corrupt, wasteful, abusive, tyrannical, incompetent governance is the bane of development. Where governance is endemically bad, rulers do not use public resources effectively to generate public goods and thus improve the productivity and well-being of their society. Instead, they appropriate these goods for themselves, their families, their parties and their cronies. Unless we improve governance, we cannot foster development."[8]

Debating the Efficacy of U.S. Democracy Aid

With the raising of democratic governance to the highest reaches of the development agenda, donor budgets for democracy programs have grown steadily. The best rough measurement of donor aid in the area of democratic governance is the government and civil society budget category maintained by the OECD's Development Assistance Committee (DAC). This broad category includes the following: economic and development policy planning, public sector financial management, legal and judicial development, government administration, strengthening of civil society, postconflict peace building, elections, human rights, demobilization, free flow of information, and land-mine clearance. According to the DAC, total aid provided by all donors (bilateral and multilateral) in this category rose from US$2.1 billion in 1991 to US$3.4 billion in 2001. During this period, the U.S. share of the total stayed relatively constant: 33 percent (US$0.7 billion) in 1991; 38 percent (US$1.3 billion) in 2001.[9]

Between 1993 and 2003, USAID's budget for democracy programs nearly tripled, rising from US$315 million in fiscal year 1993 to US$864 million in fiscal year 2003. In fiscal year 2003, this budget was divided among USAID's four geographical regions in the following manner:

—Africa: 11 percent, or US$95 million.
—Asia and the Near East: 18 percent, or US$154 million.
—Europe and Eurasia: 57 percent, or US$492 million.
—Latin America and the Caribbean: 12 percent, or US$108 million.

The remaining 2 percent, or US$15 million, was for global programs run by the Office of Democracy and Governance.

The budget is spread across USAID's four democratic-governance subsectors. In fiscal year 2001, this spread was as follows:[10]

—Rule of law: 22 percent.
—Elections and political processes: 7 percent.
—Civil society: 47 percent.
—Governance: 24 percent.

At the same time as democracy promotion budgets increased, more attention has rightfully been focused on the efficacy of international democracy aid. The founder and still-reigning dean of democracy assistance studies, Thomas Carothers, stunned the development community in early 2002 with the publication of his article "The End of the Transition Paradigm." Carothers argues that the transition paradigm, which he conceives as a set of five overoptimistic donor assumptions about the nature of democratic transition, has rendered USAID and other providers of democracy aid unable to identify the core "political syndromes" that constitute poor performance in the gray zone. In Carothers's view, the continued existence of the paradigm has resulted in unfocused and inappropriate aid programs. "A whole generation of democracy aid," he writes, "is based on the transition paradigm, above all the typical emphasis on an institutional 'checklist' as a basis for creating programs, and the creating of nearly standard portfolios of aid projects consisting of the same diffuse set of efforts all over." "This smorgasbord of democracy programs," he continues, is "based on the vague assumption that they all contribute to some assumed process of [democratic] consolidation."[11]

In the wake of this article, other authors have issued variations on the theme of Carothers's central point. Marina Ottaway, who along with Carothers co-directs the Democracy and Rule of Law Project at the Carnegie Endowment for International Peace, argues that providers of democracy aid fail to understand the "structural obstacles" to democratization in "semi-authoritarian" states.[12] Hilton Root and Bruce Bueno de Mesquita assert that donors have misunderstood how poverty is rooted in the interlinked politicoeconomic maladies of autocracy and patronage.[13] USAID's own study urges donors to base their democracy programs on a clear analysis of where a recipient country is located within a five-part typology of political regimes.[14]

Having reviewed U.S. democracy strategies during the 1990s while serving in democracy promotion posts at USAID and the State Department, I am painfully familiar with the diagnostic and prescriptive failings that Carothers and others identify. At formal Washington reviews of the multiyear strategies governing USAID's aid programs or of the State Department's country-specific annual "performance plans," I, to the chagrin of my regional bureau colleagues in both agencies, regularly voiced this refrain: "Excuse me, but did the embassy (or USAID mission) forget to include its analytical section?" Therefore, based on my own bureaucratic experience, I accept Carothers's conclusion: in my view, most democracy programs do seem to subscribe to a scattershot theory of development aid. Yet I reject Carothers's premise: the analyses underlying the programs, I find, do not necessarily consist of naïve assumptions about democratization. During my many years in the trenches of U.S. democracy promotion, I never met rose-colored notions such as the ones that Carothers alleges make up the "transition paradigm" (for example, "structural conditions won't impede democratization," "all current democratic transitions are based on functioning states," "democratization always unfolds in a strict sequence of 'opening,' 'breakthrough,' and 'consolidation'").[15]

Instead, I start from a simpler premise. That is, donor strategies for democratic governance are still rudimentary at best and inadequate at worst because the task of analyzing the "core political syndrome" of a poorly performing country is very difficult—both intellectually and practically—to carry out. While I tried (usually without success) to veto USAID democracy strategies that I deemed to be insufficient, I also wondered if I could do any better in conducting such a daunting analytical task. Once the moments of bureaucratic confrontation had passed, I would become terrified of the prospect of being invited (by the USAID mission whose strategy was in question) to the field as a "democracy expert" from headquarters, landing in Ulaanbaatar or Rabat, jet-lagged and missing my family, equipped with only my memorized eleven-part definition of liberal democracy by Larry Diamond (the leading scholar of comparative democratic development in the third wave), and expected to supply the mission with a comprehensive analysis of the country's dysfunctional political economy and a practical program of assistance—all within a few weeks![16]

In sum, where Carothers sees a nasty five-headed hydra blocking the path to democracy promotion enlightenment, I have seen—and continue to see—a still relatively new field of development assistance without anything but the most basic understandings of democracy and democratization to guide it.

In this chapter, I take stock of USAID's democracy strategies in poorly performing states from the perspective of a former insider. By democracy strategy, I specifically mean the section on democratic governance contained in the multiyear country strategies that each USAID field mission is required to submit and that USAID's headquarters, in cooperation with other U.S. foreign affairs agencies, is required to approve.[17] Thus the scope of this chapter is not as broad as that of Carothers's critique, for he believes that all democracy promotion organizations—bilateral and multilateral donor agencies as well as all of the nongovernmental implementing partners of these agencies—uniformly suffer from the misconceptions of the transition paradigm and the resulting mishmash of aid programs.[18]

Given the severity of Carothers's thesis ("much of the democracy aid based on this paradigm is exhausted"), I believe that it is important for the democracy promotion community to engage his argument in as detailed and fair a manner as possible.[19] Accordingly, in this chapter I evaluate the democracy strategies of only one organization (USAID), leaving it to others to assess the relevance of the transition paradigm to the host of other democracy promotion organizations in the governmental, intergovernmental, and nongovernmental sectors.

Like Carothers, I also believe in the fundamental importance of strategy. Many of my colleagues both within and outside the U.S. government argue that the USAID strategic plans are unimportant, perhaps even useless documents that have significance only within the foreign aid bureaucracy, wherein officials are required to justify their funding decisions using the cutting-edge but often misguided tools of contemporary management theory—including hyperrational "results frameworks" and hyperquantitative "indicators" of achievement.[20] Accordingly, my colleagues say, the real test of democracy promotion lies in the more concrete analyses, programs, and results of USAID's many implementing partners.

No doubt there is some truth to this argument: the activities of an implementing partner do bring to life the words contained in a donor's strategic plan. For that reason, an implementing partner might be in a position to remedy the flaws of USAID's strategic vagueness. However, it is nonetheless true that USAID's strategic plans identify the most critical development goals and the best methods by which the goals can be pursued. In turn, these goals and methods inform the "requests for proposals" that USAID issues to its prospective partners. To succeed, the partners must achieve the specific targets included in the strategy. Thus to a very large degree USAID strategies shape— and limit—the actions of an implementing partner, regardless of whether the partner is a nonprofit organization that has received a USAID "grant" or a for-profit consulting firm that has signed a USAID "contract." That is why the quality of democracy strategies of USAID and other donor agencies truly matters to the success or failure of the democracy promotion enterprise.

Again in the spirit of fairness and attention to detail, I attempt to measure the quality of USAID's democracy and governance strategies by using the agency's own tool for formulating such strategies as put forth in *Conducting a DG [Democracy and Governance] Assessment: A Framework for Strategy Development.*[21] I choose this document (hereafter referred to as the *DG Framework*) not only because of its general excellence but specifically because Carothers and his USAID interlocutors agree that it should be the starting point for USAID's strategic planning in the area of democratic governance.

Beneath the contentious debate about whether the transition paradigm truly exists, there has emerged an important agreement about which are the right analytical questions to ask in regard to the democratic deficits of poorly performing countries.[22] In USAID's formal response to Carothers's article, Gerald Hyman, the director of USAID's Office of Democracy and Governance, characterizes the five elements of the transition paradigm as "straw men" and points to the *DG Framework* (of which Hyman was the principal author) as prime evidence of USAID's serious approach to democratic governance. In replying to Hyman, Carothers calls the *DG Framework* "a sophisticated tool and a valuable advance"; yet, he observes, "it is only just starting to translate into significantly different programming." Carothers concludes: "In sum, Hyman and I share many views about how democracy aid can and should evolve. What we disagree about is how far along USAID is on that path."[23]

In seeking to chart progress on the path, I undertake this review as follows. I first introduce the main analytical questions posed by the *DG Framework*. Next I evaluate USAID democracy strategies from three poorly performing states (all of which have been mired in the gray zone): Haiti, Kenya, and Cambodia. Specifically, of each strategy I ask three questions:

—To what degree does the analysis address the fundamental questions posed in the *DG Framework*?

—To what degree is the program informed by such a comprehensive analysis?

—To what degree do the results of the program contribute to a solving of the basic problems of democracy (again as outlined by the *DG Framework*)?

For the democracy strategies in each case study, I find three fundamental flaws (corresponding to the three questions above):

—An unacceptably short formal analysis that barely scratches the surface of the complex analytical agenda recommended by the *DG Framework*.

—A proposed aid program that consequently lacks clarity, purpose, and verisimilitude.

—Limited programmatic results that reflect a conceptually shallow approach to democracy promotion.

In short, the documents suffer from a persisting poverty of strategic analysis and the programmatic consequences thereof. In the concluding section, I argue that the analytical poverty, programmatic vagueness, and slight results can be remedied only through a comprehensive reform of USAID's strategic planning process for democracy aid.

Introducing USAID's *Democratic Governance Framework*

The *DG Framework* defines a strategy as "an objective or set of objectives along with a general plan for the deployment of resources to achieve those objectives." Therefore, it notes, a strategy is "neither an analysis by itself nor a program by itself" but "the relation between the two."[24] The *DG Framework* lays out three main steps in the formulation of a democracy strategy: diagnosing the country's problems, identifying the country's key actors, and examining the country's political arenas.

The first step diagnoses the country's primary problems for the transition to or consolidation of democracy. In particular, it inquires into the state of five basic elements of democracy:

—Consensus: Is there a consensus about the fundamental rules of politics?

—Rule of law: Is politics governed by a rule of law?

—Competition: Is there competition in the political system (including in elections, ideas, the media, civil society, the economy, and between branches and levels of government)?

—Inclusion: Are parts of the population formally excluded from political, economic, or social participation? Is political participation high or low?

—Good governance: Is there the capacity for good governance (including transparency, accountability, and efficiency) by the state as well as by social institutions generally?[25]

According to the *DG Framework*, these five factors "define the structural basis for democracy." It states: "No country ever completely resolves the many, sometimes conflicting, elements within and between the five. . . . Nevertheless, at least minimum thresholds must be reached in each of the five in order to create the basis for a transition to, let alone the consolidation of, democracy."[26] The diagnosis thus begins not with a long, undiscriminating checklist of institutions belonging to the state and civil society but rather with an analysis of democratic processes that intersect and link a country's many governmental and nongovernmental institutions. It is the particular problems concerning these processes that collectively form the larger structural problems for a country's democratization.

Once these structural problems are diagnosed, the *DG Framework*'s second step analyzes the key actors involved in these political processes. Specifically, the strategic planners are asked to identify "the forces which support democratization, those that oppose it, and their respective interests, objectives, resources, strategies, and alliances." This analysis about the balance of political forces in the country should allow the strategic planners to determine which of the structural problems identified in the first step would benefit the most from the intervention of donors.[27]

The *DG Framework*'s third step examines the institutional arenas in which the prodemocratic actors identified in the second step are best positioned to address the structural problems identified in the first step. The *DG Framework* asks the strategic planners to analyze four broad arenas:

—The legal arena (including constitutional law, subsidiary substantive law, and the implementation of law through the judiciary).

—The competitive arena (including elections and the balance of power among branches of government).

—The governance arena (including the legislature, executive, and local government).

—The civil society arena (including its functions of aggregating interests, organizing itself within associations, and petitioning government).

While the *DG Framework* stresses that the analyst must understand how the rules governing each arena create incentives favoring or disfavoring democracy, it at the same time points out that the institutional arena is not itself the structural problem but merely the "organizational sphere" in which the problem can be addressed.[28] Again, this warning is clearly meant to steer USAID missions away from the pitfall of constructing strategies as long institutional checklists.

The remaining task would be to translate the results of this three-part strategic analysis into a concrete and focused program of democracy assistance.[29] The program's overall goal and supporting activities—or, "strategic objective" and "intermediate results," respectively, in USAID's planning lingo—would flow directly from the prior analysis.

Evaluating USAID's Democratic Governance Strategies

In this section, I evaluate the democracy strategies of USAID's missions in Haiti, Kenya, and Cambodia. I do so by judging whether the missions have analyzed the five key elements of democratic governance (including the problems, actors, and institutional arenas relevant to each element); whether the missions have based their program on this analysis; and whether the programmatic results (cited by the missions in their annual reports) have relevance to the five problems. At the end of each case study, I offer specific examples of how a fuller analysis (that is, one more in accord with the *DG Framework*) would produce a more sharply focused program and a more pertinent set of results.

As a preface to this discussion, I must point out the extreme shortness of the formal democracy analyses contained in the overall country strategies. Any description or explanation of the weakness of USAID's analysis of democratic problems must begin with this simple fact.

In spite of the central emphasis placed on democratic governance in each of the strategies (as is shown below), the democracy analyses represent only a small fraction of the space in all three documents. For Haiti, the main text of the document runs over 150 pages, but democracy analysis takes up less than 5 pages.[30] Of these 5 pages, a third are devoted to the presentation of a public opinion survey that the mission conducted as part of its strategic planning. While these data are useful, they do not constitute the mission's independent analysis of the problems. In the Kenya country strategy, the formal analysis of the democracy problem consists of just 2 pages in a document whose main text encompasses almost 180 pages. Moreover, over half of the second page is not part of the analysis per se but rather a preview of the program.[31] In the Cambodia mission's document, the democracy analysis fills the equivalent of just a single page in a document of 40 pages.[32]

To be fair to the missions, I should note that they supply some additional information regarding the state of political development in their countries in the introductory sections of the strategic plans. However, befitting an introduction, the missions present the information descriptively rather than analytically—and thus the additional material, which itself is brief, does not serve as either a substitute for or a supplement to the formal analytical sections. Simply put, the brevity of the analytical sections on democratic governance is astounding.

Haiti

The USAID strategy for Haiti discussed here covers the fiscal years 1999 to 2004. The strategy includes "strategic objectives" in five areas: economic growth, environment, health and family planning, education, and democratic governance. The overall goal of the strategy is "sustainable democracy with equitable economic growth."[33]

Submitted by the Port-au-Prince mission in early 1998, the strategy was formulated during the period in which the disputed parliamentary elections of April 1997 had resulted in a bitter political stalemate between President Andre Preval and his opponents over the appointment of a new prime minister. (A similar impasse between President Jean-Bertrand Aristide and the opposition party Democratic Convergence over the 2000 presidential and parliamentary elections resulted in a protracted crisis and ultimately in Aristide's resignation and exile in February 2004.) Thus the strategic plan is realistic about the huge challenges facing democratic governance in Haiti. "After more than 200 years of dictatorship and tyranny," the mission writes, "it is to be expected that the new state has not found its equilibrium in only its first four years of democracy." The mission envisions that the achievement of "sustainable democracy" will require "at least a generation," and it describes the level of democratic institutionalization in Haiti as "low to non-existent."[34]

Given that the mission's strategy predates the *DG Framework*'s publication by several years, the mission of course does not systematically use the concepts contained in the *DG Framework*. To facilitate a comparison of the strategies included in this study, I nevertheless evaluate the mission's democracy strategy in the context of the *DG Framework*.

CONSENSUS. The Haiti mission states that one of the major problems with Haiti's new democracy is "a lack of clear consensus on the rules of the game." As evidence of this problem, it cites the disagreements regarding the establishment of the Permanent Elections Council, the recent parliamentary elections, the lengths of terms in office, and the enabling legislation for the constitutionally mandated decentralization of authority.[35] It identifies these issues, but it provides no analysis of the nature of the problems or of the actors and institutional arenas involved in addressing the problems.

RULE OF LAW. The Haiti mission identifies "a lack of adherence to the rule of law" as another major problem. Specifically, it writes, "one of the most serious constraints to democracy in Haiti is the weakness of the judicial system." In explaining the problem, the mission points to the following aspects: lack of judges, low judicial salaries and status, political control of the judiciary by the executive, lack of lawyers for the poor, bad prison conditions, police misconduct, and outdated legal codes.[36] In this area, the mission provides a slightly more detailed picture of the problems, but it does not delve into the causes of the problems and it does not analyze the actors or arenas involved in current reform.

COMPETITION. Although the Haiti mission does not address competition directly, it does briefly discuss the weakness of various institutions that could provide competition within the political system. According to the mission, elections have not been free and fair, political parties "are not functioning to represent real interest groups or offer meaningful choices," the parliament is poorly organized and there is little interaction between the legislators and their constituents, local governments lack the funds to deliver basic services, and civil society "has yet to find its voice."[37] The mission does not expand its analysis beyond these assertions, and it does not discuss any reform initiatives regarding these problems.

INCLUSION. The Haiti mission states that another major problem is "a lack of political inclusion in which an overwhelming percentage of the population feel unrepresented and excluded from the political center." It cites as evidence the steep decline in voter turnout, from 70 percent in the 1990 presidential election to just 5 percent in the 1997 parliamentary election. The mission believes that the drop in participation is due to the lack of communication between governmental officials and their constituents and to the failure of local governments to provide services.[38] This is the extent of the mission's discussion in this area.

GOOD GOVERNANCE. The Haiti mission states that another of the major problems with Haiti's new democracy is "weak governance characterized by a lack of transparency, accountability and adherence to the rule of law."[39] But it does not provide any analysis beyond the issues discussed above.

SUMMARY OF HAITI'S DEMOCRATIC GOVERNANCE ELEMENTS. Overall, except perhaps for the rule-of-law area, the Haiti mission provides very little description or explanation of the democratic problems that Haiti faces. Given the paucity of analysis, it is not able to relate the five democratic elements to each other or to rank the problems in terms of their severity. Across all five areas, the mission provides no analysis of existing or potential reform initiatives.

DEMOCRACY PROGRAM. The Haiti mission states the strategic objective of its democracy program as "more genuinely inclusive democratic governance attained."[40] It proposes four areas of intervention: civil society, elections, governance, and rule of law.[41]

—Civil society: the mission says it will aid civil society organizations to conduct civic education, to influence public policy, and to monitor governmental institutions. It will support training to strengthen nongovermental organizations (NGOs) in terms of their management, advocacy, and knowledge of substantive issues. To simultaneously support its strategic objectives in nondemocracy sectors, the mission envisions targeting such issues as reproductive rights, property rights and economic growth, the environment, and the rule of law.

—Elections: the mission says it will support voter education, political parties, and electoral administration and monitoring. It will thus train civil society organizations to conduct education and monitoring, political parties to craft "genuine issue-oriented platforms that reflect views expressed by civil society," and electoral administrators to organize voter registration and polling.

—Governance: the mission says it will focus on the parliament and local governments. It will strengthen the ability of legislators to communicate with their constituents and respond to their needs. It will also aid the parliament in developing a research capacity. Regarding local government, the mission will train local officials in the areas of policy analysis, revenue administration, development planning, and community outreach. It will also support the completion of the legal infrastructure for decentralization.

—Rule of law: the mission says it will train judges, prosecutors, defense attorneys, and court clerks; support new case-tracking systems in model jurisdictions; and expand its existing support for legal aid to the poor. It will also work with civil society organizations to advocate for the establishment of sanctions for judicial misconduct and to monitor human rights abuses.

The glaring weakness of the mission's program is that it is not at all rooted in a specific analysis of Haiti's democratic problems. The program is at once comprehensive and superficial. Its premise seems to be that because all of Haiti's political institutions are weak, USAID should provide aid across the board. In sum, there is no real democracy strategy, just a collection of anecdotal analyses and cookie-cutter programs.

RESULTS. The prolonged political impasse arising from the flawed elections of 2000 forced the Haiti mission to alter its original program greatly. Most donor organizations ended or curtailed their assistance. From fiscal year 1999 to fiscal year 2002 USAID's budget for Haiti decreased by 60 percent. In the mission's view, the domination of the judiciary and the legislature by the executive increased and the human rights situation deteriorated. The mission cites "a growing culture of impunity and institutionalized lawlessness," yet it reports that the media and civil society persevere in the face of this repression.[42] Accordingly, the mission stopped its democracy aid to Haiti's central government (including the judiciary and the electoral administration) and focused its support on the independent media, civil society organizations, and political parties. Its revised goal was "to help Haitian society stand up to increasing authoritarianism and lawlessness and to demand greater accountability and better performance by the Haitian Government."[43]

In its annual reports of 2002 and 2003, the mission presented three major results from its pared-down democracy program.[44] First, the network of domestic electoral observers played the leading role in detecting and publicizing the fraud in the May 2000 election. Second, at the national level a coalition of civil society organizations emerged from this electoral observation network to demand that the fraud be addressed and, more generally, to check the government's move toward authoritarian rule. This movement also spawned a coalition of more than forty NGOs (spanning the commercial, legal, human rights, and media sectors) to advocate for greater judicial independence. Third, at the local level similar coalitions of NGOs successfully engaged with locally elected officials to design and implement community projects.

Overall, the lack of focus of the mission's original program was fortuitously remedied by Haiti's unfortunate political crisis. Indeed, the mission deserves much credit for the rapid revision of its democracy program in the face of an extremely tense environment. Yet even in its scaled-back program, the mission presents results whose impact on the structural problems of Haitian democracy is unclear. No doubt, the two postelection results cited by the mission—the emergence of a coalition of NGOs at the national level and the increased cooperation between NGOs and elected officials at the local level—are promising signs. But the mission would benefit from a deeper analysis of the democracy problems that it is attempting to address. This can be demonstrated by a closer look at the mission's efforts to support civil society and local governance.

In regard to its aid to the nationwide coalition of civil society organizations, the mission could have first arrived at a better understanding of the coalition's target. That is, it could have analyzed the specific ways in which the Aristide government tightened its authoritarian rule. For example, did it formally revise laws and regulations that governed the operations of the media, NGOs, and political parties? Or did it simply fail to enforce existing legal protections for these political actors? Furthermore, did the government increase its grip on economic resources both in the public and private sectors? Finally, did President Aristide politicize the use of the Haitian National Police (the creation of which, along with the dismantling of the armed forces, had earlier held great promise for democratization)?

Based on this deeper analysis, the mission could have then crafted a more targeted program. It could, for instance, have used such analysis to distinguish among the various roles being played by the media, NGOs, and political parties in checking President Aristide's monopolization of political and economic power. How were these three types of actors trying to preserve the dwindling political space in Haiti? What were the most important of the reforms they were pressing for? The mission mentions one specific example: the case of a new subcoalition advocating for judicial independence. But what reform program was this movement undertaking and how was it related to initiatives being carried out by reformist elements within the government?

Concerning the relationship between community-based NGOs and local elected officials, the mission could have made similar inquiries. It could have asked how, if at all, the increased cooperation served to remedy structural problems pertaining to local governance generally. Was local governance in Haiti part and parcel of the central government's authoritarian rule? If so, how? Specifically, how did the Aristide government control political and economic resources at the local level? And how could increased NGO-government cooperation at the local level have undermined this monopoly? Conversely, if Haiti's scheme of local governance was somehow insulated from the central government's control, how could the greater cooperation between NGOs and local officials widen this remove—or even create ripples of reform that might flow toward the national level?

Answers to these and other questions would have strengthened the mission's democracy program and have suggested more specific and more compelling indicators of structural political reform.

Kenya

During a decade of turbulent but productive political liberalization in Kenya, USAID was a key provider of aid for democratic governance by advocating political, legal, and constitutional reform. The USAID strategy for Kenya that covered the years 2001–05 expanded U.S. democracy aid to include governmental institutions. Submitted in November 2000 by the mission in Nairobi, the strategic plan contains "strategic objectives" in four areas: democratic governance, economic growth, population and health, and natural resource management.[45]

In his cover letter to the strategic plan, then U.S. ambassador Johnnie Carson notes that despite a long period of "economic decay" and "bad governance" in Kenya, "signs of new hope abound." He cites a vocal civil society, an increasingly independent legislature, and several new executive branch anticorruption measures as evidence of genuine change. "Now is the time," he writes, "to help Kenyan reformers prepare their country for a better future." In the preface to the strategy's section on democracy, the mission makes clear its view that democratic governance is the key to the entire country strategy. The guiding hypothesis of USAID's work during the first three decades after Kenya's independence in 1963, the mission states, was that "economic development is a prerequisite for democracy." Kenya's hard experience, it observes, had forced a revision of this hypothesis: "While economic growth can contribute to democratic governance, in the long run it is clearly insufficient and is itself dependent on broad popular participation and strong institutions of governance."[46]

Because the mission's strategic plan was submitted to USAID's headquarters in the same month that the headquarters issued its strategic framework for democratic governance, the mission presumably did not have the opportunity to use the new framework in the formulation of its democracy strategy. However, as with the Haiti strategy, I use the *DG Framework* as a means to measure the breadth and depth of the mission's analysis of Kenya's democratic problem.

The mission opens its analysis by stating that Kenyan politics was characterized by "personal rule rather than the rule of law." In the mission's view, Kenya's democratic problems all derived from this root problem.[47]

CONSENSUS. The mission identifies several basic problems of Kenyan politics that had yet to be resolved: "A lack of consensus [regarding these rules] is feeding the primacy of personal rule." Specifically, there was no consensus concerning how political power should be transferred, an issue that includes not only specific questions about elections (such as the registration of political parties, the size of voting districts, and the adjudication of electoral disputes) but also broader questions pertaining to "distributive justice" ("how should power be rotated among heterogeneous communities?"). There was also no consensus in regard to the legitimate roles of the executive, legislative, and judicial branches of government or to the separation of powers among them. Furthermore, Kenyan society lacked agreement regarding the relationship between the central government and local governments: "A serious disagreement over federalism or other forms of decentralized governance dates back to the independence era and to the independence constitution." Finally, the mission highlights the absence of consensus regarding the fundamental rights of individuals and the limits on governmental actions vis-à-vis individuals, civil society, and the private sector.[48]

The mission was right to identify these core issues pertaining to "consensus." However, the identification of the issues should be the starting point of the mission's analysis; instead, it was the end point. Except for a single paragraph in the overview of the entire strategy, the mission provides no analysis of the politics of constitutional reform in Kenya.[49] Who were the main advocates for constitutional reform in civil society, the parliament, and the executive branch? Who were the main opponents? What were the key substantive and procedural issues within the proreform and antireform camps? Given these issues, what types of alliance exist or were possible within each camp? What compromises were possible between the camps? How did ethnic group politics intersect with the politics of constitutional reform? In which institutional arenas (for example, civil society, parliament, the executive) could the agenda for constitutional reform have been most productively advanced? None of these basic questions are addressed.

RULE OF LAW. In the rule-of-law area, the Kenya mission devotes literally one sentence: "The selective use of law enforcement and the court system to serve the interests of the ruling political coalition results in the common citizen . . . having no confidence that public institutions will guarantee him or her justice." Earlier in the document, the mission, again using a single sentence, presents its view of the judiciary: "The judiciary is largely corrupt and inefficient." Obviously, it would be useful to know in detail about the means by which President Moi and his associates had corrupted the many parts of the legal system, the political actors pushing for legal reform, and the arenas in which such reform was being attempted.[50]

COMPETITION. The Kenya mission's analysis is equally clipped in this area. In its formal section devoted to analyzing the democratic problem, the mission mentions only one area of competition: elections. Even here, the brief discussion merely explains that past electoral manipulation by the Moi government had eroded faith in the integrity of the electoral system. There is no analysis beyond this general point, nor is there analysis of the other main areas of political competition. For example, although the strategy describes the relative freedom of the media and civil society, there is no explanation of how secure this freedom was (what is the legal structure governing the media and civil society?) and how this freedom related to the otherwise "personal rule" by which the mission characterizes Kenyan politics. Similarly, although the document refers to the system of political patronage in Kenya, there is no explanation of the structure of this system either at the national or local level, resulting in a blank analysis of the degree to which the Moi government controlled economic resources. The mission does assert that the government's "patronage base" was "shrinking," but it does not explain what opportunities for political reform might have arisen from this shrinkage. Finally, the key relationships between the parliament and the executive branch and between the central and local governments are not covered at all in the main analytical section.[51]

INCLUSION. The Kenya mission presents no analysis in the area of inclusion. Such an analysis would have been useful, given Freedom House's claims that "Kenya's politics have traditionally been divided along ethnic lines" and that "ethnically based tension continues."[52]

GOOD GOVERNANCE. The Kenya mission states that the corruption associated with personal rule resulted in a decline of the government's public services across the board: "Kenya's roads and other economic infrastructure have deteriorated, vaccination rates have fallen, schools have declined, and the time required to obtain licenses, permits, passports, and other government services has increased." It is in this area that the mission presents its fullest analysis, noting several anticorruption initiatives that were taken by the executive or the parliament since the mid-1990s. It cites as examples of reform the establishment of the Kenya Anti-Corruption Authority (which investigates corruption in the executive branch) and the parliament's Anti-Corruption Committee (which published a report naming officials involved in corruption and which drafted anticorruption legislation). The mission also identifies the government's initiatives to reform the civil service, to strengthen the Office of the Controller and Auditor General and the Office of the Attorney General, to disclose the assets of officials and to introduce conflict-of-interest rules and regulations for procurement.[53]

The review of the anticorruption initiatives is useful, but what is missing is a deeper analysis of the systemic corruption that the initiatives were attempting to address. What is also missing is the mission's analysis of the politics of these reforms and thus its assessment of which of these many anticorruption initiatives held the most promise for sustained progress. Finally, except for a brief comment that "civil society organizations generally mirror the pathologies of Kenyan society," the mission does not evaluate the capacity of civil society for governance.[54]

DEMOCRACY PROGRAM. Based on its diagnosis of "personal rule" as the root problem of democratic governance in Kenya, the mission prescribes a program whose overall objective was to diffuse the excessive power of the executive branch to the other branches of the central government, to local levels of government, and to civil society and the private sector. Accordingly, the mission formally states its "strategic objective" as the following: "Sustainable reforms and accountable governance strengthened to improve the balance of power among the institutions of governance." The achievement of this strategic objective, in the mission's view, requires two basic tasks: the creation of a social contract in the form of a new constitution and a set of other wide-ranging legal and political reforms; and governmental mechanisms that would hold the executive branch accountable for its actions in accordance with the new social contract.[55]

In regard to the first task, the mission assumes that a social contract will not be made without the continuing demand for one from civil society: "The need to support a viable, constructive, capable civil society in Kenya has been and remains the most critical element in the promotion of democracy." Hence the mission sought specifically to foster "civil-society organizations [that] effectively demand reforms and monitor government activities." In aiding civil society organizations (including the media), the mission was to help them in the areas of analysis and advocacy, management, conflict resolution, and engagement with governmental institutions (such as through hearings with parliamentary committees). Given that membership organizations wield more political clout, the mission was to focus on business associations, labor unions, religious organizations, and women's groups. Finally, because the mission believed that focusing on a handful of substantive areas would increase the impact of its civil society program, it would do so "in accordance with emerging political opportunities."[56]

The mission's second task in pursuing its strategic objective required that governmental institutions transform the demands of civil society for a new social contract into a practical reality and then hold the executive branch accountable to the new contract. In supporting this second task, the mission would aid governmental institutions "only when there is evidence that the foundations for and commitment to increasing independence are in place." The choice of institutions would be determined by the outcome of the constitutional reform process and the 2002 elections. At the time the strategy was drafted, the mission was considering the following as possible recipients of aid: parliament, the judiciary, local government, the Office of the Ombudsman, the Police Review Commission, the Office of the Attorney General, the Office of the Controller and Auditor General, and the Kenya Anti-Corruption Authority. For the selected institutions, the mission would support the establishment of their legal structure (the "enabling environment" for their independence), their knowledge of how their counterparts work in other countries, and their capacity to analyze issues and shape policy or legislation.[57]

The mission also included elections in its support for institutional mechanisms of accountability: "Regular elections are the ultimate expression of accountability." In the context of its strategy, the mission viewed elections as another means by which citizens can demand reforms and then hold the government accountable for implementing them. While the mission viewed the 1997 elections as a "major improvement" over those in 1992, it says that there was still "much room for improvement." In particular, the mission aimed to support improvement in the following areas: electoral laws and regulations, electoral administration, electoral monitoring, political parties, and voter education.[58]

In all three areas of its program—civil society, governmental institutions, and elections—the mission provides no details about the issues, actors, and institutional arenas that would constitute the focus of its work. The lack of specificity mirrors—and directly derives from—the lack of specificity of its analysis. As with the Haiti democracy strategy, the Kenya democracy strategy was merely a shell of a strategy.

RESULTS. In its 2002 and 2003 annual reports, the Kenya mission cites progress in three areas: parliament, civil society, and elections.

Two types of achievement are identified with the parliament. First, the parliament took unprecedented action to exercise oversight of the executive's annual budgets for the entire government. In 2001 it made six major amendments to the executive's proposed finance bill, whereas in the past the parliament's review of the proposed budget had been perfunctory. Second, the parliament produced more effective legislation. For example, it legislated reform in the sugar industry whereby farmers were given formal representation in the processing and marketing of their commodity.[59]

The strengthening of parliament was, according to the mission, in large measure due to the increased effectiveness of civil society. In 2002 Kenyan NGOs supported by USAID engaged parliament's budget committee on forty-four issues and successfully influenced the final budget on twenty-four of them. In addition, when the Kenyan courts ruled a key anticorruption law unconstitutional, USAID-supported NGOs established the Kenya Anti-Corruption Coalition, which includes representatives from parliament, the Office of the Attorney General, the private sector, and civil society. The coalition worked to formulate an anticorruption law that would enjoy broad political support and addressed the constitutional issues raised by the courts. Finally, in regard to the landmark elections of 2002, the mission asserts that there were improvements in the electoral laws and regulations, the electoral administration, and the monitoring by NGOs of election-related violence and intimidation.[60]

Although the mission does not elaborate on the results of its electoral programs, it no doubt provided invaluable support to that historic election. The evidence cited in support of its aid to legislators and NGOs regarding the annual budget bills is also potentially important. Yet the mission's very success—the effective budget advocacy of NGOs vis-à-vis the legislature—reveals at the same time the program's continuing lack of strategic focus. It is one thing to quantify an NGO success rate of 55 percent (twenty-four of forty-four), but what do these numbers really represent?

To be truly effective, a democracy strategy should aim to do more than merely make the legislature or civil society "more effective." The strategy should locate its aid efforts in the specific struggles for political, economic, and social reform in these societies. Beyond the citing of broad statistics, the mission would do better to develop a clear plan for bridging the gap between civil society and the government on especially promising issues of reform.

What are the forty-four issues in the mission's civil society portfolio? What do they add up to? What are the linkages between various political, economic, and social issues included in the basket of forty-four? And most important, how are these many issues related to the major currents of reform initiated by the government of President Kibaki? After all, in its strategy the mission claimed that its civil society program would focus on a few substantive areas "in accordance with emerging political opportunities." Where is the focus and what are the opportunities?

In sum, the mission's strategic plan as well as its annual reports portray an image of a donor casting many seeds to the wind in the hope that some will find fertile soil. In my view, the image that the mission should aspire to portray is of a donor that understands the theoretical linkages between political, economic, and social reform; that possesses an equally strong understanding of the current opportunities for reform in Kenya after the victory of the present leadership; and that can act on both this theoretical and practical knowledge. The mission could seek to bind together the various components of its democracy program and, moreover, to integrate that program with its support for related reforms in its economic and social programs. Simply put, the mission needs to multiply its single example of integrated success—its anticorruption work; multiply it if not by forty-four, then at least by five.

Cambodia

USAID has actively provided aid for democratic governance in Cambodia since the United Nations implemented the Paris Peace Accords of 1991. The USAID strategic plan for Cambodia that I reviewed covers the years 2002 to 2005.[61] It contains "strategic objectives" in three areas: democratic governance; population, health, and nutrition; and basic education.

In May 2002, the mission in Phnom Penh submitted the plan as an "interim" strategy. According to the mission, the reason for the interim status was that continuing U.S. congressional restrictions and Cambodia's "limited progress" in democratic governance prevented the formulation of a "full sustainable development strategy" at this time.[62] In July 1997, after Second Prime Minister Hun Sen ousted First Prime Minister Norodom Ranariddh in a violent coup, Congress banned direct U.S. assistance to Cambodia's central government. Subsequently, Congress made exceptions to this restriction in the areas of fighting drug trafficking and providing basic education.[63] Under this interim strategic plan, U.S. assistance for democratic governance therefore continues to be limited to Cambodian NGOs and local governments.

The overall strategy opens by stating that the U.S. national interest lies in making good on its investment in the 1991 peace agreement that ended decades of civil war. The main U.S. objectives in Cambodia, the mission states, are "democracy, good governance and continued improvement of human rights." In setting the context of the proposed aid program, the mission observes that there is "little sense of urgency" for political reform on the part of the Cambodian government. It also notes that most Cambodians and donors believe that "true change will only come over the course of a generation." But the mission warns that a passive stance will backfire: "Waiting for genuine political change leaves Cambodia vulnerable to renewed conflict and a deterioration of the fragile progress that has been made in improving democratic practices." The mission's assumption, then, is that the United States must seek out and support opportunities to advance democratic governance in Cambodia. It concludes that although the Cambodian government places a low priority on democracy, "there are, however, significant short-term opportunities for helping Cambodians achieve reform" in this area.[64]

Because the strategy was written several years after the publication of the *DG Framework*, the mission (in contrast to the Haiti and Kenya strategies) explicitly uses the concepts of the framework in presenting its analysis of the democratic problem in Cambodia. The brief analytical section starts by explaining that "consensus" and "inclusion" are the "least problematic" of the five elements of democracy. The mission states that of the three remaining factors in the *DG Framework* (rule of law, competition, and governance), "serious problems" exist in all three.

CONSENSUS. The mission asserts that the legitimacy of Cambodia's statehood, borders, constitution, and form of government are not in question. But it notes that regarding the basic relationship between the state and individual citizens, the existing consensus is fraying as opposition political parties and civil society activists "vie for greater voice in national life."[65] The mission's observation on this point represents a significant qualification to its overall assertion regarding a national consensus and thus warrants much more analysis than is presented. For example, where does the current consensus about the relationship between the state and the individual—which presumably allows for considerable governmental curbs on individual liberty—lie? In the constitution? In an unwritten post-1991 consensus among political elites? In Cambodia's traditional political culture? In the still lingering psychological effects of Cambodia's tragic contemporary history? Elsewhere? Without answers to this fundamental question, the mission has not made a compelling case that a strong consensus about first principles truly underlies Cambodian politics.

RULE OF LAW. According to the mission, the "rule of law" is "severely lacking" because disputes are resolved on the basis of wealth and political power rather than on the basis of impartial justice. It also states that the "structural base for rule of law is incomplete" and that existing laws are "only rarely enforced."[66] Instead of presenting an in-depth explanation of how this dysfunctional legal system works, the mission merely makes this blunt assertion. Thus, for instance, there is no analysis of how the political and economic elites wield their power over police, judges, and prosecutors. Likewise, there is no analysis of whether the ruling party (the Cambodian People's Party, or CPP) is the sole perpetrator of this corruption or whether the other main political parties (the royalist United Front for an Independent, Neutral and Free Cambodia, or FUNCINPEC, and the reformist Sam Rainsy Party, or SRP) also participate in it.

COMPETITION. The mission views "competition" in Cambodian politics as being tightly controlled. It cites the use by the ruling party of intimidation, restrictions on press coverage, and procedural manipulation to have unfairly advantaged itself in recent elections. It observes that while Cambodian civil society grew in numbers and maturity in recent years, "even the most daring [NGOs] self-regulate their activities." The written media is relatively free, the mission says, but the readership of newspapers is located mostly in the cities. The mission states that the CPP dominates FUNCINPEC in the coalition government and that the SRP has very little influence on policy. It says that legislators are beholden to their political parties rather than their constituents, resulting in the lack of "meaningful discussion" in the National Assembly. Overall, it states that the executive branch controls the legislative and judicial branches of government.[67]

In these and other areas of competition, the mission again does not provide analyses but instead only makes blanket assertions. Moreover, on two critical areas of competition—the distribution of economic resources in society and the balance of power between the central government and local governments—the mission is virtually silent. Without an analysis of the former, the mission is unable to supply an explanation of the political economy of injustice to which it alludes in its discussion of the absence of rule of law above. Without an analysis of the latter, the mission cannot back up its subsequent claim (when presenting its proposed democracy program) that opportunities for local government reform have arisen in the wake of the first-ever commune elections held in 2002.

INCLUSION. The mission leaves much analytical ground uncovered in regard to inclusion. The strategy states that while discrimination against former members of the Khmer Rouge and members of ethnic minority groups (such as the Vietnamese) no doubt remains, the members of these groups are "by and large" considered to be Cambodian citizens and can accordingly exercise the rights of citizenship. However, this conclusion sidesteps one of the largest questions in Cambodian politics: How should Cambodia bring to justice former Khmer Rouge leaders who committed genocide and crimes against humanity? Until there is resolution of the issues concerning what type of tribunal to establish and what level of former Khmer Rouge officials to try, the basic problem of inclusion will not be resolved—if only because many of the current leaders of Cambodia were complicit in the past crimes.[68]

GOOD GOVERNANCE. About the element of good governance the mission simply states that, in this regard, "Cambodia also falls very short." It notes that the Cambodian government initiated an ambitious Governance Action Plan but that progress on the plan was slow and that the initiative stemmed more from "the need to appease donors" than from "a sincere desire to change."[69] Notwithstanding the congressional ban on direct U.S. aid to the central government, the mission's strategy would have benefited from an analysis of how, for instance, key Cambodian ministries failed in the areas of transparency, accountability, and efficiency. In addition, as recommended in the *DG Framework,* the mission could have usefully evaluated the general capacity of Cambodian civil society to supply good governance, especially given the failure of the government to provide services and the congressionally mandated reliance of the U.S. aid program on Cambodian NGOs.[70]

SUMMARY OF DEMOCRATIC GOVERNANCE ELEMENTS. After its brief evaluation of the five elements of democratic governance in Cambodia, the mission presents an even shorter analysis of the initiatives for political reform in these areas and of the opposition to such reform. Rather than presenting (as suggested by the *DG Framework*) a detailed analysis of the allies and opponents of reform and an analysis of the institutional arenas in which these actors vie, the mission simply restates its observation that the Cambodian political system is corrupt. "Given the rent-seeking opportunities available in government positions," it writes, "incumbents have strong financial and personal interests in maintaining power." Fundamental change is difficult, the mission concludes, because the current power holders are entrenched, because reformers fear that if they push too hard their lives would be endangered, and because after all it has been through in past decades, Cambodian society prefers peace over a renewal of conflict that a head-on challenge to entrenched power might provoke.[71]

DEMOCRACY PROGRAM. Of the three democratic problems that it characterizes as serious, the mission rules out programmatic interventions in rule of law and governance due to the absence of political will in the Cambodian government. Thus the mission is left with the issue of competition as its focus, and it defines its overall strategic objective in the area of democratic governance as "increased competition in Cambodian political life." Specifically, the mission's goal is to strengthen the competitiveness of the reformers: that is, "to increase the power of those groups within Cambodian society who seek equitable treatment for Cambodian citizens to compete for their demands." The mission sets out four main ways in which to pursue this overall goal. As with the Haiti and Kenya programs, the Cambodia program lacks verisimilitude, given the shallow analysis upon which it is based.[72]

First, the mission seeks to establish "political processes and parties that meet international standards" by aiding political parties, electoral monitors, and electoral administrators. Regarding political parties, the strategy states that the mission will offer help to build internal democratic procedures, to strengthen organizational capacity, to sharpen the focus of campaign platforms, and to foster new leaders (especially women). While the mission will follow USAID's standard nonpartisan practice of offering aid to all political parties, the strategy, given its goal of advancing reform, notes that "both FUNCINPEC and the SRP offer alternatives [to the CPP] that could help develop a broader basis for competition on political issues." Concerning the electoral process, the mission proposes to support Cambodian NGOs in their efforts to advocate for fairer electoral rules and institutions and to monitor local and national elections; and to support international NGOs in their efforts to monitor the entire electoral process from the preelection construction of the legal framework and registration of voters to the postelection adjudication of disputes and formation of the new government. The strategy includes the possibility of aid to national electoral authorities for organizing and administering the 2003 national elections, provided that "there is genuine reason to believe that the rules will meet democratic norms and authorities will be impartial."[73]

Second, the mission aims to increase "transparency and accountability on key economic and political issues." To accomplish this end, the mission will support the efforts of Cambodian think tanks to research significant areas of corruption, foster public debate based on this research, and advocate for specific governmental measures to address the corruption. The mission will target sectors in which corruption is known to be very high, such as customs, public procurement, and the judiciary. It will also provide support to Cambodian business associations to highlight the bribery and red tape faced by entrepreneurs that try to start and maintain a business. The mission stresses that its objective is "not simply to raise public awareness about corruption but to establish the basis for enforcement."[74]

Third, the mission will support the "focused monitoring and defense of human rights." In its previous democracy strategy, the mission focused its human rights activities on the provision of basic education and legal services. Now the mission will shift beyond "general awareness raising" to support for "cutting-edge cases" that could shape government policy. Regarding these cases, the mission will encourage indigenous NGOs to collaborate with international human rights NGOs in order both to obtain a degree of protection and to ensure the application of global norms. The mission targets the areas of women's rights (including sex trafficking, rape, and domestic violence), the rights of ethnic minorities (especially in regard to the titling of their land), and the rights of workers (particularly in the important industries of textiles, construction, hotels, and teaching).[75]

Fourth, the mission seeks the "engagement of newly elected local officials with central, provincial, and district level officials on key development issues." It notes that since the local elections in February 2002 the donor community has been paying much attention to the training of the newly elected "commune" officials. Because of this attention from other donors as well as "the unclear legal and policy environment in which these new officials will work," the mission instead will focus its efforts on organizing associations of local officials. Its premise is that through these new associations local officials would be able to lobby their central government counterparts at the national, provincial, and district levels for the laws, policies, and funds needed to make Cambodian decentralization a success.[76]

RESULTS. In its 2003 annual report, the Cambodia mission does not present any results of its democracy strategy, explaining that the reporting period (2002) was devoted to completing the previous strategy.[77] Therefore, given the absence of results to evaluate, I instead suggest here how the mission could increase the prospect for meaningful results by undertaking a fuller analysis in each of its four programmatic areas.

First, regarding political parties and the electoral process, the mission's proposed assistance is neither innovative nor unsound. The proposal represents the standard package of USAID support in this area. The problem with this first area of intervention is that the mission does not base its program in any analysis and thus it cannot flesh out the program in any meaningful way. For example, concerning the political parties, what are the prospects for the emergence of reformist factions within the CPP and FUNCINPEC? What prevents the SRP from becoming a more broad-based party of reform? In the area of electoral monitoring and administration, what changes are needed in the electoral laws or administrative procedures based on the experience of flawed national elections in 1993 and 1998 and flawed local elections in 2002? Is there an existing or prospective alliance of indigenous NGOs, political parties, or individual legislators pushing for such changes? None of these basic questions are either posed or answered.

Second, given that corruption lies at the heart of the mission's analysis of the democratic problem in Cambodia, the proposed assistance to foster transparency and accountability is right on target. However, the mission does not provide any assessment of the think tanks or business associations that might carry out the intended research and advocacy. Do such organizations exist? If so, are they sufficiently capable and independent to carry out this analytically difficult and politically dangerous function? Moreover, while the mission aims to "establish the basis for enforcement" of anticorruption measures, it paints a picture of a government that would not be receptive to such initiatives. For example, the mission cites the establishment of several anticorruption units in both the executive and legislative branches. But it concludes that none of them "are sufficiently independent from the government to provide effective oversight." If that is the case, what is the mission's strategy for linking the research and advocacy of the NGOs with reform initiatives in the government?

Third, as with the aid for anticorruption efforts, the weakness of the proposed support for human rights is the lack of analysis linking these projected high-profile legal cases with current reform efforts within the government. The mission makes a passing reference to the Ministry of Women's Affairs regarding women's rights and an equally brief reference to the "new land law" regarding the rights of ethnic minorities, but there is no indication of how the ministry in the one case and the new law in the other is evidence of genuine prospects for political reform in the respective areas.

Fourth, the proposed aid to local governance no doubt has merit. USAID has had success with organizing such local government associations in many countries. Yet without a detailed analysis of the political economy of local governance (especially in the wake of the 2002 election), this initiative bears an air of unreality. After all, the CPP won 1,600 of the 1,621 communes, thereby "keeping control of local security forces and resources in the hands of trusted [CPP] officials."[78] To be fair to the mission, the other political parties won many seats on the commune councils even though they are in the minority. However, given the size of the CPP victory (coupled with the "unclear legal and policy environment"), it is incumbent on the USAID mission to present a compelling case of why, under such political and economic circumstances, local officials (especially those representing the CPP) could be expected to challenge the CPP on issues pertaining to decentralization.[79] In essence, has decentralization in general, or the CPP's electoral victory in the local elections specifically, altered the basic contours of the CPP's political and economic dominance at the local level? If so, how? If not, why not? The mission provides no answers to these fundamental questions.

Recommending a Comprehensive Reform of Strategic Planning for Democracy Aid

Needless to say, USAID's implementing partners in the area of democratic governance do excellent work through their diverse training programs. These talented and committed partners, supported by USAID funds, help thousands of struggling democrats across the developing world. What is in question here—that is, the very question of strategy—is whether USAID, through its partners, is working on the most important democracy problems, with the most effective reformers, and in the most promising institutional arenas. Unfortunately, the limited answer provided by the three case studies above is not positive: USAID's democracy strategies for poorly performing states still suffer from shallow (or absent) analysis, vague programs, and scattered results. Lack of analysis is the root of the problem. If the analysis could be strengthened, then the programs and results would follow in turn. Without better analysis, the programs and results will continue to be diffuse.

Based on my experience of having reviewed tens of USAID democracy strategies during my service in government and having read many more since, I believe that these three case studies are representative of the overall state of USAID's strategic planning for democracy. Moreover, I believe that the problem of poor analysis is so serious that it can be remedied only through a comprehensive reform of USAID's strategic planning for democracy. I thereby recommend—in the spirit of "fives" (Carothers's five assumptions of the "transition paradigm" and Hyman's five elements of democratic governance)—the following five-step program for producing more effective strategic analysis in USAID's democracy assistance.

Step One: Acknowledging the Problem of Poor Analysis

USAID must acknowledge that the lack of analysis underlying its democracy strategies is simply unacceptable. The analytical weakness not only renders its programs vague and often unjustified but also tarnishes USAID's deserved reputation as a leading donor in the field of democratic governance. In defense of their strategic plans, USAID field missions often claim that the formal presentation of their analysis is so short because it is just a summary—indeed, some missions say, the strategic plans are intended to be public relations documents. The full analysis, they argue, resides in the many commissioned studies, including ones based on the *DG Framework* and conducted by USAID's Office of Democracy and Governance, which fill up drawers and drawers of their filing cabinets. For a simple reason, I do not find this argument compelling: the commissioned studies represent the views of private consultants or experts from headquarters; they do not yet constitute the views of the missions themselves. For such a transformation to take place, the missions must filter the studies through their own understanding of the country, only then arriving at a comprehensive analysis that is wholly owned by the mission itself.

Step Two: Refining the Democratic Governance Framework

The *DG Framework* is an excellent starting point for the formulation of democracy strategies. But in several ways the framework, as currently written, might unintentionally contribute to programmatic sprawl. The framework's first step—the assessment of the five elements of democracy—does not address the thorny question regarding prioritization among the problems. In many if not most poorly performing states, serious problems exist in all five of the elements. However, the framework confidently states that "the completion of [the first step of the] analysis and inventory should point to the primary, secondary, and tertiary problems."[80] Yet it is not at all clear from the *DG Framework* which of the five elements is inherently most critical to laying the foundation of democratic governance in poorly performing states.

Moreover, the *DG Framework's* third step—the analysis of institutional arenas wherein the struggles for reform on the identified problems are taking place—asks the analyst to undertake full-scale evaluations of all the country's governmental and nongovernmental political institutions. Such a task is not only impossible practically, it also undermines the more narrow conceptual focus of the third step, which is simply to place the identified reformers in their institutional context. The broader institutional analysis would more properly belong in the *DG Framework*'s first step. However, the authors of the document choose not to do so, probably because they want to conceive of basic democracy problems as thematic (that is, cutting across multiple institutions) rather than institutional (that is, specific to a single institution). But in pushing the analysis of institutions to the third step, the authors have not resolved the tension between thematic and institutional constructions of democratic governance problems; they have merely disguised the tension. Without a satisfactory theoretical resolution of this core issue, the analyses and programs of missions will continue to produce the institutional "check-lists" and "smorgasbords" that Carothers abhors.

To help it tackle these two vexing conceptual issues—prioritizing among multiple democratic problems and synthesizing the thematic and institutional approaches to the conceptualization of democratic problems—USAID could tap the best thinkers in the booming field of comparative democratic development (as evidenced, for example, in the impressive scholarship contained in the *Journal of Democracy* since its establishment in 1990).

Step Three: Adopting the DG Framework *as USAID Policy*

Currently, USAID's headquarters only recommends that missions use the *DG Framework* as the basis of their democracy strategies.[81] To demonstrate the utility of the *DG Framework,* the Office of Democracy and Governance should undertake a formal review of the "more than two dozen" countries in which the framework had already been applied by 2002.[82] This review could also contribute to step two above by clarifying which aspects of the framework might be in need of revision. After completing the review of the framework's prior use and the refinement of its rough edges, USAID should then require its field missions to use the document as the basis for all future democracy strategies. The adoption of such a requirement would ensure that USAID headquarters and field missions are using a shared conceptual framework and a common vocabulary across the democracy sector.

Step Four: Conducting the Strategic Analysis

In addition to refining various conceptual aspects of the *DG Framework,* USAID also needs to revise upward its estimates of the time and personnel needed for formulating a democracy strategy. According to its introduction, the framework was "designed to construct a DG strategy in three weeks by a team of three people—one of whom should know the country very well."[83] Practically speaking, there is no way that the *DG Framework*'s complex analytical agenda could be carried out in such a short time and by so few people. Indeed, missions regularly allot a full year or more to prepare a new country strategy.[84] However, they are not in the practice of conducting rigorous analytical assessments of the type presented in the *DG Framework*. To produce better analysis, the missions should combine their longer time frame with the framework's more serious analytical agenda. Moreover, the missions are overly dependent on external advisers (from either headquarters or consulting firms), who have very little knowledge of the country. Instead, the mission's resident democracy officer should take the lead on conducting the strategic analysis, tapping the expertise within the country and orchestrating a wide-ranging consultation that culminates at the year's end with the drafting of the strategy.

Step Five: Reviewing the Strategic Analysis in Headquarters

The mission should be required to submit not just a summary of its analysis but rather a full-length treatment that covers the entire agenda included in the *DG Framework*. Without such a written requirement, the review of the democracy strategies by USAID's headquarters will continue to be more or less rubber-stamp affairs, during which the missions pretend to have done serious analysis and headquarters officials pretend to seriously review the mission's phantom analysis. If USAID prefers to maintain its current practice of having brief sectoral chapters within its overall country strategies, then it should require the democracy sector to submit a separate document that would be reviewed in tandem with the overall strategy. To further ensure that the review is a serious exercise, the strategies should be approved not only by the relevant regional bureaus of USAID and the State Department but also by the relevant functional bureaus (USAID's Office of Democracy and Governance and the State Department's Bureau of Democracy, Human Rights, and Labor).

Conclusion

Although the field of democracy aid is still relatively new compared to the more traditional fields of international development, the newness of the field is not the only reason that USAID's analysis of democratic governance is so weak. Instead, the problem is a much larger, even systemic one: a strategic planning revolution that has run amok. With laudably good intentions, donor organizations in general and USAID in particular have sought to counter the perennial charges of bloated and wasteful foreign aid budgets by designing and implementing systems of "results-based management." While the theory of such management may be sound, its application to USAID's democracy sector has produced the exact opposite of what it intended: shallow rather than deep analysis, generic rather than tailored programs, and minute rather than overarching indicators of achievement.

How did USAID's strategic planning revolution get so derailed? A full answer to this question is beyond the scope of this chapter. Suffice it here to say that the story of USAID's management revolution is a variation of the age-old theme of good intentions producing unintended (and often ironic) consequences. From my perspective, the entire apparatus of "results frameworks," "strategic objectives," "intermediate results," and "quantitative indicators" has served to constrain rather than liberate the creativity of USAID's able corps of field officers not only in democratic governance but across all sectors of the agency's work. In its zeal, this revolution has driven out the old-fashioned strategic pillars of full-bodied analysis and expository narrative in favor of the newfangled claptrap of multidimensional diagrams and omnipresent numbers. Thus the analytical poverty of USAID's democratic governance work is not unique within the agency. Yet given its very newness and abiding spirit of innovation, the democracy sector has the potential for leading USAID out of its current strategic planning fog.

In conclusion, the big questions regarding the promotion of democratic governance in poorly performing states can be answered only by deeper and broader strategic analysis. Which of the five elements of democracy is key for a particular poor performer can be known only through better analysis of each of the elements and of the interrelationships among the five. In such cases, whether a donor should support government or civil society (or what types of civil society organizations) is also unknowable a priori. Ditto for the overarching strategic question of whether core U.S. interests would be better protected vis-à-vis a poor performer by supporting potentially destabilizing reform initiatives or by taking a more gradualist approach. "It all depends" is perhaps never a compelling thesis. In the case of the effectiveness of USAID's current and future democracy aid, however, knowing the details would make all the difference in the world.

Notes

1. Thomas Carothers, "The End of the Transition Paradigm," *Journal of Democracy* 13, no. 1 (2002): 9. The term "third wave" was coined by Samuel Huntington. See his *The Third Wave: Democratization in the Late Twentieth Century* (University of Oklahoma Press, 1991).

2. The term "gray zone" was coined by Carothers, "The End of the Transition Paradigm," p. 9.

3. For a discussion of U.S. democracy promotion policy during this period, see Madeleine Albright, *Madam Secretary* (New York: Miramax Books, 2003), pp. 442–47.

4. For the fullest exposition of this view, see Amartya Sen, *Development as Freedom* (New York: Anchor Books, 1999).

5. UNDP, *Human Development Report 2002: Deepening Democracy in a Fragmented World* (Oxford University Press, 2002), p. v. For a further discussion of the relationship between democratic governance and poverty reduction, see UNDP, *Human Development Report 2003: Millennium Development Goals: A Compact among Nations to End Human Poverty* (Oxford University Press, 2003), esp. chap. 7.

6. United Nations, "Millennium Declaration," UN doc. A/RES/55/2, September 18, 2000, pp. 2, 6.

7. United Nations, "Final Outcome of the International Conference on Financing for Development," UN doc. A/CONF.198, March 22, 2002.

8. Larry Diamond, "Promoting Democratic Governance," in *Foreign Aid in the National Interest* (Washington: USAID, 2003), p. 33. Also see Morton H. Halperin, Joseph T. Siegle, and Michael M. Weinstein, *The Democracy Advantage: How Democracies Promote Prosperity and Peace* (London: Routledge, 2004).

9. OECD/DAC, "International Development Statistics Online" (www.oecd.org/dataoecd/50/17/5037721.htm [June 2003]).

10. All of USAID's budget figures were provided by USAID's Office of Democracy and Governance upon my request. I would like to thank Shamila Chaudhary of that office for her assistance. For an explanation of the type of aid provided in each of the four subsectors, see USAID, *Democracy and Governance: A Conceptual Framework* (Washington: 1998).

11. Carothers, "The End of the Transition Paradigm," pp. 10, 18–19.

12. Marina Ottaway, *Democracy Challenged: The Rise of Semi-Authoritarianism* (Washington: Carnegie Endowment for International Peace, 2003), esp. chap. 7.

13. Hilton Root and Bruce Bueno de Mesquita, "The Political Roots of Poverty: The Economic Logic of Autocracy," *National Interest* (Summer 2002): 27–37.

14. Diamond, "Promoting Democratic Governance," pp. 45–47. For a review of comparative democratic development in the gray zone, see Larry Diamond, "Thinking about Hybrid Regimes," *Journal of Democracy* 13, no. 2 (2002): 21–25.

15. Carothers, "The End of the Transition Paradigm," pp. 6–9. Carothers provides only anecdotal and impressionistic evidence for the existence of the five assumptions, mostly citing in USAID's public-relations-type documents what are, in my view, merely examples of self-interested and inflated donor claims of democratic progress. See, for example, pp. 20–21, nn. 4, 13. But the citation of USAID's loose usages of the adjective "democratic" does not prove that such laxity necessarily stymies USAID's capacity to diagnose a country's "particular core syndrome" or prescribe remedies for it. Carothers implicitly acknowledges the lack of documentary evidence for his thesis. The transition paradigm, he writes, is "not something I just made up after a casual perusal of the USAID website" but rather it is based on his fifteen years of experience in this field, including hundreds of interviews with aid donors and recipients in every region of the world. See Thomas Carothers, "A Reply to My Critics," *Journal of Democracy* 13, no. 3 (2002): 37.

16. For Diamond's discussion of liberal democracy, see Larry Diamond, *Developing Democracy: Toward Consolidation* (Johns Hopkins University Press, 1999), pp. 10–12.

17. For USAID's requirements for the strategic plans of its missions, see USAID, "Functional Series 200—Programming Policy, ADS 201—Planning," October 11, 2001.

18. Carothers demonstrates his argument with the use of USAID documents "because they are the most readily available practitioners' statements of guidelines and political assessments." However, he believes that his analysis "applies equally well to most other democracy promotion organizations in the United States and abroad" ("The End of the Transition Paradigm," p. 20, n. 4).

19. Ibid., p. 18.

20. For Carothers's critique of USAID's methods for reporting results, see his seminal book, Thomas Carothers, *Aiding Democracy: The Learning Curve* (Washington: Carnegie Endowment for International Peace, 1999), chap. 10.

21. Center [now Office] for Democracy and Governance, *Conducting a DG Assessment: A Framework for Strategy Development* (Washington: USAID, 2000). Hereafter referred to as *DG Framework*.

22. For a debate between Carothers and several of his critics, see section entitled "Debating the Transition Paradigm," *Journal of Democracy* 13, no. 3 (2002): 5–38.

23. For USAID's formal response to Carothers, see Gerald Hyman, "Tilting at Straw Men," *Journal of Democracy* 13, no. 3 (2002), quotations on pp. 26, 30. For Carothers's reply to Hyman, see "A Reply to My Critics," p. 38.

24. *DG Framework*, pp. 8–9.

25. For a discussion of these five elements, see ibid., pp. 2–3, 13–30.

26. Ibid., pp. 29–30.

27. For a discussion of the second step, see ibid., pp. 3, 31–35. The quotation is taken from a summary in the document's appendix B.

28. For a discussion of the third step, see ibid., pp. 3–4, 37–51.

29. The *DG Framework* actually contains a fourth step in this strategic planning process. The purpose of this step is to identify the interests, constraints, and resources of the donors themselves. The issues to be considered here include U.S. foreign policy priorities; the availability of funding and staffing for the USAID mission; the mission's existing portfolio; USAID's comparative advantages as an agency; and the interests, skills, and resources of other donors (ibid., pp. 4, 53–55). (I do not cover this fourth step because of my focus on the donor's analysis of the recipient country's democratic problems.)

30. USAID/Haiti, *Strategic Plan for Haiti, Fiscal Years 1999–2004* (Washington: USAID, 1998), pp. 80–84.

31. USAID/Kenya, *Integrated Strategic Plan, 2001–2005* (Washington: USAID, 2000), pp. 39–40.

32. USAID/Cambodia, *Interim Strategic Plan, 2002–2005* (Washington: USAID, 2002), pp. 2–3.

33. For an overview of the country strategy, see USAID/Haiti, *Strategic Plan for Haiti*, pp. 2–7.

34. Quotations from ibid., pp. 81.

35. Ibid., pp. 82, 84.

36. Ibid., pp. 83–84.

37. Ibid., pp. 82–83.

38. Ibid., pp. 82–84.

39. Ibid., p. 84.

40. Ibid., p. 80.

41. Ibid., pp. 90–91.

42. USAID/Haiti, *FY 2002 Annual Report* (Washington: USAID, 2002), pp. 6, 12.

43. USAID/Haiti, *FY 2003 Annual Report* (Washington: USAID, 2003), pp. 3–4.

44. USAID/Haiti, *FY 2002 Annual Report,* annex on "selected performance measures"; USAID/Haiti, *FY 2003 Annual Report,* pp. 12–13.

45. For an overview of the country strategy, see USAID/Kenya, *Integrated Strategic Plan,* pp. v–vii. For a brief description of the democracy strategy, see p. 37.

46. Quotations from ibid., unnumbered page at the beginning of the document and p. 37.

47. Ibid., p. 39.

48. Ibid., p. 40.

49. Ibid., p. 11.

50. For quotations, see ibid., pp. 39, 13.

51. In the "overview" section, the mission briefly comments on these two relationships, noting that the creation of the Parliamentary Service Commission might result in the financial and administrative separation of the legislature from the executive, thereby increasing the parliament's independence. "Local government is an implementing arm of the executive branch," according to the mission, "rather than an autonomous authority responsive to local communities." For sources in this paragraph, see ibid., pp. 39, 10, 11, 13.

52. Freedom House, *Freedom in the World, 2003* (New York: Rowman and Littlefield), pp. 300–01.

53. This information is presented in the strategy's introductory overview section rather than in the section on democratic governance. USAID/Kenya, *Integrated Strategic Plan,* pp. 11–12. Earlier quotation from ibid., p. 39.

54. Ibid., p. 49.

55. See ibid., pp. 40, 45.

56. See ibid., pp. 49–52.

57. Ibid., pp. 45, 52.

58. Ibid., pp. 46, 53–54.

59. USAID/Kenya, *FY 2002 Annual Report* (Washington: USAID, 2002), p. 6.

60. Ibid.; USAID/Kenya, *FY 2003 Annual Report* (Washington: USAID, 2003), p. 6.

61. For an overview of the country strategy, see USAID/Cambodia, *Interim Strategic Plan,* pp. i–iii.

62. Ibid., pp. 1–2.

63. Ibid., p. 1. The USAID mission also was allowed to use global "notwithstanding authority" to provide assistance in the areas of HIV/AIDS (and other infectious diseases) and anticorruption.

64. Ibid., pp. 1–2, 16.

65. Ibid., p. 2.

66. Ibid., pp. 2–3.

67. Ibid., p. 3.

68. Ibid., p. 2. The mission does mention in one sentence (as part of its analysis of rule-of-law issues) the need for a tribunal. But it does not raise the implications concerning inclusion.

69. Ibid., p. 3.

70. See *DG Framework,* pp. 23–26.

71. USAID/Cambodia, *Interim Strategic Plan,* p. 3.

72. Quotations from ibid., pp. 16, 18. The mission actually offers a fifth "intermediate result"—the long-term training in the United States of future Cambodian governmental and NGO leaders (ibid., p. 23). Because of the measure's generality, I do not evaluate it here.

73. Ibid., pp. 5, 19. The mission does not address the issue of whether the U.S. Congress would need to revise its ban on assistance to the central government if aid is offered to the "electoral authorities." That is, it is unclear if the mission considers the electoral authorities part of the central government or independent from it.

74. Ibid., p. 20.

75. Ibid., pp. 21–22.

76. Ibid., p. 22.

77. USAID/Cambodia, *FY 2003 Annual Report* (Washington: USAID, 2003), p. 5.

78. Freedom House, *Freedom in the World, 2003,* pp. 123–24.

79. Quotation from USAID/Cambodia, *Interim Strategic Plan,* p. 22.

80. *DG Framework,* p. 30.

81. Hyman, "Tilting at Straw Men," p. 30.

82. For the "more than two dozen" quote, see ibid.

83. *DG Framework,* p. 10.

84. For instance, the Kenya mission submitted its finished strategy in November 2000, even though it had already held its first consultation on the strategy with its local implementing partners in February 1999. USAID/Kenya, *Integrated Strategic Plan,* p. 3.

13

U.S. Military and Police Assistance to Poorly Performing States

ADAM ISACSON AND NICOLE BALL

For the last fifty years—since the United States' emergence as a global superpower, the breakup of Europe's colonial empires, and the cold war's onset—it has been a central U.S. foreign policy objective to maintain close military relationships with virtually every nonenemy country in the world. Several programs managed and funded primarily by the U.S. State and Defense Departments carry out arms transfers, training and education, joint exercises, stationing of U.S. military personnel, and "engagement" efforts, ranging from academic conferences to exchanges of entire units. The reach of these programs is extensive; in 2002, for instance, the United States sold over US$12.9 billion worth of weapons to these countries and trained 42,169 of their military and police personnel.[1]

The following stated goals guide these programs:

—Protecting U.S. security interests such as counterterrorism; or preventing rogue states from gaining control of strategic areas.

—Protecting economic interests, particularly access to natural resources, open markets, and trade routes.

—Countering narcotics and international organized crime.

—Enhancing relationships with key military officers.

—Familiarizing U.S. forces with foreign terrain and cultures.

—Easing possible future coalition efforts by improving interoperability.

—Supporting postconflict rebuilding.

—Professionalizing security forces and improving human rights, democratic governance, and civil-military relations.

Despite these understandable, and in some cases noble, objectives, U.S. military and police assistance has been a controversial subject at least since the cold war. While militaries have a monopoly of legitimate violence in all states, many of the world's armed forces routinely employ this violence in ways that hinder achievement of the objectives listed above, particularly where state institutions are weak, impunity is widespread, and societies are divided. Lethal U.S. aid to military and police bodies that abuse human rights has been a source of much contention, and such aid remains widespread today despite decades of reform and legislation seeking to limit it. Some critics question the message sent by any U.S. engagement with notoriously abusive or corrupt security forces, even when the aid in question is nonlethal or focused on governance issues.

The impact of security assistance on civil-military relations and democracy remains controversial as well, particularly when U.S. assistance appears to neglect civilian governance needs or when it aims to increase the internal role of the armed forces. Other concerns surround the potential impact that a military aid buildup might have on security balances in unstable regions and the possibility that a strengthened military might someday cease to be a U.S. ally. Meanwhile, management and oversight of U.S. military and police cooperation programs—including the degree of diplomatic and legislative control over them within the U.S. government—is an increasing point of concern.

U.S. security assistance worldwide decreased somewhat in aggregate terms during the 1990s. The number of countries receiving assistance expanded, however, as the imperative of "engagement" with foreign militaries led Washington to initiate relatively small military aid programs in dozens of new countries. For instance, the number of countries participating in one of the principal military training programs, International Military Education and Training (IMET), grew from 97 in the 1988-93 period to 122 in 2002.[2] Much of this expansion benefited the militaries of countries that fit the criteria of poorly performing states as determined by various international groups: the United Nations Development Program, the World Bank, and Freedom House (see appendix table 13A-1 for the ranking on these criteria of the world's poorly performing states). U.S. assistance to police forces, which came to a near halt in the mid-1970s as human rights concerns placed strong restrictions in foreign aid law, crept steadily upward throughout the 1990s among poor performers and elsewhere. Counternarcotics programs account for much of the renewal of police assistance, as do efforts to assist security sector reforms in postconflict or democratizing states and programs to improve border controls and investigate terrorist activity.

To determine the nature of current U.S. security assistance to poorly performing states, the authors consider the forty-seven countries that meet at least four of five criteria (see appendix table 13A-2). Though inexact, this selection method gives a useful idea of the scale and scope of U.S. military and police assistance to poorly performing states.

Because of legislative or policy bans, fifteen of the forty-seven countries listed in table 13A-2 receive almost no military or police assistance. The remaining thirty-two countries fit into three categories: seven are priority countries for the post–September 11, 2001, war on terror; twelve other countries are of strategic importance to the United States; and thirteen are lower priority countries (see appendix table 13A-3). The nature of U.S. assistance varies widely among these three categories. The poorly performing states engaged in the war on terror receive the vast majority of military and police aid: 90 percent of assistance during the five-year period 2000–04. Much of this aid closely resembles the assistance that Washington provided to developing world allies at the height of the cold war. Peacekeeping, border security, and professionalization are the primary rationales for the provision of arms and training to strategically important countries. The relative trickle of aid to lower priority countries is geared toward interdicting narcotics; rebuilding the postconflict security sector; and strengthening democracy, human rights, and civil-military relations. All military aid programs share the underlying imperative of military-to-military engagement, however. Even the poor performers legally banned from receiving assistance through standard aid channels participate in conferences, seminars, and engagement programs.

Poorly Performing States and the War on Terror

Seven poorly performing states in the sample are at the forefront of Washington's anti-terror efforts (see table 13-1). All have overwhelmingly Islamic populations. Some are frontline states bordering Afghanistan and played a critical role in helping the United States and coalition partners stage Operation Enduring Freedom and subsequent efforts to root out terrorist groups in Afghanistan. Afghanistan itself received a large amount of assistance during this period (2000 to 2004), enough to make it the world's number-three recipient of U.S. military and police aid in 2004 (after Israel and Egypt). The

Table 13-1. *Expenditures, Military and Police Assistance,*
Seven War-on-Terror States, by Year, 2000–04

US$ thousand (except as noted)

State	2000	2001	2002	2003[a]	2004[a]	Total	Reason for classification as war-on terror state
Afghanistan	0	0	179,604	348,074	829,407	1,357,085	Rebuilding security forces after war to oust Taliban and bin Laden
Pakistan	4,651	3,900	395,340	257,617	121,104	782,611	Staging area for operations in Afghanistan and hunt for terror group leaders
Uzbekistan	2,879	4,116	41,746	11,775	13,648	74,164	Staging area for operations in Afghanistan, allows use of military base
Yemen	308	338	20,871	2,877	16,138	40,532	Collaborating in attacks against al Qaeda elements
Indonesia	110	131	20,655	542	4,697	26,135	Large Islamic population, 2002 Bali bombing attributed to al Qaeda
Tajikistan	473	384	11,600	731	1,720	14,908	Front-line state bordering Afghanistan
Djibouti	228	241	1,710	204	2,247	4,630	U.S. military base, headquarters for counterterror Combined Joint Task Force on Horn of Africa
Total[b]	8,649	9,110	671,526	621,820	988,961	2,300,066	

Source: See appendix 13B.

a. At the time of this study, 2003 figures were estimates and 2004 figures were estimated at 114.3 times the 2000 figures.

b. These seven states account for 90 percent of such expenditures in the 47-state sample.

aid was part of a multinational effort, led by the United States, to build a post-Taliban army, police force, and presidential protective service. In addition, the U.S. military contingent in Kabul continues to carry out joint military operations, alongside Afghan counterparts, against Taliban and al Qaeda remnants. Across the border between Afghanistan and Pakistan, the United States cooperates on antiterror operations with Pakistan's army, which has seen a sharp increase in the amount and sophistication of U.S. security assistance since the September 11 attacks.

Afghanistan and Pakistan account for 93 percent of all aid to the seven war on terror countries, but U.S. military and police aid to all poorly performing states on the list (see table 13A-1) began to multiply in 2002. Taken together, these countries were to receive 114 times as much assistance in 2004 as they did in 2000. While much of this remarkable increase owes to jumps in aid to Afghanistan and Pakistan, U.S. aid in 2004 to the other countries reached 10 times their 2000 levels.

Beyond helping recipient governments take on al Qaeda and other terrorist and Islamic extremist groups, U.S. military aid to the seven war on terror countries seeks to achieve several other policy goals. One is to maintain good military-to-military relations in several states that do not have a long history of friendly relations with the United States. Washington hopes to foster a climate in which the U.S. military can use bases, maintain overflight rights, and rely on the antiterror information of local intelligence services. Security assistance also seeks to help governments to improve their control over porous borders, with an eye toward restricting the transit of terror cells, illegal drugs, and weapons of mass destruction. This border control assistance includes control of maritime borders for those countries with coastlines. Afghanistan and Pakistan are also receiving assistance in their efforts to eradicate opium poppy.

U.S. government documents claim that an underlying purpose of aid to all of these states is to encourage human rights and pluralistic politics. In Tajikistan, for instance, the State Department's 2004 congressional presentation for foreign aid programs holds that IMET-funded military training would "expose the armed forces and civilian officials to Western concepts of democracy, rule of law, human rights, and free markets, with the goal of exposing the Tajik military to Western standards and doctrine."[3]

The war on terror countries received very little U.S. security assistance before the September 11 attacks. Nearly all aid since 2000 (US$2.28 billion of US$2.30 billion) was appropriated or requested since the U.S. government's fiscal year 2002 (October 2001–September 2002). Of that, the U.S. Congress approved nearly all of the funds through four emergency supplemental spending measures, signed into law after September 11, 2001.[4] In fact, on September 11 three of these seven countries were legally banned from receiving U.S. security assistance. Aid to Pakistan, other than counternarcotics programs, had already been frozen by Foreign Assistance Act prohibitions on aid to countries developing nuclear weapons and countries whose government reached power through a military coup. Concerns over the Taliban regime's human rights record and sponsorship of international terrorism had frozen aid to Afghanistan. Congress had prohibited most aid to Indonesia's security forces due to serious human rights concerns. (As of 2003, nearly all of Indonesia's aid still went only to the police.) The Bush administration waived these prohibitions in the weeks following the attacks on New York and Washington.

Though not banned, the remaining countries in the war on terror category received very little military and police aid before 2002. Military-to-military relations with former Soviet republics of Central Asia were cordial but distant; to institute greater cooperation with them was not deemed worth antagonizing Russia, though all have serious human rights concerns. After the Somalia debacle, the Clinton administration gave little priority to Djibouti and most other Horn of Africa states. Relations with Yemen were warming, but this Arabian Peninsula nation of few oil reserves was undergoing a difficult political transition during the late 1990s.

Grant Aid

Aid to the war on terror countries consists of weapons and equipment, especially mobility and communications equipment, necessary to carry out joint operations in Central Asia; training in counterterror techniques and border control, offered mostly by teams of U.S. Special Forces; and a great deal of intelligence and training in intelligence gathering and analysis. Some militaries in this category, particularly those of Central Asia, are so unestablished, unprofessional, or underequipped that U.S. funds pay for such basic items as food, uniforms, and even salaries. In Afghanistan, of course, U.S. funds support an effort, in concert with France and a few other countries, to establish an Afghan national army. Other security forces, including Pakistan's army and Indonesia's police, receive more sophisticated and high-priced items such as cargo planes, helicopters, and small boats. All receive vehicles, communications equipment, ammunition, spare parts, and similar items, as the United States seeks to build or upgrade their military infrastructure.

In Pakistan, for example, the State Department indicates that it sought "better security cooperation with Pakistan as a friend, ally and strategic coalition partner" through the transfer of C-130 cargo aircraft, Cobra and Huey helicopters, and communications equipment, including air-ground radios; in addition Pakistan received P-3C airborne surveillance aircraft fighter training, ground support equipment, and high-mobility transport vehicles.[5] Table 13-2 lists the principal U.S. aid programs providing assistance to these countries. The seven war on terror countries account for the vast majority of aid from the main programs used to grant weapons and equipment. The largest

Table 13-2. *Expenditures, Military and Police Aid Programs, Seven War on Terror States, by Program 2000–04*
US$ thousand (except as noted)

State	Total	Foreign military financing	Counter-narcotics and law enforce-ment	Afghan Freedom Support Act drawdowns	Peace-keeping	Nonprolifera-tion, counter-terrorism, demining, and related programs	Inter-national military education and training	Section 1004 Defense Depart-ment counter-narcotics	Unified Marshall Center European security	Command activities (includes JCETs)	Other
Afghanistan	1,357,085	664,256	258,097	300,000	23,949	110,084	600	0	0	0	99
Djibouti	4,630	3,600	0	0	0	0	868	0	0	51	111
Indonesia	26,135	0	4,000	0	8,000	12,000	1,405	0	0	246	484
Pakistan	782,611	375,000	163,877	0	220,000	16,100	3,144	2,700	0	0	1,791
Tajikistan	14,908	4,400	0	0	0	7,900	1,009	0	1,599	0	0
Uzbekistan	74,164	59,152	0	0	0	7,230	4,721	1,144	1,800	0	117
Yemen	40,532	37,041	0	0	0	440	2,461	0	0	142	448
Total	2,300,066	1,143,449	425,974	300,000	251,949	153,754	14,208	3,844	3,399	439	3,050
Percent of 47-state sample	90.0	89.0	98.2	100	87.7	95.2	32.1	29.1	39.0	6.0	n.a.

Source: See appendix 13B.

Table 13-3. *U.S.-Funded Trainees, Seven War on Terror States, by Year, 2000–03*

State	2000	2001	2002	2003[a]	Total
Uzbekistan	67	133	224	230	654
Pakistan	44	32	92	320	488
Yemen	101	75	151	106	433
Tajikistan	38	37	64	214	353
Afghanistan	0	0	0	142	142
Djibouti	6	9	42	81	138
Indonesia	6	9	47	74	136
Total[b]	262	295	620	1,167	2,344

Source: See appendix 13B.

a. At the time of this study, 2003 figures were estimated at 4.5 multiple of 2000 trainees.

b. These seven states account for 17.2 percent of such expenditures in the 47-state sample.

single source, Foreign Military Financing, is the primary military assistance program in U.S. foreign aid law. Used heavily during the cold war, this program declined during the 1990s; until the terror war revived it, the program overwhelmingly benefited only two countries, Israel and Egypt.

Training

Though the United States trained 4.5 times as many military and police personnel from the war on terror countries in 2003 as it did in 2000, military training figures for this category still appear relatively small, accounting for only 17 percent of all trainees in the forty-seven-country sample (see table 13-3). The low numbers are in part accounted for by the fact that much training does not appear in official reports to Congress; it takes place either through joint military operations (such as the U.S. Special Forces' activities with Afghan and Pakistani forces near the border of the two countries), which are not considered training activities, or through joint training exercises, which occur frequently but go unreported to Congress because, by law, the "primary purpose" of such activities is the training of U.S. personnel, not their counterparts.

Training figures also appear low because the United States lacks a historical relationship with the militaries of most of these countries; before U.S. personnel can teach dozens or hundreds of students a year, they must first understand the structure of the forces they are training, gain their willingness to cooperate, and overcome language barriers. U.S. forces have been developing this cultural competency, and training for war on terror countries is expected to increase.

Several countries, in particular Pakistan and Uzbekistan, receive training in combat skills. Another training program frequently used is that of policing, which is funded by the State Department and the Justice Department's International Criminal Investigation Training and Assistance Program (ICITAP). This program trains Pakistani border guards, for example, and instructs Indonesian police in "civil disturbance management" and community policing skills.[6] Established in the 1980s, ICITAP is the U.S. government's principal program for encouraging police reform and improvement of technical skills.

Most other training aid to the war on terror countries is education in nonlethal, nontechnical subjects: human rights, civil-military relations, defense resource management, international law, military justice, and U.S. doctrine. Such courses, referred to as Expanded IMET courses after the subset of the IMET program that often funds them, are available to nearly all poorly performing states; the United States offers them in an effort to encourage adoption of U.S. values and doctrine as well as to develop relationships with the students who take such courses, usually low- and mid-ranking officers climbing the ranks. Some training in these subjects takes place at regional security studies schools established by the Defense Department since the late 1990s. The Africa Center for Strategic Studies, Asia-Pacific Center for Security Studies, Center for Hemispheric Defense Studies, George C. Marshall European Center for Security Studies, and Near East–South Asia Center for Strategic Studies offer courses to military and civilian personnel in defense management topics, while fostering relations between U.S. personnel and regional leaders and among the leaders and officers of each region. Finally, nearly all seven war on terror countries receive extensive English language training, since instructors lack the capability to teach skills in most recipient countries' native languages.

The following lists the number of students from the seven war on terror countries and the courses these students enrolled in during 2000–02:[7]

—Department of Defense security studies: 557 students.
—Counternarcotics course: 285 students.
—Coast Guard course: 130 students.
—English language course: 124 students.
—Health care course: 55 students.
—Leadership course: 42 students.
—Maintenance: 30 students.

—Civil-military relations: 21 students.
—Officer training: 19 students.
—Joint combined exchange training: 10 students.

Poorly Performing States of Strategic Importance to the United States

The principal U.S. interest served by security aid to the twelve countries categorized as strategically important (see table 13-4) is to maintain governments friendly to the Unites States; these countries have something the United States wishes to protect, usually natural resources, geographic location, or a position of regional leadership.

Among countries in this category, U.S. State Department documents most frequently cite the following interests:

—A geographical location considered strategic: according to the State Department, for instance, Cameroon has a "strategic location and excellent airport facilities," Tanzania is "adjacent to the Great Lakes region and just south of the conflict-prone Horn of Africa," and Georgia lies "at the crossroads of Russia, Iran and Turkey."[8]

—Volatile borders: the State Department refers to "Azerbaijan's shared border with Iran and its long-standing conflict with Armenia" and Zambia's proximity to "ongoing conflict in one of its largest neighbors (the Democratic Republic of Congo) and political and economic instability in Zimbabwe," while warning that "Chad is vulnerable to its neighbors Libya and Sudan."[9]

—Significant natural resources: oil and gas are found in Azerbaijan, Chad, and Nigeria, and pipelines run through Azerbaijan, Georgia, and Cameroon. Niger is a significant source of uranium.

—Assistance in the war on terror: the State Department maintains that Georgia "has been a strong supporter in the war on terrorism, granting the United States overflight rights and potential basing permission." For its part, "the Eritrean military is ready to assist the counterterrorism effort and has offered use of its facilities for logistical and/or operational purposes." "Ethiopia is an African frontline state in the war on terrorism, supporting efforts to apprehend terrorists in Ethiopia and beyond," while "Kenyan support for the war on terrorism has been solid and wholehearted, a reflection of national values, and a recognition that Kenya has twice been a target of al Qaeda bombs."[10]

Although the security forces of some of these countries (particularly those of Kenya, Nigeria, Azerbaijan, and Georgia) receive counterterror assistance,

Table 13-4. *Expenditures, Military and Police Assistance,*
Twelve Strategically Important States, by Year, 2000–04
US$ thousand

State	2000	2001	2002	2003[a]	2004[a]	Total	Reason for classification as strategically important state
Georgia	6,239	5,754	32,900	8,572	11,994	65,459	Fossil fuels and pipelines, strategic location, support against insurgency, overflight, possible base use
Nigeria	10,539	10,676	$9,052	8,613	7,128	46,008	Size, regional influence, Islamic population, fossil fuels
Kenya	436	3,972	15,529	2,119	7,121	29,177	Strategic location, U.S. personnel allowed to use some facilities, 1998 al Qaeda bombing
Azerbaijan	1,399	1,338	9,826	6,098	5,277	23,938	Fossil fuels and pipelines, proximity to Iran and Iraq, overflight, possible base use
Ethiopia	159	14	2,717	1,025	1,087	5,002	Strategic location
Guinea	264	3,368	313	287	377	4,609	Wars in neighboring countries
Eritrea	41	166	617	919	968	2,711	Strategic location
Cameroon	805	492	467	362	516	2,642	Oil pipeline
Zambia	370	771	827	243	252	2,463	Borders with troubled Democratic Republic of Congo and Zimbabwe
Chad	396	348	329	447	170	1,690	Oil, pipeline, proximity to Libya and Sudan
Tanzania	181	222	355	248	256	1,262	Proximity to Great Lakes and Horn of Africa regions, 1998 al Qaeda bombing
Niger	14	116	182	159	228	699	Islamic population, uranium reserves
Total[b]	20,843	27,237	73,114	29,092	35,372	185,658	

Source: See appendix 13B.

a. At the time of this study, 2003 figures were estimates and 2004 figures were estimated at 1.7 times the 2000 figures.

b. These twelve states account for 7.3 percent of such expenditures in the 47-state sample.

these poor performers are not first-tier states in the war on terror. Only a modest amount of funding from Washington's 2002-04 supplemental antiterror appropriations found its way to this group. As a result, despite their strategic significance they account for only 7.3 percent of U.S. military grant and police aid among the forty-seven most poorly performing states. Security assistance to this group is growing, but nowhere near as rapidly as in the case of the seven war on terror countries. Aid for 2004 was about 70 percent over 2000 levels.

U.S. military aid to the strategically important countries seeks to achieve several policy goals. As with the war on terror group, the defense of land and maritime borders, including export controls, is a frequently invoked mission for aid. U.S. aid encourages internal security missions as well: State Department documents mention combating insurgencies as a purpose of aid to Georgia and Chad, while interdicting narcotics flows is a stated purpose of aid to Azerbaijan and Nigeria. Perhaps the principal expressed rationale for military and police aid to these countries, however, is peacekeeping. The State Department's 2004 foreign aid requests for Azerbaijan, Chad, Ethiopia, Kenya, Niger, Nigeria, Tanzania, and Zambia called for improving the recipient country's ability to participate in peacekeeping missions, whether under the auspices of the United Nations or regional arrangements such as the Economic Community of West African States' Military Observer Group and the U.S.-funded pan-Sahel border cooperation initiative.

Peacekeeping (the deployment of military personnel to observe, verify, or enforce a negotiated cessation of hostilities) is a frequent mission in Africa. The continent is the site of most of the world's armed conflicts; since the 1993 Somalia fiasco Washington has been reluctant to commit U.S. troops to these countries. Several African recipient states have played leading roles in regional peacekeeping efforts, particularly in West Africa, while Kenya and Tanzania have provided soldiers to many UN missions worldwide. Some countries in this group participated in the Africa Crisis Response Initiative (ACRI), a State Department–managed program of training and (until recently) equipment transfers designed to improve the ability of regional leaders to mount peacekeeping missions. The program, now an Africa region version of the State Department's Peacekeeping Operations (PKO), has been christened African Contingency Operations Training and Assistance (ACOTA) and has been scaled back significantly under the Bush administration.

A key subsidiary goal of peacekeeping assistance is interoperability, the ability of recipient country militaries to work with each other and with the

United States on joint operations. Interoperability requires that militaries have similar structures and training and use similar weapons and equipment. Interoperability not only is useful for peacekeeping but also prepares armies to fight alongside the United States, if that becomes necessary. It also benefits U.S. defense industries: for a country's military equipment to be interoperable with U.S. military equipment, it must buy this equipment from the United States. At the same time, the peacekeeping mission provides the United States with a politically palatable reason for maintaining close military ties with troubled yet strategic countries. It would be difficult otherwise to convince the U.S. Congress and the international community to give tens of millions of dollars annually to the militaries of poor, unstable states to guarantee access to oil reserves or trade routes. Transferring weapons and teaching lethal skills are less controversial, however, if the goal is to create a corps of blue-helmeted guarantors of human rights and regional stability.

Beyond peacekeeping, State Department documents also cite improving civil-military relations and human rights among their goals for this group of countries. Several of these states are haltingly transitioning from dictatorship to some form of more open rule, and U.S. education programs offer several courses in such topics as the role of the military in a democratic society, military law and discipline, and defense resource management (see table 13-5).

Grant Aid

Though on a smaller scale, weapons and equipment transfers to strategically important countries resemble those provided to the war on terror countries. Aircraft and technical equipment go to countries with larger or better-established militaries, such as Ethiopia, Kenya, Nigeria, and the two former Soviet states. Others receive more basic assistance, including uniforms, spare parts, vehicles, and communications equipment. U.S. documents mention improvements to military infrastructure in Azerbaijan, Georgia, and Kenya. The ICITAP police aid program is helping to establish forensics labs in the former Soviet countries and is promoting an ambitious overhaul of Nigeria's police.

Training

Training programs (chiefly for peacekeeping, civil-military topics, and technical courses) account for much of the assistance to the strategically important countries. Due largely to peacekeeping programs like ACRI and ACOTA, this group accounted for over 57 percent of military and police trainees in the forty-seven-country sample (see table 13-6).

Table 13-5. Expenditures, Military and Police Aid Programs, Twelve Strategically Important States, by Program, 2000–04
US$ thousand (except as noted)

State	Total	Foreign military financing	International military education and training	Nonproliferation, counterterrorism, demining, and related programs	International counternarcotics and law enforcement	Unified Command Activities (includes JCETs)	Marshall Center European Security	Africa Crisis Response Initiative	Africa Center for Security Studies	Students at U.S. service academies	Other
Azerbaijan	23,938	9,500	2,027	7,775	0	2,752	1,884	0	0	0	0
Cameroon	2,642	0	1,005	0	0	59	0	0	96	1,481	0
Chad	1,690	606	769	0	0	215	0	0	100	0	0
Eritrea	2,711	1,250	1,372	0	0	0	0	0	89	0	0
Ethiopia	5,002	3,250	1,667	0	0	0	0	0	85	0	0
Georgia	65,459	55,490	4,279	0	0	1,419	3,441	0	0	0	830
Guinea	4,609	3,000	1,299	0	0	177	0	0	133	0	0
Kenya	29,177	24,000	2,551	0	0	50	0	2,470	106	0	0
Niger	699	0	544	0	0	0	0	0	139	0	16
Nigeria	46,008	36,000	3,588	0	6,280	0	0	0	140	0	0
Tanzania	1,262	0	1,116	0	0	17	0	0	129	0	0
Zambia	2,463	500	957	0	0	872	0	0	134	0	0
Total	185,658	133,596	21,174	7,775	6,280	5,561	5,325	2,470	1,150	1,481	846
Percent of 47-state sample	7.3	10.4	47.8	4.8	1.4	75.9	61.0	59.2	36.6	78.0	

Source: See appendix 13B.

Table 13-6. *U.S.-Funded Trainees, Twelve Strategically Important States, by Year, 2000–03*

State	2000	2001	2002	2003[a]	Total
Kenya	114	1,419	144	177	1,854
Guinea	127	285	1,043	51	1,506
Georgia	416	468	310	219	1,413
Azerbaijan	84	150	167	416	817
Nigeria	126	79	219	161	585
Zambia	168	136	126	49	479
Chad	125	49	74	99	347
Niger	4	16	117	109	246
Cameroon	126	18	22	57	223
Eritrea	4	8	70	88	170
Tanzania	14	12	22	63	111
Ethiopia	4	4	10	34	52
Total[b]	1,312	2,644	2,324	1,523	7,803

Source: See appendix 13B.

a. At the time of this study, 2003 figures were estimated at 1.2 times of 2000 trainees.

b. These twelve states account for 57.2 percent of such expenditures in the 47-state sample.

This group also receives the sample's largest share of training from three other programs, one under State Department management and two under the guidance and budgetary authority of the Defense Department. The IMET program funded the training of approximately 2,980 military and police personnel from strategically important countries between 2000 and 2003. This program, created in 1976 and governed by U.S. foreign aid law under diplomatic supervision, is the principal source of State Department–managed grant training.

Programs established by the Defense Department during the 1990s provide further training without explicit State Department budgetary authority or policy guidance. Every country in this group participates in the Pentagon-run security studies centers described in this chapter's discussion of war on terror countries. Another 700 or more military and police personnel from strategically important countries trained with U.S. Special Forces between 2000 and 2002 under a Pentagon program called Joint Combined Exchange Training (JCET). Established in 1991, the JCET program carries out joint exercises in foreign countries covering a wide variety of military topics, from light infantry training to internal defense to mountain warfare; the program is largely secret (the Bush administration has classified the only Pentagon report that provides any significant information to Congress on JCETs) and has been controversial, as JCETs have taken place in countries banned from receiving military aid through standard foreign aid channels.

The courses most commonly offered to the strategically important group were

—Courses provided by the Africa Crisis Response Initiative: 1,300 students.

—International law courses: 736 students.

—Courses given at the Defense Department security studies centers: 721 students.

—Courses provided by the Joint Combined Exchange Training: 708 students.

—Port security courses provided by the U.S. Coast Guard: 447 students.

—Courses in finding and destroying land mines: 217 students.

—Courses in defense resource management: 145 students.

—Infantry courses: 118 students.

—English language courses: 114 students.

—Courses in security assistance management: 74 students.

—Courses in helicopter piloting and maintenance: 58 students.

—Command and general staff officer courses (leadership training for higher-ranking officers): 55 students.

—Special operations courses: 50 students.

—Health care courses: 26 students.

Poorly Performing States of Lower Priority to the United States

With no significant terror activity, few strategic resources, and little regional political clout, the thirteen remaining countries account for only a minuscule portion of U.S. security assistance: 2.4 percent of that provided to the forty-seven-country sample. U.S. economic and social assistance outlays to these countries are far greater, totaling an estimated US$599.3 million (or 90.6 percent of all of their aid) between 2000 and 2004.

Military and police aid to this group has not increased; in fact, aid in 2004 was only 60 percent that provided in 2000. The decrease owes largely to the winding down of the UN-led postconflict rebuilding effort in East Timor, to which the United States was a significant contributor. Students from these countries received little combat-related or other sophisticated equipment and almost no combat or technical training. In fact, three countries

Table 13-7. *Expenditures, Military and Police Assistance,*
Thirteen Lower Priority States, by Year, 2000–04
US$ thousand

State	2000	2001	2002	2003	2004[a]	Total
Timor-Leste	8,500	10,296	8,146	7,136	4,159	38,237
Haiti	5,143	2,977	2,342	2,323	2,432	15,217
Lao People's Dem. Rep.	384	559	261	238	268	1,711
Papua New Guinea	244	267	327	311	392	1,541
Sierra Leone	7	144	199	285	320	955
Central African Republic	110	124	195	133	176	738
Swaziland	119	189	123	112	154	697
Solomon Islands	75	104	180	186	84	629
Lesotho	100	87	157	118	151	613
Togo	14	65	230	138	154	601
Congo	14	94	187	132	133	560
Guinea-Bissau	36	69	100	112	124	441
Gambia	14	14	98	93	130	349
Total[b]	14,760	14,989	12,545	11,317	8,675	62,287

Source: See appendix 13B.
a. At the time of this study, 2004 figures were estimated at 0.6 times the 2000 figures.
b. These twelve states account for 2.4 percent of such expenditures in the 47-state sample.

(East Timor, Haiti, and Sierra Leone) either recovering from conflict or transitioning from dictatorship account for over 87 percent of the military and police assistance to this group. Aid for these purposes was transferred largely through State Department–managed accounts: FMF, PKO, and IMET. In all three countries, U.S. assistance contributed to efforts to reestablish security forces. In East Timor, U.S. contributions to a multilateral effort (the UN Mission of Support in East Timor) included largely nonlethal equipment and extensive training for the East Timor Police Service and the East Timor Defense Force.

Narcotics interdiction is a significant mission for aid to Haiti and Laos, as indicated by significant outlays of Defense Department counternarcotics funds for the former and State Department International Narcotics Control aid to the latter. In Haiti, U.S. funds helped to establish and maintain a Haitian coast guard, with a key purpose of limiting drug transshipments to the United States. In Laos, where most U.S. narcotics assistance seeks to offer economic alternatives to opium cultivation, modest amounts of narcotics funds also help to train and maintain police antidrug units.

Table 13-8. *Expenditures, Military and Police Aid Programs, Thirteen Lower Priority States, by Program, 2000–04*[a]

US$ thousand (unless otherwise noted)

State	Total	Peace-keeping operations	Section 1004 Defense Dept. counternarcotics	Foreign military financing	International military education and training	International counternarcotics and law enforcement	Africa Center for Security Studies	Asia-Pacific Center	Center for Hemispheric Defense Studies	Unified Command Activities (including JCETs)
Central African Republic	738	0	0	0	607	0	131	0	0	0
Congo	560	0	0	0	446	0	114	0	0	0
Gambia	349	0	0	0	198	0	151	0	0	0
Guinea-Bissau	441	0	0	0	321	0	120	0	0	0
Haiti	15,217	3,891	9,365	1,330	486	0	0	0	145	0
Lao People's Dem. Rep.	1,711	0	0	0	200	1,321	0	190	0	0
Lesotho	613	0	0	0	485	0	128	0	0	0
Papua New Guinea	1,541	0	0	0	1,083	0	0	458	0	0
Sierra Leone	955	0	0	0	857	0	98	0	0	0
Solomon Islands	629	0	0	0	461	0	0	168	0	0
Swaziland	697	0	0	0	522	0	93	0	0	82
Timor-Leste	38,237	31,103	0	6,796	293	0	0	45	0	0
Togo	601	0	0	96	360	0	145	0	0	0
Total	62,287	34,994	9,365	8,222	6,319	1,321	979	860	145	82
Percent of 47-state sample	2.4	12.2	70.9	0.6	14.3	0.3	31.1	38.4	90.1	1.1

Source: See appendix 13B.

a. At the time of this study, figures for 2003 and 2004 were estimates.

Table 13-9. *U.S.-Funded Trainees, Thirteen Lower Priority States,*
by Year, 2000–03

State	2000	2001	2002	2003[a]	Total
Lesotho	73	69	62	341	545
Haiti	189	7	8	186	390
Papua New Guinea	102	89	45	60	296
Swaziland	22	75	19	136	252
Sierra Leone	2	16	87	112	217
Congo	4	4	14	128	150
Togo	5	18	80	44	147
Solomon Islands	21	36	32	33	122
Gambia	4	6	8	94	112
Central African Republic	4	5	16	14	39
Guinea-Bissau	5	6	8	16	35
Lao People's Dem. Rep.	5	0	2	6	13
Timor-Leste	0	0	0	4	4
Total[b]	436	331	381	1,174	2,322

Source: See appendix 13B.

a. At the time of this study, figures for 2003 were estimated at 2.7 of 2000 figures.

b. These thirteen states account for 17 percent of total trainees in the 47-state sample.

Nearly all of the remainder of the security-related aid to this group is in the form of education in civil-military relations, human rights, and defense and security issues. The training, usually to a handful of students a year, is intended to ease transitions to democracy, to improve the military's democratic credentials, and to build relationships with key officers. Students at the Defense Department security studies centers account for a disproportionate share of total trainees from this category of countries. The following lists the courses and number of students taking the courses in 2000-02:

—Courses in military justice: 361 students.

—Coast Guard courses: 332 students.

—Courses in civil-military relations: 247 students.

—Courses in international law: 236 students.

—Courses at Defense Department security studies centers: 206 students.

—Defense resource management courses: 119 students.

—Boat maintenance courses: 60 students.

—Courses provided by the Joint Combined Exchange Training: 40 students.

—English language courses: 22 students.

—Health care courses: 14 students.

Poorly Performing States Banned from Receiving U.S. Aid

In fifteen of the listed poorly performing states, internal political conditions or relations with Washington are poor enough to have forced a cutoff in U.S. security assistance. The Foreign Assistance Act, which governs most U.S. military and police aid, bans security assistance to states that commit gross human rights violations against their citizens, that have a communist government, that are governed by the military after a coup, that detonate nuclear weapons, that support terrorism, that are in default on their debt, and that fail to meet drug war certification conditions. The U.S. president can waive these prohibitions if he determines that to do so is in the national security interest. (Some of the largest aid recipients in the forty-seven-country sample would still be on the list of banned countries had the war on terror not occurred.)

Several of the fifteen banned countries listed are not completely cut off from aid. The Defense Department's budget, which is outside the reach of the prohibitions in foreign aid law, can provide some forms of military and police aid: chiefly, counternarcotics aid, Special Forces JCET deployments, and education at Pentagon-run security studies schools. Significant amounts of security assistance were given to some banned countries between 2000 and 2004, either because the aid cutoff took place after 2000 or because Washington expected conditions to improve sufficiently to allow aid to resume flowing in 2004 (see tables 13-10 and 13-11). The tables indicate a sharp drop in assistance beginning in 2001, as bans to Côte d'Ivoire, Zimbabwe, Uganda, and Rwanda took hold. Estimates for 2003 and 2004 creep slightly upward, as State Department estimates forecast a possibility of renewing aid to some countries.

Training

After 2000 the number of U.S.-funded trainees from banned countries dropped sharply, although not to zero (see table 13-12): 136 students attended security studies schools funded through the Defense Department budget and 78 Cambodians participated in a 2002 Defense Department–funded training event that is listed, but not described, in the State and Defense Departments' annual Foreign Military Training Report to Congress.[11] Additionally, in 2003 inauguration of an ICITAP program in Uganda was inaugurated, supported by State Department narcotics funds, to improve the Uganda police force's criminal investigation capacities.

Table 13-10. *Expenditures, Military and Police Assistance,*
Fifteen Banned Countries, by Year, 2000–04
US$ thousand

State	2000	2001	2002	2003[a]	2004[a]	Total	Reason for classification
Côte d'Ivoire	1,736	13	51	86	29	1,915	Military coup
Zimbabwe	1,222	0	34	6	14	1,276	Human rights
Uganda	261	9	51	189	223	733	Human rights
Cambodia	0	0	328	200	202	730	Human rights, POW-MIAs
Rwanda	171	9	47	170	196	593	Involvement in neighbors' conflicts
Angola	14	10	66	118	127	335	Civil war; ban is gradually ending, and Angola provides 7% of U.S. oil imports
Congo, Dem. Rep. of	0	0	62	72	121	255	Civil war
Burundi	7	8	44	69	120	248	Civil war
Comoros	7	8	48	68	70	201	Military coup
Equatorial Guinea	7	0	0	63	55	125	Human rights (US$5 billion in private U.S. oil sector investment in past five years)
Liberia	7	0	0	0	2	9	Civil war, contribution to regional instability, human rights
Myanmar	0	0	0	0	0	0	Human rights
North Korea	0	0	0	0	0	0	Human rights, communist, poor relations, nuclear proliferation
Somalia	0	0	0	0	0	0	Absence of central government
Sudan	0	0	0	0	0	0	Civil war, on list of terrorism-sponsoring states
Total[b]	3,432	57	731	1,041	1,158	6,419	

Source: See appendix 13B.

a. At the time of this study, 2003 figures were estimates and 2004 figures were 0.3 percent of 2000 figures.

b. These fifteen states account for 0.3 percent of such expenditures in the 47-state sample.

Table 13-11. *Expenditures, Military and Police Aid Programs, Fifteen Banned States, by Program, 2000–04*
US$ thousand (except as noted)

State	Total	International military education and training	Africa Crisis Response Initiative	Unified Command activities (includes JCETs)	Africa Center for Security Studies	Asia-Pacific Center
Angola	335	200	0	0	135	0
Burundi	248	150	0	0	98	0
Cambodia	730	400	0	319	0	11
Comoros	201	100	0	0	101	0
Congo, Dem. Rep. of	255	150	0	0	105	0
Côte d'Ivoire	1,915	72	1,700	0	143	0
Equatorial Guinea	125	100	0	0	25	0
Liberia	9	0	0	0	9	0
Myanmar	0	0	0	0	0	0
North Korea	0	0	0	0	0	0
Rwanda	593	489	0	0	104	0
Somalia	0	0	0	0	0	0
Sudan	0	0	0	0	0	0
Uganda	733	617	0	0	116	0
Zimbabwe	1,276	286	0	922	68	0
Total	6,419	2,564	1,700	1,241	903	11
Share of 47-country sample	0.3	5.8	40.8	16.9	28.7	0.5

Source: See appendix 13B.

Table 13-12. *U.S.-Funded Trainees, Fifteen Banned States, by Year, 2000–03*

State	2000	2001	2002	2003[a]	Total
Côte d'Ivoire	748	7	7	7	769
Uganda	24	3	7	49	83
Cambodia	0	0	79	2	81
Zimbabwe	73	0	2	2	77
Rwanda	10	2	5	46	63
Angola	4	2	6	41	53
Burundi	3	2	5	8	18
Congo, Dem. Rep. of	0	0	8	8	16
Comoros	1	3	6	4	14
Equatorial Guinea	1	0	0	3	4
Liberia	2	0	0	0	2
Myanmar	0	0	0	0	0
North Korea	0	0	0	0	0
Somalia	0	0	0	0	0
Sudan	0	0	0	0	0
Total[b]	866	19	125	170	1,180

Likely 2003 trainees, as a multiple of 2000 trainees: 0.2   (8.6% of 47-country sample)

Source: See appendix 13B.
a. At the time of this study, 2003 figures were 0.2 times the 2000 figures.
b. These fifteen states account for 8.6 percent of such expenditures in the 47-state sample.

Major Issues Raised by U.S. Security Assistance to Poorly Performing States

This overview of U.S. security assistance to poorly performing states raises several policy-relevant concerns.

—The focus on security bodies (the armed forces, the intelligence services, paramilitary forces, and the police) rather than on assistance designed to strengthen democratic accountability and the capacity to provide security for all.

—The tendency to encourage internal military roles.

—The focus on short-term U.S. interests rather than on the long-term stability and security of both aid recipients and the United States.

—The impact of U.S. assistance on regional security.

—The relatively low levels of security assistance available to most poorly performing states.

—The growing role of the U.S. Defense Department and the U.S. military in determining security assistance policies and the need for transparency and oversight of military and police aid programs.

While these concerns are not relevant to all poor performers in the same way, each of these factors does carry important consequences for U.S. policymakers.

Security Bodies

The characteristics of democratically governed bodies capable of providing security for the state and its population are outlined below. For all countries, including the United States, achieving these objectives is a work in progress. U.S. assistance rarely addresses the serious constraints that poor performers face in this regard.

—Professional security forces: professionalization encompasses doctrinal development, skill development, rule orientation, internal democratization, technical modernization, accountability, and the rule of law.

—Capable and responsible civil authorities: the relevant civil authorities in the executive and legislative branches of government have the capacity to develop security policy and to manage and oversee the security sector. They carry out these activities in a responsible manner.

—High priority for human rights protection: both civilians and members of the security forces respect human rights.

—A capable and responsible civil society: civil society has the capacity to monitor the security sector, promote change, and provide input to government on security matters. It conducts these activities in a responsible manner.

—Transparency: although it is legitimate to keep some information about the security sector confidential, basic information about security policies, planning, and resourcing is accessible both to the civil authorities and to members of the public.

—Regional approaches: countries and their populations benefit from regional approaches to shared problems.

In poorly performing states, members of security bodies typically enjoy some degree of political and economic impunity.[12] The security bodies play a direct or indirect role in politics, complicating the ability of reform-minded civilians to introduce or strengthen the rule of law or democratic practice. This political dominance enables security forces to play a considerable economic role as well. Police and military forces have a substantial advantage in competing for a share of state resources, and many are engaged in a wide range of economic activities, including trafficking in drugs and weapons and exploiting natural resources.[13] Security bodies that are heavily engaged in economic and political activities tend to be professionally weak and to prioritize regime security above the security of the state and the population.

Rather than seeking to improve the accountability of security bodies or their capacity to provide appropriate security, civilian political elites are often allied with security elites in many poor performers governed by repressive regimes. Additionally, since civilians do not have much experience in the security arena, even those who would seek greater accountability for security bodies are unable to exercise it.[14] Civil society is frequently quite weak, without much influence in the security sector. All of this perpetuates poor governance and inadequate security for the state and its population, which in turn perpetuates poor development outcomes.

Neither U.S. development assistance nor U.S. security assistance is likely to reverse this crisis of governance in poorly performing states, since neither has as a main objective greater democratic accountability of the security sector. Although there is some recognition within both the Department of Defense and USAID that unaccountable armed forces constitute a major threat to emerging democracies, neither organization is equipped to address the problem effectively and neither is committed to developing the capacity necessary to do so. The memorandum of understanding between the two departments in the late 1990s (see note 14) was limited to the State Department–guided, Defense Department–administered, expanded IMET program (a relatively small source of aid though a significant funder of training programs) and USAID's small civilian-military relations program. Excluded from this arrangement are other training and arms transfer programs,

Defense Department regional security studies schools, counternarcotics and peacekeeping programs, and JCET deployments, among others.

A good deal of U.S. security assistance to poor performers takes the form of training and equipment transfers for security bodies, especially the armed forces. Very little is aimed at strengthening democratic civil control of security bodies, and even less is directed toward civil management and oversight authorities. These latter actors are, however, critical to the quality of governance in the security sector. Most assistance is instead oriented toward military or paramilitary type activities and intelligence. The security sector consists of

—Organizations legally authorized to use force: armed forces, police, paramilitary forces, gendarmeries, intelligence services (military and civilian), secret services, coast guards, border guards, customs authorities, civil defense forces, national guards, presidential guards, militias, and others.

—Security management and oversight bodies: president or prime minister, national security advisory bodies, legislature and legislative select committees, ministries (defense, internal affairs, foreign affairs), customary and traditional authorities, financial management bodies (finance ministries, budget offices, financial audit and planning units), and statutory civil society organizations (civilian review boards and public complaints commissions).

—Justice and law enforcement institutions: judiciary, justice ministries, prisons, criminal investigation and prosecution services, human rights commissions and ombudsmen, correctional services, and customary and traditional justice systems.

Two other groups influence the quality of security sector governance:

—Nonstatutory security forces: liberation armies, guerrilla armies, private bodyguards, private security companies, and political party militias.

—Nonstatutory civil society bodies: Professional organizations and research organizations.

The U.S Department of Defense does provide some assistance to help countries build more accountable ministries of defense, but this assistance has been available to a limited number of former Warsaw Treaty Organization countries and larger Latin American states. The courses offered by the Defense Department's regional security studies centers are designed for individuals rather than organizations or institutions.[15] While changing patterns of behavior and attitudes and building skills among senior-level security force personnel, legislators, and bureaucrats is important, organizational reform is also critical.

The United States has the capacity to support police reform, but this has not been a priority for most poorly performing states. The Department of Justice's ICITAP program is intended to develop the "capacity to provide professional law enforcement services based on democratic principles and respect for human rights."[16] ICITAP could be a useful police reform tool, if carried out with executive, legislative, and citizen oversight sufficient to avoid repeating the ugly human rights consequences of past police assistance programs, such as USAID's notorious Office of Public Safety during the 1960s and 1970s.

As the first part of this chapter indicates, however, ICITAP has provided very little assistance to poor performers. Of the trickle of aid that has flowed to the forty-seven poorly performing countries studied, most has sought to improve border controls, investigative techniques, and the capacity of police forces to undertake policing based on consent rather than repression. This is central to improving the ability of the police to provide security for all. However, little assistance has focused on strengthening civil oversight and management. In the absence of high-level commitment to the concept of democratic policing and adequate civil oversight, it is doubtful that efforts to train the police officers themselves will have their desired outcome.

ICITAP has provided assistance to seven countries of the forty-seven (Azerbaijan, East Timor, Georgia, Indonesia, Kenya, Pakistan, and Uzbekistan) and is launching programs in four others (Nigeria, Tajikistan, Tanzania, and Uganda). Though these recipients encompass all four categories of poorly performing countries, the size of the programs is small (roughly US$1 million a year for each country).

In Uzbekistan, ICITAP provided forensics aid "to reorient regional law enforcement agencies toward reliance on scientific and physical evidence versus confessions as the preferred means of resolving crimes." In Indonesia, it provided instruction on strengthening police command and control capabilities, on nonconfrontational critical incident tactics, and on improving police-community relations. It hopes to develop a broader program that would help the Indonesian police make the transition to a civilian police service committed to democratic principles.[17] ICITAP is far from the only U.S. agency engaging with the Indonesian police, but these other agencies primarily focus on counterterrorism.

Development assistance suffers from a similar lack of emphasis on democratic accountability over security. The main category of USAID funding that would be expected to support democratic civil control of the security sector—democracy and governance—has a number of shortcomings. To begin with, USAID provides only limited support for strengthening executive branches in general and cannot provide any assistance to ministries of interior or defense. While it does provide support to ministries of finance, that assistance does not seek to increase their political weight vis-à-vis "power" centers, such as the ministries of defense and internal affairs and the security forces themselves. Thus ministries crucial to the democratic management of security policy do not receive USAID assistance.

USAID does provide more extensive support to oversight bodies, particularly the legislature and the judiciary. USAID also supports a range of other activities that help strengthen the rule of law, an important component of democratic governance. These include enhancing the capacity of civil society groups, including the media, political parties, and advocacy groups; strengthening the legal system; and promoting the protection of human rights. Most often, however, these activities are not directed toward the security sector. While generalized attention to oversight can help build a culture of and capacity for democratic accountability, it does not address the core problem of democratic unaccountability in the security sector, which characterizes most poor performers.

What is more, most development assistance to these countries, including those that receive the largest amount of security assistance, tends to support trade and commercial activities, basic health and education, and energy and natural resource development. Support for democracy and governance in general holds a lower priority for USAID than these other activities. USAID does give a small amount of money to work on civil-military relations.[18] A significant proportion has been channeled through the Security Sector Reform program of the National Democratic Institute, which has provided support to eight poor performers under this program: Angola, Cambodia, East Timor, Guinea, Indonesia, Lesotho, Niger, and Sierra Leone.[19]

The second major channel for USAID's civil-military relations work is the Office of Transition Initiatives (OTI) within USAID itself. OTI has pursued this work in both Indonesia and Nigeria. In Indonesia, OTI has partnered with local academics, NGOs, and international groups such as NDI and the Asia Foundation to address such critical issues as executive and legislative control over the armed forces, separation of the police from the military, the military's legal and institutional framework, and budget transparency. In September 2002, OTI funded a workshop on the issue of off-budget funding. Minister of Defense Juwono Sudarsono spoke to members of Parliament's Commission I, presenting data and material on his calculations that 70 percent of the expenditure of TNI (the Indonesian armed forces) is drawn from off-budget sources. Members of Parliament used the data to formulate questions to TNI's commander-in-chief General Endriartono Sutarto at a parliamentary hearing on September 17. This exchange was widely published by the media, with Endriartono acknowledging that TNI used off-budget funds to increase the welfare of its troops. He stopped short, however, of admitting that TNI relied heavily on extortion and illegal businesses to cover its organizational costs.[20]

Internal Military Roles

When the United States perceives a threat to its interests coming from a foreign state's own problems (anti-U.S. insurgencies, narcotics trafficking, weapons proliferators, terrorist cells), it usually does not respond with civilian police assistance programs like ICITAP. At least since the cold war, the United States has exhibited a pattern of turning to the militaries of these countries to confront the problems. U.S. officials either distrust the capacity of civilian bodies in these countries to deal with the problems or believe that developing country militaries are the only place to turn.

A classic example of this pattern is the drug war in Latin America, in which the United States has used diplomatic pressure and massive aid to encourage the region's militaries to take on an ambitious internal mission. Though the U.S. military has almost no counternarcotics role within U.S. borders, the commander of the U.S. Southern Command, General James Hill, argued in January 2003 that militarization is the only counterdrug option in the region.[21] In Chile, only the military has the assets to protect Chilean borders and land in northern Chile from drug trafficking. In Paraguay, only the military can counteract the continuous violations of Paraguayan airspace as drugs enter and exit the country. In Brazil, only the military can prevent the country's rivers from becoming highways for precursor chemicals and go-fast boats (the preferred boat of drug smugglers).

Though perhaps it promises a quicker outcome than efforts to improve police and the rule of law, militarization carries strong disadvantages. The purpose of a military in nearly every successful democracy is limited to defending against violent threats to the state. Unless organized as an opposition army, a nation's own citizens never meet this definition and thus should not be subject to military arrests, interrogations, roadblocks, surveillance, searches, and seizures. Because of the military's unique training, few democracies regularly call on them to play internal roles, from building roads to meting out justice, which civilians can easily perform.

Particularly in the war on terror countries, however, the United States is continuing to urge expanded military roles. This expansion not only increases the risk of human rights abuse but also increases the power, prestige, and impunity that militaries enjoy within their own states. This is especially damaging in weak or transitional democracies, where civilian rule is tenuous.

Short-Term U.S. Interests and U.S. Security

Before September 11, 2001, the present war on terror countries received very little in the way of U.S. support for their security sectors, but by 2003 they accounted for 94 percent of U.S. security assistance to poorly performing states and roughly one-third of security assistance worldwide, excluding Israel and Egypt. While protecting the United States against future terrorist activities may be a valid, short-term national security interest of the United States, the way in which it is being implemented may undermine U.S. security in the long term.

Weak States

If a major threat to U.S. security comes from terrorism harbored in, if not actually fostered by, weak states, U.S. security assistance policy is helping to make weak states weaker. All of the war on terror countries have extensive records of repression of civil and political liberties, human rights violations, and economic impunity on the part of civilian and security elites. The same is true of many other poor performers. Such states are extremely weak institutionally. In some cases, their governments are no more than personalized rule by authoritarian leaders backed by the security forces. Historically, governments that have focused on regime protection, that have consistently repressed political opposition, and that have engaged in serious violations of human rights are breeding grounds for internal instability and external adventurism. They are, to say the least, poor partners in the quest for security, either their own or that of the United States.

Turkmenistan, one of the United States' newest war on terror allies (though not a poor performer in the forty-seven-country sample) provides an important example. Saparmurad Niyazov, the last communist leader of the Soviet republic of Turkmenistan, has ruled this Central Asian nation since independence from the Soviet Union. A *Washington Post* article says that "the collapse of the Soviet Union did not lead, as many hoped, to democratic rule," and continues:

Early attempts by Turkmen intellectuals to establish some kind of political pluralism were short-lived. Proto-political parties such as Agzybirlik soon disappeared as political life became increasingly dominated by the former Communist Party leader, Saparmurat Niyazov. He outlawed political parties except for the Communists, renamed the Democratic Party of Turkmenistan (DPT), and established himself not just as the dominant political force, but as the embodiment of all things Turkmen. Taking on the title of Turkmenbashi (Head or Father of all Turkmens) the Great, his rule became increasingly bizarre during the 1990s, developing a cult of personality to rival those of Mao Zedong or Saddam Hussein.[22]

Not surprisingly, opposition to Niyazov has grown both within Turkmenistan and among Turkmen exiles. The state has been severely weakened and increasingly criminalized. The primary function of Turkmenistan's security bodies is to keep Niyazov in power. The rule of law is continually degraded. Under the pretext of what many believe was a staged assassination attempt against him on November 25, 2002, Niyazov changed the legal code to ensure that some of those accused of plotting against him will receive life in prison, if they survive to stand trial. Hundreds of Turkmen citizens have been arrested in connection with the assassination attempt: some are political opponents of the president, others are relatives of political opponents, still others are reportedly politically unaffiliated NGO activists.

The exile-based opposition to Niyazov has been seriously weakened by this change in the legal code as well as by internal divisions. But Niyazov will leave power at some point, and the political vacuum that he has created will inevitably produce what the International Crisis Group (ICG) terms "an unpredictable transition." What is more, there are signs that the security bodies are poised to play a direct political role. According to ICG, the main threats to the continuation of Niyazov's rule include the Presidential Guard, which is closely associated with Niyazov; the intelligence service (the KNB), which was severely purged in 2002; army officers, who are increasingly disinclined to support the regime; and finally, the people, who have begun to voice their opposition more publicly.[23] At the same time, Niyazov has accused Uzbekistan of supporting Turkmen exiles opposed to his rule, ratcheting up tension between two U.S. allies in the war on terror.

Uzbekistan, the third-largest security assistance recipient in the forty-seven-country sample, is an equally problematic ally.[24] Like his Turkmen

442 *Adam Isacson and Nicole Ball*

counterpart, Uzbek president Islam Karimov is essentially an unreconstructed Soviet leader. As in Turkmenistan, a central role of the security forces is to protect Karimov's position of power, often by engaging in serious, sustained human rights violations and religious persecution.[25] Similar assessments can be made for many other poor performers.

Some analysts believe that the United States has very little leverage over allies such as Turkmenistan and Uzbekistan and that the leverage it does have has been dissipated "by the desire to avoid regional opposition to its [Washington's] counterterrorism agenda."[26] The kind of assistance offered these countries is at best inappropriate and ineffective; at worst, it is counterproductive. During 2002, for example, much U.S. security assistance to Tajikistan went to a border security program seeking to prevent the spread of weapons of mass destruction and to interdict the trade in narcotics. However, as the State Department's annual *International Narcotics Control Strategy Report* indicates, "public speculation regarding trafficking involvement by government officials is rampant," and "the lavish lifestyles of some . . . do give some credence to corruption allegations."[27] Of course, this greatly reduces the likelihood that U.S. counternarcotics assistance will bear any results. The ICG believes that this will also undermine U.S. credibility in the region.

One of the clearest examples of how the U.S. focus on its short-term objectives can make a weak state weaker is Afghanistan. During the Taliban period, the power of the regional warlords was severely eroded. In order to minimize the number of U.S. casualties during the fighting in Afghanistan, the United States began to use some of the warlords' troops as proxy fighters in 2001 and to reward warlords who did not fight against coalition forces and the new government in Kabul. This has enabled warlords to rebuild their regional power bases and to threaten the authority of the central government.[28] Even when one part of the U.S. government (the Pentagon) decided to limit support for one or more warlords, another part of the U.S. government (the Central Intelligence Agency) continued to provide support to the same warlords in order to continue to carry out its own operations.

Proliferation of Weapons of Mass Destruction

If a major threat to U.S. security comes from rogue states with weapons of mass destruction capacity, the United States has to be concerned about two poorly performing states in particular.[29] One of these, Pakistan, was for many years a recipient of significant amounts of U.S. security assistance. This assistance was banned throughout the 1990s because U.S. legislation requires aid to be halted to countries that possess nuclear devices and whose governments come to power through a coup d'état. After September 11, 2001, Pakistan's overwhelming strategic importance in the effort to destroy al Qaeda and to remove the Taliban regime allowed the Bush administration to cite national security reasons for resuming U.S. security assistance.

The other state, North Korea, remains on the list of those banned from receiving U.S. security assistance, although Washington has shown periodic signs of reengaging with the North Korean government in an effort to prevent it from resuming its own nuclear weapons development program, to return it to the Nuclear Non-Proliferation Treaty regime, and to prevent it from becoming a source of nuclear technology for other states.

It appears that, rather than guaranteeing U.S. security, current security assistance risks becoming a zero-sum game, in which both the United States and its aid recipients become more insecure. In our view, U.S. security would be better served by an effort to enhance the quality of governance in the security sectors of key countries. This would help strengthen the states of strategically important countries, reducing the risk of generating or sustaining local or regional instability or providing havens for terrorist groups.

Regional Security

Some U.S. security assistance has the potential to enhance regional security, notably through peacekeeping training and support and through the regional security studies centers, which help foster dialogue among regional actors and provide a forum for discussing issues of common concern. Many participants in the seminars held by the Africa Center for Strategic Studies, for example, highlight the importance of bringing together Africans from across the continent to address issues of common concern. At the same time, the appropriateness of the U.S. peacekeeping model has sometimes been questioned, particularly in Africa. The same is true of the content of the courses and seminars offered by the regional security studies centers, which have been criticized for drawing too heavily on U.S. experience rather than attempting to identify or develop models more appropriate to the region.[30]

U.S. security assistance can also increase regional instability. First, disputes between states generally require political solutions reached through negotiation and accommodation rather than the use of force. By encouraging a role for the security bodies in addressing problems between states, U.S. security assistance can contribute to a tendency to use force to "resolve" disputes. Second, arms transfers can create the perception of regional imbalances, if not actual imbalances. This can encourage leaders in neighboring states to build up their arsenals as well. Arms races do not by themselves create conflict, but they do little to improve regional relations. The two nuclear powers in South Asia, India and Pakistan, came very close to war in 2002 over the disputed territory of Kashmir, for instance, raising the specter of a nuclear exchange.

Third, regional arms races can have extraregional effects, thereby helping to destabilize other objectives of U.S. assistance. For example, it was revealed in late 2002 that Pakistan was the source of a key element of North Korea's nuclear program. North Korea reportedly bartered missiles and missile technology for uranium enrichment technology. What is more, North Korea has sold missiles to Yemen, seemingly without U.S objections. As Jon Wolfsthal at the Carnegie Endowment observes, "These decisions demonstrate to the rest of the world that the U.S. war on terrorism—in which Pakistan and Yemen are key American allies—takes precedence over the fight against proliferation. As a result, states bent on acquiring weapons of mass destruction may be in a position to play this preference to their advantage, as has Pakistan."[31]

Fourth, by sending the message that security bodies are important interlocutors both domestically and between states, U.S. security assistance can undermine the civil authorities and the rule of law. While the civil authorities in many poor performers cannot be described as adherents to the democratic process, politically active security forces always complicate efforts to introduce more democratic forms of government. Countries in which the rule of law is routinely violated, either domestically or with neighboring states, are more likely to engage in activities that will destabilize the region.

Low Levels of Assistance

The attacks of September 11, 2001, ended the post–cold war decline in worldwide U.S. security-related assistance, a period during which very few countries beyond Israel and Egypt received more than US$10 million a year. Countries experiencing subsequent changes in the volume and content of their assistance include such poor performers as Pakistan, Afghanistan, and Uzbekistan. Nonetheless, for the most part, security assistance to poorly performing states has remained low. Twenty-nine of the forty-seven countries sampled received less than US$2 million in U.S. security assistance over a five-year period. U.S. economic and social assistance typically outstrips security assistance, even for most countries receiving the largest amounts of weapons and training (see appendix table 13A-2). Moreover, U.S. security assistance represents but a small portion of the resources available to the government in each of these countries. While such assistance is an important policy tool, the United States does not employ security assistance to the exclusion of other forms of engagement or assistance.

This raises the question of whether low levels of assistance will have much impact, either for good or ill. From the perspective of the U.S. government, providing even a small amount is a seemingly cost-effective method of enabling the United States to develop or maintain relations with security bodies in as many countries as possible. Since much security assistance going to the low-priority countries is for education through expanded IMET and the regional security studies centers, policymakers may argue that these resources will have a small, positive effect on civil-military relations in the world's poorest countries.

However well intentioned, even small amounts of assistance carry important risks when the recipients suffer from serious deficits of governance. Aid can confer legitimacy on corrupt or abusive security forces through the symbolic power of association or partnership with the United States. Small amounts of assistance can be enough to upset delicate civil-military balances or to prop up abusive regimes or institutions. A safe and secure environment for states and their populations is critical for sound governance, which in turn is a necessary condition for sustainable economic and political development and social well-being. If U.S. security assistance, even in small amounts, contributed to these goals, the argument of positive benefits might be tenable.

It is difficult to argue, though, that U.S. security assistance to poorly performing states is part of a concerted effort to strengthen the democratic accountability of police and military forces or to enhance their capacity to create a safe and secure environment for both the state and its population. As it is, neither U.S. development assistance nor U.S. security assistance is likely to provide sufficient support to improve democratic accountability or to provide safety and security.

Assistance Decisionmaking

"Long before September 11, the U.S. government had gown increasingly dependent on its military to carry out its foreign affairs," notes the journalist Dana Priest. "The military simply filled a vacuum left by an indecisive White House, an atrophied State Department, and a distracted Congress."[32] Foreign policy decisionmakers responsible for the "big picture," as well as legislative oversight personnel, largely abdicated the design of U.S. security assistance to those with the greatest zeal for militarization, such as regional military commands and hawkish members of Congress. Consistent losers in bureaucratic battles, if they choose to fight at all, are those charged with guaranteeing the full spectrum of U.S. interests in the region: the National Security Council, the State Department's regional bureaus, and moderates on the congressional foreign relations committees. The result is that U.S. assistance packages too often end up reflecting the concerns of agencies charged with preparing for even the most hypothetical threats to U.S. security.

Security assistance programs to poor performers show symptoms of this shift. During the cold war, nearly all U.S. military and police aid was funded through programs authorized by the Foreign Assistance Act of 1961, a law passed to rationalize military aid, to ensure that it is carried out in line with policy objectives, and to give civilians (more precisely, the State Department) the leading role in setting military aid policy. While such programs continue to provide the bulk of aid to poorly performing states, the first section of this chapter shows how the activity of programs managed by the Pentagon and funded through the defense budget have expanded.

Congressional and citizen oversight of Defense Department security assistance accounts has been difficult. While much of what these accounts pay for is classified, they are also tiny in comparison to the entire defense budget, which exceeds US$400 billion (foreign aid, by contrast, totaled about US$18 billion). Congressional oversight committees have surprisingly small staffs; the House Armed Services Committee, for instance, has a staff of forty-five people from both parties, including administrative staff, overseeing a US$400 billion annual budget, and is therefore unable to subject Defense Department counternarcotics activities to much scrutiny.[33] Even the little transparency that is available has been under assault from Secretary of Defense Donald Rumsfeld, who has placed a priority on reducing the number of annual reports the Pentagon must provide to Congress.[34]

Policy Recommendations

As the security priorities of the United States shift in the post-September 11 world, U.S. security assistance to poor performers is changing—and in many cases, expanding—quite rapidly. If it is to be effective, Washington's military and police assistance must address the crisis of governance afflicting the security sectors in recipient countries, not simply the short-term interests of counterterrorism, counternarcotics, geopolitics, or oil. In fact, these immediate interests will not be served if security assistance aggravates the political and social conditions that led many poor performers into their current crises.

This review of security assistance provides a number of lessons for policymakers focused on the capacity of police and military assistance in poorly performing states:

—Improve civilian governance of the security sector. Greatly increased resources must go toward improving civilian security and control institutions, training civilians in security planning and defense resource management, and improving access to information for legislators and civil society. The United States must also offer emphatic political support to local reformers working to increase civilian control and expertise, to end impunity, and to impose the rule of law.

—Recognize the great danger inherent in aiding the security forces that are abusive, corrupt, pose a likely threat to their neighbors, or are proliferating weapons. While the imperatives of the war on terror might force the United States into an uneasy partnership with such security forces, clear limits to cooperation (including legal restrictions on aid to security force units that commit gross human rights violations with impunity) must be strictly observed. The U.S. Congress and citizens' groups must be vigilant for indications that security assistance is strengthening leaders whose attacks on their own people and behavior toward neighbors indicate their potential to be future enemies of the United States.

—Articulate a long-term vision and encourage governments to work toward it. When hard-headed realism or security imperatives demand close cooperation, it must be clear that even when the United States has little leverage (when, for example, U.S. forces need to use an airfield or seal a border), U.S. engagement has its limits. The civilian and security elites of recipient countries must understand that the long-term security interests of the United States will be at risk if its aid is not linked to a full spectrum of economic, political, and social reforms. In cases like this, the United States may find its security assistance to be counterproductive and cut it off.

The United States is encouraging such reform to some extent in Uzbekistan. President Islam Karimov undoubtedly received a boost at home from the diplomatic attention, economic aid, and military partnership with the United States. Yet for the first time since Uzbekistan became independent, U.S. officials are also meeting regularly with a wide range of Uzbek officials and conveying strongly worded messages about the need for change. And there are signs of nascent political and economic reforms, albeit small, tentative ones.[35] Even when dealing with the states seen as most essential for the U.S. counterterror strategy, it is not in Washington's interest to simply write checks, ship weapons, and transfer lethal skills. Strong, sustained diplomatic and political engagement with recipient countries must directly link further aid and a closer relationship with clearly defined reform goals. Thus follow two more lessons:

—Assess objectively the real results that aid is achieving. Evaluations of aid programs must do more than cite process goals, like the number of students, the number of border patrols, or the frequency of engagement. Looking at intermediate achievements, and not at progress toward larger goals like security and democratic consolidation, is a product of bureaucratic inertia and the need to sustain agency budgets. A counterterror strategy should measurably reduce the ability of terror groups to operate; a counternarcotics strategy should reduce the availability of drugs on U.S. streets; and peacekeeping assistance should increase the role of recipient countries in leading peacekeeping missions. It does not matter how efficiently a strategy is being implemented if that strategy is failing to meet its larger goals. When strategies are failing, or in fact are subverting their own goals, Congress and aid agencies must be prepared to scrap them and radically alter their approaches.

—Make security assistance as transparent as possible. Assistance to foreign militaries carries significant foreign policy risks and cannot be shrouded in secrecy. Yet the Bush administration has been increasingly stingy with the information it doles out about security assistance programs, especially those that benefit the war on terror countries and those funded through the defense budget. To the extent that force protection is not compromised, congressional oversight bodies and nongovernmental monitors must have access to regular reporting about the cost, extent, goals, and nature of arms transfers, training programs, joint operations, intelligence sharing, overseas military presences, and other forms of military cooperation. Democratic control over the security sector must begin at home.

Appendix 13A: Data on Poorly Performing States

Table 13A-1. *Poorly Performing States, According to Five Criteria*

State	Fallling below the mean of the human development index in 2003	Having a gross national per capita annual income of $735 or less in 2002	Ranking in the bottom 2 quintiles of policy and insti- tutional quality in 2003	Scoring a freedom ranking greater than 7 in 2001–02	Ranking in the bottom 2 quintiles of gov- ernance indica- tors in 2002	Total
The 47 states satisfying 4 or 5 criteria						
Afghanistan	n.a.	1	n.a.	1	1	5
Angola	1	1	1	1	1	5
Azerbaijan	0	1	1	1	1	4
Burundi	1	1	1	1	1	5
Cambodia	1	1	1	1	1	5
Cameroon	1	1	1	1	1	5
Central African Republic	1	1	1	1	1	5
Chad	1	1	1	1	1	5
Comoros	1	1	0	1	1	4
Congo, Republic of	1	1	1	1	1	5
Congo, Dem. Rep. of	1	1	1	1	1	5
Côte d'Ivoire	1	1	1	1	1	5
Djibouti	1	0	1	1	1	4
Equatorial Guinea	1	1	0	1	1	4
Eritrea	1	1	0	1	1	4
Ethiopia	1	1	0	1	1	4
Gambia	1	1	1	1	1	5
Georgia	0	1	1	1	1	4
Guinea	1	1	0	1	1	4
Guinea-Bissau	1	1	1	1	1	5
Haiti	1	1	1	1	1	5
Indonesia	1	1	1	0	1	4
Kenya	1	1	1	1	1	5
Lao People's Dem. Rep.	1	1	1	1	1	5
Lesotho	1	1	1	1	0	4
Liberia	n.a	1	n.a.	1	1	5
Myanmar	1	1	n.a.	1	1	5
Niger	1	1	0	1	1	4
Nigeria	1	1	1	1	1	5
North Korea	n.a.	1	0	1	1	4
Pakistan	1	1	0	1	1	4
Papua New Guinea	1	1	1	0	1	4
Rwanda	1	1	0	1	1	4
Sierra Leone	1	1	0	1	1	4
Solomon Islands	1	1	1	1	1	5
Somalia	n.a.	1	n.a.	1	1	5
Sudan	1	1	1	1	1	5

Table 13A-1 *(continued)*

State	Fallling below the mean of the human development index in 2003	Having a gross national per capita annual income of $735 or less in 2002	Ranking in the bottom 2 quintiles of policy and institutional quality in 2003	Scoring a freedom ranking greater than 7 in 2001–02	Ranking in the bottom 2 quintiles of governance indicators in 2002	Total
Swaziland	1	1	0	1	1	4
Tajikistan	1	1	1	1	1	5
Tanzania, U. Rep. of	1	1	0	1	1	4
Timor-Leste	n.a.	1	n.a.	1	1	5
Togo	1	1	1	1	1	5
Uganda	1	1	0	1	1	4
Uzbekistan	0	1	1	1	1	4
Yemen	1	1	1	1	1	5
Zambia	1	1	0	1	1	4
Zimbabwe	1	1	1	1	1	5
The 14 states satisfying 3 criteria						
Bangladesh	1	1	0	0	1	3
Bhutan	1	1	0	1	0	3
Burkina Faso	1	1	0	1	0	3
Egypt	1	0	0	1	1	3
Kyrgyzstan	0	1	0	1	1	3
Madagascar	1	1	1	0	0	3
Malawi	1	1	0	0	1	3
Mali	1	1	0	0	1	3
Mauritania	1	1	0	1	0	3
Mozambique	1	1	0	0	1	3
Nepal	1	1	0	0	1	3
Nicaragua	1	1	0	0	1	3
São Tomé and Principe	1	1	1	0	0	3
Vietnam	0	1	0	1	1	3
The 31 states satisfying 2 criteria						
Albania	0	0	0	1	1	2
Algeria	0	0	0	1	1	2
Armenia	0	0	0	1	1	2
Belarus	0	0	0	1	1	2
Benin	1	1	0	0	0	2
Bolivia	1	0	0	0	1	2
Bosnia-Herzegovina	0	0	0	1	1	2
Botswana	1	1	0	0	0	2
Colombia	0	0	0	1	1	2
Cuba	0	0	0	1	1	2
Gabon	1	0	0	1	0	2
Ghana	1	1	0	0	0	2
Guatemala	1	0	0	0	1	2

State	Fallling below the mean of the human development index in 2003	Having a gross national per capita annual income of $735 or less in 2002	Ranking in the bottom 2 quintiles of policy and institutional quality in 2003	Scoring a freedom ranking greater than 7 in 2001–02	Ranking in the bottom 2 quintiles of governance indicators in 2002	Total
Honduras	1	0	0	0	1	2
India	1	1	0	0	0	2
Iran	0	0	0	1	1	2
Iraq	0	0	0	1	1	2
Kazakhstan	0	0	0	1	1	2
Lebanon	0	0	0	1	1	2
Libya	0	0	0	1	1	2
Macedonia	0	0	0	1	1	2
Moldova	0	1	0	0	1	2
Mongolia	1	1	0	0	0	2
Morocco	1	0	0	1	0	2
Russia	0	0	0	1	1	2
Senegal	1	1	0	0	0	2
Syria	0	0	0	1	1	2
Tonga	0	0	0	1	1	2
Turkmenistan	0	0	0	1	1	2
Ukraine	0	0	0	1	1	2
Venezuela	0	0	0	1	1	2
The 21 states satisfying 1 criterion						
Argentina	0	0	0	0	1	1
Bahrain	0	0	0	1	0	1
Brunei	0	0	0	1	0	1
China	0	0	0	1	0	1
Ecuador	0	0	0	0	1	1
Jordan	0	0	0	1	0	1
Kiribati	0	0	1	0	0	1
Kuwait	0	0	0	1	0	1
Malaysia	0	0	0	1	0	1
Maldives	0	0	0	1	0	1
Namibia	1	0	0	0	0	1
Oman	0	0	0	1	0	1
Paraguay	0	0	0	0	1	1
Qatar	0	0	0	1	0	1
Saudi Arabia	0	0	0	1	0	1
Singapore	0	0	0	1	0	1
Tunisia	0	0	0	1	0	1
Turkey	0	0	0	1	0	1
United Arab Emirates	0	0	0	1	0	1
Vanuatu	1	0	0	0	0	1
Yugoslavia	0	0	0	0	1	1

Source: See appendix B.
n.a. Means datum is not available and is scored as 1.

Table 13A-2. *U.S. Aid to Forty-Seven Poorly Performing States,*
by Category, 2000–04[a]

US$ thousand unless noted otherwise

State	Military and police aid	Economic and social aid	Military/police aid share (percent)
Afghanistan	1,357,085	1,537,999	47
Pakistan	782,611	1,387,394	36
Uzbekistan	74,164	246,006	23
Georgia	65,459	473,716	12
Nigeria	46,008	324,069	12
Yemen	40,532	43,468	48
Timor-Leste	38,237	111,495	26
Kenya	29,177	331,654	8
Indonesia	26,135	665,349	4
Azerbaijan	23,938	216,763	10
Haiti	15,217	303,562	5
Tajikistan	14,908	193,573	7
Ethiopia	5,002	522,024	1
Djibouti	4,630	8,501	35
Guinea	4,609	143,149	3
Eritrea	2,711	64,444	4
Cameroon	2,642	17,232	13
Zambia	2,463	244,742	1
Côte d'Ivoire	1,915	13,818	12
Lao People's Dem. Rep.	1,711	28,859	6
Chad	1,690	17,123	9
Papua New Guinea	1,541	2,257	41
Zimbabwe	1,276	101,128	1
Tanzania, U. Rep. of	1,262	149,646	1
Sierra Leone	955	111,462	1
Central African Republic	738	1,434	34
Uganda	733	396,418	0
Cambodia	730	169,103	0
Niger	699	43,886	2
Swaziland	697	2,885	19
Solomon Islands	629	1,097	36
Lesotho	613	11,829	5
Togo	601	10,516	5
Rwanda	593	149,786	0
Congo, Republic of	560	0	100
Guinea-Bissau	441	2,276	16
Gambia	349	11,590	3
Angola	335	191,045	0
Congo, Dem. Rep. of	255	139,459	0

State	Military and police aid	Economic and social aid	Military/police aid share (percent)
Burundi	248	40,565	1
Comoros	201	0	100
Equatorial Guinea	125	0	100
Liberia	9	250,202	0
Myanmar	0	34,985	0
North Korea	0	0	0
Somalia	0	55,770	0
Sudan	0	316,871	0
Addendum			
War on terror states	2,300,066	4,082,290	36
Strategically important states	185,658	2,548,448	7
Lower priority states	62,287	99,262	9
Banned states	6,419	1,859,150	0
Total	2,554,430	8,589,150	22

Source: See appendix B.

a. These figures represent the authors' best estimates based on U.S. government sources. Some countries may secretly receive additional military assistance from U.S. intelligence agencies. Economic and social assistance does not include emergency humanitarian aid, such as food drops to Afghanistan and funds from regional accounts.

Table 13A-3. *U.S. Programs Providing Military and Police Assistance to Forty-Seven Poorly Performing States, 2000–04*[a]

Program	War on terror states	Strategically important states	Lower priority states	Banned states	Total
Foreign military financing					
US$ thousand	1,143,449	133,596	8,222	0	1,285,267
Percent to these states	49.7	72.0	13.2	0.0	50.3
International narcotics and law enforcement					
US$ thousand	425,974	6,280	1,321	0	433,575
Percent to these states	18.5	3.4	2.1	0.0	17.0
Afghan Freedom Support Act drawdowns					
US$ thousand	300,000	0	0	0	300,000
Percent to these states	13.0	0.0	0.0	0.0	11.7
Peacekeeping operations					
US$ thousand	251,949	340	34,994	0	287,283
Percent to these states	11.0	0.2	56.2	0.0	11.2
Nonproliferation, antiterrorism, demining, and related programs					
US$ thousand	153,754	7,775	0	0	161,529
Percent to these states	6.7	4.2	0.0	0.0	6.3
International military education and training					
US$ thousand	14,208	21,174	6,319	2,564	44,265
Percent to these states	0.6	11.4	10.1	39.9	1.7
Defense Department regional security studies institutes					
US$ thousand	5,320	6,491	1,984	914	14,709
Percent to these states	0.2	3.5	3.2	14.2	0.6
Defense Department counternarcotics (sec. 1004)					
US$ thousand	3,844	0	9,365	0	13,209
Percent to these states	0.2	0.0	15.0	0.0	0.5
Unified command activities (includes JCETs)					
US$ thousand	439	5,561	82	1,241	7,323
Percent to these states	0.0	3.0	0.1	19.3	0.3
Africa Crisis Response Initiative					
US$ thousand	0	2,470	0	1,700	4,170
Percent to these states	0.0	1.3	0.0	26.5	0.2
U.S. service academies					
US$ thousand	418	1,481	0	0	1,899
Percent to these states	0.0	0.8	0.0	0.0	0.1

Program	War on terror states	Strategically important states	Lower priority states	Banned states	Total
Excess defense articles					
US$ thousand	366	460	0	0	826
Percent to these states	0.0	0.2	0.0	0.0	0.0
Exchanges					
US$ thousand	276	0	0	0	276
Percent to these states	0.0	0.0	0.0	0.0	0.0
Aviation Leadership Program					
US$ thousand	69	30	0	0	99
Percent to these states	0.0	0.0	0.0	0.0	0.0
Total (US$ thousand)	2,300,066	185,658	62,287	6,419	2,554,429

Source: See appendix B.

a. See note to table 13A-2.

Appendix 13B: Sources for Tables

U.S. Department of State, Bureau of International Narcotics and Law Enforcement Affairs, *Fiscal Year 2004 Budget Congressional Justification;* Office of Management and Budget, *Reports on Expenditures from the Emergency Response Fund, 2003;* Office of Management and Budget, *Supplemental #4—Operation Iraqi Freedom, 2003;* Office of Management and Budget, *2004 Supplemental: Iraqi/Afghanistan War—9/17/03;* U.S. Congress, *Conference Report 108-76;* U.S. Congress, *Conference Report 108-337;* White House, *FY 2002 Foreign Operations Emergency Supplemental Funding Justifications;* U.S. Department of State, *FY 2003 Congressional Budget Justification for Foreign Operations;* U.S. Department of State, Department of Defense, *Foreign Military Training and DoD Engagement Activities of Interest: Joint Report to Congress 2003;* U.S. Congress, *Conference Report 107-593;* U.S. Department of State, Bureau of International Narcotics and Law Enforcement Affairs, *Fiscal Year 2003 Budget Congressional Justification;* U.S. Department of State, *FY 2002 Congressional Budget Justification for Foreign Operations.*

Notes

1. U.S. Department of State, *FY 2004 Congressional Budget Justification for Foreign Operations* (Washington: 2003); U.S. Department of State, U.S. Department of Defense, *Foreign Military Training and DoD Engagement Activities of Interest: Joint Report to Congress* (Washington: 2003). These numbers do not include significant but smaller amounts of police assistance provided by the U.S. Department of Justice through the International Criminal Investigative Training Program (ICITAP) and a number of U.S. Defense Department military exercises and unified command activities.

2. John A. Cope, "International Military Education and Training: An Assessment," McNair Paper 44 (Washington: Institute for National Strategic Studies, 1995); U.S Department of State, *FY 2004 Congressional Budget Justification for Foreign Operations*.

3. U.S. Department of State, *FY 2004 Congressional Budget Justification for Foreign Operations*, p. 380.

4. H.R. 2888, signed into law September 18, 2001; H.R. 4775, signed into law August 2, 2002; H.R. 1559, signed into law April 16, 2003; and H.R. 3289, signed into law November 6, 2003.

5. U.S. Department of State, *FY 2004 Congressional Budget Justification for Foreign Operations*, p. 436.

6. U.S. Department of Justice, *International Criminal Investigative Assistance Training Program* (Washington: 2003).

7. U.S Department of State, U.S. Department of Defense, *Foreign Military Training and DoD Engagement Activities of Interest: Joint Report to Congress* (Washington: 2001, 2002, 2003).

8. U.S. Department of State, *FY 2004 Congressional Budget Justification for Foreign Operations*, pp. 202, 263, 340.

9. Ibid., pp. 206, 268, 322.

10. Quotations from ibid., pp. 340, 216, 217, 226.

11. U.S. Department of State, U.S. Department of Defense, *Foreign Military Training and DoD Engagement Activities of Interest*.

12. Poorly performing states are not, however, the only countries in which security forces exercise political and economic impunity. That problem is far more widespread.

13. For example, on Indonesia, Niger, and Pakistan, see the papers presented at a conference organized by the Bonn International Centre for Conversion, "Soldiers in Business: The Military as an Economic Player" (www.bicc.de/budget/events/milbus/confpapers.html). On Indonesia, see also M. Riefqi Muna, "Money and Uniform: Corruption in the Indonesian Armed Forces in Stealing from the People: 16 Case Studies of Corruption in Indonesia," in *The Big Feast: Soldier, Judge, Banker, Civil Servant,* edited by Richard Holloway (Jakarta: Aksara Foundation, 2002).

14. "A continuing threat to many emerging democracies is military control of, or inappropriate intervention in, the government decision-making process. Without effective civilian control and legitimacy, democracies falter, instability thrives, and economic and political development is impeded. To counter the threat of military dominance, there must be a shift in the ways that militaries define their responsibilities and an improvement in the ways that civilians exercise theirs." Memorandum of Understanding between the Department of Defense, Defense Security Cooperation Agency, Agency for International

Development, Center for Democracy and Governance, and Office of Transition Initiatives on the Conduct of Building Democracy Programs.

15. "The specific purpose" of the senior leader seminar, according to the website of the Africa Center for Strategic Studies, "is to afford African policymakers an opportunity to consider and evaluate alternative approaches to the pressing challenge of 'democratic defense.'" The course in democratic civil-military relations "examines the nexus between democratic societies and security organs. It includes a broad assessment of the appropriate ways in which executive branches, legislatures, judicial institutions, and civil society relate to security forces and suggests mechanisms through which an acceptable balance can be maintained. The imperatives of civilian control over the military and the responsibilities of each party and organization responsible for national security are a critical part of this module." The course in national security strategy "examines the concept of national interests in a democratic society and identifies the various instruments of national power which can be harnessed to protect those interests. The various instruments of national power—diplomacy, economic, informational, and military—are examined in detail." The course in defense economics "addresses the efficient allocation of national resources between security and nonsecurity related requirements. It examines how national security is financed in a democracy and addresses the relationship between economic growth, development, and security, particularly under emerging market conditions" (www.africacenter.org/english/e3100_senior.htm).

16. According to the U.S. Department of Justice (DOJ) website, "ICITAP'S mission is to serve as the source of support for U.S. criminal justice and foreign policy goals by assisting foreign government in developing the capacity to provide professional law enforcement services based on democratic principles and respect for human rights. It was created by DOJ in 1986 to respond to a request from the Department of State for assistance in training police forces in Latin America. Since then, ICITAP's activities have expanded to encompass two principal types of assistance projects: (1) the development of police forces in the context of international peacekeeping operations, and (2) the enhancement of capabilities of existing police forces in emerging democracies. Assistance is based on internationally recognized principles of human rights, rule of law and modern police practices. ICITAP's training and assistance programs are intended to develop professional civilian-based law enforcement institutions. This assistance is designed to: (1) enhance professional capabilities to carry out investigative and forensic functions; (2) assist in the development of academic instruction and curricula for law enforcement personnel; (3) improve the administrative and management capabilities of law enforcement agencies, especially their capabilities relating to career development, personnel evaluation, and internal discipline procedures; (4) improve the relationship between the police and the community it serves; and (5) create or strengthen the capability to respond to new crime and criminal justice issues" (www.usdoj.gov/criminal/icitap/).

17. U.S. Department of Justice, *ICITAP Project Overviews: Indonesia* (Washington: 2003). Some observers feel that ICITAP is spreading itself too thin in Indonesia.

18. U.S. Agency for International Development, *USAID Civil-Military Programs* (Washington: 2003).

19. National Democratic Institute for International Affairs, *Global Programs: Security Sector Reform* (Washington: 2003). The institute's website provides this overview of the program in Cambodia: "The goal of this program is to work with Cambodian NGOs,

supporting them by enhancing their understanding of the role of the armed forces in a democratic society, by initiating dialogue about the role of the military in Cambodia, and by providing advice and financial assistance to their current efforts to improve civil-military relations in the country. NDI has chosen not to work directly with the Cambodian government in demobilization efforts or to assist the military. Instead, by working directly with civil society organizations, NDI hopes to begin to build civil society's familiarity with the discourse on civil-military relations, to raise the confidence of these civil society organizations as they engage in discussions with the government and military about security issues, and to encourage civil society organizations to eventually advocate for responsible security policy. In the future, NDI hopes to provide technical assistance to NGOs involved in reviewing defense proposals or to help them develop advocacy efforts on military reform issues" (www.ndi.org/globalp/civmil/programscm/cambodia/cambodia_202.asp).

20. See www.usaid.gov/hum_response/oti/country/indones/rpt0902.html.

21. General James Hill, U.S. Southern Command, "Comments before the Council of the Americas, November 1, 2003" (www.ciponline.org/colombia/03010901.pdf).

22. Robert G. Kaiser, "'Dribs and Drabs' of Information Keep Turkmen Plot in Shadows," *Washington Post,* January 13, 2003, p. A16. The International Crisis Group writes that "Turkmenistan has become a major drugs transit state, with the connivance of the authorities, including President Niyazov himself. The government's close relations with the Taliban regime in Afghanistan, combined with corruption in the security forces, has reportedly allowed Taliban and al Qaeda fighters to escape from Afghanistan across the border. Further decline will merely increase the risk of Turkmenistan becoming a failed state that poses a serious threat to regional and international security." ICG, "Cracks in the Marble: Turkmenistan's Failing Dictatorship," Asia Report 44 (Brussels: 2003), p. ii.

23. ICG, "Cracks in the Marble," p. ii.

24. The 2001 *U.S. Human Rights Report on Uzbekistan* claims that its "human rights record remained very poor. . . . Citizens cannot exercise the right to change their government peacefully; the Government does not permit the existence of opposition parties." It goes on to claim that treatment by security forces resulted in the deaths of citizens in custody and that the police and other security forces "tortured, beat, and harassed persons. Prison conditions were poor, and pretrial detention can be prolonged. The security forces arbitrarily arrested and detained persons, on false charges, particularly Muslims suspected of extremist sympathies, frequently planting narcotics, weapons, or banned literature on them." Furthermore, "the judiciary does not ensure due process and often defers to the wishes of the executive branch," allowing the police and security forces to infringe "on citizens' privacy, including the use of illegal searches and wiretaps. Those responsible for documented abuses rarely are punished. The Government severely restricts freedom of speech and the press, and an atmosphere of repression stifles public criticism of the Government. Although the Constitution expressly prohibits it, censorship is practiced widely. The Government limits freedom of assembly and association. The Government continued to ban unauthorized public meetings and demonstration . . . and continued to deny registration to opposition political parties as well as to other groups that might be critical of the Government; unregistered opposition parties and movements may not operate freely or publish their views. . . . The Government restricted local nongovernmental organizations working on human rights and refused to register the two main human rights organizations. Security forces abused human rights activists. The Office of the Human Rights

Ombudsman reported that it assisted hundreds of citizens in redressing human rights abuses, the majority of which involve allegedly unjust court decisions and claims of abuse of power by police. . . . Violence against women, including domestic violence, was a problem, and there continued to be significant traditional, societal discrimination against women. Workplace discrimination against some minorities persisted. There are some limits on worker rights. Some children, particularly in rural areas, are forced to work during the harvest season. Trafficking in women and girls to other countries for the purpose of prostitution was a problem." Bureau of Democracy, Human Rights, and Labor, "Uzbekistan: Country Reports on Human Rights Practices—2001."

25. Uzbekistan does have a short history of military collaboration with the United States. Since the 1998 bombings of the U.S. embassies in Kenya and Tanzania, the two countries have shared intelligence and conducted joint covert operations aimed at capturing al Qaeda leader Osama bin Laden. See, for example, Thomas E. Ricks and Susan B. Glasser, "U.S. Operated Secret Alliance with Uzbekistan," *Washington Post,* October 14, 2001.

26. ICG, "Cracks in the Marble," p. 33.

27. U.S. Department of State, *International Narcotics Control Strategy Report* (Washington: 2003).

28. For example, see Thomas Carothers, "Promoting Democracy and Fighting Terror" (www.foreignaffairs.org/20030101faessay10224/thomas-carothers/promoting-democracy-and-fighting-terror.html ([January 30, 2003]).

29. The United States has given considerable attention since the late 1990s to the possibility of terrorist use of weapons of mass destruction, especially chemical and biological agents. There are reasons to believe that a focus on nonstate actors is misplaced and that any genuine threat will come from state actors. See, for example, Milton Leitenberg, "An Assessment of the Threat of the Use of Biological Weapons or Biological Agents," in *Biosecurity and Bioterrorism,* edited by Maurizio Martellini (Como, Italy: Landau Network Centro Volta, 2000); Milton Leitenberg, "Biological Weapons in the Twentieth Century: A Review and Analysis," *Critical Reviews in Microbiology* 27, no. 4 (2001): 267–320.

30. An example of programs is the yearly conferences held at the Marshall Center. The center's website describes the program as "divided between bilateral, single nation seminars and multinational and regional conferences," the latter focusing on security and economic concerns, "giving participants the opportunity to hear from experts and to discuss with their peers impacts and concerns" (www.marshallcenter.org/Conference%20Center/default.htm).

31. Jon Wolfsthal, "U.S. Non-Proliferation Policy," Proliferation Brief, January 6, 2003 (www.ceip.org/files/nonprolif/templates/Publications.asp?p=8&PublicationID=1144 [January 30, 2003]).

32. Dana Priest, *The Mission: Waging War and Keeping Peace with America's Military* (New York: W. W. Norton, 2003), p. 14.

33. Personal communication from House Armed Services Committee staff, May 29, 2003.

34. See, for instance, Donald H. Rumsfeld "Defense for the 21st Century," *Washington Post,* May 22, 2003, p. A35.

35. Carothers, "Promoting Democracy and Fighting Terror."

Contributors

NICOLE BALL
Center for International Policy

SUSAN BURGERMAN
Columbia University

SHEILA CARAPICO
University of Richmond

PIERRE ENGLEBERT
Pomona College

ADAM ISACSON
Center for International Policy

CAROL LANCASTER
Georgetown University

PETER M. LEWIS
American University

ANDREW MACINTYRE
Australian National University

THEODORE H. MORAN
Georgetown University

MARTHA BRILL OLCOTT
*Carnegie Endowment for
International Peace*

ARVIND PANAGARIYA
Columbia University

DAVID I. STEINBERG
Georgetown University

MILAN VAISHNAV
Columbia University

JEREMY M. WEINSTEIN
Stanford University

DAVID W. YANG
United Nations Development Program

Index

Abacha, Sani, 33, 87, 90–91, 93, 100–01, 106. *See also* Nigeria
Abioloa, M. K. O., 93, 105, 106. *See also* Nigeria
Abubakar, Abdulsalami, 91, 106. *See also* Nigeria
Accords, 32, 33, 396. *See also* Cambodia; El Salvador; Guatemala; Nicaragua
Aceh (Indonesia), 121, 123, 134
ACOTA. *See* African Contingency Operations Training and Assistance
ACP countries. *See* African, Caribbean, and Pacific countries
ACRI. *See* Africa Crisis Response Initiative
AFDL. *See* Alliance of Democratic Forces for the Liberation of Congo
Afghanistan: al Qaeda and, 1, 231, 415; Buddhist statues in, 233; Central Asia and, 147, 175; crime, conflict, and corruption in, 163, 167, 224; economic issues of, 47; as a failed state, 292; military and police issues, 417, 419; political issues of, 2, 174; reconstruction of, 175; recruitment and training of terrorists, 1, 3–4, 146; U.S. assistance to, 39, 175, 286, 301, 414–17, 418, 444; U.S. disengagement from, 1; warlords in, 442; Yemen and, 184. *See also* Taliban
AFPFL. *See* Anti-Fascist People's Freedom League

Africa: flow of arms to, 4; democratization in, 289; educational levels in, 352–53; peacekeeping in, 423, 443; poorly performing countries in, 10, 11–12, 13; reversal of state failure in, 302–03; social sectors in, 56; trade issues, 322–23, 327; underdevelopment in, 95; U.S. aid to, 286, 288, 290. *See also individual countries*
Africa Center for Strategic Studies, 420, 443
Africa Crisis Response Initiative (ACRI; U.S.), 423, 424, 427
African, Caribbean, and Pacific (ACP) countries, 318
African Contingency Operations Training and Assistance (ACOTA), 423, 424
African Growth and Opportunity Act (AGOA; *2000, 2003*), 6, 37, 317, 318, 320, 322–23, 345
African Leadership forum, 107
Agence Nationale des Renseignements (ANR; Congo), 61
Aggarwal, Mita, 349–50
AGOA. *See* African Growth and Opportunity Act
Agro Management, 359
AIG risk insurance, 355
Akayev, Askar, 152, 156, 162–63, 172. *See also* Kyrgyzstan
Albright, Madeleine, 229

Alemán, Arnoldo, 270. *See also* Nicaragua
Alien Tort Claims Act (ATCA; *1789*), 336
Alliance for Progress, 288
Alliance of Democratic Forces for the Liberation of Congo (AFDL), 70
Al Qaeda: Afghanistan and, 1, 231, 415; Congolese view of, 71; in Kenya, 421; massacres of, 231; Pakistan and, 443; in the Philippines, 230; in Singapore, 230–31; in Somalia, 4; U.S. and, 415; Yemen and, 183, 184, 186. *See also* Terrorism and terrorists
Andean region, 5. *See also individual countries*
Andean Trade Preferences Act (ATPA; *1991*), 317
Angola: AGOA and, 6; Congo and, 57, 59, 73; Nigeria and, 104; security sector reform in, 438; U.S. aid for, 432–33
ANR. *See* Agence Nationale des Renseignements
Anti-Fascist People's Freedom League (AFPFL; Burma), 210
Apparel and textiles, 37–38, 318, 335, 341, 350, 351, 359
Arab Fund for Social and Economic Development, 199
Arabia Felix, 189
Arab-Israeli conflict, 192
Arakan Rohingya National Organization (Myanmar), 231
ARENA. *See* National Republican Alliance
Aristide, Jean-Bertrand, 41, 385, 389–90. *See also* Haiti
Arms and weapons: arms transfers and races, 443–44; Chinese assistance to Myanmar, 227–28; illicit trade networks and, 4; North Korea and, 443; Saudi assistance to Yemen, 193; U.S. sales of, 412; U.S. security sector assistance and, 39, 442; USSR assistance to Yemen, 191, 192, 197; weapons of mass destruction, 1–2, 44, 442–44
ASEAN. *See* Association of Southeast Asian Nations
Asia: FDI of, 337; financial crisis of *1997*, 30–31, 123, 126, 128–30, 139, 218, 226, 228, 235, 337; flow of arms to, 4; U.S. assistance to, 3, 13. *See also individual countries*
Asia, Central. *See* Central Asia

Asia, East, 329
Asia Foundation, 438
Asian Development Bank, 211, 347, 355–56
Asia-Pacific Center for Security Studies, 420
Asia, South, 314
Asia, Southeast, 212, 230, 347
Assessing Aid (World Bank; report), 289
Association of Southeast Asian Nations (ASEAN), 216–17, 226, 227, 228, 231, 235, 237–38
ATCA. *See* Alien Tort Claims Act
ATPA. *See* Andean Trade Preferences Act
Aung San (General), 219. *See also* Myanmar
Aung San Suu Kyi, 209, 216, 225, 226, 229, 230, 234, 238. *See also* Myanmar; National League for Democracy
Authoritarian regimes. *See* Political issues
Azerbaijan: aid to, 422, 424, 425, 426t; corruption in, 152; economic issues, 151; ICITAP and, 437; peacekeeping and, 423; strategic importance of, 421, 422

Babangida, Ibrahim, 87, 90, 93, 100, 105. *See also* Nigeria
Baker, James, 195
Bali nightclub bombing, *2002*, 33, 230
Ball, Nicole, 39, 40, 44, 45, 46, 412–60
Bangladesh, 218, 221, 232–33, 313, 345, 349, 357
Banque du Zaire, 56
BCP. *See* Burma Communist Party
Belgium, 66, 71, 76
Bhagwati, Jagdish, 326
Biafran civil war. *See* Nigeria
Biggs, Tyler, 352–53
Bin Laden, Osama, 1, 71, 163, 184, 231–32
Blair, Dennis, 239
Blair (Tony) government, 112
Bolaños, Enrique, 270. *See also* Nicaragua
Bolivia, 5, 42, 293
Botswana, 20, 288, 298. *See also* Africa
BP. *See* British Petroleum
Brazil, 132, 328, 439
Bretton Woods, 102–03, 310, 311
British Petroleum (BP), 194
Brown, Mark Malloch, 377
Brussels Round Table (*1960*), 65
BSPP. *See* Burma Socialist Programme Party
Buddhism, 210, 219, 220, 221, 222
Bueno de Mesquita, Bruce, 379

Buhari, Muhammadu, 87, 90, 100. *See also* Nigeria
Bureau of International Narcotics and Law Enforcement (U.S.), 44
Burgerman, Susan, 32, 245–84
Burma. *See* Myanmar
Burma Communist Party (BCP), 225
Burma Socialist Programme Party (BSPP), 210, 211, 216, 224
Burmese Freedom and Democracy Act of *2003* (U.S.), 234
Burundi, 6, 70, 73, 297, 298, 302, 432–33
Bush, George H. W., 66, 194
Bush (George H. W.) administration, 68, 251, 265, 273
Bush, George W., 74, 107, 287
Bush (George W.) administration: ACOTA and, 423; categorization of states by performance, 291; interest in Myanmar, 233–34; interest in Yemen, 182, 187; intervention in failing states, 301; JCETs and, 426–27; Millennium Challenge Account and, 5–6, 8, 10, 76, 285, 377; National Security Strategy for Africa (*2005*), 3; trade issues, 322, 331; U.S. security issues, 45, 417, 443, 448

Cadot, Olivier, 325
CAFTA. *See* Central America Free Trade Agreement
Cambodia: civil war and peace accords, 397; crime, conflict, and corruption in, 398, 399, 400–01, 402; economic issues, 213; ethnic and minority issues, 399; performance struggles of, 13; postconflict rebuilding, 18; security sector reform in, 438; social and civil issues, 215, 397, 398; training issues, 431, 432–33; USAID strategy for, 41, 44, 385, 396–403
Cambodian People's Party (CPP), 398, 400, 402–03
Cameroon, 421, 422, 425–26
Canada, 74, 314, 355, 356, 358
Canadian Occidental, 194
Carapico, Sheila, 28, 30, 182–208
Career Judicial Service Act (Guatemala), 264
Caribbean Basin Trade Partnership Act (CBTPA; *2000*; U.S.), 317
Carnegie Endowment and Fund for Peace, 293

Carnegie Endowment for International Peace, 379
Carothers, Thomas, 379–82, 403
Carrington, Walter, 106
Carson, Johnnie, 390
Carter (Jimmy) administration, 66, 67, 272
CART Tajikistan (airline company), 166
CBTPA. *See* Caribbean Basin Trade Partnership Act
CDU. *See* United Democratic Center
CEMEX cement factory (Indonesia), 128
Center for Global Development, 321–22
Center for Hemispheric Defense Studies, 420
Central African Republic, 428t, 429, 430t
Central America: crime, conflict, and corruption in, 275; democracy and democratization in, 275–76; emigration from, 275; free trade accords, 32; government and governance in, 275–76; overview of postconflict period, 247–52; peace accords in, 265; political issues in, 275–76; postconflict reconstruction in, 32, 34; regional peace process, 253, 276; social and civil issues, 276; terrorism and, 252; trade issues in, 327; U.S. and, 246, 249, 251–52, 265, 275. *See also* Latin America; *individual countries*
Central America Free Trade Agreement (CAFTA), 252, 275
Central Asia: aid to, 152, 153t, 172, 417; cause of poor performance of, 152–57; collapse of the Soviet Union and, 144, 145, 150; crime, conflict, and corruption in, 152–53; demographic factors of, 150; economic issues in, 145–46, 147–48, 149, 151–52, 156–57, 158, 172, 175–76; ethnic and minority issues of, 145; foreign aid to, 251; government and governance in, 154–55, 156; international attitudes and effectiveness, 28, 148–49, 152, 172–76; military and police issues in, 417; political issues in, 149–50, 172; population of, 157; reform trajectories in, 28, 29, 148–49, 176; security issues of, 146–47; trade issues of, 156–57, 169, 175–76; U.S. assistance to, 39, 174. *See also individual countries*
Central Asian Cooperation Organization, 156
Central Intelligence Agency (CIA; U.S.): in Afghanistan, 442; in Guatemala, 265;

Mobutu, Joseph and, 67; in Myanmar (Burma), 224; in Nicaragua, 267, 273; Office of the Coordinator for Reconstruction and Stabilization and, 35; strategies for failing states, 301; study of failed states, 21

Cerezo, Vinicio, 265. *See also* Guatemala

Chad, 336, 421, 422, 423, 425–26

Chamorro, Violeta, 267–68, 269, 271, 272, 273. *See also* Nicaragua

Cheney, Dick, 186

Chile: drug trafficking in, 439; economic issues, 43, 313, 329, 336; human rights issues, 297, 323; trade issues, 323, 326, 327

China: economic issues of, 130, 313; formation of the People's Republic of China, 223–24; investment in Mauritius, 341; Kuomintang Nationalist government in, 223; Kyrgyzstan and, 161; Myanmar and, 215, 218, 220, 221, 223–24, 225, 226, 227, 236; Soviet Union and, 224; trade issues of, 169, 328, 329; U.S. and, 232, 236; Yemen and, 191, 192, 193

Christian Democratic Party (PDC; El Salvador), 253, 255

Chuaan Leekpai, 228. *See also* Thailand

CIA. *See* Central Intelligence Agency

CIS. *See* Commonwealth of Independent States

Civil society. *See* Social and civil issues; *individual countries*

Civil wars, 245. *See also individual countries*

Climate, 19

Cline, William, 37

Clinton, Bill, 107

Clinton (Bill) administration: Africa and, 417; Central America and, 251, 265; intervention in failing states, 301; Myanmar and, 229; Nigeria and, 66, 70, 105, 106

CNN, 231

Cold war: Burma and, 213, 214, 223; Mobutu, Joseph and, 56, 68; Nigeria and, 104; U.S. strategies after, 135, 444; U.S. strategies during, 3, 27, 66, 68, 251, 446; Yemen and, 190–92, 193

Cole. See USS *Cole*

Collier, Paul, 20

Colombia, 296, 297

Colonies, 20

COMIEX, 60

Commonwealth Eminent Persons Group, 107

Commonwealth of Independent States (CIS), 167, 169

Communist Party, 120, 124, 441

Comoros, 432–33

Competition. *See* Political issues

"Conflict diamonds," 297

Congo. *See* Democratic Republic of Congo

Consensus, 393, 386, 391, 397–98

Contadora process (Central America), 253

Contras (counterrevolutionaries), 267, 268, 270, 271, 272, 273. *See also* Nicaragua

Corruption Perceptions Index (Transparency International; *2003*), 152, 153

Costa Rica, 267, 288

Côte d'Ivoire, 4, 13, 18, 102, 318–19, 431, 432–33

Cotonou Agreement (*1994*), 318, 326

Country studies, 25–34. *See also individual countries*

CPP. *See* Cambodian People's Party

Crime, conflict, and corruption: conflict prevention in failing states, 295–99; conflict vulnerability analyses, 295; democracy and, 22; drug and narcotics trafficking, 44, 103, 154, 163, 165, 167, 224–25, 227, 228, 234, 252, 265, 275, 414, 423, 428, 435, 439, 442; Dutch disease and, 98; economic effects of conflict, 24, 329; in failed and failing states, 16–17, 27, 293; FDI and, 335, 336, 357–58; geography and, 19; lowering of violent crime, 277; military issues, 413; money laundering, 35, 85, 103–04, 225, 246; poorly performing states and, 4–5, 10, 11–12, 13, 14, 15, 16, 18, 277; postconflict environments, 32, 45–46; poverty and, 20; privatization of state resources for personal gain, 25–27; state sovereignty and, 63; U.S. security sector assistance and, 40. *See also* International Criminal Investigation Training and Assistance Program; Military and police issues

Crime, conflict, and corruption—specific countries: Afghanistan, 163, 167, 224; Cambodia, 398, 399, 400–01, 402; Central America, 252; Congo, 54, 55, 58, 59–66, 77; El Salvador, 245, 246, 248,

249, 250, 253, 254, 255, 256, 258, 277;
Guatemala, 245, 246, 248, 249, 250,
259, 261, 262–63, 264, 265, 266, 277;
Haiti, 428; Indonesia, 27, 29, 118,
121–22, 123, 125–27, 134, 136, 437,
439; Kenya, 41, 30, 392–93, 290, 395;
Kyrgyzstan, 152, 154, 158, 159–60,
162–63, 173; Laos, 428; Myanmar, 212,
218, 221, 224–25, 226, 227, 228, 229,
232, 233, 234, 238; Nicaragua, 245, 246,
249, 250, 268, 269–70, 271, 272,
274–75; Nigeria, 85, 86, 87, 89, 90–91,
93–94, 100, 101, 103–04, 105–06, 111,
112, 423; Russia, 163; Tajikistan, 44,
152, 154, 155, 163, 164, 165, 167,
172–73, 442; Thailand, 226, 227;
Uganda, 431; United States, 412; Uzbekistan, 152, 154, 169–70, 437; Yemen,
184, 187, 189, 190, 194, 200, 201
Cristiani, Alfredo, 253–54. *See also*
El Salvador

DAC. *See* Development Assistance
Committee
Darfur, 102
Defense, Department of (U.S.): budget of,
446; counternarcotics funds, 428, 446;
Office of the Coordinator for Reconstruction and Stabilization and, 35; military
exercises of, 273; oversight of, 446;
reforms of, 36; regional security studies
schools, 420, 427, 430, 431, 435–36,
443, 445; security sector policies and, 40,
45, 434, 445; state failure and, 300;
training programs, 426, 436; U.S. military objectives and, 412
Defense Science Board, 36
Defense Services Institute (Myanmar), 213
Definitions: communal competition, 96;
democracy strategies, 380; democratic
governance, 377; Dutch disease, 98;
failed and failing states, 285, 291–92,
293, 294; foreign aid, 286; fragile states,
285, 293; geography, 18–19; institutions,
19; less-developed countries, 322–23;
low-income countries and states, 246;
313; military and police aid, 431; peacekeeping, 423; pivotal studies, 3–4; poorly
performing states and governments, 2–3,
8, 13, 16, 313; rentier states, 97, 98–99;

social dilemmas, 94; state bankruptcy, 98;
state deterioration and failure, 16, 19
Democracy and democratization: bargaining
and compromise in, 131–32; basic elements and structural areas of, 383–84;
civil society and, 393–94; decline in liberal democracies, 24; democratic governance, 377, 378, 380; development and,
289, 377; difficulties of, 131; electoral
reform, 278; foreign aid and, 289–90,
378–79, 430; governance and, 387;
growth in elections, 23–24; military and
police issues in, 437, 439–40; prevention
of state failure and, 295; promotion of,
40–42, 43–44; security issues of, 434–39,
444; semi-authoritarianism and, 22;
stages of, 379–80; strategies for, 395–96;
third wave of, 376; transition to, 22, 296,
383; USAID assistance for, 41–42, 44,
277, 289, 299, 378–406, 438; U.S. foreign policies and, 377, 413. *See also individual countries*
Democracy and Governance framework
(USAID), 41, 42, 44, 381, 382–84, 386,
391, 397, 399, 404–06
Democracy and Rule of Law Project, 379
Democratic Convergence (political party;
Haiti), 385
Democratic Party of Turkmenistan (DPT), 441
Democratic Republic of Congo (DRC;
Congo): aid to, 58, 63–64, 66–68, 70,
74, 76–77, 78, 432–33; crime, conflict,
and corruption in, 3, 54, 55, 58, 59–66,
77; democratization of, 55, 56, 58–59,
64, 65, 68, 73–74, 75; economic issues
of, 26, 29, 54–56, 58, 59–60, 61–62, 64,
67–68, 70; foreign direct investment in,
68–69; government and governance of,
26, 62–63, 75; independence of, 57, 66;
international attitudes toward, 27, 76;
military and police issues, 428t, 429,
430t; minorities of, 63, 77, 78; natural
resources of, 54, 58, 59, 60, 68, 72; Nigeria and, 102; nuclear materials in, 72;
political issues in, 56–59, 68, 75, 77–78;
predation and privatization, 59–66; public opinion in, 70–71; rebel and insurgent
groups in, 56–57, 58, 59, 65, 72; reforms
for strategic planning for democracy aid,
403–06; regime changes of, 31, 33, 57,

58, 59, 66; repression in, 58, 61; secessionist and partition movements in, 64,
65, 75–76, 77; social issues of, 56, 64–65,
73, 75; sovereignty of, 62, 63, 64, 75, 77,
78; state performance, 26, 53–59, 62, 63,
65, 72–75; trade issues, 68–70, 72; U.S.
and, 33, 54, 58, 66–78; Zaireanization
policies in, 55, 63, 67; Zambia and, 421
Developed countries, 312, 314, 324, 325,
354–60. *See also individual countries*
Developing countries: arms trade in, 4; collapse of governments in, 2; economic factors of, 36, 312–14; foreign aid to,
187–91; foreign investment in, 126, 340,
344–45, 348–54; GATT and, 309–10;
isolationist policies of, 42; military and
police issues of, 439; Millennium Challenge Account in, 6, 8–10; population,
313; promotion of development in, 287;
spillover effects in, 4; state weakness in, 2,
3–4; trade issues in, 309–31; U.S. policy
in, 3. *See also* Least developed countries;
Poorly performing states and governments; *individual countries*
Development Assistance Committee (DAC),
378. *See also* Organization for Economic
Cooperation and
Development
DG. *See* Democracy and Governance
framework
Diamond, Larry, 380
Djibouti, 415t, 418
Doe, Samuel K., 296. *See also* Liberia
Doha Ministerial Declaration, 328
Doha Round of trade negotiations, 312, 328,
329, 331
Dominican Republic, 342–43, 347, 348,
349, 350, 351, 353
Domino strategy and theory, 3
DPT. *See* Democratic Party of Turkmenistan
DRC. *See* Democratic Republic of Congo
Drugs. *See* Crime, conflict, and corruption;
Pharmaceuticals
Duarte, José Napoleón, 253, 257, 265
"Dutch disease," 98, 336

East Germany, 192, 193, 197
East Pakistan, 232
East Timor: human rights issues, 123;
ICITAP and, 437; secessionist movement

in, 121, 135; security sector reform in,
438; as a state in recovery, 18, 427–28;
UN-supervised referendum, 129. *See also*
Indonesia
EBA. *See* Everything but Arms initiative
EBRD. *See* European Bank for Reconstruc-
tion and Development
ECOMOG. *See* ECOWAS Monitoring
Group
Economic Community of West African
States (ECOWAS), 102, 423
Economic, Financial, and Administrative
Reform Program (EFARP), 19
Economic issues: business and corporate
issues, 39, 99; crises, 94–95; determinants
of economic performance, 21, 95; Dutch
disease, 98; effectiveness of U.S. aid, 6;
eligibility for MCA funds, 8; employ-
ment, 359–60; foreign aid, 287–91; frag-
ile and failing states, 295, 301; geography,
19–20, 95; institutions and development,
21; per capita income, 14, 15, 16;
poverty and poverty traps, 7, 14, 20, 21,
22–23, 24, 28, 30, 94, 379; state failure,
294, 295–96; state income, 19
ECOWAS. *See* Economic Community of
West African States
ECOWAS Monitoring Group (ECOMOG),
102
Educational issues. *See* Social and civil issues
EFARP. *See* Economic, Financial, and
Administrative Reform Program
EFTA. *See* European Free Trade Association
Egypt, 40, 184, 286, 414, 440, 444
EITI. *See* Extractive Industries Transparency
Initiative
Elections, 387, 394, 395, 398, 401, 402
Elf Aquitaine, 194
El Salvador: civil war in, 247, 253–54, 257,
258, 268; crime, conflict, and corruption
in, 245, 246, 248, 249, 250, 253, 254,
255, 256, 258, 277; democracy and
democratization in, 250, 252–55, 258,
260; economic issues of, 246, 247–48,
249, 250, 252, 255–56, 258, 275; FDI
in, 345; government and governance in,
247, 249, 296; immigration to the U.S.,
252; military and police issues in, 32,
249–50, 252–53, 255–56, 257; political
issues of, 32, 246, 247, 249, 252–55,

258; as a poorly performing country, 245; postconflict peace accords, 247, 253–54, 255, 256, 257, 268, 271–72; postconflict reconstruction in, 32; rule of law in, 255–57, 296; social and civil issues of, 247, 257–58; trade issues, 252, 275; U.S. and, 246, 251, 257–58, 264, 267, 275, 296. *See also* Central America; Latin America

Eminent domain, 201

Encarnation, Dennis, 338

"End of the Transition Paradigm, The" (Carothers), 379

Endriartono Sutarto, 439

Englebert, Pierre, 26, 31, 33, 53–82

Environmental issues, 326, 328, 356, 359

EPS. *See* Sandinista Popular Army

EPZs. *See* Export processing zones

Equatorial Guinea, 432–33

Eritrea, 421, 422, 425–26

Esquipulas II (peace process), 253, 259, 267

Ethiopia, 13, 421, 422, 423, 424

Ethnic and minority issues, 22. *See also individual countries*

Euro-Mediterranean Partnership, 326

European Bank for Reconstruction and Development (EBRD), 168, 169, 170, 355–56

European Commission, 318

European Community, 237, 325

European Free Trade Association (EFTA), 325

European Union (EU): Central America and, 252; Congo and, 74; Nigeria and, 105; trade issues, 37, 311–12, 314, 317, 318, 320–21, 326, 327, 328; Yemen and, 196

Europe, Central, 148, 150, 151

Europe, Eastern, 192, 286, 289

Europe, Western, 192, 193, 223

Everything but Arms initiative (EBA; *2001*; EU), 37, 314, 317, 321, 330

Expanded IMET courses. *See* International Military Education and Training program

Export Development Canada, 356, 360

Export processing zones (EPZs): FDI and, 38, 347, 340–45, 347–49; unions and treatment of workers in, 349–52; U.S. companies and, 359. *See also* Foreign Direct Investment; Trade issues; *individual countries*

Extractive Industries Transparency Initiative (EITI), 112

Exxon and Exxon Mobil, 194, 195, 336

Failed and failing states: assistance models for, 290–91, 300; conflict prevention and termination in, 295–99; definition of, 285, 291–92, 293, 294; identification of, 294–95; international collaboration toward, 302–03; reversal of, 300, 302; U.S. policies toward, 293–303. *See also* Poorly performing states and governments

Farabundo Martí National Liberation Front (FMLN; El Salvador), 253, 254, 255, 258

FCS. *See* Foreign Commercial Service

FDI. *See* Foreign direct investment

FDNG. *See* New Guatemala Democratic Front

Fernandes, George, 227. *See also* India

FIAS. *See* Foreign Investment Advisory Service

Financial Times, 74, 322

Flores, Francisco, 254. *See also* El Salvador

FMF. *See* Foreign Military Financing

FMLN. *See* Farabundo Martí National Liberation Front

Food and Drug Administration (FDA; U.S.), 342

Foreign aid (U.S.): amounts of, 446, 452–55; approaches to recipient choice and change and, 287–99; risks of, 445, 447; selectivity and preconditions of, 6–7. *See also* African Growth and Opportunity Act; Democracy and democratization; Foreign direct investment; Millennium Challenge Account; United States; *individual countries*

Foreign Assistance Act (1961; U.S.), 40, 416, 431, 446

Foreign Commercial Service (FCS; U.S.), 39, 360

Foreign Corrupt Practices Act (*1977*), 359

Foreign direct investment (FDI): amounts, by country, 361–70; arbitration and dispute settlement, 337–38, 356–57; bribery and corruption, 357–58, 359; decline in, 126; economic effects and factors of, 38, 335–36, 337, 338–39, 352, 353, 354, 359–60; educational issues of, 352–53,

354; good conditions for, 340; indigenous linkages and spillovers, 342, 343, 344, 352–54; in infrastructure, 337–38; international sovereignty and, 63; investment promotion agencies, 347–48, 354; labor and union issues, 349–52; locational subsidies and assistance, 358; measures for attracting most beneficial FDI, 340–54; model of investment promotion, 345–49; in natural resources, 335–36; in nonextractive, noninfrastructure sectors, 338–39; political issues of, 337; in poorly performing countries, 38–39, 46, 334–35; provision of most beneficial FDI, 354–58; risks and risk insurance, 337–38, 346, 354, 355–56, 358–59; taxation issues of, 357, 358, 359; trade issues of, 338–39, 352, 355. *See also* Export processing zones; *individual countries*

Foreign Investment Advisory Service (FIAS), 346, 348–49

Foreign Military Financing (FMF), 428

Foreign Service (U.S.), 39

Fragile States Strategy (USAID), 36

France, 74, 102, 341, 417

Freedom House, 188, 392

Freedom House Gastil Index, 56

Freeport mining company (Indonesia), 127

Free Trade Area of the Americas, 327, 331

Free trade areas and agreements, 325–27, 331, 343–45. *See also individual agreements*

FRG. *See* Guatemalan Republican Front

From Bullets to Ballots: Electoral Assistance to Postconflict Societies (Kumar and Ottaway), 299

FSLN. *See* Sandinista National Liberation Front

FUNCINPEC. *See* United Front for an Independent, Neutral and Free Cambodia

Gambia, 428t, 429, 430t

GATT. *See* General Agreement on Tariffs and Trade

Gazprom (Russian gas company), 154, 162

Gécamines (Congo), 61

General Agreement on Tariffs and Trade (GATT), 309–11, 312, 319, 324, 325

Generalized System of Preferences (GSP; U.S.): AGOA and, 317, 318; effects of, 38, 319; Enabling Clause of, 309–10,

324, 320–21, 325; reform of, 324; trade liberalization and, 311, 323–24

General People's Congress (Yemen), 186

George C. Marshall European Center for Security Studies, 420

Georgia: crime, conflict, and corruption in, 291; ICITAP and, 437; military and police assistance to, 422, 423, 424, 425, 426t; strategic importance of, 421; transition of, 150, 151

German Finance Company for Investments in Developing Countries, 348

Germany, 102, 196, 211, 341, 358

Ghana, 42, 293, 349

Global and Inclusive Agreement (Congo; *2002*), 56, 65, 74

Globalization, 352

Golkar Party (Indonesia), 121, 129

Gore, Al, 294

Government and governance: AGOA and, 320; NGOs and, 389–90; reforms and, 289; security and, 435, 440, 445; state failure and, 294; USAID and, 402–03. *See also* States and nations; *individual countries*

Gowon, Yakubu, 89, 92. *See also* Nigeria

Graham, Edward, 350–51

Great Mining State of South Kasai (Congo), 64

Group of Eight, 336

G-7 countries, 102

GSP. *See* Generalized System of Preferences

GTE. *See* Verizon

Guatemala: civil war in, 247, 268; crime, conflict, and corruption in, 245, 246, 248, 249, 250, 259, 260–61, 262–63, 264, 265, 266, 277; democracy and democratization in, 250, 259–61, 263, 265, 266; economic issues of, 246, 248, 249, 250; ethnic and minority issues of, 249; government and governance in, 247, 248, 249, 265; institutional changes in, 32; military and police issues in, 249–50, 258–59, 261–65, 266; political issues of, 246, 247, 249, 258–61, 263, 275; as a poorly performing country, 245; postconflict peace accords, 247, 248, 251, 259–60, 261–62, 266, 268, 271–72; postconflict reconstruction in, 32; rule of law in, 261–64; social and civil issues of, 248, 249, 252, 265–66;

trade issues of, 258; U.S. and, 246, 251, 264–66. *See also* Central America
Guatemalan National Revolutionary Unity (URNG), 259, 263
Guatemalan Republican Front (FRG), 261, 263
Guinea, 4, 422, 425–26, 438
Guinea-Bissau, 428t, 429, 430t
Gulf Cooperation Council, 195
Gulf War of *1990-1991*, 30, 87, 186, 190, 195. *See also* Kuwait War

Habibie, Bacharuddin Jusuf, 131. *See also* Indonesia
Haiti, 41, 286, 301, 385–90, 427–28, 429, 430t
Haitian National Police, 389
Hamoudi, Amar, 321–22
Harmonized system 6 (HS6), 317
Harvard Center for International Development, 352
Heavily indebted poor countries (HIPCs), 74, 102–03, 111
Herbst, Jeffrey, 75
Hill, James, 439
HIPCs. *See* Heavily indebted poor countries
Hizbut Tahrir (Islamic group), 163
Holmes, Peter, 325
Honduras, 267, 345
Hong Kong, 42–43, 312–13, 341
HS 6. *See* Harmonized system 6
Hudec, Robert, 323
Human Development Report *2002* (UNDP), 377
Human rights: application of human rights law, 297; Foreign Assistance Act and, 431; police and security reforms and, 413–14, 432–33, 434, 437; USAID and, 401, 402, 438; use of the military and, 440; in war-on-terror states, 416, 440
Human rights—specific countries: Cambodia, 401, 402; Chile, 297, 323; East Timor, 123; Guatemala, 252; Indonesia, 417
Human Rights and Reconciliation Program (Guatemala; USAID), 252
Hun Sen, 396
Hunt Oil Company (Texas), 185, 194, 195
Hurricane Mitch (*1998*), 248, 257, 274
Hyman, Gerald, 382, 403

ICG. *See* International Crisis Group
ICITAP. *See* International Criminal Investigation Training and Assistance Program
ICSID. *See* International Center for the Settlement of Investment Disputes
IDA. *See* International Development Association
IDB. *See* Inter-American Development Bank
Idiagbon, Tunde, 90, 100. *See also* Nigeria
ILO. *See* International Labor Organization
IMET. *See* International Military Education and Training program
IMF. *See* International Monetary Fund
Immigration, 252
India: aid to, 286; Burma and, 219, 220, 221; economic issues of, 18, 43, 313; Kashmir and, 444; MCA and, 13; Myanmar and, 227, 228; trade issues of, 328, 329; U.S. and, 228, 286
Indonesia: aid to, 136–38, 286, 417, 418; Asian financial crisis and, 30–31, 33; banking in, 126, 130; crime, conflict, and corruption in, 27, 29, 118, 121–22, 123, 125–27, 134, 136, 439; democratization and democratic reforms of, 33, 117, 118–19, 126, 129, 131–32, 133, 134, 136–37; developmental record of, 118–28, 134–40; economic issues in, 28, 29, 30–31, 117, 118–19, 120, 121–25, 126, 128–30, 132–33, 135–36, 137, 139–40, 313, 329; ethnic and minority issues of, 118, 126–27, 136; government and governance in, 118–19, 120, 124, 127–28, 129, 130–32, 139; international attitudes toward, 27, 124; investment in, 126, 130, 337; military and police issues, 120, 127, 134, 137–38, 139, 417, 437, 438; Muslim population in, 118, 127, 128, 135, 136, 137–38, 230; natural resources of, 118, 128; oil of, 121–22; performance struggles of, 124–40; political issues in, 29–31, 117, 118, 119–21, 124, 125, 126–28, 129, 130, 131–34, 137; population of, 118, 125; regime changes of, 119, 120, 124–25, 129; security sector reform in, 438; shocks of the *1990s*, 29, 128–29; social and civil issues, 121, 122, 125, 126, 220; terrorism and, 33, 127, 135, 136, 137–38, 230, 437; trade issues of, 43, 122, 130, 138; U.S.

and, 108, 121, 124, 134–38, 139, 140, 235, 286, 415t, 417
Indonesian Bank Restructuring Agency, 130
Insurgents and insurgencies, 19, 20–21. *See also individual countries*
Intellectual property, 320, 330–31
Inter-American Development Bank (IDB), 256, 273, 347, 355–56
Inter-Congolese Dialogues (*1999, 2002*), 65, 74
Inter-Governmental Group on Indonesia, 134
International Bank for Reconstruction and Development, 355
International Center for the Settlement of Investment Disputes (ICSID), 337–38
International community. *See individual countries*
International Conference on Financing for Development (*2002*), 377
International Criminal Investigation Training and Assistance Program (ICITAP), 251–52, 277, 420, 424, 431, 437. *See also* Justice, Department of
International Crisis Group (ICG), 441
International Development Association (IDA), 8, 160, 192, 196, 198, 201, 313, 331. *See also* World Bank
International Finance Corporation, 355
International Labor Organization (ILO), 349, 350, 351
International Military Education and Training (IMET) program: Expanded IMET courses, 420, 435, 445; growth in, 413; policy objectives of, 416, 428; use of, 137, 251–52, 426
International Monetary Fund (IMF): Congo and, 74; Indonesia and, 28–29, 121, 134; Kyrgyzstan and, 156, 160; Nicaragua and, 269; Nigeria and, 87, 107, 111; Tajikistan and, 156; Uzbekistan and, 156, 167–68, 175; Yemen and, 186, 195, 196
International Narcotics Control Strategy Report (U.S. State Department), 442
International Rescue Committee, 73
IPAnet, 347
Iran, 1–2, 421
Iran-contra scandal, 273. *See also* Contras; Nicaragua
Iraq: efforts to procure nuclear material, 72; doctrine of preemption and, 1–2; recon-

struction of, 175; U.S. aid to, 286; Yemen and, 193. *See also* Gulf War of *1990–1991*
Ireland, 358
Isacson, Adam, 39, 40, 44, 45, 46, 412–60
Islam and Muslim populations: shari'a law, 92, 93, 103, 136; Taliban and, 1; terrorists and, 1; U.S. anti-terror efforts, 414
Islam and Muslim populations—specific countries: Afghanistan, 414; Congo, 71, 72; Indonesia, 118, 127, 128, 135, 136, 137; Kyrgyzstan, 163; Myanmar, 210, 218, 219–20, 221, 222, 231–33; Nigeria, 84, 91, 92–93, 96, 103; Uzbekistan, 29, 155, 156, 172; Yemen, 184, 200, 201, 202–03
Islamic Movement of Uzbekistan, 156
Israel, 184, 186, 192, 286, 414, 440, 444
Ivory Coast. *See* Côte d'Ivoire

Jakarta Initiative (Indonesia), 137
Jamaica, 318–19
Jane's, 228
Japan: China and, 228; civil rights issues, 357; economic issues, 126, 130; Indonesia and, 121; labor issues of, 349; Myanmar and, 211, 222–23, 237; Nigeria and, 102; political risk insurance, 355; trade issues of, 314; Yemen and, 192, 193
Joint Combined Exchange Training (JCET; U.S.), 426–27, 430, 431, 435–36
Joint Declaration for Cooperation to Combat International Terrorism (*2002*; U.S.-ASEAN), 232
Jordan, 286, 311, 312
Journal of Democracy, 405
Justice, Department of (U.S.), 35, 40, 277, 420. *See also* International Criminal Investigation Training and Assistance Program
Justice systems, 277

Kabila, Joseph, 27, 59, 60, 63, 74. *See also* Democratic Republic of Congo
Kabila, Laurent Désiré: assassination of, 72, 59; background of, 72; investment and, 68; leadership and rule of, 26, 31, 59, 60; U.S. backing for, 27, 66, 70. *See also* Democratic Republic of Congo
Kagame, Paul, 74. *See also* Rwanda

Karimov, Islam: economic policies of, 151, 155–56; leadership of, 29, 156, 169–70, 174, 442; U.S. aid and, 447. *See also* Uzbekistan

Kasavubu, Joseph, 57, 64, 65. *See also* Democratic Republic of Congo

Katanga province (Congo), 64

Kazakhstan: aid to, 153t; crime, conflict, and corruption in, 152, 153–54, 173; economic issues of, 145, 147t, 148t, 149, 151–52, 154, 158t, 172, 173, 176; foreign investment in, 173; legal reforms in, 173; natural resources of, 153–54; oil industry, 153, 173; political issues of, 172, 174; reform trajectory of, 29, 155; social and civil issues of, 166; trade issues of, 156, 161; World Bank view of, 145. *See also* Central Asia

Kennedy, John F., 66, 288

Kennedy Round of trade negotiations, 309

Kenya: crime, conflict, and corruption in, 41, 30, 290, 392–93, 395; democratization in, 18, 41, 46; military and police issues, 423, 424, 425–26, 437; social and civil issues in, 390, 393–94, 395; trade issues in, 331, 339; USAID strategy for, 385, 390–96; U.S. foreign aid for, 423; War on Terror and, 4, 421, 422

Kenya Anti-Corruption Authority, 393, 394

Kenyan Anti-Corruption Coalition, 41, 395

Khin Nyunt, 235, 237. *See also* Myanmar

Khmer Rouge, 399

Kibaki, Mwai, 46, 396. *See also* Kenya

Kimberley process, 35

Kirkpatrick, Jeane, 66

KMT. *See* Kuomintang

Korea, 290, 292, 319, 349, 357. *See also* North Korea; Republic of Korea; South Korea

Korean War, 218

Koskinen, Matti, 325

Kumar, Krishna, 299

Kuomintang (KMT; Chinese Nationalist government), 223, 224

Kuwait, 191, 193, 195

Kuwait Foreign Petroleum Exploration Corporation, 195

Kuwait Fund, 198

Kuwait War (*1990–91*), 186, 190. *See also* Gulf War

Kyrgyzstan: aid to, 152, 153t, 158, 159–60, 161, 162–63, 173, 175; crime, conflict, and corruption in, 152, 154, 158, 159–60, 162–63, 173; economic issues of, 146, 147t, 148t, 149, 151–52, 154, 157–64, 169, 172, 173, 176; food production in, 160; government and governance in, 159, 160–61, 162; hydroelectric projects in, 161–62; international views of, 159, 160; legal reforms in, 173; Muslim population of, 163; natural resources of, 161; political issues of, 162–64, 172; reform trajectory of, 29, 155; security issues of, 159; social and civil issues of, 166; trade issues of, 155–56, 160, 161, 166; World Bank view of, 145, 157. *See also* Central Asia

Labor, Department of (U.S.), 350

Labor issues, 326, 328, 349–50, 356, 357

Lall, Sanuaya, 338

Lancaster, Carol, 34–35, 36, 42, 44, 45, 285–305

Lao People's Democratic Republic, 428t, 429, 430t

Laos, 213, 215, 428

Latin America: democracy and democratization in, 288; drug trafficking in, 301, 439; foreign direct investment in, 337, 347; political issues in, 290; reversal of state failure in, 302; trade issues of, 312, 329. *See also* Central America; *individual countries*

Law and legal issues. *See* Military and police issues; Rule of law

LDCs. *See* Least developed countries

Least developed countries (LDCs), 313–29, 331, 359. *See also* Developing countries; Poorly performing states and governments

Leopold II (King of Belgium), 76

Lesotho: economic issues of, 43; FDI in, 345; labor issues in, 351; security sector issues, 428t, 429, 430t, 438; trade issues of, 37–38, 318. *See also* Africa

Lesotho Clothing and Allied Workers Union, 351

Lesotho National Development Corporation, 348

Lewis, Peter, 26, 30, 31, 83–116

Liberal Constitutionalist Party (PLC; Nicaragua), 270

Liberia: breakdown of, 4; exclusion from for-
eign assistance, 6; Nigeria and, 84, 85,
102; peace in, 47; U.S. aid and assistance
to, 286, 296, 301, 302, 432–33. *See also*
Africa
Libya, 1–2, 71, 421
LICUS. *See* Low-income countries under
stress
Lloyds of London risk insurance, 355
Lomé IV Convention, 318
Lovanium conference (*1961*), 65
Low-income countries under stress (LICUS),
13, 293
Lumumba, Patrice, 57, 64, 66. *See also*
Democratic Republic of Congo
Lusaka Cease Fire Agreement (*1999*), 65

MacIntyre, Andrew, 27, 28, 29, 30, 33,
117–43
Madagascar, 43, 318, 345, 350
Mai-Mai (Congo), 57
Malaysia, 119–20, 126, 130, 313, 329, 349
Marshall Plan, 223
Mahathir bin Mohamad, 230, 235. *See also*
Malaysia
Mauritius: economic issues of, 46, 318–19;
educational levels and, 353; EPZs and
FDI in, 38, 340–42, 343, 344, 345, 350,
351
Mbeki, Thabo, 74
MCA. *See* Millennium Challenge Account
MCC. *See* Millennium Challenge
Corporation
McCalla, Alex, 329
McConnell, Mitch (R-Ky.), 234
Media, 41
Megawati Sukarnoputri, 126, 131. *See also*
Indonesia
Mexico, 3, 108, 234, 325–26, 345
MFA. *See* Multifiber Agreement/
Arrangement
MFN status. *See* Most-favored-nation status
MidAmerican Corporation, 337, 338
Middle East, 290. *See also individual countries*
MIGA. *See* Multilateral Investment Guaran-
tee Agency
Military and police issues: fragile states and,
294; military government, 213; purpose
of the military, 439; security sector assis-

tance, 39–40; U.S. assistance priorities
and, 277; U.S. military and police
assistance, 412–55. *See also individual
countries*
Millennium Challenge Account (MCA),
5–10, 76, 285, 286, 290, 313, 377
Millennium Challenge Corporation (MCC),
286
"Millennium Declaration" (*2000*), 377
Milosevic, Slobodan, 77
MLC. *See* Mouvement de Libération du
Congo
MPLA. *See* Popular Movement for the Liber-
ation of Angola
Mobutu, Joseph (Mobutu Sese Seko): dicta-
torship of, 26; economic issues, 29, 31,
55; governance by, 62; pacification of
Congo by, 57–58; political power of,
58–59, 60, 63; political violence and, 57;
U.S. and, 27, 66, 67, 68, 70; West's need
for, 31; Zaireanization policies and, 55,
67. *See also* Democratic Republic of
Congo
Moi, Daniel arap, 290, 392. *See also* Kenya
"Monterrey Consensus" (*2002*), 377
Moran, Theodore H., 38–39, 43, 46,
334–75
Morocco, 327
Most-favored-nation status (MFN status),
317, 326–327
Mouvement de Libération du Congo (MLC),
56–57, 74
Mouvement Populaire de la Révolution
(MPR; Congo), 58
Mozambique, 348, 349
MPR. *See* Mouvement Populaire de la Révo-
lution
Mugabe, Robert, 47, 297. *See also* Zimbabwe
Multi-Donor Group for Yemen Water, 201
Multifiber Agreement/Arrangement (MFA;
1974), 226, 310, 321, 324, 345
Multilateral Investment Guarantee Agency
(MIGA), 347, 355–56
Multinational organizations, 339, 340,
345–46
Murtala Muhammad, 89–90, 100. *See also*
Nigeria
Muslim Liberation Organization of Burma,
231

Muslims. *See* Islam and Muslim populations

Myanmar (Burma): Buddhist population in, 210, 219, 220, 221, 222, 232; crime, conflict, and corruption in, 212, 218, 221, 224–25, 226, 227, 228, 229, 232, 233, 234, 237, 238; democracy and democratization in, 211, 212, 213, 225, 229–30, 233–34, 235, 237–38; economic issues, 27, 29, 209, 211–12, 213–15, 216, 217–19, 220–21, 225–26, 228–29, 232, 234–35, 236, 238–39; ethnic and minority issues, 209, 210, 211, 212, 215, 219–20, 221–22; foreign assistance, influence, and investment, 217–18, 221. 222–23, 226–29; future issues for, 235–39; government and governance in, 27, 209, 210–11, 213, 215–17, 219, 220, 222, 225, 231; history of, 209, 210, 212–14, 219–20, 221–22, 223–24; HIV-AIDS in, 226, 235; insurgent and rebel groups in, 224–25, 226, 232; military and police issues, 210, 211, 213, 215, 216–17, 219, 220, 221, 222, 225, 229, 236–38; Muslim population of, 210, 218, 219–20, 221, 222, 231–33; natural resources of, 212, 225–26; performance struggles of, 211–12, 213–23, 235–39; political issues, 209, 210–11, 215–17, 219, 220–21, 222, 226, 228, 229–30, 236–37; social and civil issues of, 210, 211, 212, 214, 215–16, 217, 218, 219, 220, 221, 224–25, 227; terrorism and, 230–35, 239; trade issues of, 212, 216–17, 218, 220, 221, 226, 234; U.S. relations and assistance to, 33, 211, 214, 218, 221, 223–35, 237–39, 432–33

Myanmar Economic Corporation, 216

Myanmar Economic Holdings Corporation, 216

NAFTA. *See* North American Free Trade Agreement

Namibia, 73, 348, 349

Narcotics. *See* Crime, conflict and corruption

Nationalism, 149–50

National Civilian Police (El Salvador), 255, 257

National Civil Police (Guatemala), 262

National Council of the Judiciary (El Salvador), 256

National Democratic Institute (NDI; U.S.), 438

National Endowment for Democracy (U.S.), 276

National League for Democracy (NLD; Myanmar), 209, 216, 225, 226, 230, 235, 236. *See also* Aung San Suu Kyi

National Opposition Union (UNO; Nicaragua), 267–69

National Republican Alliance (ARENA; El Salvador), 253–54, 255

National Security Council (NSC; U.S.), 35, 45, 301, 445–46

National Security Strategy for Africa (*2005*), 3

National Water and Sewerage Authority (NWASA; Yemen), 200

Natsios, Andrew, 290, 292

Natural disasters, 248, 257, 274, 279n3

Natural resources, 19, 21, 26, 297, 334, 335–36, 421. *See also individual countries*

Nazarbayev, Nursultan, 153, 156, 173, 174. *See also* Kazakhstan

NDI. *See* National Democratic Institute

Near East-South Asia Center for Strategic Studies, 420

NEPAD. *See* New Partnership for African Development

Netherlands, 192, 196, 199, 201

New Guatemala Democratic Front (FDNG), 259

Ne Win, U, 210, 211, 237. *See also* Myanmar

New International Economic Order (NIEO; UN), 104, 310, 311

New Partnership for African Development (NEPAD), 102

New Zealand, 329, 356

NGOs. *See* Nongovernmental organizations

Nicaragua: civil war in, 247, 250, 266–67, 268, 271, 273, 274; crime, conflict, and corruption in, 245, 246, 249, 250, 268, 269–70, 271, 272, 274–75; democracy and democratization in, 267–68, 269–70, 271, 274; economic issues in, 246, 248, 249, 250, 266–67, 269, 272, 273–74; government and governance in, 247, 248, 249, 275; military and police issues, 250,

270–71, 272, 274; political issues of, 246, 247, 249, 266–70, 273–75; as a poorly performing country, 245; postconflict peace accords, 32, 247, 268, 271, 272; rule of law in, 270–72, 275; social and civil issues, 267, 274; U.S. and, 246, 249, 251, 272–75. *See also* Central America; Latin America

Nicaraguan National Police, 250

NIEO. *See* New International Economic Order

Niger, 421, 422, 423, 425–26, 438

Nigeria: AGOA and, 37; aid to, 107, 423; Biafran civil war, 30, 86, 89, 92, 104; colonial period of, 96; crime, conflict, and corruption in, 85, 86, 87, 89, 90–91, 93–94, 100, 101, 103–04, 105–06, 111, 112, 423; democratization and democratic reforms of, 33, 84, 85–86, 89, 90, 91–92, 101, 105, 106, 109, 112; developmental failure of, 83, 86–94; economic issues, 29, 83, 84, 85–89, 91, 94–95, 96, 97–100, 101, 102–03, 111; foreign affairs of, 84, 104; government and governance of, 26, 83–84, 86, 89–91, 92, 94, 95, 99–101, 108; HIV-AIDS in, 85, 104; as an influence for security, 5; institutional decline in, 99–101; international attitudes toward, 27; military and police issues, 100, 103, 105, 112, 423, 424, 425–26, 437, 438; minority and ethnic issues, 89, 91, 92–93, 95–97; Muslim population in, 84, 91, 92–93, 96, 103; oil industry of, 26, 33, 83, 84, 85, 86–88, 92, 95, 97–100, 102, 104, 106, 109–10, 112, 336, 421; performance struggles of, 13, 18, 83, 87–88, 91, 94–101, 108–13; political issues, 30, 31, 33, 83, 84, 91–94, 96–97, 99, 105, 106–09; population of, 102; regime changes of, 31, 87, 89–91, 93, 100, 104, 105, 106, 108; security issues, 85; social and civil issues in, 84–86, 88, 91–94, 101, 108, 110, 112–13; trade issues, 84, 85, 87, 88–89, 97–98, 102, 105–06; U.S. and, 84–86, 101–03, 104–07, 109–11, 423; War on Terror and, 421, 422. *See also* Africa

Nixon, Richard M., 66

Niyazov, Saparmurad, 154, 156, 174, 440–41. *See also* Turkmenistan

NLD. *See* National League for Democracy

Nongovernmental organizations (NGOs): in Cambodia, 396, 398, 400, 401; in Chad, 336; in Haiti, 41, 388, 389–90; in Indonesia, 438; in Kenya, 41, 395; in Myanmar, 227, 229, 235, 238–39; in Nigeria, 86, 111–12; in Tajikistan, 164; in Turkmenistan, 441

North American Free Trade Agreement (NAFTA), 311, 325–26

Northern People's Congress (NPC; Nigeria), 96

North Korea, 1–2, 220, 432–33, 443, 444

North Yemen, 183, 184, 188, 191, 192–93, 195–96, 197. *See also* Yemen

North Yemen Central Planning Organization, 198

NPC. *See* Northern People's Congress

NSC. *See* National Security Council

Nuclear Non-Proliferation Treaty (*1968*), 443

Nu, U, 210, 214, 221, 224. *See also* Myanmar

NWASA. *See* National Water and Sewerage Authority

OAS. *See* Organization of American States

Obasanjo, Olusegun: coup plot of, 105; economic issues of, 102; effectiveness of, 18, 31, 90, 101; election of *2000*, 106; political issues of, 18, 89, 91, 107–08; U.S. leaders and, 107. *See also* Nigeria

OECD. *See* Organization for Economic Cooperation and Development

Office of Conflict Management and Mitigation (USAID), 295, 301

Office of the Coordinator for Reconstruction and Stabilization (U.S.), 35–36

Office of Democracy and Governance (USAID), 378, 382, 404, 405

Office of the U.S. Trade Representative, 38

Office of Transition Initiatives (OTI; USAID), 299, 301, 438

OIC. *See* Organization of Islamic Conference

Oil. *See individual countries*

Olcott, Martha Brill, 28, 29, 144–81

Oman, 184

OPEC. *See* Organization of Petroleum Exporting Countries

Operation Enduring Freedom, 414

OPIC. *See* Overseas Private Investment Corporation

Organization for Economic Cooperation and Development (OECD), 20, 37, 286, 328, 358, 360, 378

Organization of American States (OAS), 271

Organization of Islamic Conference (OIC), 93

Organization of Petroleum Exporting Countries (OPEC), 102, 193, 310

Ortega, Daniel, 270. *See also* Nicaragua

OTI. *See* Office of Transition Initiatives

Ottaway, Marina, 24, 299, 379

Overseas Development Institute, 13

Overseas Private Investment Corporation (OPIC; U.S.), 38–39, 46, 337, 355, 356, 359–60

Ozden, Caglar, 323, 325

Pakistan: as an influence for security, 5; Kashmir and, 444; labor issues in, 349; MCA and, 13; military and police issues, 419, 420, 437; North Korea and, 444; signs of future conflict, 18, 47; U.S. aid to, 39, 286, 415–16, 417, 418, 420; U.S. security assistance to, 442–43, 444

PAN. *See* Partido de Avanzada Nacional

Panagariya, Arvind, 36, 37, 38, 42, 46–47, 309–33

Pan-Sahel border cooperation initiative, 423

Papua New Guinea, 428t, 429, 430t

Paraguay, 439

Paris Club, 74, 102, 111, 158, 164, 199

Paris Peace Accords (*1991*), 396

Park Chung Hee, 42, 292. *See also* South Korea

Partido de Avanzada Nacional (PAN; Guatemala), 261

Partido de Conciliacion Nacional (PCN; El Salvador), 255

PDC. *See* Christian Democratic Party

PDRY. *See* People's Democratic Republic of Yemen

Peace Corps, 36

Peacekeeping, 423–24, 435–36, 443, 448

Peacekeeping Operations (PKO; U.S.), 423, 428

People's Democratic Republic of Yemen (PDRY), 183–84, 191, 192, 193, 195–96. *See also* North Yemen; South Yemen; Yemen

People's Republic of China (PRC). *See* China

Pharmaceuticals, 330–31, 342

Philippines, 223, 230, 344, 345, 347, 349, 351

Philips, 347

Pinochet, Augusto, 297. *See also* Chile

Pivotal states, 3–4

PKO. *See* Peacekeeping Operations

PLC. *See* Liberal Constitutionalist Party

Police. *See* Military and police issues; *individual countries*

Political issues: authoritarian and semi-authoritarian regimes, 14, 22, 24, 31; clientelism, 23; collective welfare, 94; competition for power, 31, 386, 392, 398, 400; development, 377; dynamics of transition, 22, 30–31; failed and failing states, 296; foreign aid, 289–91; fragile and failing states, 294, 301–02; inclusion, 386–87; neopatrimonialism, 23; policy choices, 29–30; political risk insurance, 355–56; postconflict peace accords and changes, 32, 33; poverty, 7, 22–23; public policies, 7; security bodies and, 435; social dilemmas, 94; trade, 324, 326, 327, 328; use of assistance funds, 6. *See also* Democracy and democratization; *individual countries*

Poorly performing states and governments: categorizations and criteria of, 290–91, 313, 449–51; causes and stages of state deterioration, 16–25, 245; changes in domestic policies and practices, 33, 34; civil liberties and political rights, 14–16; crime and conflict in, 4–5, 10, 13, 14, 15, 16, 435; definitions and names for, 2–3, 8, 13, 16; democratic governance and, 377, 381–82, 445; dimensions of performance, 9; economic issues, 8, 14, 15, 16, 34, 36, 43–44, 318, 435; endogenous shocks and, 30; foreign assistance and, 34–36, 42–43, 287–91, 292–93, 452–55; foreign direct investment in, 5–6, 334–70; governance in, 42–45; inclusion and exclusion of MCA in, 7, 8–16; key characteristics of, 10–16; lower priority states; 427–30; MCA and, 285; military and police issues, 35, 412–60; political issues, 43–44, 380, 435; regional insecurity and, 5; security bodies in, 435;

security sector assistance to, 39–40,
412–60; spillover effects of, 4–5; states
banned from receiving aid, 431–33; state
failure in, 17–25; states of strategic
importance to the U.S., 421–27; trade
issues of, 14, 15, 36–38, 309–31; U.S.
and, 5, 7–8, 14, 16, 34–47, 108, 277,
287–91, 292–93, 311, 434–40, 444; War
on Terror states and, 414–21. *See also*
Developing countries; Failed and failing
states; Least developed countries; *individual countries*
Popular Movement for the Liberation of
Angola (MPLA), 104
Portillo, Alfonso, 261. *See also* Guatemala
*Postconflict Elections, Democratization, and
International Assistance* (Kumar), 299
PRC (People's Republic of China). *See* China
Preval, Andre, 385
Priest, Dana, 445
Privatization, 29

Quad countries, 314, 316. *See also* Canada;
European Union; Japan; United States

Radelet, Steve, 291
Rahmonov, Emomali, 154, 167, 172–73. *See
also* Tajikistan
Ramachandran, Vijaya, 352–53
Ranariddh, Norodom, 396. *See also*
Cambodia
Rassemblement Congolais pour la Démocra-
tie (RCD-Goma; Congo), 5– 57, 61
Razafindrakoto, Mireille, 350
RCD-Goma. *See* Rassemblement Congolais
pour la Démocratie
Reagan, Ronald, 66
Reagan (Ronald) administration, 68, 251,
253, 257, 272–73
Rebuilding Societies after Civil War (Kumar),
299
Reform Party (Yemen), 186
Reinhardt, Eric, 323, 325
Rentier states, 97, 98–99
Republic of Korea, 312–13
Reuber, Grant, 338
Rhee, Syngman, 288. *See also* South Korea
Ríos Montt, Efraín, 261, 263. *See also*
Guatemala
Rodrik, Dani, 21, 350

Roosevelt, Franklin D., 223
Root, Hilton, 379
Roubaud, François, 350
Rule of law: in Cambodia, 44, 398; in Haiti,
386, 388; in Kenya, 391–92; security
issues and, 434, 444, 447; in Turkmenistan, 441; USAID and, 438
Rumsfeld, Donald, 36, 446. *See also* Defense,
Department of
Russia: aid to, 3; energy issues of, 162;
Kazakhstan and Kyrgyzstan and, 161;
nationalism in, 149–50; Tajikistan and,
166; Turkmenistan and, 174; U.S. relations with, 108, 417, 421; Uzbekistan
and, 170, 174
Rwanda: crime, conflict, and corruption in,
3, 297, 301; Congo and, 57, 59, 70, 71,
73, 77; performance struggles of, 18; U.S.
and, 302, 431, 432–33. *See also* Africa

Sachs, Jeffrey, 24, 94, 95, 98
Salih, Ahmad 'Ali Abdallah, 187. *See also*
Yemen
Salih, Ali Abdallah, 185. *See also* Yemen
Sam Rainsy Party (SRP; Cambodia), 398,
400, 402
Sana'a University (Yemen), 201–02
Sanchez de Lozada, Gonzalo, 5. *See also*
Bolivia
Sandinista National Liberation Front (FSLN;
Nicaragua), 251, 267, 268, 269–70,
272–73, 274
Sandinista Popular Army (EPS; Nicaragua),
270
SAP. *See* Structural Adjustment Program
Sapir, Andre, 327
Saro-Wiwa, Ken, 93, 105–06. *See also*
Nigeria
Saudi Arabia, 184, 185, 186, 191, 192–93,
195, 197, 201–02
Security Council. *See* United Nations
Security Sector Reform program, 438
Security sectors: public security and rule of
law, 276–77; regional security, 443–44;
security bodies, 434–39; state failure and,
16; U.S. military and police assistance
and, 39–40, 45; weak states and, 440–42;
weapons of mass destruction and,
442–43. *See also* Military and police
issues; *individual countries*

Senegal, 349

September *11, 2001*: effects of, 1, 33, 70–71, 85, 135, 146, 230, 293; U.S. security assistance and, 416, 444

Shah, Manju Kedia, 352–53

Shephard, G., 325

Shinawatra, Thaksin, 228. *See also* Thailand

Siemens (USA, Canada), 360

Sierra Leone: civil war in, 4; military and police aid to, 427–28, 429, 430t; Nigeria and, 84, 85, 102; security sector reform in, 438

Simpson, Daniel, 70

Singapore, 42–43, 138, 312–13, 326, 327, 341

Sino-Indian War (*1962*), 227

SLORC. *See* State Law and Order Restoration Council

Slovak Republic, 150l

Social and civil issues, 287–88, 293, 295, 296, 352–53, 434–35, 436, 438. *See also* *individual countries*

Socialist Party (Yemen), 192

Social services, 39

Sol, Armando Calderón, 254. *See also* El Salvador

Solomon Islands, 428t, 429, 430t

Somalia, 4, 6, 297, 298, 417, 423, 432–33. *See also* Africa

Somaliland, 75–76. *See also* Africa

Somoza García, Anastasio, 266, 267. *See also* Nicaragua

Soros, George, 336

South Africa: AGOA and, 37, 322; Congo and, 74; HIV-AIDS in, 104; Lesotho and, 345; Nigeria and, 104; U.S. aid to, 286

South Korea: economic recovery of, 126, 130; as a "good performer," 288; trade policies of, 42–43; U.S. and, 42, 223, 288; Yemen and, 194. *See also* Korea

South Yemen, 183–84, 190, 191, 192, 197. *See also* People's Democratic Republic of Yemen; Yemen

Sovereign National Conference (*1991–93*), 65, 68

Soviet Union (USSR): China and, 224; collapse and division of, 31, 58, 76, 144, 145, 150–51, 289, 440; demographic factors, 150; economic issues of, 146, 151; Nicaragua and, 267; Nigeria and, 104;

withdrawal from Afghanistan, 1; Yemen and, 191, 192, 194, 197. *See also* Commonwealth of Independent States; Russia; *individual countries*

SPDC. *See* State Peace and Development Council

SRP. *See* Sam Rainsy Party

State, Department of (U.S.): ACRI and, 423; assessment of Central America, 265; assessment of Myanmar, 233; International Narcotics Control, 428; military issues, 412, 420; Pakistan and, 417; Peacekeeping Operations, 423; reporting on narcotics trade, 225; training programs, 426; U.S. leadership for weak and failing states, 35, 45, 300–01; U.S. security sector assistance and, 40, 44, 45, 445–46. *See also* International Military Education and Training program

State Economic Enterprises (Myanmar), 216

State Failure Task Force (CIA), 21, 44, 294

State Law and Order Restoration Council (SLORC; Myanmar), 211, 219

State Peace and Development Council (SPDC; Myanmar), 209, 211, 228

States and nations: categorization by performance, 291–92; causes and stages of state deterioration and failure, 16–25, 30–31; definition of state failure, 16; development of, 21; diplomacy of external actors and, 33; economic factors, 20–21, 22–23, 24, 28–29, 31, 33; geography of, 18–20, 21, 22; illicit transnational networks and, 3–4; institutions of, 19, 20, 21–24, 31–32; lower-priority states, 427–30; political factors, 30–34, 443; security issues, 434–39, 443; sovereignty of, 33–34; state collapse and security, 3–4, 36, 146–47; states banned from receiving U.S. aid, 431–33; strategically important states, 421–27; war-on-terror states, 414–21, 440. *See also* Government and governance; Poorly performing states and governments

Steinberg, David, 27, 209–44

Streeten, Paul, 338

Structural Adjustment Program (SAP), 87, 100. *See also* Nigeria

Sudan: Chad and, 421; exclusion from foreign assistance, 6; expulsion of bin Laden,

1; as an influence for security, 5; peace in, 47; U.S. aid to, 286, 432–33

Sudarsono, Juwono, 438–39

Suharto (Soeharto, Haji Mohammad): breakdown of Suharto regime, 29, 30, 123, 128–29; corruption and, 126; effectiveness of, 27, 123, 125, 139; government of, 120–22, 128, 132; macroeconomic program, 28–29, 124; radical Islam and, 230; rise to power of, 120; U.S. and, 135, 235. *See also* Indonesia

Sukarno: chaotic dictatorship of, 124, 138–39; onset of authoritarian rule, 119–20; removal from power, 139. *See also* Indonesia

Sun City Inter-Congolese Dialogue (*2002*), 74

Suvannabumi (the Golden Land), 212

Swaziland, 428t, 429, 430t

Syria, 1–2

Taiwan, 42–43, 223–24, 312–13, 319, 341

Tajikistan: agriculture in, 165; aid to, 153t, 172–73, 418; civil war in, 155, 164–65; crime, conflict, and corruption in, 152, 154, 155, 163, 164, 165, 167, 172–73, 442; democracy and democratization of, 416; economic issues of, 146, 147t, 148t, 154, 157, 158t, 164–67, 169, 172–73, 176; foreign investment in, 167; government and governance in, 155, 165; hydroelectric projects of, 162, 166; military and police issues, 437; political issues of, 150, 167, 172–73, 174; social and civil issues of, 166; trade issues of, 155–56, 165, 166; U.S. security assistance to, 44, 415t, 416, 418, 442; World Bank view of, 145. *See also* Central Asia

Taliban, 1, 231, 233, 292, 415, 416–17, 443

Thant, U, 214. *See* Myanmar

Tanzania: FDI in, 348; military and police issues, 422, 425–26, 437; reforms in, 293; strategic importance of, 421; U.S. aid to, 42, 423

Taxation, 357, 358, 359

Taylor, Charles, 4, 102. *See also* Liberia

Technoexport, 194, 195

Terrorism and terrorists: anti-terrorism pacts, 231; counterterror strategies, 448; in failed and failing states, 293; in front-line

states, 39–40; Muslim radicalization, 85; strategically important states, 421–27; training camps, 231; U.S. aid and, 286, 414–21, 431; U.S. allies in, 44, 228; weak states and U.S. security and, 3–4, 39, 235, 440–42. *See also* Al Qaeda; Bin Laden, Osama; September *11, 2001*; Taliban; USS *Cole*; World Trade Center bombing

Terrorism and terrorists—specific countries and areas: Afghanistan, 1, 3–4, 146, 231, 415; Armenia, 421; Azerbaijan, 421, 422; Cameroon, 421, 422; Central America, 252; Chad, 421, 422; Eritrea, 421, 422; Ethiopia, 421, 422; Georgia, 421, 422; Guinea, 422; Kenya, 421, 422; Myanmar, 230–35; Nicaragua, 274; Niger, 421, 422; Nigeria, 103, 421, 422; Tanzania, 421, 422; Vietnam, 231; Zambia, 421, 422

Texaco, 194

Texas Instruments, 347

Textiles and clothing. *See* Apparel and textiles

Thailand: crime, conflict, and corruption in, 226, 227; economic issues of, 126, 313, 329; foreign investment in, 349; Myanmar and, 218, 221, 228, 237

Than Shwe, 228, 235, 237. *See also* Myanmar

Timor-Leste, 428t, 429, 430t

Togo, 6, 428t, 429, 430t

Tokyo Round of trade negotiations (*1974–79*), 310–11

Total, 194, 195

Toyota, 347

Trade and Development Act (*2000*), 317

Trade issues: agricultural products, 321, 328–29, 331, 355; aid through trade, 309–31; antidumping actions, 327, 355; barriers to trade, 313–16, 326, 328; economic effects of, 319–20, 327, 329–30; exports of primary commodities, 14, 15; free trade areas and two-way preferences, 325–27, 331, 343–45; General Agreement on Tariffs and Trade, 309–11; geography, 19–20; illicit networks, 4; liberalization of trade, 37, 46–47, 309–31, 355; multilateral liberalization, 327–29, 330, 331, 355; one-way trade preferences, 317–25; political factors, 324, 326, 327,

328, 330; reforms, 324–25; rules of origin, 322–23, 325–27, 330; side conditions, 326, 328, 330; state collapse, 21; tariffs, 314, 315, 318, 322–23, 325, 326–27, 330–31; trade and market access of developing countries, 36–38, 95, 309–31. *See also* African Growth and Opportunity Act; Export processing zones
Trade-Related Aspects of Intellectual Property Rights (TRIPS) Agreement, 330–31
Tran Duc Luong, 231. *See also* Vietnam
Transition paradigm, 379–82
Transparency International, 107, 152, 291
Treasury, Department of (U.S.), 35
TRIPS Agreement. *See* Trade-Related Aspects of Intellectual Property Rights Agreement
Trust Fund for the Guatemalan Peace Process, 264
Tun Sri Razali Ismail, 230
Turkey, 319, 421
Turkmenbashi the Great. *See* Niyazov, Saparmurat
Turkmenistan: aid to, 153t; crime, conflict, and corruption in, 152, 153, 154, 441; economic issues of, 145, 147t, 148t, 154, 174, 176; food production in, 160; foreign direct investment in, 173; gas industry in, 154, 174; government and governance in, 155, 174, 441; military and police issues of, 441; political issues of, 150, 174, 440–41; social and civil issues of, 166; U.S. security assistance to, 44. *See also* Central Asia
Turzunsade Aluminum Smelter (Tajikistan), 165
Tutsis, 77

UES (Russian energy company), 162, 166
Uganda: Congo and, 57, 59, 70, 73; economic issues of, 18, 313; foreign investment in, 348, 349, 359; military and police issues of, 437; trade issues of, 43, 329; U.S. aid to, 286, 431, 432–33. *See also* Africa
UNCITRAL. *See* United Nations Center for International Trade Law
UNCTAD. *See* United National Conference on Trade and Development
UN Development Program (UNDP), 175; El Salvador, 256; Guatemala, 264;

Myanmar, 227; Yemen, 188, 198, 200, 201
Unión Nacional Independiente, 261 (UNI; Guatemala)
Union of Burma, 210
Union Solidarity and Development Association (USDA; Myanmar), 216, 227
United Democratic Center, 255 (CDU; El Salvador)
United Front for an Independent, Neutral and Free Cambodia (FUNCINPEC), 398, 400, 402
United Kingdom (U.K.): investment in Mauritius, 341; Myanmar and, 218, 219, 220, 221; Nigeria and, 102, 105; political risk insurance, 355; promotion of transparency in extractive industries, 336
United Nations (UN), 40, 293, 423
United Nations—specific countries and areas: Central America, 251, 252, 259; Congo, 57, 60, 65, 66, 74; East Timor, 427, 428; El Salvador, 255, 256, 271; Guatemala, 260, 262, 263, 271; LDCs, 31; Myanmar, 228–29, 232–33; Nicaragua, 271; Nigeria, 104; Somalia, 4; U.S., 251; Yemen, 188, 192, 195
United Nations Center for International Trade Law (UNCITRAL), 337–38
United Nations Conference on Trade and Development (UNCTAD), 309–10, 313, 317, 353
United States: anticommunism in, 223; assistance decisionmaking, 445–46; democracy assistance by, 41, 43–44, 45; disengagement from Afghanistan, 1; disengagement from Somalia, 4; doctrine of preemption, 1–2; economic issues of, 130; failed and failing states and, 293, 301–02; foreign assistance of, 6, 7–8, 33, 34, 45–46, 174, 276, 286–91; foreign direct investment and, 38–39, 349–50, 358–60; foreign policy objectives, 412, 416, 420, 423, 424, 430, 435, 446; geopolitical strategies, 5, 27; health assistance to Africa, 104; military and police issues, 412–60; Nigerian immigrants to, 103, 104; organizational changes within, 35; petroleum issues, 70, 102; policies toward poor performers, 34–47; policy recommendations, 446–48 for; role in

Africa, 4, 5; security issues of, 5, 7–8, 36, 39–40, 44, 45, 230–35, 413–14, 434–48; trade and trade policies of, 37–38, 68–70, 138, 311–31. *See also* Terrorism and terrorists; *individual foreign countries*
University of Central America, 254
University of Kinshasa (Congo), 72
University of Maryland, 294
UNO. *See* National Opposition Union
URNG. *See* Guatemalan National Revolutionary Unity
Uruguay Round of trade negotiations (*1986*), 311, 321, 332n3
U.S. Agency for International Development (USAID): aid policies of, 292; conflict vulnerability analyses, 295; democracy assistance and, 41–42, 44, 277, 289, 299, 378–407; evaluation of, 384–407; fragile and failing states and, 36, 294–95, 301; mission of, 41, 44; Office of the Coordinator for Reconstruction and Stabilization and, 35; qualifications for aid, 290–91; recommendations for, 403–06; reports and studies of, 299; risk factors for state failure, 44; security sector assistance and, 40, 435, 437–38; strategic plans and strategies of, 204–05, 302, 380–406; views of democratic governance, 377–78. *See also* Democracy and Governance framework; Office of Transition Initiatives
U.S. Agency for International Development—individual countries and areas: Cambodia, 396–403; Central America, 246, 252; Central Asia, 173; the Congo, 70, 73–74; El Salvador, 254, 256, 257–58, 277; Guatemala, 264, 265–66, 277; Indonesia, 136–37; Haiti, 385–90; Kenya, 390–96; Nicaragua, 274, 277; Yemen, 192, 201
U.S. Coast Guard, 427
USDA. *See* Union Solidarity and Development Association
U.S. Foreign Service, 360
U.S.-Jordan Free Trade Agreement, 311, 312, 326
USS *Cole*, 184, 185, 186, 204
U.S.–South Africa Free Trade Agreement, 331

U.S. Special Forces, 417, 419, 426, 431
USSR. *See* Soviet Union
Uzbekistan: agriculture in, 167, 168, 169–70, 171; aid and assistance to, 44, 153t, 174–75, 415t, 418, 420; crime, conflict, and corruption in, 152, 154, 169–70, 437; economic issues of, 146, 147t, 148t, 151, 155, 158t, 167–72, 174, 176; ethnic and minority issues of, 155; military and police issues, 420, 437, 441–42; Muslim population of, 155, 156, 163, 172; political issues of, 150, 151, 168–69, 174, 442; reform trajectory of, 29, 167, 169–70; regime change of, 31; social and civil issues of, 166, 169, 174; trade issues of, 155–56, 166, 167, 168, 169, 175, 176; Turkmen exiles in,441; U.S. security assistance to, 444, 447. *See also* Central Asia

Vaishnav, Milan, 1–50
Valdes, Alberto, 329
Van de Walle, Nicolas, 23
Verizon, 342, 347
Vietnam: economic issues of, 42, 43, 313, 329; FDI in, 345; Myanmar and, 231; U.S. aid to, 42, 223, 293
Vietnam War, 224

Wahid, Abdurrahmar, 131. *See also* Indonesia
War-transition countries. *See* El Salvador; Guatemala; Nicaragua
Wasow, Bernard, 339
Weapons of mass destruction (WMD). *See* Arms and weapons
Weinstein, Jeremy M., 1–50
Wells, Louis, 338
West Africa, 4–5, 33, 47, 84, 102, 423. *See also individual countries*
West Germany, 192, 198
Westinghouse, 342, 347
West Papua (Indonesia), 121, 123
Whalley, John, 319
WHO. *See* World Health Organization
WMD (weapons of mass destruction). *See* Arms and weapons
Wolfsthal, Jon, 444
Wolpe, Howard, 297
World Bank: Central Asia and, 145; Chad and Exxon Mobil and, 336; concessional

lending window, 313; Congo and, 74; El Salvador and, 256–57; good governance and effective aid, 40; Indonesia and, 134; LICUS program of, 13, 293; Myanmar and, 209, 211; Nicaragua and, 246, 269, 273; Nigeria and, 87, 107; reports and studies of, 20, 118, 289; trade issues and, 328, 329, 331; Uzbekistan and, 145, 167, 168, 170–71, 175; Yemen and, 188, 189, 190, 191, 192, 193, 196, 197, 198, 201, 202, 203. *See also* International Development Association

World Bank Group, 346, 347

World Economic Forum, 352

World Health Organization (WHO), 200, 226

World Trade Center bombing (*1993*; U.S.), 274

World Trade Organization (WTO), 161, 175, 189, 312, 324, 328

World War II, 210, 212, 223

WTO. *See* World Trade Organization

Yang, David, 41, 42, 44, 376–411

Yemen: agriculture in, 201; civil war of *1994*, 184, 186, 190, 195–96, 199; crime, conflict, and corruption in, 184, 187, 189, 190, 194, 200, 201; democracy and democratization in, 183, 184, 185, 186, 187, 188, 202, 204; development finance of, 190–202; economic issues, 30, 182–83, 187, 188–202; electric power, 198–99, 203; ethnic and minority issues in, 187; foreign aid to, 28, 30; geography of, 190; government and governance in, 183, 184, 185, 187–88, 190, 202–03; history of, 183–84, 190–97; international attitudes toward, 28, 196–202; militant groups in, 182, 183, 184, 187; military and police issues in, 187; Muslim population of, 184, 200, 201, 202–03; North Korea and, 444; oil industry in, 183,

185–86, 188, 189, 190, 193, 194–95, 196; performance struggles of, 188, 202–04; political issues, 30, 184, 192, 199, 202; public sector growth of, 197–202; qualification for MCA, 13; regime change of, 31; security issues of, 183–88; social and civil issues of, 188, 189–90, 191, 196, 201–02; terrorism and, 183, 184–85, 186, 187, 203; trade issues of, 189, 201; unification of, 30; U.S. relationship with and assistance to, 182, 185–86, 187, 191, 192, 193, 197, 203–04, 415t, 418; vote against Gulf War of *1990–91*, 30, 195; water management in, 28, 189, 197, 199–201, 203. *See also* North Yemen; People's Democratic Republic of Yemen; South Yemen; USS *Cole*

Yemen Arab Republic, 183, 199

Yemen Company for Investment in Oil and Mineral Resources, 195

Yemen General Electric Company (YGEC), 199

Yemeni Socialist Party (Yemen), 186

Yerodia, Abdoulaye, 77. *See also* Democratic Republic of Congo

YGEC. *See* Yemen General Electric Company

Yudhyono, Susilo Bambang, 30. *See also* Indonesia

Yugoslavia, 133

Zaire. *See* Democratic Republic of Congo

Zaireanization episode. *See* Democratic Republic of Congo

Zimbabwe: Congo and, 57, 59, 73; effectiveness of foreign aid, 43, 297; instability of, 421; labor issues of, 349; Nigeria and, 102; performance struggles of, 13; political issues of, 18; potential failure of, 47; trade issues of, 318–19; U.S. aid to, 431, 432–33. *See also* Africa

Zambia, 421, 422, 425–26. *See also* Africa

Zurich risk insurance, 355

Past Publications from the
CENTER FOR GLOBAL DEVELOPMENT

A New Era at the Inter-American Development Bank: Six Recommendations for the New President
January 2006 ISBN 1-933286-08-3

Reality Check: The Distributional Consequences of Privatization in Developing Countries
John Nellis and Nancy Birdsall
October 2005 ISBN 1-933286-00-8

The United States as a Debtor Nation: Risks and Policy Reform
William R. Cline
September 2005 ISBN 0-881323-99-3

Give Us Your Best and Brightest: The Global Hunt for Talent and Its Impact on the Developing World
Devesh Kapur and John McHale
September 2005 ISBN 1-933286-03-02

The Hardest Job in the World: Five Crucial Tasks for the New President of the World Bank
Nancy Birdsall et al.
June 2005 ISBN 1-933286-04-0

Does Foreign Direct Investment Promote Development?
Theodore H. Moran, Edward M. Graham, and Magnus Blomström, eds.
April 2005 ISBN 0-88132-381-0

Making Markets for Vaccines: Ideas to Action
Owen Barder, Michael Kremer, and Ruth Levine
April 2005 ISBN 1-933286-02-4

Overcoming Stagnation in Aid-Dependent Countries
Nicolas van de Walle
March 2005 ISBN 1-933286-01-6

A Better Globalization: Legitimacy, Governance, and Reform
Kemal Dervis, assisted by Ceren Özer
March 2005 ISBN 0-8157-1763-6

Millions Saved: Proven Successes in Global Health
Ruth Levine and the What Works Working Group, with Molly Kinder
November 2004 ISBN 0-88132-372-1

Financing Development: The Power of Regionalism
Nancy Birdsall and Liliana Rojas Suarez
September 2004 ISBN 0-88132-353-5

On the Brink: Weak States and US National Security
Jeremy M. Weinstein, John Edward Porter, and Stuart E. Eizenstat
June 2004

Trade Policy and Global Poverty
William Cline
June 2004 ISBN 0-88132-365-9

From Social Assistance to Social Development: Targeted Education Subsidies in Developing Countries
Samuel Morley and David Coady
September 2003 ISBN 0-88132-357-8

The Other War: Global Poverty and the Millennium Challenge Account
Lael Brainard, Carol Graham, Nigel Purvis, Steven Radelet, and Gayle Smith
June 2003 Paper, ISBN 0-8157-1115-8
Cloth, ISBN 0-8157-1114-x

Challenging Foreign Aid: A Policymaker's Guide to the Millennium Challenge Account
Steven Radelet
May 2003 ISBN 0-88132-354-3

Delivering on Debt Relief: From IMF Gold to a New Aid Architecture
Nancy Birdsall and John Williamson, assisted by Brian Deese
April 2002 ISBN 0-88132-331-4